WordPerfect® Made Easy,
Series 5 Edition

WordPerfect®
Made Easy,
Series 5 Edition

Mella Mincberg

Osborne **McGraw-Hill**
Berkeley New York St. Louis San Francisco
Auckland Bogotá Hamburg London Madrid
Mexico City Milan Montreal New Delhi
Panama City São Paulo Singapore
Sydney Tokyo Toronto

Osborne **McGraw-Hill**
2600 Tenth Street
Berkeley, California 94710
U.S.A.

For information on translations and book distributors outside of the U.S.A., write to Osborne **McGraw-Hill** at the above address.

A complete list of trademarks appears on page 641.

234567890 DOCDOC 89

ISBN 0-07-881358-1

CONTENTS

APPENDIXES

ACKNOWLEDGMENTS

As with several of my previous books, I relied on a certain trio at Osborne/McGraw-Hill to coordinate the job of publishing *WordPerfect Made Easy, Series 5 Edition:* Cindy Hudson, editor-in-chief; Ilene Shapera, associate editor; and Dusty Bernard, project editor. Thanks, once again, for your support and expertise. Thanks also to other folks who worked diligently on this book, including Peggy Naumann, technical reviewer, for making sure that what I wrote was accurate; Gaen Murphree, copy editor, for making sure that what I wrote made sense; and Jeffrey Folsom, typesetter, for doing a nice job with the book's layout.

I wish to thank my friends, particularly Scott, for helping me regain my perspective at times when I let this book control me rather than the other way around. I am also grateful to my mother for her continual interest in my progress on each chapter.

Finally, I wish to acknowledge the readers of my previous computer books   including the first edition of *WordPerfect Made Easy.* Your kind words, encouragement, and comments let me know that someone is actually turning the pages. Keep those cards and letters coming in (care of Osborne/McGraw-Hill).

INTRODUCTION

Get ready to roll up your sleeves and learn how to use the most popular word-processing package on the market today. WordPerfect version 5 will edit your words, rearrange your paragraphs, and print your text with speed and sophistication. And its impressive array of features—like a 115,000-word spell checker, a thesaurus, outlining and footnoting capabilities, and the ability to combine text with graphics images, to name only a few—will help you produce slick-looking documents with ease.

IS THIS BOOK FOR YOU?

This book is for the beginning or intermediate WordPerfect version 5 user—those who fall into one of these categories:

- You are just beginning to use a personal computer.

- You've worked previously with a personal computer, but never used it as a word processor.

- You know word processing, but you're new to WordPerfect version 5.

- You are familiar with WordPerfect, but want to use it more effectively and take advantage of its more sophisticated features.

Moveover, this book is for the person who has little interest in the theoretical, but instead wants to learn the practical—how to employ WordPerfect for everyday word processing tasks. You'll learn what WordPerfect is capable of and exactly which keys to press so that you tap those capabilities. To that end, each chapter offers

- Thorough, straightforward explanations of WordPerfect concepts and features
- Step-by-step procedures to help you put those concepts and features into action on your computer
- Review exercises to help you build confidence as you become proficient using WordPerfect
- A review that summarizes what you've learned and serves as a quick chapter reference guide

While reading, you may feel as if you're sitting in a WordPerfect training class; that's because I used my experience in teaching personal computer users when writing this book.

HOW THIS BOOK IS ORGANIZED

The book begins with a chapter titled "Getting Started," which you should read if you've never before used a computer or never before started up WordPerfect on your computer. It describes the computer equipment, shows you how to use the computer keyboard, and provides directions for starting and ending a WordPerfect session.

The main chapters of the book are divided into two parts. Part I explains the fundamentals. You'll learn how to type, edit, save, and print documents. You'll also discover how to perform such essential tasks as altering margins and tab settings; inserting headers and footers on a page; moving a paragraph from one location to another; underlining, boldfacing, and centering text; and checking your document for spelling errors. If you're new to WordPerfect, you should probably read Part I from beginning to end, since the exercises in each chapter build on previous chapters.

Part II covers WordPerfect's special word processing features. These include file management capabilities for properly organizing documents on disk, as well as features for outlining, footnoting, creating text columns, merging form letters, and using fancy fonts and graphics for desktop publishing. You'll also find that macros and styles (Chapter 14) are wonderful time-savers, not to be ignored. The last chapter discusses those features that go beyond the bounds of typical word processing, into such areas as WordPerfect's math and sorting capabilities. Part II's chapters can be read in any order and will make you a sophisticated WordPerfect user.

The book concludes with four appendixes. Appendixes A and B describe how to install WordPerfect to work with your computer and your printer(s)—important topics if you've just purchased the WordPerfect program or a printer. Appendix C explains how to customize the WordPerfect program for your equipment or for particular formatting needs. Finally, Appendix D offers sources for additional support in using WordPerfect.

BOOK NOTATION

A specific notation is used in this book to indicate what keys you press to activate each WordPerfect feature.

- All keys are shown in SMALL CAPITALS, such as PGUP, PGDN, DEL, HOME, and CTRL.

- A plus sign (+) between keys indicates that you press them together. For example, CTRL + PGDN means that, while holding down the CTRL key, you also press PGDN. Then release both keys.

- A comma between keys indicates that you press them sequentially. For example, HOME, LEFT ARROW means press HOME and release it; then press LEFT ARROW and release it.

- WordPerfect assigns a name to each function key. The function key names are listed in FULL CAPITALS, followed in parentheses by the corresponding key(s), such as SAVE (F10) or CENTER (SHIFT + F6), or MERGE CODES (SHIFT + F9).

The keystrokes used in this book are based on the version of WordPerfect created for IBM personal computers and compatibles. If you are using another type of computer, the keystrokes to activate a given command might be slightly different. Check your manual for details.

A SPECIAL NOTE TO BEGINNERS

Getting over the hurdle of learning something new can feel uncomfortable and takes both time and practice, so you must be patient as you learn WordPerfect. Work at your own pace. Tackle a chapter or two every day or every week—whatever is appropriate for you. And since the best way to learn is by doing, make sure that you don't just read the chapters, but that you follow along on the computer, step by step. Pretty soon you'll be using WordPerfect like a pro.

The benefits in learning WordPerfect are innumerable and far outweigh any initial discomfort. Don't worry if at first you feel awkward with the WordPerfect concepts. Give yourself time to gain skill with the basics. Give yourself the freedom to experiment with the more advanced features. Above all, as you use *WordPerfect Made Easy, Series 5 Edition*, give yourself the latitude to have some fun.

—Mella Minceberg

GETTING STARTED

This chapter allows you to become comfortable using your computer with WordPerfect. It begins with a quick overview of computer equipment for those of you who are unfamiliar with the basic parts of a computer, and then provides step-by-step directions for starting up WordPerfect on your computer.

Once in WordPerfect, you'll discover how it offers a comfortable word processing environment. Its Typing screen is clear of distracting messages so that you can focus not on WordPerfect but on your goal— writing and typing documents. You'll be instructed to type one line of text and see how WordPerfect operates using all the different sections of the keyboard. And you'll learn how to use WordPerfect's Help feature, so that if you can't remember how to accomplish a task, you can get your answer by tapping a few keys on the keyboard.

At the end of the chapter, you'll learn how to leave the Word-Perfect program when you're done for the day. Exiting WordPerfect is swift and easy and will soon become as habitual as closing a door behind you when you leave a building.

For those of you who have just purchased WordPerfect but have yet to prepare your copy to work with your computer, turn now to Appendix A, "Installing WordPerfect," before you read further.

For those of you who have worked with WordPerfect before, you may already be familiar with the information provided in this chapter. Skim over its contents, and then read through the "Review" section at the end of the chapter to reinforce the information that you already know.

YOUR COMPUTER EQUIPMENT

If you're facing a computer for the first time, you're probably unfamiliar with the equipment occupying your desk. Let's briefly examine the basic computer components you need to know about, illustrated in Figure GS-1.

With the computer *keyboard,* you provide information and instructions to the computer. There are different keyboard models, with keys located in different places and with varying numbers of keys. Later on in this chapter, after you have started up WordPerfect, you will learn about the functions of each of the keys.

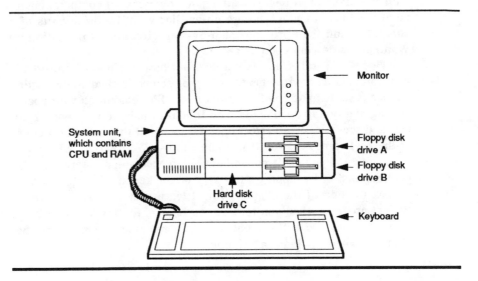

FIGURE GS-1   The computer components

The computer *monitor,* which resembles a television screen, displays messages from the computer and also displays any characters that you type on the keyboard. A *cursor,* which resembles a line that blinks, acts like your pointer on the monitor screen. A monochrome monitor displays one-color characters (most often green or amber) on a black background screen. A color monitor can display numerous colors. Most monitors have an 80-column by 25-line display, which means that at any one time you can see 80 characters across the width of the screen and 25 lines of text across the length of the screen.

The computer *system unit* contains the heart of the computer system. Inside the system unit is the *central processing unit* (CPU), often referred to as the brain of the computer because the CPU interprets all instructions and performs all necessary computations.

Also inside the system unit is the computer's *random-access memory* (RAM). RAM is circuitry where the computer temporarily stores information that needs to be processed by the CPU. For example, when you type on the keyboard, the characters that appear on your monitor are also placed in RAM. A computer comes with a certain amount of RAM installed; your computer must be equipped with at least 384 kilobytes of RAM (meaning that RAM can hold approximately 384,000 characters of information at one time) to operate WordPerfect—although 512 kilobytes are recommended. When you turn off your computer, all the information stored in RAM (and all characters displayed on the monitor screen) disappear.

The computer *disk drives* take information that resides in RAM and store that information for future use. For example, suppose you type a document using WordPerfect. That document is shown on the computer monitor and is stored in RAM. But the document will disappear as soon as you turn off the computer. Thus, you must direct the computer to store that document by means of a disk drive if you wish to review or edit that document tomorrow or next month.

One type of disk drive stores information onto *floppy diskettes (disks),* which are removable. If your computer has two floppy disk drives, then the one on the left or on top is referred to as drive A, and the second one is referred to as drive B. Another type of disk drive stores information onto a *hard disk,* which is made of metal and is fixed inside the computer. If your computer has a hard disk, it is usually referred to as drive C.

Figure GS-1 shows an example of a computer system with two floppy disk drives and one hard disk drive. WordPerfect will operate only if your computer is equipped with, at a minimum, either two floppy disk drives or one floppy disk drive and one hard disk drive. Think of a floppy or hard disk as your file cabinet, where you store programs (such as WordPerfect) and where you store your own documents that you will want to use later on. A hard disk holds many times more information than a floppy disk. As a result, a hard disk is usually segregated electronically into separate parts, called *directories,* so that particular groups of information can be kept together. Think of a directory as a separate file drawer of your file cabinet. (Chapter 8, "Managing Files on Disk," offers information on how to create new directories or delete old ones.)

START THE WORDPERFECT PROGRAM

When you work with WordPerfect, you are also working with another program called DOS, which stands for Disk Operating System. DOS acts like an interpreter at the United Nations, taking what you type during a WordPerfect session and converting it into a language the computer can understand. If your computer is not equipped with a hard disk, then after you install WordPerfect to work with your computer hardware (Appendix A), both DOS and WordPerfect are housed on the WordPerfect 1 disk. If your computer is equipped with a hard disk, then after you install WordPerfect (Appendix A), both DOS and Word-Perfect are housed on the hard disk. (As mentioned at the beginning of this chapter, if you just purchased WordPerfect and no one has yet installed your copy of WordPerfect to work with your computer, you must turn to Appendix A, "Installing WordPerfect," before you read further.)

Whenever you wish to use WordPerfect, you must start up DOS on your computer first and start up WordPerfect second. The computer's RAM will contain both DOS and WordPerfect, and you will be ready to use WordPerfect.

When starting up DOS and WordPerfect on your computer, there are two keys on the keyboard you should know about:

- The ENTER key, also called the return key, is used to register instructions into the computer. It is usually on the right side of the keyboard, marked with the word "ENTER" or the word "RETURN" or with a symbol of a crooked arrow pointing to the left: ↵. (Some of you may have two ENTER keys on your keyboard.)

- The BACKSPACE key is used to correct a mistake when you accidentally type the wrong character. It is usually just above the ENTER key, marked with the word "BACKSPACE" or with a symbol of a long, straight arrow pointing to the left: ←.

With these two keys in mind, let's start up DOS, a procedure known as *booting up* the computer:

1. Floppy disk users should place the WordPerfect 1 disk in drive A—usually the disk drive on the left or on the top—and close the disk drive door. Place a data disk where you will store your documents in drive B—usually the disk drive on the right or on the bottom—and close the disk drive door. (For information on formatting a blank disk so that it becomes a data disk to be used to store documents, see Appendix A.) Now turn on the computer. If you have a color monitor, you may have to turn on the monitor separately.

    Hard disk users don't need to insert disks in the floppy disk drives because WordPerfect is stored on the hard disk, which is fixed inside the computer; simply turn on the computer. If you have a color monitor, you may have to turn it on separately.

    It will take a few moments for the computer to warm up and begin working.

2. For some of you, the computer will respond with a request for the current date; type it in. For example, if today's date is December 9, 1988, type **12-09-88**; if the date is January 15, 1989, type **01-15-89**. Be sure to use real zeros and real ones on the keyboard; a computer will not accept the letters "o" or "l" as substitutes.

    If you make a typing mistake when typing the date, simply press the BACKSPACE key to erase the error, and then type the correct character(s).

3. If you typed in the correct date, press the ENTER key.

4. For some of you, the computer responds with a request for the current time; type it in. The computer works on military time (a 24-hour clock); so if the correct time is, for example, 7:30 A.M., type **7:30**, or if the correct time is 4:30 P.M., type **16:30**.

5. If you typed in the correct time, press the ENTER key.

You are now ready to start up WordPerfect on the computer, a procedure referred to as *loading* WordPerfect. How you load WordPerfect depends on (1) whether or not your computer is equipped with a hard disk, and (2) whether or not you or someone else has written a batch file (a set of computer instructions written in DOS, as described in Appendix A) for your computer so that WordPerfect can be loaded automatically.

Floppy disk users who have written a batch file as described in Appendix A to automatically load WordPerfect should proceed as follows:

1. Because of the automatically activated batch file, WordPerfect automatically begins loading WordPerfect for you. In a few moments, a WordPerfect screen appears with the following message:

   Insert diskette labeled "WordPerfect" and press any key.

2. Take out your WordPerfect 1 disk from drive A, place it back in its protective envelope, and insert your WordPerfect 2 disk into drive A.

3. Press ENTER to continue loading WordPerfect.

Floppy disk users who have not written a batch file should proceed as follows:

1. After DOS is loaded, you will see the DOS prompt A> appear on the screen, signaling that DOS has been loaded into RAM and that the active drive is drive A. Your cursor should be located just to the right of the A>.

2. Type **b:** (uppercase or lowercase makes no difference), and press ENTER. Now the DOS prompt reads B>. This means that the default drive—the drive for storing and retrieving files— has been changed to drive B, where the data disk is stored. (This step is necessary so that WordPerfect knows to store your documents not on the same disk where the WordPerfect program is housed, but rather on a separate disk. Storing programs and your documents on separate disks is a good idea so that you have an uncluttered space just for your documents

and to reduce the chances of inadvertently erasing or damaging the WordPerfect program.)

3. Type **a:wp**, and press ENTER. The WordPerfect program begins to load into the computer's RAM. In a few moments, a Word-Perfect screen appears with the following message:

   Insert diskette labeled "WordPerfect 2" and press any key

4. Take out your WordPerfect 1 disk from drive A, place it back in its protective envelope, and insert your WordPerfect 2 disk into drive A.

5. Press ENTER to continue loading WordPerfect.

Hard disk users who have written a batch file as described in Appendix A should proceed as follows:

1. You will see a DOS prompt such as C> or C:\> appear on screen, signaling that DOS has been loaded into RAM and that the active drive is drive C, the hard disk. Your cursor should be located just to the right of the C> or C:\>.

2. Type **wp5** (uppercase or lowercase makes no difference), which is the name of the batch file.

3. Press ENTER to activate the batch file; WordPerfect will be loaded for you.

Hard disk users who have installed WordPerfect without writing a batch file should proceed as follows:

1. You will see a DOS prompt such as C> or C:\> appear on screen, signaling that DOS has been loaded into RAM and that the active drive is drive C, the hard disk. Your cursor should be located just to the right of the C> or C:\>.

2. You must issue a CD (Change Directory) command to switch to the directory on the hard disk where the WordPerfect program instructions are housed. For example, suppose that the WordPerfect program files are housed in a directory named \WPER (as suggested in Appendix A). Then, type **cd \wper** and press ENTER. This tells the computer to change directories to \WPER so that WordPerfect can be started.

3. Type **wp** and press ENTER. Now the WordPerfect program loads into the computer's RAM.

4. Keep in mind that this procedure for loading WordPerfect causes the default directory (the directory that WordPerfect assumes for saving or retrieving your documents) and the directory housing the WordPerfect program to be one and the same. This is not a good idea. A better idea is to store your documents in a different directory from where the WordPerfect program is housed, thus allowing for better organization of information on the hard disk and reducing the chances of accidentally erasing or damaging the WordPerfect program. Once you begin working extensively with WordPerfect to type documents, you might want to see Appendix A to learn how to create a separate directory named \WPER\DATA to store your documents and how to write a batch file to load WordPerfect, making this directory the default. Or you might want to see Chapter 8 to learn how to create new directories and how to change the default directory once WordPerfect is loaded.

Note: Whether you're a floppy or hard disk user, you should know that you have the ability to load WordPerfect in a slightly different way to activate options that might make your WordPerfect session more productive. For instance, you may be able to load WordPerfect in a way that speeds up its operations on your computer. Refer to the last section of Appendix A, "Startup (Slash) Options," for more details.

EXAMINE THE TYPING SCREEN

Whether you use a floppy disk or hard disk, you will know that Word-Perfect has successfully started when your computer screen resembles Figure GS-2, which shows the WordPerfect Typing screen.

The Typing screen is almost totally blank, so that there is little to distract you from your typing. A blinking line sits at the top left corner of the screen. This is your WordPerfect cursor, which acts like a position marker or pencil point on the screen. A character that you type will appear wherever the cursor is located. The bottom line on the screen, called the *status line,* provides information on the cursor's present location. On a clear Typing screen, the cursor is in the upper left corner and the status line reads

Doc 1 Pg 1 Ln 1" Pos 1"

Doc 1 indicates that the cursor is in document 1; this is important information when you begin working with two documents at once, referred to as Doc 1 and Doc 2, as described in Chapter 3, "Typing Enhancements."

Pg 1 informs you that the cursor is on page 1 of the document. In WordPerfect, a document can be many pages long.

Ln 1" signifies that the cursor is positioned one inch down from the top of the page. In other words, whatever you type on Ln 1" will appear one inch from the top edge of a piece of paper when you print out what you've typed, so that your printed document has a one-inch top margin. The one-inch top margin is an assumption, called a *default* or *initial setting,* that WordPerfect makes about how you wish your document produced. A related default setting is for a one-inch bottom margin. You will learn in Chapter 5 how you can change these top and bottom margin settings for any document.

Pos 1" means that the cursor is located one inch from the left edge of the page. In other words, whatever you type at Pos 1" will appear

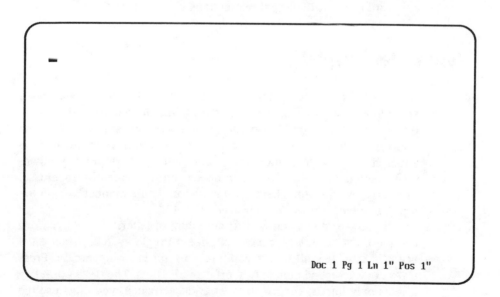

Doc 1 Pg 1 Ln 1" Pos 1"

FIGURE GS-2   The WordPerfect Typing screen

one inch from the left edge of a piece of paper when you print out what you've typed, so that your printed document has a one-inch left margin. This one-inch left margin is another default setting; a related setting is for a one-inch right margin. You will learn in Chapter 4 how to change these left and right margin settings for any document.

Note: If your status line reads something other than **Ln 1"** or **Pos 1"** then someone has changed either the default settings for your copy of WordPerfect or the units of measure on the status line. Look to the sections "Initial Settings" and "Units of Measure" in Appendix C for further explanation.

USE THE KEYBOARD IN WORDPERFECT

Let's explore how the computer keyboard works with WordPerfect. Most keyboards consist of three distinct sections: the typewriter keypad, the cursor movement/numeric keypad, and the function keypad. Figures GS-3 and GS-4 illustrate two of the most common keyboard types, with these three sections indicated.

Typewriter Keypad

In the center of the computer keyboard are the standard typing keys—a SPACEBAR at the bottom, letters on the middle three rows, numbers on the top row. Just as on a typewriter, letters will appear in lowercase as you type unless you press either of the two SHIFT keys, located on either side of the SPACEBAR, and, while holding the SHIFT key down, type a letter. That letter will then appear on the screen in uppercase. Similarly, use the SHIFT key in combination with a number key on the top row to type a symbol, such as @, #, or !.

If you wish to capitalize a whole group of letters at once, you can use the CAPS LOCK key, which acts like a toggle switch. When CAPS LOCK is activated, all letters you type will appear in uppercase. Press CAPS LOCK a second time to turn off capital letters. The CAPS LOCK key affects only letters; even with CAPS LOCK activated, you must use the SHIFT key to produce symbols. You can easily tell when CAPS LOCK is active: the **Pos** indicator on the status line appears in uppercase—**POS**. (There is also an indicator on some keyboards that lights up when CAPS LOCK is active.)

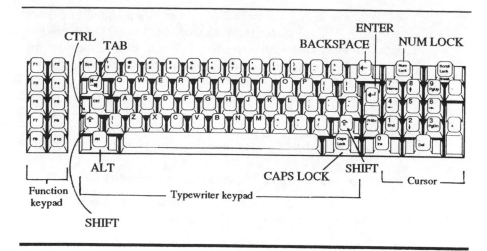

FIGURE GS-3   The IBM standard keyboard

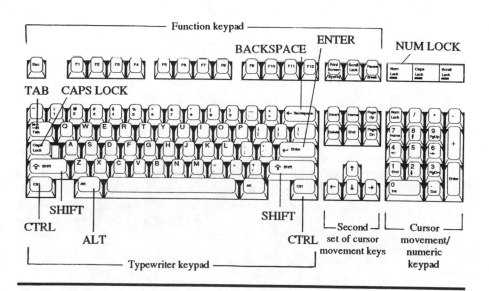

FIGURE GS-4   The IBM enhanced keyboard

The TAB key, with the symbol of two arrows pointing in opposite directions, moves the cursor from tab stop to tab stop. The default setting for tab stops is one tab stop every 0.5 inch. Every time you press TAB, the cursor jumps to the next tab stop location, so that the next character you type will be fixed at that location.

To get a feel for the keyboard, try the following. If you make a typing mistake, press BACKSPACE to erase it, and then type the correct character. (You learned about BACKSPACE previously; it is usually marked with a symbol of a long, straight arrow pointing to the left.)

1. Press TAB one time. The cursor jumps 0.5 inch to the right.

2. Type **Hello!!!** Remember to use the SHIFT key when typing the "H" and the three exclamation points.

3. Press the SPACEBAR once to insert an empty space.

4. Press CAPS LOCK. When you do, notice that the position indicator on the status line at the bottom of the computer screen now reads **POS** rather than **Pos**, indicating that uppercase has been activated.

5. Type **WELCOME**. All the letters appear in uppercase without your using the SHIFT key. (Remember, however, that to type symbols like the exclamation point, even with CAPS LOCK activated, you must still use the SHIFT key.)

6. Press CAPS LOCK. Now the status line reads **Pos**, since uppercase has been deactivated. The screen reads

   Hello!!! WELCOME_

Did you notice how the cursor moved to the right as you typed each new character? The cursor is now just to the right of the last "E" in "WELCOME." The status line always reflects the change in the cursor's position. If you look at the status line, you'll notice that it indicates a new cursor position. For example, when the cursor is at position 3.1" (meaning 3.1 inches from the left edge of the page), then the status line reads

Doc 1 Pg 1 Ln 1" Pos 3.1"

Cursor Movement/Numeric Keypad

The section located on the right side of the computer keyboard serves two purposes. First, this section can act as the cursor movement keypad, controlling the whereabouts of your cursor. The LEFT ARROW key (marked with a left arrow and with the number 4), for example, moves the cursor to the left, and the RIGHT ARROW key (marked with a right arrow and with the number 6) moves the cursor to the right. Or this section may act as a numeric keypad, allowing you to type the numbers shown on those keys, so that when you press the LEFT ARROW key, for example, you insert the number 4 on your screen, and the RIGHT ARROW key inserts the number 6. Those of you who frequently type on a ten-key adding machine may prefer to type numbers using this section of the keyboard, rather than using the top row on the typewriter keypad.

The NUM LOCK key controls whether you're using this keyboard section for cursor movement or for typing numbers. The NUM LOCK key, like the CAPS LOCK key, is a toggle switch. When it is active, the keypad inserts numbers. Press NUM LOCK again to return this keyboard section to a cursor movement keypad. You can tell when NUM LOCK is active: the **Pos** indicator on the status line blinks. (There is also an indicator on some keyboards that lights up when NUM LOCK is active.)

Those of you with the standard keyboard (Figure GS-3) will find that you must use the NUM LOCK key constantly if you wish to switch between the cursor movement and numeric keys (unless you decide to type in numbers using the typewriter keypad only). Those of you with the enhanced keyboard (Figure GS-4) have a second set of arrow keys on your keyboard, enabling you to keep NUM LOCK activated all the time and use the second set of cursor movement keys for moving the cursor around the screen.

Try the following for practice in using the NUM LOCK key:

1. With NUM LOCK inactive, press the LEFT ARROW (number 4) key five times. The cursor now moves five spaces to the left, and the position indicator on the status line indicates the change in location.

2. Press the RIGHT ARROW (number 6) key five times. The cursor now moves five spaces to the right.

3. Press NUM LOCK. Notice that the position indicator on the status line blinks. This indicates that the numeric keypad has been activated.

4. Press the LEFT ARROW (number 4) key five times. Notice that you have typed the number 44444.

5. Press the RIGHT ARROW (number 6) key five times. Now you have typed the number 66666.

6. Press NUM LOCK. This deactivates the numeric keypad. Now if you press LEFT ARROW, for example, you'll see that you can again move the cursor; you've switched back to the cursor movement keypad. Now the screen reads

   Hello!!! WELCOME4444466666_

You can move the cursor only within that part of the screen in which you've already typed characters or pressed the SPACEBAR; the cursor movement keypad won't relocate the cursor to a place in the screen where you've yet to type. To move the cursor down to an empty portion of the screen, you use the ENTER key. For example:

1. With the cursor located just past the last character you typed, press RIGHT ARROW. Notice that the cursor refuses to move past the section of the screen where you've typed.

2. Press DOWN ARROW (number 2). The cursor still won't move past the typed line.

3. Press ENTER. The cursor moves down to the beginning of a new line. Notice that the status line indicates that the cursor is at the left margin on the next line.

   Doc 1 Pg 1 Ln 1.16" Pos 1"

Now whatever you type on this second line will print 1.16 inches from the top of the page.

Note: You may find that after you press ENTER, the status line indicates that your second line will print in a spot other than 1.16 inches from the top of the page. For instance, the status line may indicate that your second line is at 1.15" or 1.17". This is a result of the variation in how different printers operate. Some printers automatically allow for 0.16 inch between lines, while others allow for 0.15 inch or 0.17 inch. Thus, the height of each line depends on the printer that is selected to print out your WordPerfect documents when your copy of WordPerfect is installed. Appendix B describes how you select a printer in Word-Perfect. Chapter 9 discusses how this line-height setting can be altered for your printer.

Function Keypad

The third section of the keyboard is the function keypad. Depending on your keyboard, the function keypad sits either on the left with keys labeled F1 through F10 (as shown in Figure GS-3) or on top with keys labeled F1 through F12 (as shown in Figure GS-4).

WordPerfect's special features are controlled via the function keypad, by pressing one of the first ten function keys either by itself or in combination with one of three other keys: CTRL (control), ALT (alternate), and SHIFT. Each function key can thus be used in four different ways. For example, you can press F1 on its own; you can press the ALT key and, while holding it down, press F1 (denoted from now on as ALT + F1); you can press SHIFT + F1; or you can press CTRL + F1. Each key combination invokes a different command; therefore, there are 40 commands at your fingertips on the function keypad.

To remind you which function keys perform which command, the WordPerfect package comes with two plastic templates. One template is shaped like a rectangular donut and is for those keyboards where the function keys are on the left side. The other template is shaped like a ruler and is for those keyboards where the function keys are at the top. The templates indicate function key names, to help you know which function keys perform which special features. *Before you continue, be sure to place the template that is appropriate for your keyboard next to your function keys.* You can also look to Table GS-1 for an alphabetical list of function key names.

The templates are color-coded. Functions listed in black are selected by pressing the function key alone; in blue, by pressing ALT + function key; in green, by pressing SHIFT + function key; and in red, by pressing CTRL + function key.

When you press a function key to select a command, WordPerfect responds in different ways:

- WordPerfect may respond with a message on the status line, called a *prompt,* asking for further information before activating a feature. You would enter the appropriate information and then the command would be carried out.

- WordPerfect may provide you with a list of choices, called a *menu;* this menu may appear at the bottom of the screen, temporarily replacing the status line, or on the full screen, temporarily replacing the Typing screen. You would select a menu item by either selecting the number or the mnemonic character that corresponds to your selection.

- WordPerfect may simply turn on or off a feature, inserting a symbol called a *code* into the text of your document. (Codes are described in further detail in the next chapter.)

If you press a function key inadvertently and a prompt or a menu appears, you can clear the prompt or menu from the screen by pressing CANCEL, the F1 function key. (The SPACEBAR or ENTER key can usually also clear a prompt or menu.) Sometimes you must press CANCEL (F1) more than once to completely back out of a command. If you press a function key and a feature is turned on, you can cancel the feature by pressing the BACKSPACE key and erasing the code you inserted.

Here's a chance for you to practice reading the template and viewing different prompts and menus. We'll use the CANCEL (F1) and BACKSPACE keys to back out of the commands.

1. Find the EXIT key on the template (or in Table GS-1). You'll find it located next to the F7 function key. Since the word "Exit" is written in black on the template, you know that the EXIT feature is accessed with the F7 key alone.

2. Press the EXIT (F7) key. The following prompt appears on the status line (bottom of the screen) asking for further information:

Save Document? (Y/N) <u>Yes</u>

(**Y/N**) indicates that WordPerfect is waiting for you to type **Y** to indicate "Yes, I wish to save this document" or **N** to indicate "No, I do not wish to save this document." WordPerfect is suggesting a response, as the "Yes" at the end of the prompt indicates.

Function Key Name	Key Combination
BLOCK	ALT + F4
BOLD	F6
CANCEL	F1
CENTER	SHIFT + F6
DATE/OUTLINE	SHIFT + F5
EXIT	F7
FLUSH RIGHT	ALT + F6
FONT	CTRL + F8
FOOTNOTE	CTRL + F7
FORMAT	SHIFT + F8
GRAPHICS	ALT + F9
HELP	F3
→INDENT	F4
→INDENT←	SHIFT + F4
LIST FILES	F5
MACRO	ALT + F10
MACRO DEFINE	CTRL + F10
MARK TEXT	ALT + F5
MATH/COLUMNS	ALT + F7
MERGE CODES	SHIFT + F9
MERGE R	F9
MERGE/SORT	CTRL + F9
MOVE	CTRL + F4
PRINT	SHIFT + F7
REPLACE	ALT + F2
RETRIEVE	SHIFT + F10
REVEAL CODES	ALT + F3
SAVE TEXT	F10
SCREEN	CTRL + F3
→SEARCH	F2
←SEARCH	SHIFT + F2
SETUP	SHIFT + F1
SHELL	CTRL + F1
SPELL	CTRL + F2
STYLE	ALT + F8
SWITCH	SHIFT + F3

TABLE GS-1   Alphabetical List: WordPerfect Function Key Names

Function Key Name	Key Combination
TAB ALIGN	CTRL + F6
TEXT IN/OUT	CTRL + F5
THESAURUS	ALT + F1
UNDERLINE	F8

TABLE GS-1   Alphabetical List: WordPerfect Function Key Names (*continued*)

3. Press the CANCEL (F1) key. The prompt disappears, and the command is canceled.

4. Find the FOOTNOTE key on the template. You'll find the word also located next to the F7 key, but in red, meaning that the FOOTNOTE key is CTRL + F7.

5. Press the FOOTNOTE (CTRL + F7) key. The following menu appears on the status line:

   1 Footnote; 2 Endnote; 3 Endnote Placement: 0

   WordPerfect is waiting for you to make a footnote menu selection by typing a number or by typing a mnemonic character. For instance, you could choose option 1, Footnote, by pressing either the number 1 or the letter "F." The mnemonic characters on a menu are usually indicated on your computer screen in boldface; in the text of this book, however, mnemonic characters are indicated with an underline for clarity.

6. Press the CANCEL (F1) key. The menu disappears.

7. Find the FORMAT key on the template. You'll find it next to the F8 key, in green, meaning that the FORMAT key is SHIFT + F8.

8. Press the FORMAT (SHIFT + F8) key. A menu appears, this time on the entire screen, as shown in Figure GS-5. Here you have four items from which to select by either typing a number or a mnemonic character.

9. Press the CANCEL (F1) key. The menu disappears, and the Typing screen reappears, with the characters that you previously typed intact.

10. Find the UNDERLINE key on the template. You'll find it next to the F8 key, in black, meaning that the UNDERLINE key is F8.

11. Press the UNDERLINE (F8) key. No menu appears, but you have turned on the Underline feature; a special, hidden code has been inserted in the text.

12. Press BACKSPACE to cancel the Underline feature. WordPerfect prompts for confirmation, asking whether you wish to do so:

Delete [UND]? (Y/N) No

13. Type **Y**. The prompt clears and the Underline feature has been canceled.

```
Format

     1 - Line
                 Hyphenation                    Line Spacing
                 Justification                  Margins Left/Right
                 Line Height                    Tab Set
                 Line Numbering                 Widow/Orphan Protection

     2 - Page
                 Center Page (top to bottom)    New Page Number
                 Force Odd/Even Page            Page Numbering
                 Headers and Footers            Paper Size/Type
                 Margins Top/Bottom             Suppress

     3 - Document
                 Display Pitch                  Redline Method
                 Initial Codes/Font             Summary

     4 - Other
                 Advance                        Overstrike
                 Conditional End of Page        Printer Functions
                 Decimal Characters             Underline Spaces/Tabs
                 Language

Selection: 0
```

FIGURE GS-5 The Format menu

ACCESS WORDPERFECT'S HELP FACILITY

One of the most useful function keys, especially for beginning users, is the HELP (F3) key. With the HELP key, you can discover what features are available to you and which function keys control those features. It's like having an abbreviated version of the WordPerfect manual on screen.

There are two ways to use the Help facility. Once you press the HELP (F3) key, either press a letter key to view an alphabetical index of features and commands starting with that letter, or press a function or cursor movement key to view an explanation of that key's purpose. To exit Help, press either the ENTER key or the SPACEBAR.

Suppose you wish to know how to center text between your margins (a task you will actually perform in Chapter 3) and also how to exit WordPerfect (a task you will perform at the end of this chapter). Let's use the HELP facility to find out how to perform each task.

1. Press the HELP (F3) key. Hard disk users will view the screen shown in Figure GS-6, which describes how to use the Help feature. Floppy disk users will view the following message at the bottom of the same screen:

   WPHELP.FIL not found. Insert disk and press drive letter:

   This message means that WordPerfect cannot find the Help facility, which is stored in two files on disk named WPHELP.FIL and WPHELP2.FIL. Floppy disk users should remove the disk currently in drive B, replace it with the Word-Perfect Help disk that you created when you followed the directions in Appendix A (or the original WordPerfect 1 disk if you didn't follow Appendix A), close the drive door, and type **B**. The message will disappear.

2. To learn how to center text, type the letter **C** (for "Center"). The Help index beginning with the letter "C," which is shown in Figure GS-7, appears on the screen. Notice that halfway down the page, in the middle column, is listed the feature "Center Text." The first column indicates that the key that controls the Center Text feature is SHIFT + F6 (abbreviated on screen as Shft-F6). The last column indicates that the key name is CENTER. (At the bottom of Figure GS-7, WordPerfect

```
Help                                              WP 5.0   07/11/88


    Press any letter to get an alphabetical list of features.

        The list will include the features that start with that letter,
        along with the name of the key where the feature is found.  You
        can then press that key to get a description of how the feature
        works.


    Press any function key to get information about the use of the key.

        Some keys may let you choose from a menu to get more information
        about various options.  Press HELP again to display the template.

    Press Enter or Space bar to exit Help.
```

FIGURE GS-6   The Introductory Help screen

```
    Key           Feature                          Key Name

    Alt-F7        Calculate Math                   Math/Columns
    F1            Cancel                           Cancel
    Home "/"      Cancel Hyphenation Code          Home "/"
    Shft-F7       Cancel Print Job(s)              Print,4
    Shft-F3       Capitalize Block (Block On)      Switch
    Alt-F9        Caption Number Style             Graphics,1,4
    Shft-F7       Cartridges and Fonts             Print,S,3
    Shft-F3       Case Conversion (Block On)       Switch
    Shft-F6       Center Text                      Center
    Shft-F8       Center Page (Top to Bottom)      Format,2
    Shft-F8       Center Tabs                      Format,1
    F5            Change Default Directory         List Files,7
    Shft-F5       Change Outline Numbering Style   Date/Outline,6
    Shft-F5       Change Text to Comment (Block On) Text In/Out
    Ctrl-V        Character Set                    Compose
    Ctrl-F1       Clipboard                        Shell
    Alt-F3        Codes, Reveal                    Reveal codes
    Shft-F1       Colors/Fonts/Attributes          Setup,3
    Alt-F7        Column On/Off                    Math/Columns

                        Type 1 for more help: 0
```

FIGURE GS-7   The Help index starting with "C"

is informing you that for more features beginning with the letter "C," type **1**; this means that there are more features and commands starting with the letter "C" than can display on one screen.)

3. Press the CENTER (SHIFT + F6) key. Figure GS-8 appears, telling you how to center text between margins or over columns.

4. To learn how to exit WordPerfect, type the letter **E**. A new Help index appears, beginning with the letter "E," informing you that to exit you must use the EXIT (F7) key.

5. Press the EXIT (F7) key. Now the Help facility offers an explanation for the uses of the EXIT (F7) key.

6. Press the ENTER key or SPACEBAR to leave the Help facility. The Typing screen reappears.

7. Floppy disk users can now remove the Help disk from drive B and replace it with the disk that was there previously.

```
Center

     Centers one or several lines between margins or over columns.

Between margins
     a.  To center a line, place the cursor at the left margin and press
         Center.  Any text typed will automatically be centered until Tab or
         Enter is pressed.
     b.  With an existing line of text, press Center at the beginning of the
         line.  The line will be centered after down arrow is pressed.

Over columns
     a.  Over a text column, press Center at the column's left margin and
         type the text.
     a.  Over a column created with tabs or indents, tab to where you want
         the text centered, press Center and type the text.

Several lines can be centered by blocking the text then pressing Center.
```

FIGURE GS-8   Help information on the CENTER (SHIFT + F6) key

Help is useful only for a brief explanation of a feature. Nevertheless, it comes in handy when you are typing a document and want a quick reminder of how to accomplish a specific task.

CLEAR THE TYPING SCREEN

As you work at your desk throughout the day, there are times when you clear it of paper. You have two basic alternatives: put the paper in a file folder and slip the folder into your file cabinet, or crumple up the paper and throw it away. Once you've cleared off your desk, you have another set of options: start a new project, or leave your office.

You have the same options in WordPerfect. When you select the EXIT (F7) key, WordPerfect first asks whether you wish to either store the document currently on screen onto a disk for use in the future or to just simply "throw it away," clearing the text from RAM. Then WordPerfect asks whether you wish to end your session for the day or to remain in WordPerfect.

To practice with the EXIT key, let's assume that since what appears on your screen right now is just practice material you wish to throw it away, but you wish to remain in WordPerfect.

1. Press the EXIT (F7) key. WordPerfect responds with

   Save document? (Y/N) Yes

   WordPerfect always makes an assumption when it prompts for a yes/no answer. Since the prompt ends with **Yes**, WordPerfect is assuming you wish to save the text. That is incorrect in this case.

2. Type **N**, which overrides the suggestion; WordPerfect understands that you don't wish to save the document. Next WordPerfect responds with

   Exit WP? (Y/N) No

   Since the prompt ends with **No,** WordPerfect is assuming you wish to remain in WordPerfect, which is indeed what you want.

3. Press the ENTER key (or type **N**, or press any letter key other than **Y**) to accept the suggestion. The screen clears, and you

remain in WordPerfect. Now you have "fresh paper" for a new project.

EXIT WORDPERFECT

You may have worked with other word processing packages in which, to end the session, you simply turned off the computer. But whenever you finish using WordPerfect for the day, you should never simply turn off the computer! Rather, you must exit the WordPerfect program first. Only then should you turn off the computer (or load another software program). The EXIT (F7) key accomplishes this task.

Why must you exit WordPerfect before you turn off the computer? If you don't, the program has no opportunity to manage its operations and to delete special temporary files (such as overflow files) that it creates so you can use WordPerfect. You could, over time, harm the WordPerfect program on disk. Let's exit WordPerfect properly.

1. Press the EXIT (F7) key. WordPerfect responds with

   Save document? (Y/N) Yes

   Since the prompt ends with **Yes**, WordPerfect is assuming you wish to save the text. However, the screen is blank, so you have nothing to save.

2. Type **N**. WordPerfect responds with

   Exit WP? (Y/N) No

   The prompt ends with **No**; WordPerfect is assuming you wish to remain in WordPerfect. That is not true in this case.

3. Type **Y**. If you are a floppy disk user, the DOS prompt (A> or B>) will appear on screen and you will have successfully exited the program, or WordPerfect will prompt as follows:

   Insert disk with COMMAND.COM in drive A
   and strike any key when ready

   WordPerfect is requesting that you reinsert the WordPerfect 1 disk in drive A (the WordPerfect 1 disk contains COMMAND.COM, a part of the DOS program). Take out your WordPerfect 2 disk from drive A, place it back in its protective envelope, and insert your WordPerfect 1 disk into drive A. Then press ENTER (or any other key). The DOS prompt (such as A> or B>) appears on screen, which means you have successfully exited the program. Now, if you have finished working with the computer for today, you can turn it off.

If you are a hard disk user, DOS is stored on the hard disk, so that the DOS prompt (such as C> or C:\>) appears on screen in moments; you have successfully exited the program. Now, if you have finished working with the computer for today, you can turn it off.

What happens if you or a colleague forgets to exit WordPerfect before turning off the computer? (This should be a rare occurrence.) Or what if the power in your building flickers and the computer is shut off because of forces beyond your control? The next time you load the WordPerfect program, a prompt such as the following will appear on the screen:

Are other copies of WordPerfect currently running? Y/N

Type **N.** The WordPerfect Typing screen will appear, and you will be ready to begin working with WordPerfect again.

REVIEW

- You must load DOS and WordPerfect into the computer's RAM each time you wish to use the WordPerfect program. When WordPerfect's Typing screen appears, you are ready to begin typing.

- The cursor acts like a pointer on the Typing screen, and the status line at the bottom reports the cursor's current location.

- The CAPS LOCK key is a toggle switch. If you press CAPS LOCK to turn it on, all the letters you type using the typewriter keypad will appear in UPPERCASE. Press CAPS LOCK again to turn it off and the letters you type will appear in lowercase.

- The NUM LOCK key is a toggle switch. If you press NUM LOCK to turn it on, the right section of the keyboard acts as a numeric keypad for numbers typing. Press NUM LOCK again to turn it off, so that the right section of the keyboard serves as a cursor movement keypad, moving the cursor on the Typing screen. You can move the cursor only within the area of the screen where you've already typed characters.

- The function key template fits beside the function keypad. The template is a plastic card that lists the names of the features available with each function key, accessed by either pressing the function key by itself or in combination with CTRL, ALT, or SHIFT. A list of key names can also be found in Table GS-1.

- The HELP (F3) key provides on-screen assistance with Word-Perfect features.

- You must always use the EXIT (F7) key to quit WordPerfect before you turn off your computer at the end of a working session. Alternatively, the EXIT (F7) key allows you to clear the Typing screen but keep working in WordPerfect.

Part I

BASIC FEATURES

Typing, Cursor Movement, and Editing
Retrieving, Saving, and Printing
Typing Enhancements
Changing Margins, Tabs, and Other Line Formats
Working with Multiple-Page and Page Format Features
Moving, Searching, and Editing Enhancements
The Speller and The Thesaurus

1

TYPING, CURSOR MOVEMENT, AND EDITING

Once you know how to start up WordPerfect on your computer, you're ready to type a business report, write a short memo, or create "the great American novel." While Chapter 1 won't start you on the path to novel writing, it will have you typing a short document for a fictitious organization (named the R&R Wine Association). You'll see that typing and editing text with WordPerfect is even simpler than using a typewriter.

You'll also learn what goes on behind the scenes when you type. WordPerfect hides certain symbols, called codes, from you. These codes control how your words appear, and so they are important to be aware of. You will uncover the codes from their hiding places and see how a simple code insertion or deletion can reshuffle paragraphs. Don't let the term "code" make you uncomfortable; in no time you'll be inserting and deleting codes easily.

This chapter also includes a discussion of one of WordPerfect's most essential features, the Block command. With this command, you can mark a section of text (whether it's 1 character or 15 paragraphs in size) in order to perform an operation on just that block—such as deleting it. The review exercise that concludes the chapter will prove to you that after one short lesson, you have the skill to type and edit documents on your own

TYPE A DOCUMENT

One of the major timesaving features of a word processor happens automatically at the end of a line. With a typewriter, you slow down and listen for the sound of a bell at the end of every line so that you know when to press the carriage return. With WordPerfect, there's no need to slow down. When the cursor bumps up against the right margin as you type, a feature called *word wrap* takes over: the next word that would otherwise extend past the right margin is wrapped around to the left margin of the next line for you.

Where WordPerfect performs word wrap depends on how you wish the document to appear when printed. As discussed in "Getting Started," WordPerfect starts with the assumption that you desire 1-inch left and right margins. Another WordPerfect default setting is that you wish to print your text on standard-sized paper: 8.5 inches wide by 11 inches long. As a result, WordPerfect will wrap a word down to the next line when your cursor is approximately 7.5 inches from the left edge of the page (in other words, 1 inch from the right edge of the page).

Word wrap allows you to focus on your paragraphs rather than on the sound of a bell. You need to press the ENTER key only when you wish to do one of the following:

- End a paragraph

- End a short line of text

- Insert a blank line

To practice typing text, make sure you have started WordPerfect (as explained in "Getting Started") so that you are viewing the Typing screen. Follow the steps below to type a document regarding the fictitious R&R Wine Association. If you type a wrong character, remember that you can press BACKSPACE to erase it and then retype, just as described in "Getting Started." But don't worry too much about typing mistakes; you will learn various ways to edit your text soon. The final outcome of your typing is shown in Figure 1-1.

```
Two of the major wine-producing countries in Europe are France and
Italy.  France produces a wide variety, and Bordeaux is often
considered one of the centers of fine wine,  In Italy, wine
production takes place in just about every region,  Other countries
in Europe that produce wine include:

Spain
Germany
Portugal
Switzerland
Austria
Hungary
Greece


For more information on wine from all over Europe and the rest of
the world, CONTACT THE R&R WINE ASSOCIATION at (415) 444-1234,  Or,
write to us at the following address:

              R&R Wine Association
              3345 Whitmore Drive, #505
              San Francisco, CA  94123

  _                                  Doc 1 Pg 1 Ln 4.83" Pos 1"
```

FIGURE 1-1   Sample text to be typed

Note: As you are typing, you may notice that your words wrap differently than what is shown in Figure 1-1. This is a result of the variations in how different printers place characters on the page. Exactly where WordPerfect wraps a word depends on the printer you select to print out your WordPerfect documents. (Appendix B describes how you select a printer in WordPerfect.)

1. Type the following paragraph. Remember, do *not* press the ENTER key at all while typing the paragraph. Just keep typing, and watch word wrap go to work.

   Two of the major wine-producing countries in Europe are France and Italy. France produces a wide variety, and Bordeaux is often considered one of the centers of fine wine. In Italy, wine production takes place in just about every region. Other countries in Europe that produce wine include:

2. Press ENTER to end the paragraph and to move the cursor to the beginning of the next line.

3. Press ENTER to insert a blank line.

4. Type **Spain**.

5. Press ENTER to end the short line of text.

6. Type the following countries, making sure to press ENTER after each so that you type one country on each line:

   Germany
   Portugal
   Switzerland
   Austria
   Hungary
   Greece

   Your cursor should now be on a blank line below "Greece."

7. Press ENTER three times to insert three blank lines.

8. Type the following paragraph. Remember not to press the ENTER key within the paragraph; instead, let word wrap work for you. Also remember from "Getting Started" that the CAPS LOCK key is available for typing a group of words in uppercase letters. Also remember from "Getting Started" that you should type real ones and zeros, rather than o's and l's, when typing numbers.

For more information on wine from all over Europe and the rest of the world, CONTACT THE R&R WINE ASSOCIATION at (415) 444-1234. Or, write to us at the following address:

9. Press ENTER twice.

10. Press TAB three times. (Remember from "Getting Started" that each time you press TAB, the cursor jumps to the next tab stop, which is 0.5 inch to the right.)

11. Type **R&R Wine Association**.

12. Press ENTER.

13. Press TAB three times. Type **3345 Whitmore Drive, #505**.

14. Press ENTER.

15. Press TAB three times. Type **San Francisco, CA 94123**.

16. Press ENTER.

Congratulations to those of you who have just completed your very first WordPerfect document! You've probably noticed that word wrap has helped you type faster, whether you type 5 or 85 words per minute.

MOVE THE CURSOR BETWEEN WORDS AND LINES

On a standard-size monitor, you can see up to 24 lines of WordPerfect text on the screen at one time. (The 25th is occupied by the status line.) The document you just typed is 24 lines long, so with such a monitor you can see all of it at one time.

There are various methods for moving the cursor between words and lines. You learned in "Getting Started" that the LEFT and RIGHT ARROW keys move the cursor horizontally one character at a time. Similarly, the UP and DOWN ARROW keys move the cursor vertically one line at a time.

To move more quickly, press and hold down on any of the arrow keys and the key will repeat automatically. Also, if you press RIGHT or LEFT ARROW when the cursor is where you previously pressed the TAB key, the cursor will jump to the next or previous tab stop, respectively. Remember from "Getting Started," however, that the cursor can move only in that part of the screen where you've previously typed characters, pressed the SPACEBAR, or used the ENTER key.

1. Press and hold down the UP ARROW key and watch the cursor zoom up until it stops at the top of the document.

2. Press and hold down the RIGHT ARROW key for a few moments to watch the cursor speed to the right. When the cursor reaches the end of the first line of text, word wrap moves the cursor down to the beginning of the next line, and the cursor continues speeding along.

3. Use the LEFT ARROW key to position the cursor at the left margin (position "1").

4. Press and hold down the DOWN ARROW key until the cursor moves to the left margin of the line containing the address "3345 Whitmore Drive."

5. Press RIGHT ARROW three times. Since you pressed the TAB key before you began typing the address, the cursor jumps from tab stop to tab stop.

6. Press LEFT ARROW three times. The cursor hops between tab stops to the left margin.

There are also quick ways to move by combining the arrow keys with other keys. One key combination uses the CTRL key. When you hold down the CTRL key and press LEFT ARROW (denoted as CTRL + LEFT ARROW), the cursor moves to the first letter of the word to the left; CTRL + RIGHT ARROW moves the cursor to the first letter of the word to the right.

Another key combination uses the HOME key, which is located on the cursor movement/numeric keypad. Whenever a key combination involves the HOME key, you press the HOME key first, release it, and press the second key. To move to the left edge of the text, press the HOME key once, and then press the LEFT ARROW key once. This is denoted as HOME, LEFT ARROW. Similarly, HOME, RIGHT ARROW positions the cursor at the right end of the text. (When the line of text is no wider than the screen, the END key works just like HOME, RIGHT ARROW.)

Either HOME, UP ARROW or the MINUS key (−) on the cursor movement/numeric keypad moves the cursor to the top line of text on the screen. HOME, DOWN ARROW or the PLUS key (+) on the cursor movement/numeric keypad moves the cursor to the bottom line of visible text.

1. Press HOME, DOWN ARROW, or press PLUS. The cursor moves down to the bottom line on the screen.

2. Press HOME, UP ARROW, or press MINUS. The cursor moves to the top line.

3. Press CTRL + RIGHT ARROW. The cursor jumps one word to the right.

4. Press the CTRL key, and, while holding it down, press the RIGHT ARROW key five times. The cursor moves five more words to the right.

5. Press HOME, LEFT ARROW. The cursor moves to the left edge of the text on screen.

6. Press HOME, RIGHT ARROW, or press END. The cursor moves to the right edge of the text.

7. Press HOME, DOWN ARROW, or press PLUS. The cursor moves to the bottom of the screen.

DELETE CHARACTERS

Once you know how to control the location of the cursor, you are ready to edit your text. Editing text is easy with WordPerfect because your words appear on the computer screen rather than on a piece of paper. You don't have to reach for an eraser or whiteout when you want to fix a typing mistake. And you don't have to start typing all over again if you forget to include a paragraph or two at the top of the document. You just press certain keys on the keyboard and the text is changed right on the screen.

The BACKSPACE and DEL keys will erase text character by character; which one you use depends on where your cursor is located. As you've already learned, to erase a character you've just typed (and that is therefore just to the *left* of the cursor), use the BACKSPACE key. To erase a character *at* the cursor, press the DEL (delete) key. If you press and hold down on the BACKSPACE or DEL key, it will repeat automatically (just like the arrow keys), so that you can erase many characters in a row.

There are fast ways to delete entire words or groups of words. To erase one word, position the cursor anywhere within that word or on the empty space to its right and press CTRL + BACKSPACE. To erase all or part of a line of text, position the cursor on the first character closest to the left edge of the page that you wish to erase and press CTRL + END; this is referred to as "DELETE EOL (end of line)." For instance, position the cursor on the first character in a line and press CTRL + END to clear the entire line of text. To erase all or part of a page of text, position the cursor on the first character closest to the top of the page that you wish to erase and press CTRL + PGDN; this is referred to as "DELETE EOP (end of page)." For instance, position the cursor on the first character on a page and press CTRL + PGDN to clear the entire page of text.

There are also two options for deleting part of a word: to erase characters left of the cursor through the first letter of that word, press HOME, BACKSPACE; to erase characters right of the cursor to the next word, press HOME, DEL.

When you delete characters, word wrap adjusts the remaining text to fit properly inside the right margin boundary. If you delete several words from the text, you may need to *rewrite* the screen by pressing DOWN ARROW once or more than once to adjust the remaining paragraph within the margins.

Here's a chance to delete some characters, words, and lines in your text:

1. Position the cursor just to the right of the "3" in the ZIP code "94123" near the bottom of the screen. Press BACKSPACE five times. You have erased the ZIP code.

2. Press UP ARROW to position the cursor on the comma in ", #505". Press DEL six times to erase that string of characters.

3. Press HOME, LEFT ARROW once and then press UP ARROW as many times as necessary until the cursor is positioned on the "F" in "For more information." Now press CTRL + END. The entire line of text is erased.

4. If necessary, press CTRL + BACKSPACE to erase any additional words that precede the phrase "CONTACT THE R&R WINE ASSOCIATION."

5. Press DOWN ARROW once. The revised paragraph readjusts within the margins. The bottom of your document now reads as follows:

CONTACT THE R&R WINE ASSOCIATION at (415) 444-1234. Or, write to us at the following address:

R&R Wine Association
3345 Whitmore Drive
San Francisco, CA

RECOVER DELETED TEXT

Probably, you will one day erase a word, line, paragraph, or page accidentally. Fortunately, rather than retyping the text, you can use WordPerfect's *Undelete* feature to restore a previous deletion. A deletion is considered to be a group of text you erase before typing again or moving the cursor again in the document. For instance, suppose you press CTRL + END to delete a line; that's one deletion. Suppose you then resume typing and press DEL twice in a row; that's another deletion. And assume you move the cursor to the top of the document and press CTRL + BACKSPACE four times in a row; that's a third deletion. Any of your three most recent deletions can be restored with Undelete.

Undelete is accessed with the CANCEL (F1) key. You learned in "Getting Started" that if you inadvertently press a function key and then wish to clear the menu or prompt that appears, you can simply press the CANCEL (F1) key to clear the menu or prompt. When *no* menu or prompt appears on the screen, the CANCEL key controls the Undelete menu. The most recent deletion reappears in reverse video wherever the cursor is currently located, and a menu appears on the screen enabling you to either restore ("undelete") the text at the current cursor position or view a previous deletion. If, instead, you press CANCEL (F1) again, the Undelete menu clears. WordPerfect remembers your last three deletions until you leave WordPerfect using the EXIT (F7) key.

Let's delete and then undelete a line of text.

1. Position the cursor in the upper left corner of the screen on the "T" in "Two."

2. Press CTRL + END to erase that first line of text.

3. Press the CANCEL (F1) key. That most recent deletion reappears in reverse video, and the Undelete menu appears at the bottom of the screen, as shown in Figure 1-2. The selections are

   Undelete: 1 _Restore; 2 _Previous Deletion: 0

4. Select Previous Deletion (2 or P). Your next-to-last deletion now appears in reverse video.

5. Select Previous Deletion (2 or P). Your third-to-last deletion now appears in reverse video.

6. Select Previous Deletion (2 or P). Since WordPerfect remembers only your last three deletions, the line of text that you erased most recently reappears.

7. Select Restore (1 or R). The line is reinserted into the text at the current cursor position, and the menu clears.

```
Two of the major wine-producing countries in Europe are France and
Italy.  France produces a wide variety, and Bordeaux is often
considered one of the centers of fine wine.  In Italy, wine
production takes place in just about every region.  Other countries
in Europe that produce wine include:

Spain
Germany
Portugal
Switzerland
Austria
Hungary
Greece


CONTACT THE R&R WINE ASSOCIATION at (415) 444-1234.  Or, write to
us at the following address:

                    R&R Wine Association
                    3345 Whitmore Drive
                    San Francisco, CA


Undelete: 1 Restore; 2 Previous Deletion: 0
```

FIGURE 1-2   Undelete menu

INSERT CHARACTERS

WordPerfect is normally in *Insert mode*. This means that any character you type will be inserted at the current cursor position, and any text following that new character will move to the right to accommodate the insertion. Just as for a deletion, word wrap adjusts the text when you make an insertion so that your paragraph fits properly within the margins. If you insert many words, it may appear that your already-existing text is disappearing off the right edge of the screen, but that is not so. As soon as you press DOWN ARROW to rewrite the text on screen, word wrap will bring the "disappeared" words back into view, adjusting the paragraph within the margins.

An alternative way to insert characters is to switch to *Typeover mode*, where any new character you type will replace whatever character is currently located at the cursor. The INS (insert) key activates Typeover mode. Press it once and Typeover mode toggles on; the message **Typeover** appears on the status line. Press INS again and Typeover mode is turned off.

Let's add some text to the document to watch how the Insert and Typeover modes operate:

1. Position the cursor at the top left corner of the screen, on the "T" in "Two."

2. Type the following: **Fine wines are produced all over the world.** The text is inserted at the cursor.

3. Press the SPACEBAR twice to insert two spaces. It may appear that text has disappeared to the right.

4. Press DOWN ARROW. Word wrap rewrites the paragraph for you.

5. Position the cursor on the "O" of "Other" in the last sentence of the first paragraph.

6. Type the following:

   In fact, Italy has been known to yield more wine per year than any other country in the world. Though white wines are manufactured here, it is Italy's red wines that have achieved a special reputation.

7. Press the SPACEBAR twice to insert two spaces.

8. Press DOWN ARROW. Word wrap rewrites the paragraph for you.

9. Position the cursor on the "C" of "CONTACT," near the bottom of the screen.

10. Press INS one time and notice that **Typeover** appears in the left-hand corner on the status line. You have just toggled into Typeover mode.

11. Type **Contact**. Notice how, in Typeover mode, text is replaced character for character.

12. On the same line, position the cursor on the "1" of "1234" in the phone number.

13. Type **5678**. The old numbers are replaced.

14. Press INS one time to turn off Typeover mode. The message **Typeover** disappears from the status line.

After inserting characters, the screen should now resemble Figure 1-3.

Fine wines are produced all over the world. Two of the major wine-producing countries in Europe are France and Italy. France produces a wide variety, and Bordeaux is often considered one of the centers of fine wine. In Italy, wine production takes place in just about every region. In fact, Italy has been known to yield more wine per year than any other country in the world. Though white wines are manufactured here, it is Italy's red wines that have achieved a special reputation. Other countries in Europe that produce wine include:

Spain
Germany
Portugal
Switzerland
Austria
Hungary
Greece

Contact THE R&R WINE ASSOCIATION at (415) 444-5678._ Or, write to us at the following address:

R&R Wine Association

Doc 1 Pg 1 Ln 4.33" Pos 6"

FIGURE 1-3 Sample text after insertions

MOVE THE CURSOR BETWEEN SCREENS

Notice that after you have inserted additional sentences in your document, the address is no longer visible at the bottom of the screen. This is simply because your document is now longer than 24 lines. The text is still there, but not all of it can be viewed on screen at one time. All you need to do is move the cursor down until the additional text comes into view. This is referred to as *scrolling* down the screen.

Press and hold down the DOWN ARROW key; as you scroll down the screen, the address will come into view and the top lines of the document will disappear. You must grow accustomed to seeing only 24 lines of text at a time. Approximately two and a half screens of single-spaced text are equal to one printed page.

Now that your text can no longer fit on one screen, let's look at some quick ways to move the cursor. You learned previously that to move to the top of a screen, you press HOME, UP ARROW or the MINUS key (−) on the cursor movement/numeric keypad. To move to the next screen above, simply press HOME, UP ARROW or MINUS a second time. To move to the very top of the document, no matter how many screens above, press HOME, HOME, UP ARROW (that is, press HOME twice and then press UP ARROW). Similarly, press HOME, DOWN ARROW or the PLUS key (+) on the cursor movement/numeric keypad to move to the next screen below, and press HOME, HOME, DOWN ARROW to move to the bottom of the document.

1. With the cursor located at the bottom of the document, press HOME, UP ARROW. The cursor moves to the top of the screen.

2. Press HOME, UP ARROW again. The cursor scrolls up one full screen to the top of the document.

3. Press HOME, DOWN ARROW. Your cursor is now at the bottom of the screen.

4. Press HOME, DOWN ARROW again to scroll down a screen. Since only a few lines of the second screen are occupied, most of that screen is blank.

5. Press HOME, HOME, UP ARROW. The cursor is again at the top of the document.

You've now learned how to move the cursor quickly between words, lines, and screens. Methods for moving the cursor between pages and when lines are very long are discussed in Chapter 5.

REVEAL CODES

Hidden from view, codes were inserted as you typed the document now on screen. A code is a command telling the computer how text should be displayed on the screen, how it should be printed, or both. Codes are created whenever you press keys that determine how the text will appear. For instance, in "Getting Started," you learned that when you press the UNDERLINE (F8) key, a code is inserted in the text; you'll learn more about this Underline code in Chapter 3. As another example, when you press TAB, a **[Tab]** code is inserted at the cursor. Similarly, when you press ENTER, the code **[HRt]**, which stands for hard carriage return, is inserted. The carriage return is called "hard" because it will not disappear as text readjusts. One code that WordPerfect creates on its own is **[SRt]**, which is inserted whenever word wrap moves a word down to the left margin of a line. **[SRt]** stands for soft carriage return—"soft" because it will readjust as you insert or delete text. In WordPerfect, codes are represented as words or phrases enclosed in square brackets [ ].

The codes are hidden from you so as not to clutter the Typing screen. As you type, you need not be concerned with where codes are hiding. However, when you wish to change the appearance of your text on screen, understanding the location of codes becomes vital. You uncover codes with the REVEAL CODES (ALT + F3) key.

Note: If your computer is equipped with a keyboard containing 12 function keys, then you can reveal codes by pressing either ALT + F3 or, more simply, by pressing F11. Both are referred to as the REVEAL CODES key and produce the same effect.

The REVEAL CODES key splits the screen into two separate windows. The top window displays 11 lines of text just as it normally appears on the Typing screen—with codes hidden. The bottom window displays ten lines of text—with codes revealed. Separating the top and bottom windows is the status line as well as a *ruler line* (also called a tab ruler), a solid bar that displays the document's current margin and tab settings. You press the REVEAL CODES (ALT + F3) key a second time to clear the Reveal Codes screen, returning to the Typing screen.

When viewing the Reveal Codes screen, you can move the cursor by using the arrow keys, just as on the Typing screen, or by using any of the other cursor movement keys. For example, press HOME, UP ARROW to move the cursor up a screen (only ten lines at a time in the Reveal Codes screen), or press HOME, HOME, UP ARROW to move to the top of the document.

You can also insert or delete characters on the Reveal Codes screen just as if you were on the Typing screen. In fact, you can type a whole document with codes revealed (though the main advantage to revealing codes is when you wish to edit, rather than type, your document).

In addition, you can select features on the Reveal Codes screen just as you do on the Typing screen. But if you press a function key and a prompt or menu appears, the prompt or menu is displayed between the top and bottom windows on the Reveal Codes screen, instead of at the bottom of the screen.

Figure 1-4 shows how the Reveal Codes screen appears when the screen is clear of all text and codes and you press REVEAL CODES (ALT + F3). The cursor appears twice—once in each window. In the top window, it looks identical to the cursor on the Typing screen; in the bottom, it is represented as a highlighted block as tall as a standard

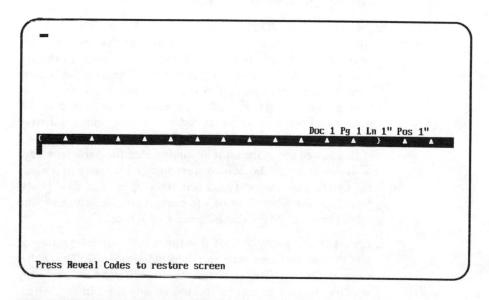

FIGURE 1-4   A clear Reveal Codes screen

character. The ruler line between the two windows contains triangles that represent tab stop locations, a left brace { that represents the left margin where a tab is also located, and a right brace } that represents the right margin where a tab stop is also located. From the ruler line you can see the defaults that were discussed previously: left margin of 1 inch from the left edge of the page, right margin of 1 inch from the right edge, and tab stops every 0.5 inch. Knowing how a blank Reveal Codes screen displays will help you orient yourself to seeing it when full of text.

Let's reveal codes on the document you just typed. Be warned that while the Typing screen is clutter free, the Reveal Codes screen can confuse the beginning WordPerfect user. All of a sudden your screen is split into two windows, with some of the same text repeated in both windows. All of a sudden, all sorts of strange codes are surrounding your text in the lower window. And all of a sudden, a thick ruler line is crossing the middle of the screen. But after examining text on the Reveal Codes screen, you will become comfortable with its appearance and quickly see how invaluable it is in controlling exactly how you want the text of a document to appear.

1. Press HOME, HOME, UP ARROW to position the cursor at the very top left corner of the document.

2. Press REVEAL CODES (ALT + F3). The Reveal Codes screen will appear as shown in Figure 1-5. Notice that your text appears twice, in both the top and bottom windows. In the top window, the cursor is under the "F" in "Fine"; in the bottom window, the cursor highlights the "F." Also notice that in the bottom window where codes are revealed each line of the paragraph ends with an [SRt] code, indicating that word wrap took effect at the end of every line in this paragraph. In addition, you can see in the bottom window that the paragraph ends with two [HRt] codes, which were inserted where you pressed the ENTER key as you typed this document. The first [HRt] ends the last, short line of the paragraph, while the second [HRt] creates a blank line between paragraphs.

3. Press DOWN ARROW at least five times and watch how the top and bottom windows start to move independently. This is because the cursor behaves differently in each window: in the top window, the cursor can be located on any line; in the bottom window, WordPerfect always maintains the cursor on the third

line (unless the cursor is on the first or second line in the document).

4. Press DOWN ARROW until the cursor is on the line just above the word "Spain," as shown in Figure 1-6. In the top window, it looks as if the cursor is on a blank line. But check the bottom window. The cursor is actually on an **[HRt]** code. When the cursor in the bottom window is on a code, that code becomes highlighted in reverse video. Notice also in the bottom window the short lines ending with **[HRt]** codes, which were inserted where you pressed ENTER.

5. Press HOME, HOME, DOWN ARROW so that the cursor moves to the bottom of the document. Notice that in the lower window you can view a string of three **[Tab]** codes on those lines where you pressed the TAB key three times before typing in R&R Wine Association's address. Those same lines end with **[HRt]** codes, where you pressed ENTER to end these short lines.

```
Fine wines are produced all over the world.  Two of the major
wine-producing countries in Europe are France and Italy.  France
produces a wide variety, and Bordeaux is often considered one of
the centers of fine wine.  In Italy, wine production takes place
in just about every region.  In fact, Italy has been known to yield
more wine per year than any other country in the world.  Though
white wines are manufactured here, it is Italy's red wines that
have achieved a special reputation.  Other countries in Europe that
produce wine include:

Spain
                                          Doc 1 Pg 1 Ln 1" Pos 1"
[   ▲   ▲   ▲   ▲   ▲   ▲   ▲   ▲   ▲   ▲   }   ▲   ▲
Fine wines are produced all over the world.  Two of the major[SRt]
wine-producing countries in Europe are France and Italy.  France[SRt]
produces a wide variety, and Bordeaux is often considered one of[SRt]
the centers of fine wine.  In Italy, wine production takes place[SRt]
in just about every region.  In fact, Italy has been known to yield[SRt]
more wine per year than any other country in the world.  Though[SRt]
white wines are manufactured here, it is Italy's red wines that[SRt]
have achieved a special reputation.  Other countries in Europe that[SRt]
produce wine include:[HRt]
[HRt]

Press Reveal Codes to restore screen
```

FIGURE 1-5   Reveal Codes screen at top of document with cursor highlighting a character

```
Fine wines are produced all over the world.  Two of the major
wine-producing countries in Europe are France and Italy.  France
produces a wide variety, and Bordeaux is often considered one of
the centers of fine wine.  In Italy, wine production takes place
in just about every region.  In fact, Italy has been known to yield
more wine per year than any other country in the world.  Though
white wines are manufactured here, it is Italy's red wines that
have achieved a special reputation.  Other countries in Europe that
produce wine include:

Spain
                                         Doc 1 Pg 1 Ln 2.5" Pos 1"
{   ▲    ▲    ▲    ▲    ▲    ▲    ▲    ▲    ▲    ▲    ▲    }  ▲    ▲
have achieved a special reputation.  Other countries in Europe that[SRt]
produce wine include:[HRt]
[HRt]
Spain[HRt]
Germany[HRt]
Portugal[HRt]
Switzerland[HRt]
Austria[HRt]
Hungary[HRt]
Greece[HRt]

Press Reveal Codes to restore screen
```

FIGURE 1-6   Reveal Codes screen with cursor highlighting a code

6. Press UP ARROW once and then repeatedly press RIGHT ARROW to watch the cursor in the bottom window as it moves past **[Tab]** codes and characters.

7. Press REVEAL CODES (ALT + F3) to again hide the codes from view. You undoubtedly can now appreciate the Typing screen; it hides all these distracting codes.

It will now appear as if most of your text has disappeared along with the codes. But remember, all you need to do is scroll up using the cursor movement keypad to again view the full text. Press HOME, HOME, UP ARROW, and the cursor returns to the top of the document.

INSERT CODES

You insert codes just as you insert characters when in Insert mode: position the cursor, then type. (Even when you've switched to Typeover mode by pressing INS, any codes you insert operate as if in Insert mode; codes will never replace text at the current cursor position on screen, nor will text replace codes. Typeover only operates if you wish to replace one character with another character.) Codes can be inserted either on the Typing screen or on the Reveal Codes screen. After codes are inserted, press DOWN ARROW so that the text readjusts to fit within the margin boundaries, just as when you insert text.

For example, suppose you wish to indent the first paragraph of your document. To do so, we will precede the paragraph with a Tab code, so that the paragraph is indented to the next tab stop, which is set by default as 0.5 inch from the left margin. It is better to use tabs rather than spaces to indent a paragraph because text may not always line up properly when printed if preceded by spaces. Let's indent the paragraph on the Typing screen.

1. Position the cursor at the top left corner of the document on the "F" in "Fine."

2. Press TAB once. A hidden **[Tab]** code is inserted.

3. Press DOWN ARROW to readjust the **[SRt]** codes and, thus, rewrite the text on screen.

Suppose you wish to separate the first paragraph into two separate ones. To do so, we will split the paragraph using the ENTER key. Let's do so on the Reveal Codes screen.

1. Position the cursor on the "I" at the start of the sentence that begins with "In Italy."

2. Press REVEAL CODES (ALT + F3) to view the Reveal Codes screen.

3. Press ENTER. An **[HRt]** is inserted at the cursor location, so the text that follows moves down to the next line. You see this code if you glance at the bottom window on screen.

4. Press ENTER again. Another **[HRt]** has been inserted, creating a blank line.

```
      Fine wines are produced all over the world.  Two of the major
wine-producing countries in Europe are France and Italy.  France
produces a wide variety, and Bordeaux is often considered one of
the centers of fine wine.

      In Italy, wine production takes place in just about every
region.  In fact, Italy has been known to yield more wine per year
than any other country in the world.  Though white wines are
manufactured here, it is Italy's red wines that have achieved a
special reputation.  Other countries in Europe that produce wine
include:

Spain
Germany
Portugal
Switzerland
Austria
Hungary
Greece


Contact THE R&R WINE ASSOCIATION at (415) 444-5678.  Or, write to
us at the following address:
                                           Doc 1 Pg 1 Ln 2" Pos 1.5"
```

FIGURE 1-7   Sample text after paragraphs re-formed

5. Press TAB. Now the second paragraph is indented.

6. Press DOWN ARROW to readjust the text.

7. Press REVEAL CODES (ALT + F3) to return to the Typing screen.

Figure 1-7 shows the results after splitting a large paragraph into two small paragraphs in the sample text.

DELETE CODES

There are two approaches to deleting codes. You can make the codes visible using the REVEAL CODES (ALT + F3) key and then delete as desired. When codes are revealed, the BACKSPACE key erases the character or code to the cursor's left, while the DEL key erases the character or code highlighted by the Reveal Codes cursor (the cursor in the bottom window on the Reveal Codes screen). Alternatively, you can delete a code on the Typing screen—if you know where the code is "hiding." Over time, you will be able to detect the location of many codes without needing to reveal them.

Suppose you wish to take the first two paragraphs and combine them back into one. You must delete the [Tab] and [HRt] codes just inserted. Let's do so on the Reveal Codes screen.

1. Position the cursor at the first letter of the second paragraph, which is the "I" at the start of the sentence "In Italy."

2. Press REVEAL CODES (ALT + F3). Notice in the bottom window that the cursor is just to the right of a [Tab] code.

3. Press BACKSPACE to erase the [Tab] code. Notice that the cursor is just below an [HRt] code. Because of the word wrap feature, the BACKSPACE key can wrap back up to the previous line and erase that code.

4. Press BACKSPACE to erase the [HRt] code.

5. Press BACKSPACE again to erase another [HRt] code. The paragraphs have been combined.

6. Press REVEAL CODES (ALT + F3) to return to the Typing screen.

Now you're probably starting to develop an intuitive sense of where codes are positioned in the text. Let's use that intuition to erase some codes on the Typing screen without revealing them first.

1. Position the cursor on the "C" in "Contact," near the bottom of the screen.

2. Realize that since the line above is blank, there must be an [HRt] code hidden there.

3. Press BACKSPACE. The line your cursor is on moves up as an [HRt] code is erased.

4. Position the cursor on the "F" in "Fine" at the very top of the document.

5. Realize that the line is indented because you inserted a [Tab] there.

6. Press BACKSPACE. The **[Tab]** is erased.

7. Press DOWN ARROW to see if WordPerfect needs to rewrite the text, adjusting it within the margins.

DELETE BLOCKS OF CHARACTERS AND CODES

WordPerfect provides speedy ways to erase a whole chunk of text at once, no matter what its content—characters, codes, or both—and no matter what its size—six words, six lines, or six paragraphs.

In WordPerfect, a chunk of text is referred to as a *block*. If that block is either a sentence ending with a period and a space, a paragraph ending with an **[HRt]** code, or a page ending with a page break (more on page breaks in Chapter 5), the deletion can be accomplished quickly with the MOVE (CTRL + F4) key. You can position the cursor anywhere within the sentence, paragraph, or page and press MOVE. WordPerfect prompts with the Move menu, and you can select that the block be a sentence, paragraph, or page. When you make a selection, WordPerfect highlights the block in reverse image and prompts

1 <u>M</u>ove; 2 <u>C</u>opy; 3 <u>D</u>elete: 4 <u>A</u>ppend: 0

Select Delete (3 or D) to erase the text (Chapter 6 discusses the Move and Copy options and Chapter 2 the Append option).

If the block is not a sentence, paragraph, or page, you must manually define for WordPerfect the block's contents and dimensions, using the BLOCK (ALT + F4) key. Position the cursor on the first character or code of the block you want to delete and press BLOCK (ALT + F4). The message **Block on** blinks in the left-hand corner on the status line, indicating that the Block feature is active. Also, the Pos number in the right-hand corner is displayed in reverse video. You then move the cursor, using the arrow keys, just past the last character or code of the block. WordPerfect highlights the block in reverse video. With the block defined, you may press either BACKSPACE or DEL. WordPerfect prompts you to verify the deletion before completing it. If the block you wish to delete is correctly highlighted, type **Y**.

Note: If your computer is equipped with a keyboard containing 12 function keys, you can access the Block command by pressing either ALT + F4 or, more simply, by pressing F12. Both are referred to as the BLOCK key and produce the same effect.

Suppose you wish to erase the first sentence of the document that is currently on your Typing screen. Here, the MOVE key is appropriate.

1. Position the cursor anywhere within the document's first sentence.

2. Press the MOVE (CTRL + F4) key. WordPerfect responds with the Move menu:

   Move: 1 Sentence; 2 Paragraph; 3 Page; 4 Retrieve: 0

3. Select Sentence (1 or S). WordPerfect highlights the sentence in reverse video, as shown in Figure 1-8, and prompts

   1 Move; 2 Copy; 3 Delete: 4 Append: 0

4. Select Delete (3 or D). Watch the sentence disappear.

5. Press DOWN ARROW to rewrite the text on screen.

Now suppose you wish to erase the last three countries from the list in the middle of the document. These three do not compose a sentence, paragraph, or page; therefore, you must use the BLOCK key to erase them all quickly in one command.

1. Position the cursor on the "A" in "Austria," the first character of the block.

2. Press BLOCK (ALT + F4). **Block on** flashes in the left-hand corner on the status line.

3. Press RIGHT ARROW until the cursor is just to the right of the lowercase "a." "Austria" is now highlighted.

4. Press DOWN ARROW twice to also highlight the last two countries listed. The screen will appear as shown in Figure 1-9.

5. Press DEL or BACKSPACE. WordPerfect responds with

   Delete Block? (Y/N) No

```
Fine wines are produced all over the world.  Two of the major
wine-producing countries in Europe are France and Italy.  France
produces a wide variety, and Bordeaux is often considered one of
the centers of fine wine.  In Italy, wine production takes place
in just about every region.  In fact, Italy has been known to yield
more wine per year than any other country in the world.  Though
white wines are manufactured here, it is Italy's red wines that
have achieved a special reputation.  Other countries in Europe that
produce wine include:

Spain
Germany
Portugal
Switzerland
Austria
Hungary
Greece


Contact THE R&R WINE ASSOCIATION at (415) 444-5678.  Or, write to
us at the following address:

            R&R Wine Association
            3345 Whitmore Drive
1 Move; 2 Copy; 3 Delete; 4 Append; 0
```

FIGURE 1-8   A highlighted sentence

```
Two of the major wine-producing countries in Europe are France and
Italy.  France produces a wide variety, and Bordeaux is often
considered one of the centers of fine wine.  In Italy, wine
production takes place in just about every region.  In fact, Italy
has been known to yield more wine per year than any other country
in the world.  Though white wines are manufactured here, it is
Italy's red wines that have achieved a special reputation.  Other
countries in Europe that produce wine include:

Spain
Germany
Portugal
Switzerland
Austria
Hungary
Greece


Contact THE R&R WINE ASSOCIATION at (415) 444-5678.  Or, write to
us at the following address:

            R&R Wine Association
            3345 Whitmore Drive
            San Francisco, CA
Block on                                Doc 1 Pg 1 Ln 3.5" Pos 1.6"
```

FIGURE 1-9   A highlighted block

6. Type **Y** to erase the block. The rest of the text moves up because, along with the text, you deleted **[HRt]** codes contained in the block.

HIGHLIGHT BLOCKS

In later chapters, you will find that it is often necessary to mark off blocks of text for purposes other than deletion. For example, you may wish to boldface a chunk of text, center it, or underline it. You will use the BLOCK key to mark that chunk. There are a variety of shortcuts to use when manually highlighting a block of text. You can use all four directional arrow keys—UP, DOWN, RIGHT, or LEFT ARROW—as shown in the preceding example, or you can use other cursor movement keys. You can also type the character or code that appears at the end boundary of the block. If you've highlighted too much text by accident, simply move the cursor in the opposite direction, or press CANCEL (F1) to erase all the highlighting and turn Block off.

Here's some practice in highlighting text and then removing the highlighting.

1. Position the cursor in the upper left corner of the screen, on the "T" in "Two."

2. Press BLOCK (ALT + F4). **Block on** flashes on the status line.

3. Type **.** (period). Notice that the first sentence is now highlighted.

4. Type **.** again. Now the first two sentences are highlighted.

5. Type **j**. WordPerfect highlights all the way up to and including the "j" in "just."

6. Press ENTER. WordPerfect highlights up to the end of the first paragraph, where an invisible **[HRt]** code is located.

7. Type **C** (in uppercase). WordPerfect highlights to the "C" in "Contact."

8. Press HOME, RIGHT ARROW, or press END. WordPerfect highlights to the end of the line.

9. Press UP ARROW several times and notice that WordPerfect removes the reverse video from the text as you move up.

10. Press the CANCEL (F1) key. The highlighting disappears, and Block is turned off.

You have not actually done anything to the text that you just highlighted; you just practiced with the Block command. Why become proficient at blocking a section of text? You will see in later chapters that it is often necessary to block a section of text in order to perform a specific operation on only that section—whether it's printing, underlining, or centering on the page. Therefore, the practice you just had will soon come in handy.

SAVE THE TEXT AND CLEAR THE SCREEN

So far, everything that you typed has been stored temporarily in RAM and displayed on the Typing screen. If the computer power shut off suddenly, you would lose the document you have just created; the only way to use the document again would be to retype it.

So that you can use this document later, let's save it on a disk. Remember from the explanation in "Getting Started" that a disk acts like your filing cabinet, storing documents for future use. Documents are saved on disk in separate files, each with a different *filename,* just as paper documents are saved in a filing cabinet in separate file folders. Let's save the document you just created and edited into a file with the name "SAMPLE." (In the chapter that follows, you will learn more about saving files on disk.) After the document is saved, we'll clear the screen. The EXIT (F7) key allows you to perform both tasks.

1. Press the EXIT (F7) key. WordPerfect responds with

   Save document? (Y/N) Yes

   Since the prompt ends with "Yes," WordPerfect is assuming you wish to save the text. That is correct.

2. Press the ENTER key (or type any key on the typewriter keypad other than **N**). WordPerfect responds with

   Document to be saved:

WordPerfect is requesting a filename.

3. Type **SAMPLE** (uppercase or lowercase letters make no difference), making sure not to press the SPACEBAR at all when
typing in the filename.

4. Press ENTER. WordPerfect indicates that the file is now being
saved. Then WordPerfect prompts

Exit WordPerfect? (Y/N) No

Since the prompt ends with "No," WordPerfect is assuming
you wish to remain in WordPerfect.

5. Press the ENTER key (or type **N** or any letter key other than **Y**)
to accept the suggestion.

Now the screen is clear. It seems as if you've just typed a document
that no longer exists. But in fact the document does exist—it is resid-
ing on disk. You'll see in the next chapter how quickly you can bring it
back to the screen anytime you wish.

REVIEW EXERCISE

So far you've learned quite a bit about typing and editing in Word-
Perfect. To make sure you're comfortable using the skills you've just
learned, follow the instructions below to create and edit a new document, a letter to Mr. Barrett Smith. Refer back to the information in
this chapter for guidance. The letter that you complete will be used in
Chapter 2 as you learn more about saving documents and printing
documents on paper.

1. Once the Typing screen is clear, type the letter shown in Figure
1-10. (*Hint:* Use the TAB key to indent the list of names and anniversary dates.)

2. Practice moving the cursor to specific locations in the document as quickly as possible using the arrow keys along with
the HOME and CTRL keys.

3. Edit the document as shown in Figure 1-11. (*Hint:* Use both
the Insert and Typeover modes for quick editing.)

4. Use the EXIT (F7) key to save this document under the filename LETTER.

5. If you're done for the day, exit WordPerfect by typing **Y** in response to the EXIT key prompt **Exit WP? (Y/N) No**. If, instead, you're ready to proceed to Chapter 2, just clear the Typing screen but remain in WordPerfect by pressing ENTER or typing **N** in response to that prompt.

```
February 3, 1989


Mr. Barrett Smith
FST Accounting
1801 S. Harmon Street
Oakland, CA  94130


Dear Mr. Smith:

     As you requested, here are a list of full-time employees who
elected to accept the new vacation option, along with their
anniversary dates with us.  There are only three employees who
chose the plan.  Please add their names to your record.

          Antonio Abbot        May 13th
          Lois Chang           April 27th
          Paul McClintock      August 7th

The new accrued vacation system should begin for these employees
immediately.


Sincerely,


Sandy Peterson
R&R Wine Association


P.S.  I've enclosed a copy of our quarterly newsletter for your
enjoyment.
```

FIGURE 1-10   Review exercise text

February 3, 1989

Mr. Barrett ^*P.* Smith
FST Accounting
1801 S. Harmon Street
Oakland, CA 94~~130~~ *413*

Dear ~~Mr. Smith:~~ *Barrett*

   As ~~you requested~~ *we discussed*, here ~~are~~ a ^*is* list of full-time employees who *complete* elected to accept the new vacation option, along with their anniversary dates with us. ~~There are only three employees who chose the plan~~. Please add their names to your record.

                Antonio Abbot   May ~~13th~~ *31st*
Tim Fingerman → Lois Chang   April 27th ← *May 20th*
                Paul McClintock   August 7th

The new accrued vacation system should begin for these employees immediately. *Thank you* ⊗

Sincerely,

Sandy Peterson ← *President*
R&R Wine Association

P.S.   I've ~~enclos~~ed *includ* a copy of our quarterly newsletter for your enjoyment.

FIGURE 1-11   Review exercise text to be edited

REVIEW

- Two of WordPerfect's default settings are for left and right margins of one inch. As you type, press the ENTER key only to end a paragraph or a short line of text or to insert a blank line. Otherwise, let word wrap automatically adjust text within the margin boundaries.

- The LEFT, RIGHT, UP, and DOWN ARROW keys move the cursor one character or line at a time. In addition, quick methods for moving the cursor are shown in Table 1-1.

- There is a variety of methods for deleting text, as shown in Table 1-2. Any of your last three deletions can be recovered using the CANCEL (F1) key.

- Insert mode is a WordPerfect default setting. Characters that you type will be inserted at the current cursor location, and existing text will move to accommodate the new characters. Word wrap will ensure that paragraphs are readjusted after an insertion.

- The INS key is a toggle that switches the Typing screen from Insert mode into Typeover mode. In Typeover mode, existing characters are replaced with new characters that you type. Press INS again to return to Insert mode.

- Codes are inserted as you type, determining how text will appear on screen and on the printed page. The codes are hidden from view, but the REVEAL CODES (ALT + F3) key switches you onto the Reveal Codes screen, enabling you to locate hidden codes.

- You can type and edit text either on the Typing screen or on the Reveal Codes screen. The advantage to inserting or deleting on the Reveal Codes screen is that you can view various codes as they are inserted or deleted.

- A large chunk of text, containing both characters and codes, can be deleted either using the MOVE key (for a sentence, paragraph, or page) or the BLOCK key. When using the BLOCK key, you must manually mark off the beginning and end of the block. You can mark the end of a block by using the cursor movement keys or by typing the character or code that appears at the end of the block.

Key Combination	Cursor Movement
CTRL + LEFT ARROW	First letter of word to the left
CTRL + RIGHT ARROW	First letter of word to the right
HOME, LEFT ARROW	Left edge of text on screen
HOME, RIGHT ARROW or END	Right edge of text on screen
HOME, UP ARROW, or MINUS	Top of screen (or, if cursor is at the top, the screen above)
HOME, DOWN ARROW, or PLUS	Bottom of screen (or, if cursor is at the bottom, the screen below)
HOME, HOME, UP ARROW	Top of document
HOME, HOME, DOWN ARROW	Bottom of document

TABLE 1-1   Cursor Movement Between Words, Lines, and Screens

Key Combination	Text Deleted
BACKSPACE	Character (or code) left of the cursor
DEL	Character (or code) at the cursor
CTRL + BACKSPACE	Word at the cursor
HOME, BACKSPACE	Characters left of cursor to word boundary
HOME, DEL	Characters right of cursor to word boundary
CTRL + END	Characters right of the cursor to line end (DELETE EOL)
CTRL + PGDN	Characters right of the cursor to page end (DELETE EOP)
MOVE (CTRL + F4)	Sentence, paragraph, or page
BLOCK (ALT + F4), DEL or BACKSPACE	Characters and codes in a marked block
CANCEL (F1)	Undo a previous deletion

TABLE 1-2   Deletion Options

2

RETRIEVING, SAVING, AND PRINTING

You have little to show for all your hard work in the last chapter: neither of the two documents you created is on screen, and neither has been printed. That is now going to change. In this chapter you will learn more about how to store files on disk and how to get a listing of the stored files. And you'll retrieve your documents back to the screen for review.

You'll also learn how to transform your words from glowing characters on a computer screen to printed characters on paper. In the pages that follow, you'll print your documents using several different methods. As you settle into using WordPerfect, you will probably learn to rely on only one or two of the five possible methods of printing. In this chapter you will also learn how to cancel a print job.

For those of you who recently purchased WordPerfect but have yet to define and select a printer, turn now to Appendix B, "Selecting Printers," before you read further.

LEARN ABOUT NAMING AND STORING FILES

In Chapter 1, you typed and then saved two documents for future use: the document with the filename SAMPLE and the review exercise document named LETTER. Both documents were placed in a file and stored in a specific place on a disk. Unless you specify otherwise, a file is stored in the default drive or directory, which you determined based on how you loaded WordPerfect. The default is drive B (denoted as **B:** or **B:**) for floppy disk users who followed the directions for loading in "Getting Started." The default is the directory called **\WPER\DATA** on the hard disk (denoted as **C:\WPER\DATA**) for hard disk users who installed WordPerfect according to Appendix A. (If you wish to save files to another place or to change the default drive or directory, refer to Chapter 8.) SAMPLE and LETTER were both stored in your default drive or directory.

As you work more and more with WordPerfect, you will save literally hundreds of files on disk for future use, each with a different filename. When you name files, you must abide by the following rules:

- A filename can contain from one to eight characters followed by an optional period and a one- to three-character extension.

- Acceptable characters in a filename and its optional extension include all letters and numbers and any of the following characters:

  ! @ # $ % & ( ) - { } ` ' ^ ~

- A filename cannot contain spaces.

The filenames SAMPLE and LETTER are acceptable filenames. Other acceptable filenames include

SAMPLE1	SAMPLE1.SWJ	SAMPLE1.01
BRADY#1	BRADY#1.LTR	BRADY(1).LTR
007	RPT007	RPT!.007

Examples of invalid filenames are

FIRSTSAMPLE	(Too many characters in filename)
SAMPLE.4232	(Too many characters in extension)
BOB SMIT	(Contains a blank space)
LETTER*.1	(Contains *, an unacceptable character in a
filename)	

Establishing an orderly naming system for files is essential for identifying documents easily. It is wise to develop a descriptive system based on the type of documents you create. An appropriate naming system if you type different types of documents might specify a document's type in its filename extension. For example, all correspondence could end with the extension .LET, standing for "letter," all reports could end with the extension .RPT, and so on. An alternative naming system if you share a hard disk with other users might indicate a document's author in its filename extension. For example, if your initials are MRM, you could assign .MRM as the extension for all documents you write; a document discussing the 1989 budget could be called BUD89.MRM. Or a document's author might be included as the first three letters of the filename, with no file extension used. For instance, the budget document could be named MRMBUD89. Whatever naming system you choose, be sure to plan now, before you accumulate too many files.

DISPLAY A LIST OF FILES

You can direct WordPerfect to display a complete list of files stored in a specific drive or directory by pressing the LIST FILES (F5) key and then pressing ENTER. An example of the List Files screen is shown in Figure 2-1. At the very top of the List Files screen, in the first line of the List Files header, WordPerfect lists the current date and time (provided that you properly entered the current date and time as described in "Getting Started" or that your computer is equipped with an internal clock) and the name of the drive and/or directory for which

```
02/09/89  13:59           Directory C:\WPER\DATA\*.*
Document size:       0   Free:  3911680   Used:   591942        Files:  39

. <CURRENT>    <DIR>                    .. <PARENT>    <DIR>
005     .CRG       993  02/16/88 23:41  1001     .CRG     48173  06/16/88 15:55
5008    .CRG      1312  07/22/88 02:08  5012     .CRG     35605  10/04/88 20:41
5020    .CRG     29573  10/04/88 20:42  88NNN    .RPT     21212  02/09/88 11:23
88NNN2  .RPT     35597  10/04/88 20:41  88NNN3   .RPT     35597  10/04/88 20:41
88RENT  .        43544  06/16/88 15:56  ACCOUNTS .        36762  02/21/88 15:41
BBS009  .1       21212  02/09/88 11:23  BBS009   .2        4751  02/09/88 12:45
BBS009  .3        2703  04/04/88 19:56  BKGROUND .88        778  02/23/88 13:28
BOOKKEEP.         1838  02/24/88 02:43  BUDMIN   .         1961  05/22/88 21:32
BUDMIN88.        28120  10/04/88 20:43  C2       .LTR      1551  02/09/89 11:05
CBS&RP  .         2666  02/18/88 10:59  CE01     .MMO       942  12/21/88 11:15
DOCLIS2 .MS       3241  10/04/88 20:40  DOCLIST1 .MS     40756  10/04/88 20:39
FON     .        28120  10/04/88 20:43  GAIN     .LTR      1598  02/09/89 11:05
J&B     .MMO      2317  09/16/88 20:36  JONES1   .MMO      1356  07/22/88 00:56
JONES2  .MMO      5936  02/11/88 01:01  LETTER   .          858  08/05/88 00:33
LINKER  .MS       1206  09/16/88 20:36  LINKER2  .        35597  10/04/88 20:40
MEYERS-1.MS       1206  09/16/88 20:36  P&L      .        35597  10/04/88 20:40
ROGERS  .LTR       714  02/15/88 03:21  SALVA    .         4537  09/16/88 20:37
SALVA:  .        29573  10/04/88 20:43 ▼ SAMPLE   .         1099  08/05/88 00:21

1 Retrieve; 2 Delete; 3 Move/Rename; 4 Print; 5 Text In;
6 Look; 7 Other Directory; 8 Copy; 9 Word Search; N Name Search: 6
```

FIGURE 2-1   List Files screen

files are listed. For example, **C:\WPER\DATA*.*** in Figure 2-1 indicates that the files listed are from the directory \WPER\DATA in drive C, the hard disk. As another example, **B:*.*** would indicate that the files listed are those in drive B, the default for floppy disk users. (The notation *.* means that WordPerfect will display all files in the default drive/directory, no matter what their filenames or extensions.) The second line of the header provides the following information:

- *Document size*   This is the size of the document on the Typing screen when you first pressed the LIST FILES key. For instance, if the Typing screen was clear when you pressed LIST FILES, then the document size will read 0 (as shown in Figure 2-1). If the Typing screen contained text, then WordPerfect reports the size of the text on screen in *bytes,* a computer term of measurement equal to a number, letter, space, or piece of punctuation. For comparison purposes, keep in mind that approximately 1500 to 2000 bytes equals one double-spaced page of text.

- *Free*   This is the amount of free space still available to store files on the floppy or hard disk. This is also measured in bytes.

- *Used*   This is the amount of space occupied by files on the floppy disk or on the directory of your hard disk, also measured in bytes.

- *Files*   This is the total number of files on the floppy disk or in the directory of your hard disk.

Below the List Files header, filenames are displayed in two columns and are alphabetized row by row. Filenames that begin with numbers are listed first, followed by filenames that begin with letters, and then by filenames that begin with symbols. Notice in Figure 2-1 that you can see an alphabetized list of files, two of which are SAMPLE and LETTER.

Only 36 filenames can be displayed at one time on the List Files screen. If there are more than 36 files in the drive/directory, then an arrow appears at the bottom of the screen between the two columns (as shown in Figure 2-1). You must then use the arrow keys or the other cursor movement keys to scroll the cursor down to the filenames on the screen below. On the List Files screen, the cursor covers the full width of one column.

Next to each document's filename, the List Files screen provides other useful information. The number just to the right of each filename indicates its size, again in bytes. Notice in Figure 2-1, for example, that the size of both SAMPLE (1099 bytes) and LETTER (850 bytes) indicates that the text of each fills up less than a full page. Word-Perfect also lists next to each file the date and the time that the file was last saved to disk. By glancing at a file's date and time, you can tell when you or someone else made the most recent typing and editing changes to that document.

At the bottom of the List Files screen is a menu of options for managing files. Three of the options—Retrieve (1 or R), Print (4 or P), and Look (6 or L)—are described later in this chapter. Additional file-management capabilities are described in Chapter 8.

You can clear the List Files menu and return to the Typing screen at any time using the CANCEL (F1) key—the same way you back out of any command where WordPerfect displays a menu or prompt.

Here's how to list the files in your default drive or directory and move the cursor on the List Files screen:

1. Press the LIST FILES (F5) key. WordPerfect lists your default drive or directory. Floppy disk users should see

   Dir B:*.*

For hard disk users whose default directory is WPER\DATA\, the prompt reads

DIR C:\WPER\DATA*.*

2. Press ENTER. In moments, a list of files in the default drive is displayed on the screen. The cursor is a full column in width and is positioned on the phrase "<CURRENT> <DIR>."

3. Press DOWN ARROW. The cursor moves down to the first file listed in the first column.

4. Press RIGHT ARROW. The cursor moves to the first file listed in the second column.

5. Press and hold down the DOWN ARROW key until the cursor reaches the last file in column two. (There may be only two files—LETTER and SAMPLE—on your List Files screen, so that the cursor can move down no further.)

6. Press HOME, UP ARROW. The cursor moves up to the file listed in the upper left corner on screen. If you have already stored many files in this drive or directory, it may be necessary to continue pressing HOME, UP ARROW until the cursor is back to the very top, on the phrase "<CURRENT> <DIR>."

7. Press the CANCEL (F1) key. The List Files screen disappears.

You can also list files in a drive or directory other than the default. Press the LIST FILES (F5) key, and when WordPerfect suggests the default, type in another drive or directory before pressing ENTER. For instance, if you are a hard disk user and wish to view a list of files on the floppy disk in drive A, press LIST FILES (F5) and, when Word-Perfect prompts you with

Dir C:\WPER\DATA*.*

type the drive letter followed by a colon, writing over the prompt in order to edit it. Type A:. (There's no need to type A:*.* because, unless you specify otherwise, WordPerfect assumes you wish to list every file in that drive.) Now the prompt reads

Dir A:

Press ENTER. The List Files screen now displays a list of files on the floppy disk in drive A.

As another example, suppose you wish to view a list of files in a directory named \WPER\SUE. Press LIST FILES (F5) and, when WordPerfect prompts you with

Dir C:\WPER\DATA*.*

edit the prompt to read

Dir C:\WPER\SUE*.*

(Or you can edit the prompt to read DIR C:\WPER\SUE.) Press ENTER. The List Files screen now displays a list of the files in that directory.

RETRIEVE A DOCUMENT TO THE SCREEN

In order to review or edit a document stored on disk, you must retrieve that document file to the screen. What you retrieve is actually a copy of the file: the original version remains stored safely on the disk. Therefore, if you retrieve a document for review, but make no editing changes to the document, you can simply clear the screen when you are finished reviewing it.

It is critical that before retrieving a document, you make sure that the Typing screen contains no other document. This is trickier than you may think. Many WordPerfect users have accidentally combined documents on screen because the Typing screen wasn't truly blank. While the screen may look clear, a document may be on screen but not in view until you press the UP ARROW key to scroll up to the text. When a Typing screen is completely void of text and codes, the cursor does not move when you press any of the arrow keys, and the status line reports that the cursor is at Pg 1 Ln 1" Pos 1".

What happens if the Typing screen is not clear when you retrieve a document? WordPerfect inserts the contents of a retrieved file wherever the cursor is located. For instance, suppose you typed three paragraphs of text. With your cursor below the third paragraph, if you retrieve a file, the contents of that file will be added onto the end of the three paragraphs. So unless you want to combine text from dif-

You can retrieve a file in one of two ways: with the RETRIEVE (SHIFT + F10) key or with the LIST FILES (F5) key. Using the RE-TRIEVE key is swift and easy, provided that you remember the name of the file you wish to retrieve. On a clear Typing screen, press the RETRIEVE (SHIFT + F10) key, type in the document's full name (including a period and its extension if it has one), and press ENTER. WordPerfect checks the default drive or directory for that file and recalls a copy of its contents onto the Typing screen. Should Word-Perfect be unable to locate that file on disk, it responds

ERROR: File not found

If you made a typing mistake, you now have the opportunity to retype or edit the filename you just typed and press ENTER to retrieve the correct file. If the wrong floppy disk is in the default drive, then you can insert the correct disk and press ENTER. Or, if you wish to back out of the Retrieve command, press CANCEL (F1).

When using the RETRIEVE key, there may be times that you wish to retrieve a file from other than the default drive or directory. In that case, you must precede the document's filename with the drive or directory where WordPerfect will find the file. For instance, suppose that your default directory is \WPER\DATA, but that the file named SAMPLE is stored in the directory on the hard disk named \WPER\SUE. After pressing the RETRIEVE key, you would type **C:\WPER\SUE\SAMPLE** and press ENTER. Or suppose that the file named SAMPLE is stored on drive A. After pressing the RETRIEVE key, you would type **A:\SAMPLE** (or more simply, **A:SAMPLE**) and press ENTER. (See Chapter 8 for more on altering the default drive/directory.)

Using the LIST FILES key to retrieve files is handy if you have forgotten the document's filename (a likely occurrence once you've accumulated numerous files on your disk), or if you are a slow typist and prefer to use the cursor rather than typing in a filename. On a clear Typing screen, use the LIST FILES (F5) key to list the files in the correct drive or directory. Next, position the cursor on the file to be retrieved. Finally, select Retrieve (1 or R) from the menu of options at the bottom of the List Files screen. A copy of the file's contents appears on the Typing screen.

Suppose you wish to review a document and you know that its filename is SAMPLE. Proceed as follows:

1. The screen should be completely clear. If not, clear the screen by pressing the EXIT (F7) key and then typing **N** twice.

2. Press the RETRIEVE (SHIFT + F10) key. WordPerfect responds with

   Document to be retrieved:

3. Type **SAMPLE** (uppercase or lowercase makes no difference) and then press ENTER. WordPerfect checks the default drive or directory for a file named SAMPLE. In seconds, a copy of that file appears on the screen for you to read and/or edit.

Suppose after reading through the file named SAMPLE, you wish to retrieve another file, whose filename you forgot. Let's clear the screen and then retrieve that other file.

1. Press the EXIT (F7) key.

2. Since the file named SAMPLE is still safely on disk and you did not revise it on screen, you don't need to save it again. In fact, you'll see the message (**Text was not modified**) in the lower right corner of the status line, verifying that the version on screen is identical to the version on disk. Simply type **N** twice to clear the screen.

3. Press the LIST FILES (F5) key.

4. Press ENTER. The List Files menu appears, showing the names of files in your default drive or directory.

5. Use the cursor movement keys to position the cursor on the filename LETTER.

6. Select Retrieve (1 or R). In seconds, a copy of the file is retrieved to the screen.

You'll find that whenever you retrieve to the screen a document previously saved to disk, the drive or directory location where it is stored, followed by its filename, is listed in the lower left corner of the status line. For instance, if you use a floppy disk system and LETTER has been stored on the disk in drive B, when you retrieve that file, the lower left corner of the status line reads

B:\LETTER

A hard disk user whose default directory is \WPER\DATA will see

C:\WPER\DATA\LETTER

This information helps remind you of the name of the file you are working on. (Should you find the filename distracting when listed on the status line, you can ask WordPerfect to hide the filename. See the information under the heading "Display" in Appendix C.)

LOOK AT THE CONTENTS OF A FILE

You've learned that the Retrieve feature is used when you wish to recall a file to the screen for review or editing. WordPerfect offers a related feature, the Look feature, whereby you can review (but not edit) the contents of a file *without actually recalling the text to the screen*. Look is handy when you don't wish to disrupt the text currently on the Typing screen but want to take a quick glance at the contents of another document.

You initiate the Look feature from the List Files screen by positioning the cursor on the file you wish to take a peek at and then either selecting Look (6 or L) or pressing the ENTER key. (Pressing the ENTER key is the alternative because, as shown in Figure 2-1, the assumed menu option—at the end of the List Files menu at the bottom of the screen—is number 6, Look.) You can then use the up and down cursor keys to scroll through the document on the Look screen. The cursor keys that ordinarily position the cursor left and right do not operate on the Look screen because the Look feature allows you only to read the text, not to edit it. Press CANCEL (F1) or EXIT (F7) when you wish to return to the List Files screen.

Let's take a glance at the file named SAMPLE, even though the file named LETTER is currently on screen.

1. Press the LIST FILES (F5) key.

2. Press ENTER. The List Files menu appears, showing the names of files in your default drive or directory.

3. Position the cursor on the filename SAMPLE.

4. Press ENTER. Or select Look (6 or L). A Look screen appears, displaying the contents of the file named SAMPLE, as shown in Figure 2-2. Notice the header at the top of the screen indicating the filename and the file size. Below the header, WordPerfect displays the text of that file.

5. Use the keys that position the cursor up and down (UP ARROW, DOWN ARROW, MINUS, and PLUS on the cursor movement keypad) and watch as you move to different lines in the file.

```
Filename C:\WPER\DATA\SAMPLE                    File size:      1099

Two of the major wine-producing countries in Europe are France and
Italy.  France produces a wide variety, and Bordeaux is often
considered one of the centers of fine wine.  In Italy, wine
production takes place in just about every region.  In fact, Italy
has been known to yield more wine per year than any other country
in the world.  Though white wines are manufactured here, it is
Italy's red wines that have achieved a special reputation.  Other
countries in Europe that produce wine include:

Spain
Germany
Portugal
Switzerland



Contact THE R&R WINE ASSOCIATION at (415) 444-5678.  Or, write to
us at the following address:

              R&R Wine Association
              3345 Whitmore Drive

Press Exit when done                    (Use Cursor Keys for more text)
```

FIGURE 2-2   Look screen showing the contents of the file named SAMPLE

6. Press CANCEL (F1) twice—once to exit the Look screen and a second time to exit the List Files screen. You are returned to the Typing screen. Notice that the text on screen has been un-affected by your having looked quickly at the contents of another file.

SAVE A DOCUMENT AT REGULAR INTERVALS

After you've retrieved a document to screen and revised it, you must remember to save it again if you want to keep a copy of the revised document. As in retrieving, there are two methods for saving a document to disk, one using the EXIT (F7) key and the other using the SAVE (F10) key.

Use the EXIT (F7) key if you wish to save the document and you've finished working with it for the moment; using this key allows you either to start something new or to end your WordPerfect session. (In Chapter 1, you were introduced to this method for saving files.) When you press the EXIT (F7) key, WordPerfect responds with

Save document? (Y/N) Yes

When you press ENTER or type any key other than **N** to save the document, WordPerfect prompts

Document to be saved:

After you type in a filename and press ENTER, the document is saved on disk, and WordPerfect prompts

Exit WP? (Y/N) No   **(Cancel to return to document)**

Type **Y** to exit WordPerfect, or press ENTER or type any key other than **Y** to clear the screen and remain in WordPerfect. Either way, you will exit the document. If you decide instead to return to the document after saving it, you should press the CANCEL (F1) key when you see the **Exit WP?** prompt as suggested on the right side of the prompt.

Use the SAVE (F10) key if you wish to save the document in its present form and continue working on it. Why save a document to disk before you're done? Remember that every word you type is temporarily stored in RAM: unless you save your text to a disk, it will disappear forever as soon as you clear the screen or should you experience a power failure. Just imagine having typed and edited a ten-page document for four hours, only to have the electricity go off with just one more paragraph to go. If you haven't saved any part of that document to disk, you'll have lost a full four hours of work! On the other hand, if you saved your work 15 minutes before the blackout, you'll have lost only your last 15 minutes of work.

Thus, as you begin to spend long hours typing and editing documents, you should acquire the habit of saving documents to disk at regular intervals of 15 to 30 minutes—not just when you have finished typing or editing them. Because the SAVE key automatically returns you to your document after storing it on disk, using the SAVE key is a quick and easy way to periodically safeguard against losing your new text.

When you press the SAVE (F10) key, there are fewer prompts to contend with than when using the EXIT (F7) key. WordPerfect will simply respond with

Document to be saved:

You should type in a filename and press ENTER. The document is saved on disk; at the same time, it remains on screen.

After the first time you store a document on disk, WordPerfect knows the document by its filename; every time thereafter that you begin to save the same document—whether using the SAVE (F10) key or the EXIT (F7) key—WordPerfect suggests the known name. If you press ENTER to accept the known name, WordPerfect requests verification to replace the file stored on disk with the current version shown on screen, in which case you'll store on disk just one copy of a document, the most current version. If you instead type in a new filename, the current version will be stored as a separate file with that new filename, and the earlier version will remain unchanged.

Note: You have the ability in WordPerfect to change the way in which documents are saved. Using the Fast Save option, you can speed up the time it takes WordPerfect to store your text. The tradeoff, however, is that the Fast Save option restricts how you can print your documents. Refer to the "Fast Save" section of Appendix C for more on this option.

Pretend that you've just spent 20 minutes revising the letter now on screen. Let's again save the document under the filename LETTER to safeguard against a power failure and then leave the document on screen for further editing.

1. Press the SAVE (F10) key. WordPerfect assumes you wish to save the file under the known name, so it responds with that name. For floppy disk users, the prompt reads

   Document to be saved: B:\LETTER

   For hard disk users, the prompt reads

   Document to be saved: C:\WPER\DATA\LETTER

2. Press ENTER to accept the suggestion. WordPerfect prompts for verification that you wish to replace the original screen file with the current screen version. For floppy disk users, the prompt reads

   Replace B:\LETTER? (Y/N) No

   The prompt ends with **No** because WordPerfect assumes that you wish *not* to replace the old version—to be as conservative as possible so that you don't inadvertently overwrite a file.

3. Type **Y**. WordPerfect saves the file on disk, replacing the old file with the current version of the letter, while displaying a message that, for floppy disk users, reads

   Saving B:\LETTER

Now you can continue editing, knowing that if the power goes out, you'll be able to retrieve this file to the screen when the power comes back on and have lost none of your revisions.

Religiously save files to disk every 15 to 30 minutes and you will avoid disaster. If you think you won't remember to save to disk that often, give WordPerfect the responsibility. WordPerfect has an automatic backup option that saves the file on screen into a temporary file at regular intervals. You activate this option when you load WordPerfect. To learn how to set up timed backup, refer to the section entitled "Backup" in Appendix C.

SAVE A PORTION OF A DOCUMENT

Sometimes you may wish to save to disk just a portion of what's on the screen. With WordPerfect, you can save a block of text into a separate file, referred to as a Block Save, or to the tail end of a file already existing on disk, referred to as a Block Append.

A Block Save is useful when you've typed text on screen as part of a document and realize that you wish to save that text separately. For instance, you may wish to store a paragraph into its own file so that it can later be used independently from the rest of the letter. First use the BLOCK (ALT + F4) key to highlight the portion of text you wish to save. The message **Block on** is displayed, flashing at the bottom of the screen. When you press the SAVE (F10) key, a special prompt appears:

Block name:

WordPerfect is requesting a filename to save this text under. Type in a filename and press ENTER. If a file by that name already exists, WordPerfect will ask whether you wish to replace the existing file. Type **Y** to replace the old version on disk, or type **N** and enter in a different filename.

Block Append comes in handy if you have text, such as a paragraph, typed on screen that you want to add as text in a file already stored on disk. You first use the BLOCK (ALT + F4) key to highlight the portion of text you wish to append. The message **Block on** flashes on the status line. Next, press the MOVE (CTRL + F4) key, and WordPerfect prompts with the Move menu:

Move: 1 Block; **2** Tabular Column; **3** Rectangle: **0**

Select Block (1 or B). (See Chapter 6 for a discussion of tabular columns and rectangles, the second and third options on the Move menu.) WordPerfect highlights the block in reverse video and prompts

1 Move; **2** Copy; **3** Delete; **4** Append: **0**

If you select the Append option (4 or A), WordPerfect prompts

Append to:

Type in the name of the existing file and press ENTER; the text is attached to that file (or, if WordPerfect cannot locate that file, a new file by that name is created). At the same time, the text remains on screen.

Currently on your monitor screen is a letter addressed to Mr. Barrett P. Smith. Suppose that you frequently use Mr. Smith's name and address when typing letters or documents. You may wish to save his name and address in a separate file so that in the future you won't have to retype them. Use the Block Save feature as follows:

1. Position the cursor on the "M" in "Mr. Barrett P. Smith," near the top left corner of the document on the screen.

2. Press the BLOCK (ALT + F4) key. The message **Block on** appears on the status line.

3. Press DOWN ARROW four times. The inside address is highlighted, as shown in Figure 2-3.

February 3, 1989

Mr. Barrett P. Smith
FST Accounting
1801 S. Harmon Street
Oakland, CA 94413

Dear Barrett:

        As we discussed, here is a complete list of full-time
employees who elected to accept the new vacation option, along
with their anniversary dates with us. Please add their names to
your record.

                Antonio Abbot   May 31st
                Lois Chang   April 27th
                Tim Fingerman   May 28th
                Paul McClintock   August 7th

The new accrued vacation system should begin for these employees
immediately. Thank you.
Block on   Doc 1 Pg 1 Ln 2.33" Pos 1▊

FIGURE 2-3   A highlighted block to be saved into its own file

4. Press the SAVE (F10) key. WordPerfect responds with

Block name:

5. Type **SMITH.ADD** (a name that reminds you that this file will contain Mr. Smith's address) and press ENTER. WordPerfect saves the block independently under that filename.

Nothing on the screen has changed. And yet, you've also created a new, separate file on disk that contains only Smith's name and address.

PRINT FROM THE SCREEN

Once you've typed and edited a document so that it says exactly what you want it to, you will want not only to save that document but to print it on paper as well.

When you print a document, WordPerfect must know what type of printer you are using. Is it an IBM Proprinter? An Epson LQ-1000? A Diablo 630? In addition, the program must know what type of paper you are using. Will you feed single sheets manually? Do you have a sheet feeder that feeds single sheets for you? Are you using continuous-feed paper (a long stack of paper separated by perforations)? The following discussions on printing assume that you have already defined and selected your printer(s) for WordPerfect as described in Appendix B. You can tell whether or not a printer has previously been selected by pressing the PRINT (SHIFT + F7) key and then checking the column to the right of the Select Printer option. If a printer is listed in the second column—for example, the HP LaserJet Series II is shown in Figure 2-4—then one has previously been selected and you can read on. If no printer is listed, then turn to Appendix B before you read further.

When a document is already on screen, printing it is quick and easy. To print the entire document or just one page, press the PRINT (SHIFT + F7) key. A full screen menu appears, as shown in Figure 2-4 (with the HP LaserJet Series II as the selected printer). Select Full Document (1 or F) to print the entire document or select Page (2 or P) to print only the page on which the cursor is located. If the document is only one page long, as is the case for the document currently on your screen, then these two selections are identical.

You can also print a block of text—perhaps just one paragraph from a screenful of text. First, press the BLOCK (ALT + F4) key and highlight the block. With Block on, press the PRINT (SHIFT + F7) key. Now instead of displaying the Print screen, WordPerfect prompts

Print block? (Y/N) No

Type **Y** to print the block; type **N** or press ENTER to abort the print.

For sheet-feeder and continuous-paper users, when the paper is present in the printer the printing will begin immediately. If the paper is not initially in the printer or your printer has been defined for manually fed paper, the computer pauses and sounds a beep, indicating that it is waiting for a signal that you have placed a fresh piece of paper in the printer. To give it that signal, press the PRINT (SHIFT + F7) key again, select Control Printer (4 or C), and then select Go (Start Printer) (4 or G). (For more information on the Control Printer screen see the last section of this chapter.) Continue to insert a new sheet of paper and select Go for each page to be printed. Then press CANCEL (F1) to return to the Typing screen.

```
Print

     1 - Full Document
     2 - Page
     3 - Document on Disk
     4 - Control Printer
     5 - Type Through
     6 - View Document
     7 - Initialize Printer

Options

     S - Select Printer          HP LaserJet Series II
     B - Binding                 0"
     N - Number of Copies        1
     G - Graphics Quality        Medium
     T - Text Quality            High




Selection: 0
```

FIGURE 2-4   Print screen

Here's some practice printing the document that is currently on the screen.

1. Turn your printer on and insert paper. Sheet-feeder users should place a stack of sheets into the feeder. Continuous-feed users should insert the paper and line up the top of one sheet (at the perforation) with the printhead (the mechanism that creates the characters on paper). Manual-feed users should insert a sheet of paper and roll it up just above the printhead.

2. Press the PRINT (SHIFT + F7) key. The Print screen appears, as shown in Figure 2-4.

3. Select Full Document (1 or F). Alternatively, you can instead select Page (2 or P).

4. The printing should begin. If, however, WordPerfect sounds a beep, your printer has been defined for hand-fed paper or with the paper not initially present.

Manual-feed-paper users should then proceed as follows:

1. Press the PRINT (SHIFT + F7) key.

2. Select Control Printer (4 or C).

3. Select Go (4 or G), and the printing begins.

4. Press the CANCEL (F1) key to clear the Control Printer screen and return to your document.

Note: Your printer may fail to print for reasons having nothing to do with the insertion of paper. If your printer refuses to print, refer to the "Control Print Jobs" section further on in this chapter to learn how to uncover problems and correct them.

Now let's print only the list of names and dates found in the middle of the letter (that is, print a block of text from the screen):

1. Make sure that the printer is turned on and paper is inserted.

2. Position the cursor at the left margin of the line that reads "Antonio Abbot...."

3. Press the BLOCK (ALT + F4) key.

4. Press DOWN ARROW four times. All four names are highlighted.

5. Press the PRINT (SHIFT + F7) key. WordPerfect prompts

   Print Block? (Y/N) No

6. Type **Y** to print the block.

7. The printing should begin. If, instead, WordPerfect sounds a beep, your printer has been defined for manual-feed paper or as not initially present. In that case, follow the procedure for manual-feed paper as described previously.

Printing all or part of a document directly from the screen is handy, especially because you will most often want to print a document when you've finished editing it and the document is still on screen. In fact, you'll probably find yourself printing in this way more times than not.

Printing from the screen is also versatile. You can print text without ever saving it to disk. For instance, perhaps you want to type and distribute a short memo. If you will have no future use for this memo, don't bother storing it on disk where it will occupy space. Just type the letter, print it from the screen, and then clear the screen. You've produced the memo, and you haven't taken up valuable storage space.

PRINT A FILE FROM DISK

In addition to printing the document on screen, you can print a document directly from disk, which is convenient when you wish to print a long document that isn't on screen or when you have many documents to print. Rather than retrieving and printing each one in turn, print directly from the disk. It makes no difference whether the Typing screen is clear or contains a document. There are two methods for printing from disk: using the Print screen, which is convenient when you remember a document's filename, or using the List Files screen, which is effective if you can't remember a document's filename or are a slow typist.

To print from disk using the Print screen, press the PRINT (SHIFT + F7) key and, from the menu illustrated in Figure 2-4, select Document on Disk (3 or D). WordPerfect prompts

Document name:

Type in the file's name, including a period and the extension if that file has one, and press ENTER. Next, WordPerfect wants to know how many pages of the document you wish to print, prompting with

Page(s): (All)

WordPerfect assumes that you wish to print the entire document. You have four alternatives:

- Press ENTER to print the entire document (all pages).

- Type in any page number and press ENTER to print that specific page.

- Type in page numbers joined by a hyphen (no spaces) and press ENTER to print a range of consecutive pages.

- Type in numbers separated by commas and press ENTER to print nonconsecutive pages.

For instance, to print pages 5 through 10, type **5-10**. To print pages 1 through 5, type **1-5** or **-5** (page 1 is assumed). To print pages 14 through the end of the document, type **14-** (the last page is assumed). To print pages 5 and 9, type **5,9**. And you can even combine hyphens and commas in the same command: to print pages 5 through 10 and page 20, type **5-10,20**.

The printing begins immediately, except when paper is manually fed or defined as not initially present, in which case you must follow the previously outlined procedure for printing with manually fed paper.

To print from disk using the List Files screen, press the LIST FILES (F5) key and press ENTER to display a list of files. Next, position the cursor on the file to be printed and select Print (4 or P) from the menu of options at the bottom of the screen. WordPerfect prompts

Page(s): (All)

With the List Files screen, you have the same four options for indicating which pages you wish to print as you do when using the Print menu's Document on Disk option. Indicate the pages you wish to print and press ENTER. Press CANCEL (F1) to return to the Typing screen.

Let's print the file named SAMPLE. It doesn't matter that another file is currently on the Typing screen since you'll be printing directly from disk.

1. Make sure that the printer is turned on and paper has been inserted.

2. Press the PRINT (SHIFT + F7) key. WordPerfect responds with the Print screen.

3. Select Document on Disk (3 or D). WordPerfect responds with

   Document name:

4. Type **SAMPLE** and press ENTER. (If SAMPLE is stored on other than the default drive or directory, indicate where the file is stored. For example, type **B:SAMPLE** and press ENTER.) WordPerfect responds with

   Page(s): (All)

5. Press ENTER to print all the pages (here, just one page).

6. The document will begin printing. (Again, if WordPerfect sounds a beep, you must signal that paper has been inserted into the printer as described previously in this section.)

7. Press the CANCEL (F1) key to clear the Control Printer menu and return to the Typing screen.

Note: If you attempt to print from disk and WordPerfect refuses to print your document, displaying the error message **Document was Fast Saved—Must be retrieved to print**, then a default setting has been changed as to how WordPerfect stores documents on disk. Refer to Appendix C to learn about the Fast Save feature and how the default setting for this feature can be altered. Or your printer may not operate for another reason; in that case, refer to the next section, "Control Print Jobs."

Pretend you wish to print a file whose name you can't remember. In that case:

1. Turn your printer on and insert paper.

2. Press the LIST FILES (F5) key. WordPerfect prompts you with your default drive or directory.

3. Press ENTER. A list of files in the default drive or directory is displayed on the screen. Now you can find the name of the file you forgot.

4. Position the cursor on the filename SAMPLE.

5. Select Print (4 or P). WordPerfect responds with

   Page(s): (All)

6. Press ENTER to print all the pages (here, just one page).

7. The document will begin printing. (Again, if WordPerfect sounds a beep, you must signal that paper has been inserted into the printer as described previously in this section.)

8. Press the CANCEL (F1) key to clear the List Files screen and return to the Typing screen.

Keep in mind that printing from screen and printing from disk are distinct commands. Whatever is currently on screen will be ignored should you decide to print from disk. For example, let's suppose that you retrieve to the screen and edit the document named SAMPLE and now wish to print out the edited version. You can either resave the edited document and print it from disk or print directly from the screen. But if you print from disk *before resaving,* you'll be printing the old, unedited version of SAMPLE, instead of the document on screen containing the revisions.

CONTROL PRINT JOBS

Every time you ask WordPerfect to print a document, no matter whether you're printing from screen or from disk, a *print job* is created, assigned a job number, and added to the list of jobs waiting their turn to be printed. As a result, you don't have to wait until one document has finished printing before continuing to work with WordPerfect. After you've sent one job to the printer, you can either continue to request additional print jobs or you can return to the Typing screen and perform a nonprinting task like editing another document. Or you can do both. For instance, request three print jobs so that the printer will print three documents one after another in the order that they were created in the job list; then, while the printer is working in the background, retrieve and start editing a fourth document. Keep in mind, however, that if you do perform an editing task while documents are printing, WordPerfect will proceed a bit more slowly because it is performing two tasks at once.

At any time you can check the status of your print jobs. To do so, press the PRINT (SHIFT + F7) key and then select Control Printer (4 or C). Using the Control Printer menu, you can also cancel a job so that it won't print, or you can change the order in which jobs will be printed.

The Control Printer screen is separated into three sections. Figure 2-5 illustrates the Control Printer screen when no jobs have been sent to the printer; Figure 2-6 shows the same screen with three jobs listed. The top section of the screen provides information on the current job (the one being sent to the printer). Notice in Figure 2-5 that Word-Perfect reports "No print jobs" next to the heading "status." In Figure 2-6, on the other hand, WordPerfect indicates that (1) job 1 is printing, (2) WordPerfect assumes 8.5- by 11-inch paper for the print job, (3) the paper is fed continuously into the printer, (4) no action is required, (5) page 1 is printing, and (6) only one copy of the job has been requested (see Chapter 9 for directions on how to direct WordPerfect to

```
Print: Control Printer

Current Job

Job Number: None                        Page Number:  None
Status:     No print jobs               Current Copy: None
Message:    None
Paper:      None
Location:   None
Action:     None


Job List

Job  Document              Destination        Print Options




Additional Jobs Not Shown: 0



  1 Cancel Job(s); 2 Rush Job; 3 Display Jobs; 4 Go (start printer); 5 Stop: 0
```

FIGURE 2-5   Control Printer screen with no print jobs

print multiple copies of a document, one of the options on the Print screen).

The middle section offers information about the job list of all jobs that have been sent to the printer. For instance, Figure 2-6 indicates that (1) job 1 is being printed from screen, while jobs 2 and 3 are specific files on disk, (2) all three jobs are being sent to the printer attached to LPT 1 (the specific plug at the back of the computer to which that printer is attached, as described in Appendix B), and (3) no print options have been activated (refer to Chapter 9 for more on print options). Only three jobs are shown on the list at one time, so Word-Perfect also indicates how many additional jobs are not shown; the "0" in Figure 2-6 means that there are only three jobs in the job list.

The third section provides a menu of five options for controlling the print jobs in the job list. Perhaps you accidentally sent the wrong document to the printer, the paper has jammed in the printer, or the printer isn't working at all. The Control Printer menu provides the following options:

```
Print: Control Printer

Current Job

Job Number: 1                              Page Number:  1
Status:      Printing                      Current Copy: 1 of 1
Message:     None
Paper:       Standard 8.5" x 11"
Location:    Continuous feed
Action:      None


Job List

Job  Document            Destination      Print Options
 1   (Screen)            LPT 1
 2   C:\WPER\DATA\SAMPLE LPT 1
 3   C:\WPER\DATA\BUDMIN LPT 1

Additional Jobs Not Shown: 0




 1 Cancel Job(s); 2 Rush Job; 3 Display Jobs; 4 Go (start printer); 5 Stop: 0
```

FIGURE 2-6 Control Printer screen showing three print jobs in the job list

- *Cancel Job(s) (1 or C)*   This option erases from the job list a print job. If you're currently printing job 1, then when you type **1** or **C**, WordPerfect responds with

  Cancel which job? (*=all jobs) 1

  To cancel the current job, press ENTER. Or, type in a different job number and press ENTER. If more than one print job is in the job list and you wish to cancel every one, type an asterisk (*). WordPerfect asks for verification, prompting

  Cancel all print jobs? (Y/N) No

  Type **Y** to verify that you wish to cancel all jobs.

  Rush Job (2 or R)   This option rearranges the order of print jobs listed. For instance, suppose you had jobs 1, 2, 3, and 4 in the job list to be printed. As job 1 is printing, type **2** or **R**, and WordPerfect prompts

  Rush which job? 2

  WordPerfect assumes you wish to rush the next print job listed. Press ENTER, and job 2 is printed next, or type in another job number and press ENTER to move that job ahead of the others. WordPerfect will also ask whether you wish to interrupt the current job; type **Y** to do so, or type **N** to print the rush job after the current job is completed.

- *Display Jobs (3 or D)*   This option shows a complete list of jobs waiting to be printed, temporarily replacing the Control Printer screen. As many as 24 jobs in the list are displayed at one time. Press any key to return to the Control Printer screen.

- *Go (Start Printer) (4 or G)*   This option resumes printing after a pause to insert paper or a new print wheel or cartridge or re-starts the printer after you've selected the stop option (see the next item in this list).

- *Stop (5 or S)*   This option stops the printer temporarily, without actually canceling the print job, which is useful in case of a paper jam or if the ribbon runs out. When you're ready to begin printing again, select the Go option. The printing begins at the beginning of the document unless page 1 has already been printing, in which case WordPerfect prompts you for the page number to begin with.

Depending on your printer, you may find that even when you attempt to stop or cancel a print job, the printing continues for a while. Because the computer has already sent part or all of the text to the printer, the printing continues for the text that has been sent. To cancel the current print job immediately, first turn off the printer, and then cancel the print job as described previously. Turn the printer back on when you are ready to print again.

If you ever issue a print command and the printer doesn't print, don't issue another print command. Instead, always check the top section on the Control Printer screen. Indication of a printing problem or error is listed next to the heading "Message." For instance, Figure 2-7 shows the following information next to "Message": **Printer not accepting characters**. This usually means that the connection between the computer and the printer is inoperative. Perhaps the printer is turned off or the cable connecting the two pieces of equipment is worn, cracked, or plugged in incorrectly. The information next to the heading "Action" indicates possible solutions: **Check cable, make sure printer is turned ON**. Once you've read the information under "Current Job," you can correct the problem, or select an item from the Control Printer menu.

```
Print: Control Printer

Current Job

Job Number: 1                              Page Number.  None
Status:       Initializing                 Current Copy: None
Message:      Printer not accepting characters
Paper:        None
Location:     None
Action:       Check cable, make sure printer is turned ON


Job List

Job  Document              Destination      Print Options
 1   (Screen)              LPT 1
 2   C:\WPER\DATA\SAMPLE   LPT 1
 3   C:\WPER\DATA\BUDMIN   LPT 1

Additional Jobs Not Shown: 0




1 Cancel Job(s): 2 Rush Job; 3 Display Jobs: 4 Go (start printer): 5 Stop: 0
```

FIGURE 2-7 Control Printer screen showing an error message

As you can see, WordPerfect allows enormous control over print jobs. Feel free to send jobs to the printer one after another. There's no need to print only one document at a time if there's a whole group to print. You can follow the progress of each job and manage them by displaying the Control Printer menu.

Note: WordPerfect offers a variety of special options for printing out your document. For instance, you can request that WordPerfect print a specific number of copies of your document. Or you can request that WordPerfect initialize the printer, downloading special fonts into the printer. Or you can even use an option called View Document, whereby you can preview how your document will appear on the printed page. Look to Chapter 9 for more details on special print options and enhancements.

REVIEW EXERCISE

In the following exercise you will practice saving and printing a document. Find a short memo or report around your office that you want to practice on. The document should be a simple one, without any fancy features or enhancements like underlining or centered text—you will learn these features in future chapters. If you encounter problems during printing, don't forget to press PRINT (SHIFT + F7) and select Control Printer (4 or C) to uncover the problem and to manage the print job.

1. Clear the screen by pressing EXIT (F7) and typing **N** twice. Then type the first several paragraphs of one of your own documents.

2. Assume that 15 minutes have elapsed. Use the SAVE (F10) key to save the document on disk to safeguard against a power failure. Select a filename that abides by the rules for naming files discussed at the beginning of this chapter.

3. Print your short document. (*Hint:* As long as the document is on screen, you can print directly from the screen by pressing the PRINT (SHIFT + F7) key and selecting Full Document (1 or F) or Page (2 or P)).

4. Add another paragraph or so to your document.

5. After another 15 minutes have elapsed, you must again save the current version of your text to disk. But suppose this time you wish to save the document and clear the screen. Use the EXIT (F7) key to do so. (*Hint:* After pressing the EXIT (F7) key, type **Y** to save the document, press ENTER to use the same filename, and type **Y** to replace the file on disk. Then type **N** to clear the screen without leaving WordPerfect.)

6. Print the document. (*Hint:* Since the document is no longer on screen, print it from disk using either the PRINT (SHIFT + F7) key and selecting the Document on Disk option or the LIST FILES (F5) key and selecting the Print option.)

REVIEW

- You can store an entire document on disk using either the EXIT (F7) key or the SAVE (F10) key. The EXIT key is convenient when you wish to save a document and then immediately clear the screen or exit WordPerfect. The SAVE key is convenient when you wish to save a document and then continue working to type or edit that same document.

- Remember to save a file on disk frequently as you're typing and editing it—not just when you've completed the final product. This protects against your losing hours of work because of a power failure or human error. The SAVE (F10) key is most convenient for doing so.

- You can store any portion of a document on disk. First, use the BLOCK (ALT + F4) key to highlight a block of text. Then, use the SAVE (F10) key to save the block into its own file or use the MOVE (CTRL + F4) key to append the block to an existing file.

- The LIST FILES (F5) key displays information about your floppy or hard disk and about the documents you've stored there, including each document's filename, size (measured in bytes), and the date and time it was last saved to disk.

- If you wish to retrieve a file to screen and you remember its name, use the RETRIEVE (SHIFT + F10) key. If you don't remember the file's exact name, retrieve it using the List Files menu, accessed via the LIST FILES (F5) key.

- When you wish to glance at the contents of a file but don't wish to retrieve that file to screen, you can employ the Look feature. The Look feature is available via the List Files menu.

- WordPerfect enables you to print either directly from the screen or from a file on disk. Printing options are described in Table 2-1.

- If you have a printing problem, check the Control Printer screen for information on the status of print jobs or for print errors. Make changes to print jobs by selecting from the menu of options at the bottom of the Control Printer screen.

Sequence of Keystrokes	Printing Task
PRINT (SHIFT + F7), **1** or **F**	Entire document from screen
PRINT (SHIFT + F7), **2** or **P**	One page from screen
Block Text, PRINT (SHIFT + F7), **Y**	Block of text from screen
PRINT (SHIFT + F7), **3** or **D**	Entire document or range of pages from disk (by typing in a filename)
LIST FILES (F5), ENTER, **4** or **P**	Entire document or range of pages from disk (by positioning the cursor on a filename)

TABLE 2-1   Printing Options from Screen or Disk

3

TYPING ENHANCEMENTS

This chapter covers the extras that make your readers notice words you want to stand out from the rest. You'll learn how to position words centered or flush at the right margin, how to boldface and underline words, how to switch between uppercase and lowercase in seconds, and how to indent whole paragraphs on a tab stop.

You'll also learn WordPerfect features that make the job of typing easier. One example, the Date feature, inserts the current date or time in a document for you. Another provides the ability to work simultaneously with two separate documents, jumping from one to the other as often as you like. You'll also discover how to split the screen in half to view two independent documents at the same time. You'll type several documents and use all these special typing features along the way.

CENTER AND FLUSH RIGHT TEXT

WordPerfect text is typically aligned flush left, meaning that each line starts flush against the left margin. As an alternative, you can have any short line of text centered between the left and right margins, such as this line:

Journey to the Center

You can also align text flush right, meaning that the last character of the line sits at the right margin, such as the following date:

June 16, 1989

You can reposition text either as you type or after you've typed. To center text that you are about to type, press the CENTER (SHIFT + F6) key. The cursor jumps to the center of the line. Now type the text and press ENTER to end the line. The text is centered between the margins. Similarly, if you wish to align text flush right, you press the FLUSH RIGHT (ALT + F6) key. The cursor jumps to the right edge of the line. Type the text and then press ENTER to end the line.

You can type flush left, centered, and flush right text all on the same line. For example, with the cursor at the left margin of a blank line, you could type **Anita Robbins**, press the CENTER (SHIFT + F6) key, type **President**, press the FLUSH RIGHT (ALT + F6) key, and type **ABC Company** to get the following results:

Anita Robbins   **President**   **ABC Company**

If you align text in different ways on one line, make sure that each segment of text is short; otherwise, text will overlap, and it will seem as if some of the text has disappeared.

To center or align flush right a line of text you've already typed, place the cursor at the left margin of a short line of text that you wish to reposition. Press CENTER or FLUSH RIGHT. Then press DOWN ARROW to rewrite the screen so that the text is centered or aligned flush right.

You can also center or align flush right many lines of text at once. From lines typed like this:

Wine Tasting
Through the Ages
by
Jan Miller

You can produce this:

Wine Tasting
Through the Ages
by
Jan Miller

You must first use the BLOCK (ALT + F4) key to highlight the lines. Then if you want to center them, press the CENTER (SHIFT + F6) key. WordPerfect prompts you for verification that you wish to center the block; you type **Y** for "Yes" to do so. Similarly, if you want to align the block of text flush right, press the FLUSH RIGHT (ALT + F6) key and, at the prompt, type **Y**.

What keeps text centered or aligned flush right is a pair of hidden codes inserted around the text. Like a pair of bookends, an On code precedes the text to be centered or aligned flush right, and an Off code follows the text. The following pair of hidden codes surrounds centered text: **[Cntr]** and **[C/A/Flrt]**. The following pair of hidden codes surrounds text aligned flush right: **[Flsh Rt]** and **[C/A/Flrt]**. (Notice that the Off code is identical whether you've centered or aligned flush right. C/A/Flrt stands for "Center/Align/Flush right.") But remember from Chapter 1 that codes are always hidden; you must use the REVEAL CODES (ALT + F3) key to view the codes.

If you change your mind and decide to cancel the centering or flush right aligning of text on a line, you must locate and delete the codes that surround the text. You need only erase one code in each pair—WordPerfect automatically erases the other. You can erase a code on the Reveal Codes screen or on the Typing screen. Erasing on the Reveal Codes screen allows you to view the code you are deleting. Erasing on the Typing screen means that you must deduce where one of the pair of codes is hiding (which is quite straightforward since the code pair surrounds the text). For instance, on the Typing screen you can position the cursor on the first character of centered text and press BACKSPACE. The **[Cntr]** code is deleted; as a result, WordPerfect automatically deletes the accompanying **[C/A/Flrt]** code, and the text returns to the left margin, no longer centered.

Let's practice centering and aligning text flush right.

1. Clear the Typing screen with the EXIT (F7) key. The cursor should now be at the top left corner of an empty screen.

2. Press the CENTER (SHIFT + F6) key.

3. Type **Urgent Notice**. This title is automatically centered as you type.

4. Press ENTER twice to end the line and insert a blank line.

5. Type **To: All Employees**.

6. Press the FLUSH RIGHT (ALT + F6) key.

7. Type **From: Sandy Peterson**.

8. Press ENTER to move down one line.

9. Press HOME, HOME, UP ARROW to position the cursor at the top of the document, and then press the REVEAL CODES (ALT + F3) key to view the codes inserted to center and align the text flush right.

Figure 3-1 illustrates how your screen will appear once on the Reveal Codes screen. The top window shows centered and flush right text. The bottom window shows the codes instead of the actual positioning of the text. Notice, for example, that the title is surrounded by Center codes on the Reveal Codes screen.

[Cntr]Urgent Notice[C/A/Flrt]

Suppose you wish to cancel the centering of the phrase "Urgent Notice." Remain in the Reveal Codes screen so that you can watch as the code pair is deleted:

1. Check the bottom window in the Reveal Codes screen to make sure the cursor is positioned on the [Cntr] code.

2. Press DEL. Notice that both the [Cntr] and [C/A/Flrt] codes disappear and that the text is no longer centered.

Now suppose you change your mind and decide to center the title after all. Remain in the Reveal Codes screen so that you can watch as the code pair is reinserted:

1. The cursor should already be positioned under the "U" in "Urgent." Press the CENTER (SHIFT + F6) key.

2. Press DOWN ARROW to rewrite the screen. The title is again centered.

3. Press REVEAL CODES (ALT + F3) to exit the Reveal Codes screen.

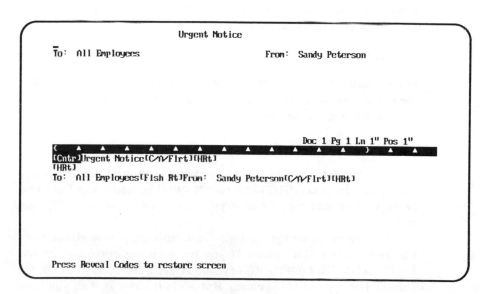

FIGURE 3-1   Reveal Codes screen showing Center and Flush Right codes

INSERT THE DATE OR TIME

Your computer knows the current date and time if either of the following two conditions are met: (1) you entered the date and time before loading WordPerfect (as described in "Getting Started"), in which case the computer keeps track of the correct date and time until you turn it off again; or (2) your computer has an internal, battery-operated clock, so it automatically keeps track of the correct date and time whether it is on or off.

If your computer knows the correct date and time, you can let WordPerfect insert the date or the time into the text of a document for you. The DATE/OUTLINE (SHIFT + F5) key controls this feature. When you press the DATE/OUTLINE (SHIFT + F5) key, the following menu is displayed:

1 Date Text; 2 Date Code; 3 Date Format; 4 Outline; 5 Para Num; 6 Define: 0

Menu options 1, 2, and 3 relate to the Date feature.

The first menu option, Date Text, simply inserts the date at the current cursor position. WordPerfect's default for the appearance of the date in your text is as follows:

Month #, 19##

For example, if the date is the 9th of May, 1989, then, unless you alter the default for the format of the date (as described further on), Word-Perfect will display the date as

May 9, 1989

To insert the date, position the cursor where you want the date to appear, press the DATE/OUTLINE (SHIFT + F5) key, and select Date Text (1 or T). The date appears as if you had typed it out yourself, only faster.

The second menu option, Date Code, appears at first glance to be identical to the first option. If you position the cursor, press the DATE/OUTLINE (SHIFT + F5) key, and select Date Code (2 or C), the current date appears at the cursor. But while it looks as if all you have done is insert text, you actually have inserted a hidden code. If the Date format is the default (Month #, 19##), then the code you have inserted is **[Date: 3 1, 4]**, with the code **3 1, 4** standing for month, day, and year (all four digits), respectively. (As described below, the numbers 3 1, 4 are derived from the Date Format menu, shown in Figure 3-2.) Of course, the code is hidden, and what you see is the text instead.

Because you inserted the code with the Date Code option, the date will automatically be updated when you next retrieve the document to the screen or print it from disk. For example, suppose that tomorrow you retrieve to the screen a letter that contains a date code. The letter will appear with tomorrow's date. Or suppose that the week after next, you print the same letter from disk. The printed result will show the current date. This feature is especially handy when included in a header or footer—the current date can be printed on every page, whenever you print (headers and footers are discussed in Chapter 5).

The third menu option, Date Format, enables you to select a different default style for the display of the date, tailoring it to meet your needs. When you select Date Format (3 or D), the screen shown in Figure 3-2 appears. Here you can select exactly how the date will appear when inserted automatically. Notice that the bottom of the screen indicates that the current date format is **3 1, 4**—the default pattern. The two columns in the center of the Date Format menu indicate your other format choices; you can pick and choose as you like. You can insert not only the month, the day of the month, and the year, but also

```
Date Format

     Character    Meaning
         1        Day of the Month
         2        Month (number)
         3        Month (word)
         4        Year (all four digits)
         5        Year (last two digits)
         6        Day of the Week (word)
         7        Hour (24 hour clock)
         8        Hour (12 hour clock)
         9        Minute
         0        am / pm
         %        Used before a number, will:
                     Pad numbers less than 10 with a leading zero
                     Output only 3 letters for the month or day of the week


     Examples:   3 1, 4      = December 25, 1984
                 %6 %3 1, 4  = Tue Dec 25, 1984
                 %2/%1/5 (6) = 01/01/85 (Tuesday)
                 8:90        = 10:55am


Date format: 3 1, 4
```

FIGURE 3-2   Date Format menu

the current hour, the current minute, and the day of the week. You can also include symbols or words in the format pattern, so long as the date format does not exceed 29 characters. A percentage symbol (%) can be used to insert a leading zero for numbers less than ten or to shorten the month or day of the week to three letters. Table 3-1 shows some date format examples, assuming that today is Monday, May 9, 1989, and that the time is 1:30 P.M.

When you change the date format, no codes are inserted into the text. Instead, you are directing how information will appear every time you use the DATE/OUTLINE (SHIFT + F5) key to insert the date— either as text or as a code—until you change the date format again or exit WordPerfect. (Next time you load WordPerfect, the default Date format returns.) Suppose, for example, that you change the date format to **2-1 at 8:9 0**. When you select Date Text (1 or T) the following appears at the current cursor position:

5-9 at 1:30 pm

Or, if you select Date Code (2 or C), the same information appears, but tucked behind this text would be the hidden code **[Date:2-1 at 8:9 0]**,

Date Format Pattern	Display of Date on Screen
2/1/5	5/9/89
2-1-4	5-9-1989
%2-%1-4	05-09-1989
Time—8:9 0	Time—1:30 pm
Time—7:9	Time—13:30
6, 3 1, 4	Monday, May 9, 1989
%6, 3 1, 4	Mon, May 9, 1989
Signed on 3 1, 4	Signed on May 9, 1989
Signed on 3 1 at 8:9 0	Signed on May 9 at 1:30 pm

TABLE 3-1   Formatting the Date

and the date and time would update automatically the next time you retrieved or printed the document.

Remember that in order for the DATE/OUTLINE (SHIFT +F5) key to work properly, the computer must know the correct date and time; otherwise, the wrong date will be inserted. If your computer is not equipped with a battery-operated clock and you forgot to enter the current date and time before starting WordPerfect, you can exit Word-Perfect, turn off your computer, and then reload WordPerfect all over again—this time making sure to enter the proper date and time when prompted. An easier alternative is to exit to DOS temporarily in order to enter the date and time (a procedure described in the "Go to DOS" section in Chapter 8).

Let's change the date format to include the date and the day of the week and then insert that information into the memo on the Typing screen.

1. Press HOME, HOME, DOWN ARROW to position the cursor at the bottom of the document, where you left off typing the document on screen.

2. Press ENTER to insert a blank line.

3. Press the DATE/OUTLINE (SHIFT + F5) key. WordPerfect responds with

    1 Date Text; 2 Date Code; 3 Date Format; 4 Outline; 5 Para Num; 6 Define: 0

4. Select Date Format (3 or D). The Date Format menu appears, as shown in Figure 3-2.

5. Type (6) 3 1, 4, and press ENTER. The Date menu returns to the bottom of the screen.

6. Select Date Text (1 or T). Watch as WordPerfect inserts the date for you, in a fraction of a second, in the following format:

    (Day) Month #, 19##

Remember that the date format will remain as you specified it until you alter it again or exit WordPerfect.

Note: You can permanently change the default setting for the date format from Month #, 19## to something else. See the "Initial Settings" section of Appendix C for details.

UNDERLINE AND BOLDFACE

If you wish to stress important words, you can underline them, or you can make them **boldface** (darker than the rest of the text). You can underline text or make it boldfaced either as you type or after you type.

To underline as you type, press the UNDERLINE (F8) key and type all the text you want underlined. Then press the UNDERLINE (F8) key again to turn off the feature. Similarly, you make text boldface by pressing the BOLD (F6) key, typing the text, and then pressing the BOLD (F6) key a second time to turn the feature off. You can also create an underscore without text by using the UNDERLINE (F8) key: turn on the Underline feature, press the SPACEBAR until the line is as long as you desire, and press the key again to turn underline off.

You can tell if underline or boldface is active by checking the Pos number on the status line. Normally, the Pos number is the only number not boldfaced on the status line, as follows:

Doc 1 Pg 1 Ln 2" Pos 3.2"

On a monochrome monitor, when you press the UNDERLINE (F8) key to turn on the feature, the Pos number on the status line is underscored as follows:

Doc 1 Pg 1 Ln 2" Pos 3.2"

When you press the BOLD (F6) key to turn on boldfacing, the Pos number becomes boldfaced, like the rest of the status line.

Doc 1 Pg 1 Ln 2" Pos 3.2"

On a color monitor, the Pos number changes color when either feature is activated. When you turn off these features, the status line returns to normal.

To underline or boldface text you've already typed, use the BLOCK (ALT + F4) key to highlight the portion of text you wish to underline or change to boldface. Then, with **Block on** flashing, press either the UNDERLINE (F8) or the BOLD (F6) key. WordPerfect activates the feature for just the highlighted text and turns Block off automatically.

Whether you underline or boldface text, a code pair surrounds that portion of text, just like when you center or align text flush right. The code pair [UND] and [und] are inserted to mark the boundaries of the underlined text. For boldfaced text, the codes are [BOLD] and [bold]. Of course, the codes are shown only on the Reveal Codes screen. To remove the underlining or boldface, you must delete the codes. Although they come in pairs, you need only delete one of the codes; the other will be erased automatically by WordPerfect.

How underlined and boldfaced text is displayed on the Typing screen depends on your monitor. If you have a monochrome monitor, the underline appears as a line below your text, and boldfaced words appear brighter than regular text. (If boldface does not appear on your monochrome monitor, adjust the contrast and brightness knobs.) If you have a color monitor, the underlined and boldfaced text appears in different colors than the rest of the text; color monitor users can see the actual underlining and boldfacing only on the printed page.

Note: WordPerfect lets you change how text with enhancements—such as underlining and boldfacing—is displayed on the Typing screen. In fact, some color monitor users may even be able to view underlining on screen. Refer to the "Display" section of Appendix C for more details.

Let's continue with the "Urgent Notice" memo, underlining and creating boldfaced text along the way (Figure 3-3 shows the result).

1. Your cursor should be just to the right of today's date. Press ENTER twice to insert a blank line.

2. Type the following:

   As you know, we announced on September 15th a new vacation option for employees who are

3. Press the SPACEBAR once, and then press the UNDERLINE (F8) key to turn on the Underline feature.

4. Type **full-time**.

5. Press the UNDERLINE (F8) key to turn off the Underline feature, and press the SPACEBAR once.

6. Type **or who work**.

7. Press the SPACEBAR once, and then press the UNDERLINE (F8) key to turn on underlining.

8. Type **more than twenty hours per week**.

9. Press the UNDERLINE (F8) key to turn off underlining. Then type a period, press the SPACEBAR twice, and type the following:

   Here is the list of those employees who have

10. Press the BOLD (F6) key to turn on the boldface feature.

11. Type **already signed up**.

12. Press the BOLD (F6) key to turn off the boldface feature, and type **for the new option:**.

13. Press ENTER twice to insert a blank line.

14. Press the UNDERLINE (F8) key to turn on underlining and type **Name**.

15. Press TAB five times and type **Department**.

16. Press the UNDERLINE (F8) key to turn underlining off.

17. Type the remainder of the document as shown in Figure 3-3. (When typing the two columns of information under the headings "Name" and "Department," remember to use the TAB key. That is, type the information under the heading "Name," then

---

```
                    Urgent Notice

To:  All Employees                  From:  Sandy Peterson

(Monday) October 2, 1989

As you know, we announced on September 15th a new vacation option
for employees who are full-time or who work more than twenty hours
per week.  Here is the list of those employees who have already
signed up for the new option:

Name                        Department

Antonio Abbott              Distribution, East Coast
Lois Chang                  Personnel
Tim Fingerman               Public Relations
Paul McClintock             Distribution, West Coast

If you wish to sign up, but your name is not on the list, then you
must telephone our Personnel Director, John Sansone, by October
15th at (415) 333-9215.  Thank you._


                                Doc 1 Pg 1 Ln 4.33" Pos 4.5"
```

FIGURE 3-3   Sample document for underlining and boldfacing

press TAB five times, then type in the information under the heading "Department," and then press ENTER. As discussed previously, using the TAB key is more effective than pressing the SPACEBAR when moving the cursor by a certain increment to the right so that text under a heading such as "Department" lines up evenly in columns when printed.)

Now that the document has been typed, suppose you decide to underline the name John Samsone and change the date, October 15th, to boldface in the last paragraph. Since the information has already been typed, you must use the BLOCK (ALT + F4) key, as follows:

1. Position the cursor on the "J" in "John Samsone."

2. Press the BLOCK (ALT + F4) key, and type **e** to highlight the first and last names. (Remember from Chapter 1 that you can quickly move the cursor to the end of a block simply by typing the last character in the block.)

3. Press the UNDERLINE (F8) key. The name becomes underlined.

4. Position the cursor on the capital "O" in "October 15th."

5. Press the BLOCK (ALT + F4) key, and then type **h** to highlight the date.

6. Press the BOLD (F6) key. The date becomes boldfaced.

In addition to underlining and boldfacing, there are many other alternatives for changing the appearance of characters to make text stand out. For instance, you can increase or decrease the size of characters or use italics. Or you can direct WordPerfect to underline with a double underscore rather than a single underscore. Refer to Chapter 10 for more on using the FONT key to change the appearance of characters.

CHANGE THE UNDERLINE STYLE

Depending on the capability of your printer, you can change the style with which WordPerfect underlines text when printed. The default setting is for WordPerfect to underline all spaces located between the On

Underline and Off Underline codes, but not to underline any tabs. Examples of this and of other options are shown in Figure 3-4.

To change the underline style, position the cursor at the left margin of the line where you want to change the style. Press the FORMAT (SHIFT + F8) key and select Other (4 or O). The Other Format menu, as shown in Figure 3-5, appears. Notice that the default settings—underlining spaces but not tabs—are indicated on this menu. Next, select Underline (7 or U) and then type **Y** or **N** to determine whether spaces and/or tabs are to be underlined. As a last step, press EXIT (F7) to return to the Typing screen.

When you alter the underline style, a code is inserted at the cursor location. For instance, if you decide to change the style so that both spaces and tabs are underlined, the code inserted is [**Undrln:Spaces,Tabs**]. Or, if you decide to underline only tabs, the code inserted is [**Undrln:Tabs**].

An underline style code affects all underlined text from the location where it is inserted all the way to the end of the document, or until another underline style code is encountered farther forward in the document. For instance, suppose you decide to underline both spaces and tabs starting at the top of the document. Position the cursor at the top of the document and use the FORMAT key to insert the code [**Un-**

```
Spaces Underlined: Yes

Tabs Underlined: No

                  Last Name      First Name     Employee Number

Spaces: No

Tabs: Yes

                  Last Name      First Name     Employee Number

Spaces: No

Tabs: No

                  Last Name      First Name     Employee Number

Spaces: Yes

Tabs: Yes

                  Last Name      First Name     Employee Number
```

FIGURE 3-4   Underline styles

drln:Spaces,Tabs]. Farther forward in the text, suppose you select to underline only tabs. Then reposition the cursor where you want to change the style and insert the code **[Undrln:Tabs].**

Suppose you want WordPerfect to underline the tabs between the headings "Name" and "Department." Remember that WordPerfect assumes you wish to underline only spaces and not tabs. Thus, we must insert an Underline style code just above these two headings.

1. Position the cursor on the blank line above the "N" in "Name."

2. Press the FORMAT (SHIFT + F8) key.

3. Select Other Format (4 or O). The menu shown in Figure 3-5 appears.

4. Select Underline (7 or U).

5. Type **Y** twice to indicate that you desire both spaces and tabs underlined.

6. Press EXIT (F7) to leave the Other Format menu and return to the Typing screen.

```
Format: Other

    1 - Advance

    2 - Conditional End of Page

    3 - Decimal/Align Character          ,
        Thousands' Separator             ,

    4 - Language                         US

    5 - Overstrike

    6 - Printer Functions

    7 - Underline - Spaces               Yes
                    Tabs                 No




Selection: 0
```

FIGURE 3-5 Other Format menu

```
                          Urgent Notice

  To:  All Employees                From:  Sandy Peterson

  (Monday) October 2, 1989

  As you know, we announced on September 15th a new vacation option
  for employees who are full-time or who work more than twenty hours
  per week.  Here is the list of those employees who have already
  signed up for the new option:

  Name                      Department

  Antonio Abbott            Distribution, East Coast
  Lois Chang                Personnel
  Tim Fingerman             Public Relations
  Paul McClintock           Distribution, West Coast

  If you wish to sign up, but your name is not on the list, then you
  must telephone our Personnel Director, John Sansone, by October
  15th at (415) 333-9215.  Thank you.



                               Doc 1 Pg 1 Ln 2.66" Pos 1"
```

FIGURE 3-6   Sample document with underline style changed to underscore tabs

Monochrome monitor users will see that the tabs are now underlined, continuing from the heading "Name" to the heading "Department," as shown in Figure 3-6.

Color monitor users who view underlined text in a different color rather than with an underscore will see the change only on the printed page; print out the page if you wish to verify the change in the underline style. You can also verify the alteration by revealing codes so that you can view the Underline style code that you inserted. If you erase the Underline style code, then the underline style for the entire document (and not just for the top portion of the document) returns to the default underline style: spaces underlined but tabs not underlined.

A REMINDER: SAVE THE DOCUMENT PERIODICALLY

As you've been reading this chapter and typing the practice document, 15 minutes or so have probably gone by. Remember from the discussion in Chapter 2 that you must save to disk regularly; otherwise, you risk losing your text to a power failure or an operator error. Let's take a moment to save the typing done so far.

1. Press the SAVE (F10) key. WordPerfect requests a document filename.

2. Type **URGNOTE** (standing for urgent notice) and press EN-TER. (Remember to type the correct drive/directory designation in front of URGNOTE if you want that file stored somewhere other than the default—for example, B:URGNOTE.)

You can now continue, knowing that a copy of the text you've typed is safely stored on disk. If you experience a power failure, you can reload WordPerfect, retrieve the document named URGNOTE, and continue from this point.

REPEAT A KEYSTROKE WITH THE ESCAPE KEY

The ESC (ESCAPE) key, usually located on the top row of the keyboard, can be used in WordPerfect to repeat a character a specified number of times—a quick typing aid. The default repeat value is 8. Therefore, to repeat a character eight times, position the cursor where you want that character to appear and press ESC. WordPerfect responds with

Repeat Value = 8

Press any character to insert it eight times. For instance, if you press the PLUS key, the following appears:

++++++++

When you want a character repeated more or less than eight times, press ESC, type in the desired repeat value, and type the character.

Suppose that you wish to insert eight exclamation points after the words "Thank you" at the end of the "Urgent Notice" document.

1. Position the cursor at the period just to the right of the words "Thank you," and press DEL to erase the period.

2. Press ESC. WordPerfect prompts

   Repeat Value = 8

3. Type !. WordPerfect inserts eight exclamation points.

Now let's draw a blank line 20 spaces long at the bottom of the document as a place for a signature. What that means is that you will want to turn on the underline feature, insert 20 spaces, and turn underlining off. The ESC key makes this easy.

1. Press ENTER twice to move to a blank line.

2. Press the UNDERLINE (F8) key to turn on the feature.

3. Press ESC. WordPerfect prompts

   Repeat Value = 8

4. Type **20**. Now the prompt reads

   Repeat Value = 20

5. Press SPACEBAR. Twenty spaces are now inserted, all underlined.

6. Press the UNDERLINE (F8) key to turn off the Underline feature.

You can also alter the repetition number for an entire working session. Suppose you were typing a document where, every page or so, you inserted a row of 35 asterisks. You could change the repetition number to 35 for the working session and insert those asterisks quickly. To change the default repeat value, press ESC, type in a new repetition number, and press ENTER. From then on until the end of the working session, every time you pressed ESC, the prompt would reflect the new number:

Repeat Value = 35

The ESC key can be used not only to repeat a specific character, but to repeat a cursor movement or deletion operation as well. For instance, press ESC and then press the RIGHT ARROW key to move 8 places to the right. Or, press ESC, type **12**, and press DEL to delete 12 characters in a row, just as if you pressed the DEL key 12 times. Besides the arrow keys and DEL, other keys that work with the ESC key include

- CTRL + LEFT ARROW and CTRL + RIGHT ARROW, to move the cursor by a specific number of words

- PGUP and PGDN, to move the cursor by a specific number of pages

- MINUS and PLUS (on the cursor movement/numeric keypad), to move the cursor by a specific number of screens

- CTRL + BACKSPACE, to delete a specific number of words

- CTRL + END, to delete a specific number of lines

CONTROL WORD WRAP WITH SPACES AND HYPHENS

Sometimes word wrap will break a line at an awkward or inappropriate spot, as in the following examples:

```
According to my calendar, Mr. Patterson is due back on September
14th.  He will call you then.

Ms. Cindy Ballenger can be reached in New York City at (212) 455-
1299.
```

You can control how word wrap operates so that you can keep dates, telephone numbers, or names together on one line. Your lines can look like the following instead:

```
According to my calendar, Mr. Patterson is due back on
September 14th.  He will call you then.

Ms. Cindy Ballenger can be reached in New York City at
(212) 455 1299.
```

To keep together words that are separated by a space, you must create a "hard" space—one that glues words together. Type the first word, press HOME, press SPACEBAR, and type the second word. You have thus created a Hard Space code, which, on the Reveal Codes screen, looks like [ ]. The two words on either side of the hard space will be kept on the same line. If you had already typed the words that you wanted kept together, you would delete the space between them before pressing HOME, SPACEBAR.

To keep together words joined by a hyphen, the process is similar. Type the first word, press HOME, press the HYPHEN key, and type the second word. You have created a Hyphen code, which on the Reveal Codes screen resembles an ordinary hyphen: -. (If you press the HYPHEN key without first pressing HOME, you insert an ordinary hyphen, and the code inserted is [-]. This ordinary hyphen *won't* protect two words from being split by word wrap.)

Notice that the date "October 15th" in the last paragraph is separated onto two separate lines in Figure 3-6. (This may also be the case on your computer screen, though not necessarily. Remember from Chapter 1 that the printer you defined to work with WordPerfect determines where word wrap will break a line; thus, your words may wrap differently than what is shown in Figure 3-6.) Suppose you wish to make sure that WordPerfect keeps "October 15th" on the same line, and you wish to ensure that the phone number "(415) 333-9215," stays together on one line as well.

1. Position the cursor on the blank space after "October."

2. Press DEL to delete the space. The text readjusts.

3. Press HOME, SPACEBAR. A hard space code is inserted in the text.

4. Press DOWN ARROW to readjust the text. "October 15th" is treated like one word for purposes of word wrap; the two words remain together on one line, even though, for some of you, the word "October" could, by itself, fit at the end of the line above.

5. Position the cursor on the blank space after "(415)."

6. Press DEL to delete the space.

7. Press HOME, SPACEBAR. A hard space code is inserted in the text.

8. Position the cursor on the hyphen after "333."

9. Press DEL to delete the hyphen.

10. Press HOME, HYPHEN. A hard hyphen is inserted, keeping the complete phone number on one line.

Now no matter how you edit your text, neither the date nor the phone number will be split by word wrap. You may wish to experiment by inserting or deleting random words to verify that word wrap will no longer split the date or phone number on separate lines. WordPerfect will leave extra space at the end of a line instead.

CONVERT LOWERCASE AND UPPERCASE LETTERS

WordPerfect provides a slick feature that lets you change uppercase text that you've already typed to lowercase or vice versa. You first use the BLOCK (ALT + F4) key to highlight the text you wish to convert between lowercase and uppercase. Next, with **Block on** flashing, press the SWITCH (SHIFT + F3) key and select to switch all letters to either uppercase or lowercase. (If you select lowercase and the block of text you highlighted contains any sentences, then the first letter of each sentence remains in uppercase automatically.)

Let's change the words "Urgent Notice" to all uppercase letters:

1. Press HOME, HOME, UP ARROW, and then press RIGHT ARROW to position the cursor on the "U" in "Urgent Notice."

2. Press the BLOCK (ALT + F4) key.

3. Press END to highlight the text to the end of the line.

4. Press the SWITCH (SHIFT + F3) key. WordPerfect prompts

   1 Uppercase; 2 Lowercase: 0

5. Select Uppercase (1 or U). The title is switched to uppercase letters—URGENT NOTICE. The Block feature is turned off automatically.

CREATE DOCUMENT COMMENTS

WordPerfect offers the Comment feature, whereby you can type information that will appear in a double-line box in the document on screen, but will not appear on the printed page. This is convenient if you wish to leave within a document a mental reminder for yourself or someone else who will be viewing this document on screen. A comment is also handy for indicating what information should be typed at a specific location in a document or form you may have designed using WordPerfect.

To insert a document comment, position the cursor where you wish the comment to appear, press the TEXT IN/OUT (CTRL + F5) key, and select the Comment option (5 or C). WordPerfect then displays the following Comment menu:

Comment: 1 Create; 2 Edit; 3 Convert to Text: 0

Next, select Create (1 or C). A comment box appears on screen, in which you can type up to 1157 characters. When you are done typing, you must press the EXIT (F7) key. The comment appears in your document in a double-line box. If you reveal codes, you'll see that the hidden code **[Comment]** is inserted in the text; this code creates the double-line box and contains the comment text.

A document comment can be deceiving. While the comment may occupy various lines on screen, it occupies no space at all in the actual printed document. As a result, the status line ignores the position of the comment. When the cursor is located just before or after the comment box, simply use the LEFT and RIGHT ARROW keys to pass over the code (and the box) in one keystroke.

Suppose you wish to insert a reminder to yourself that employees must receive the "URGENT NOTICE" memo by Tuesday. Proceed as follows:

1. Press HOME, HOME, HOME, UP ARROW to position the cursor at the top left corner of the document.

2. Press the TEXT IN/OUT (CTRL + F5) key. The following menu appears on screen:

   1 DOS Text; 2 Password; 3 Save Generic; 4 Save WP 4.2; 5 Comment: 0

3. Select Comment (5 or C). A new menu appears:

   Comment: 1 Create; 2 Edit; 3 Convert to Text: 0

4. Select Create (1 or C). An empty document comment box appears on screen, as shown in Figure 3-7.

5. Type the following:

   Make sure employees receive memo by Tuesday. Special courier to distribution centers on the East Coast.

6. Press the EXIT (F7) key. You are returned to the Typing screen, with the comment at the top of the screen, as Figure 3-8 shows.

7. Press LEFT ARROW. The cursor moves before the **[Comment]** code, so that on the Typing screen the cursor is above the comment.

8. Press RIGHT ARROW. The cursor moves below the comment.

Remember that the comment will not appear when you print this document; it is solely an on-screen feature. You may wish to print this document to verify that, in fact, the comment doesn't appear as part of the printed document.

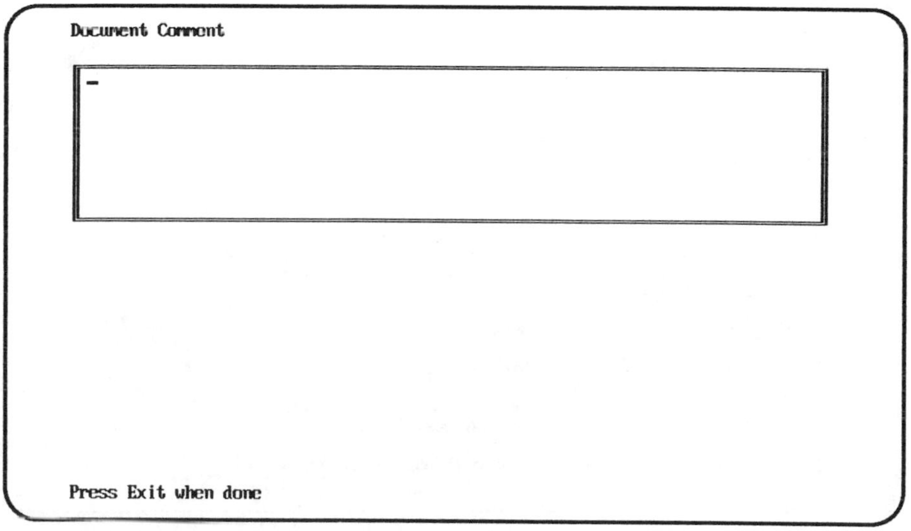

FIGURE 3-7   Document comment box

You can edit the contents of the comment box at any time by positioning the cursor below the comment, following steps 2 and 3 above, and then selecting the Edit Option (2 or E). The comment appears on the screen for editing. Press the EXIT (F7) key when you have completed editing the comment.

You can also convert the contents of the comment box into standard text. For instance, suppose you typed text into a Comment box and now decide you want that text incorporated into the document. Position the cursor just below the comment, follow steps 2 and 3 above, and then select Convert to Text (3 or T). The double-line box disappears, but the comment text remains in the document.

Conversely, you can convert a portion of text into a comment. As an example, suppose you type a sentence in a document and then realize that the sentence is more appropriate as a comment; that is, text that appears only when the document is on screen. Use the BLOCK (ALT + F4) key to highlight the sentence, and with **Block on** flashing, press the TEXT IN/OUT (CTRL + F5) key. WordPerfect prompts

Create a comment? (Y/N) No

Type **Y** to convert that text into a comment, or type **N** or press ENTER to abort the command but leave Block on.

```
┌─────────────────────────────────────────────────────────────────┐
│  ╔═══════════════════════════════════════════════════════════╗   │
│  ║ Make sure employees receive memo by Tuesday.  Special courier to  ║   │
│  ║ distribution centers on the East Coast.                   ║   │
│  ╚═══════════════════════════════════════════════════════════╝   │
│  ▬               URGENT NOTICE                                    │
│                                                                   │
│  To: All Employees                    From: Sandy Peterson        │
│                                                                   │
│  (Monday) October 2, 1989                                         │
│                                                                   │
│  As you know, we announced on September 15th a new vacation option│
│  for employees who are full-time or who work more than twenty hours│
│  per week.  Here is the list of those employees who have already  │
│  signed up for the new option:                                    │
│                                                                   │
│  Name                     Department                              │
│                                                                   │
│  Antonio Abbott           Distribution, East Coast               │
│  Lois Chang               Personnel                               │
│  Tim Fingerman            Public Relations                        │
│  Paul McClintock          Distribution, West Coast               │
│                                                                   │
│  If you wish to sign up, but your name is not on the list, then you│
│  C:\WPER\DATA\URGNOTE                      Doc 1 Pg 1 Ln 1" Pos 1"│
└─────────────────────────────────────────────────────────────────┘
```

FIGURE 3-8   Sample document with an on-screen comment

If you wish to erase a comment, including the comment text, you must delete the **[Comment]** code. For instance, with your document on the screen, you can press the REVEAL CODES (ALT + F3) key, position the cursor to the right of the code, and press BACKSPACE.

One final option allows you to hide the display of all document comments. The default setting is to display comments; to change the default, refer to the "Display" section in Appendix C.

DUAL DOCUMENT TYPING

With WordPerfect, you can work on two Typing screens at one time, each containing a separate document. Both documents remain in the computer's RAM; you simply switch between them at will using the SWITCH (SHIFT + F3) key. The first Typing screen is referred to as the Doc 1 window, while the second is the Doc 2 window. Both windows are always available to you; so far, we haven't accessed the Doc 2 window.

Why work with two documents at one time? Doc 1 might contain an outline you wish to refer to periodically when creating a report in Doc 2. Or Doc 1 might contain a memo you wish to refer to when typing a letter in the other Doc window. Or Doc 2 could be reserved for your random thoughts as you type a report in Doc 1. Also, dual document typing is especially handy when you want to copy a paragraph from one document to another. You can retrieve one document in the Doc 1 window and copy text from it to the Doc 2 window. (The Move/Copy command is described in Chapter 6.)

All of WordPerfect's features operate the same in the Doc 2 window as in the Doc 1 window. For instance, you could retrieve a document into the Doc 2 window in the usual manner—using the RETRIEVE (SHIFT + F10) or the LIST FILES (F5) key. You must make sure the cursor is in the Doc 2 window before retrieving.

Suppose that while working on the "URGENT NOTICE" memo, you have a brainstorm regarding another memo you wish to write. Let's switch between the Doc 1 and Doc 2 windows.

1. Press the SWITCH (SHIFT + F3) key. Now the screen becomes blank. Notice at the bottom of the screen that the status line reads **Doc 2**. You have switched to the second Typing screen.

2. Press the SWITCH (SHIFT + F3) key. You are returned to Doc 1 and the memo it contains. When you switch between documents in separate Typing screens, you don't lose any text from either one.

3. As this chapter continues, you will create a memo in the Doc 2 window. The "URGENT NOTICE" memo in Doc 1 will remain in RAM. But because you have substantially edited the memo in Doc 1 since you last saved it, it is a good idea to again save the contents of what's in the Doc 1 window, just in case there's a power failure. Press the SAVE (F10) key, press ENTER, and type **Y** to save the document in the Doc 1 window.

4. Press the SWITCH (SHIFT + F3) key. You are returned to Doc 2, ready to work on a new document.

LEARN ABOUT TAB STOP KEYS

You learned previously that as a default setting tab stops are set every 0.5 inch. When you wish to jump to a tab stop, you press the TAB key; a **[Tab]** code is inserted, and the line of text that you type following that code will be aligned at the tab stop.

In addition to the TAB key, the →INDENT, ←INDENT→, ←MARGIN RELEASE, CENTER and TAB ALIGN keys move the cursor from tab stop to tab stop as well. As illustrated in Figure 3-9, each key has a slightly different effect on the text.

Indent

While the TAB key indents a single line, the →INDENT (F4) key indents an entire paragraph. Each time you press the →INDENT (F4) key, an **[→Indent]** code is inserted, indenting all lines to the next tab stop until an **[HRt]** code is encountered. This key widens the left margin for a single paragraph. If you edit the text of the paragraph, the margins are readjusted so that the paragraph remains indented.

A related key is the →INDENT← (SHIFT + F4) key, which indents both the left and right edges of all lines in a paragraph by an equal amount. This key widens both the left and right margins for a single paragraph, such as a long quotation. An **[→Indent←]** code is inserted.

Tab stop
↓

When you use the TAB key, only one line is indented. As a result, the TAB key is commonly used to indent the first line of a paragraph.

When you press the ->INDENT (F4) key and type a paragraph, the entire paragraph is indented to the next tab stop, no matter how many lines that one paragraph contains.

When you press the ->INDENT<- (SHIFT + F4) key, the whole paragraph is indented not only from the left side, but from the <u>right</u> side as well -- quite a convenient feature if you wish to type a long, indented quote.

You can create a hanging paragraph by first pressing the ->INDENT (F4) key, pressing the <-MARGIN RELEASE (SHIFT + TAB) key, and then typing your text. The first line of the paragraph hangs out farther than the remaining lines of the paragraph.

↑
Tab stop

Centered on the Tab ↓	Tab Aligned on a Decimal ↓	Tab Aligned on a Dollar Sign ↓
This	44.55	$44.55
is	3.40	$3.40
centered	112.0	$112.00
on	1500.05	$1500.89
a tab stop.	33.44	$2.33

FIGURE 3-9   Different keys that work on tab stops

Margin Release

The ←MARGIN RELEASE (SHIFT + TAB) key is used to move a single line of text back one tab stop to the left. It has the reverse effect of the TAB key, and it will even move text to the left of the left margin. An [←**Mar Rel**] code is inserted.

When you press the ←MARGIN RELEASE (SHIFT + TAB) key immediately after pressing the →INDENT (F4) key, you create a hanging paragraph, whereby the first line of a paragraph begins one tab stop to the left of the remaining paragraph lines. The hanging paragraph style is useful for indicating that each paragraph discusses a separate topic.

Center

The CENTER (SHIFT + F6) key can center a short entry on a tab stop. To center text you must first press TAB to position the cursor on the correct tab stop. Then press the CENTER (SHIFT + F6) key and type the entry. Now press TAB to move to the next tab stop or ENTER to move down to a new line. The following pair of Center codes is inserted around the text like bookends: [**Cntr**] and [**C/A/Flrt**].

Tab Align

The TAB ALIGN (CTRL + F6) key lines up all the text at a tab stop on a specific character. The default character is the decimal point (period) so that you can easily align numbers in a column on a decimal, as shown in the second column at the bottom of Figure 3-9. When you use this key, the following pair of Align codes is inserted around the text that precedes the decimal point: [**Align**] and [**C/A/Flrt**].

When you press the TAB ALIGN (CTRL + F6) key, the cursor jumps to the next tab setting, and WordPerfect prompts

Align char = .

reminding you that the align character is the period (decimal point). You can type in text or a number, including a period. Then press TAB or the TAB ALIGN (CTRL + F6) key if you wish to move to the next tab stop, or you can press ENTER to move down to the next line. If you type text that didn't contain a period before moving to the next tab stop or line, that text will be right justified, meaning that the right edge of the text will be aligned on the tab stop.

The Tab Align feature is quite flexible because you can alter the character that aligns on the tab for a particular document. For example, perhaps you want the tab stop to align with the colon (:). Or perhaps you wish to align numbers on the dollar sign ($), as shown in the third column at the bottom of Figure 3-9. If so, you must change the alignment character *before* using the TAB ALIGN (CTRL + F6) key. Position the cursor where you want the new alignment character to take effect. Then press the FORMAT (SHIFT + F8) key and select Other (4 or O). The Other Format menu, as shown in Figure 3-5, appears. Notice that the period (.) is indicated as the default decimal/align character. Select Decimal/Align Character (3 or D), and type the new character on which you want the text to align. Then press ENTER to bypass changing the thousands' separator (which is related to the Math feature). As a last step, press EXIT (F7) to return to the Typing screen. A code is inserted in the text at the current cursor position. For instance, if the align character is changed to the dollar sign ($), the code inserted is **[Decml/Algn Char:$,,]**. The code determines what character will be aligned on the tab when you use the Tab Align feature at any point following the location of the code.

WORK WITH TAB STOP KEYS

Here's a chance to practice with various keys that operate on a tab stop. You'll create a bulleted list using the →INDENT (F4) key, and then type two columns, the first aligned on the decimal point and the second with the text centered on the tab. The result of your typing is shown in Figure 3-10.

1. Your cursor should be in Doc 2, a blank screen. If you are still in Doc 1, press the SWITCH (SHIFT + F3) key.

2. Type the following:

   I spoke to John Samsone on January 3rd about our financial situation. He reported the following highlights:

3. Press ENTER twice.

4. Type **o**, to represent a bullet dot, and press the →INDENT (F4) key.

5. Type the following:

   He is meeting with a venture capitalist next week who is interested in investing with us.

6. Press ENTER twice.

7. Type **o** and press the →INDENT (F4) key.

8. Type the following:

   Our debt stands at $159,000 as of December 31st, 10% lower than we anticipated. Financial forecasts project that we'll be out of debt in two years time. Here are the debt figures (in thousands):

9. Press ENTER twice.

10. Press TAB twice, and then press the CENTER (SHIFT + F6) key.

11. Type **Amount Owed**, and watch as the heading is centered on the tab stop.

12. Press TAB four times, and then press the CENTER (SHIFT + F6) key.

13. Type **Name of Bank**, and watch as the heading is centered on the tab stop.

14. Press ENTER twice.

15. Press TAB once, and then press the TAB ALIGN (CTRL + F6) key. WordPerfect responds with

    Align char = .

16. Type **$48.5**. When you press the period (decimal), the prompt at the bottom of the screen disappears.

17. Press TAB five times, and then press the CENTER (SHIFT + F6) key.

18. Type **Floyd Interstate** and press ENTER.

19. Continue (starting again at step 15) until you've completed typing the document shown in Figure 3-10.

If you wish to cancel an indent, margin release, center, or tab align, you must delete the code or code pair that you inserted. Suppose

```
I spoke to John Samsone on January 3rd about our financial
situation. He reported the following highlights:

o    He is meeting with a venture capitalist next week who is
     interested in investing with us.

o    Our debt stands at $159,000 as of December 31st, 10% lower
     than we anticipated. Financial forecasts project that we'll
     be out of debt in two years time. Here are the debt figures
     (in thousands):

     Amount Owed              Name of Bank

       $48.5                  Floyd Interstate
         9.8                     Center Bank
       100.7                  Bank of Stevenson_
```

Doc 1 Pg 1 Ln 3.5" Pos 5.4"

FIGURE 3-10   Sample document for working with tab stop keys

you wished to erase an indent. You could either press the REVEAL
CODES (ALT + F3) key, position the cursor just to the right of the
[→**Indent**] code, and press BACKSPACE or, on the Typing screen, position the cursor just to the right of where the indent took effect and
press BACKSPACE.

SPLIT THE SCREEN IN HALF

While practicing with tab stops, did you forget about the document
still occupying the Doc 1 screen? The document is still there. In fact,
with WordPerfect, not only can you work with two documents on
separate screens, but you can view and edit two documents on the
same screen! To do this, you must reduce the size of either the Doc 1
or Doc 2 Typing screen's window by pressing the SCREEN (CTRL +
F3) key and selecting Window (1 or W). Then, as prompted by Word-
Perfect, type the desired size (in number of lines) for the Typing screen
you are now viewing, and press ENTER.

You can size both windows evenly or make one window larger than the other. You learned previously that WordPerfect displays 24 lines of text on a standard-sized monitor, with the 25th serving as the status line. If you shrink a Typing screen to an 11-line window, the screen splits in half: Doc 1 and its Status line appear in the top 12 lines, and Doc 2 and its status line appear on the bottom. A ruler line splits the two windows (the same ruler line that appears to split the windows on the Reveal Codes screen). Or you can make one window larger than the other by sizing it at a number larger than 11 but smaller than 23. Once the screen is split, you can type, edit, and move the cursor in one window while referring to text in the other window.

Suppose that in Doc 2 you wish to insert a phone number that you haven't memorized but that you know can be found in the document located in the Doc 1 window. Let's split the screen in half to work with both documents at the same time. You'll first position the cursor at the top of each document.

1. With Doc 2 on the Typing screen, press HOME, HOME, UP ARROW.

2. Press the SWITCH (SHIFT + F3) key to go to Doc 1.

3. Press HOME, HOME, UP ARROW.

4. Press the SCREEN (CTRL + F3) key. WordPerfect responds with the following menu:

   0 Rewrite; 1 Window; 2 Line Draw: 0

5. Select Window (1 or W). WordPerfect prompts

   Number of lines in this window: 24

6. Type **11** and press ENTER. The screen splits in half, and a ruler line appears in the middle of the screen, as shown in Figure 3-11. Notice that the tab stop markers (triangles) on the ruler line are pointing upward. This indicates that the cursor is currently in Doc 1.

7. Press DOWN ARROW until John Samsone's phone number comes into view in the top window. Now that you can view the phone number, you're ready to type it into Doc 2.

8. Press the SWITCH (SHIFT + F3) key. Now the tab stop markers are pointing downward; the cursor is in Doc 2.

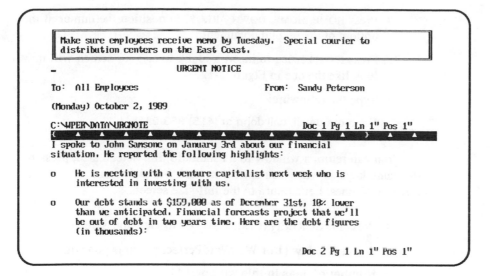

FIGURE 3-11   A split screen, displaying the Doc 1 and Doc 2 windows

---

```
Name                     Department

Antonio Abbott           Distribution, East Coast
Lois Chang               Personnel
Tim Fingerman            Public Relations
Paul McClintock          Distribution, West Coast

If you wish to sign up, but your name is not on the list, then you
must telephone our Personnel Director, John Sansone, by
October 15th at (415) 333-9215.  Thank you!!!!!!!!

C:\WPER\DATA\URGNOTE                          Doc 1 Pg 1 Ln 4.5" Pos 1"
{  ▼    ▼    ▼    ▼    ▼    ▼    ▼    ▼    ▼    }   ▼    ▼
   than we anticipated. Financial forecasts project that we'll
   be out of debt in two years time. Here are the debt figures
   (in thousands):

   Amount Owed           Name of Bank

     $18.5               Floyd Interstate
       9.8               Center Bank
     100.7               Bank of Stevenson


 _                                            Doc 2 Pg 1 Ln 3.83" Pos 1"
```

FIGURE 3-12   A split screen, with the cursor in the bottom (Doc 2) window

9. Press HOME, HOME, DOWN ARROW to position the cursor at the bottom of the second document.

10. Press ENTER twice to insert a blank line. Your screen will now look like the one in Figure 3-12.

11. Type the following:

    For more detail, call John at (415) 333-9215.

You can return a window to its standard, full-screen size, pressing the same keys as when you split it in half, but sizing one of the windows at 24 lines. Let's return to the full-size screen.

1. Press the SCREEN (CTRL + F3) key to view the Screen menu.

2. Select Window (1 or W). WordPerfect prompts you with

   Number of lines in this window: 11

3. Type **24** and press ENTER. Now only Doc 2 is displayed because that's the window the cursor was located in when you returned the screen to full size. Doc 1 is still in RAM, but it cannot be displayed on the screen unless you use the SWITCH (SHIFT + F3) key to switch to it.

EXIT FROM TWO SCREENS

WordPerfect keeps track of whether or not you've been working with two Typing screens. If both Typing screens contain text, when you use the EXIT (F7) key to clear a screen or exit WordPerfect the prompts are a bit different. WordPerfect won't allow you to exit the program until you decide on the fate of both documents. Rather than asking whether you wish to exit WordPerfect, the prompt asks whether you wish to leave the document you're currently in. Once you have exited one of the screens, you can then exit the other in the usual manner.

Suppose you've completed both memos. You wish to save the memo in Doc 2 under the name FINANCE and save the memo in Doc 1 under the name URGNOTE again.

1. If you're not viewing Doc 2, press the SWITCH (SHIFT + F3) key to do so.

2. Press the EXIT (F7) key, and save the document under the name FINANCE. Notice that WordPerfect prompts you with the following after you save the document to a file:

Exit Doc 2? (Y/N) No

3. Type **Y** to leave Doc 2. The screen switches to Doc 1—Doc 2 has been cleared. (Alternatively, you could type **N**, in which case WordPerfect would remain in Doc 2, but the screen would clear.)

4. Press the EXIT (F7) key and resave the document in the Doc 1 window under the name URGNOTE by pressing ENTER to accept the suggested name and typing **Y** to replace the earlier file on disk. Now WordPerfect prompts you with

Exit WP? (Y/N) No

This is because the second document screen is clear.

5. Type **N** so that you may remain in WordPerfect and proceed with the review exercise that follows.

REVIEW EXERCISE

The following steps will help you to gain skill in using enhancements as you type a document. Find a document containing several paragraphs of text that you can practice with. You will perform tasks such as underlining and boldfacing. Then you will work with two documents at once—each in a different Typing screen window.

1. On a clear Typing screen, begin to type the document. As you do so, practice underlining and boldfacing words and sentences. Also practice centering and aligning flush right as you type, and use the →INDENT (F4) key and other keys that work on tab stops as you type paragraphs or type text in columns aligned on tabs.

2. Using the DATE/OUTLINE (SHIFT + F5) key, change the date format to display the current date and time as follows: Month ##, 19## at #:## am. Then position the cursor where you would like the date and time to appear. Press the DATE/OUT-LINE (SHIFT + F5) key, and insert the date and time as text.

3. Switch to the Doc 2 Typing screen. Make sure that the screen is clear, and retrieve the file named SAMPLE.

4. Practice underlining and boldfacing individual words and sentences in SAMPLE. (*Hint:* Since the text has already been typed, you must use the BLOCK (ALT + F4) key to highlight the text that you want to underline or boldface.)

5. Center all of the countries that are listed on individual lines in the document. (*Hint:* Use the BLOCK (ALT + F4) key to highlight the list of countries, and then press the CENTER (SHIFT + F6) key to center them all at once.)

6. Use the EXIT (F7) key to exit WordPerfect *without* saving the documents on screen. (*Hint:* Since you have text on both the Doc 1 screen and the Doc 2 screen, WordPerfect won't allow you to exit the program until you decide on the fate of both documents. So after pressing the EXIT (F7) key, type N, indicating that you do not wish to resave the file named SAMPLE. Next, type Y to exit the Doc 2 screen. Now you must repeat this procedure—press EXIT (F7), type N, and type Y— to exit the Doc 1 screen and WordPerfect.)

REVIEW

- The CENTER (SHIFT + F6) key centers text between the left and right margins. You can press the CENTER (SHIFT + F6) key before typing the text. Or, to center text that's already been typed, use the BLOCK (ALT + F4) key to highlight the text, and then press the CENTER (SHIFT + F6) key.

- The FLUSH RIGHT (ALT + F6) key aligns text against the right margin. You can press the FLUSH RIGHT (ALT + F6) key before typing the text. Or, to align text that's already been typed, use the BLOCK (ALT + F4) key to highlight the text, and then press the FLUSH RIGHT (ALT+ F6) key.

- The UNDERLINE (F8) key underscores text. Press the UNDERLINE (F8) key once, type the text, and then make sure to press UNDERLINE a second time to turn off the feature. You can also type the text first, then use the BLOCK (ALT + F4) key to highlight the text you want underlined, and finally press the UNDERLINE (F8) key. You can decide whether you wish spaces and tabs underlined using the FORMAT (SHIFT + F8) key.

- The BOLD (F6) key boldfaces text. Press the BOLD (F6) key once, type the text, and then make sure to press BOLD again to turn off the feature. You can also type the text first, then use the BLOCK (ALT + F4) key to highlight the text you want boldfaced, and finally press the BOLD (F6) key.

- The DATE/OUTLINE (SHIFT + F5) key automatically inserts the date at the cursor position—either as text or as a code that changes the date automatically when you retrieve or print the document containing that date code. You can also specify the format in which the date will appear. The computer must know the correct date and time in order for the Date feature to function properly.

- The ESC key can be used to repeat a character a specific number of times or to repeat a cursor movement or a deletion a certain number of times. The default repeat value is 8.

- The HOME key helps you control where word wrap breaks a line of text. Press HOME, SPACEBAR to ensure that two words separated by a space remain together on a line. Press HOME, HYPHEN to ensure that two words separated by a hyphen remain together on a line.

- Convert text from lowercase to uppercase by pressing the BLOCK (ALT + F4) key to highlight the text, pressing the SWITCH (SHIFT + F3) key, and responding to the prompt for uppercase or lowercase.

- On-screen comments that will never be printed can be incorporated into a document. The TEXT IN/OUT (CTRL + F5) key allows you to access the Document Comments feature.

- A number of keys in addition to TAB can affect how text is positioned on a tab stop: the →INDENT (F4) key indents an entire paragraph to the next tab stop; the →INDENT← (SHIFT + F4) key indents from both the left and the right; the ←MARGIN RELEASE (SHIFT + TAB) key moves one line of text back to the previous tab stop; the TAB ALIGN (CTRL + F6) key aligns text on a specific character at the tab stop; and the CENTER (SHIFT + F6) key centers text on a tab stop if you press the TAB key first.

- WordPerfect lets you work with two documents at the same time. Keep each document on a separate Typing screen, and press the SWITCH (SHIFT + F3) key to go from the Doc 1 to the Doc 2 window. Or split the Typing screen's window with the SCREEN (CTRL + F3) key to view the Doc 1 and Doc 2 windows simultaneously.

4

CHANGING MARGINS, TABS, AND OTHER LINE FORMATS

When you make decisions about how text will appear on the printed page, you are said to be setting the document's format. You made no format decisions when you worked with documents in the preceding chapters, and as a result WordPerfect assumed the initial or default format settings—settings that the designers of the WordPerfect program established for you.

You don't have to abide by the default settings: you can customize the appearance of each document you create, and you can do so at any time—before you start typing a document, while you're typing it, or when you're done.

You'll learn in this chapter what the default settings are for left and right margins, tabs, and other basic settings that affect each line of text. Using one of the documents you created in a previous chapter, you'll establish new margins. You'll also work with the justification and hyphenation settings and make the whole document double rather than single spaced. To help you become skillful with tabs, step-by-step instructions will show you how to change tab stop locations. By the chapter's end, you will have become skilled at working with the hidden codes inserted into your document whenever you make margin, tab, and other line format changes.

INITIAL LINE FORMAT SETTINGS

The initial settings for formatting each line of text in a document are as follows:

Left and right margins	1-inch borders on either side of the printed page
Right justification	On, meaning that WordPerfect will adjust the spacing between characters when printing the text to establish a right margin that is even
Hyphenation	Off, meaning that WordPerfect will wrap a long word that extends beyond the right margin down to the next line rather than split the word with a hyphen
Spacing	Single
Tab stops	One every 0.5 inch

If you do not specify otherwise, the above defaults will take effect in each line you type, providing a printed result as illustrated in Figure 4-1.

Note: The above are the defaults as initially set up at WordPerfect Corporation. If some of your default settings appear different, then a coworker may have altered these default settings for your copy of WordPerfect. The procedure to alter the standard defaults is described in the "Initial Settings" section of Appendix C.

You can change any or all of the format defaults for a particular document by inserting format codes within the document. These codes serve to override the default settings.

Placement of format codes is critical. Any code that you insert in a document controls all text from that location *forward,* all the way to either the end of the document or up to the next code of its type farther down in the document. For instance, position the cursor at the top of a document to change margins for the entire document. Or position the cursor just before the third paragraph to change margins for paragraph three and all succeeding paragraphs; paragraphs one and two will abide by the original margin settings.

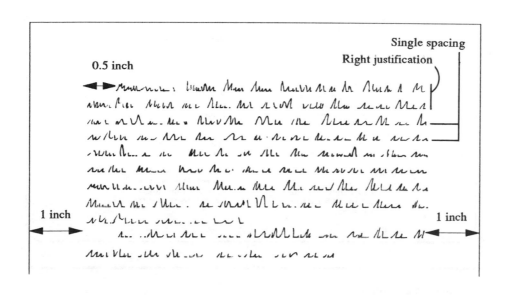

FIGURE 4-1 Printed page using default line format settings

You insert a format code in a document by pressing the FORMAT (SHIFT + F8) key. When you do so, the menu in Figure 4-2 appears. Notice in Figure 4-2 that there are four types of format changes that can be made: line format changes, which will be discussed in this chapter; page format changes, which affect the layout of text on a page and will be discussed in the next chapter; document format changes, which are special and affect an entire document (one of which will also be discussed in this chapter); and other format changes, which cover special formatting, such as a document's underline style (as described in Chapter 3). You select the appropriate menu option to change a format; a format code is inserted at the current cursor position, which is displayed in the document when you reveal codes.

You will insert various format codes as this chapter continues. Remember that if you lose your bearings as you press function keys and select menu items, press CANCEL (F1) until you back out of the menus and then start again. (In a few circumstances, CANCEL won't back you out of a menu, and you must press EXIT (F7) instead, as is usually indicated at the bottom of the menu screen.)

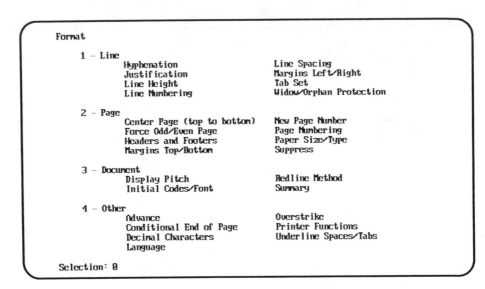

FIGURE 4-2 Format menu

CHANGE LEFT AND RIGHT MARGINS

WordPerfect's initial left and right margin settings are 1 inch. This means that WordPerfect will insert 1 inch of white space on both the left and right edges of the printed page. Since WordPerfect assumes that you will be printing on 8.5- by 11-inch paper (paper size is another assumption that can be changed, as discussed in the next chapter), this means that WordPerfect assumes you want each line of text to be 6.5 inches long—8.5 inches minus 1-inch left margin minus 1-inch right margin.

Note: If you followed the directions in Chapter 2 to print your document but your printed result had left/right margins other than 1 inch, then the paper may have been improperly aligned in your printer. For example, if the paper has been placed in the printer too far to the right, the right margin would be wider than the left. Try printing again by shifting where paper is inserted into the printer.

You can set new margins, thus increasing or decreasing the width of each line of text. To set new margins, position the cursor at the beginning of the line where you want the new margins to take effect. For example, you would position at the very top left corner of page 2 to change margins starting on that page. Positioning the cursor is critical: remember that a margin change will take effect from the cursor position on down.

Once the cursor is properly positioned, press the FORMAT (SHIFT + F8) key. The Format menu shown in Figure 4-2 appears. Select Line (1 or L), and the Line Format menu as shown in Figure 4-3 appears. Select Margins Left and Right (7 or M), and then enter both your left and right margin settings in inches. Finally, press EXIT (F7) to return to the Typing screen, or press CANCEL (F1) to return to the Format menu.

When you alter margins within a document, a Left and Right Margin code is inserted at the current cursor position. For instance, if you changed left and right margins to 2 inches, then the code inserted is **[L/R Mar:2",2"]**. As with any other code placed in a document, a Left/ Right Margin code is visible only when you reveal codes. This code affects margins from that point and forward or up to another **[L/R Mar:]** code located farther down in the document.

Let's alter margins for an entire document. We'll set the left margin to 1.5 inches and the right margin to 1 inch.

```
Format: Line

    1 - Hyphenation                      Off

    2 - Hyphenation Zone - Left          18%
                           Right         4%

    3 - Justification                    Yes

    4 - Line Height                      Auto

    5 - Line Numbering                   No

    6 - Line Spacing                     1

    7 - Margins - Left                   1"
                  Right                  1"

    8 - Tab Set                          0", every 0.5"

    9 - Widow/Orphan Protection          No



Selection: 0
```

FIGURE 4-3   Line Format menu

1. On a clear Typing screen, retrieve the file named SAMPLE by using either the LIST FILES (F5) or the RETRIEVE (SHIFT + F10) key. (Both methods for retrieving a document are described in Chapter 2.)

2. Make sure the cursor is at the top left corner of the document.

3. Press the FORMAT (SHIFT + F8) key. The Format menu appears.

4. Select Line (1 or L). The Line Format menu appears, as shown in Figure 4-3. Notice that option 7, Margins, indicates that the current default settings are 1 inch for both the left and right margins.

5. Select Margins Left and Right (7 or M).

6. Type **1.5** and press ENTER to set a left margin. (WordPerfect automatically assumes inches and inserts the " symbol.)

7. Type 1 and press ENTER to set a right margin.

8. Press EXIT (F7) to return to the Typing screen.

9. Press DOWN ARROW to readjust the text on screen.

Word wrap has readjusted the text to fit properly within the new margin settings. Notice that with the cursor at the left margin the position indicator on the status line now reads **Pos 1.5"** indicating a new left margin setting. This is because the Margin code **[L/R Mar:1.5",1"]** has been inserted at the top of the document. This code overrides the default settings. Since it is the only margin code in the document and is at the top, it affects the entire document.

What if you wish the bottom portion of the text to have different margins? In that case, you would insert a second Margin code farther down in the text. Let's set the bottom portion of the text to wider margins of 2.5 inches on both the left and the right.

1. Position the cursor on the "C" at the left margin on the line that reads "Contact THE R&R WINE...."

2. Press the FORMAT (SHIFT + F8) key. The Format menu appears.

3. Select Line (1 or L). The Line Format menu appears. Notice on your screen that option 7, Margins, indicates that the current settings are 1.5 inches for the left margin and 1 inch for the right margin. This is a result of the Margin code we previously inserted at the top of the document.

4. Select Margins Left and Right (7 or M).

5. Type **2.5** and press ENTER to set a left margin. (WordPerfect automatically assumes inches and inserts the " symbol.)

6. Type **2.5** and press ENTER to set a right margin.

7. Press EXIT (F7) to return to the Typing screen.

8. Press DOWN ARROW to rewrite the text on screen.

You have just inserted a second Margin code **[L/R Mar:2.5", 2.5"]** into the text so that the first and second halves of the document have different margin settings. The first Margin code stays in control of the text up to the point where the second code appears. Though the codes are invisible, they can be viewed if you reveal codes.

EDIT MARGIN CODES

It is common to change your mind once you've reset your margins (or changed any other format). If you wish to cancel a margin change, you must find and erase the **[L/R Mar:]** code that controls it. Remember from Chapter 1 that to uncover the location of a code, you can use the REVEAL CODES (ALT + F3) key. If you don't know where the Margin code is hiding, the Reveal Codes screen enables you to find it quickly. Let's reveal codes to view those codes you just set and erase the second Margin code:

1. Position the cursor on the "C" in "Contact THE R&R...."

2. Press the REVEAL CODES (ALT + F3) key. In the bottom window, you should be able to spot the **[L/R Mar:2.5",2.5"]** code.

3. If the cursor is just to the right of the Margin code, press BACK-SPACE to delete the code. If the cursor is on the Margin code, press DEL to delete the code.

4. Press REVEAL CODES (ALT + F3) to return to the Typing screen.

5. Press HOME, HOME, UP ARROW to move to the top of the document. As you can see, the bottom portion of the document has been adjusted to abide by the only Margin code in the text, which is located at the top of the document, dictating left and right margins of 1.5 inches and 1 inch respectively.

Now suppose that you wish to return the document to the default left and right margin settings of 1 inch. To do so, we must erase the **[L/R Mar:1.5",1"]** code located at the top of the document; when WordPerfect finds no Margin codes in the text, the default margins will again take effect. Remember from Chapter 1 that you don't necessarily have to erase a code using the Reveal Codes screen. If you know where a code is hiding, you can erase it on the Typing screen. When you attempt to erase a format code on the Typing screen, you'll find that WordPerfect always prompts to verify the deletion—just in case you don't realize that there's a format code that you're about to erase. If you wish to erase the code, type **Y**. If you bumped up against the code accidentally and don't wish to erase it, press ENTER or type **N** or any key other than **Y**.

Let's erase the remaining Margin code on the Typing screen.

1. Press HOME, HOME, UP ARROW to position the cursor at the top of the document.

2. Press BACKSPACE. WordPerfect prompts

    Delete [L/R Mar:1.5",1"]? (Y/N) No

    WordPerfect is informing you that you have bumped up against a hidden code. Notice from the prompt that Word-Perfect is assuming that you do not wish to delete this code, with the suggestion "No" at the end of the prompt line.

3. Type **Y**. The margin code is deleted.

There are now no Margin codes in the text; if you press DOWN ARROW to rewrite the screen, the text returns to the default settings.

But suppose you change your mind one more time; that is, you decide that you *did* want a left margin of 1.5 inches. In other words, you wish to reinstate the Margin code you just deleted. To do so, there are two alternatives. You could use the FORMAT (SHIFT + F8) key over again to insert a new Margin code. An easier way, however, is to simp-ly recover the deleted code using the Undelete feature, which you learned about in Chapter 1. (See the "Recover Deleted Text" section of Chapter 1 for a refresher.) The Undelete feature will work because you just deleted the Margin code:

1. Move the cursor to the top of the document, where you wish to reinsert the margin code.

2. Press CANCEL (F1). No prompts or menus are on screen, so the Undelete menu appears:

    Undelete: 1 Restore; 2 Previous Deletion: 0

    No text appears in reverse video on screen because you just deleted a code—not text.

3. Select Restore (1 or R). The **[L/R Mar:1.5",1"]** code is recovered, when you use DOWN ARROW, and the text readjusts for the new margins.

If you find the Undelete feature mysterious when working with codes, just remember that on the Typing screen a code is hidden. You may wish to erase the Margin code again and this time press the REVEAL CODES (ALT + F3) key before you use the Undelete feature. In that way, you can view the Margin code as it reappears in the text.

TURN RIGHT JUSTIFICATION ON/OFF

WordPerfect's default setting is for right justification on. This means that text in paragraphs will be justified at both the left and right margins when printed; extra spaces will be inserted between words to justify the text. The alternative is to turn justification off; in this case, no extra spaces are inserted and the right margin is ragged. When right justification is on, it is not shown on the Typing screen; it takes effect only at the printer. Figure 4-4 shows examples of printed text when justification is on and when it is off.

```
RIGHT JUSTIFICATION OFF:

Two of the major wine-producing countries in Europe are France
and Italy.  France produces a wide variety, and Bordeaux is often
considered one of the centers of fine wine.  In Italy, wine
production takes place in just about every region.  In fact,
Italy has been known to yield more wine per year than any other
country in the world.  Though white wines are manufactured here,
it is Italy's red wines that have achieved a special reputation.


RIGHT JUSTIFICATION ON:

Two of the major wine-producing countries in Europe are France and
Italy.  France produces a wide variety, and Bordeaux is often
considered one of the centers of fine wine.  In Italy,  wine
production takes place in just about every region. In fact, Italy
has been known to yield more wine per year than any other country
in the world.  Though white wines are manufactured here, it is
Italy's red wines that have achieved a special reputation.
```

FIGURE 4-4   The printed result with justification on and off

As with margins, you change the justification for a document on the Line Format menu. The current setting is indicated with the "Yes" or "No" next to option 3, Justification; for instance, the "Yes" in Figure 4-3 indicates that justification is on. You can type N to turn justification off or, if it had been off previously, you would type **Y** to turn it on. The code **[Just Off]** or **[Just On]** is inserted.

Let's turn off justification for the entire document now on screen.

1. Press HOME, HOME, UP ARROW to position the cursor at the top of the document.

2. Press the FORMAT (SHIFT + F8) key.

3. Select Line (1 or L). The Line Format menu appears.

4. Select Justification (3 or J).

5. Type **N** to turn off justification.

6. Press EXIT (F7) to return to the text of your document.

Remember that the text on screen will look no different whether right justification is on or off (although, depending on your printer, word wrap may readjust the lines slightly). But if you reveal codes, you'll see the **[Just Off]** code you inserted. And if you print out your document, you'll see that WordPerfect no longer inserts spaces between letters and words; the right margin is ragged.

To return to justification on starting at the the top of the document, erase the **[Just Off]** code; the default setting, justification on, becomes active. (Another way to return to justification is to move to the top of the document and use the FORMAT (SHIFT + F8) key to insert a **[Just On]** code. Then you'd have two codes sitting side by side: **[Just Off][Just On]**. The code farther to the right, the Justification On code, overshadows the first code, and so justification would be on. However, this method is not advisable since these two redundant codes only serve to clutter the screen.)

TURN HYPHENATION ON/OFF

Whether right justification is on or off, hyphens at the ends of lines can improve the look of the printed page. Figure 4-5 shows the line-

```
HYPHENATION OFF:


Here is a standard paragraph to show the
noticeable effects of hyphenation in your
documents.  Hyphenation is off as the default
but can be turned on easily enough.
Hyphenation is preferred by some people but
disliked by others.



HYPHENATION ON:


Here is a standard paragraph to show the no-
ticeable effects of hyphenation in your docu-
ments.  Hyphenation is off as the default but
can be turned on easily enough.  Hyphenation
is preferred by some people but disliked by
others.
```

FIGURE 4-5   How hyphenation affects line format

by-line differences for identical text with and without hyphenation. (How hyphenation affects a document when printed depends on the right justification setting: with justification turned off, hyphens make the right margin less ragged; with justification turned on, hyphens reduce the number of extra spaces necessary to make the right margin straight. Figure 4-5 compares a document with and without hyphenation when justification is off.) You can have WordPerfect assist you in hyphenating, or you can hyphenate on your own.

WordPerfect-Assisted Hyphenation

The default is for hyphenation off; WordPerfect will automatically wrap down to the next line any word that extends too far beyond the right margin. However, you can request that WordPerfect hyphenate long words.

You can turn hyphenation on before, after, or while typing a document. First move the cursor to the line where you want hyphenation to begin. Then press the Line option on the Format menu and select Hyphenation (1 or H). A Hyphenation menu appears at the bottom of the Line Format menu:

1 Off; 2 Manual; 3 Auto: 0

Off (1 or F) turns off hyphenation if it had been turned on previously. Manual (2 or M) turns on hyphenation whereby WordPerfect prompts, asking for confirmation or for you to indicate where to position the hyphen in each word to be hyphenated; this allows you total control over the location of a hyphen in a word. Auto (3 or A) turns on hyphenation whereby WordPerfect uses a special formula to determine the positioning of the hyphen and prompts for a hyphenation decision only when WordPerfect cannot determine it.

A **[Hyph Off]** code is inserted when you turn off hyphenation, while a **[Hyph On]** code is inserted when you turn on hyphenation—whether the hyphenation is manual or automatic. For text already typed after the code, WordPerfect checks from the current cursor position forward for any hyphenation candidates. For any new text you add below the code, it checks for hyphenation candidates as you type.

How does WordPerfect decide what words are candidates for hyphenation when you turn on this feature? It depends on what's called the *hyphenation zone* (*H-Zone*). An H-Zone extends from a certain measurement before the right margin setting to a certain measurement after the right margin, expressed as a percentage of a line's length. It is preset with a left H-Zone setting of 10% of the line length and a right H-Zone setting of 4% of the line length. For instance, suppose that a line is 6.5 inches long (as in the case where all the default settings are intact—your paper width is 8.5 inches and left/right margins are 1 inch). In that case, the H-Zone starts 0.65 inch (10% of 6.5 inches) from the right margin, and the right H-Zone extends 0.26 inch (4% of 6.5 inches) past the right margin. If a word starts on or before the left H-Zone setting and extends past the right H-Zone setting, it is a candidate for hyphenation. Figure 4-6 illustrates two words that are candidates for hyphenation: "Approximately" and "Volleyball." The other two words are not: "Dictionary" does not go beyond the right H-Zone, so it would remain at the end of the current line; "Personal"

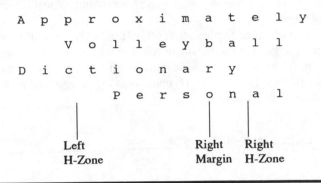

FIGURE 4-6 The H-Zone determining that only the first two words are hyphenation candidates

begins after the start of the H-Zone, so it would be wrapped down to the next line.

The narrower the H-Zone, the more words are hyphenated. With justification on a narrower H-Zone reduces the number of spaces between words; with justification off a narrower H-Zone reduces the raggedness of the right margin when a document is printed.

To alter the H-Zone, you select Hyphenation Zone (2 or Z) on the Line Format menu and type in new percentages for the left and right H-Zone boundaries. Suppose you change the left and right H-Zone to 5% and 0%. Then the code **[H-Zone:5%,0%]** is inserted. (Changing the right H-Zone to 0% means that you won't allow characters to extend at all beyond the right margin during hyphenation. With an H-Zone greater than 0%, as in the case of the default setting, text can extend a bit beyond the right margin, which allows for a more reliable average right margin.)

Let's narrow the H-Zone for the document on screen and then turn on manual hyphenation, where we can confirm the hyphenation of each word. Just as with margins and justification, it is critical to position the cursor before turning on hyphenation:

1. Make sure that the cursor is at the top of the document so that hyphenation will be turned on for the entire document.

2. Press the FORMAT (SHIFT + F8) key.

3. Select Line (1 or L). Notice that, as shown in Figure 4-3, hyphenation is off and the current H-Zone is 10%,4%.

4. Select Hyphenation Zone (2 or Z).

5. Type **6** and press ENTER to change the left H-Zone. (Word-Perfect assumes you are entering the H-Zone as a percentage, so it is unnecessary to type the **%** symbol.)

6. Type **0** and press ENTER to change the right H-Zone.

7. Select Hyphenation (1 or Y). The following menu appears at the bottom of the Line Format screen:

   1 Off; 2 Manual; 3 Auto: **0**

8. Select Manual (2 or M). The word "Manual" now appears at the top of the Line Format menu.

9. Press EXIT (F7) to return to the Typing screen.

You have now inserted both an **[H-Zone:6%,0%]** and a **[Hyph On]** code at the top of the document. Since already-existing text appears below that code, WordPerfect immediately begins checking for hyphenation candidates. If a word requires hyphenation, WordPerfect sounds a beep and displays that word at the bottom of the screen (you may be unable to see where that word is located in the actual text), asking for confirmation regarding where to position the cursor. For instance, you may now see the following at the bottom of the screen:

Position hyphen; Press ESC Fra-nce

Note: Remember from Chapter 1 that word wrap may operate differently on your screen because of the variation in how printers place characters on the page. Thus, WordPerfect may prompt you for a different hyphenation candidate or may not need to prompt for a hyphenation candidate at all.

When WordPerfect prompts for hypenation, you have three choices:

- To accept the hyphen location suggestion, you simply press ESC; the hyphen is inserted wherever suggested by Word-Perfect.

- To reject the suggestion (WordPerfect's suggestions are sometimes grammatically incorrect) and reposition the hyphen, you use the RIGHT or the LEFT ARROW key to relocate the hyphen and then press ESC; the hyphen is inserted wherever you indicated.

- To cancel hyphenation for that one word, press the CANCEL (F1) key; the hidden Cancel Hyphenation code [/] is inserted before that word, and the entire word is wrapped down to the beginning of the next line.

Let's respond to WordPerfect's prompts. The first prompt may be

Position hyphen; Press ESC Fra-nce

1. Press CANCEL (F1), since it is inappropriate to hyphenate a one-syllable word. Another beep sounds and WordPerfect may prompt with

Position hyphen; Press ESC Bor-deaux

2. In this case, press ESC to hyphenate the word in the location suggested by WordPerfect. Now WordPerfect may prompt with

Position hyphen; Press ESC Eur-ope

3. Press the LEFT ARROW key several times and then the RIGHT ARROW key several times to watch as the hyphen is repositioned as you move. Notice that the hyphen moves only so far in the word; WordPerfect only allows you to move the hyphen within the range of the hyphenation zone.

4. Position the cursor where you wish to insert a hyphen and press ESC. (Or you can press CANCEL to refuse hyphenation of that word.)

5. Continue responding to the hyphenation prompts until your cursor returns to the document text, meaning that all hyphenation candidates have been processed.

When using manual hyphenation, you can even relocate a hyphen after it has been inserted by WordPerfect. Simply position the cursor on the hyphen and press DEL. WordPerfect will again prompt for a hyphenation location so that you can reposition the hyphen and press ESC or press CANCEL (F1) to refuse hyphenation for that word.

Whenever WordPerfect assists you in hyphenation, whether you use manual or automatic hyphenation, soft hyphens are inserted—

"soft" because a hyphen disappears if you edit your text in such a way that the word containing the hyphen no longer requires hyphenation. For instance, if you edited the second line on the screen by erasing the word "wide," then when you pressed DOWN ARROW to adjust the text, the hyphen in "Bordeaux" would disappear.

```
Two of the major wine-producing countries in Europe are
France and Italy.  France produces a wide variety, and Bor-
deaux is often considered one of the centers of fine wine.
```

would become

```
Two of the major wine-producing countries in Europe are
France and Italy.  France produces a variety, and Bordeaux
is often considered one of the centers of fine wine.   In
```

WordPerfect might then need to request a new hyphenation candidate.

The soft hyphen remains as a hidden code even if the text is readjusted so that the hyphen doesn't appear on the Typing screen; it stays around just in case you edit further and the hyphen again becomes needed. A soft hyphen can be viewed by revealing codes. On the Reveal Codes screen, a soft hyphen appears as a boldface hyphen character (-).

Note: As mentioned previously, WordPerfect attempts to position hyphens properly in a word using a special formula (algorithm). If you plan to employ hyphenation for most of your documents, and especially if you plan to use the automatic hyphenation feature, you should know that WordPerfect Corporation offers a hyphenation module. With this module, words are hyphenated according to a hyphenation dictionary, making hyphenation more accurate than with the algorithm. The hyphenation module is sold separately from WordPerfect; contact WordPerfect Corporation for details.

Unassisted Hyphenation

Perhaps you dislike hyphenation as a general rule but find there are occasions when, as you type a long word at the end of a line, you wish to hyphenate without WordPerfect's assistance. To insert a soft hyphen on your own with hyphenation off, hold down the CTRL key and type a hyphen; in other words, press CTRL + HYPHEN. The hyphen will appear at that place in the word only if the word falls at the end of a line.

If you press the HYPHEN key without also pressing CTRL, you are inserting a regular hyphen, not a soft hyphen. A regular hyphen remains in the word no matter where the word falls on a line. The hyphen in "wine-producing" is an example: regardless of where it appears on a line, that phrase will remain hyphenated. On the Reveal Codes screen, a regular hyphen looks as follows: [-]. For instance, if you press the REVEAL CODES (ALT + F3) key to view the document now on your screen, you'll see "wine-producing" in the top window but "wine[-]producing" in the bottom window. A regular hyphen will not disappear if you edit your text, so make sure to use CTRL + HYPHEN to insert a soft hyphen when hyphenating a word at the end of the line that is not otherwise hyphenated—or else you could get awkward results if you edit the document later on. (Also remember from Chapter 3 that there's an additional way to insert a hyphen. If you press HOME and then type the hyphen, you insert a special hyphen that always stays in the text and, at the same time, glues two words together so that they will not be separated on two different lines by word wrap.)

MODIFY LINE SPACING

Line spacing increases or decreases the amount of space between lines. WordPerfect assumes you want all your text single spaced. To alter spacing, you must position the cursor at the left margin of the line where you want to make the change, and, as with margins, justification, and hyphenation, use the Line Format menu to make the change. Select Line Spacing (6 or S), and then enter the spacing you desire— providing that your printer supports the spacing increment you entered. For instance, you can type **2** to request double spacing, or **1.5** to change to one-and-one-half-line spacing. Some printers will even support fractional spacing such as **1.25** or **1.1**, allowing you the flexibility to refine the spacing between lines.

The screen can show spacing only to the nearest whole number. If you selected one-and-one-half-line spacing, for example, the screen will show double spacing, but when printed, the text will have one-and-one-half spacing. A **[Ln Spacing:]** code is inserted when you change line spacing, affecting all text down to the next spacing code or the end of the document.

Here's the step-by-step procedure to double space the document that is currently on screen.

1. Press HOME, HOME, UP ARROW. The cursor moves to the top of the document.

2. Press the FORMAT (SHIFT + F8) key.

3. Select Line (1 or L). Notice that, as shown in Figure 4-3, the number 1 appears next to the Line Spacing option. The **1** indicates that the document is currently single spaced.

4. Select Line Spacing (6 or S).

5. Type **2** and press ENTER.

6. Press EXIT (F7) to return to the document. The entire document is now double spaced.

Note: Technically, WordPerfect determines the spacing between lines of text on the printed page by multiplying line spacing by a feature called line height, which is the amount of space assigned to a single line. For instance, a common line height is 0.16 inch. As a result, 0.16 inch times single spacing means that lines will be printed 0.16 inch apart, so that there will be six lines per one vertical inch. Or, 0.16 inch times double spacing means that lines will be printed 0.32 inch apart. See Chapter 10 for more on the Line Height feature and your ability to control the amount of space assigned to each line of text.

CHECK FORMAT CODES AND PRINT

When your documents become intricate, with numerous format codes throughout, it becomes difficult to remember what changes you have made and where they take effect. You can find out by using the REVEAL CODES (ALT + F3) key. You can reveal codes and scroll down through the document to survey the location of format codes.

And, of course, you can erase any codes you no longer desire or that you inserted by accident.

In fact, inserting extra or unwanted codes is quite common, especially for beginning users. For example, you may set margins and then, realizing you made a typing mistake in entering the margins, insert another Margin code to reset them. You would then have two codes side by side in the text.

[L/R Mar:2.5",2.5"][L/R Mar:1.5",1.5"]

Remember that a format code's effect on a document is canceled as soon as another code of the same type is encountered farther on in the text. As a result, the first Margin code's effect on the text is overshadowed by the second code; in the example, the 1.5-inch margins will control the text. Nonetheless, you will still want to delete that first, unnecessary code.

Why delete extra codes? They have a tendency to create problems. For instance, if you happened to position the cursor between two **[L/R Mar:]** codes and then began typing, the first code would affect the new text, and the results might be awkward. Therefore, always tidy up your documents by erasing unwanted codes.

Let's reveal codes to check the format settings. Once you have verified that the format settings are correct, you'll print the document to see the changes.

1. Press HOME, HOME, UP ARROW to position the cursor at the top of the document.

2. Press the REVEAL CODES (ALT + F3) key. You should see a long string of codes in the bottom window, as shown in Figure 4-7. (Your codes may appear in a different order.)

3. Check your screen against Figure 4-7. If there are extra codes shown in the bottom window, delete them. Position the cursor just to the right of an unwanted code and press BACKSPACE, or position it on the code and press DEL.

4. If any codes are missing, insert them as described earlier in this chapter. (If the Justification code refuses to appear, it may be that the default for your copy of WordPerfect has been set for right justification off. If so, it would be unnecessary to insert a **[Just Off]** code.)

5. Turn on your printer, insert paper, and print the page by pressing the PRINT (SHIFT + F7) key and selecting Page (2 or P). (You can be displaying the Reveal Codes screen when you print, or you can press REVEAL CODES (ALT + F3) to return to the Typing screen before printing.)

You should see the following results:

Left and right margins	1.5 inch and 1 inch, respectively
Right justification	Off
Hyphenation	On, with various words hyphenated according to the new H-Zone setting
Spacing	Double

These format changes affect only the document currently on screen. If you clear the screen to begin typing a new document, the new document starts out with all the default settings.

```
Two of the major wine-producing countries in Europe are

France and Italy.  France produces a wide variety, and Bor-

deaux is often considered one of the centers of fine wine.

In Italy, wine production takes place in just about every

region.  In fact, Italy has been known to yield more wine

per year than any other country in the world.  Though white
C:\WPER\DATA\SAMPLE                                Doc 1 Pg 1 Ln 1" Pos 1.5"
{   ▲   ▲   ▲   ▲   ▲   ▲   ▲   ▲   ▲   ▲   ▲   }   ▲   ▲
[L/R Mar:1.5",1"][Just Off][HZone:6%,0%][Hyph On][Ln Spacing:2]Two of the major
wine[-]producing countries in Europe are[SRt]
[/]France and Italy.  France produces a wide variety, and Bor-
deaux is often considered one of the centers of fine wine. [SRt]
In Italy, wine production takes place in just about every[SRt]
region.  In fact, Italy has been known to yield more wine[SRt]
per year than any other country in the world.  Though white[SRt]
wines are manufactured here, it is Italy's red wines that[SRt]
have achieved a special reputation.  Other countries in Eur-
ope that produce wine include:[HRt]

Press Reveal Codes to restore screen
```

FIGURE 4-7 Numerous format codes on the Reveal Codes screen

PLACE CODES ON THE DOCUMENT INITIAL CODES SCREEN

As shown in Figure 4-7, you can amass many format codes together on a certain line in a document. In Figure 4-7, they are all located at the top of the document.

WordPerfect offers the ability to place many format codes that would otherwise appear at the top of the document on a special screen, the Document Initial Codes screen. By inserting format codes on this screen rather than in the document yourself, you (1) reduce the clutter at the top of the document, and (2) safeguard against accidentally moving or erasing a code, something that is all too easy to do when a code is in the document itself.

Place a format code on the Document Initial Codes screen only if you wish to change a document's format starting *at the top* of the document. Any format codes of the same type found in the document itself override any codes on the Document Initial Codes screen. Thus, the hierarchy of how a document is formatted is as follows: (1) when a document is first created, WordPerfect assumes default settings, (2) if a format code is located on the Document Initial Codes screen, then the default setting is overridden by that format code, (3) if a format code is located in the text of the document itself, then the format code on the Document Initial Codes screen is overriden by the code in the text, from the point where that code is located until the end of the document or until the next code of its type farther forward in the text.

You can access the Document Initial Codes screen with your cursor positioned anywhere on screen. Press the FORMAT (SHIFT + F8) key to display the menu in Figure 4-2, and then select Document (3 or D), in which case the Document Format menu shown in Figure 4-8 appears. Select Initial Codes (2 or C). A screen that resembles a Reveal Codes screen appears. Then proceed as if you were placing a code within the document itself, by again using the FORMAT (SHIFT + F8) key. When you exit the Document Initial Codes screen using the EXIT (F7) key, your cursor repositions at the top of the document on screen.

Codes inserted on the Document Initial Codes screen are never displayed when you reveal codes in a document. You can see the codes only when you return to the Document Initial Codes screen.

Let's view the current Document Initial Codes screen for the file named SAMPLE:

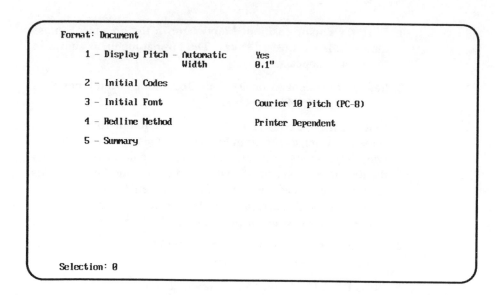

FIGURE 4-8 Document Format menu

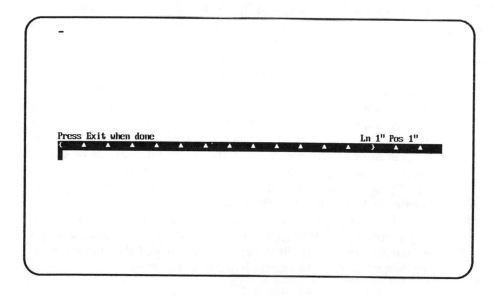

FIGURE 4-9 A blank Document Initial Codes screen

1. With the cursor positioned anywhere in the document, press the FORMAT (SHIFT + F8) key. The Format menu, as shown in Figure 4-2, appears.

2. Select Document (3 or D). The Document Format menu, as shown in Figure 4-8, appears.

3. Select Initial Codes (2 or C). The Document Initial Codes screen appears, as shown in Figure 4-9. This screen is split into two windows and separated by a tab ruler line (which shows the default margin and tab settings), just like the Reveal Codes screen. The Document Initial Codes screen is blank. If there were codes on this screen, however, the codes would be hidden in the top window and displayed in the bottom window.

4. As noted in Figure 4-9, press the EXIT (F7) key to exit the Document Initial Codes screen.

5. Press EXIT (F7) to return to your document.

Because the Document Initial Codes screen is blank, you can tell that no changes have yet been made to the default settings. As a result, the document is formatted with all default settings, unless format codes are found in the text to override the defaults.

Note: If on your screen, you find that one or more codes appear in the bottom window of the Document Initial Codes screen, then a coworker has altered certain default settings for the copy of WordPerfect you are using. Besides changing default formats for particular documents, you also have the ability to change the default format settings permanently—for all documents that you create from that point on. For instance, you can permanently change the justification default to off, so that justification is never activated in a document unless you specify otherwise for a particular document. See the "Initial Settings" section in Appendix C to learn more about this ability.

Now that you know about the Document Initial Codes screen and the advantage to keeping the amount of codes within a document to a mimimum, let's erase all the codes at the top of the document and reinsert them on the Document Initial Codes screen.

1. Press REVEAL CODES (ALT + F3) to display the codes at the top of the document.

2. Use the BACKSPACE or DEL key to erase the five codes at the top of the document. The default settings now take effect for this document—left/right margins of 1 inch, justification on, no hyphenation, single spacing.

3. Press REVEAL CODES again to return to the Typing screen.

4. Press the FORMAT (SHIFT + F8) key.

5. Select Document (3 or D). The Document Format menu, as shown in Figure 4-8, appears.

6. Select Initial Codes (2 or C). The Document Initial Codes screen appears, as shown in Figure 4-9. It is currently blank. Let's insert the codes in the same order as they were inserted previously.

7. Press the FORMAT (SHIFT + F8) key.

8. Select Line (1 or L). The Line Format menu appears.

9. Select Margins Left and Right (7 or M).

10. Type **1.5** and press ENTER and then type **1** and press ENTER to set margins.

11. Select Justification (3 or J).

12. Type **N** to turn off justification.

13. Select Hyphenation Zone (2 or Z).

14. Type **6** and press ENTER and then type **0** and press ENTER to change the H-Zone.

15. Select Hyphenation (1 or Y). The following menu appears at the bottom of the Line Format screen:

    1 Off; 2 Manual; 3 Auto: 0

16. Select Manual (2 or M). The word "Manual" now appears at the top of the Line Format menu.

17. Select Line Spacing (6 or S).

18. Type **2** and press ENTER.

19. Press EXIT (F7) to exit the Line Format menu. You are returned to the Document Initial Codes screen. Notice that the five codes you inserted are on the screen, as shown in Figure 4-10.

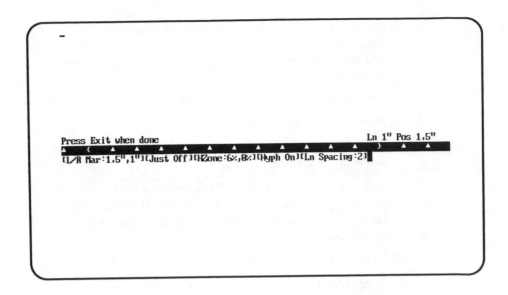

FIGURE 4-10   Document Initial Codes screen after format codes are inserted

20. Press EXIT (F7) two more times to return to the text of your document. Whenever you return to the text from the Document Initial Codes screen, the cursor repositions at the very top of the document.

21. Press DOWN ARROW to readjust the text on screen.

Notice that the text has been readjusted for the new format settings. If you reveal codes using the REVEAL CODES (ALT + F3) key, however, you'll find that no codes are displayed at the top of the document. All the codes are on the Document Initial Codes screen. If you wish to view or edit the codes, you must return to that screen.

Format changes made on the Document Initial Codes screen affect only the one document to which the changes were made—just like format changes made within the text of the document itself. If you clear the screen to begin typing a new document, the new document starts out with all the default settings.

Let's save this document on disk with the changes made to it and then clear the screen:

1. Press the EXIT (F7) key, type **Y**, and press ENTER to save the document on screen under the filename SAMPLE.

2. Type **Y** when WordPerfect asks whether you wish to replace SAMPLE.

3. Type **N** when WordPerfect asks whether you wish to exit the program.

The screen is clear, and the revised document is safely stored on disk, format codes and all. You are returned to the default settings on the Typing screen, ready to begin a new document. Notice, for example, that with the cursor at the left margin of the blank screen, the status line indicates **Pos 1"**: 1 inch is the default left margin setting.

CHANGE TAB STOP LOCATIONS

The default for tab stop locations is every 0.5 inch across the full width of a page. The default tab style is left justified. This means that text positioned on the tab is aligned with its left edge at the tab stop. This is the most commonly used tab style (it indents the first line of a paragraph). Other tab stop styles include

Right justified	The right edge of the tab entry aligns on the tab stop
Decimal align	The decimal point aligns on the tab stop
Center	The entry is centered on the tab stop

Except for center tabs, each style can be set so that it is preceded by a dot leader, meaning that when you press TAB, a row of dots will be inserted as the cursor jumps to the next tab stop. Figure 4-11 shows the effects of the various styles.

You can change the number, frequency, and style of tab stops. You can, for example, set left-justified tab stops only at positions 1.5" and 3", or you can set numerous, evenly spaced tab stops. To set tab stops, move the cursor to the position where you want the new tab stops to take effect. For instance, position the cursor midway down a page in order to change tabs and type a table at that location. Or, to change tab stop locations for an entire document, position the cursor on the Document Initial Codes screen. Then press the FORMAT (SHIFT + F8) key to access the Line Format menu and from that menu select Tab Set (8 or T). WordPerfect displays a Tab menu with one row of dots and the default tab stop locations indicated with Ls at the bottom of the Typing screen, as shown below; "L" stands for left-justified tab, the default style.

```
L....L....L....L....L....L....L....L....L....L....L....L....L....L....L...
 !    ^    !    ^    !    ^    !    ^    !    ^    !    ^    !    ^    !    ^
 1"       2"       3"       4"       5"       6"       7"       8"
Delete EOL (clear tabs); Enter Number (set tab); Del (clear tab);
Left; Center; Right; Decimal; .= Dot Leader
```

Once viewing the Tab menu, there are two ways to delete tab stops. To delete a single tab stop, use the RIGHT ARROW or the LEFT ARROW key to position the cursor on the tab stop and press DEL. To delete *all* tab stops from the current cursor position to the end of the row, position the cursor on the first tab stop you wish to delete and press DELETE EOL (CTRL + END).

There are several ways to insert tab stops, depending on the number and style of tabs you wish to set:

- To insert a single, left-justified tab stop, you have two choices. You can either (1) move the cursor to the location where you want a tab stop and then type **L** or **T** or press TAB to insert a left-justified tab, or (2) type a location (in inches) where you want a tab to appear and press ENTER; for instance, type **1.4** and press ENTER to place a tab at position 1.4".

- To insert a row of evenly spaced, left-justified tab stops, type the starting tab stop location, type a comma, type the incremental spacing, and press ENTER. For instance, to set tabs starting at the 1.5" position and every inch after that, you would type **1.5",1"** and press ENTER. (Or, more simply, you would type **1.5,1** and press ENTER; WordPerfect assumes inches.)

- To insert a single tab stop using a style other than left justified or using a dot leader, move the cursor to the location where you want a tab stop and type **R** to insert a right-justified tab, type **D** to insert a decimal tab, type **L** to insert a left-justified tab, or type **C** to insert a center tab. Then if you wish to create a dot leader type a period; the "L" or "R" or "D" on screen appears in reverse video, signifying a tab with a dot leader.

- To insert a row of evenly spaced tab stops using a style other than left justified, first set a single tab at the starting tab stop location. Then enter the starting tab stop location and the incremental spacing, separated by a comma. For example, to set decimal tabs every inch starting at position 2.4", first set a

---

```
WITHOUT DOT LEADERS:

   CENTER        LEFT            RIGHT           DECIMAL

      ^            ^                ^                ^

      1          June            Smith         $  33.66
    222          Peter            Wild             5.00
  33333          Marilyn          Gold         1,236.17
4444444          Kim            Wallens           14.50


WITH DOT LEADERS:

                 LEFT            RIGHT           DECIMAL

                   ^                ^                ^

1............. June............ Smith .......... $33.66
2............. Peter........... Wild ............  5.00
3............. Marilyn......... Gold ........ 1,236.17
4............. Kim.......... Wallens ..........  14.50
```

^ represents tab stop location

FIGURE 4-11   Tab stop styles

single decimal tab at position 2.4". Then type **2.4,1** and press
ENTER.

Once tab stops are set to your specifications, press the EXIT (F7)
key to leave the Tab menu. A **[Tab Set:]** code is inserted into the text,
listing each tab stop that you set. For instance, if you inserted two tab
stops only, at positions 2" and 3.4", then the code inserted is **[Tab
Set:2",3.4"]**. Or, if you inserted tab stops starting at 1.5" and every
inch after that, the code inserted is **[Tab Set:1.5", every 1"]**. The code
does not indicate the style of each tab stop, only the location. Of
course, the code is hidden on the Typing screen; you must press the
REVEAL CODES (ALT + F3) key to examine it.

As you learned previously, you use the TAB key to move the cursor
to the next tab stop. Remember also from Chapter 3 that you can use
other keys on tab stops. →INDENT (F4), the most popular alternative
to the TAB key, enables you to indent a full paragraph (not just a single
line) at a tab stop location. →INDENT← (SHIFT + F4), ←MARGIN
RELEASE (SHIFT + TAB), CENTER (SHIFT + F6), and TAB ALIGN
(CTRL + F6) are other keys that work on tab stops as well. (In fact, by
using the CENTER and TAB ALIGN keys, you can create the same effects as the center, right-justified, or decimal tabs even when the tab
style for that tab stop is left aligned.) Review Chapter 3 for details on
the various tab stop keys.

```
     Here are the names that were left off the list of deliveries
to the Northwestern territory.  Please make sure to add these names
immediately:

Customer        City          Order #       Cases

Chou            Seattle       AB-1          34 cases from container
                                            744; 25 cases from 333

Goldberg        Seattle       AB-12         2 cases from container
                                            744; 8 cases from 334

Johnson         Portland      AL-12         88 cases from
                                            containers 100 and 142
```

FIGURE 4-12   Sample text to be typed

Suppose you want to type the document shown in Figure 4-12. Follow the steps below to practice setting individual tabs and typing a table on the newly defined tab stops.

1. Starting with a clear Typing screen, press TAB. So far, the default settings are in effect: the cursor moves 0.5 inch to the right.

2. Type the following paragraph:

   Here are the names that were left off the list of deliveries to the Northwestern territory. Please make sure to add these names immediately:

3. Press ENTER twice to insert empty lines. The cursor is now positioned where you will modify tab stops. (Since you want to change tabs in the middle of the document and not at the top of the document, you will insert the Tab Set code in the document itself, not on the Document Initial Codes screen.)

4. Press the FORMAT (SHIFT + F8) key. WordPerfect responds with the Format menu.

5. Select Line (1 or L) to display the Line Format menu, indicating the default tab stop settings.

6. Select Tab Set (8 or T). The tab ruler appears.

7. Press LEFT ARROW until the cursor moves all the way to the left edge of the page, which is position 0" according to the Tab menu. (You can also press HOME, LEFT ARROW to move to the left edge of the Tab menu more quickly.)

8. Press CTRL + END to delete all tabs starting from position 0" (the current cursor position).

9. Set three tab stops as follows: type **2.5** and press ENTER; type **4** and press ENTER; type **5.4** and press ENTER.

10. Press the EXIT (F7) key twice to return to the document. A **[Tab Set:2.5",4",5.4"]** code is inserted in the document. This determines tab stop locations from the current cursor location down. (The Tab Set code is invisible on the Typing screen, of course.)

11. To begin the table, type in the first heading, "Customer," at the left margin. Press TAB to move to the first tab stop, and type in the heading "City." Continue, pressing TAB and typing the remaining headings. After typing "Cases," press ENTER twice to end the line and to insert one blank line.

12. Type each line of customer entries until you've completed the table. As discussed in Chapter 3, you'll want to press →INDENT (F4) rather than TAB before typing the last entry for each customer (under the "Cases" heading) so that the entry is indented to the correct tab stop as it extends beyond one line.

For example, here's how you would proceed in typing the first group of entries: type **Chou**, press TAB; type **Seattle**, press TAB; type **AB-1**, press →INDENT (F4); type **34 cases from container 744; 25 cases from 333**, and press ENTER.

After typing the table, suppose you wish to return tab stops to their default settings, one every 0.5 inch. To do so, you must insert another Tab Stop code below the table. Here's the quick procedure for doing so.

1. Press ENTER twice to position the cursor below the table, at the left margin of a blank line.

2. Press the FORMAT (SHIFT + F8) key. WordPerfect responds with the Format menu.

3. Select Line (1 or L) to display the Line Format menu, indicating the default tab stop settings.

4. Select Tab Set (8 or T). The tab ruler appears.

5. Press CTRL + END to delete all tabs starting from position 1″ (the current cursor position).

6. Type **1,0.5**. Notice that what you just typed now appears in the lower right corner of the tab ruler. (WordPerfect assumes inches when you type **1,0.5**, so there's no need to type **1", 0.5".**)

7. Press ENTER. Tab stops now appear every 0.5 inch.

8. Press the EXIT (F7) key twice. A **[Tab Set:1", every 0.5"]** code is inserted in the document. This determines tab stop locations from the current cursor location down. (The Tab Set code is invisible on the Typing screen, of course.)

9. Press TAB. Notice that the default settings are in effect; the cursor jumped 0.5 inch to the next tab stop.

10. Type the following sentence:

    I should have a list for the Northeastern territory by tomorrow morning.

KEEP TRACK OF TABS AND MARGINS

When your document contains many different Tab Set codes, it becomes difficult to remember which portion of text is affected by which tab settings. Some word processing packages maintain a ruler line on screen so that you can quickly check your current tab and margin settings. This feature is available in WordPerfect, but at a price: it reduces the number of text lines you can see on the screen. The ruler line that appears is the same one displayed between windows on the Reveal Codes screen, with symbols to represent tab stops as well as margins. Triangles represent tab stop locations, a square bracket [or] represents a margin setting, and a curly brace { or } represents a margin where a tab stop is also located.

The standard monitor, which displays 24 lines of text, must be reduced to 23 lines for the ruler line to appear. You would press the SCREEN (CTRL + F3) key, select Window (1 or W), and when WordPerfect prompted you for the window size, either press UP ARROW or type **23** and press ENTER. (This is similar to how you split screens, a feature discussed in Chapter 3; the difference is that to insert a ruler line, you reduce the screen by only one line.)

Let's display the ruler line right now. The cursor can be located anywhere in the document:

1. Press the SCREEN (CTRL + F3) key. WordPerfect responds with the Screen menu:

   0 Rewrite; 1 Window; 2 Line Draw: 0

2. Select Window (1 or W). WordPerfect prompts you with

   Number of lines in this window: 24

3. Type **23** and press ENTER. (Or you can press UP ARROW and then press ENTER.)

A ruler line is now fixed at the bottom of the screen. If you move the cursor through the text, you'll find that the tab markers on the ruler line change to reflect the different tab settings in the document. Within the table, there are only three triangles on the ruler line, representing the three tab stops you set, as shown in Figure 4-13. But when you move the cursor either above or below the table, there are many more tab stops where the tab setting is the default.

The ruler line remains on the screen—regardless of what document is on screen, even if the screen is clear. If you're used to another word processing package that continually displays margin and tab settings, you may welcome the ruler line. To type and edit your text with the ruler line always on screen, shrink your window by one line at the beginning of each WordPerfect session. The ruler line will remain on screen until you return the window to full size or until you exit WordPerfect.

FIGURE 4-13   A ruler line on screen

On the other hand, you may find the ruler line distracting. To return the window to full size, you would follow the steps outlined above, specifying a window size of 24. Let's save the document you just typed under the filename LIST, clear the screen, and then get rid of the ruler line.

1. Press the EXIT (F7) key, type **Y**, and save the document under the filename LIST.

2. Type **N** when WordPerfect asks whether you wish to exit the program. Notice that while the screen is clear, the ruler line remains.

3. Press the SCREEN (CTRL + F3) key. WordPerfect responds with the Screen menu:

   0 _Rewrite; **1** _Window; **2** _Line Draw: **0**

4. Select Window (1 or W). WordPerfect prompts you with

   Number of lines in this window: 23

5. Type **24** and press ENTER. (Or, you can press DOWN ARROW and then press ENTER.)

If you dislike keeping the ruler line on screen as you type, you have, of course, other alteratives for keeping track of tab stops. First, you can position the cursor on the line where you wish to check tabs, then return to the Line Format menu, and select Tab Set to view the tab ruler line. Then press the CANCEL (F1) key to back out of the tab command. (Be sure to press CANCEL and not EXIT. If you press EXIT (F7), you will insert an extra, unneeded Tab Set code.) Another way to keep track of tab stops is to reveal the Tab Set code. Press the REVEAL CODES (ALT + F3) key, and move the cursor until the **[Tab Set:]** code appears on the screen. The code reports the location of each tab stop.

REVIEW EXERCISE

You have now explored a number of ways to control the overall design of a document. The following exercise has you working with the letter that you typed to Mr. Barrett Smith in Chapter 1. You will make format changes in the letter and print it out.

1. On a clear screen, retrieve the file named LETTER in order to make format changes.

2. For the whole document, change the left margin to 1.5 inches and the right margin to 1.5 inches. (*Hint:* Since you are changing margins for the whole document, place the Margin code on the Document Initial Codes screen.)

3. Turn off justification for the whole document. (*Hint:* Again, since you are changing the justification default for the whole document, place the Justification Off code on the Document Initial Codes screen.)

4. Reset tabs for the list of names and dates so that the first tab stop is at position 3" and other tab stops appear in increments of 0.5 inch. (*Hint:* Position the cursor at the left margin of the line that reads "Antonio Abbot" and then set tabs in the document itself. Also, make sure that when you view the Tab menu, you delete the old tab stops before setting new ones. Then set new ones by typing **3,0.5** and pressing ENTER.)

5. Double space only the list of names. (*Hint:* Again, position the cursor at the left margin of the line that reads "Antonio Abbott," and set double spacing. Then position the cursor at the left margin of the line that reads "The new accrued...," and set line spacing back to single spacing.)

6. Return to the Document Initial Codes screen to ensure that the Margin and Justification codes are correct.

7. Reveal codes to make sure that the Tab Set and Line Spacing codes are correct.

8. Print the document to see the final product, save the document on disk, and clear the screen.

REVIEW

- Default format settings control each document you create until you insert format codes to override the defaults.

- Format codes can be inserted on the Document Initial Codes screen to affect the format for the whole document or in the document itself to affect a specific portion of a document. When you insert a format code in the document itself, it overrides any code of the same type found on the Document Initial Codes screen and stays in effect up to the next code of its type farther forward in the document. It is critical to position the cursor carefully before inserting a format code.

- The Line Format menu, accessed from the FORMAT (SHIFT + F8) key, enables you to change left and right margins, tab stop locations, and line spacing. It also enables you to turn hyphenation on (manual or automatic) and off and to turn justification on or off.

- It is good practice to periodically check format codes that you insert in a document. Check the Document Initial Codes screen to view any format codes inserted there, and check your Reveal Codes screen periodically to view any format changes inserted within a document itself. Delete from a document unwanted or unnecessary codes that might cause formatting problems when you print.

- The SCREEN (CTRL + F3) key can establish a ruler line at the bottom of the screen. This is useful when you change margins and/or tabs frequently in a document and wish to keep track of which part of the text is governed by which margin or tab set change.

5

WORKING WITH MULTIPLE-PAGE AND PAGE FORMAT FEATURES

The documents you created in the previous chapters were all less than one page in length. Few documents, however, are limited to one page. In this chapter, you'll add text to a document you've already created and watch as WordPerfect breaks that document into distinct pages automatically. You'll also see how you can control exactly where one page ends and another begins. You'll find that most of WordPerfect's page features are on the Page Format menu, accessed via the FORMAT (SHIFT + F8) key.

Farther on in the chapter, you'll establish headers and footers, which are standard lines of text at the top and bottom of each page in the document. You'll also activate the Page Numbering feature—and never have to number pages manually again! And you'll discover how to change the size of paper on which you plan to print so that you can print out envelopes, mailing labels, or any documents on odd-sized paper. WordPerfect's Page Format features allow you to design page layout with ease.

INITIAL PAGE FORMAT SETTINGS

The initial settings for how each page of text is formatted in a document are as follows:

Top and bottom margins	1-inch borders on the top and bottom of the printed page
Paper	Standard, 8.5 inches wide by 11 inches long
Headers and footers	None
Page numbering	None

If you do not specify otherwise, the preceding defaults will take effect in each document you type, providing a printed result as illustrated in Figure 5-1.

As you learned in the last chapter, you can change any or all of the format defaults for a particular document by inserting format codes within the document. These codes serve to override the default settings. Also remember from the last chapter that the placement of format codes is critical. Any code that you insert in a document controls all text from that location *forward,* all the way to either the end of the document or to the next code of its type further down in the document. And many page format codes can be inserted on the Document Initial Codes screen if you wish to change the format starting at the top of the document.

TYPE A MULTIPLE-PAGE DOCUMENT

WordPerfect automatically breaks your text into pages as you type. This Page Break feature is as much a timesaver as is word wrap: there's no need to keep track of whether you're typing more lines than can fit on one page.

When does WordPerfect break pages? WordPerfect's default is for a top margin of 1 inch and a bottom margin of 1 inch. WordPerfect as-

FIGURE 5-1 Printed page using default page format settings

sumes you will be printing on 11-inch-long paper, so the program will break to a new page after 9 inches of text have been typed—11 inches minus 1 inch top margin minus 1 inch bottom margin. Thus, after you type text to approximately 9.8 inches (the exact line position depends on your printer) of page 1 and your cursor moves down to the next line, the status line does *not* indicate **Doc 1 Pg 1 Ln 10" Pos 1"**. Instead, it indicates the top of a new page—**Doc 1 Pg 2 Ln 1" Pos 1"**.

Where a page break occurs, WordPerfect inserts an [SPg] code, which stands for soft page—"soft" because it will adjust as you insert or delete text. (This is comparable to the [SRt] code created by word wrap at the end of a line.) Like all codes, [SPg] is hidden from view on the Typing screen. To indicate that a new page has begun on the Typing screen, WordPerfect draws a page bar (a line of hyphens) just below the last line of the page. A new page begins below the page bar.

Let's retrieve a document you've already created and add some text so that it becomes long enough to break into pages.

1. Retrieve the document saved under the filename SAMPLE. This document is double spaced, with a left margin of 1.5 inches and a right margin of 1 inch. Justification is off and manual hyphenation is on. This is all because of the line format codes you inserted into that file's Document Initial Codes screen as you followed the directions in Chapter 4.

2. Press HOME, HOME, DOWN ARROW to move to the bottom of the document.

3. Press ENTER to insert a blank line.

4. Type the following paragraph to add length to the text:

   R&R WINE ASSOCIATION, established in 1982, boasts a membership of over 100 outstanding wineries from California, New York, Europe, South America, and Australia. We disseminate information about wine tasting, production, and enjoyment. In addition, we distribute wine produced by our member wineries.

   (As you type, WordPerfect may prompt asking for confirmation on the location of a hyphen; review Chapter 4 if you need a refresher on the possible responses to the hyphenation prompt.)

Notice that as you typed, a page bar appeared across the screen. Figure 5-2 shows the page bar. (Your page break may occur at a different spot, depending on how many blank lines you inserted in your document and on how WordPerfect wraps words in your document based on your printer selection.) This page bar is accompanied by a hidden **[SPg]** code. If you reveal codes and position the cursor at the top of page 2, you will see the **[SPg]** code, as illustrated in Figure 5-3.

If you add lines of text to a page, the page bar will automatically adjust to retain only nine vertical inches of text on that page. You are free from concern about adjusting page breaks yourself. To illustrate WordPerfect's page break readjustment, here you'll add five short lines of text to page 1.

1. Position the cursor at the end of the line that reads "Switzerland," just to the right of the "d."

2. Press ENTER and type **Austria**.

```
        R&R Wine Association

        3345 Whitmore Drive

        San Francisco, CA


R&R WINE ASSOCIATION, established in 1982, boasts a member-

ship of over 100 outstanding wineries from California, New

York, Europe, South America, and Australia.  We disseminate
----------------------------------------------------------------
information about wine tasting, production, and enjoyment.

In addition, we distribute wine produced by our member wine-

ries.

C:\WPER\DATA\SAMPLE                      Doc 1 Pg 2 Ln 2" Pos 1.5"
```

FIGURE 5-2 A dotted line indicating a soft page break

```
    ship of over 100 outstanding wineries from California, New

    York, Europe, South America, and Australia.  We disseminate
    _____
    information about wine tasting, production, and enjoyment.

    In addition, we distribute wine produced by our member wine-

    ries.
    C:\WPER\DATA\SAMPLE                       Doc 1 Pg 2 Ln 1" Pos 1.5"
    {   ▲    ▲    ▲    ▲    ▲    ▲    ▲    ▲    ▲    ▲    }   ▲    ▲
    ship of over 100 outstanding wineries from California, New[SRt]
    York, Europe, South America, and Australia.  We disseminate[SPg] ←
    [I]nformation about wine tasting, production, and enjoyment.[SRt]
    In addition, we distribute wine produced by our member wine-
    ries.[HRt]



    Press Reveal Codes to restore screen
```

FIGURE 5-3   A soft page break on the Reveal Codes screen

3. Press ENTER and type **Hungary**.

4. Press ENTER and type **Greece**.

5. Press ENTER and type **Romania**.

6. Press ENTER and type **Yugoslavia**.

7. Press DOWN ARROW until the page bar comes into view. Notice that the page bar has relocated.

As you can see, when you create a lengthy document, you can just keep typing along without worry; WordPerfect inserts page breaks every nine vertical inches automatically for you.

CHANGE TOP AND BOTTOM MARGINS

WordPerfect's initial top and bottom margin settings are 1 inch. This means that WordPerfect will roll the paper up in the printer so that the first line of text begins 1 inch below the top edge of the page and because of WordPerfect's automatic page breaks, a page will stop printing 1 inch from the bottom edge of the page.

Note: If you followed the directions in Chapter 2 to print your document but your printed result had top/bottom margins other than 1 inch, then the paper may have been improperly aligned in your printer. For example, if the paper had been rolled up too far from the printhead, the top margin would be larger than one inch. Try printing again by shifting the location where paper is inserted into the printer.

```
Format: Page

    1 - Center Page (top to bottom)    No

    2 - Force Odd/Even Page

    3 - Headers

    4 - Footers

    5 - Margins - Top                  1"
                  Bottom               1"

    6 - New Page Number                1
          (example: 3 or iii)

    7 - Page Numbering                 No page numbering

    8 - Paper Size                     8.5" x 11"
          Type                         Standard

    9 - Suppress (this page only)

Selection: 0
```

FIGURE 5-4 Page Format menu

You can set new margins, thus increasing or decreasing the white space at the top and bottom of the printed page. To set new margins, position the cursor at the beginning of the page where you want the new margins to take effect. For instance, place the cursor on the Document Initial Codes screen to change top/bottom margins starting at page 1. Or position at the very top left corner of page 3 to change margins starting on that page. Positioning the cursor is critical: remember that a margin change will take effect from the cursor position on down. If you position the cursor in the middle of page 2 and then change the top/bottom margins, the change will not take effect until printed page 3!

After positioning the cursor, press the FORMAT (SHIFT + F8) key. The Format menu appears. Select Page (2 or P) and the Page Format menu as shown in Figure 5-4 appears. To change these margins, select Margins Top and Bottom (5 or M), and then enter both your top and bottom margin settings in inches. Finally, press EXIT (F7) to return to the Typing screen or press CANCEL (F1) to return to the Format menu.

When you alter top and bottom margins within a document, a Top/Bottom Margin code is inserted at the current cursor position. For instance, if you changed top and bottom margins to 2 inches, then the code inserted is **[T/B Mar:2",2"]**. This code affects margins from that point forward or up to another **[T/B Mar:]** code located further down in the document.

Let's change the top margin of the document on the screen to 2 inches and leave the bottom margin at 1 inch. Remember from the previous chapter that since we want the change in the top margin to begin at the start of the document it is advisable to place the **[T/B Mar:]** code on the Document Initial Codes screen.

1. Press the FORMAT (SHIFT + F8) key.

2. Select Document (3 or D). The Document Format menu appears.

3. Select Initial Codes (2 or C). The Document Initial Codes screen appears, containing the five codes that you inserted after following the instructions in the previous chapter.

4. Press the FORMAT (SHIFT + F8) key.

5. Select Page (2 or P). The Page Format menu appears as shown in Figure 5-4.

6. Select Margins Top and Bottom (5 or M). Notice that top and bottom margins of 1 inch are currently indicated.

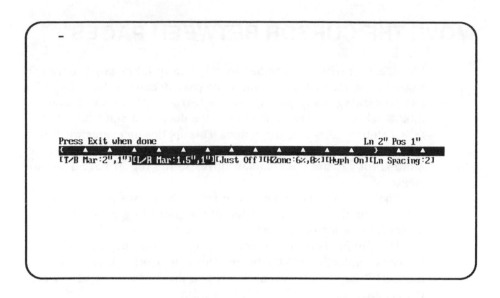

FIGURE 5-5   Document Initial Codes screen with six format codes inserted

7. Type **2** and press ENTER and then type **1** and press ENTER to set margins.

8. Press EXIT (F7) to exit the Line Format menu. You are returned to the Document Initial Codes screen. Notice that there are now six codes on this screen, as shown in Figure 5-5, including the Top/Bottom Margin code, which is shown at the far left in the figure.

9. Press EXIT (F7) two more times to return to the text of your document.

Notice that with the cursor at the top of the document the status line indicates **Ln 2"**. This is because the new top margin setting of 2 inches is now in effect. Because of this top margin change, Word-Perfect also readjusted the text so that now only 8 inches of text appear on each page (11 inches minus 2-inch top margin minus 1-inch bottom margin).

MOVE THE CURSOR BETWEEN PAGES

WordPerfect offers a number of ways to quickly move between pages—of small significance for a two-page document, but critical for one containing many pages. You've learned that HOME, HOME, UP ARROW takes the cursor to the top of the document and HOME, HOME, DOWN ARROW takes it to the bottom. This applies no matter what page the cursor is on. If you are on page 18 and you press HOME, HOME, UP ARROW, for example, the cursor moves to the top of page 1 in moments.

The PGUP and PGDN keys also move the cursor between pages. PGUP moves the cursor to the top of the preceding page, and PDGN moves it to the top of the next page.

In addition, there are a variety of ways to move page by page with the key combination CTRL + HOME. This combination is referred to as the GOTO key combination. When you press CTRL + HOME, WordPerfect prompts

Go to

Move to the top of the current page (the page where the cursor is currently located) by pressing CTRL + HOME, UP ARROW. Similarly, move to the bottom by pressing CTRL + HOME, DOWN ARROW. Or move to the top of a specific page by pressing CTRL + HOME and, when prompted, entering the desired page number.

The document on screen contains only two pages. Nevertheless, try the following to become comfortable moving from page to page in a document:

1. Press HOME, HOME, UP ARROW to move to the top of the document, page 1.

2. Press PGDN. The cursor moves to the top of page 2.

3. Press PGUP. The cursor moves back to the top of page 1.

4. Press CTRL + HOME, and when you see the prompt

   Go to

   press DOWN ARROW. The cursor moves to the bottom of the page, page 1.

5. Pretend for the moment that the cursor is on page 15 of a long document and you wish to move to the top of page 2. Press CTRL + HOME, and, when prompted, type **2** and press ENTER. The cursor moves to the top of page 2.

CONTROL SOFT PAGE BREAKS

Unfortunately, sometimes WordPerfect's Automatic Page Break feature creates a page end at an awkward spot. Fortunately, you do have some control over the location of soft page breaks.

Widow and Orphan Protection

When a paragraph's first line appears at the bottom of the preceding page, it is called a *widow*. When a paragraph's last line appears at the top of the following page, it is called an *orphan*. You can request protection against one line of a paragraph being left stranded. By asking for widow/orphan protection, you are giving WordPerfect the license to break one line earlier or later than it might otherwise.

To protect against "family" separations, position the cursor at the top of the page where you want to activate the feature. Then press the FORMAT (SHIFT + F8) key. The Format menu appears. Select Line (1 or L) and the Line Format menu shown in Figure 5-6 appears. Notice in Figure 5-6 that option 9, Widow/Orphan Protection is off, as indicated by "No." This is the default setting. Select Widow/Orphan Protection (9 or W), and then type **Y** to turn on the feature (or type **N** to turn it off if it had been turned on for previous pages in the document). Finally, press EXIT (F7) to return to the Typing screen or press CANCEL (F1) to return to the Format menu. A **[W/O On]** code is inserted at the current cursor position if you turned the feature on, and **[W/O Off]** is inserted if you turned it off.

```
Format: Line
      1 - Hyphenation              Off

      2 - Hyphenation Zone - Left  10%
                          Right    4%

      3 - Justification            Yes

      4 - Line Height              Auto

      5 - Line Numbering           No

      6 - Line Spacing             1

      7 - Margins - Left           1"
                    Right          1"

      8 - Tab Set                  0", every 0.5"

      9 - Widow/Orphan Protection  No


Selection: 0
```

FIGURE 5-6   Line Format Menu

Keep Lines Together

You can also protect against a particular group of lines being split by a page break. For instance, suppose you commonly type a heading followed by two hard returns and then a paragraph. You can request that WordPerfect keep the heading, the blank lines, and the first few lines of the paragraph on the same page, without the threat of their being split by a page break. Or suppose you included a table in a document, and you want to make sure that WordPerfect inserts a page break either above or below the table, but not through the table. You have your pick of two features to keep specific lines together: Conditional EOP (end of page) and Block Protect.

Conditional EOP is most useful for keeping a specified number of lines together where the contents of those lines may change—such as a heading and the first two lines of the paragraph that follows. To use Conditional EOP, you must count the number of lines you wish to keep together—for example, a one-line heading, two blank lines, and two lines of text equal five lines. Then move the cursor to the line *just above* where you want the feature to take effect; for example, the line above the heading. Press the FORMAT (SHIFT + F8) key, select Other Format (4 or O), and select Conditional End Of Page (2 or C). Word-Perfect prompts at the bottom of the Other Format menu:

Number of Lines to Keep Together:

Type in the number of lines you wish to keep together, press ENTER, and then press EXIT (F7) to return to your text. A code is inserted in the text. For example, if you wish to keep five lines together, the **[Cndl EOP:5]** code is inserted at the cursor.

Block Protect is simpler because you don't have to count the number of lines to be kept together. Also, the advantage of Block Protect is that you can add lines within the block, and the entire block will remain protected from a page break. Thus, Block Protect is most useful for keeping together tables, charts, or other portions of a document where you may later add more lines. To use Block Protect, highlight the text you want kept together with the BLOCK (ALT + F4) key and then press the FORMAT (SHIFT + F8) key. Because Block is on, instead of displaying the Format menu, WordPerfect will ask you whether you wish to protect the highlighted block with the following prompt:

Protect block? (Y/N) No

Type **Y** to protect the block and WordPerfect inserts a **[Block Pro:On]** code in front of the block and a **[Block Pro:Off]** code at the end of the block, marking off the lines that must not be separated by a page break. Or type **N** or ENTER to cancel the Block Protect command.

As practice, suppose that you plan to edit the document on screen. You want to make sure, however, that R&R Wine Association's phone number and address are always kept together on the same page. To protect them from being split between different pages, proceed as follows, using the Block Protect feature:

1. Move the cursor to the left margin of the line that reads "Contact THE R&R...."

2. Press the BLOCK (ALT + F4) key and highlight the text up to and including "San Francisco, CA" as shown in Figure 5-7. (If you'll remember from Chapter 1, one quick method to highlight the text would be to type A—in uppercase—until the entire block is highlighted up to and including the "A" in "San Francisco, CA.")

3. Press the FORMAT (SHIFT + F8) key. WordPerfect prompts you with

   Protect block? (Y/N) No

4. Type **Y**. WordPerfect inserts the **[Block Pro:On]** and **[Block Pro:Off]** codes around the block like bookends.

If you press the REVEAL CODES (ALT + F4) key, you can locate the two codes that now surround the block. If the association's phone number and address had previously been split by a page break, the text is now readjusted to fall below the page break. Whether you add text above the address or below, those lines of text will not be split by a page break as long as the **[Block Pro:]** codes border those lines.

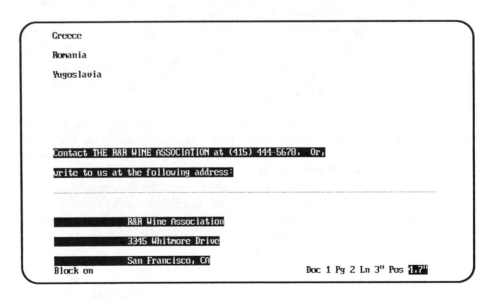

FIGURE 5-7   Highlighting text for a block protect

INSERT HARD PAGES

There are instances when you will want even more control over page breaks—for example, when you wish to end a short page of text and begin typing a new page. You might want a title page, a table of contents, and a list of illustrations each on a distinct page of a report. That control is available to you.

To end a short page of text, position the cursor where you want a page bar to appear and simply press CTRL + ENTER. A Hard Page code **[HPg]** is inserted. The code is "hard" because the page end will not adjust, no matter how you edit the text; a page boundary will always be located at that spot. Of course, the code is hidden on the Typing screen. You will see a page bar of *equal signs* rather than hyphens so that you can distinguish a hard page from a soft page on the Typing screen.

Suppose that you want to place the last paragraph of the document that you've been working with on a separate page. Proceed as follows:

1. Move the cursor to the left margin of the line that begins "R&R WINE ASSOCIATION, established in 1982...."

2. Press CTRL + ENTER. A page bar appears, and the status line now indicates that the cursor is on page 3.

   Doc 1 Pg 3 Ln 2" Pos 1.5"

   You have ended page 2 early so that the description of the wine association appears on a separate page.

In general, it is wise to allow WordPerfect's automatic page break feature to work for you, inserting soft pages that will readjust as you edit your text. Reserve hard pages for those times when you want to end a short page of text or have a page break at a specific point no matter how the document changes. Otherwise, you may find that if you use hard pages and then substantially edit a document, pages end at awkward places.

Should you decide to cancel a hard page, you must erase the **[HPg]** code just as you would any other code—either on the Reveal Codes screen or on the Typing screen. Since the page bar gives its location away, an **[HPg]** code can be erased easily on the Typing screen; position the cursor just below the page bar and use the BACK-SPACE key to delete the code.

CENTER PAGE TOP TO BOTTOM

WordPerfect offers a feature that will center a short page of text vertically. Maybe you've typed a short letter that you wish to center, or perhaps you've typed a title page and want it to be centered. To do so, you

THE EXCITEMENT
OF WINE TASTING

presented by

The R&R Wine Association

FIGURE 5-8   A page centered vertically

would move to the top of that page, before any other format codes that may be located there. Then press the FORMAT (SHIFT + F8) key and select Page (2 or P). The first option, Center Page Top to Bottom, is defaulted at N for "No," but as soon as you select Center Page Top to Bottom (1 or C), this setting changes to "Yes." Press EXIT (F7) to return to the document. A [Center Pg] code is inserted in the text. For just that one page (*and only that one page*—unlike how most codes operate), the top and bottom margin settings are overridden. The centering occurs only at the printer, not on screen. Figure 5-8 shows a printed page centered in this way.

As an example, let's vertically center the last page of the document on screen:

1. Position the cursor at the very top of page 3.

2. Press the FORMAT (SHIFT + F8) key to display the Format menu.

3. Select Page (2 or P) to display the Page Format menu.

4. Select Center Page (1 or C).

5. Press EXIT (F7) to return to the Typing screen.

Remember that the vertical centering is not displayed on screen but takes effect at the printer. To prove that the page will, in fact, center when printed, you can reveal codes to view the [Center Pg] code you just inserted. Or you can print the page. Remember that the quickest way is to press PRINT (SHIFT + F7) and select Page (2 or P).

INSERT HEADERS/FOOTERS

A *header* prints the same line or lines of text at the top of every page, while a *footer* prints text at the bottom of every page. WordPerfect offers a feature whereby you can create a header or footer. In fact, you can create different headers or footers for alternating pages. For example, in a report, you can insert your company's name at the top of even-numbered pages and the report's topic at the top of odd-numbered pages. An example is shown in Figure 5-9. A header or footer can be one, two, or many lines long.

R&R Wine Association

Wine Tasting

FIGURE 5-9   Alternating headers

To create a header or footer you must position the cursor at the very top of the first page on which you want the header or footer to appear, before any text. If you want a header or footer to start at page 1, position the cursor at the top of the document; unlike most other format codes, headers and footers are *not allowed* on the Document Initial Codes screen.

Once the cursor is positioned, press the FORMAT (SHIFT + F8) key, select Page (2 or P), and then select either Headers (3 or H) or Footers (4 or F). WordPerfect provides a menu with two choices, asking whether you wish to choose a header/footer A or B. For instance, if you select Headers (3 or H), then the following menu appears at the bottom of the Page Format menu:

1 Header A̲; 2 Header B̲: 0

Select the type you want—Header A or B, or Footer A or B. Always select Header or Footer A first. Select Header or Footer B only if, for example, you've already created one header or footer in the document on even-numbered pages and you wish to create a second one on odd-numbered pages. Next, WordPerfect offers options on the frequency with which the header or footer should occur: should WordPerfect print it on every page? on even-numbered pages? The following menu appears:

1 Discontinue; 2 Every Page; 3 Odd Pages; 4 Even Pages;
5 Edit: 0

Select an option (2, 3, or 4) to choose the pages on which you want the header or footer to appear.

WordPerfect then provides a blank screen on which you would type the header or footer just as you want it to appear. You can use enhancements when typing a header or footer. For instance, use the CENTER (SHIFT + F6) key if you wish to center the header/footer on each page. Or use the UNDERLINE (F8) key to underscore all or part of the header/footer text. After typing the header or footer, press EXIT (F7) to leave the Header/Footer screen. You are returned to the Page Format menu. The Page Format menu will now indicate the frequency of occurrence of any headers or footers that you created. For instance, next to option 3, Headers, WordPerfect might insert on the Page Format menu "HA Every Page," standing for Header A, Every Page.

When you press EXIT (F7) to return to your document, a Header or Footer code will be inserted in the text, indicating the type and frequency of the header or footer, as well as up to the first 50 characters contained in the header or footer. For instance, suppose you insert a Header A on every page that reads "R&R Wine Association Annual Report." In that case, the code inserted is **[Header A:2;[UND]R&R Wine Association Annual Report[und]]**.

Headers and footers appear on the printed page but not on the Typing screen. When printed, a header will start on the first text line of a page and be followed by one blank line to separate it from the first line of the text. A footer will appear on the last text line on each page, preceded by a blank line. For more than one line separating a header from the rest of the page, insert hard returns below the text when you create the header. Similarly, you can insert hard returns above the text of the footer. Top and bottom margins are preserved even when you insert headers or footers in your text; WordPerfect adjusts its soft page breaks to accommodate any headers or footers.

You can also edit the text of a header or footer once you've created it. Suppose, for example, that you inserted a header and now realize that you'd like to change it. Position the cursor after the **[Header:]** code and follow the procedure described above to return to the following menu:

1 Discontinue; 2 Every Page; 3 Odd Pages; 4 Even Pages;
5 Edit: 0

Then select Edit (5 or E). The Header/Footer screen appears, with the text of your header displayed. When you have corrected the header, press the EXIT (F7) key to save the editing changes.

And you can discontinue a header or footer. Position the cursor at the top of the page where the header/footer will be terminated, return to the Header/Footer menu, and select Discontinue (1 or D). A code such as **[Header A:1]** is inserted; this code signifies that header A is discontinued for the rest of the document.

Here's an opportunity to practice creating a header in the top left corner on every page of the document on screen.

1. Press HOME, HOME, UP ARROW.

2. Press the FORMAT (SHIFT + F8) key.

3. Select Page (2 or P) to display the Page Format menu.

4. Select Headers (3 or H). The following menu appears:

   1 Header A; 2 Header B: 0

5. Select Header A (1 or A). Another menu appears:

   1 Discontinue; 2 Every Page; 3 Odd Pages; 4 Even Pages;
   5 Edit: 0

6. Select Every Page (2 or P). A blank Header/Footer screen now displays in order for you to type the header just as it should appear on every page.

7. Type **R&R Wine Association**.

8. Press the EXIT (F7) key to return to the Page Format menu. Notice that this menu now indicates "HA Every Page" next to the heading "Headers."

9. Press EXIT (F7) to return to the Typing screen.

If you now press the REVEAL CODES (ALT + F3) key, you'll see that the following code has been inserted at the top of the document:

[**Header A:2;R&R Wine Association**]. Remember that a header or footer is never displayed on the Typing screen. If you desire, you can print any one or all three of the pages to find that the header appears on each page, with one line (double spaced, since the whole document is double spaced) separating it from the body of the text.

INSERT PAGE NUMBERS

WordPerfect is capable of numbering pages consecutively when you print your document, but only when you direct the program to do so. The page numbers that are printed correspond to the **Pg** number as indicated on the status line. There are two different page numbering methods.

Numbering in Headers/Footers

If you wish to combine text with your page numbers, you will need to insert the symbol ^B within the text of a header or footer. You insert the ^B on the Header/Footer screen where you want the page number to be printed. For instance, if you want the bottom of each page to read "Page 1," "Page 2," and so on, type **Page ^B** as the footer text. Or, to be more complicated, the footer might read "R&R Wine Association (Page ^B)." The ^B character is automatically replaced by the appropriate page number when the document is printed.

You create a ^B symbol by pressing CTRL + B. Do not create the ^B by typing a caret (^) and then typing **B**; it looks the same on screen, but CTRL + B is the correct special symbol that WordPerfect recognizes for page numbering in a header or footer.

Choosing a Page Number Position

A second way to number pages is useful if you want a page number to appear *without any accompanying text*. You can select exactly where the page number will appear—whether at the top, bottom, left, right, or center of a page. To do so, position the cursor at the very top of the page on which you want numbering to start, press the FORMAT (SHIFT

+ F8) key, select Page (2 or P), and then select Page Numbering (7 or P). The menu in Figure 5-10 appears, providing options for where you want page numbers to appear on each printed page. Six of the options are for page numbering in the same position on every page; for instance, type **2** to insert page numbers in the top center of every page. Two other options are for alternating page number locations; for example, type **4** to insert page numbers in the top left corner on even-numbered pages and in the top right corner on odd-numbered pages. Then press EXIT (F7) to return to your text. A code is inserted at the current cursor position. For example, if you selected page numbering at the bottom center of every page, the code inserted is **[Pg Numbering: Bottom Center]**.

Like headers and footers, page numbers added to a document with the Page Numbering feature appear on the printed page but not on the Typing screen. Also like headers and footers, a page number at the top of the page is followed by one blank line, and a page number at the bottom is preceded by one blank line. Soft page breaks adjust to accommodate the page numbering.

Be cautious that you don't create conflicts when choosing both a header or footer and a page number position option. For instance,

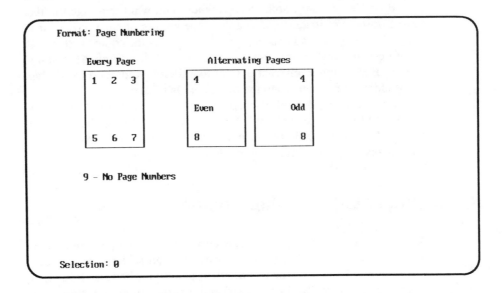

FIGURE 5-10   Page Numbering menu

since you've already created a header that will print in the top left corner of every page for the document on screen, you shouldn't also select page numbers at the top left of every page. Instead, let's insert page numbers at the bottom center of every page:

1. Press HOME, HOME, UP ARROW to move to the top of the document.

2. Press the FORMAT (SHIFT + F8) key.

3. Select Page (2 or P) to display the Page Format menu.

4. Select Page Numbering (7 or P). The menu shown in Figure 5-10 appears.

5. Type **6** to center page numbers at the bottom of every page. You are returned to the Page Format menu. Notice that this menu now indicates "Bottom Center" next to the heading "Page Numbering."

6. Press EXIT (F7) to return to the document.

The code **[Pg Numbering: Bottom Center]** is inserted at the top of the document. You've now activated WordPerfect's Automatic Page Numbering feature for each page of this document when printed.

RENUMBER PAGES AND FORCE ODD/EVEN PAGES

The New Page Number feature allows you to reset page numbers so that you can print out whatever page numbers you choose. For instance, you may have written a book with each chapter saved into its own file. When you print, you will want to number the pages sequentially. Perhaps Chapter 1 ends with page 50; you'll want Chapter 2 to begin at page 51.

When you renumber pages, WordPerfect offers you a choice between Arabic numerals (1,2,3...) and lowercase Roman numerals (i, ii, iii...). In that way, a table of contents, abstract, appendix, or bibliography can be numbered with Roman numerals, while the body of your book can be numbered with Arabic numerals.

To renumber pages, position the cursor at the top of the page where you want to start the renumbering (before any Page Numbering or Header/Footer codes already inserted on that page) and select New Page Number (6 or N) from the Page Format menu. Then type in the new page number in either Arabic style or as a Roman numeral and press ENTER. Press EXIT (F7) to return to the document.

WordPerfect inserts a Page Numbering code in the text. For instance, **[Pg Num:51]** indicates page 51 in Arabic style, while **[Pg Num:i]** indicates page 1 in Roman numeral style. When the cursor is to the right of or below that Page Numbering code, the **Pg** indicator on the status line reflects the new page number—but not the numbering style. The status line shows Arabic numerals on screen even when you choose Roman—the Roman numerals appear only at the printer. All subsequent pages are renumbered consecutively to the end of the document or up to the next **[Pg Num:]** code found farther forward in the document.

Besides renumbering pages, WordPerfect allows you to dictate that a certain page be assigned an odd or even number. This is useful, for instance, to ensure that the first page of a report or book chapter is

```
Format: Suppress (this page only)

     1 - Suppress All Page Numbering, Headers and Footers

     2 - Suppress Headers and Footers

     3 - Print Page Number at Bottom Center    No

     4 - Suppress Page Numbering               No

     5 - Suppress Header A                      No

     6 - Suppress Header B                      No

     7 - Suppress Footer A                      No

     8 - Suppress Footer B                      No




Selection: 0
```

FIGURE 5-11   Suppress (this page only) menu

an odd-numbered page. To use the Force Odd/Even Page feature, make sure that the cursor is at the top of the page, before any Page Numbering or Header/Footer codes that may be located on that page. Select Force Odd/Even (2 or O) on the Page Format menu. WordPerfect responds by displaying the following menu at the bottom of the screen:

1 Odd; 2 Even: **0**

Select from these two options and then press EXIT (F7) to return to your document. A **[Force:Odd]** or **[Force:Even]** code is inserted on that page. You may find that WordPerfect inserts a blank page as a result of this feature. If, for example, you insert a **[Force:Odd]** code at the top of page 2, then the page is renumbered to page 3 and a blank page is inserted as page 2. If, however, you insert a **[Force:Even]** code at the top of page 2, the page retains its number since it is, in fact, an even-numbered page.

SUPPRESS HEADERS, FOOTERS, AND PAGE NUMBERING

What if you wish to print a header, a footer, or page numbers on all but a select page? You can suppress those features on specific pages. For instance, you can insert a Header code on page 1 and then also suppress that code on page 1; a header will appear on all but the first page of the document.

To suppress headers, footers, and/or page numbers, position the cursor at the top of the page on which you wish to suppress a feature, and from the Page Format menu select Suppress (9 or U). The menu in Figure 5-11 appears. Next indicate what feature or combination of features you want to suppress. For instance, select Suppress Page Numbering (4 or P) and type **Y** so that page numbers do not appear on that page—although headers and footers will appear (as well as page numbers if inserted in a header or footer using ^B). Or select Suppress Header A (5 or H) and type **Y** to suppress only header A on that page. Or select Suppress Headers and Footers (2 or S) to suppress all headers and footers on that page—although page numbers will appear. (When you select options 1 or 2 on the Suppress menu, it is unnecessary to type **Y** or **N**; WordPerfect changes "No" to "Yes" where appropriate.) Now press EXIT (F7) to return to the Typing screen.

When you suppress headers, footers, and/or page numbering on a specific page, a [**Suppress:**] code is inserted. For instance, if you elect to suppress headers and footers, then the code inserted is [**Suppress:HA,HB,FA,FB**]. Unlike most other codes, this one takes effect *only for the current page*.

Suppose you wish to suppress the page numbering, headers, and footers for the first page of your document on screen:

1. Press HOME, HOME, UP ARROW.

2. Press the FORMAT (SHIFT + F8) key.

3. Select Page (2 or P) to display the Page Format menu.

4. Select Suppress (9 or U). The menu shown in Figure 5-11 appears.

5. Select Suppress All Page Numbering, Headers, and Footers (1 or A). Notice that WordPerfect changes "No" to "Yes" for options 4 through 8.

6. Press EXIT (F7) to return to the Typing screen.

If you now reveal codes, you'll view the following new code that you inserted: [**Suppress:PgNum,HA,HB,FA,FB**]. Print page 1 and you'll see that, in fact, there is no page number or header on the page. In fact, print all three pages. Since the start of this chapter, you've inserted various page format codes into the text. You'll find when you print that there are page numbers and headers on pages 2 and 3 and that page 3 is centered vertically.

Note: You should know that there is a method for previewing the format of your document before it is actually printed. The View Document feature displays a replica of each page of your document, showing the current settings for margins, headers, footers, and page numbers. For instance, if you use the View Document feature with the document currently on your computer screen, you can see pages with top and bottom margins as you set them earlier in this chapter and with page numbers and headers on pages 2 and 3. This feature enables you to save paper, printing a document only after checking to make sure that the format of your document meets your approval. Refer to Chapter 9 for more on the View Document feature.

ALTER THE PAPER SIZE/TYPE FOR ODD-SIZED PAPER, ENVELOPES, AND LABELS

WordPerfect assumes that you wish to print on standard-sized paper 8.5 inches wide by 11 inches long. This is WordPerfect's initial *paper size* setting. Your margins operate based on this setting. For instance, if your left margin is set to 1 inch and your right margin to 1 inch, then that means that 6.5 inches of text will fit vertically across the page (8.5 inches minus 1 inch minus 1 inch). Similarly, if your top margin is set to 1 inch and your bottom margin is set to 1 inch, then this means that 9 inches of text will fit vertically on the page (11 inches minus 1 inch minus 1 inch).

You can establish a different paper size, thus indicating to Word-Perfect that you wish to print on different-sized paper. For instance, you may wish to turn the paper sideways (referred to as standard landscape size, where the paper dimensions are 11 inches wide by 8.5 inches long) to print a wide chart. Or you may wish to print a legal document on 8.5- by 14-inch legal-sized paper. Or you may wish to print out an envelope. You must change the paper size setting so that WordPerfect can adjust margins based on the correct paper size.

If you change your paper size, then the text on screen readjusts to maintain your margins. For instance, suppose you select the standard envelope size, which is 9.5 inches wide by 4 inches long. In that case, assuming default margins, the text readjusts so that 7.5 inches of text can fit across the page (9.5 inches minus 1 inch minus 1 inch) and only 2 inches of text can fit down the page (4 inches minus 1 inch minus 1 inch).

Associated with paper size is another feature called *paper type*. In WordPerfect, you have various methods for selecting the paper on which your document will be printed and the location for that paper. You indicate special instructions to WordPerfect when you define the forms you plan to use with your printer, as described in Appendix B. These instructions fall into several categories:

- *Initially Present*   Is the paper present in the printer so that printing can begin immediately; or should WordPerfect pause when printing on this paper type in order for you to feed the paper into the printer and then signal to WordPerfect that it can begin to print?

- *Location*   Will WordPerfect find this paper type in a specific sheet feeder bin, will it be fed continuously, or will it be hand-fed?

- *Orientation*   Should the characters be printed parallel to how the paper is inserted into the printer (portrait mode) or perpendicular to how it is inserted into the printer (landscape mode)? This is relevant for laser printer owners, who are unable to insert the paper sideways and, in order to print sideways on the page, must rely on the printer to print the information that way using special fonts.

- *Offset*   Does the paper type need an offset value so that the paper aligns properly in the printer? For example, should the printhead move down three extra inches every time it prints out this paper type?

At least one form type is automatically defined for you when you select your printer—the standard type, used for 8.5- by 11-inch paper. You can change the special instructions set up as defaults by Word-Perfect for this form type (the defaults depend on your printer) and you can define many more form types. For instance, suppose you plan to print out envelopes on your printer. In that case, look to Appendix B for help in defining the form type for envelopes, so that WordPerfect will know how to print them out. (Laser printer owners: You *can* print out envelopes, even though you can't feed the envelope into the printer sideways, because of the special instruction regarding orientation, as described above.)

Paper type tells WordPerfect which previously defined form type you wish to use when printing. The default is the standard type. When you specify another paper type in a document, WordPerfect checks this request against the form types you previously defined for your printer. If a match is found, then WordPerfect uses the special printing instructions based on the matching form type. If no match is found, Word-Perfect either uses the form called [ALL OTHERS], as described in Appendix B, or finds the closest match and indicates such on the Page Format menu with a message such as "requested form is unavailable."

You insert a Paper Size/Type code in your document whenever you want to print out using a size other than 8.5 inches by 11 inches and/or using other than the standard type. Position the cursor at the top of the page where you want the new paper size or type instructions to begin and press the FORMAT (SHIFT + F8) key and select Page (2 or P) to display the Page Format menu. Next select Paper Size/Type (8 or S). The Paper Size menu in Figure 5-12 appears, from which you select the appropriate paper size. (If the paper size on which you wish to print is not listed as a menu item, select the last option, Other (0 or O), and then type in the appropriate paper dimensions.) Next Word-Perfect displays the Paper Type menu, as illustrated in Figure 5-13, from which you select the appropriate paper type. (If the form type you wish to select is not listed, then select the last option, Other (8 or O), and then choose from the list of special form types you previously defined to operate with your printer.) You are returned to the Page Format menu, where your selections will be indicated next to the heading "Paper Size" (and where, if no match is found for the paper type you indicated and the previously defined form types, you will find the mes-

```
Format: Paper Size

    1 - Standard                (8.5" x 11")

    2 - Standard Landscape      (11" x 8.5")

    3 - Legal                   (8.5" x 14")

    4 - Legal Landscape         (14" x 8.5")

    5 - Envelope                (9.5" x 4")

    6 - Half Sheet              (5.5" x 8.5")

    7 - US Government           (8" x 11")

    8 - M                       (210mm x 297mm)

    9 - M Landscape             (297mm x 210mm)

    0 - Other


Selection: 1
```

FIGURE 5-12 Paper Size menu

sage "requested form is unavailable"). Press EXIT (F7) to return to your document. WordPerfect inserts a Paper Size/Type code at that location. For instance, suppose you select envelope size (9.5 inches by 4 inches) and envelope type. Then the code inserted is **[Paper Sz/Type:9.5" x 4",Envelope]**.

Let's retrieve another document that you typed in a previous chapter and saved under the name LIST. Then we'll change the paper size to 11 inches by 8.5 inches, as if planning to print sideways on the page.

1. Press SWITCH (SHIFT + F3) to shift to the Doc 2 screen. This screen should be clear. (For a review of Dual Document typing, whereby you use both the Doc 1 and Doc 2 screens, refer to Chapter 3).

2. Retrieve to the Doc 2 screen the file named LIST.

3. Press the FORMAT (SHIFT + F8) key.

```
Format: Paper Type

     1 - Standard

     2 - Bond

     3 - Letterhead

     4 - Labels

     5 - Envelope

     6 - Transparency

     7 - Cardstock

     8 - Other




Selection: 1
```

FIGURE 5-13   Paper Type menu

4. Select Page (2 or P) to display the Page Format menu.

5. Select Paper Size/Type (8 or S). The menu shown in Figure 5-12 appears.

6. Select Standard Landscape (2 or T). The menu shown in Figure 5-13 appears.

7. Select Standard (1 or S). The Page Format menu reappears.

   Note: Selecting Standard allows you to see the effects of changing the paper size on your screen, no matter what printer you are using. However, choosing standard paper type is technically correct at the printer only for those of you with printers that allow you to place your paper sideways into the printer and where the standard type is defined for manually fed paper to give you the opportunity to insert the paper sideways before printing. If you can feed paper sideways but the paper is defined for continuous feed, then to actually print this document sideways on the page, you need to (1) define a form type where you feed the paper manually, so that the printer will pause for you to insert the paper, and (2) select that corresponding paper type rather than Standard. If you are a LaserJet owner, where the printer doesn't allow you to feed the paper sideways, then to actually print this document sideways, you need to (1) define a form where the printer prints in a landscape orientation, and (2) select that corresponding paper type rather than Standard. See Appendix B for details on defining form types.

8. Press EXIT (F7) to return to the document.

9. Press DOWN ARROW to readjust the text; WordPerfect rewrites the screen based on the margins that relate to the new paper size.

You have inserted the code **[Paper Sz/Typ:11" × 8.5";Standard]** into the text. This code can be displayed if you reveal codes. (Depending on your printer and the limitations with regard to the type of forms it can print on, the code you insert may say something else.)

Once you return to your document, notice that it appears as if some of the text disappears off the right edge of the screen, as shown in Figure 5-14. This is because the margins are now such that a line is longer than what can display on screen; only a portion of each line is displayed at one time on a standard, 80-column monitor.

```
        Here are the names that were left off the list of deliveries to the Northw
    territory. Please make sure to add these names immediately:

    Customer        City         Order #       Cases

    Chou            Seattle      AB 1          34 cases from container 744: 25 cas

    Goldberg        Seattle      AB 12         2 cases from container 744: 8 cases

    Johnson         Portland     AL 12         88 cases from containers 100 and 14

        I should have a list for the Northeastern territory by tomorrow morning.




    C:\WPER\DATA\LIST                               Doc 2 Pg 1 Ln 1" Pos 1"
```

FIGURE 5-14   LIST after a paper size/type change, where the length of a line
is longer than the width of the screen

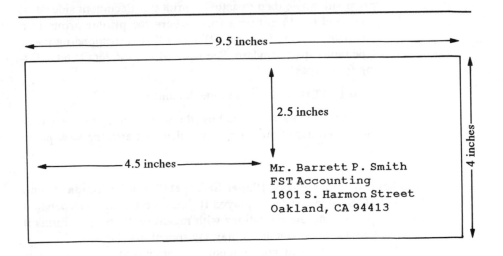

FIGURE 5-15   Paper size/type and margin changes to print an envelope

Remember that when you change paper size, it is often necessary to also alter your margin settings so that the text prints at the proper spot on the page. For instance, if you change your paper size to 9.5 inches by 4 inches in order to print an envelope but maintain a top margin of 1 inch, the name and address will print too high on the envelope. Most offices use business-size envelopes, with the company's return address already printed. In that case, type the name and address on a clear screen and then try the following settings for printing out the envelope (on your particular printer, different margin settings may be more appropriate):

Paper size and type	If the envelopes you use are standard business size, which is 9.5 inches by 4 inches, use Envelope size and type. If the envelopes you use are a size other than 9.5 inches by 4 inches, use Other size—and type in the dimensions of your envelope—and Envelope type. (Remember, you must define an envelope form type before you attempt to print out envelopes so that WordPerfect knows special instructions in relation to printing out envelopes. See Appendix B for details.)
Left and right margins	4.5 inches as a left margin, 0 inches as a right margin (to allow room for a lengthy line in an address)
Top and bottom margins	2.5 inches as a top margin, 0 inches as a bottom margin (If you insert the envelope into the printer yourself, you can simply roll up the envelope in the printer about two inches and set the top margin to 0.)

When you print, you'll get a result such as that shown in Figure 5-15. The review exercise at the end of this chapter provides the opportunity to practice formatting and printing an envelope.

In order to print out a label, you must also change your paper size/type and margin settings. Try these settings:

Paper size and type	Other size, where you indicate the label's dimensions in inches, and

	Labels type (Remember to define a label form type before you print a label so that WordPerfect knows special instructions for printing labels.)
Left and right margins	0.5 inch as a left margin, 0 inches as a right margin (to allow room for a lengthy line in an address)
Top and bottom margins	0.25 inch as a top margin, 0 inches as a bottom margin

Once you know how to define form types for your printer, how to alter your document's paper size/type, and how to alter margin settings, you have the tools to properly print out envelopes and/or mailing labels on your printer.

Note: In addition to printing out the occasional envelope or mailing label, you may have the need to print numerous envelopes and mailing labels at one time, perhaps for a special mailing. Refer to Chapter 13 for information on producing letters and corresponding envelopes or mailing labels for a list of individuals, using WordPerfect's Merge feature.

MOVE THE CURSOR WHEN LINES ARE LONG AND FORMAT CODES ARE PRESENT

As shown in your document now on screen, there are times when you alter the paper size such that the width of a line is greater than what can be displayed across the width of your computer screen. If this is the case, you must grow accustomed to viewing on a standard, 80-column monitor only a portion of a line at one time and to scrolling to the left or the right to see the rest of the text.

The number of times you press HOME before tapping an arrow key determines whether the cursor goes to the end of the screen or to the end of the line—an important distinction if your line is longer than the screen. HOME, LEFT ARROW moves the cursor to the left edge of the current screen, as previously discussed in Chapter 1. But if you press HOME one extra time—pressing HOME, HOME, LEFT ARROW—the cursor moves to the left edge of the *line,* rather than the left edge of the *screen.* Similarly, HOME, RIGHT ARROW moves the cursor to the right

edge of the screen, while HOME, HOME, RIGHT ARROW (or END) moves
it to the right edge of the line.

There's even the opportunity to move the cursor to the left edge of
the line or to the top of the document *before any format codes,* based
on the number of times you press the HOME key. Press HOME three
times in a row to move before format codes, a distinction that can be
seen on the Reveal Codes screen. For instance, suppose that you've
placed a Paper Size/Type code at the beginning of a line. If you press
HOME, HOME, LEFT ARROW, the cursor moves to the left edge of the
line of text, but stops to the right of the Paper Size/Type code.

```
[Paper Sz/Typ:11" x 8.5",Standard][Tab]Here are the names that were left off the
list of deliveries to the Northwestern[SRt]
```

If you press HOME, HOME, HOME, LEFT ARROW instead, the cursor
moves to the complete left edge of the line, so that the cursor rests on
the **[Paper Sz/Typ:]** code.

```
[Paper Sz/Typ:11" x 8.5",Standard][Tab]Here are the names that were left off the
list of deliveries to the Northwestern[SRt]
```

Similarly, HOME, HOME, UP ARROW moves to the top of the document
but stops to the right of any format codes located there. On the other
hand, HOME, HOME, HOME, UP ARROW moves to the top of the document and to the left of any format codes.

These differences in cursor movement on a line containing codes
are subtle. In fact, you cannot tell whether the cursor is to the left or
the right of codes on the Typing screen. The difference is apparent
only on the Reveal Codes screen. As you work more and more with
WordPerfect, and as you type documents with more and more codes,
precise cursor control will become important, especially when you accumulate a number of format codes at one spot in a document.

To illustrate cursor movement differences, proceed as follows.
Start with the cursor at the top of the document, on the "H" in "Here
are the names":

1. Press HOME, RIGHT ARROW to move to the right edge of the
   screen. The cursor does not move beyond the screen, even
   though the line extends farther.

2. Press HOME, RIGHT ARROW again. Now you scroll to the next screen to the right, so the end of the line comes into view.

3. Press HOME, LEFT ARROW to move to the left edge of the screen.

4. Press HOME, LEFT ARROW to scroll to the next screen to the left, so that you can again view the beginning of each line.

5. Press HOME, HOME, RIGHT ARROW. Notice that the cursor moves all the way to the right edge of the line in one command.

6. Press HOME, HOME, LEFT ARROW to move to the left edge of the line in one command.

7. Press REVEAL CODES (ALT + F3). Notice that the cursor stops just before the Paper Size/Type code.

8. Press HOME, HOME, HOME LEFT ARROW. Notice that the cursor is now on the Paper Size/Type code.

9. Press SWITCH (SHIFT + F3) to view the document currently on the Doc 1 screen. You should still be viewing a screen with codes revealed.

10. Press HOME, HOME, UP ARROW and notice that the cursor moves to the top of the document, but stops before the Header, Page Numbering, and Suppress codes.

11. Press HOME, HOME, HOME, UP ARROW and notice that the cursor moves before these codes, so that it is positioned on the first of these codes.

Before moving on to the review exercise, save the documents on both the Doc 1 and Doc 2 screens and clear the screen. To do so

1. Press the EXIT (F7) key, and save the document under the name SAMPLE by pressing ENTER to accept the suggested name and typing **Y** to replace the older file on disk with the revision on screen. Notice that WordPerfect prompts you with the following after you save the document to a file:

Exit Doc 1? (Y/N) No

2. Type **Y** to leave Doc 1. The screen switches to Doc 2.

3. Press the EXIT (F7) key and save the document in the Doc 2 window under the name LIST by pressing ENTER to accept the suggested name and typing **Y** to replace the older file on disk with the revision on screen. Notice now what WordPerfect prompts you with

   Exit WP? (Y/N) No

   This is because the second document screen is clear.

4. Type **N** so that you may remain in WordPerfect and proceed with the review exercise that follows.

REVIEW EXERCISE

You are now ready to tackle a document of any length! For practice, find a two- to three-page document that's on your desk and follow the suggestions below. You'll reassure yourself that you can easily format pages any way you desire.

1. Clear the screen.

2. For the document that you're about to type, change the top and bottom margins to 1.5 inches. (*Hint:* Since you are changing top/bottom margins starting at the top of the documents, insert the Top/Bottom Margin code on the Document Initial Codes screen.

3. Turn on Widow/Orphan Protection so that WordPerfect is given flexibility in inserting page breaks.

4. Type and edit your multiple-page document. Now WordPerfect inserts automatic page breaks after 8 inches of text are typed (11 inches minus 1.5 inches minus 1.5 inches).

5. Create the following header, which will insert a page number on every page:

   Review Exercise —^B

   (*Hint:* Before pressing the PAGE FORMAT (ALT + F8) key to insert the header, be sure to move to the very top of the document. [**Header:**] and [**Footer:**] codes cannot be inserted on the

Document Initial Codes screen. And remember to use CTRL + B to create the "^B" character.)

6. Scroll through the document. Notice that since you created the header, page breaks have adjusted to accommodate the one-line header and its accompanying blank line.

7. Print the document to examine the final results of your work and then clear the screen (making sure to save your document if you plan to edit, print, or reuse the document later on).

8. If you haven't already done so, define an envelope form type so that you can print out envelopes using your printer. Look to Appendix B for assistance. (If you don't plan on using your printer to print envelopes, then you may wish to stop the review exercise at this point.)

9. On a clear screen, retrieve the file SMITH.ADD. (This is a file you created in Chapter 2 using the Block Save feature; it contains only a name and an address.)

10. Make the proper format changes to print out the name and address onto an envelope. (*Hint:* Position the cursor at the top of the document and insert a Paper Size/Type code for envelopes, and then change your left/right and top/bottom margins.)

11. Print the envelope to examine the final results of your work and clear the screen.

REVIEW

- WordPerfect automatically inserts soft page breaks after a certain amount of text is typed on a page. Where the soft page break occurs depends on your paper size and top/bottom margin settings. Assuming default settings, WordPerfect inserts a soft page break after 9 vertical inches of text have been typed on a page—11 inches page length minus 1 inch top margin minus 1 inch bottom margin.

- You can alter default page format settings, such as top/bottom margins and paper size/type, using the Page Format menu, accessed via the FORMAT (SHIFT + F8) key.

- To print out an envelope or mailing label, you should have already defined an envelope or label form type (see Appendix B). Insert the appropriate Paper Size/Type and Margin codes on a separate page in your text. Type the name and address to appear on the envelope or label and print it out.

- You can control where WordPerfect inserts soft page breaks by using the following features: Widow/Orphan Protection, which guards against the *first or last line* of a paragraph being separated by a page break from the rest of the paragraph; Block Protect, which defends against *a block of text* being separated by a page break; or Conditional End of Page, which protects against a *certain number of lines* being separated by a page break. Or you can insert a hard page break on your own by positioning the cursor where you want a page break to occur and pressing CTRL + ENTER.

- WordPerfect offers the ability to center a page top to bottom vertically when printed. This is useful for printing out title pages or a short letter that you wish to center on the page.

- WordPerfect assumes that you do not desire headers, footers, or page numbers when printing out a document. Use the Page Format menu to include headers, footers, or page numbers in your document. Be aware that unlike most Page Format features, Header, Footer, and Page Numbering codes cannot be inserted on the Document Initial Codes screen—but only within the document itself. Also, features are available to suppress headers, footers, and page numbers on a specific page, to renumber pages, and to force a page to have an odd or even number.

- There are a number of alternatives for moving the cursor quickly between pages. These are summarized in Table 5-1.

- Press the HOME key one extra time to maneuver the cursor in front of format codes that are located at the beginning of a line or at the top of a document. Press HOME, HOME, HOME, LEFT ARROW to position the cursor at the left edge on the line where the cursor is positioned and before any codes that may be located there. Press HOME, HOME, HOME, UP ARROW to position the cursor at the top of the document and before any codes that may be located there.

Key Combination	Cursor Movement
PGUP	Top of preceding page
PGDN	Top of following page
CTRL + HOME, UP ARROW	Top of current page
CTRL + HOME, DOWN ARROW	Bottom of current page
CTRL + HOME, [page number]	Top of a specific page

TABLE 5-1   Cursor Movement Between Pages

6

MOVING, SEARCHING, AND EDITING ENHANCEMENTS

Search for Characters in Text
Search for Codes in Text
Replace Text and/or Codes
Move/Copy a Block of Text
Compare Documents After Editing
Review Exercise
Review

Reworking words, rearranging sentences, reordering paragraphs—
these are some of the constants in document editing. WordPerfect
makes the rewriting process less arduous with some special editing enhancements. One editing timesaver is the Search feature. WordPerfect
can look through a long document and position the cursor on the
specific word or phrase you can't seem to locate, or it can find a hidden code that is elluding you. A related feature is Replace, whereby
WordPerfect locates a certain word or phrase everywhere it occurs and
swaps it for another phrase of your choice.

Another handy feature enables you to perform a cut-and-paste procedure—moving text from one part of the document to another—
without having to use scissors or tape. You can also copy text from one
place to another.

Should you decide to edit your document and keep track of editing changes, you can ask that WordPerfect compare the edited version of a document on screen with the old version on disk. This is useful if you want to contrast an original contract with a revision, or the draft of a report with the final version. In this chapter, the various editing features will be explained, and you will practice using them with documents that you created in previous chapters.

SEARCH FOR CHARACTERS IN TEXT

Searching through the text for a specific character, word, or phrase can be a time-consuming process. Imagine, for instance, needing to reread a 30-page report just to find one reference to wine sales in San Francisco. Rather than scroll through the document screen by screen, you can start with the cursor at the top of the document and request that WordPerfect find the phrase "San Francisco." WordPerfect moves the cursor to that phrase in moments. A character, phrase, or word that you are searching for is referred to as a *string*.

The GOTO Key

If the string is just one character in length, than you can use the GOTO key combination, CTRL + HOME, to move there. Chapter 5 describes how, if you press CTRL + HOME and then enter a number, WordPerfect moves the cursor to the top of that page. Similarly, if you press CTRL + HOME and, at the prompt,

Go to

you type a letter or a symbol (such as !, *, or %), the cursor moves just to the right of the first occurrence of that letter or symbol—as long as it appears within the next 2000 characters. The GOTO key combination only moves the cursor forward in the text, so you must position the cursor before the character you seek.

The Search Feature

If the string you want to locate is more than 1 character long but less than 59 characters long, you will rely on the Search feature. With the Search feature, you're not limited to looking within the next 2000 characters; rather, an entire document can be scanned. You can search either forward from the current cursor position with the →SEARCH (F2) key or backwards with the ←SEARCH (SHIFT + F2) key. To search an entire document, for example, move the cursor to the top of the document and press the →SEARCH (F2) key, or move the cursor to the bottom of the document and press the ←SEARCH (SHIFT + F2) key. WordPerfect prompts asking for the string of characters for which you wish to search. The prompt contains an arrow pointing to the right for a forward search:

→Srch:

And it contains an arrow pointing to the left for a backward search:

←Srch:

At the search prompt, type in the string and then press either the →SEARCH (F2) key or the ←SEARCH (SHIFT + F2) key or the ESC key to execute the command. Or press the CANCEL (F1) key to abort the search. When you initiate a search and the search string is found, the cursor will move just to the right of the first occurrence of the string. Otherwise, WordPerfect will prompt with

* Not found *

In a search string, WordPerfect is sensitive to uppercase letters. An uppercase string will match only uppercase in the text, while a lowercase string will match either. For instance, suppose your string is "CHAMPAGNE". WordPerfect will stop after "CHAMPAGNE" but not after "champagne" or "Champagne". However, if the string is "champagne", then it will stop after any of the three variations. Be careful of typos, however. If the string you typed is "hcampagne", the word would not be found in the text, and WordPerfect would respond with a * **Not found** * message.

You have several options when performing a search. One is to execute an Extend Search, whereby WordPerfect searches through headers, footers, and footnotes as well as the main body of text. To do so, press HOME before pressing the →SEARCH (F2) or the ←SEARCH (SHIFT + F2) key. Then type in the search string and press the →SEARCH (F2) or the ←SEARCH (SHIFT + F2) key again. A second option is to search through only a specific part of your document. You would press the BLOCK (ALT + F4) key and highlight that specific block before you pressed the →SEARCH (F2) or ← SEARCH (SHIFT + F2) key.

Furthermore, you can include a "wild card" in the search string to represent any single character, as long as the wild card isn't the first character in the string. To include a wild card, you would press CTRL + V and then press CTRL + X. The wild card character ^X is inserted. So, for example, "wa^Xt" would match "wait", "walt", "want", "wart" and "watt".

As an example, let's first move the cursor using the GOTO key. You'll search in the short document you edited in Chapters 4 and 5. (Be aware that the time savings in using the Search feature are even more dramatic on a long document.)

1. On a clear Typing screen, retrieve the file named SAMPLE.

2. With the cursor at the top of the document, suppose you want to move the cursor to the end of the first full sentence. Press CTRL + HOME. WordPerfect prompts you with

   Go to

3. Type a period (.). The cursor moves past the end of the sentence in an instant.

4. Press CTRL + HOME again.

5. Type a colon (:). The cursor moves to the end of the first paragraph, where the colon is located.

Here's some practice using the →SEARCH (F2) key. Suppose you're searching through the entire document for a reference to "R&R," the name of the wine association. You know that the reference to it appears further forward in the document, so you will search in the forward direction.

1. Press the →SEARCH (F2) key. WordPerfect responds with

   →Srch:

2. Type **R&R**.

3. Press the →SEARCH (F2) key to initiate the search.

In seconds, the cursor flies down the document, just to the right of "R&R." If you typed the string wrong (such as inserting spaces so that the search string is "R & R"), WordPerfect would be unable to locate the string and would prompt you with

* Not Found *

If that prompt appeared on screen, try again, being sure to type the name correctly in step 2.

Each time you complete a search, WordPerfect remembers the search string that you typed. The next time you press the →SEARCH (F2) or the ←SEARCH (SHIFT + F2) key, the same string appears in the prompt. If you want to again search for the next occurrence of that string, simply press the →SEARCH (F2) key again. If you want to search for another word or phrase, you could type the new string right over the old one before pressing the →SEARCH (F2) key a second time.

1. Press the →SEARCH (F2) key. WordPerfect responds with

   →Srch: R&R

   Notice that WordPerfect remembers the last search string, and so suggests it again.

2. Press the →SEARCH (F2) key to initiate the search. The cursor moves just past the next occurrence of "R&R."

3. Repeat steps 1 and 2 until WordPerfect prompts *** Not found ***, meaning that the search string "R&R" does not appear farther forward in the document.

4. Press the ←SEARCH (SHIFT+F2) key. WordPerfect responds with a backwards search prompt, still remembering the most recent search string:

   ←Srch: R&R

5. Suppose you wish to search for the reference to Spain. Type **Spain**. As soon as you begin typing the new search string, the old one is erased—you don't even need to use the BACKSPACE or DEL key. Now the prompt reads

←Srch: Spain

6. Press the ESC key to initiate the search. Now the cursor moves backwards in the text and stops just past the occurrence of "Spain."

The Search feature can be used as a convenient way to leapfrog from one section of a document to the next. For instance, suppose you are writing a report but must talk to several experts before you include some statistics. At each place in the document where you are missing a statistic, you can type a string of characters that you would not otherwise find in the document, such as **??**. After you have talked to the experts, you can use the Search feature to move quickly to the places where you must fill in the statistics.

Be sure that you don't use the ENTER key to try to execute a search. If you do, you'll insert an **[HRt]** code in the search string rather than execute the search. For instance, suppose you press the →SEARCH (F2) key and type **Europe**. The prompt reads

→Srch: Europe

Now if you press ENTER the search doesn't begin! Instead, you have added an **[HRt]** code to the search string. WordPerfect believes that you wish to find the phrase "Europe" only when it is followed by a hard return. The prompt appears as

→Srch: Europe[HRt]

To correct the problem, press BACKSPACE to erase the **[HRt]** code from the search string and then press the →SEARCH (F2) key or ESC key to execute the search. The next section describes more about how you can locate codes such as **[HRt]** using the Search feature.

SEARCH FOR CODES IN TEXT

One of the Search command's most compelling features is the ability to quickly locate hidden codes, either by themselves or along with text. This frees you from having to reveal codes and then move slowly through the text to find a code you're looking for. For instance, what if you printed out a document only to find that the margins shifted unexpectedly on page 3. By now you know that the culprit is most likely a **[L/R Mar]** code or perhaps an **[→Indent]** code that you accidentally placed on that page. With the Search command, you could find that troublesome code instantly and use the BACKSPACE key to erase it, since WordPerfect positions the cursor just to the right of the code you're seeking.

To include a code in a search string, you use the same function key combination as when you inserted that code in the text in the first place. For instance, you would press the ENTER key to search for a Hard Return code **[HRt]**, or press the BOLD (F6) key to search for a beginning Bold code **[BOLD]** or press BOLD (F6) twice and then erase the beginning Bold code to search for an ending Bold code **[bold]**. Or use the FORMAT (SHIFT + F8) and then follow the procedure as if changing left/right margins to search for a Left/Right Margin code **[L/R Mar]**. Although any WordPerfect code can be part of a search string, there's no way to specify a particular parameter within a code. For example, you can search for a Left/Right Margin code, but not for only those Left/Right Margin codes with margins of 1.5 inches.

As an example, let's recall a different document to the screen and then search for **[Tab]** codes.

1. Clear the screen by pressing EXIT (F7) and then typing **N** twice. Then retrieve the file named LIST to the Typing screen.

2. Make sure that the cursor is at the top of the document. Suppose you wish to locate any Tab codes located in the document.

3. Press the →SEARCH (F2) key. WordPerfect responds with

   →Srch: Spain

   Notice that WordPerfect remembers the last string you searched for. You can type right over that string.

4. Press the TAB key. Now the search string reads

   →Srch: [Tab]

5. Press the →SEARCH (F2) key to begin the search. The cursor
   moves just to the right of a **[Tab]** code. You can verify this by
   pressing REVEAL CODES (ALT + F3) so that the codes are displayed on screen.

6. Press →SEARCH (F2) twice and watch how the cursor jumps
   just past the next **[Tab]** code located forward in the document.

7. Repeat step 6 above several more times and watch how the
   cursor jumps to each **[Tab]** code. You may wish to switch to
   the Reveal Codes screen as you use the Search feature, so that
   you can watch as the cursor repositions just to the right of each
   successive Tab code. (If WordPerfect doesn't pause at a spot
   where you believe a Tab code is located, reveal codes; you
   may find that an **[→Indent]** code is located there instead.)
   Once WordPerfect responds with * **Not found** *, then you have
   verified the absence of any more Tab codes located forward
   from the cursor.

Suppose that you now wish to position the cursor next to any **[Tab
Set]** code that may exist in the document and erase one of those codes.

1. Press HOME, HOME, HOME, UP ARROW to move the cursor to the
   top of the document. (Remember from Chapter 5 that pressing
   HOME three times before pressing UP ARROW ensures that the
   cursor moves to the top of the document, before any codes that
   may be located there.)

2. Press the →SEARCH (F2) key. WordPerfect responds with

   →Srch: [Tab]

   WordPerfect remembers the last code you searched for.

3. Press the LINE FORMAT (SHIFT + F8) key (the function key that enables you to insert Tab Set codes into a document). Because you are in the midst of a search, a slightly different menu appears than when you actually changed margins. This menu is

   1 Line; 2 Page; 3 Other: 0

   WordPerfect is asking whether the code you wish to search for is inserted into the document using the Line Format, Page Format, or Other Format menu.

4. Select Line (1 or L). The following menu appears:

   1 Hyphen; 2 HZone; 3 /; 4 Justification; 5 Line; 6 Margins;
   7 Tab Set; 8 W/O: 0

   Each of these options represents a different type of Line Format code.

5. Select Tab Set (7 or T). The search prompt reappears and reads

   →Srch: [Tab Set]

6. Press the →SEARCH (F2) key again. The cursor moves forward in the text. If you reveal codes by pressing REVEAL CODES (ALT + F3), you'll see that the cursor is now just to the right of a [Tab Set] code.

7. Press the →SEARCH (F2) key twice; the cursor moves to the next [Tab Set] code in the text.

8. Press BACKSPACE to erase this second Tab Set code. If you're viewing the Typing screen, WordPerfect asks for verification:

   Delete [Tab Set:1", every 0.5"]? (Y/N) No

9. Type **Y** and the code will disappear; once you move the cursor to rewrite the screen, the last sentence will abide by the tab settings controlled by the first Tab Set code in the text.

Table 6-1 provides a complete list of codes—even some codes that have yet to be discussed but that will be covered in future chapters. Using this table, you can more easily identify codes as you edit your text and as you include codes in a search string. Refer to this table when you find a code on the Reveal Codes screen that you can't identify so that you can look up the associated feature, learn how the code will affect the text when printed, and decide whether or not to delete or move it.

REPLACE TEXT AND/OR CODES

The Replace feature goes one step further than Search. Not only will WordPerfect locate an occurrence of a specific string, but it can also automatically substitute a new phrase for that string, continuing along until all such occurrences in the document are found and replaced. For example, you could search for all the places where you referred to "ABC Company" in a proposal and change them to "XYZ Company"—tailoring the proposal to a different organization in moments.

In a Replace, there are the following two strings:

Search string	The phrase that you are looking for
Replace string	The phrase that will be substituted for the search string

Both the search and replace strings can include text, codes, or both, up to 59 characters in length.

There are two ways that the Replace feature can operate. First, you can request the Replace with confirmation, meaning that when the search string is found, WordPerfect pauses and asks if you wish to substitute the replace string. Alternatively, you can request Replace without confirmation, whereby WordPerfect performs the substitution of all search strings found in the document without stopping.

Depending on what the replace string is, it can serve as a straight substitution, an insertion, or a deletion. For example, if you searched for "Joe Smith" and replaced with "Hanna Jones", that would be a straight substitution. If you searched for "Joe Smith" and replaced it with "Joe Smith, Sr.", that would be more like an insertion. If you searched for an Underline code and left the replace string blank, you can effectively delete all underlining from the text.

You can execute the Replace in either the forward or the backward direction from the current cursor position. First position the cursor. Next press the REPLACE (ALT + F2) key. WordPerfect prompts you with

w/Confirm? (Y/N) No

-	Soft Hyphen
^M	Merge (M=merge code letter, as in ^E or ^R)
/	Cancel Hyphenation
[-]	Hard Hyphen
[ ]	Hard Space
[+]	Subtotal Calculation (Math)
[=]	Total Calculation (Math)
[*]	Grand Total Calculation (Math)
[!]	Formula Calculation (Math)
[N]	Calculation treated as negative (Math)
[t]	Subtotal Entry (Math)
[T]	Total Entry (Math)
[AdvDn:]	Advance Down
[AdvLft:]	Advance Left
[AdvRgt:]	Advance Right
[AdvToPos:]	Advance To Position
[AdvToLn:]	Advance to Line
[AdvUp:]	Advance Up
[Align][C/A/Flrt]	Tab Align (begin and end)
[Block]	Beginning of Highlighted Block (in Reveal Codes)
[Block Pro:On][Block Pro:Off]	Block Protection (begin and end)
[BOLD][bold]	Bold (begin and end)
[Box Num]	Caption in Graphics Box
[C/A/Flrt]	End of Center, Tab Align, or Flush Right
[Center Pg]	Center Page Top to Bottom
[Cntr][C/A/Flrt]	Center (begin and end)
[Cndl EOP:]	Conditional End of Page
[Col Def:]	Text Columns Definition
[Col Off]	Text Columns Off (end)
[Col On]	Text Columns On (begin)
[Comment]	Document Comment
[Color:]	Print Color
[Date:]	Date/Time Format
[DBL UND][dbl und]	Double Underline (begin and end)
[Decml/Algn Char:]	Decimal Align and Thousands Separator Characters
[Def Mark:Index]	Index Definition

TABLE 8-1   WordPerfect Codes

[Def Mark:List,n]	List Definition (n=list number)
[Def Mark:ToA,n]	Table of Authorities Definition (n=section number)
[Def Mark:ToC,n]	Table of Contents Definition (n=ToC level)
[DSRt]	Deletable Soft Return
[EndDef]	End of Index, List, or Table (after generation)
[EndMark:List,n]	End marked text for List(n=list number)
[EndMark:ToC,n]	End marked text for Table of Contents (n=ToC level)
[End Opt]	Endnote Options
[Endnote:n;[Note Num]text]	Endnote (n=note number)
[Endnote Placement]	Endnote Placement
[EXT LARGE][ext large]	Extra Large Print (begin and end)
[Figure:n;]	Figure Box (n=box number)
[Fig Opt]	Figure Box Options
[FINE][fine]	Fine Print (begin and end)
[Flsh Rt][C/A/Flrt]	Flush Right (begin and end)
[Footnote:n;[Note Num]text]	Footnote (n=note number)
[Font:]	Base Font
[Footer N:n;text]	Footer (N=type, A or B) (n=frequency)
[Force:]	Force Odd or Force Even
[Ftn Opt]	Footnote Options
[Header N:n;text]	Header (N=type, A or B) (n=frequency)
[HLine:]	Horizontal Line
[HPg]	Hard Page
[HRt]	Hard Return
[Hyph Off]	Hyphenation Off
[Hyph On]	Hyphenation On
[HZone:n,n]	Hyphenation Zone (n=left,right)
[→Indent]	Indent
[→Indent←]	Left/right Indent
[Index:heading;subheading]	Index Entry
[ISRt]	Invisible Soft Return
[ITALC][Italc]	Italics Print (begin and end)
[Just Off]	Right Justification Off

TABLE 6-1   WordPerfect Codes (*continued*)

[Just On]	Right Justification On
[Just Lim:]	Justification Limits for Word/Letter Spacing
[Kern:Off]	Kerning Off
[Kern:On]	Kerning On
[L/R Mar:]	Left and Right Margins
[Lang:]	Language (for Speller, Thesaurus, Hyphenation module)
[LARGE][large]	Large Print (begin and end)
[Ln Height:]	Line Height
[Ln Num:Off]	Line Numbering Off
[Ln Num:On]	Line Numbering On
[Ln Spacing:]	Line Spacing
[←Mar Rel]	Left Margin Release
[Mark:List,n][EndMark:List,n]	List Entry Mark (n=list number) (begin and end)
[Mark:ToC,n][EndMark:ToC,n]	Table of Contents Entry Mark (n=ToC level) (begin and end)
[Math Def]	Math Columns Definition
[Math Off]	Math Columns Off (end)
[Math On]	Math Columns On (begin)
[New End Num:]	New Endnote Number
[New Fig Num:]	New Figure Box Number
[New Ftn Num:]	New Footnote Number
[New Tab Num:]	New Table Box Number
[New Txt Num:]	New Text Box Number
[New Usr Num:]	New User-Defined Box Number
[Note Num]	Footnote/Endnote Reference Number
[Open Style:name]	Open Style (n=style name)
[OUTLN][outln]	Outline Print (begin and end)
[Ovrstk:]	Overstrike
[Paper Sz/Typ:s,t]	Paper Size and Type (s=size, t=type)
[Par Num:Auto]	Paragraph Number, Automatic
[Par Num:n]	Paragraph Number (n=paragraph level)
[Par Num Def]	Paragraph Numbering Definition
[Pg Num:]	New Page Number
[Pg Numbering:]	Page Numbering Position
[Ptr Cmnd:]	Printer Command
[REDLN][redln]	Redline (begin and end)

TABLE 6-1 WordPerfect Codes (*continued*)

[Ref(name) t]	Automatic Reference (name=target name) (t=what reference is tied to)
[SHADW][shadw]	Shadow Print (begin and end)
[SM CAP][sm cap]	Small Caps (begin and end)
[SMALL][small]	Small Print (begin and end)
[SPg]	Soft Page
[SRt]	Soft Return
[STKOUT][stkout]	Strikeout (begin and end)
[Style On:name][Style Off:name]	Paired Style (begin and end) (name=style name)
[Subdoc:]	Subdocument in a Master Document
[Subdoc Start:][Subdoc End:]	Subdocument after being generated (begin and end)
[SUBSCRPT][subscrpt]	Subscript (begin and end)
[SUPRSCPT][suprscpt]	Superscript (begin and end)
[Suppress:]	Suppress Page Format Options
[T/B Mar:]	Top and Bottom Margins
[Tab]	Tab
[Tab Set:]	Tab Set
[Table:n;]	Table Box (n=box number)
[Target(name)]	Target in Auto Reference (name=target name)
[Tbl Opt]	Table Box Options
[Text Box:n;]	Text Box (n=box number)
[ToA:;text]	Table of Authorities Short Form (text=text of Short Form)
[ToA:n;text];Full Form]]	Table of Authorities Full Form (n=section number) (text=text of Short Form)
[Txt Opt]	Text Box Options
[UND][und]	Underlining (begin and end)
[Undrln:]	Underline Spaces and/or Tabs
[Usr Box:n;]	User-Defined Box (n=box number)
[Usr Opt]	User-Defined Box Options
[VLine:]	Vertical Line
[VRY LARGE][vry large]	Very Large Print (begin and end)
[Wrd/Ltr Spacing:]	Word and Letter Spacing
[W/O Off]	Widow/Orphan Off
[W/O On]	Widow/Orphan On

TABLE 6-1   WordPerfect Codes (*continued*)

The prompt ends with "No" because WordPerfect assumes that you want the Replace command to work on the document without confirmation. Type **N** or press ENTER to accept this assumption, or type **Y** to perform the Replace with confirmation. After you type **Y** or **N**, Word-Perfect assumes you wish to proceed in the forward direction and prompts for a search string with an arrow pointing to the right:

→Srch:

To perform a backward replace, press the UP ARROW key. Now the prompt reads

←Srch:

Next type the search string and press any of the following keys to register the search string: REPLACE (ALT + F2) key, →SEARCH (F2), ←SEARCH (SHIFT + F2), or ESC. Now a prompt appears for the replace string:

Replace with:

Type in the replace string and then press REPLACE (ALT + F2), →SEARCH (F2), ←SEARCH (SHIFT + F2), or ESC to execute the replacement (or press the CANCEL (F1) key to abort it).

For a replacement without confirmation, the substitutions occur in moments.

For a replacement with confirmation, WordPerfect pauses with the cursor at the first occurrence of the search string and prompts

Confirm? (Y/N) No

Type **Y** to make the substitution or type **N** or press ENTER to skip over that string and to look for the next occurrence. This would continue to the end of the text unless you pressed the CANCEL (F1) key during the Replace to stop the procedure.

Some of the same options apply to the Replace command as to the Search command. For instance, both the search string and the replace string are sensitive to uppercase letters. You can also perform an Extended Replace, including headers, footers, and footnotes in the command, by pressing the HOME key before pressing the REPLACE (ALT + F2) key. And you can block a section of text and execute a Replace on only that portion of text.

As an example, the document currently on your Typing screen contains the word "territory" several times, as in "Northwestern territory". Suppose that you decide to refer to a section of the country as a "region", rather than as a "territory".

1. Position the cursor at the top of the document.

2. Press the REPLACE (ALT + F2) key. WordPerfect prompts

   w/Confirm? (Y/N) No

3. Type N. Now WordPerfect prompts

   →Srch: [Tab Set]

   Notice that even though you are performing a replace, Word-Perfect remembers your last search string.

4. Type **territory**. The prompt reads

   →Srch: territory

5. Press the ESC key. Now WordPerfect asks for the replace string.

   Replace with:

6. Type **region**.

7. Press the ESC key.

In moments, WordPerfect makes the substitution everywhere that the word "territory" appears on screen and then rewrites the screen so that when "region" is inserted the document adjusts within the margins. It doesn't matter whether a replace string is shorter or longer than the search string; WordPerfect adjusts the text accordingly once the substitutions are made.

Let's perform another replace. If you reveal codes for the document on screen, you'll notice that there are several places where there is an [→Indent] code. This is because you originally typed this document assuming paper 8.5 inches wide, so that, in order to align information in the "Cases" column, it was necessary to press →INDENT (F4) rather than TAB before typing information into that column. Since the paper is now 11 inches wide (remember that you inserted a Paper Size/Type code in an earlier chapter), the information in the "Cases" column now fits on one line. Let's replace every occurrence of [→**Indent**] with a [**Tab**] code.

1. Position the cursor at the top of the document.

2. Press the REPLACE (ALT + F2) key. WordPerfect prompts

   w/Confirm? (Y/N) No

3. Type **N**. Now WordPerfect prompts

   →Srch: territory

   Notice that even though you are performing a replace, Word-Perfect remembers your last search string.

4. Press →INDENT (F4). The prompt reads

   →Srch: [→Indent]

5. Press the ESC key. Now WordPerfect asks for the replace string.

   Replace with:

6. Press TAB. The prompt reads

   Replace with: [Tab]

7. Press the ESC key. In moments the substitution is complete. If you reveal codes, you can see that your document no longer contains any [→**Indent**] codes.

Some of the best uses for the Replace command occur when you want to eliminate codes. For instance, you can use Replace to delete unnecessary hard returns or to delete any underlining or boldfacing from a document that you already typed. Indicate in the search string the code or codes you are searching for. For instance, the search string could read →**Srch: [BOLD]**. Then leave the replace string blank.

You can execute the reverse operation as well—that is, search for a specific word or phrase that you wish to underline or boldface throughout a document. For example, to underline the word "immediately" everywhere it occurs in a document, the search string would be

   →Srch: immediately

When WordPerfect prompts for a replace string, press the UNDER-LINE (F8) key, type **immediately**, and press the UNDERLINE (F8) key again to create the replace string. The prompt would be

   Replace with: [UND]immediately[und]

As discussed previously, although any WordPerfect code can be part of the search string, there's no way to specify a particular parameter within a code. For example, you can search for a Left/Right Margin code, but not for only those Left/Right Margin codes with margins of 1.5 inches. Because you cannot specify a particular parameter within a code, format codes cannot be included in a replace string. The codes that can be included in a replace string include

Center	Hard Space	Math On/Off
Center Page	Hyphen	Math Operators
Columns On/Off	Hyphenation Cancel	Merge Codes
Flush Right	→Indent	Soft Hyphen
Font Appearance	→Indent←	Tab
Font Size	Justification On/Off	Tab Align
Hard Page	←Margin Release	Widow/Orphan On/Off

Be careful when you execute a Replace without confirmation. WordPerfect replaces *every* occurrence of a string—even if it's a part of another word—and you may be surprised at the results. For instance, if you replaced all occurrences of "pen" with "ballpoint", you'd also change "*pen*cil" to "*ballpoint*cil", and you'd swap "indis-*pen*sable" with "indis*ballpoint*sable." An alternative would be to search for "pen" both preceded and followed by a blank space. But then WordPerfect wouldn't find the word if it were followed by a period at the end of a sentence—or by any other punctuation—or if it were the first word in a paragraph (where it is usually preceded by a Tab code and not a space). The safest method for replacing a fairly common character string is to execute with confirmation.

MOVE/COPY A BLOCK OF TEXT

WordPerfect can move a whole block of text, meaning that it will erase the text from its current location and reinsert it at another location in your document. The program can also copy a block so that the text remains at the current location but is also placed in a new location. There are several methods for moving/copying a block of text, depending on the size of the block.

Move/Copy a Complete Sentence, Paragraph, or Page

If the block you wish to move or copy is either a sentence ending with a period, question mark, or exclamation point, a paragraph ending with an [HRt] code, or a page ending with a Hard Page code [HPg] or a Soft Page code [SPg], then the procedure can be accomplished using only the MOVE (CTRL + F4) key. There are two stages: indicating what text you wish to move or copy, and indicating where you want that text moved or copied to.

In stage one, you position the cursor anywhere within the sentence, paragraph, or page and press the MOVE (CTRL + F4) key. Word-Perfect then prompts with the Move menu:

Move: 1 Sentence; **2** Paragraph; **3** Page; **4** Retrieve: **0**

Choose one of the first three options, and WordPerfect highlights that block in reverse video and prompts you with

1 Move; **2** Copy; **3** Delete; **4** Append: **0**

If you select Move (1 or M), the block disappears from the screen and is placed in WordPerfect's *buffer,* which is like a holding tank in RAM, until you indicate where you want the text inserted. If you select Copy (2 or C), the block remains, but a copy is placed in the buffer. (You learned about the Delete option in Chapter 1 and about the Append option in Chapter 2.) A prompt at the bottom of the screen now reads

Move cursor; press Enter to retrieve.

In stage two, you have two choices. If you're ready to recall the text from the buffer onto the screen, position the cursor where you want the block to be inserted and press ENTER. You can then press DOWN ARROW to readjust the text within the margin settings. If you're not quite ready to retrieve the text into another location, then *instead* of pressing ENTER, press the CANCEL (F1) key. The prompt "Move cursor; press **Enter** to retrieve" disappears. Whenever you're ready to retrieve that block, position the cursor where you want the block inserted on screen and press the MOVE (CTRL + F4) key, select Retrieve (4 or R), and then choose Block (1 or B). The text that had been stored in the move/copy buffer reappears on screen. (In fact, since a block of text remains in the buffer until you wish to move/copy another block, you can retrieve the same block of text many times; reposition the cursor and then again press MOVE, select Retrieve, and select Block.)

There are a fair number of keys you must press to move or copy text, so becoming comfortable with the process takes a few tries. Let's practice on a document you've already typed and stored under the filename FINANCE, which contains two bullet-dotted, indented paragraphs. Pretend that you want to reverse the order of the two paragraphs. Since you're moving a paragraph, you can use the MOVE (CTRL + F4) key to do so.

1. Press the SWITCH (SHIFT + F3) key to shift to the Doc 2 Typing screen. This screen should be clear. (For a review of Dual Document typing, whereby you can use both the Doc 1 and Doc 2 screens, refer to Chapter 3.)

2. Retrieve the file named FINANCE into the Doc 2 screen.

3. Position the cursor anywhere on the first bullet-dotted item. For example, position the cursor on the "v" in "venture capitalist."

4. Press the MOVE (CTRL + F4) key. WordPerfect responds with the Move menu:

   Move: 1 Sentence; 2 Paragraph; 3 Page; 4 Retrieve: 0

5. Select Paragraph (2 or P). WordPerfect highlights the paragraph in reverse video, as shown in Figure 6-1, and prompts

   1 Move; 2 Copy; 3 Delete; 4 Append: 0

6. Select Move (1 or M). Now the sentence has disappeared—but not for long. A prompt at the bottom of the screen reads

   Move cursor; press **Enter** to retrieve.

7. Position the cursor on the last line of text, on the "F" in "For more detail."

8. Press the ENTER key. The result of the move is shown in Figure 6-2.

Imagine what a timesaver the MOVE (CTRL + F4) key is for restructuring whole pages of text. Also imagine how powerful the MOVE (CTRL + F4) key is in working between two different documents on the Doc 1 and Doc 2 screens. For instance, suppose that you want to write a

```
I spoke to John Samsone on January 3rd about our financial
situation. He reported the following highlights:

o    He is meeting with a venture capitalist next week who is
     interested in investing with us.

o    Our debt stands at $159,000 as of December 31st, 10% lower
     than we anticipated. Financial forecasts project that we'll
     be out of debt in two years time. Here are the debt figures
     (in thousands):

     Amount Owed              Name of Bank

        $48.5                 Floyd Interstate
          9.8                    Center Bank
        100.7                 Bank of Stevenson

For more detail, call John at (415) 333-9215.




1 Move; 2 Copy; 3 Delete; 4 Append: 0
```

FIGURE 6-1   A paragraph highlighted with the MOVE key

```
I spoke to John Samsone on January 3rd about our financial
situation. He reported the following highlights:

o    Our debt stands at $159,000 as of December 31st, 10% lower
     than we anticipated. Financial forecasts project that we'll
     be out of debt in two years time. Here are the debt figures
     (in thousands):

     Amount Owed              Name of Bank

        $48.5                 Floyd Interstate
          9.8                    Center Bank
        100.7                 Bank of Stevenson

o    He is meeting with a venture capitalist next week who is
     interested in investing with us.

For more detail, call John at (415) 333-9215.




C:\WPER\DATA\FINANCE                          Doc 2 Pg 1 Ln 3.33" Pos 1"
```

FIGURE 6-2   Sample text after a paragraph is moved

report based on a letter you had already created. You could retrieve the letter into the Doc 1 window and begin writing the report in the Doc 2 window, copying selected paragraphs from the letter as needed. For instance, in the Doc 1 window, you would use the MOVE (CTRL + F4) key to copy a paragraph from the letter. Then you would press the SWITCH (CTRL + F3) key to jump to the Doc 2 window, position the cursor where you wanted the paragraph to appear in the report, and press ENTER to retrieve the text. Thus, you can assemble one document quickly by copying text from another.

Move/Copy Blocks of Other Sizes, Including Columns and Rectangles

What if the block you wish to move or copy is not a sentence, paragraph, or page? Perhaps you wish to move just three words, three paragraphs, or half a page. This requires an extra step. *Before* you press the MOVE (CTRL + F4) key, you must define for WordPerfect the block's contents and dimensions.

When WordPerfect typically highlights a block of text, the block includes the first and last characters you define and all characters on every line in between. In that way, you can highlight just three words or three paragraphs.

But there may be times when you wish to move or copy (or even delete or append) just a portion of each line in a highlighted block. WordPerfect enables you to move or copy just one tabular column, where the column entries are aligned on the left margin or on a tab stop with a [Tab] code. You can also cut or copy a rectangular block, where opposing corners of the rectangle are composed of the first and last characters in that block. Figure 6-3 illustrates the differences between highlighted blocks, tabular columns, and rectangles.

To move or copy a block that is not a complete sentence, paragraph, or page, you first use the BLOCK (ALT + F4) key to highlight the text you want to move or copy.

- For a standard block, highlight it just as you've learned previously—position the cursor on the first character in the block, press BLOCK (ALT + F4), and then position the cursor one past the last character in the block.

Standard Block:

> Our debt stands at $159,000 as of December 31st, 10% lower
> than we anticipated. Financial forecasts project that we'll
> be out of debt in two years time. Here are the debt figures
> (in thousands):

Tabular Column:

Customer	City	Order #
Chou	Seattle	AB-1
Goldberg	Seattle	AB-12
Johnson	Portland	AL-12

Two Separate Rectangles:

> Our debt stands at $159,000 as of December 31st, 10% lower
> than we anticipated. Financial forecasts project that we'll
> be out of debt in two years time. Here are the debt figures
> (in thousands):

Customer	City	Order #
Chou	Seattle	AB-1
Goldberg	Seattle	AB-12
Johnson	Portland	AL-12

FIGURE 6-3   Examples of a highlighted block, a column, and rectangles

- For a tabular column, position the cursor anywhere on the first line in the column you wish to move or copy, press BLOCK (ALT + F4), and then position the cursor anywhere on the last line in that same column. (Do not be confused by the fact that WordPerfect highlights the entire block instead of only that column; WordPerfect will highlight only that column when you select Tabular Column in the next step.)

- For a rectangular block, position the cursor on the character that sits at the upper left corner of the rectangle, press BLOCK (ALT + F4), and then position the cursor one past the character that sits at the lower right corner of the rectangle. (Do not be confused by the fact that WordPerfect highlights the entire block instead of only that rectangle; WordPerfect will highlight only that rectangle when you select Rectangle in the next step.)

Now, press the MOVE (CTRL + F4) key. With **Block on** flashing, a different menu appears:

Move: 1 Block; **2** Tabular Column; **3** Rectangle: **0**

Choose one of the three options, and WordPerfect highlights that block in reverse video and prompts

1 Move; **2** Copy; **3** Delete; **4** Append: **0**

If you select Move (1 or M), the block disappears from the screen and is placed in WordPerfect's buffer until you indicate where you want the text inserted. If you select Copy (2 or C), the block remains, but a copy is placed in the buffer. (You learned about the Delete option in Chapter 1 and about the Append option in Chapter 2.) A prompt at the bottom of the screen now reads

Move cursor; press **Enter** to retrieve.

In stage two, you have the same two choices as when moving/copying a sentence, paragraph, or page—either position the cursor where you want the block to be inserted and press ENTER or press the CANCEL (F1) key, in which case the prompt "Move cursor; press **Enter** to retrieve" disappears. Whenever you're ready to retrieve that block, position the cursor where you want the block inserted on screen, press the MOVE (CTRL + F4) key and select Retrieve (4 or R). WordPerfect prompts

Retrieve: 1 Block; **2** Tabular Column; **3** Rectangle: **0**

Choose one of the three options; the text that had been stored in the move/copy buffer you specified (block, tabular column, or rectangle) reappears on screen.

Note: Some WordPerfect users have reported a problem when attempting to move a tabular column. After placing the tabular column in the computer's buffer and just before retrieving the column, the computer system freezes; the keyboard won't respond and the only way to continue working is to reboot the computer and start Word-Perfect all over again. Thus, before attempting to move a tabular column, be sure to save the document that is on screen to disk. If your computer freezes, restart your computer, reload WordPerfect, retrieve the document to screen, and try to move the tabular column again— this time using the Rectangle option on the Move menu.

Suppose you wish to change the order of words in the sentence on the Doc 2 screen that reads, "Our debt stands at $159,000 as of December 31st, 10% lower than we anticipated." You will reverse the order of words and change the sentence to read, "Our debt as of December 31st stands at $159,000, 10% lower than we anticipated." The three words you will be moving do not comprise a complete sentence; therefore, you must use the BLOCK (ALT + F4) key and select to move a block.

1. Position the cursor on the blank space between "debt" and "stands." The space will be the first character of the block.

2. Press the BLOCK (ALT + F4) key. **Block on** flashes on the status line.

3. Press RIGHT ARROW until the cursor is highlighting "stands at $159,000" as shown in Figure 6-4.

4. Now press the MOVE (CTRL + F4) key. WordPerfect prompts

   Move: 1 Block; **2** Tabular Column; **3** Rectangle: **0**

5. Select Block (1 or B). Another prompt appears:

   1 Move; **2** Copy; **3** Delete; **4** Append: **0**

6. Select Move (1 or M). The highlighted text disappears from the screen and WordPerfect reminds you

   Move cursor; press Enter to retrieve.

```
I spoke to John Samsone on January 3rd about our financial
situation. He reported the following highlights:

o   Our debt stands at $159,000 as of December 31st, 18% lower
    than we anticipated. Financial forecasts project that we'll
    be out of debt in two years time. Here are the debt figures
    (in thousands):

    Amount Owed              Name of Bank

     $48.5                   Floyd Interstate
      9.8                    Center Bank
    100.7                    Bank of Stevenson

o   He is meeting with a venture capitalist next week who is
    interested in investing with us.

For more detail, call John at (415) 333-9215.



Block on                              Doc 2 Pg 1 Ln 1.5" Pos 1.2"
```

FIGURE 6-4   A portion of a sentence highlighted for a move

7. Position the cursor on the comma (,) in the middle of the sentence.

8. Press ENTER. You have now reordered words in a sentence without needing to retype.

Now suppose that you wish to edit the table on the Doc 1 screen. The first three columns appear as follows:

Customer	City	Order #
Chou	Seattle	AB-1
Goldberg	Seattle	AB-12
Johnson	Portland	AL-12

Assume that you want to move the third column, "Order #," over one column to the left. You can't use the Block option on the move menu as you did for the previous example because, in addition to moving the third column, WordPerfect will also move parts of other columns. But you can use either the Tabular Column option (because each column is aligned on a tab) or the Rectangle option. Let's use the Rectangle option to move the third column. (You may wish to try using the Tabular Column option; however, keep in mind that, as mentioned previously, some WordPerfect users have reported that their computers freeze when they attempt to move a tabular column.)

1. Press SWITCH (SHIFT + F3) to return to the document named LIST that appears on the Doc 1 screen.

2. Position the cursor on the "O" in the heading "Order #."

3. Press the BLOCK (ALT + F4) key.

4. To define the rectangle, first press DOWN ARROW until your cursor sits on the last line in the table. Then press RIGHT ARROW until your cursor is located on the first character in the fourth column:

```
Customer      City        Order #      Cases
Chou          Seattle     AB-1         34 cases from container 744; 25 cas
Goldberg      Seattle     AB-12        2 cases from container 744; 8 cases
Johnson       Portland    AL-12        88 cases from containers 100 and 14
```

By positioning the cursor on the first character in the fourth column, you are also highlighting the Tab code that follows each entry in the second column. You must move Tab codes in the block so that the columns will align properly when moved.

5. Press the MOVE (CTRL + F4) key. WordPerfect prompts

   Move: 1 Block; 2 Tabular Column; 3 Rectangle: 0

6. Select Rectangle (3 or R). Now WordPerfect highlights only the portion of text that forms a rectangle, including the **[Tab]** code that follows each entry.

```
Customer      City        Order #      Cases
Chou          Seattle     AB-1         34 cases from container 744; 25 cas
Goldberg      Seattle     AB-12        2 cases from container 744; 8 cases
Johnson       Portland    AL-12        88 cases from containers 100 and 14
```

Another prompt appears:

1 <u>M</u>ove; 2 <u>C</u>opy; 3 <u>D</u>elete; 4 <u>A</u>ppend: 0

7. Select Move (1 or M). The highlighted text disappears from the screen and you are left with the following:

Customer	City	Cases
Chou	Seattle	34 cases from container 744; 25 cases from 333
Goldberg	Seattle	2 cases from container 744; 8 cases from 334
Johnson	Portland	88 cases from containers 100 and 142

The following prompt appears at the bottom of the screen:

Move cursor; press ENTER to retrieve.

8. Now you're ready to reinsert the deleted rectangle. Position the cursor on the "C" in "City" since you want the rectangle you cut to come just before the "City" column.

9. Press ENTER. Now the first three columns appear as follows:

Customer	Order #	City
Chou	AB-1	Seattle
Goldberg	AB-12	Seattle
Johnson	AL-12	Portland

Besides being used to move or copy one column, the Rectangle option is also useful if you wish to move/copy more than one tabular column or just a portion of tabular column. The following is an example of a rectangular portion of a column just before it is moved:

Order for	Chou	AB-1	Seattle
Order for	Goldberg	AB-12	Seattle
Order for	Johnson	AL-12	Portland

When you move or copy a block that you define using the BLOCK key—whether a standard block, a tabular column, or a rectangle—make sure to include in the block any hidden codes you want to take along in the process. For instance, it was important to include the [Tab] codes in the last example so that, when moved, the rectangle would align properly. As another example, if you were copying a table to another place, you would want to include in the block the **[Tab Set:]** code that may precede the table to reset tab stops. Thus, it is often a good idea to perform the move or copy procedure when viewing the Reveal Codes screen, rather than the Typing screen, so that you can position the cursor precisely, including or excluding codes depending on what you are moving/copying.

Also, keep in mind that working with columns and rectangles can be tricky. In standard editing, WordPerfect operates from line to line. Any insertions are made on one particular line, and all text already on the screen that follows the insertion is pushed out of the way. Working with columns and rectangles, however, WordPerfect operates with a whole group of lines; if you insert a column, you are actually inserting text on many lines at once, and many individual lines of text need to be pushed out of the way. This can cause word wrap to readjust text in unexpected ways. Therefore, make sure that you have stored a file on disk before you start moving and copying columns and rectangles. If the text is reshuffled so extremely that a document is ruined, you can always retrieve the file from disk and try again.

COMPARE DOCUMENTS AFTER EDITING

WordPerfect offers a feature whereby any editing changes made to a document on screen can be compared to the original version on disk. The documents are compared phrase by phrase, where a phrase is defined as text between punctuation marks like a period, colon, question mark, exclamation point, or comma. The Document Compare feature is useful when you wish to compare an edited article or contract with the original.

On-screen text that has been added so that it does not exist in the file on disk is redlined; the codes **[REDLN]** and **[redln]** are inserted around that text. Once you print the on-screen text, redline on your printer may result in shading that appears over characters, such as in this example:

```
The last three words of this sentence are redlined.
```

Redline may also appear as a vertical bar in the left margin or in a different color than the rest of your text. How redline appears on the printed page depends on your printer.

On-screen text that has been deleted is recalled onto the screen and marked with strikeout; the codes [STKOUT] and [stkout] are inserted around that text. Strikeout on your printer may result in a solid line through the characters, such as in this example:

The last three words of this sentence ~~contain strikeout marks.~~

Strikeout may also appear as a broken line through the characters. As with redline, how strikeout appears depends on your printer.

Moreover, any on-screen text that has been moved from one location to another compared to the text on disk is bordered by two messages on screen—"THE FOLLOWING TEXT WAS MOVED" and "THE PRECEDING TEXT WAS MOVED."

Note: Neither the redline nor the strikeout marks are visible on the Typing screen; they appear only on the printed page. But you can decide exactly how the text should appear on screen. Color monitor users can select a specific color for redline and another for strikeout. Monochrome monitor users can choose to show redline or strikeout in any combination of a blinking, underlined, boldfaced, or reverse video image. To determine how redline and strikeout will appear on screen, refer to the "Display" section of Appendix C. (You can also mark sections of text for redline and strikeout by yourself, inserting the redline and strikeout codes manually. In addition, you can change the redline method used when your printer prints out your document; see Chapter 10 for details.)

To compare an edited document to the original on disk, make sure that the edited version is on screen. Then press the MARK TEXT (ALT + F5) key. The following menu appears:

1 Auto Ref; 2 Subdoc; 3 Index; 4 ToA short form; 5 Define;
6 Generate: 0

Select Generate (6 or G) and the Generate menu, as shown in Figure 6-5, appears. Select Compare Screen and Disk Documents and Add Redline and Strikeout (2 or C). WordPerfect prompts for a filename (usually the name of the file you retrieved to the screen before initiating the Document Compare).

Other document:

Press ENTER to accept the suggested filename or type a filename and then press ENTER.

In moments, WordPerfect marks the on-screen document. On-screen text that does not exist in the file on disk is redlined. Text in the file on disk that does not exist in the document on screen is copied to the on-screen document with Strikeout codes inserted.

After WordPerfect has compared the two documents, you have a variety of options. First, you can simply print out the result. That way you can see the changes quite clearly and can even solicit suggestions for the final version of your document by distributing the printed text.

Second, you can move the cursor phrase by phrase to each Redline or Strikeout code in the text and decide which version of that phrase you prefer. (The Search feature is convenient for moving the cursor to each **[REDLN]** or **[STKOUT]** code; see Chapter 10 for the procedure to insert one of these codes individually, so that you'll know how to include one in the search string.) Delete the rejected text along with the accompanying Redline or Strikeout codes.

```
Mark Text: Generate

    1   Remove Redline Markings and Strikeout Text from Document

    2 - Compare Screen and Disk Documents and Add Redline and Strikeout

    3 - Expand Master Document

    4 - Condense Master Document

    5 - Generate Tables, Indexes, Automatic References, etc.




Selection: 0
```

FIGURE 6-5   The Generate menu

Third, you can decide to remove all the Redline codes and strikeout text from the document. In that way, you are returning the on-screen text to the way it appeared before WordPerfect performed a Document Compare for you—meaning that you prefer the on-screen version as compared to the disk version of the document. To remove all the Redline codes and strikeout text, return to the Generate menu (as shown in Figure 6-5). Then select Remove Redline Markings and Strikeout Text from Document (1 or R). To verify, WordPerfect prompts with the following:

Delete redline markings and strikeout text? (Y/N) No

Type **Y** and in moments all redline marks will be gone, and all strikeout text will be deleted. Or type **N** or press ENTER and the command is aborted.

Here's an example. Your Doc 2 screen contains an edited version of the file named FINANCE. Following instructions found in earlier sections of this chapter, you edited the document by moving a paragraph and several words. Let's take a look at the changes:

1. Press SWITCH (SHIFT + F3) to return to the document named FINANCE that appears on the Doc 2 screen.

2. To view the redline and strikeout more clearly, edit a few more words in the document. For example, in the first sentence, change "spoke" to "talked." In the last sentence, change "John" to "him."

3. Press the MARK TEXT (ALT + F5) key to display the following menu:

   1 Auto Ref; 2 Subdoc; 3 Index; 4 ToA short form; 5 Define; 6 Generate: 0

4. Select Generate (6 or G). The Generate Mark Text menu appears, as shown in Figure 6-5.

5. Select Compare Screen and Disk Documents for Redline and Strikeout (2 or C). WordPerfect prompts for the name of the document on disk, assuming it is the same document as you retrieved before editing. For instance, floppy disk users will see

   Other document: B:\FINANCE

6. Press ENTER to accept the suggested filename.

7. Print out the document. You'll get a result similar to Figure 6-6 (depending on how you edited the document and also depending on how your printer handles redline and strikeout).

Notice in Figure 6-6, for example, that WordPerfect indicates that one paragraph of text was moved. Also notice that WordPerfect redlined "call him at (415) 333-9215." and marked for strikeout "call John at (415) 333-9215." because the phrase is different on screen—"John" has been changed to "him."

Now suppose that after reviewing the editing changes you wish to return the text on screen to the edited version. You wish to remove all the Redline codes and all the text marked for strikeout. Proceed as follows:

1. Press the MARK TEXT (ALT + F5) key to display the following menu:

1 Auto Ref; 2 Subdoc; 3 Index; 4 ToA short form; 5 Define; 6 Generate: 0

```
I talked to John Samsone on January 3rd about our financial
situation. I spoke to John Samsone on January 3rd about our
financial situation. He reported the following highlights:

o    Our debt as of December 31st stands at $159,000, 10% lower
     than we anticipated. Financial forecasts project that we'll
     be out of debt in two years time. Here are the debt figures
     (in thousands):

     Amount Owed              Name of Bank

       $48.5               Floyd Interstate
         9.8                 Center Bank
       100.7              Bank of Stevenson


THE FOLLOWING TEXT WAS MOVED
o    He is meeting with a venture capitalist next week who is
     interested in investing with us.

o    Our debt stands at $159,000 as of December 31st,
THE PRECEDING TEXT WAS MOVED
For more detail, call him at (415) 333-9215. call John at (415)
333-9215.
```

FIGURE 6-6   Redline and Strikeout on the printed page, the result of comparing documents

2. Select Generate (6 or G). The Generate Mark Text menu appears, as shown in Figure 6-5.

3. Select Remove Redline Markings and Strikeout Text from Document (1 or R). To verify, WordPerfect prompts with the following:

Delete redline markings and strikeout text? (Y/N) No

4. Type **Y**. The document returns to its edited version, with Redline and Strikeout codes no longer in the text.

REVIEW EXERCISE

Practice some editing tasks as suggested below. You will then be quite ready to revise any document that comes your way.

1. Clear the documents that are currently on the Doc 1 and Doc 2 screen. You don't need to bother resaving either document, since the editing changes you made were just for practice. (*Hint:* In other words, press EXIT (F7), type **N** so you don't resave the first document, and then type **Y** to exit the first Doc screen. Then press EXIT (F7), and type **N** twice so that you don't resave the second document but remain in WordPerfect.)

2. On a clear Doc 1 Typing screen, retrieve the file named URGNOTE, which you created in Chapter 3.

3. The "Urgent Notice" memo's date is near the top of the document. Move it down to the bottom left corner of the document. (*Hint:* Since the date is a short line of text ending with an **[HRt]** code, you can move it as if it were a paragraph.)

4. Delete the column entitled "Department" from the memo. (Hint: If this column is aligned on tabs, it can be deleted by using the Tabular Column option; otherwise, use the Rectangle option.)

5. Substitute the word "plan" for the word "option" every time it occurs in the document. (*Hint:* Use the Replace feature to perform this task quickly.)

6. Use the Document Compare feature to view the changes that you've made to this document, and print out the results.

7. Return the document on screen to its edited version with no Redline or Strikeout codes. (*Hint:* Use the Generate menu to perform this task quickly.)

8. Suppose that you plan to write another "Urgent Notice" memo. Copy the top of the memo—just the block that includes "URGENT MEMO" and the "To:" and "From:" lines—to the Doc 2 window. (*Hint:* After you use the BLOCK and MOVE keys to copy these lines of text, WordPerfect will prompt "Move cursor; Press ENTER to Retrieve." At that point, press the SWITCH (SHIFT + F3) key to shift to the Doc 2 screen; then press ENTER to retrieve a copy of those lines.) Then go ahead and type a new memo of your own creation in the Doc 2 window.

9. Save these documents to disk and clear the screen. You can resave the text in the Doc 1 window again under the name URGNOTE. Select your own filename for the practice document in the Doc 2 window.

REVIEW

- The MOVE (CTRL + F4) key allows you to move or copy a complete sentence, paragraph, or page from one location to another.

- Use the BLOCK (ALT + F4) key in combination with the MOVE (CTRL + F4) key to move or copy a block of text of any size or to move or copy a tabular column or a rectangle.

- The GOTO key combination (CTRL + HOME) can move you to the next occurrence of one letter or symbol.

- The →SEARCH (F2) key locates the next occurrence of a string containing characters, codes, or both in a forward direction, while the ←SEARCH (SHIFT + F2) key locates a string in a backward direction.

- The REPLACE (ALT + F2) key finds a string each time it occurs in the text and substitutes another one in its place. You can have WordPerfect execute the replacement without stopping or have it pause for your confirmation each time the string is located.

- The Search and Replace commands are useful in finding or eliminating codes from the text. Include a code in a string by pressing the same key combination as when you insert that code in the text.

- The Document Compare feature reminds you of editing changes you've made in a document. The text on screen is compared to a document on disk. Redline marks are inserted around text added on screen. Strikeout marks are inserted around text deleted on screen. These features are options on the Generate menu, accessed via the MARK TEXT (ALT + F5) key. Use the same menu to remove the redline markings and strikeout text from the on-screen document.

7

THE SPELLER AND THE THESAURUS

When proofreading a document, you can easily miss spelling errors—especially if you're the author and all too familiar with the material. WordPerfect offers a comprehensive spelling checker packed with more than 100,000 words in its dictionary. The Spell feature makes sure that all the words in a document are spelled correctly by comparing each word with those in its dictionary. You can thus ensure that there are no misspellings before you print.

Another bonus is WordPerfect's Thesaurus feature, which helps you find just the right phrase as you're writing a document. It is also useful when you're not sure of the exact meaning of a word: it provides synonyms and antonyms for some 10,000 common words. In this chapter, you'll learn how to access a dictionary and thesaurus as you write your documents by tapping keys rather than by lifting heavy books.

SPELL CHECK A WORD

WordPerfect's Spell feature lets you verify the spelling of a word before you type it or check spelling in a document that you've finished typing. WordPerfect's dictionary is split into two separate lists: a common word list of 2500 words and a main word list of 115,000 words. The latter is quite comprehensive—it even includes some technical terms, such as "endocrinology," and some proper nouns, such as "John" and "Smith." When you use the spell checker, the common word list is always checked first; this makes for a speedy spelling check.

The dictionary is stored on the Speller disk, in a file called WP{WP}US.LEX. (If you purchased one of the first releases of version 5, then your dictionary may be in a file named WP{WP}*EN*.LEX, rather than WP{WP}*US*.LEX. When WordPerfect Corporation first released version 5, the United States English dictionary was identified with the letters "EN," which stood for "English," and was later changed to "US".) To have access to the dictionary, floppy disk users must insert the Speller disk into drive B. Hard disk users should already have the dictionary stored on the hard disk. (If not, hard disk users can insert the Speller disk in a disk drive or turn to Appendix A to learn how to install the dictionary onto your hard disk.) You are now ready to use the Spell feature.

Note: You have the ability to purchase additional dictionaries (at an additional charge) in British English (UK), Canadian French (CA), Danish (DA), Dutch (NE), Finnish (SU), French (FR), German (DE), Icelandic (IC), Italian (IT), Norwegian (NO), Portuguese (PO), Spanish (ES), and Swedish (SV). Each foreign language dictionary comes stored in a file similar to how the United States version is stored. For instance, the French dictionary is stored on disk in a file named WP{WP}FR.LEX. Contact WordPerfect Corporation if you wish to purchase a foreign language dictionary.

When you wish to use a foreign language dictionary in a certain document, you must inform WordPerfect by using the Language feature, which inserts a Language code in the text. Position the cursor where another dictionary should be used during the spell check, press FORMAT (SHIFT + F8), select Other (4 or O), select Language (4 or L), and then enter the two letters representing that language (such as FR for French). WordPerfect inserts a Language code into the text, such as **[Lang:FR]**, which informs WordPerfect which language to use from that point forward in the document.

Check a Word Before You Type

Suppose you're typing a document and you aren't sure how to spell a word. You're probably used to reaching over to a shelf of books and grabbing *Webster's*. Instead, you can rely on WordPerfect. When you are about to type the word, press the SPELL (CTRL + F2) key. Word-Perfect prompts you to wait as it accesses the dictionary. The following menu then appears on the screen:

Check: 1 Word; 2 Page; 3 Document; 4 New Sup. Dictionary;
5 Look Up; 6 Count: 0

Select Look Up (5 or L), and WordPerfect responds with

Word or word pattern:

You must provide WordPerfect with some indication of the word you want to look up so that it can respond with some correctly spelled words from the dictionary. You have two alternatives. First, you can type in the word *as you think it should be spelled*. Where there are letters you aren't sure of, you can use the wild cards ? and *. The question mark (?) substitutes for one letter, while the asterisk (*) substitutes for any number of letters. For example, if you can't remember how to spell "hippopotamus," you can type **hippo*** and then press ENTER. A double line of dashes appears in midscreen, and below that line WordPerfect provides a list of possibilities, as shown in Figure 7-1. If you don't remember which vowels are where in the word "repetition," you can type **r?p?t?tion** and press ENTER. WordPerfect responds with "repetition" and "reputation." Alternatively, if you have no idea how a word is spelled, you can type in the word *as it sounds*—that is, spell it out phonetically. For instance, suppose you didn't remember how to spell the word "cinnamon." You can sound it out and type what you hear—for example, "sinomon." If you try the word pattern "fobea," you'd find out how to spell "phobia" and "phoebe."

When you are done verifying the spelling of a word, press the CANCEL (F1) key, ENTER, or SPACEBAR twice—once to return to the Spell menu and a second time to exit the Spell feature. Now you can type the word you just looked up and continue writing your document.

Note: If you attempt to use the Spell feature and WordPerfect cannot find where the dictionary is stored, the following menu appears.

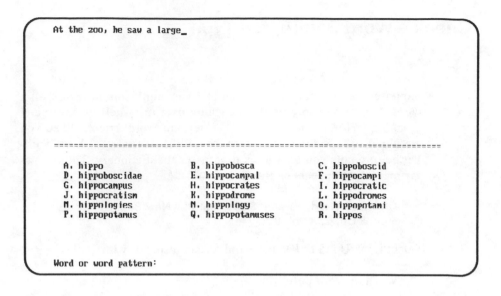

FIGURE 7-1   Speller screen when looking up "hippo*"

WP{WP}US.LEX not found: 1 Enter <u>P</u>ath; 2 <u>S</u>kip Language; 3 <u>E</u>xit Spell: 3

Select Enter Path (1 or P), type in the drive and/or directory where the dictionary can be found (such as **B:** if the Speller disk is in the B drive or **C:\WPER\SPELL** if the dictionary has been stored in a directory on the hard disk named \WPER\SPELL), and press ENTER. Then proceed with the Spell feature.

For practice, suppose you can't remember how to spell the word "embarrassment." Let's use the Spell feature and sound out the word phonetically.

1. *Floppy disk users:* Replace the disk currently in drive B with the Speller disk. *Hard disk users:* Proceed directly to step 2.

2. Press the SPELL (CTRL + F2) key. After a few moments, Word-Perfect responds with

   Check: 1 <u>W</u>ord; 2 <u>P</u>age; 3 <u>D</u>ocument; 4 <u>N</u>ew Sup. Dictionary; 5 <u>L</u>ook Up; 6 <u>C</u>ount: 0

3. Select Look Up (5 or L). WordPerfect responds with

Word or word pattern:

4. Type **imbaresment** (one possible guess as to how the word sounds) and press ENTER. After a few moments, WordPerfect lists the word "embarrassment," the only word in its dictionary that sounds like the word pattern you typed. After a few more moments of checking its dictionary, WordPerfect asks for a new word pattern.

5. Press the CANCEL (F1) key twice to exit the Spell feature.

6. *Floppy disk users:* Remove the Speller disk from drive B and reinsert the disk used to store your documents. (When done using the Spell feature, floppy disk users should always remember to remove the Speller disk from drive B and reinsert the disk previously stored there; otherwise, when you later save a document to disk, you could accidentally store a file on the Speller disk, which you don't want to do. You will want to leave any available room on the Speller disk to store some of your own dictionary words in a supplementary dictionary, described later in this chapter.)

Check a Word Already Typed

If you wish to check the spelling of a word that has already been typed on screen, position the cursor anywhere within that word and press the SPELL (CTRL + F2) key. The Spell Check menu appears; select Word (1 or W).

When that word is found in the dictionary (meaning that it is properly spelled), the word is passed over; the cursor simply jumps to the next word on screen, and the Spell Check menu remains at the bottom of the screen. You can then either select another option from the menu or press the CANCEL (F1) key to exit the Spell feature.

When that word is not in the dictionary, it will be highlighted in reverse video at the top of the screen. Just as when you were finding out how to spell "embarrassment," a double line of dashes appears midscreen. Below that line, WordPerfect suggests replacements for the highlighted word, guessing at what you had intended to type. Another menu appears at the very bottom of the screen.

```
I spke to John Samsone on January 3rd about our financial
situation. He reported the following highlights:

o    He is meeting with a venture capitalist next week who is
     interested in investing with us.

o    Our debt stands at $159,000 as of December 31st, 18% lower
     than we anticipated. Financial forecasts project that we'll
     be out of debt in two years time. Here are the debt figures
     (in thousands):

================================================================================

     A. sake              B. spike              C. spoke
     D. spca              E. spcc

Not Found: 1 Skip Once; 2 Skip; 3 Add; 4 Edit; 5 Look Up; 6 Ignore Numbers: 0
```

FIGURE 7-2   Speller screen with alternatives for "spke"

> **Not Found: 1 Skip Once; 2 Skip; 3 Add; 4 Edit; 5 Look Up;
> 6 Ignore Numbers: 0**

An example is shown in Figure 7-2, where WordPerfect cannot find
the word "spke" in the dictionary. From here, you have several
choices.

*If the word is misspelled and WordPerfect has suggested a proper
replacement,* you can press the corresponding letter to select that
word. For instance, Figure 7-2 shows that WordPerfect suggests five
possible replacements for the misspelled "spke." Type **C** and Word-
Perfect will replace "spke" with "spoke." The cursor will then jump to
the next word on the screen, preparing for a spell check of the next
word.

*If the word is misspelled but WordPerfect has not suggested the
correct replacement,* then you have two possible options available on
the Not Found menu displayed at the bottom of the screen:

- *Edit (4)*   Select this option to correct the word yourself. (Or you can select the Edit option by pressing the LEFT ARROW or RIGHT ARROW.) The cursor moves up to the word in the text so that you can correct the misspelling using all the standard editing keys, such as DEL or BACKSPACE. You then press EXIT (as would be indicated at the bottom of the screen) to continue with the spell check.

- *Look up (5)*   Select this option to request a new list of replacement words. WordPerfect prompts you for a word pattern; you can then spell out the word as best you can, using the asterisk (*) to substitute for any number of characters and the question mark (?) to substitute for one character, as described previously. WordPerfect will provide a new list of possible replacements. Choose a word from the new list, type in a new word pattern, or press the CANCEL (F1) key or ENTER to return to the Spell menu.

If the highlighted word is spelled correctly, then it is most likely a technical word or a proper noun that the dictionary doesn't contain. It might also be a word containing numbers; WordPerfect doesn't spell check words containing only numbers (such as 200 or 9555), but does check words containing a mix of letters and numbers (such as 555A or AB14). You'd want to select from among the remaining options on the Not Found menu:

- *Skip Once (1)*   Select this option to skip the word once—the spell check continues without tampering with the word, even though it is not listed in the dictionary. This option is an appropriate selection if the highlighted word is spelled correctly and is used just once in the document.

- *Select Skip (2)*   Select this option to skip the word for the remainder of the spell check. Spell check will treat the word as correctly spelled for the rest of the spell check. The cursor jumps to the next word, and the Spell menu remains on screen. This option is an appropriate selection if the word is spelled correctly and is repeated throughout the document.

- *Add (3)*   Select this option to add the word to a supplementary dictionary. This option is appropriate if you wish WordPerfect to recognize a certain technical word, proper name, or other word as correctly spelled permanently—every time that you use the spell check feature from this day forward. The word is stored on disk, added to a supplemental dictionary file named WP{WP}US.SUP, which is distinct from the main dictionary file. (Technically, the first time you add a word to the supplemental dictionary, the file is actually created; from then on, words are added to that file.)

- *Ignore Numbers (6)*   Select this option to have WordPerfect ignore occurences of words containing numbers. From this point on and until you press CANCEL (F1) to exit the spell check, WordPerfect will skip over any words that are a combination of letters and numbers, such as 334AB or AMT334.

Whichever of the Not Found menu options you choose, the cursor jumps to the next word, and the Spell menu returns to the screen, so that you can select to spell check another word, select another option, or press CANCEL (F1) to exit the Spell feature.

SPELL CHECK MORE THAN ONE WORD

In addition to spell checking a single word, you can wait until you've finished typing a document and then check all or part of that document for spelling mistakes. You can spell check just one page, the whole document, or a block of text. In addition, you can ask that WordPerfect spell check using the main dictionary and a special supplementary dictionary or you can perform a simple word count.

Spell Check a Page, Document, or Block

Checking a page or a document is similar to checking one word. You must make sure that the page or the document you wish to check is on the screen. To spell check the whole document, you can place the cursor anywhere; to check a page, you must place the cursor on that page. Then press the SPELL (CTRL + F2) key so that the Spell Check menu appears:

Check: 1 Word; 2 Page; 3 Document; 4 New Sup. Dictionary; 5 Look Up; 6 Count: 0

Select Page (2 or P) or Document (3 or D). Each word on the page or in the document will be checked. If a certain word is not found in the dictionary, then the Not Found menu appears, just as in a word check (Figure 7-2). You have the same six options to choose from on the Not Found menu as described previously.

Once you decide what to do about the first highlighted word, the spell check continues with the next unrecognized word until Word-Perfect has highlighted and you have dealt with all the occurrences of words not found in the Speller's dictionaries. After a page check, WordPerfect lists the total number of words on that page. Press any key to return to the Spell menu. Then you can either select a new option from the Spell menu or press the CANCEL (F1) key to exit the Spell feature. After a document check, WordPerfect also provides a word count, but it does not return you to the Spell menu. When you press any key, you are exited automatically from the Spell feature.

You can also spell check just a portion of a document or a page by using the BLOCK (ALT + F4) key in combination with the Speller. First, use the BLOCK (ALT + F4) key to highlight the text you wish to spell check. Next, press the SPELL (CTRL + F2) key. WordPerfect immediately begins to check that block for spelling mistakes in the same way that it checks through a page or a document. After a block check, WordPerfect provides a word count of that block. Press any key to exit automatically from the Spell feature.

If a word appears twice in a row when you spell check a page, a document, or a block, the Speller stops to highlight both occurrences of that word and provides a different Not Found menu, from which you can skip over the double word, delete the second of the two words, edit the document, or disable double-word checking for the rest of the spell check. Figure 7-3 shows an example of the screen when a double word is encountered.

The Speller will automatically check any headers, footers, footnotes, or endnotes that are located in the page, document, or block to be checked. If a word in a note is misspelled, the footnote or endnote screen will appear, with the misspelled word highlighted for your correction. WordPerfect will then return to the main text to continue the spell check.

You can stop a spell check at any time by pressing CANCEL (F1). You may need to press CANCEL (F1) two or three times to completely back out of the Spell feature.

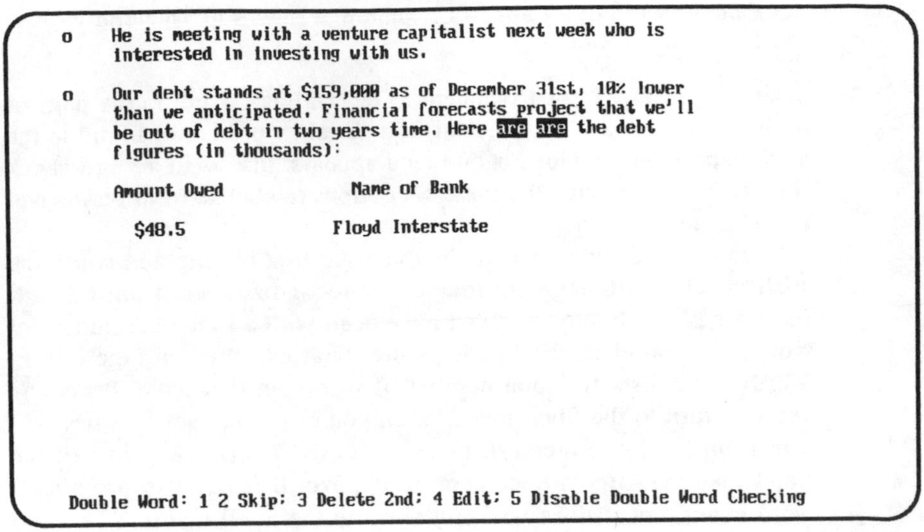

```
o    He is meeting with a venture capitalist next week who is
     interested in investing with us.

o    Our debt stands at $159,000 as of December 31st, 10% lower
     than we anticipated. Financial forecasts project that we'll
     be out of debt in two years time. Here are are the debt
     figures (in thousands):

     Amount Owed              Name of Bank

      $48.5                   Floyd Interstate
```

```
Double Word: 1 2 Skip; 3 Delete 2nd; 4 Edit; 5 Disable Double Word Checking
```

FIGURE 7-3   Speller screen paused at a double word

Keep in mind that a spell check is no substitute for a final proof-reading. The program will not catch grammatical errors. For instance, it cannot check for homonyms such as "no" and "know" or "see" and "sea." For example, suppose one sentence in your document reads as follows.

I hope to sea you soon.

WordPerfect won't pause during the spell check, even though the sentence should read "*see* you soon."

Nor can WordPerfect figure out whether a sentence makes sense. For instance, suppose your document contained the following sentence:

We hope to distribute bonus cheeks by December 15th.

You undoubtedly realize that the sentence was meant to read "bonus *checks*" and not "bonus cheeks." But since "cheeks" is in the dictionary, WordPerfect won't pause during the spell check to alert you to a problem in the sentence. While the spell check will catch all your misspellings, it is no substitute for a final proofreading.

Let's spell check the document named LETTER, which you created back in Chapter 1 and have revised in other chapters. The file is only one page long, so the result will be the same whether you select spell check for a page or for the whole document.

1. On a clear screen, retrieve the file named LETTER. To make the spell check more interesting, purposely misspell some words. In the first paragraph, remove the last "s" in "discussed" and the "p" in "complete" so that the sentence begins "As we *discused,* here is a *comlete* list ...."

2. *Floppy disk users:* Replace the disk currently in drive B with the Speller disk. *Hard disk users:* Proceed directly to step 3.

3. Press the SPELL (CTRL + F2) key. After a few moments, Word-Perfect responds with

   Check: 1 Word; 2 Page; 3 Document; 4 New Sup. Dictionary; 5 Look Up; 6 Count: 0

4. Select Page (2 or P). WordPerfect highlights "Barrett" and, in moments, suggests numerous replacement words, as shown in Figure 7-4. (In fact, notice that the screen is full of replacement words—so full that not all of them can fit on one screen; thus, the bottom of the screen indicates to press ENTER if you wish to view more replacement words.) "Barrett" is correctly spelled and appears more than once in this document.

5. Select Skip (2). WordPerfect highlights "FST." Suppose that the correct name of the accounting firm is FSST accounting.

6. Select Edit (4).

7. Edit "FST" to read "FSST" and then press EXIT (F7), as indicated at the bottom of the screen, to return to the spell check. WordPerfect again highlights "FSST," because this newly edited word is still not in its dictionary.

8. Select Skip Once (1). WordPerfect highlights the word "Harmon." Suppose that this is correctly spelled.

9. Select Skip Once (1). WordPerfect highlights the word "discused" and suggests replacements at the bottom of the screen. (Notice that WordPerfect skips over the second occurrence of the word "Barrett" because you previously selected the option

10. Type **B** to insert the correctly spelled word, which is "discussed." WordPerfect highlights "comlete" and suggests alternatives.

11. Type **B** to insert the correct word, which is "complete." WordPerfect highlights the word "31st."

12. Select Ignore Numbers (6). WordPerfect will no longer pause at words such as "27th" that are found further down in the document. WordPerfect highlights the word "Lois." Suppose that you frequently type letters containing the name "Lois"— perhaps that's your boss's first name.

13. Select Add (3). The word will be added to your supplementary dictionary (if a supplementary dictionary does not yet exist, it will be created).

14. Continue until the spell check ends. WordPerfect will provide a word count at the bottom of the screen with a message indicating to press any key.

```
February 3, 1989


Mr. Barrett P. Smith
FST Accounting
1001 S. Harmon Street
Oakland, CA  94413


Dear Barrett:

================================================================================

    A. barrette          B. bard              C. bared
    D. baret             E. barite            F. barred
    G. beard             H. beareth           I. beirut
    J. berate            K. beret             L. berried
    M. berth             N. bewared           O. bird
    P. birth             Q. biuret            R. board
    S. borate            T. bored             U. borrowed
    V. bort              W. buret             X. burette
Press Enter for more words

Not Found: 1 Skip Once; 2 Skip; 3 Add; 4 Edit; 5 Look Up; 6 Ignore Numbers: 0
```

FIGURE 7-4   Speller screen paused with numerous alternatives for "Barrett"

15. Press any key to return to the Spell menu.

16. Press CANCEL (F1) to exit the Spell feature. (If you decided to spell check the document, rather than just a page, then the Spell feature is exited automatically.)

17. *Floppy disk users:* Remove the Speller disk from drive B and reinsert the disk used to store your documents.

You can count the number of words in a document in a way that bypasses the spell check process. Simply press the SPELL (CTRL + F2) key and select Count (6 or C). In moments, a word count for the whole document appears on screen. You can then press any key to return to the Spell menu. Select a new option or press CANCEL (F1) to exit the Spell feature.

WORK WITH SUPPLEMENTARY DICTIONARIES

The file WP{WP}US.SUP contains all the words you added by selecting Add (3), from the Not Found menu. Sometimes you can accidentally select Add by mistake, including in the supplement an improperly spelled word. You will want to delete this word. In addition, you may know of certain words that you'd like to include in the supplement.

To delete or insert words in the supplement, clear the screen and retrieve the supplementary dictionary, which is the file named WP{WP}US.SUP, in the same way you'd retrieve any WordPerfect file. You'll notice that each word is on its own line, followed by an **[HRt]** code. You can delete a word and the **[HRt]** code that follows it. Or you can move the cursor to a blank line, type in a word, and press ENTER to insert an **[HRt]** code. Now resave the file.

Do not try this method with the dictionary, but only with the supplement! (See the next section regarding ways to add or delete words from the main dictionary.)

You may find it appropriate to create more than one supplementary dictionary. Perhaps you wish to create one to check legal documents and another to check personal documents. To create a supplementary dictionary, start with a clear Typing screen. Type each word on a separate line. Then save this file. (The next section describes how you can also create a new supplementary dictionary using the Spell utility.)

When you're ready to use a supplementary dictionary other than WP{WP}US.SUP, press the SPELL key and select New Supplementary dictionary (4 or N). Type in the filename of the new supplementary dictionary (preceded by the appropriate drive/directory) and press ENTER. Now when you initiate a word, page, or document check, WordPerfect will use the file you specified as the supplement.

Note: In WordPerfect you can indicate where the main and supplementary dictionary can be found whenever you initiate the Spell feature. You will want to take advantage of this Location of Auxiliary Files feature if WordPerfect displays a menu specifying "WP{WP}US.LEX not found" every time you use the Spell feature. This feature is also convenient for hard disk users to indicate one location where the supplementary dictionary is found; otherwise, WordPerfect creates the supplementary dictionary in the default directory and will be unable to locate the original supplement when you change the default. Refer to the "Location of Auxiliary Files" section of Appendix C for more on this feature.

SPELLER UTILITY

WordPerfect provides a separate program that can help manage WordPerfect's dictionary. You can add or delete words, display words in the common word list, or check to see if a word is in the main dictionary. You can also create your own dictionary.

A specific use of the Speller Utility is to transfer the words you created during a spell check from the supplementary dictionary to the main dictionary. In general, this will be necessary only if you compile so many words in the supplement that when you attempt to add another word the message **Dictionary Full** appears on screen during a spell check. You could add these supplementary words to the main dictionary and then begin a new supplementary dictionary. (On the other hand, if you wanted simply to erase the supplementary dictionary, you would not use the Speller Utility; you would just erase the file named WP{WP}US.SUP from your floppy or hard disk.)

Do not use the Speller Utility casually! Adding or deleting just a few words from the dictionary is impractical, because the process could take up to 20 minutes. Moreover, you could accidentally erase

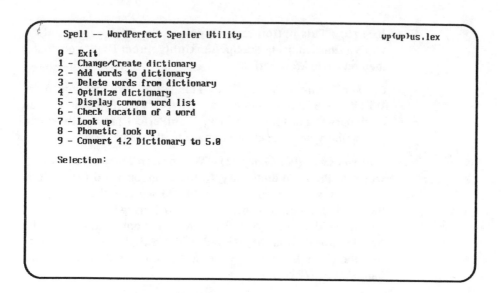

```
    Spell -- WordPerfect Speller Utility                        wp{wp}us.lex
 0 - Exit
 1 - Change/Create dictionary
 2 - Add words to dictionary
 3 - Delete words from dictionary
 4 - Optimize dictionary
 5 - Display common word list
 6 - Check location of a word
 7 - Look up
 8 - Phonetic look up
 9 - Convert 4.2 Dictionary to 5.0

 Selection:
```

FIGURE 7-5   Speller Utility main menu

part of the dictionary when shuffling words. In general, you will rarely (if ever) need to use the utility. Nevertheless, this feature is briefly discussed below.

The Speller Utility can be accessed only when you are working in DOS. You can either exit to DOS temporarily with the SHELL (CTRL + F1) key (as described in Chapter 8) or exit WordPerfect with the EXIT (F7) key. At the DOS prompt, floppy disk users should (1) place the Speller disk in drive A and a data disk in drive B (which may be blank or contain a supplementary dictionary that you wish to combine into the main dictionary); (2) type A: and press ENTER so that the DOS prompt reads A; and (3) type **SPELL** and press ENTER. Hard disk users should (1) switch to the directory where the file SPELL.EXE is stored (which is generally where the WordPerfect program is stored); and (2) type **SPELL** and press ENTER.

In a few moments, you'll see the Speller Utility main menu, as shown in Figure 7-5. Notice that the upper right corner says "WP{WP}US.LEX," meaning that you're working with the main dictionary. The options on this menu are as follows.

- *Exit (0)* This option returns you to the DOS prompt after you've finished using the Speller Utility. From DOS, you could then return to WordPerfect.

- *Change/Create dictionary (1)* This option switches you from WP{WP}US.LEX to another dictionary. If the filename of that dictionary is not found on disk, WordPerfect prompts whether you wish to create a new dictionary by the name indicated.

- *Add words to dictionary (2)* This option allows you to add words to the main dictionary, to the common word list, or to a dictionary you created. You would add words either by typing the words from the keyboard or by transferring them from a file where you'd already typed the words. This option allows you to transfer words from the file WP{WP}US.SUP, the supplement, into the main dictionary. Afterwards, you would erase the file named WP{WP}US.SUP.

- *Delete words from dictionary (3)* This option is similar to option 2, but is used for deleting words.

- *Optimize dictionary (4)* This option is used after you've created a dictionary to reshuffle it into alphabetical order.

- *Display common word list (5)* This option shows you the common word list screen by screen.

- *Check location of a word (6)* This option allows you to determine whether a word is in the dictionary, and, if so, whether it is in the common word list or the main word list.

- *Look up (7)* This option enables you to look up a word based on its spelling, using a question mark (?) or asterisk (*) in those places where you're unsure of a word's spelling (same as the Look Up option on the Not Found menu).

- *Phonetic look up (8)* This option enables you to look up a word based on how that word sounds.

- *Convert 4.2 to 5.0 (9)* This option provides the ability to convert a dictionary you created using WordPerfect version 4.2 into version 5.0 format.

Floppy disk users should be sure to remove the Speller disk from drive After using the Speller Utility.

USE THE THESAURUS

The Thesaurus feature can help you to learn the meaning of a word or find an alternative that fits better in your text. You can look up synonyms and antonyms for over 10,000 words. A synonym is a word with the same meaning as the word you're looking up, an antonym has an opposite meaning. For instance, a synomym for the word "dark" is "unlit"; an antonym for the word "dark" is "light."

Each of the 10,000 words that can be looked up is called a *headword*. The headwords, along with their synonyms and antonyms, are stored on the Thesaurus disk in a file called WP{WP}US.THS. (If you purchased one of the first releases of version 5, then your thesaurus may be in a file named WP{WP}*EN*.THS, rather than WP{WP}*US*.THS. As with the Spell feature, you have the ability to purchase additional thesauri at an additional charge in several foreign languages. You would use the Language feature to insert a Language code in the text; see the note at the beginning of this chapter for details.) If a word is not a headword, WordPerfect cannot provide synonyms or antonyms for that word; you must try looking up another word instead.

To have access to the Thesaurus, floppy disk users should place the Thesaurus disk in drive B. Hard disk users should have copied the Thesaurus file onto the hard disk. You then position the cursor on the word you wish to look up and press the THESAURUS (ALT + F1) key. If the word is a headword, the screen divides. The top displays four lines of your text and highlights the word you are looking up. The bottom of the screen lists alternative words in up to three columns, grouping them into verbs (v), nouns (n), adjectives (a), and antonyms (ant). The following menu appears at the bottom of the screen:

   1 Replace Word; 2 View Doc; 3 Look Up Word; 4 Clear Column: 0

For instance, Figure 7-6 illustrates the Thesaurus screen for the word "accept." There are two columns of references for this word.

You might find an appropriate word in one of the columns. If you find the right word in the first column, you can select Replace Word (1) from the menu. WordPerfect then prompts you with

   Press letter for word

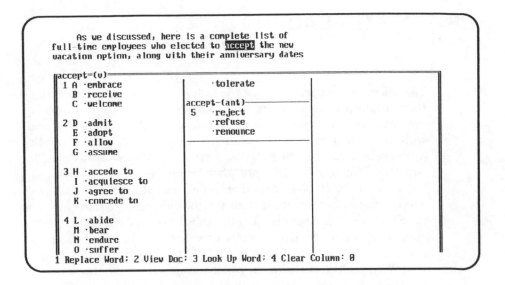

```
        As we discussed, here is a complete list of
full-time employees who elected to accept the new
vacation option, along with their anniversary dates

accept=(v)
  1 A ·embrace              ·tolerate
    B ·receive
    C ·welcome          accept-(ant)
                           5   ·reject
  2 D ·admit                   ·refuse
    E ·adopt                   ·renounce
    F ·allow
    G ·assume

  3 H ·accede to
    I ·acquiesce to
    J ·agree to
    K ·concede to

  4 L ·abide
    M ·bear
    N ·endure
    O ·suffer
1 Replace Word; 2 View Doc; 3 Look Up Word; 4 Clear Column: 0
```

FIGURE 7-6   Thesaurus screen for the word "accept"

You simply type the letter that corresponds to the word you wish to substitute. That word replaces the original word and the Thesaurus screen clears.

If you find the right word in another column, you must press RIGHT ARROW before selecting to replace the word, so that the highlighted letters move over to that column. Then you can press Replace Word (1) and make a letter selection. There may be more alternatives offered by WordPerfect for a certain word than can fit in the three columns; you can press DOWN ARROW to see the rest of the words.

You have other choices as well. Perhaps you haven't found exactly the word you were looking for. All the words preceded by dots are also headwords. In Figure 7-6, every alternative offered is a headword, and thus can also be looked up in the Thesaurus. Any synonyms or antonyms not preceded by a dot are not headwords and cannot be looked up.

To continue looking up headwords, simply type the letter corresponding to that word (without first selecting an item from the menu at the bottom of the screen). Alternatives for the first word are restricted to the first column while replacements for the new headword are displayed in the second (and perhaps third) column. Alternatives for up to three different words could be placed side by side in columns in this way. For instance, Figure 7-7 shows the Thesaurus suggesting alternatives not only for "accept" but also for "adopt." You can move between columns with the LEFT and RIGHT ARROW keys and up and down a column with the UP and DOWN ARROW keys or with PGUP and PGDN. (When you have alternatives for two or three words on screen, WordPerfect can only display a partial list of alternatives for each word and so moving the cursor up and down a column becomes important.) When you want to clear the last column and again view alternatives for the previous word, you can press BACKSPACE or select Clear Column (4).

You can also look up a word not found in one of the columns. Select Look Up Word (3). WordPerfect prompts you with

Word:

and you can type the word and press ENTER.

A last alternative is to exit the Thesaurus temporarily. You can select View Doc (2); the Thesaurus screen remains, but the cursor moves to the text at the top of the screen. You can then use the cursor movement keys to reposition the cursor as you read through the text

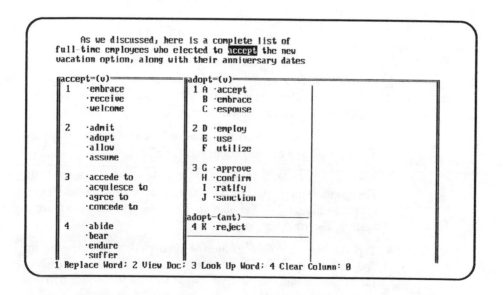

FIGURE 7-7   Thesaurus screen for the words "accept" and "adopt"

before deciding on a replacement word or move to another word that you wish to look up. But you cannot edit your text when you leave the Thesaurus temporarily. Press the EXIT (F7) key to return to the Thesaurus and to make a selection from the menu at the bottom of the screen.

If you wish to leave the Thesaurus at any time, press the CANCEL (F1) key.

Note: If you attempt to use the Thesaurus feature and WordPerfect cannot find where on disk the Thesaurus is stored, the following prompt appears:

ERROR: File not found — WP{WP}US.THS

Floppy disk users should check to make sure that the Thesaurus disk is in the default drive. Hard disk users should make sure that the Thesaurus file has been copied onto the hard disk. For hard disk users where the Thesaurus file is located somewhere other than where the WordPerfect program files are stored, you must indicate to Word-Perfect where the Thesaurus can be found; see the "Location of Auxiliary Files" section of Appendix C.

The document LETTER should be on screen. Let's use it to find an alternative for the word "begin."

1. Position the cursor anywhere within the word "begin" in the sentence near the bottom of the letter that reads "The new accrued vacation system should begin for...."

2. *Floppy disk users:* Place the Thesaurus disk in drive B. *Hard disk users:* Proceed directly to step 3.

3. Press the THESAURUS (ALT + F1) key. In moments, the Thesaurus screen appears with suggestions for alternatives as shown in Figure 7-8. Suppose that you wish to find more alternatives, this time for "start."

4. Type O. Now the first column is restricted to alternatives for "begin" and the second and third columns contain alternatives for "start." Supppose that you wish to find more alternatives, this time for "initiate."

5. Press RIGHT ARROW. The letters move to the next column.

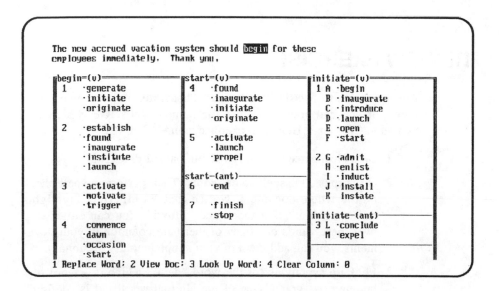

```
The new accrued vacation system should begin for these
employees immediately.  Thank you.

begin=(v)
  1 A ·generate          begin-(ant)
    B ·initiate          5    ·conclude
    C ·originate              ·dissolve
                              ·halt
  2 D ·establish             ·end
    E ·found
    F ·inaugurate
    G ·institute
    H ·launch

  3 I ·activate
    J ·motivate
    K ·trigger

  4 L  commence
    M ·dawn
    N ·occasion
    O ·start
1 Replace Word; 2 View Doc; 3 Look Up Word; 4 Clear Column: 0
```

FIGURE 7-8   Thesaurus screen for the word "begin"

```
The new accrued vacation system should begin for these
employees immediately.  Thank you.

begin=(v)            start=(v)            initiate=(v)
  1  ·generate         4   ·found           1 A ·begin
     ·initiate             ·inaugurate        B ·inaugurate
     ·originate            ·initiate          C ·introduce
                           ·originate         D ·launch
  2  ·establish                               E ·open
     ·found           5   ·activate          F ·start
     ·inaugurate          ·launch
     ·institute           ·propel          2 G ·admit
     ·launch                                 H ·enlist
                     start-(ant)             I ·induct
  3  ·activate         6   ·end              J ·install
     ·motivate                               K  instate
     ·trigger          7   ·finish
                           ·stop           initiate-(ant)
  4   commence                              3 L ·conclude
     ·dawn                                   M ·expel
     ·occasion
     ·start
1 Replace Word; 2 View Doc; 3 Look Up Word; 4 Clear Column: 0
```

FIGURE 7-9   Thesaurus screen with each column occupied with alternatives
           for a different word

6. Type **B**. Now all three columns contain alternatives for different headwords, as shown in Figure 7-9. The third column contains alternatives for "initiate." Suppose you wish to clear the last column.

7. Select Clear Column (4). Now you wish to review all the alternatives for "start" in column 2.

8. Press PGUP to see the complete list of alternatives for "start." Since column 3 has been cleared, alternatives for "start" can spill over into that column.

9. Select Replace Word (1). WordPerfect prompts for the letter corresponding to the replacement word.

10. Type **K**. The word "commence" is inserted in place of "begin," and the Thesaurus is exited automatically.

11. *Floppy disk users:* Remove the Thesaurus disk from drive B and reinsert the disk used to store your documents.

Get accustomed to using the Thesaurus, and you may find that your writing improves dramatically.

REVIEW EXERCISE

You may wish to use the Speller and Thesaurus on your own documents, or you can practice on the file named FINANCE, which you created in Chapter 3. Here's an exercise using FINANCE.

1. On a clear screen, retrieve the file named FINANCE.

2. On purpose, misspell some words. Then perform a spell check on the whole document. Notice that WordPerfect highlights names such as "Samsone" and "Floyd." You can either skip over these words or, if any of them are common in your documents, you can add them to your supplementary dictionary.

3. Look up synonyms for the word "debt," which is a word in a bulleted paragraph. One of the alternatives listed is "deficit"; go ahead and look up alternatives for that word as well. Then clear the column of alternatives for "deficit" and select "deficit" as the replacement word.

REVIEW

- With the SPELL (CTRL + F2) key, you can check the spelling of one word, one page, or one document. In addition, if you combine the use of the BLOCK (ALT + F4) and SPELL (CTRL + F2) keys, you can check the spelling of a block of text of any size.

- WordPerfect highlights a word during a spell check when that word is not listed in either the WordPerfect dictionary (which is separated into a common word list and a main word list) or a supplementary dictionary that you create for specialized terms or proper nouns found often in your document.

- When WordPerfect highlights a word not found in its dictionary, you can edit the word, choose from a list of suggested alternatives, or skip over the word. Another option is to add it to your own supplementary dictionary so that from that point on WordPerfect will recognize that word.

- If you don't know how to spell a word, sound out the word phonetically or spell the word using the wild cards * and ? in places where you're not sure of the spelling. Then request that WordPerfect look up that word in its dictionary.

- The Speller cannot check for grammatical errors and is thus no substitute for a final proofreading.

- The Speller Utility is an independent program that can add your supplementary dictionary words to the main dictionary, verify whether a word is in the dictionary, and display the common word list. It can also be used to create a supplementary dictionary file with specialized terms. But the Speller Utility should never be used to make minor changes in a dictionary.

- The THESAURUS (ALT + F1) key provides access to synonyms and antonyms for over 10,000 words. Using the Thesaurus, you can acquire a better understanding of a word's meaning or find an appropriate substitute.

Part II

SPECIAL FEATURES

Managing Files on Disk
Print Options and Enhancements
Changing Fonts and Inserting Graphics for Desktop Publishing
Creating Text Columns
Outlining, Paragraph Numbering, Footnoting
Producing Repetitive Documents and Merge
Using Macros and Styles
WordPerfect Extras

8

MANAGING FILES ON DISK

Change the Default Drive/Directory
Work with Directories
Organize Files on Disk
Go to DOS
Lock Files with a Password
Create Document Summaries
Search for Specific Files on the List Files Screen
Review Exercise
Review

By now, after following the instructions in Part I of this book, you've created as many files on disk as chapters that you've read. You've seen how easy it is to accumulate files. In fact, you will find that within weeks of working with WordPerfect, you'll have more files on disk than you can remember. WordPerfect offers many sophisticated features for working with files, helping you to manage the documents that stack up in no time. This chapter explores those features.

The first sections of this chapter explain how to work with various disks and directories, including how to change the default drive or directory for storing and retrieving files, keep track of available disk storage space, and create new directories. You'll also learn how to reorganize files already on disk, whether by deleting, renaming, or copying. The Copy feature deserves some extra attention; this command can be used to make backup copies of your files—thus averting disaster should your original file disappear because of a mechanical problem or human error. WordPerfect's ability to temporarily exit to DOS, an option that you'll appreciate if you're comfortable using DOS commands to manage files on disk, is also described. You'll also discover WordPerfect features allowing you to lock up a file with a secret password; create a Document Summary, which lets you keep a record of the status of a document; and search through a list of files to quickly find the one you're looking for.

CHANGE THE DEFAULT DRIVE/DIRECTORY

You learned in Chapter 2 that the default drive is the drive to which WordPerfect assumes you wish to save files and from which you wish to retrieve files. For floppy disk users, it is drive B; files are stored on a floppy disk placed in that drive. For hard disk users, it is generally drive C; files are stored on the hard disk fixed permanently inside the computer. Moreover, because WordPerfect supports directories, whereby a hard disk is subdivided electronically into separate sections, hard disk users also have a default directory. For instance, if you're a hard disk user who followed the installation instructions in Appendix A, then the default directory is \WPER\DATA.

There may be times when you want to store files to or retrieve files from another drive or directory, as a way of organizing your files. This is most often an issue for hard disk users. Perhaps you just typed a document on a special topic and wish to store it in a directory different from where you usually store your files. Or maybe you typed a confidential document and want to store it on the floppy disk in drive A, rather than on the hard disk, for greater security. You can change the default for an individual file or a working session or change it more permanently.

Change the Default for an Individual File

You can direct WordPerfect to a different drive or directory when saving or retrieving a single file. To do so, precede a filename with the intended drive and the directory path. For instance, suppose you wish to save a file named LIST onto the disk in the A drive, even though the default is the hard disk. The drive is indicated by the drive letter followed by a colon, such as A:, B:, or C:. Thus, to save a file onto drive A, you press the SAVE (F10) key or the EXIT (F7) key, and when WordPerfect prompts for the document to be saved, type **A:LIST** and press ENTER. This tells WordPerfect that the filename is LIST, but rather than saving that file on the default drive, WordPerfect should save it on the disk in drive A. If you simply type **LIST** and press ENTER, then the file is stored, instead, on the default drive/directory.

Suppose you wish to retrieve a file named QUARTER that is not in the default directory but in a directory named C:\WPER\BUD. A backslash (\) always precedes each directory name and also precedes the filename when following a directory name; when you retrieve the file, press the RETRIEVE (SHIFT + F10) key, and when WordPerfect prompts for the document to be retrieved, type **C:\WPER \BUD\ QUARTER** and press ENTER. (If the default is drive C, you don't have to include the drive letter. The file could be indicated more simply as WPER\BUD\QUARTER.) If you don't indicate a directory but simply type **QUARTER**, WordPerfect automatically looks to the default directory for that file and won't be able to find it.

Change the Default for a Particular Working Session

You can change the default until you turn off the computer at the end of the day or until you change it later on in the current working session. For instance, perhaps you share a computer with two other colleagues. Each of you stores your WordPerfect files in a directory designated by your first name. You can use the LIST FILES (F5) key to change the default to the directory named after you for the whole time that you are working on the computer.

There are two ways to change the default for a working session. One option is available while you're on the Typing screen. You begin by pressing the LIST FILES (F5) key. WordPerfect responds with the current default listed on the left side of the status line and with a prompt instructing you to change the default on the right side. For instance, for a hard disk user, the prompt after pressing the LIST FILES (F5) key might be

Dir C:\WPER\DATA*.*   **(Type = to change default Dir)**

To change the default, press the EQUAL (=) key. WordPerfect responds by asking for a new default, suggesting the current one:

New directory = C:\WPER\DATA

Type over or edit this prompt to reflect the new default drive or directory and then press ENTER. For instance, you might simply type over the current directory, changing it to read

New directory = A:

Or you might edit the current directory (using the cursor movement and editing keys) to read

New directory = C:\WPER\KIM

Then press ENTER again. WordPerfect will confirm the new default with the prompt such as

Dir A:*.*

or

Dir C:\WPER\KIM*.*

You have now changed the default. To see a list of files in the new default, press ENTER. To clear the prompt and continue on the Typing screen instead, press the CANCEL (F1) key. The next time you save a new document, it will be saved to the default (such as drive A or the subdirectory \WPER\KIM on the hard disk); the next time you retrieve a document, WordPerfect will search that same default for the file.

The second option for changing the default for a working session is available when you are actually viewing the List Files screen, as shown in Figure 8-1. Select Other Directory (7 or O) and WordPerfect prompts with the current default, such as

New directory = C:\WPER\DATA

```
03/06/89  11:00              Directory C:\WPER\DATA\*.*
Document size:      1400   Free:  2734080   Used:    600985        Files:  45

, <CURRENT>     <DIR>                    .. <PARENT>     <DIR>
005      .CRG      993  02/16/88 23:41   1001     .CRG    48173  06/16/88 15:55
5008     .CRG     1312  07/22/88 02:08   5012     .CRG    35605  10/04/88 20:41
5028     .CRG    29573  10/04/88 20:42   88ANN    .RPT    21212  02/09/88 11:23
88ANN2   .RPT    35597  10/04/88 20:41   88ANN3   .RPT    35597  10/04/88 20:41
88RENT   .        43544  06/16/88 15:56   ACCOUNTS.        36762  02/21/88 15:41
BBS009   .1       21212  02/09/88 11:23   BBS009   .2       4754  02/09/88 12:45
BBS009   .3        2703  04/04/88 19:56   BKGROUND.88       778  02/23/88 13:28
BOOKKEEP.          1830  02/24/88 02:43   BUDMIN   .        1961  05/22/88 21:32
BUDMIN88.         28120  10/04/88 20:43   C2       .LTR     1551  02/09/89 11:05
CBS&RP   .         2666  02/10/88 10:59   CEO1     .MMO      942  12/21/88 11:15
DOCLIS2  .MS       3241  10/04/88 20:40   DOCLIST1.MS      40756  10/04/88 20:39
FINANCE  .         1866  09/01/88 10:00   FON      .        28120  10/04/88 20:43
GAIN     .LTR      1598  02/09/89 11:05   J&B      .MMO     2317  09/16/88 20:36
JONES1   .MMO      1356  07/22/88 00:56   JONES2   .MMO     5936  02/11/88 01:01
LETTER   .         1629  08/24/88 17:05   LETTER   .WPM       57  08/24/88 16:48
LINKER   .MS       1206  09/16/88 20:36   LINKER2  .        35597  10/04/88 20:40
LIST     .         1799  08/22/88 11:23   LIST     .NEW     1939  08/21/88 21:43
MEYERS-1.MS       1206  09/16/88 20:36 ▼ P&L      .        35597  10/04/88 20:40

1 Retrieve; 2 Delete; 3 Move/Rename; 4 Print; 5 Text In;
6 Look; 7 Other Directory; 8 Copy; 9 Word Search; N Name Search: 6
```

FIGURE 8-1   List Files screen for C:\WPER\DATA

Type in the drive or directory you wish for the default and press ENTER. The default is altered; press ENTER again and a list of files in the new default is displayed.

Change the Default for Every Working Session

There's one final way to change the default—for every working session. If you find that no one using the computer ever saves documents to the default—it is consistently wrong—then you will want to change the default permanently. To do so, you must alter the way in which WordPerfect is loaded. See Appendix A to learn about creating a batch file for loading WordPerfect that can change the default permanently.

WORK WITH DIRECTORIES

The hard disk starts out with what is referred to as the *root directory*. This is split up into various directories, which are usually organized by topic or person. These directories, in turn, can be split into subdirectories, and so on. The directory to be divided is referred to as the *parent directory*. Here's an example of part of a hard disk structure.

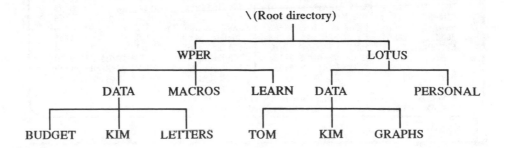

Hard disk users must split a hard disk into separate directories. Storing a maximum of about 200 files in each directory creates an organized, efficient filing system; if instead, you create no directories, you'll have hundreds of files in one directory, which will bog down WordPerfect's List Files screen and make it quite difficult to search for and find a file.

Assuming that you installed WordPerfect as suggested in Appendix A, then, as you know, you have already created at least two directories: one called \WPER, where the WordPerfect program files are stored, and a subdirectory named \WPER\DATA, where all your data (document) files are stored. When you begin to accumulate a large quantity of files in \WPER\DATA (or in any directory), it is time to consider creating additional directories and reorganizing files.

Using the List Files screen within WordPerfect, you can look at the contents of any directory, create a new one, or delete an old one.

Look at the Contents

You can move up the hierarchical structure and look at the contents of a parent directory. Position the cursor on the first item in the right-hand column, which reads "..<PARENT> <DIR>." Then select Look

(6 or L) or press ENTER. (You can press ENTER because WordPerfect assumes that if you press ENTER without selecting a menu item, you wish to activate the Look feature.) WordPerfect prompts for confirmation that you wish to view the parent directory. For instance, if the List Files screen currently shows files in C:\WPER\DATA (as in Figure 8-1) and you position the cursor on "..<PARENT> <DIR>" and press ENTER, WordPerfect prompts

Dir C:\WPER*.*

Press ENTER. The List Files screen is rewritten to show the contents of the parent directory, as shown in Figure 8-2.

The subdirectories of a directory are noted on the List Files screen wherever <DIR> appears instead of a file size. For instance, Figure 8-2 indicates that the directory \WPER has three subdirectories: \WPER\DATA, \WPER\MACROS, and \WPER\LEARN.

You can also check the contents of a subdirectory. Position the cursor on the subdirectory name and select Look (6 or L) or press ENTER. For instance, in Figure 8-2, position the cursor on the second

```
03/06/89  11:09              Directory C:\WPER\*.*
Document size:      1400   Free:  3100672   Used:    501541        Files:  46

. <CURRENT>   <DIR>                      .. <PARENT>   <DIR>
DATA     .    <DIR>    06/16/88 15:52    LEARN    .    <DIR>    03/06/89 11:02
MACROS   .    <DIR>    04/21/88 18:25    AIRPLANE.WPG     8404   07/01/88 14:50
ALTK     .WPM      145 08/15/88 12:32    ALTRNAT .WPK      919   07/01/88 13:17
ALTU     .WPM       85 02/13/88 15:00    AMD     .WPG     1978   07/01/88 14:50
ANNOUNCE.WPG     5388   07/01/88 14:50   APPLAUSE.WPG     1522   07/01/88 14:50
ARROW1   .WPG      366  07/01/88 14:50   ARROW2  .WPG      738   07/01/88 14:50
AWARD    .WPG     1746  07/01/88 14:50   BADNEWS .WPG     3750   07/01/88 14:50
BOOK     .WPG     1800  07/01/88 14:50   BORDER  .WPG    13518   07/01/88 14:50
CHARACTR.DOC    67149   07/01/88 13:17   CHARMAP .TST    15239   07/01/88 13:17
CHECK    .WPG     1074  07/01/88 14:50   CLOCK   .WPG     6234   07/01/88 14:50
CONFID   .WPG     2242  04/04/00 11:04   CONFIDEN.WPG     3226   07/01/00 14:50
CONVERT  .DOC     3968  04/04/88 11:06   CONVERT .EXE    80937   07/01/88 13:17
FIXBIOS  .COM       50  07/01/88 13:17   FLAG    .WPG      730   07/01/88 14:50
GAVEL    .WPG      856  07/01/88 14:50   GENIUS1 .WPD     4692   07/01/88 14:50
GENIUS2  .WPD     4735  07/01/00 14:50   GOODNEWS.WPG     4242   07/01/88 14:50
GRAB     .COM    15161  07/01/88 14:50   GRAPH   .WPG     1198   05/13/88 09:26
GRAPHCNV.EXE    77312   07/01/88 13:17   HAND    .WPG     1054   07/01/88 14:50
HOURGLAS.WPG     1834   07/01/88 14:50 ▼ HPLASEII.PRS   18926   07/20/88 21:14

1 Retrieve; 2 Delete; 3 Move/Rename; 4 Print; 5 Text In;
6 Look; 7 Other Directory; 8 Copy; 9 Word Search; N Name Search: 6
```

FIGURE 8-2   List Files screen for C:\WPER

item in the left-hand column, which reads "<DATA> . <DIR>." Press ENTER twice. The List Files screen will be rewritten to show the contents of that subdirectory (as shown in Figure 8-1).

Create a Subdirectory

WordPerfect can split a directory into separate subdirectories using the List Files screen. Suppose that you wish to create a subdirectory called BUDGET within the \WPER\DATA directory; that subdirectory will contain a specific type of WordPerfect document—those pertaining to the budget. In other words, you want to create the subdirectory \WPER\DATA\BUDGET.

To do so, position the cursor in the List Files screen on the item that reads ".<CURRENT> <DIR>" and select Other Directory (7 or O). If you are viewing the list of files for C:\WPER\DATA, the prompt reads

New Directory = C:\WPER\DATA

Edit this prompt to read

New Directory = C:\WPER\DATA\BUDGET

Next press ENTER. WordPerfect will ask whether you wish to create a new directory. Type **Y** for yes. Now you can begin storing files in this new directory or copy already existing files to it.

Delete a Subdirectory

WordPerfect will delete a directory for you, but only if that directory contains no files. If the directory contains even one file, WordPerfect will not remove the directory until you delete the file.

Make sure that you are viewing the list of files for the parent directory of the one you wish to delete. For instance, if you wish to delete the directory C:\WPER\DATA\BUDGET, then make sure you're viewing the List Files screen for C:\WPER\DATA. Next position the cursor on the directory you want to delete, such as the item "BUDGET .<DIR>," and select Delete (2 or D) from the List Files menu. WordPerfect will prompt for confirmation; type **Y** to confirm the deletion.

ORGANIZE FILES ON DISK

You need to give files attention to keep your disks neat and orderly and free of unnecessary files. WordPerfect provides a number of features to help you maintain an orderly system for storing all your important documents, whether you store them on floppy disks or in separate directories on a hard disk.

Monitor Disk and File Capacity

Because disk capacity is limited, it is important (especially for floppy disk users) to keep track of how much space is still available on a disk for saving files. How much information can one disk hold? It depends on your disk. The most common floppy disk—5 1/4-inch double sided, double density—is used on computers such as the IBM PC, the IBM XT, and compatibles (and sometimes on the IBM AT). One of these disks can hold about 362,000 bytes of information (362 kilobytes) in a maximum of 112 files. That's equivalent to about 150 to 200 pages of double-spaced text. The other common floppy—double sided, quad density—is used in the quad-density drives of the IBM AT. This disk holds four times as much information, or 1,200,000 bytes (1.2 megabytes).

Hard disks hold many times more information than floppy disks. The *smallest* hard disk holds 10,000,000 bytes (10 megabytes), which is about as much information as 29 double-density disks can store.

WordPerfect indicates the amount of free disk space available on the floppy or hard disk for storing files next to the heading "Free" at the top of the List Files screen. Check this heading periodically, to know when you're approaching your storage capacity.

Floppy disks fill to capacity quickly, so you should watch to see when a disk is becoming full. As a general rule, you should switch to another floppy disk or delete some obsolete files from the floppy before the amount of free disk space becomes smaller than the largest file on disk. (The deletion procedure is described in the next section.) For instance, if you want room to revise files and the largest file on your disk is 20,000 bytes, you need *at least* 20,000 bytes of free disk space because WordPerfect temporarily saves the original and the revision on disk when saving a revised file.

Hard disks take longer to fill up, but they, too, will reach capacity eventually. It is good practice, therefore, to check the available storage on your hard disk periodically. When near capacity, consider deleting files or moving rarely used files to a floppy disk. (The procedures for deleting and moving files are described in the next section.)

Besides monitoring storage capacity, it's also a good idea to watch the size of a document you're typing. WordPerfect indicates the size of the file currently on screen next to the heading "Document Size" at the top of the List Files screen.

When does a document become so large that it should be split into two separate files? That depends on your computer's RAM and storage capacity. For instance, a file may become cumbersome to edit on some computers if it becomes larger than 64,000 bytes in size.

Delete a File

A disk can become cluttered quickly with obsolete files. Not only does a cluttered disk make the work of finding a particular file more cumbersome, but it also takes space away from other files that could be stored there.

You can delete files directly from the List Files screen by positioning the cursor on the file you wish to delete and selecting Delete (2 or D). WordPerfect prompts for confirmation that you wish to delete that file. Type **Y** to delete it or type any other character to abort the deletion. You should think carefully before typing **Y** to confirm a deletion. Once a file is deleted, it is removed from that disk for good.

Here you'll see how quickly a file can be deleted from a disk. Let's delete the file named LIST, which you used frequently to practice various features in the first part of this book.

1. Press the LIST FILES (F5) key, and then press ENTER to view those files in the default drive or directory.

2. To position the cursor on the file named LIST, type **N** to initiate a Name Search, then type **LI**, the first letters of the filename, and then press ENTER to end the Name Search. (Instead of using the Name Search feature, you can simply use the cursor movement keys to move the cursor to the file named LIST.)

3. Select Delete (2 or D). WordPerfect prompts you for verification. For instance, floppy disk users will see

    Delete B:\LIST? (Y/N) No

4. Type **Y**, and the file will be deleted from disk permanently.

Once a file is deleted, it is no longer listed as a file on the disk. The only way you could work with the LIST file would be to create it all over again.

When you delete files, be very careful not to accidentally erase files you wish to refer to in the future. And don't erase WordPerfect files—files that on a hard disk are stored in the directory \WPER and on a floppy disk system are stored on drive A. Most WordPerfect program files begin with the letters WP. For instance, the file WP.EXE is the WordPerfect program file; make sure that you don't tamper with that file, or you could erase the program.

Rename/Move a File

After saving various files on disk, you may change your mind about your naming system. Perhaps the filenames aren't descriptive enough, or maybe you want to add file extensions such as .LTR or .MMO to some of them. You can rename files quickly. Position the cursor on the file you wish to rename and select Move/Rename (3 or M) on the List Files screen. WordPerfect prompts you for a new name, listing the current drive/directory and filename, such as

New name: C:\WPER\DATA\FINANCE

Edit the WordPerfect prompt by typing in the new filename and pressing ENTER. For instance, edit the prompt to read

New name: C:\WPER\DATA\FINANCE.MMO

When you press ENTER, the name change (to FINANCE.MMO) is reflected in moments on the List Files screen. Don't forget that there are rules for naming files (as discussed in Chapter 2), such as a limit of eight characters in a filename and three characters in a filename extension.

You may use this same option to move a file to a different drive or directory. For instance, suppose you wish to move the file named LET-TER stored on the hard disk to the disk in drive A. Position the cursor on the filename LETTER and select Move/Rename (3 or M) from the List Files screen. WordPerfect prompts

New name: C:\WPER\DATA\LETTER

Edit the prompt, leaving the filename the same but changing the drive onto which it is stored so that it reads

New name: A:\LETTER

When you press ENTER, the file is copied to the disk in the A drive, and the file named LETTER is erased from the List Files screen.

You must make sure that if you're moving a file to the disk in a different drive, a formatted disk is inserted in that drive before you give the Move/Rename command. (Appendix A describes how to format a disk.) If you're moving a file from one directory to another, both directories must already have been created on the hard disk.

Copy a File

Unfortunately, disks are not indestructible. On occasion, a hard disk will crash, meaning that it will lose all the information stored on it, whether 5 documents or 500. Or someone in your office (not you, of course!) will accidentally pour coffee on a floppy disk, ruining it and all its files—a tragedy of large proportions. What if you had completed seven chapters of a book, only to have your disk lose them!

The key to avoiding this disaster is to regularly make backup copies of all your important files. Hard disk users usually store backups on floppy disks (though some hard disk users employ tape backup systems), while floppy disk users should maintain a second set of floppies. With backups, if your hard disk crashed with all seven chapters aboard, you would have another copy on floppy to bail you out.

To copy a file, display the List Files screen, position the cursor on the file you wish to copy, and select Copy (8 or C). WordPerfect responds with

Copy this file to:

Now you must type in the drive or directory to which you wish to save a copy of this file. Make sure to type a colon (:) after the drive letter and to type backslashes (\) to separate the different directories on a hard disk. For instance, if you want a copy stored on the disk in drive A, you would type

A:

Or if you wanted a copy stored on the directory named \WPER\KIM on the hard disk, you would type

C:\WPER\KIM

Then press ENTER. The copy is stored under the same filename as the original.

You must make sure that if you're copying to a different drive, a formatted disk is inserted in that drive before you activate the Copy command (again, Appendix A describes how to format a disk). If you're copying a file from one directory to another, both directories must already have been created on the hard disk.

It is also possible to copy a file to the same drive or directory so that you have two copies of that file in the same location. For instance, perhaps you have a file on disk containing a letter. You wish to write a similar letter to a different person. You can copy the letter using a different filename. For instance, when WordPerfect prompts

Copy this file to:

you can enter

JONES2.LTR

Now you have two identical files (until you edit one of them) on the same drive or directory—one under the original filename and one under the filename JONES2.LTR.

Mark Files

You can mark a group of files on the List Files screen so that the group can be deleted, printed, moved, or copied in one command. By marking files, you can, for example, delete three files at once or copy ten files to another disk as a backup.

To mark files one by one, move the cursor to a file you wish to mark and type an asterisk (*). An asterisk appears next to the file's size indicator. Continue to mark as many files as you desire. You can

```
03/06/89  11:04              Directory C:\WPER\DATA\*.*
Document size:     65791   Free:   2721792   Used:     201679        Marked: 10

. <CURRENT>    <DIR>                   .. <PARENT>    <DIR>
005      .CRG      993* 02/16/88 23:41    1001     .CRG   48173* 06/16/88 15:55
5008     .CRG     1312* 07/22/88 02:08    5012     .CRG   35605  10/04/88 20:41
5028     .CRG    29573  10/04/88 20:42    88ANN    .RPT   21212  02/09/88 11:23
88ANN2   .RPT    35597* 10/04/88 20:41    88ANN3   .RPT   35597  10/04/88 20:41
88RENT   .       43544* 06/16/88 15:56    ACCOUNTS.       36762* 02/21/88 15:41
BBS009   .1      21212  02/09/88 11:23    BBS009   .2      4754  02/09/88 12:45
BBS009   .3       2703  04/04/88 19:56    BKGROUND .88      778  02/23/88 13:20
BOOKKEEP .        1830  02/24/88 02:43    BUDMIN   .       1961  05/22/88 21:32
BUDMIN88 .       28120  10/04/88 20:43    C2       .LTR    1551  02/09/88 11:05
C8FIGT1  .PIX     2914* 03/06/89 11:00    CBS&RP   .       2666* 02/10/88 10:59
CE01     .MMO      942  12/21/00 11:15    DOCLIS2  .MS     3241  10/04/00 20:40
DOCLIST1 .MS     40756  10/04/88 20:39    FINANCE  .       1866  09/01/88 10:00
FON      .       28120* 10/04/88 20:43    GAIN     .LTR    1598* 02/09/89 11:05
J&B      .MMO     2317  09/16/88 20:36    JONES1   .MMO    1356  07/22/88 00:56
JONES2   .MMO     5936  02/11/88 01:01    LETTER   .       1629  08/24/88 17:05
LETTER   .WPM       57  08/24/88 16:48    LINKER   .MS     1206  09/16/88 20:36
LINKER2  .       35597  10/04/88 20:40    LIST     .       1799  08/22/88 11:23
LIST     .NEW     1939  08/21/88 21:43 ▼  MEYERS-1 .MS     1206  09/16/88 20:36

Copy marked files? (Y/N) No
```

FIGURE 8-3   Marked files about to be copied

---

also remove the marking from a file. The * key acts like a toggle switch: press it once to mark a file, press it a second time to unmark the file.

You can also use the MARK TEXT (ALT + F5) key to mark and unmark files. If no files are marked when you press the MARK TEXT (ALT + F5) key, all the files become marked. You can then unmark individual files. If some files are already marked when you press the MARK TEXT (ALT + F5) key, all the files become unmarked.

Once files are marked, you can choose to delete, print, move, or copy them by selecting the appropriate option from the menu at the bottom of the List Files screen. WordPerfect prompts you to verify that you wish to perform the operation on the marked files. For instance, suppose that you mark certain files and then select Copy (8 or C). Figure 8-3 shows the marked files. Notice that the upper right corner of the screen indicates how many files are marked. Also, a prompt appears at the bottom of the screen.

Copy marked files? (Y/N) No

If you type **Y**, WordPerfect responds with

```
03/06/89  11:19            Directory C:\WPER\DATA\*.*
Free:  3436544

. <CURRENT>    <DIR>                     .. <PARENT>      <DIR>
005      .CRG      993    02/16/88 23:41   1001     .CRG   48173    06/16/88 15:55
5008     .CRG     1312    07/22/88 02:08   5012     .CRG   35605    10/04/88 20:41
5028     .CRG    29573    10/04/88 20:42   88ANN    .RPT   21212    02/09/88 11:23
88ANN2   .RPT    35597    10/04/88 20:41   88ANN3   .RPT   35597    10/04/88 20:41
88RENT   .       43544    06/16/88 15:56   ACCOUNTS.        36762    02/21/88 15:41
BBS009   .1      21212    02/09/88 11:23   BBS009   .2      4754    02/09/88 12:45
BBS009   .3       2703    04/04/88 19:56   BKGROUND.88       778    02/23/88 13:28
BOOKKEEP.         1830    02/24/88 02:43   BUDMIN   .       1961    05/22/88 21:32
BUDMIN88.        28120    10/04/88 20:43   C2       .LTR    1551    02/09/89 11:05
CBS&RP   .        2666    02/10/88 10:59   CEO1     .MMO     942    12/21/88 11:15
DOCLIS2  .MS      3241    10/04/88 20:40   DOCLIST1.MS     40756    10/04/88 20:39
FINANCE  .        1866    09/01/88 10:00   FON      .      28120    10/04/88 20:43
GAIN     .LTR     1598    02/09/89 11:05   J&B      .MMO    2317    09/16/88 20:36
JONES1   .MMO     1356    07/22/88 00:56   JONES2   .MMO    5936    02/11/88 01:01
LETTER   .        1629    08/24/88 17:05   LETTER   .WPM      57    08/24/88 16:48
LINKER   .MS      1206    09/16/88 20:36   LINKER2  .      35597    10/04/88 20:40
LIST     .        1799    08/22/88 11:23   LIST     .NEW    1939    08/21/88 21:43
MEYERS-1.MS       1206    09/16/88 20:36   P&L      .      35597    10/04/88 20:40
ROGERS   .LTR      714    02/15/88 03:21   SALVA    .       4537    09/16/88 20:37
SALVA%   .       29573    10/04/88 20:43   SAMPLE   .       1879    08/19/88 09:34
SMITH    .ADD      153    08/10/88 12:59   SS-45    .      40970    10/04/88 20:40
T18      .MMO      921    04/04/88 19:58   T6       .MMO    1463    02/22/88 11:31
URGNOTE  .        1670    08/12/88 00:13
```

FIGURE 8-4   A printout of the List Files screen

Copy all marked files to:

Type in the drive/directory path and press ENTER. WordPerfect will copy the marked files in the order listed. On the other hand, if you type N or another key, WordPerfect ignores the file markers and assumes that you want to copy only the file that the cursor is currently highlighting.

Print the List Files Screen

You can print a copy of the List Files screen as a way of keeping track of files on disk. To do so, display the List Files screen that you wish to print and then simply press the PRINT (SHIFT + F7) key. A sample is shown in Figure 8-4. This printout lists the current date and time, the amount of free disk space, and lists each file stored in the specified drive/directory.

GO TO DOS

Most of the basic file-management and disk-management operations described previously—such as creating a subdirectory, deleting a file, copying a file—can be performed directly from DOS (Disk Operating System). Other operations, such as formatting a floppy disk, can *only* be accomplished when you exit WordPerfect to DOS.

You can exit WordPerfect to DOS temporarily if you prefer using DOS to copy files, create subdirectories, and the like (though you will probably discover that using the List Files screen is easier), or if you wish to perform an operation not available through WordPerfect. To do so, press the SHELL (CTRL + F1) key and select Go to DOS (1 or G). (If you use WordPerfect Library in addition to WordPerfect, then you must first select Go to Shell; from here, you can exit to DOS.)

WordPerfect temporarily disappears, and a screen like that shown in Figure 8-5 takes its place. The DOS prompt (such as B> or C> or C:\WPER\DATA>) will indicate that you are in DOS, working from the default drive. Now you can type in DOS commands. (See your DOS manual for a full discussion of DOS commands.)

```
Microsoft(R) MS-DOS(R)  Version 3.20
          (C)Copyright Microsoft Corp 1981-1986


Enter 'EXIT' to return to WordPerfect
C:\WPER\DATA>_
```

FIGURE 8-5   DOS screen after temporarily exiting WordPerfect

For instance, suppose that you neglected to enter the correct date at the beginning of the day's session, and the computer had no internal clock to automatically tell it the correct date when you turned it on. To inform the computer of the date, you could type **DATE** at the DOS prompt and press ENTER. The computer responds with what it believed to be the correct date and prompts you with

ENTER new date

Type in the current date and press ENTER. The DOS prompt returns to the screen, ready for your next command.

Certain DOS commands require access to files that reside on the DOS disk. One such command is FORMAT. To format a disk, floppy disk users must insert the DOS disk in the default drive and a blank disk to be formatted in the second drive. Hard disk users may need to switch the default to the directory containing the DOS files.

You should always be very careful when you format a disk—the Format command is dangerous! When you format a disk, you prepare it to store files. In the process, everything previously stored on that disk is erased. So if you're not cautious, you can accidentally erase important files!

As a general rule, don't simply type **Format** without specifying a drive. If you wish to format a brand-new disk in drive A, the correct command is

format a:

meaning specifically that the disk in drive A should be formatted. If you put that brand-new disk in drive B, the correct command is

format b:

Without specifying a drive, floppy disk users could destroy all the files on the DOS disk, and hard disk users could delete all the hundreds of files that might be stored on the hard disk!

When you are ready to return to WordPerfect, simply type **Exit** at the DOS prompt and then press ENTER. (Actually type the word "exit." Do not press the EXIT key instead; the EXIT key operates only when in WordPerfect, not in DOS.)

It is easy to forget about WordPerfect and, after exiting to DOS temporarily, simply turn off the computer. But then you are not exiting WordPerfect properly. Therefore, remember that if you go to DOS in the middle of a WordPerfect session, you need to return to Word-

Perfect and exit properly (using the EXIT key) before turning off the computer.

Your computer must be equipped with sufficient RAM to exit to DOS. You might find that WordPerfect won't allow you to exit because you have insufficient memory to do so.

LOCK FILES WITH A PASSWORD

Some documents typed in an office are confidential, to be read only by yourself or by a specific group of individuals. When you find yourself typing a top-secret document, WordPerfect offers the ability to save a file with a password. Only the individuals who know the file's password can retrieve it or print it from disk. This is especially handy for those of you who store files on a hard disk and do not have the option of locking the hard disk in a desk drawer as you can with a floppy disk.

To lock a file with a password, make sure the file is on screen, press the TEXT IN/OUT (CTRL + F5) key, and then select Password (2 or P). WordPerfect displays the following Password menu:

Password: 1 Add/Change; 2 Remove: 0

Select Add/Change (1 or A). WordPerfect prompts for you to enter a password, which can contain up to 25 characters and can include numbers, letters, symbols, or spaces. As you type the password, your typing is invisible on screen—a precaution against someone looking over your shoulder to read the password.

Once you type a password and press ENTER, WordPerfect prompts you to reenter the password. You are always asked to enter a password twice to verify that you typed the password exactly as you intended. Type in the password a second time and press ENTER. If the two passwords are different, WordPerfect displays an error message and prompts you to start again, entering and then reentering the password. If the two attempts at typing a password match, the password is registered. As a last step, you must remember to resave your document, either using the SAVE key or the EXIT key. When you do, the password is attached to that file.

After a file is locked with a password, WordPerfect will ask for that password whenever you try to view the contents of that file— whether by using the Look option on the List Files menu, by retrieving that file (using the RETRIEVE key or the Retrieve option on the List Files menu), or by printing a document from disk (using the PRINT key or the Print option on the List Files menu). Enter the correct password in order to view, retrieve, or print the file. Enter an incorrect password, however, and WordPerfect aborts the command, with a prompt such as

ERROR: File is Locked

Don't forget your password! If you do, you'll be locked out of your own file. Keep a written copy of each password somewhere convenient (perhaps in your appointment calendar or wallet), or use a password that you won't easily forget (like your social security number or your mother's birthdate) but that an office mate won't figure out.

You can change a file's password at any time. Make sure you retrieve the file to the Typing screen. Then follow the same steps as outlined above, again selecting Add/Change (1 or A) from the Password menu. Type in the new password twice and make sure to resave your file after changing the password so that the new password takes effect.

You can also remove the password at any time. Again, make sure that the document is on screen. Display the Password menu as outlined above and then select Remove (2 or R). The password is erased. Once you resave the file, the password will become unattached and the file will be unlocked.

Here's an opportunity for you to lock a file. Suppose that the document on screen is one that you want accessed by you alone. Pretend that your ZIP code at home is 90046. Let's use that ZIP code as the password. Then we'll resave the file so that the password is attached.

1. On a clear screen, retrieve the file named FINANCE.

2. Press the TEXT IN/OUT (CTRL + F5) key. The following menu appears on screen:

   1 DOS Text; 2 Password; 3 Save Generic; 4 Save WP 4.2;
   5 Comment: 0

3. Select Password (2 or P). A new menu appears:

   Password: 1 Add/Change; 2 Remove: 0

4. Select Add/Change (1 or C). WordPerfect prompts

   Enter Password:

5. Type 90046 (the numbers will not appear as you type) and press ENTER. WordPerfect prompts

Re-Enter Password:

6. Type **90046** and press ENTER. The password has been registered.

7. Use the EXIT (F7) key to resave this file under the name FINANCE and to clear the screen (but remain in WordPerfect).

As proof that the file has been locked, let's attempt to retrieve the document.

1. Press the RETRIEVE (SHIFT + F10) key. WordPerfect prompts

Document to be retrieved:

2. Type **FINANCE** and press ENTER. WordPerfect responds with

Enter Password (FINANCE):

3. Type **99999** (an incorrect password) and press ENTER. Since the password is incorrect, WordPerfect responds with an error message indicating that the file is locked and then offers the opportunity to try again, assuming that you still wish to retrieve the same file, with the prompt

Document to be retrieved: FINANCE

4. Press ENTER to accept WordPerfect's suggestion that you wish to retrieve the file named FINANCE. WordPerfect prompts

Enter Password (FINANCE):

5. Type **90046** and press ENTER. Now the file is retrieved.

CREATE DOCUMENT SUMMARIES

The Document Summary feature attaches a summary form to a file. The form helps you keep track of the contents of or progress on a document. It is also handy for searching for a file based on its content, subject, author, or typist. A document summary is used on screen only; WordPerfect will not print out the summary when you print out the document.

```
Document Summary

      System Filename              C:\WPER\DATA\FINANCE

      Date of Creation             January 5, 1989

   1 - Descriptive Filename

   2 - Subject/Account

   3 - Author

   4 - Typist

   5 - Comments

   ┌─────────────────────────────────────────────────────────────┐
   │ I spoke to John Samsone on January 3rd about our financial situation. He │
   │ reported the following highlights:  o He is meeting with a venture       │
   │ capitalist next week who is interested in investing with us.  o Our debt │
   │ stands at $159,000 as of December 31st, 10% lower than we anticipated.   │
   │ Financial forecasts project that we'll be out of debt in two years time. │
   └─────────────────────────────────────────────────────────────┘

Selection: 0
```

FIGURE 8-6   Document Summary screen

You can create the summary before or after you complete the document or while you're working on it. However, if you want the date that WordPerfect automatically inserts on the document summary form to reflect the day you actually started the document, remember to create a summary on the same day.

Your cursor can be anywhere in the document when you create a document summary. To begin, press the FORMAT (SHIFT + F8) key, select Document (3 or D), and then, on the Document Format menu, select Summary (5 or S). A Document Summary screen appears, as shown in Figure 8-6, which contains a predesigned document summary form. (Figure 8-6 shows the summary when FINANCE is on screen.) WordPerfect fills out four of the items on this form automatically:

- *System Filename* The name with which you stored this document on disk, along with the drive/directory where it is stored, is inserted. (If you haven't yet stored this document on disk, the phrase "Not named yet" appears on the document summary form until you store the document on disk.)

- *Date of Creation*   Today's date is inserted. (As discussed in Getting Started, the computer knows today's date only if your computer is equipped with an internal clock or you indicate the current date when you turn on your computer to load Word-Perfect.)

- *Subject/Account*   WordPerfect searches the first 400 bytes (approximately 400 characters) of the document for the characters "RE:". If the characters are found, WordPerfect inserts the text that follows "RE:", either up to the next hard return or until 39 characters have been inserted, whichever comes first. If the characters are not found, the item Subject/Account remains blank.

- *Comment*   If text has been entered into the document, the first 400 characters are inserted in a double-line box at the bottom of the form. If no text has yet been entered for the document, the comments box remains clear of text.

You can enter or edit five items on the summary form. These include

- *Descriptive Filename (1 or D)*   This item allows you 39 characters with which to describe what the system filename stands for. As an example, if the system filename is 88ANN2.RPT, you can fill out the descriptive filename as "1988 Annual Report, Part 2."
    If you enter a descriptive filename before the file has been stored on disk, WordPerfect suggests a system filename. For instance, suppose you enter the descriptive filename "Status Report on 1989 Budget." WordPerfect will suggest the system filename STATREPO.ON on screen and when you store the file on disk. You can accept the suggestion or type in a system filename of your own.

- *Subject/Account (2 or S)*   This item allows you 39 characters to indicate the document's subject or the pertinent account number.

- *Author (3 or A)*   This item allows you 39 characters for typing the author of the document.

- *Typist (4 or T)*   This item allows you 39 characters for indicating who is typing the document.

- *Comments (5 or C)*   This item allows you up to 780 characters in the comments box at the bottom of the screen. You can edit text that WordPerfect automatically inserted or erase that text and insert your own comments. Only five lines of text can be displayed in the box at one time; use the cursor movement keys (such as DOWN ARROW and UP ARROW) to view additional text.

Select an item, type in the appropriate information, and then press EXIT (F7) or ENTER before selecting another option. For instance, select Author (3 or A), type in a name up to 39 characters in length, and press the EXIT key. (When you select the Comments option, you must press EXIT (F7) when done editing the comment; pressing ENTER will insert a hard return in the comments box.) Once you fill in information for some or all of these five items, press EXIT (F7) to return to the Typing screen.

After you create a document summary, save that document on disk. The document summary becomes attached to that file.

The document summary does not display on the Typing screen. To review or edit the contents of a document summary, simply proceed as if you intend to create a summary for the first time by selecting Summary (5 or S) from the Document Format menu. The form that you previously filled out appears on screen. Now you can select an item for editing or simply press EXIT (F7) to return to the Typing screen.

In addition, you can review (but not edit) a document summary when you use the Look feature to peek into the contents of documents. You'll remember from Chapter 2 that the Look feature is accessed from the List Files screen by positioning the cursor on the file whose contents you wish to peruse and either selecting Look (6 or L) or pressing the ENTER key. The Look screen first displays the document summary for a file (if that file has one); to display the actual file contents press DOWN ARROW.

Suppose you've decided that you want to create a document summary for each of your important documents. That way you'll know a document's contents and status from a quick glance at the summary. Let's create a summary for the file named FINANCE, which is now on your Typing screen, and fill out several pieces of information.

1. With the cursor positioned anywhere in the document, press the FORMAT (SHIFT + F8) key. The Format menu appears.

2. Select Document (3 or D). The Document Format menu appears.

3. Select Summary (5 or S). The Document Summary screen appears, as shown in Figure 8-6. WordPerfect has inserted the system filename, the current date, and filled in the comments box with the first 400 characters of text.

4. Select Subject/Account (2 or S), type **Financial Status**, and press ENTER.

5. Select Typist (4 or T), type your name, and press ENTER.

6. Select Comments (5 or C). The cursor moves into the comment box.

7. Press ENTER twice to insert two blank lines and then press UP ARROW twice to move to the top of the box.

8. Type **Confidential memo to the CEO.**

9. Press the DOWN ARROW key until the cursor moves no further. Then press UP ARROW to move back up to the top of the box. Notice how you can scroll up and down the comment box, even though only five lines can be displayed at one time.

```
Document Summary

        System Filename          C:\WPER\DATA\FINANCE

        Date of Creation         January 5, 1989

   1 - Descriptive Filename

   2 - Subject/Account          Financial Status

   3 - Author

   4 - Typist                   Scott White

   5 - Comments
 ┌─────────────────────────────────────────────────────────────────┐
 │ Confidential memo to the CEO.                                     │
 │                                                                   │
 │ I spoke to John Sansone on January 3rd about our financial situation. He │
 │ reported the following highlights:  o He is meeting with a venture │
 │ capitalist next week who is interested in investing with us.  o Our debt │
 └─────────────────────────────────────────────────────────────────┘

   Selection: 0
```

FIGURE 8-7   Document Summary screen after entering information

10. Press EXIT (F7) to exit the comment box. Your screen will now resemble Figure 8-7.

11. Press the EXIT (F7) key to return to your document.

12. Use the EXIT (F7) key to resave this file under the name FINANCE and to clear the screen (but remain in WordPerfect).

With the screen clear, suppose that you wish to use the Look feature to peruse the contents of the file named FINANCE. (Remember from Chapter 2 that the Look feature lets you peek at the contents of a file without actually retrieving that file to the screen.) Proceed as follows:

1. Press the LIST FILES (F5) key. WordPerfect prompts with the default drive/directory, for instance, **Dir B:*.*** or **Dir C:\WPER \DATA*.***.

2. Since FINANCE is stored in the default drive/directory, press ENTER. The List Files menu appears, showing the names of files in your default drive or directory. (If FINANCE is not stored in the default, type in the correct drive/directory before pressing ENTER.)

3. Position the cursor on the filename FINANCE.

4. Press ENTER or select Look (6 or L). Because this file is locked, WordPerfect asks for the password, with a prompt such as

   Enter Password: C:\WPER\DATA\FINANCE

5. Type **90046** and press ENTER. A Look screen appears as shown in Figure 8-8. Notice the header at the top of the screen indicating the filename and the file size. Below the header, WordPerfect displays not the contents of the file, but the document summary, since a summary had previously been created for the file named FINANCE.

6. Press DOWN ARROW. Now the Look screen shows the actual contents of the file, as shown in Figure 8-9.

7. Press EXIT (F7) or CANCEL (F1) twice—once to exit the Look screen and a second time to exit the List Files screen. You are returned to the Typing screen.

```
┌─────────────────────────────────────────────────────────────────┐
│ Filename C:\WPER\DATA\FINANCE                    File size:   2270 │
│  ┌──────────────────────────────────────────────────────────┐    │
│  │ January 5, 1989                                           │    │
│  │                                                           │    │
│  │ Financial Status                                          │    │
│  │                                                           │    │
│  │ Scott White                                               │    │
│  │ Confidential memo to the CEO.                             │    │
│  │                                                           │    │
│  │ I spoke to John Samsone on January 3rd about our financial situation. He │
│  │ reported the following highlights:  o He is meeting with a venture │
│  │ capitalist next week who is interested in investing with us.  o Our debt │
│  │ stands at $159,000 as of December 31st, 10% lower than we anticipated. │
│  │ Financial forecasts project that we'll be out of debt in two years time. │
│  └──────────────────────────────────────────────────────────┘    │
│                                                                   │
│ Document Summary                       (Use Cursor Keys for more text) │
└─────────────────────────────────────────────────────────────────┘
```

FIGURE 8-8   Look screen showing the FINANCE document summary

```
┌─────────────────────────────────────────────────────────────────┐
│ Filename C:\WPER\DATA\FINANCE                    File size:   2270 │
│ I spoke to John Samsone on January 3rd about our financial        │
│ situation. He reported the following highlights:                  │
│                                                                   │
│ o    He is meeting with a venture capitalist next week who is     │
│      interested in investing with us.                             │
│                                                                   │
│ o    Our debt stands at $159,000 as of December 31st, 10% lower   │
│      than we anticipated. Financial forecasts project that we'll  │
│      be out of debt in two years time. Here are the debt figures  │
│      (in thousands):                                              │
│                                                                   │
│      Amount Owed            Name of Bank                          │
│                                                                   │
│         $48.5               Floyd Interstate                      │
│          9.8                  Center Bank                         │
│        100.7                Bank of Stevenson                     │
│                                                                   │
│ For more detail, call John at (415) 333-9215.                     │
│                                                                   │
│                                                                   │
│ Press Exit when done                   (Use Cursor Keys for more text) │
└─────────────────────────────────────────────────────────────────┘
```

FIGURE 8-9   Look screen showing the contents of FINANCE

As you will learn farther on in this chapter, document summaries can be used when you are seeking a certain file or group of files. Therefore, it is worth your while to devise a systematic method for filling out information in a summary. For instance, you may decide that the Subject/Account for all documents related to your company's finances will be "Financial Status," so that you can search for all documents related to finances.

Note: WordPerfect offers two features that change how the Document Summary feature operates. First, you can direct WordPerfect to display a document summary form when a document is saved for the first time. In this way, you can rely on WordPerfect to remind you to fill out a summary for each new document, rather than attempting to remember yourself. Second, you can change the text for which WordPerfect searches when attempting to fill in the "Subject/Account" heading. As described previously, the default search text is "RE:". But if you type memorandums using the term "MEMO TOPIC:" instead, you can alter the subject search text accordingly. Refer to the "Initial Settings" section in Appendix C for further details on both of these options.

SEARCH FOR SPECIFIC FILES ON THE LIST FILES SCREEN

No matter how diligent you are at assigning each file a unique filename, once numerous files are accumulated on disk, it becomes difficult to remember which file contains which document. You could stare at the List Files screen for hours and still not remember the name of the file you're looking for. But you don't have to retrieve each file one by one until you find the one you want; WordPerfect offers several features to help you keep track of those files and quickly narrow down the search on the List Files screen.

Specify Filenames or File Extensions

As you know, when you first press the LIST FILES (F5) key, you see a prompt such as

Dir B:*.*

or

Dir C:\WPER\DATA*.*

The *.* means that WordPerfect will display all files in that drive or directory. When you press ENTER, a List Files screen appears containing all the files in that drive/directory.

But you can temporarily narrow down the display of files in a drive/directory to those with similar names by using the wild card characters * and ?. Those of you familiar with DOS will recognize these wild cards. The asterisk (*) represents any number of characters, while the question mark (?) represents just one character—that's why *.* means that all files will be displayed, no matter what their filenames or extensions.

You can edit the *.* and thereby limit what files are displayed. For example, perhaps you know that the file you are looking for ends with the file extension .LTR. You can display all files, with any filename, that have the file extension .LTR. You must edit the prompt when you first press the LIST FILES (F5) key so that instead of *.*, the prompt reads

Dir C:\WPER\DATA*.LTR

When you press ENTER, the List Files screen shows only those files with the extension .LTR.

Or suppose you are looking for a document named JONES, but can't remember its extension (or even whether it had one). To list all files with the filename JONES and with any extension, change the prompt to read

Dir C:\WPER\DATA\JONES.*

When you press ENTER, WordPerfect will list files such as JONES, JONES.IHM, or JONES.44.

Or suppose you are looking for documents with any filename whose extension starts with any character and ends with "MM." Then change the prompt to read

Dir C:\WPER\DATA*.?MM

before pressing ENTER.

Here's an example whereby you can narrow the List Files screen only to files with the extension ADD.

1. Press the LIST FILES (F5) key. WordPerfect prompts with the default drive/directory, for instance, **Dir B:*.*** or **Dir C:\WPER\DATA*.***.

2. Press the RIGHT ARROW key until the cursor won't move any farther (or you can press END to move the cursor more quickly); the cursor will be located just to the right of the very last character, which is the second asterisk (*).

3. Press BACKSPACE to erase that asterisk.

4. Type **ADD** (uppercase or lowercase makes no difference). Now the prompt will read **Dir B:*.ADD** or **Dir C:\WPER\DATA*.ADD**.

5. Press ENTER. A List Files screen like that shown in Figure 8-10 appears. Notice that the top of the screen indicates that the files listed are from C:\WPER\DATA*.ADD, which means files stored on the hard disk in the directory \WPER\DATA,

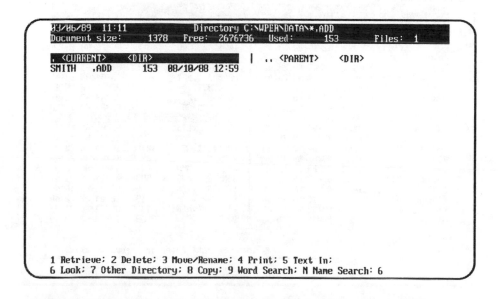

```
03/06/89  11:11              Directory C:\WPER\DATA\*.ADD
Document size:      1378   Free:  2676736   Used:      153      Files:  1

. <CURRENT>    <DIR>                    |  .. <PARENT>      <DIR>
SMITH   .ADD       153  08/10/88 12:59




















   1 Retrieve; 2 Delete; 3 Move/Rename; 4 Print; 5 Text In;
   6 Look; 7 Other Directory; 8 Copy; 9 Word Search; N Name Search: 6
```

FIGURE 8-10   List Files screen for a specific group of files with the extension .ADD

with any filename and with the extension ADD. Only one file
fits that description, and so only that one file is displayed.

6. Press EXIT (F7) or CANCEL (F1) to return to the Typing
   screen.

Name Search

Once you're viewing the List Files screen, you can use the Name
Search feature to move the cursor to a file quickly. Instead of using the
cursor movement keys to scroll through the files, type the letter **N** or
press the →SEARCH (F2) key. This activates the Name Search. The
List Files menu at the bottom of the screen is temporarily replaced by
the message (**Name Search; Enter or arrows to Exit**). Instead of
using the cursor movement keys, type the first few characters of the
document's filename. The cursor will move to the filename that begins
with those characters (or most closely matches them). For instance, if
you type **b**, the cursor moves to the first filename starting with the let-

```
03/06/89  11:14              Directory C:\WPER\DATA\*.*
Document size:    1378   Free:  2664448   Used:    600985        Files:  45


.  <CURRENT>   <DIR>                    .. <PARENT>   <DIR>
005      .CRG       993  02/16/88 23:41   1001     .CRG     40173  06/16/88 15:55
5008     .CRG      1312  07/22/88 02:08   5012     .CRG     35605  10/04/88 20:41
5028     .CRG     29573  10/04/88 20:42   88ANN    .RPT     21212  02/09/88 11:23
88ANN2   .RPT     35597  10/04/88 20:41   88ANN3   .RPT     35597  10/04/88 20:41
88BRENT  .        43544  06/16/88 15:56   ACCOUNTS.         36762  02/21/88 15:41
BBS009   .1       21212  02/09/88 11:23   BBS009   .2        4754  02/09/88 12:45
BBS009   .3        2703  04/04/88 19:56   BKGROUND .88        778  02/23/88 13:28
BOOKKEEP .         1830  02/24/88 02:43   BUDMIN   .         1961  05/22/88 21:32
BUDMIN88 .        20120  10/04/88 20:43   C2       .LTR      1551  02/09/89 11:05
CBS&RP   .         2666  02/10/88 10:59   CEO1     .MMO       942  12/21/88 11:15
DOCLIS2  .MS       3241  10/04/88 20:40   DOCLIST1 .MS      40756  10/04/88 20:39
FINANCE  .         1866  09/01/88 10:00   FON      .        20120  10/04/88 20:43
GAIN     .LTR      1598  02/09/89 11:05   J&B      .MMO      2317  09/16/88 20:36
JONES1   .MMO      1356  07/22/88 00:56   JONES2   .MMO      5936  02/11/88 01:01
LETTER   .         1629  08/24/88 17:05   LETTER   .WPM        57  08/24/88 16:48
LINKER   .MS       1206  09/16/88 20:36   LINKER2  .        35597  10/04/88 20:40
LIST     .         1799  08/22/88 11:23   LIST     .NEW      1939  08/21/88 21:43
MEYERS-1 .MS       1206  09/16/88 20:36 ▼ P&L      .        35597  10/04/88 20:40


bu                              (Name Search; Enter or arrows to Exit)
```

FIGURE 8-11   List Files screen during a name search

ter "B." If you then type **u**, the cursor moves to the first filename starting with "bu"—which in the example shown in Figure 8-11 would be
the file BUDMIN. As indicated at the bottom of Figure 8-11, press
ENTER or an arrow key to end the search. The menu of ten options
returns to the bottom of the List Files screen. Here's an example:

1. Press the LIST FILES (F5) key. WordPerfect prompts with the
   default drive/directory, for instance, **Dir B:*.*** or **Dir C:\
   WPER\DATA*.*.**

2. Press ENTER to display the list of files.

3. Type **N** to activate Name Search.

4. Type **U**. The cursor moves down to the first file beginning with
   the letter "U"; on your screen, this may be the file named
   URGNOTE that you created in a previous chapter.

5. Press ENTER to exit Name Search.

6. Press CANCEL (F1) to exit the List Files screen.

Word Search

The Word Search feature can hunt down files by looking not at each
document's filename but at its contents. To use this feature, you must
first display the List Files screen for the files that you wish involved in
the search. For instance, if you wish to search through all the files in
the default drive/directory, press LIST FILES (F5) and press ENTER. Or
type in another drive/directory and press ENTER. When viewing a list
of files, you can also narrow down the search even further by marking
those files you wish to search with an asterisk.

Next, select Word Search (9 or W) from the List Files menu at the
bottom of the screen. The following menu appears:

Search: 1 Doc Summary; 2 First Page; 3 Entire Doc;
4 Conditions; 0

There are two different categories for the Word Search. First, you
can indicate a *word pattern,* which can be a certain word, several
words, or a phrase of up to 20 characters. For instance, you could find
all those documents in which the word "computer" is mentioned.
WordPerfect will search multiple files for that word pattern in every

document summary, the first page of each document, or all pages of each document, whichever you specify. Select from the first three options on the Search menu and WordPerfect prompts

Word pattern:

In the word pattern, you can use the wild card character * to represent any number of characters or ? to represent a single character. For instance, the word pattern

computer

will find documents that contain the words "microcomputer," "microcomputers," "minicomputer," "minicomputers," "computer," and "computers," just to name a few. The word pattern

m?re

will find documents that contain the words "mare," "mere," "mire," "more," or "mure."

If the word pattern contains two or more words, you can separate the words by a space or a semicolon (;) to represent the logical operator AND and separate the words by a comma (,) to represent the logical operator OR. If you type the words in quotation marks, the words are treated as a distinct phrase that must be located. For instance, the word pattern

wine price

will locate files that contain *both* the word "wine" and the word "price." The pattern

wine,price

will locate files that contain *either* word. The pattern

"wine price"

will locate files that contain the phrase "wine price."

After you type in a word pattern, press ENTER. A prompt at the bottom of the screen indicates that the search is progressing. When the search is complete, WordPerfect will either rewrite the List Files screen, displaying an asterisk next to those files that contain the

```
Word Search

    1 - Perform Search on           All 45 File(s)

    2 - Undo Last Search

    3 - Reset Search Conditions

    4 - File Date                    No
        From (MM/DD/YY):             (All)
        To   (MM/DD/YY):             (All)

                  Word Pattern(s)

    5 - First Page
    6 - Entire Doc
    7 - Document Summary
        Creation Date (e.g. Nov)
        Descriptive Name
        Subject/Account
        Author
        Typist
        Comments

  Selection: 1
```

FIGURE 8-12   Word Search screen

specified word pattern, or prompt * **Not found** *, meaning that the word pattern was not found in any files.

The second Word Search method is to search for certain *conditions*. Using the conditions method, you can specify that WordPerfect search based on a word pattern or based on a date that you last saved a file on disk. And you can search on more than just one condition. For instance, you can search for files created in February, 1989 that contain the phrase "wine opener" in the first page of the document.

To use the conditions method, select Conditions (4 or C) on the Search menu, and the Word Search screen (as shown in Figure 8-12) appears. Four options on this menu allow you to specify what you wish to search for:

- *File Date (4 or D)*   This option allows you to search for files last saved on specific dates. When you select this option, Word-Perfect changes the "No" to "Yes" next to the heading "File Date." Press ENTER. Insert a "From" date and press ENTER. Insert a "To" date and press ENTER again.

When typing a date, use the format mm/dd/yy (though leading zeros are unnecessary, for instance, **12/15/89** or **6/9/90**). You can leave the month, day, or year unspecified, but be sure to type the slashes. For instance, suppose you wish to search for files last saved in February 1989. Enter the "From" and "To" categories as **2//89**. Or, to search for files last saved since 1989, type in the "From" date as **//89** and leave the "To" date empty by pressing ENTER (in which case WordPerfect assumes "All" dates).

- *First Page (5 or F)*   This option allows you to type in a word pattern, just as when you select the First Page option directly from the Search menu as described above.

- *Entire Doc (6 or E)*   This option allows you to type in a word pattern, just as when you select the Entire Doc option directly from the Search menu as described above.

- *Document Summary (7 or S)*   This option allows you to type in a word pattern, just as when you select the Doc Summary option on the Search menu. If you type a word pattern next to the category "Document Summary" in Figure 8-12, WordPerfect checks the entire summary. If you type a word pattern next to another category (such as "Typist"), WordPerfect checks only that category in each document summary for the word pattern.

After you set all conditions, select Perform Search On (1 or P) to initiate the search. (You can also press ENTER, since WordPerfect always assumes that your selection is option 1, as shown at the bottom of Figure 8-12, unless you specify otherwise.) A prompt at the bottom of the screen indicates that the search is progressing. When the search is complete, WordPerfect will either rewrite the List Files screen, displaying an asterisk next to those files that contain the specified word pattern, or WordPerfect will prompt * **Not found** *, meaning that the word pattern was not found.

Here's an example that requires you to use the Word Search feature. Pretend you want to find those files that mention a person named "samsone" in the document.

1. Press the LIST FILES (F5) key and then press ENTER to display a list of files in the default drive or directory.

2. Select Word Search (9 or W). WordPerfect responds with the following menu.

Search: 1 <u>D</u>oc Summary; 2 <u>F</u>irst Page; 3 <u>E</u>ntire Doc;
4 <u>C</u>onditions; 0

3. Select Entire Document (3 or E). WordPerfect prompts for a word pattern.

4. Type **samsone** and press ENTER.

5. As it is checking each file, WordPerfect will prompt for the password for FINANCE; otherwise, WordPerfect won't perform a search on that file. Type **90046** and press ENTER. The search continues in other files.

6. After several moments, WordPerfect marks the two files that contain that name, placing an asterisk just to the right of the file size for the documents named FINANCE and URGNOTE.

Once you've found the file you were looking for, you are ready to perform whatever task is at hand—whether you peruse the content of each of the marked documents using the Look feature, retrieve one of the marked documents, or print one of them. Or you can perform another word search. From the List Files screen, with certain files marked with an asterisk because of the previous word search, again select Word Search (9 or W) and Conditions (4 or C). The Word Search menu reappears, but instead of performing the search on all the files, WordPerfect will assume you wish to perform the next search on just the marked files. For instance, notice in Figure 8-12 that next to the heading "Perform Search on" the screen reads "All 45 File(s)" (because, in this example, 45 files are stored in the directory that is to be searched). After a search, suppose WordPerfect marked 9 files as meeting the search conditions; when you return to the Word Search menu, the screen will read "9 Marked File(s)." Select Undo Last Search (2 or U) to again perform a search on 45 files; do not select this option in order to perform the search on only the 9 marked files.

Keep in mind that WordPerfect remembers the search conditions you set until you change them or exit WordPerfect. Therefore, when you wish to perform a completely different search, select Reset Search Conditions (3 or R) on the Word Search menu. The conditions are reset to their original status, as shown in Figure 8-12. Then proceed to set new search conditions and perform another word search.

As soon as you exit the List Files screen after a word search, the asterisks disappear. For instance, your screen is now displaying the List Files screen with two marked files:

1. Press CANCEL (F1) to return to the Typing screen.

2. Press the LIST FILES (F5) key and press ENTER to display a list of files in the default drive or directory. Notice that no files are marked.

3. Press CANCEL (F1) to again return to the Typing screen.

REVIEW EXERCISE

If you are systematic in how you manage files on disk, you'll have little difficulty finding a file when you need it. Practice by performing the following tasks, and you'll be ready to maintain order for the hundreds of files that will soon find their way onto your hard disk or floppy disks.

1. Remove the password from the file named FINANCE. (*Hint:* To retrieve that file to the screen, remember that the password is 90046. Also, don't forget to resave the file after you remove the password from it.)

2. The file named SMITH.ADD is a file you no longer need to store on disk. Delete this file. (*Hint:* If you have other files to delete as well, mark these files with asterisks on the List Files screen and delete them all at once.)

3. Pretend that the files named URGNOTE and FINANCE are important files that you must maintain a record of. To safeguard against a disk malfunctioning, place copies of these two files on a floppy disk. (*Hint:* Make sure that you have a formatted disk and that you insert that disk in drive A. Also, mark these two files with asterisks and copy them at one time to A:.)

4. Print out a list of files in your default drive/directory.

REVIEW

- You can alter the default drive or directory where a file is stored to or retrieved from. To change the default for one file, precede the filename with the new drive or directory when saving or retrieving the file. To change the default for a working session, use the LIST FILES (F5) key.

- The List Files screen offers hard disk users the ability to manage directories by creating, deleting, or looking at the contents of different directories. In addition, it offers hard disk and floppy disk users the tools for managing files by deleting, copying, moving, or renaming files. Copying files protects against the unfortunate possibility of a disk (hard or floppy) that contains important documents malfunctioning or being destroyed.

- Floppy disk users should acquire the habit of checking the List Files screen to see whether a disk is near storage capacity.

- Print a list of files in a given drive or directory by pressing the PRINT (SHIFT + F7) key when displaying the List Files screen for that drive or directory.

- The SHELL (CTRL + F1) key can temporarily switch you to DOS. You can then execute DOS commands to manage directories or files. Type **Exit** and press ENTER to return to Word-Perfect.

- WordPerfect lets you lock a file so that only those who know the file password can retrieve or print that file. You lock a file by selecting the Password option after pressing the TEXT IN/OUT (CTRL + F5) key.

- A document summary can be created for each file stored on disk, containing information on the summary's date of creation, author, and typist, and any comments that you want noted about that document. A summary appears only on screen and not on the printed page. The Document Format menu provides access to this feature.

- Several features are available to help you locate a file quickly from the List Files screen. You can restrict the display to files with similar names by using the wildcards * and ?. Or, once the List Files screen is displayed, you can initiate a Name Search to locate a file by name quickly or initiate a word search so that WordPerfect lists only those files that contain a certain word or phrase or that were saved on a specific date.

- You can delete, print, or copy more than one file, and you can specify which files are to be included in a word search by marking those files on the List Files screen with asterisks before performing the task.

9

PRINT OPTIONS AND ENHANCEMENTS

Change Print Options
Use Your Printer Like a Typewriter
View a Document Before Printing
Initialize Your Printer for Soft Fonts
Test Your Printer Capabilities
Advance the Printer to an Exact Position On the Page
Number Lines at the Printer
Insert Printer Commands
Review Exercise
Review

In Chapter 2, you learned the basics of printing a document. This chapter covers some of the special features offered by WordPerfect for when you wish to direct the printer to do something special. You'll learn about all the options on the Print menu, such as how to switch between printers (if you have more than one), or how to print a specific number of copies of the print job. Other special print features include Type Through, which causes your text to be printed as you type it, and View Document, which offers a preview of how your document will appear on the printed page. You will also direct the printer to a precise location on the page before it prints. And you will use a special document provided by WordPerfect to test whether or not your printer has the capability to activate these fancy print features.

CHANGE PRINT OPTIONS

Print options deal with some of the more mechanical aspects of printing. As described previously, you can print a document directly from screen using the Full Document or Page options on the Print menu, or you can print a document from disk using the Document on Disk option on the Print menu or the Print option on the List Files menu. Whatever method you use to print, WordPerfect always makes assumptions for each print job about how the printer will operate with respect to the selected printer, binding, number of copies, and graphics and text quality. You can check these defaults by pressing the PRINT (SHIFT + F7) key and reading the bottom portion of the Print screen, below the heading "Options," as shown in Figure 9-1. Any number of these defaults can be changed before you send a print job to your printer.

Select Printer

The Select Printer option has two main functions. First, it allows you to define the printer(s) attached to your computer so that they will work properly with WordPerfect. As part of the installation procedures, all the printers attached to your computer must be defined to work with WordPerfect. Every time you attach a new brand of printer to your computer, you must define it for WordPerfect. The method for defining printers, which is part of the installation procedures, is described in Appendix B.

Second, the Select Printer option enables you to select the printer that you wish to use for each document from among the defined printers. The printer that you choose for a given document is recorded when the document is stored on disk. The next time you retrieve that document, WordPerfect also recalls the selected printer.

The default printer is whatever printer you last selected. For example, suppose that the selected printer is the HP LaserJet Series II. When you begin to type a new document, WordPerfect will assume that you wish to use the LaserJet to print your document. The currently

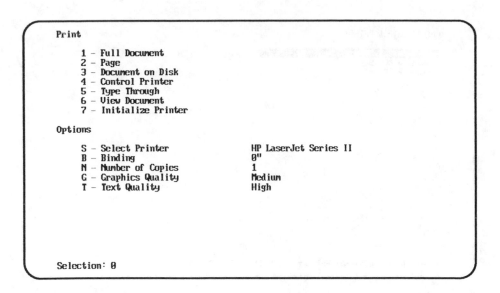

```
Print

        1 - Full Document
        2 - Page
        3 - Document on Disk
        4 - Control Printer
        5 - Type Through
        6 - View Document
        7 - Initialize Printer

Options

        S - Select Printer          HP LaserJet Series II
        B - Binding                 8"
        N - Number of Copies        1
        G - Graphics Quality        Medium
        T - Text Quality            High




Selection: 0
```

FIGURE 9-1   Print screen

selected printer is always shown on the Print screen. In Figure 9-1, for example, the HP LaserJet Series II is indicated as the selected printer.

If you have defined only one printer, then that one printer would have been selected during the installation procedures; it will be unnecessary for you to change that selection.

However, if you have more than one printer attached to your computer and have defined all your printers to work with WordPerfect, then you will want to consciously select a printer for each new document you type. Make sure that the document for which you wish to select a new printer is on screen. (Or, the screen may be clear because you intend to type a new document as soon as you select a printer.) Then press the PRINT (SHIFT + F7) key to view the Print screen as shown in Figure 9-1. The printer listed next to the heading "Select Printer" indicates the currently selected printer, which will be used for this document if you make no change. If you wish to change the printer selection, then choose Select Printer (S). The Select Printer screen appears, listing all the printers that you defined to work with your computer. A sample is shown in Figure 9-2. An asterisk appears next to the currently selected printer. Position the cursor on the name

```
Print: Select Printer

* HP LaserJet Series II
  Okidata ML 192+
  Standard Printer
```

```
1 Select: 2 Additional Printers: 3 Edit: 4 Copy: 5 Delete: 6 Help: 7 Update: 1
```

FIGURE 9-2   Select Printer menu

of the new printer you wish to use for your document and choose
Select (1 or S) from the menu at the bottom of the screen. You are
automatically returned to the Print screen, and the printer listed next to
the heading "Select Printer" reflects the change.

Once you select a different printer, that printer stays in effect for
the current document *and all future documents* that you create until
you select a new printer. Documents already created and stored on disk
are unaffected by the new printer selection, since a printer selection is
stored on disk along with the document.

You can, however, change your mind as to the printer you wish to
use for a given document. Suppose that you retrieve a document to
screen, press the PRINT (SHIFT + F7) key, and notice on the Print
screen that the document has been saved with a printer you no longer
wish to use. Simply select a different printer using the procedure
described above and print your document. If you resave your document, the newly selected printer will be saved along with the document. If you don't resave the document, then the next time you
retrieve it, the old printer selection will be in effect.

Binding

A second printing option default shown in Figure 9-1 is that the binding width is 0"—meaning that there is no provision for documents that you plan to have bound in book format. But what if you wish to print two-sided pages so that they can be bound? In that case, you'll want to reset the binding width, shifting the text of even-numbered pages to the left and the text of odd-numbered pages to the right, leaving extra space for where the book will be bound. (If you plan to bind one-sided pages, you can retain the binding setting as 0" and simply increase the left margin for the entire document to accommodate the binding.)

Binding width is measured in inches. If you want the text of each page shifted 0.5 inch to accommodate the binding, for example, you would change the binding width to 0.5 inch. To do so, select Binding (B) from the Print screen. Then type in the desired binding width, such as 0.5, and press ENTER. Once changed, binding takes effect for every print job until you change it again or until you turn off the computer. Therefore, if you wish to print out several print jobs and you want a binding width only for the first one, remember to reset the binding back to 0" before printing the second job. The next time you load WordPerfect, a binding of 0" is again assumed.

Number of Copies

WordPerfect also assumes that you wish to print only one copy of each print job. This is often correct, but you may occasionally wish to print multiple copies of one document. Rather than create multiple print jobs, you can create one print job requesting that WordPerfect print a specific number of copies.

Print many copies at once by selecting Number of Copies (N) from the Print screen, typing in a number, and pressing ENTER. Like the Binding option, the Number of Copies option takes effect for every print job until you change it again or turn off the computer. The next time you load WordPerfect, the Number of Copies value returns to 1.

Graphics and Text Quality

WordPerfect's last two options on the Print screen dictate the quality with which your text and graphics are printed. If your document contains graphics (refer to Chapter 10 for a discussion of inserting graphics images into your document), WordPerfect assumes you wish to print out the graphics in medium quality. For text, WordPerfect assumes high quality. With most printers, a better quality means a better resolution on the printed page; the better the quality, the longer it takes for the printer to print out graphics or text. (Be aware, however, that on some printers, changing the quality has no effect on the printed result.)

To alter the quality, or to request that the graphics or text not be printed during a print job, select Graphics Quality (G) or Text Quality (T) from the Print screen. WordPerfect displays a menu with four options. For instance, the Graphics Quality menu reads

Graphics Quality: 1 Do Not Print; 2 Draft; 3 Medium; 4 High: 3

The same four options are available for text quality. Select one of the options; the change is reflected on the Print screen. Like the Binding and Number of Copies options, the Graphics and Text Quality options remain in effect until you change them again or exit WordPerfect.

USE YOUR PRINTER LIKE
A TYPEWRITER

Type Through is a special feature for controlling the printer whereby you can turn your keyboard and printer into a typewriter. Whatever you type on the keyboard will be sent immediately to the printer. Type Through is particularly handy for completing preprinted forms: you can place a preprinted form in your printer and use Type Through to fill it out. You might also use Type Through to produce short notes.

The Type Through feature is accessed from the Print screen. Press the PRINT (SHIFT + F7) key and select Type Through (5 or Y). You are then given two choices for how Type Through should operate:

Type Through by: 1 Line; 2 Character: 0

If you select Type Through by line, you have the opportunity to edit each line of text before sending it to the printer. The screen in Figure 9-3 appears. You can type up to 250 characters on a line. The line of text appears at the top of the screen. Word wrap is inoperative;

```
 _

Line Type Through printing

Function Key      Action

Move              Retrieve the previous line for editing
Format            Do a printer command
Enter             Print the line
Exit/Cancel       Exit without printing




                                                        Pos 1
```

FIGURE 9-3   Line Type Through printing screen

the words you type continue to appear on one line. You can edit that line of text using the standard editing keys. When you are ready to send the line of text to the printer, press ENTER. Or, to cancel the printing of that line, press the EXIT (F7) or CANCEL (F1) key.

You can control where the line of text will appear vertically and horizontally on the page. To position the paper vertically, you can use the ENTER key before you type the line of text. Each time you press ENTER when no characters appear on the Line Type Through printing screen, WordPerfect moves the paper vertically in the printer. To position the paper horizontally, use the SPACEBAR as you type a new line of text. For example, you can press the SPACEBAR ten times and then type a line of text in order to print that line starting farther to the right.

The MOVE (CTRL + F4) key recalls a line that you had just printed for editing; the edited line can then be printed again. The FORMAT (SHIFT + F8) key allows you to insert a special command to the printer before typing characters, such as a command to change to another color on a multicolored ribbon. (Printer commands are described in more detail farther on in this chapter.)

Type Through by character works in the same way, except that you have no chance to edit what you type. As soon as you press a key on the keyboard, it will be printed.

After you have finished using the Type Through feature, press the EXIT (F7) key or the CANCEL (F1) key to return to the Typing screen.

Not all printers support Type Through; if that's the case, then when you select this option, WordPerfect prompts

Feature not available on this printer

Other printers support Type Through by line but not by character. Test this feature on your printer to see whether and how it operates. (If you wish to fill out a preprinted form and your printer can't use Type Through, an alternative is to use the Advance feature, described farther on in this chapter.)

VIEW A DOCUMENT BEFORE PRINTING

The View Document feature will show you as close in appearance as possible how your document will appear on the printed page. It displays many features not shown on the Typing screen, including margins, headers, footers, page numbers, footnotes, endnotes, and right justification of your text. With monitors that have graphics capabilities, it can also display graphics images as well as various font attributes such as small caps or large print and proportional spacing (see Chapter 10). It is also a convenient way to check the layout and format of your document before you actually print.

To preview a document before printing, the document must be on screen. Position the cursor on the first page you wish to view, press the PRINT (SHIFT + F7) key and select View Document (6 or V). In moments, WordPerfect rewrites the screen, showing the full page on which your cursor is located, an example of which is shown in Figure 9-4. WordPerfect offers four options at the bottom of the View Document screen:

1 100%   2 200%   3 Full Page   4 Facing Pages: 3

For a look at a portion of the page at its actual size, enabling you to read the text, select 100% (1). For a look at a portion of the text at twice its actual size, select 200% (2). Or, for a look at an even-numbered page

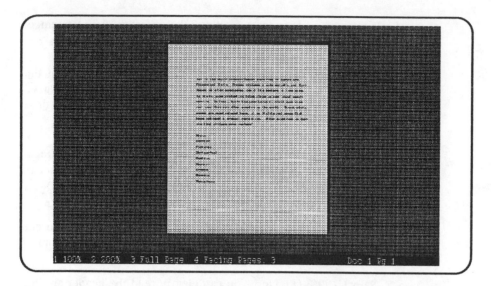

FIGURE 9-4   View Document screen showing a full page

and an odd-numbered page at the same time, select Facing Pages (4). To return to a full page look, select Full Page (3).

You can use the cursor movement keys to view a different portion of the document. For instance, if you're looking at the top portion of a page using the 100% option and wish to view the bottom portion, press HOME, DOWN ARROW or press PLUS (on the cursor movement/numeric keypad). Press DOWN ARROW to move down one line at a time. If you're looking at a full page and wish to view the next page, press PGDN. Another way to move to a specific page is to press CTRL + HOME and when WordPerfect prompts "Go to," enter a page number. The lower right corner of the screen always indicates the current page you're viewing and whether it's on the Doc 1 or Doc 2 screen.

After examining the text on the View Document screen, press the CANCEL (F1) key to return to the Print screen or press the EXIT (F7) key to return to the Typing screen.

Let's retrieve a file to the screen and then use the View Document feature.

1. Retrieve the file named SAMPLE. You worked with this document in Chapter 5 to practice features such as headers, footers, and page numbering.

2. Press the PRINT (SHIFT + F7) key.

3. Select View Document (6 or V). In moments, the View Document screen appears, as shown in Figure 9-4. The bottom of the screen indicates that you are looking at page 1 in the Doc 1 window. Notice that you can view the margins on that page.

4. Press PGDN. Now you're viewing page 2. Notice that you can see the header at the top and the page number at the bottom of the page.

5. Select 100% (1). Now you can clearly read the header and the top portion of text.

6. Press the PLUS key (+) on the cursor movement/numeric keypad. Now you can view the bottom portion of the page, which contains only a page number.

7. Select Facing Pages (4). Page 2 is now shown on the left and page 3 on the right side of the View Document screen.

8. Select Full Page (3). Page 2 is now the only text displayed.

9. Press EXIT (F7) to return to the Typing screen.

INITIALIZE YOUR PRINTER
FOR SOFT FONTS

A variety of printers allow for soft fonts, which you can use to print using fancy type styles and sizes. (See Chapter 10 for a detailed explanation of the set of characteristics that define a given font.) Soft fonts are stored on disk and must be downloaded to the printer before they can be used, which means that the instructions for how to print using those fonts is sent from disk to the printer's memory.

If you have soft fonts for your printer, you must inform Word-Perfect which ones you have available for your printer and where they are stored on disk. You can designate certain fonts as *always present* when a print job begins and other soft fonts as *available to be loaded* for a particular print job. You will find these procedures described in Appendix B.

The fonts that you designate as always present must then be downloaded the first time that you wish to use them—each time that you turn on the printer. Press the PRINT (SHIFT + F7) key and check the Print screen to see that the currently selected printer is the one that accepts soft fonts; if not, select the correct printer. Then select Initialize Printer (7 or I). WordPerfect sends a print job to the printer, which downloads the fonts; other fonts that were previously loaded into the printer's memory are erased.

TEST YOUR PRINTER CAPABILITIES

All printers are not created equal. Some can double underline and some cannot. Some can support spacing in half-line increments and some cannot. Some can support certain font changes or proportional spacing (described in the next chapter) and some cannot.

The WordPerfect package includes a file that, when printed, helps you test how WordPerfect and your printer work together. This file comes on the WordPerfect Conversion disk and is named PRINTER.TST. Figures 9-5 and 9-6 show how the two pages of this document appear when printed on an HP LaserJet Series II printer. Notice at the top half of Figure 9-5 that you can tell that the HP LaserJet supports different size attributes and the double underline (features discussed in Chapter 10). Notice at the bottom of Figure 9-5 that the LaserJet supports the Advance feature (discussed in the next section of this chapter). In Figure 9-6 notice that the LaserJet prints graphics (also discussed in Chapter 10).

Let's print this test file so that you can see whether and how various features operate on *your* printer. (The copy of PRINTER.TST on your Conversion disk may be slightly different from the one shown in Figures 9-5 and 9-6. This is because WordPerfect Corporation constantly changes the test file as it improves on the program.) You can first retrieve PRINTER.TST to the screen to examine its contents and then print. Floppy disk users should proceed as follows.

WordPerfect 5.0
Printer Test Document

In this paragraph, each word associated with a feature is printed with that feature (e.g., **bold**, ᵍᵘᵖᵉʳscript, ₛᵤᵦscript, and ~~strikeout~~). Print attributes have been expanded in WP 5.0 to include fine, small,

normal, **large**, very large, and **EXTRA LARGE** sizes of print. Some further additions to the list are _italics_, **shadow**, outline, and SMALL CAPS. The default redline method should have a shaded background or a dotted line under the characters.

If a feature described does not appear on your printout, your printer may not have that capability.

<u>Continuous</u>   <u>Double underlining</u>   Text
<u>Non-Continuous</u>   <u>Double underlining</u>   can be
<u>Continuous</u>   <u>Single underlining</u>   flush
<u>Non-Continuous</u>   <u>Single underlining</u>   right
<u>You may also choose to not underline spaces</u>

| Left | Decim.al | Center . . . . . Right |
| Tabs | T.abs | Tabs . . . . . . Tabs |

This text is left/right indented. Notice that the text is indented from both margins according to the tab settings. The indenting will continue until the "Enter" key is pressed.

(Double spacing) WordPerfect 5.0 integrates text and graphics.

A graphic image can be placed anywhere on the page. The image can

easily be scaled, moved, and rotated.

(1.5 spacing) Fonts may be mixed and changed randomly without affecting margins, tabs or column definitions.
Normal text.   Advanced up .08".   Normal text.
Normal.   Advanced down .08".
Advance can be used to SPREAD characters out, or change how they APPEAR. Back to the normal baseline.

FIGURE 9-5   Page 1 of PRINTER.TST (HP LaserJet Series II)

```
1   IMPROVED PARALLEL COLUMNS        Parallel columns now extend past a
2                                    page break.  Script writers and
3                                    others will find this feature to be
4                                    especially convenient.
5
6   MASTER DOCUMENTS                 The master document feature combines
7                                    files (e.g., chapters in a book,
8                                    files on a network) for generating
9                                    tables of contents, etc.
10
```

This paragraph is printed in 8 LPI. We can place this in eight
lines per inch by going into Shift F8 and using fixed line height.
The rest of the document's line height is fixed at 6 LPI. Already
the worlds most powerful word processor, WordPerfect continues its
tradition of excellence by adding several new features.

INTEGRATED TEXT AND GRAPHICS

The smooth integration of text and graphics in WordPerfect 5.0 makes designing newsletters, reports, and professional documents much easier. A graphic image can be scaled, moved, and rotated. You can also indicate the style and thickness of the border, and include a caption. The graphic image can be placed anywhere on the page, inserted in a line, tied to a paragraph, or included in a header or footer. The program also is shipped with a utility that allows you to capture the screen from any graphics program, converting it to a WordPerfect Graphics image file. You can then use the image within WordPerfect. This facilitates the use of various graphics programs to create graphics to be used within WordPerfect. 5.0 is designed to work with many of the most popular graphics programs available on the market. The preview feature now lets you display an entire page of text and graphics at once, zoom in for a detailed look, or view facing pages together.

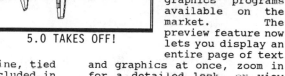

5.0 TAKES OFF!

---

[1] WordPerfect is the number 1 selling word processor in the U.S., in Canada, and in six European countries. Research estimates now show that Wordperfect sales account for approximately 40% of the market share for word processors.

Here is a test of line draw, single, double and mixed:

FIGURE 9-6   Page 2 of PRINTER.TST (HP LaserJet Series II)

1. Insert the Conversion disk in drive B.

2. Retrieve the file named PRINTER.TST.

3. Print from screen.

Hard disk users can proceed in one of two ways. If you followed the installation procedures in Appendix A, then PRINTER.TST is in the same directory as the majority of the WordPerfect files. Assume that directory is named \WPER. In that case:

1. Retrieve the file named C:\WPER\PRINTER.TST.

2. Print from screen.

Hard disk users who cannot locate the PRINTER.TST file on the hard disk can do the following instead:

1. Insert the Conversion disk in drive A.

2. Retrieve the file called A:PRINTER.TST.

3. Print from screen.

After printing the test file, you will have a great deal of knowledge of how your printer and WordPerfect work together and whether or not certain fancy printing functions are available to you.

One other way to learn more about your printer's available functions is to access the Printer Helps and Hints screen for your printer. Press the PRINT (SHIFT + F7) key and choose Select Printer (S); the menu shown in Figure 9-2 appears. Position the cursor on the name of the printer that you wish to learn more about and select Help (6 or H) from the menu at the bottom of the screen. A Printer Helps and Hints screen appears for that printer, providing you with information about how your printer and WordPerfect work together, such as what fonts aren't available, what limits the printer has on certain features, or what special print features (such as Type Through) aren't supported. The screen helps you understand more about your printer's idiosyncrasies, strengths, and limitations. After reading through the helps and hints, press EXIT (F7) or CANCEL (F1) to return to the Select Printer screen. Not all printers have a Printer Helps and Hints screen available. If not, WordPerfect displays the message "No help available."

ADVANCE THE PRINTER TO AN EXACT POSITION ON THE PAGE

The Advance feature allows you to indicate exactly where a certain section of a document should begin printing. This feature is useful as a substitute for pressing the SPACEBAR or TAB key repeatedly to position text horizontally and as a substitute for pressing the ENTER key to position text vertically. It is useful for printing on a preprinted form, for printing two sections of a document (such as a paragraph of text and a shaded graphics box) in the same location, or for spreading out characters in a title or heading.

You can use the Advance Up or Down options to position the printer vertically a certain number of inches from the current cursor position. Or use the Advance To Line option to position the printer up or down a certain number of inches from the top of the page. (Not all printers have the ability to advance back up the page.) Similarly, use the Advance Left or Right options to position the printer horizontally a certain number of inches from the current cursor position. Or use the Advance To Position option to position the printer left or right a certain number of inches from the left edge of the page.

Move the cursor just before the character or section of a document where you want the Advance feature to take effect. Press the FORMAT (SHIFT + F8) key, select Other (4 or O), and select Advance (1 or A). WordPerfect prompts with the Advance menu at the bottom of the screen:

Advance: 1 Up; 2 Down; 3 Line; 4 Left; 5 Right; 6 Position: 0

Choose an Advance option and then enter a distance. For instance, to position the printer 3 inches down from the current cursor position, select Down (2 or D), type 3, and press ENTER. Or, to position the printer 0.5 inch down from the top of the page, select Line (3 or I), type .5, and press ENTER. Then press EXIT (F7) to return to the Typing screen.

WordPerfect inserts an Advance code at the current cursor position. The code indicates the Advance option you selected, as well as the measurement that you specified. Here are examples for all six Advance options: **[AdvUp:3"] [AdvDn:1.5"] [AdvToLn:4.16"] [AdvLft:2"] [AdvRgt:2"] [AdvToPos:.5"]**. Text that follows such a code will be printed at the location specified in the code.

The cursor will not change its position on the screen following an Advance code. The status line, however, will reflect the change. For instance, suppose that in the middle of the line that is 5 inches from the top of the page, you insert a code to advance down 1.5 inches. The code inserted would be [**AdvDn:1.5"**]. With the cursor just after the code, the status line will read

Doc 1 Pg 1 Ln 6.5" Pos 1"

If you press LEFT ARROW to move just before the Advance Down code, the status line will read

Doc 1 Pg 1 Ln 5" Pos 1"

There would be no extra space between the two parts of the line on the Typing screen, but the status line would inform you that once the document is printed, there will be 1.5 inches between the two halves of the line. If you preview your document using the View Document feature, you will be able to see where on the page your text will print.

The Advance feature is often used to position text that will be inserted on a preprinted form. You must first use a ruler to measure exactly where on the form the blanks you wish to fill in are located. As you type the information, use the Advance feature to position the information on the blank lines.

For instance, suppose you wish to print a person's name in the blank line provided on a preprinted form. You measure the form to discover that in order to sit on the blank line the name must be printed 4 inches in from the left edge and 3.5 inches down from the top of the page. (When you measure from the top of the page, keep in mind that you should measure down to where the *top of the line* will be printed and not to its baseline.) Position the cursor where you are about to type the person's name. Use the Advance to Position option and enter a measurement of 4. Then, use the Advance to Line option and enter a measurement of 3.5. Now type in the person's name. When you insert the preprinted form and print, the person's name should fill in the appropriate blank.

A similar application involves letterhead. When you type a letter, the first page is often printed on letterhead, while the following pages are printed on blank sheets of the same paper stock. You can use the Advance feature to position the first page of the letter below the letterhead logo.

For instance, suppose that your letterhead logo occupies the first 2 inches of a page. You want an additional 0.5 inch of white space between the logo and the first line of a letter you are about to print. Proceed as follows to start the letter 2.5 inches from the top of the page:

1. Clear the Typing screen and retrieve the file named LETTER.

2. Position the cursor at the top of the document.

3. Press the FORMAT (SHIFT + F8) key to display the Format menu.

4. Select Other (4 or O). The Other Format menu appears.

5. Select Advance (1 or A). The following appears at the bottom of the screen:

   Advance: 1 Up; 2 _Down; 3 L_ine; 4 _Left; 5 _Right; 6 _Position: 0

6. Select Line (3 or L). WordPerfect prompts

   Adv. to line 1"

   This means that the cursor is currently at line 1", which is the current top margin.

7. Type **2.5** and press ENTER.

8. Press EXIT (F7) to return to the document. Notice that the status line now indicates that this line of text will print on Ln 2.5". This is because of the **[AdvToLn:2.5"]** code you inserted.

You can print out this document to see that, in fact, it will begin 2.5 inches from the top of the form.

NUMBER LINES AT THE PRINTER

WordPerfect offers the ability to print line numbers on a page. If you've already printed out the file named PRINTER.TST, then, depending on the contents of your file, you may see an example of the Line Numbering feature in action, as shown at the top of Figure 9-6. Line numbering is common in legal documents and can be used to create the same effect as legal pleading paper. It can also be useful for when you distribute handouts and wish to call attention to a specific

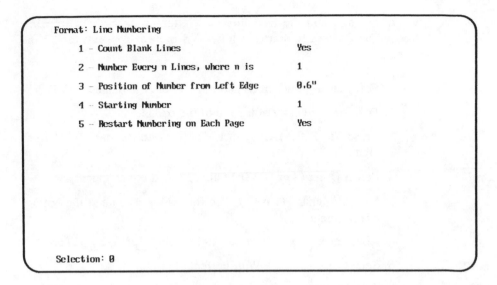

```
Format: Line Numbering
     1 - Count Blank Lines                    Yes
     2 - Number Every n Lines, where n is     1
     3 - Position of Number from Left Edge    0.6"
     4 - Starting Number                      1
     5 - Restart Numbering on Each Page       Yes




Selection: 0
```

FIGURE 9-7 Line Numbering menu

line. For example, you could say, "Please turn your attention to the sentence on line ten."

To insert line numbers, position the cursor at the left margin of the line where you want line numbering to begin. Then press the FORMAT (SHIFT + F8) key, select Line Format (1 or L), and select Line Numbering (5 or N). Type **Y** to turn line numbering on or type **N** to turn it off. If you turn the feature on, then the Line Numbering menu appears, as shown in Figure 9-7. As shown in Figure 9-7, the Line Numbering feature is preset with a variety of defaults that determine how the numbers appear:

- Blank lines are included in the line count and are numbered. To exclude blank lines from the line count, select Count Blank Lines (1 or C) and type **N**.

- A number is printed on every line. If you wish to print numbers in other increments, select Number Every n Lines (2 or N) and enter an increment. For instance, to number every other line, type **2** and press ENTER.

- The line numbers are positioned 0.6 inch from the left edge of the page. You can select another position by selecting Position of Number from Left Edge (3 or P) and entering a measurement. For instance, to position the numbers 0.5 inch from the left edge, type .5 and press ENTER.

- The numbering starts at 1. If you want to start numbering with another number, select Starting Number (4 or S) and enter in the new starting number.

- The numbering restarts at 1 on every page. If you want the numbering to continue—so that, for example, if page 1 ended at line 56, page 2 will begin at line 57—select Restart Numbering on Each Page (5 or R) and type N.

Once you've made selections on this menu, press EXIT (F7) to return to your document. A [LnNum:On] code is inserted into the text when you turn the feature on. Conversely, a [LnNum:Off] code is inserted if the feature had been on and you are now turning it off.

Line numbers appear on the printed page but not on the Typing screen. The feature will display on your screen, however, if you use the View Document feature.

Be aware that line numbering is dependent on the line spacing selection. For instance, when a document is double-spaced, then line numbers are also double-spaced. If you want line numbering to be in one spacing even if the text of the document is in another, then print the line numbers first; that is, insert hard returns all the way down a page, insert a Line Numbering code at the top of the page, and print. Then reinsert the same page to print out the document. (If you wish to create legal pleading paper, you can also insert a vertical graphics line down the left margin of the page next to the line numbers, as described in Chapter 10.)

INSERT PRINTER COMMANDS

There may be features that your printer supports but that you cannot access by any of the methods discussed so far. WordPerfect allows you to send special commands to your printer to tap such features. You must find these commands in your printer manual. They will be numbers, letters, or a combination of numbers and letters, where the numbers are surrounded by angle brackets <>. Most printer commands start with the ESCAPE control code; in that case, the first part of the command will be <27>. Thus, a printer command for your printer may be <27>A or <27><15>.

To insert a printer command into the text, position the cursor where you want the command to take effect. Then press the FORMAT (SHIFT + F8) key, select Other (4 or O), select Printer Functions (6 or P), and select Printer Command (2 or P). WordPerfect prompts

1 Command; 2 Filename: 0

Select Command (1 or C) and enter the command. Or you can create a file on disk that contains printer commands, in which case you would then select Filename (2 or F) and enter in the correct filename. Word-Perfect inserts a hidden code in the text, such as [PtrCmnd:<27>A]. During printing this code will be sent to the printer.

Needless to say, you must rely on your printer manual to tell you the right command. In general, unless your printer has a capability that you're not able to access using WordPerfect codes, there's no need to employ this feature.

REVIEW EXERCISE

Many of the features explained in this chapter depend on your printer's capabilities. Certain other features, such as Number of Copies, should work no matter what type of printer you use and no matter how many printers are attached to your computer.

1. Retrieve the file named FINANCE to a clear Typing screen.

2. Print three copies of the document in one print job. (*Hint:* Set the Number of Copies option on the Print screen to 3 before sending the print job to the printer.)

3. Reset the Number of Copies option on the Print screen back to 1; otherwise you'll get three copies of everything you print until the next time you reload WordPerfect.

4. Insert line numbers so that only lines containing text are numbered. (*Hint:* On the Line Numbering menu, change the Count Blank Lines option to "No.")

5. Use the View Document feature to preview how the document will appear when printed. (Your printer may not support line numbering.)

6. Print the file named FINANCE to see line numbers on the printed page.

7. Save this document to disk and clear the screen.

REVIEW

- Features under the heading "Options" on the Print screen allow you to change WordPerfect's assumptions for each print job. The Select Printer option allows you to select a different printer for a document; the current printer selection is always saved with a document. The Binding option establishes a binding width for binding a document like a book. The Number of Copies option allows you to produce multiple copies of a print job. The Graphics/Text Quality options determine the quality used to print out text and graphics. If you alter a print option for a particular print job, remember to return it to the previous setting once the print job is complete unless you want to maintain that new setting for future print jobs.

- Use your computer like a typewriter with the Type Through feature. You can direct the printer to print a character as you type it or print a line as you complete it. This can be convenient for filling out preprinted forms. Be aware, however, that many printers do not support this feature.

- The View Document feature allows you to preview how a document will appear on the printed page. It displays features that don't appear on the Typing screen, such as margins, headers, footers, and page numbers. By using the View Document feature regularly, you can save on the cost of paper and printer ribbons, printing out a document only when you know it will print with the formatting specifications you want.

- If you use soft fonts, you must initialize your printer in order to use those fonts defined as initially present in your printer.

- You can print a file named PRINTER.TST to test how WordPerfect and your printer work together to produce special print features like different type sizes, double underlining, and graphics printing.

- WordPerfect provides a Hints and Help screen for certain printers, which will explain certain limitations in how your printer works with WordPerfect. This screen is accessed via the Print screen.

- With the Advance feature, you can position the printer at an exact horizontal or vertical position on the page. This is useful for positioning text on preprinted forms or for spreading out characters in a heading.

- The Line Numbering feature, available on the Line Format menu, numbers lines in the left margin. It can be used, for example, to create legal pleading paper.

- If WordPerfect does not directly support a feature available on your printer, you can insert a printer command into a document to activate that feature. The Printer Command feature is accessed via the Other Format menu.

10

CHANGING FONTS AND INSERTING GRAPHICS FOR DESKTOP PUBLISHING

Modify the Initial or Base Font
Modify a Font Attribute
Adjust the Character Spacing
Insert Graphics Lines
Insert Graphics Boxes
Edit Graphics Boxes
Change Graphics Box Default Options
Review Exercise
Review

With the advent of desktop publishing, computers have created a publishing revolution. Desktop publishing is the ability to control the writing and publishing process using the computer equipment that sits on your desk. You will be interested in WordPerfect's desktop publishing abilities if, instead of sending your text to a designer, typesetter, and printer, you want to produce newsletters, business reports, company publications, or manuals by yourself.

This chapter describes the features that WordPerfect offers in order to undertake desktop publishing. You'll learn how to print characters using fancy fonts. For instance, you can print all headings in a large type size and in italics, while printing the main body of the text in a smaller type size, with a Courier typeface and proportional spacing. Font changes offer true sophistication in enhancing different sections of your text and giving your documents a slick, professional look.

You'll also insert graphics into your documents. With Word-Perfect, you can effectively merge pictures with text—such as inserting a map of the United States near a discussion of the R&R Wine Association's national growth. And you can insert graphics lines or shaded boxes in your text to emphasize certain sections of text.

Be aware that the desktop features available to you depend on the capabilities of your printer. Laser printers usually offer the most features for desktop publishing; they can produce printed documents of nearly typeset quality using a variety of fancy fonts and can print graphics of good quality.

MODIFY THE INITIAL OR BASE FONT

In WordPerfect, a font is a set of attributes that defines how text will print, as shown in Figure 10-1. These attributes include

- *Typeface*   This is the style of the characters, such as Courier, Times Roman, Presentation, or Helvetica.

- *Pitch*   This is the density of characters per inch (CPI) on a line. The larger the pitch size, the smaller or more tightly packed the character; for instance, a pitch of 10 CPI means that 10 characters fit in 1 inch of vertical space on a page, while a pitch of 12 CPI means that 12 characters are squeezed into that same inch. The smaller the pitch, the wider or farther apart the characters. Standard text usually prints in 10, 11 or 12 pitch.

- *Horizontal spacing*   This is how characters are spaced on a line. *Monospacing* means that each character occupies the same amount of space. *Proportional spacing* means that each character occupies a different amount of space in proportion to its width, so that a narrow letter like "i" is alloted less space on the page than a wide letter like "w." Proportional spacing gives documents a more typeset look.

Courier typeface, monospaced, pitch of 10 CPI, type size of 12-point.   Courier is the most common typeface.

Times Roman typeface, proportionally spaced. Proportional spacing provides a more professional look to the text.

Times Roman typeface, proportionally spaced, with italics appearance. Italics means that letters are slanted to provide a cursive effect.

PRESENTATION TYPEFACE, BOLDFACE APPEARANCE, PITCH OF 10 CPI, TYPE SIZE OF 14-POINT. NOTICE THAT THE INCREASE IN TYPE SIZE RESULTS IN A TALLER CHARACTER.

PRESENTATION TYPEFACE, BOLDFACE APPEARANCE, PITCH OF 6.5 CPI, TYPE SIZE OF 18-POINT. NOTICE THAT THE ADDITIONAL INCREASE IN TYPE SIZE RESULTS IN A STILL TALLER CHARACTER. ALSO, THE DECREASE IN PITCH MEANS THAT FEWER CHARACTERS CAN FIT ON EACH LINE.

FIGURE 10-1   Examples of different fonts

- *Type style or appearance*   This is the specific style of characters to add emphasis or contrast, such as italics, boldface, shadow, or small caps. The style applies for a particular typeface.

- *Character set*   This is the collection of symbols and characters that can be printed in the selected font, such as Roman Eight, Legal, or Math.

- *Type size*   This is the size or height of characters, typically measured in points, where approximately 72 points equal 1 vertical inch. Standard text usually prints in type sizes of 8, 10, or 12 points.

At installation an *initial font* is assigned to each printer. (The process for defining printers, as well as for establishing the initial font for a particular printer, is described in Appendix B.)

You are not limited to using the initial font, however. Most printers offer a variety of font options. Some printers have many different fonts built in. With other printers, you can have access to more fonts by purchasing printer extras. For instance, most laser printers allow you to insert cartridges containing additional fonts. Laser printers also allow for soft fonts, which are fonts stored on disk that must be read by the printer (downloaded) before they can be used.

Note: If you acquire additional cartridges or soft fonts for your printer, you must inform WordPerfect before you attempt to use them by redefining your printer; refer to Appendix B for details. Moreover, before printing a document that uses soft fonts, you must initialize your printer, which means that WordPerfect will download the fonts to your printer so that they will be available for use; refer to the "Initialize Your Printer for Soft Fonts" section in Chapter 9 for details.

For laser printer users, your alternative font options also depend on the paper size and type you are using. If WordPerfect assumes that you will print the characters parallel to how the paper is inserted into the printer (portrait mode), then only the fonts that print in portrait mode are available. If you insert a Paper Size/Type code so that the characters print perpendicular to how the paper is inserted into the printer (landscape mode), then only the fonts that print in landscape mode are available.

For each document, you can ascertain a document's initial font, display a list of other fonts available, and/or change the initial font. With the document on screen, press the FORMAT (SHIFT + F8) key and select Document Format (3 or D). The Document Format menu, as shown in Figure 10-2, appears. Next to the heading Initial Font, Word-Perfect indicates the initial font for your document. If you wish to retain that initial font, simply press CANCEL (F1) until you return to the Typing screen. If you wish to change the initial font, select Initial Font (3 or F) from the Document Format menu. A screen appears listing the available fonts for your printer; an example for the HP LaserJet Series II (with several cartridges defined) is shown in Figure 10-3. WordPerfect displays an asterisk next to the currently selected initial font. Position the cursor on the font you wish to select either by using the cursor movement keys (such as DOWN ARROW and PGDN) or by typing N to select the Name Search option, typing the first few letters of the font name until the cursor moves to that font, and pressing ENTER. Now choose Select (1 or S). You are returned to the Document Format screen, where your new font selection is now indicated next to "Initial Font."

When you alter the initial font, WordPerfect assumes the change begins at the top of the document and will affect not only the main body of text, but also headers, footers, endnotes, and footnotes. No

```
Format: Document

    1 - Display Pitch - Automatic        Yes
                        Width            8.1"

    2 - Initial Codes

    3 - Initial Font                     Courier 18 pitch (PC-8)

    4 - Redline Method                   Printer Dependent

    5 - Summary




Selection: 8
```

FIGURE 10-2   Document Format menu

```
Document: Initial Font

* Courier 10 pitch (PC-8)
  Courier 10 pitch (Roman 8/ECMn)
  Courier Bold 10 pitch (PC-8)
  Courier Bold 10 pitch (Roman 8/ECMn)
  Helv 14.4pt Bold (B)
  Letter Gothic 14pt 10 pitch (Legal) (R)
  Letter Gothic 14pt 10 pitch (R)
  Line Draw (R)
  Line Draw 10 pitch
  Line Printer 16.66 pitch (PC-8)
  Line Printer 16.66 pitch (Roman-8/ECMn)
  PC Line Draw (R)
  Presentation 14pt Bold 10 pitch (Legal) (R)
  Presentation 14pt Bold 10 pitch (R)
  Presentation 16pt Bold 8.1 pitch (Legal) (R)
  Presentation 16pt Bold 8.1 pitch (R)
  Presentation 18pt Bold 6.5 pitch (Legal) (R)
  Presentation 18pt Bold 6.5 pitch (R)
  Solid Line Draw 10 pitch
  Tms Rmn 08pt (B)
  Tms Rmn 10pt (B)

1 Select: N Name search: 1
```

FIGURE 10-3   A Document Initial Font screen for the HP LaserJet Series II and several cartridges

code is inserted in the text. If you change your mind and wish to select a different initial font, you must again return to the Initial Font screen.

In addition to changing the font starting at the top of a document, you can also change a font for a specific section of your document. When you do so, you are altering the *base font* of your document. The procedure is quite different from the method for altering the initial font. First, you must position the cursor wherever you want the font change to take effect. For instance, if you want the change to start on page 2, position the cursor at the top of page 2. Press the FONT (CTRL + F8) key. WordPerfect displays the Font menu:

1 Size; **2** Appearance; **3** Normal; **4** Base Font; **5** Print Color: **0**

Select Base Font (4 or F). WordPerfect displays the Base Font screen, listing the available fonts for your printer. This screen is identical to the Document Initial Font screen for a given printer, except that the top of the screen reads "Base Font" rather than "Document: Initial Font." An asterisk appears next to the currently selected font. To change that font, position the cursor on the font you wish to select either by using the cursor movement keys (such as DOWN ARROW and PGDN) or by typing **N** to select the Name Search option, typing the first few letters of the font name until the cursor moves to that font, and pressing ENTER. Now choose Select (1 or S). You are returned to the Typing screen.

You can alter the base font as many times as you desire in the same document. Each time, WordPerfect inserts a Font code at the current cursor position. For instance, suppose that your printer has available the Times Roman, 10-point font, which you select. The following font code is inserted: **[Font:Tms Rmn 10pt]**. The font change occurs following that hidden code until the end of the document or until another Font code inserted farther forward in the text.

A base font change will affect the main body of the text and Header and Footer codes that follow the Base Font code. If you change your mind and decide to cancel the base font change, then erase the hidden font code—in the same way you would erase a format code, such as a Margin or Tab Set code.

When you change your initial or base font, the characters on screen will appear the same, but line and page breaks may readjust if the font's pitch, horizontal spacing, and/or type size changes. For instance, suppose you change from a font with a pitch of 10 CPI to a font with a pitch of 12 CPI. Now more characters can fit on a line when printed, so the Soft Return codes at the end of lines readjust. In fact, you may no longer be able to see a full line of text at one time across the width of your screen, but will need to press HOME, RIGHT ARROW to view the end of the line. (Refer to Chapter 5 for more on moving the cursor when lines are long.) The document becomes shorter as soft page breaks readjust. Conversely, if you change to a pitch of 6.5 CPI, then fewer characters can fit on a line and on each page; the length of each line may extend only halfway across the width of the screen.

As another example, suppose that you change from a font with a type size of 12 points to a font of 18 points. Since the characters will now be taller when printed, WordPerfect automatically adjusts the height of each line of text. Fewer lines can fit on a page, so page breaks readjust. (Line height is discussed in more detail farther on in this chapter.)

Let's retrieve a document and then change the font for the middle portion. Since we will make a font change starting somewhere other than at the top of the document, we'll use the FONT key to make the change.

1. On a clear screen, retrieve the file named FINANCE.

2. Position the cursor on the blank line above the first bulleted paragraph.

3. Press the FONT (CTRL + F8) key. WordPerfect displays the Font menu:

   1 _Size; 2 _Appearance; 3 _Normal; 4 Base _Font; 5 Print _Color: **0**

4. Select Base Font (4 or F). WordPerfect displays a Base Font screen, which lists the available fonts for your printer. An asterisk appears next to the font assumed for your printer. Notice the name of the initial font that WordPerfect assumes for your printer.

5. Use the DOWN ARROW key and position the cursor on any other font selection of your choosing.

6. Choose Select (1 or S) to select that font. You are now returned to the Typing screen. If your font change resulted in a different pitch or type size, then when you move the cursor, Word-Perfect rewrites the screen, readjusting the line and page breaks for text below that code on screen. If you reveal codes, you can view the Font code you just inserted.

7. To return the bottom portion of the document to the initial font, position the cursor on the blank line below the second bulleted paragraph, and repeat steps 3 through 6, but this time selecting the initial font.

If you reveal codes, you can view the Font codes that you just inserted.

WordPerfect will again readjust the text if your font change resulted in a different pitch or type size. In fact, you may find that your margins on screen appear quite different in the middle of the document, where the font change has an effect. Remember that this is because WordPerfect is showing you how many characters will actually fit across each line when the document is printed using the font selected. You may wish to manually readjust text based on the new font changes. When you print out this document, you can see the font change take effect for the middle portion of the text.

You learned in Chapter 9 that you can select a new printer for a document at any time. When you select a different printer for a document that contains a Font change code, WordPerfect selects a font available for the newly selected printer that most closely matches the font for the previous printer.

MODIFY A FONT ATTRIBUTE

To add emphasis to a section of text, you can alter one or more attributes of a font for that section without actually asking WordPerfect to change the font itself. In WordPerfect, there are two categories of font attributes that you can control for each font.

The first attribute relates to a font's type size. Each font is assigned a specific normal size. You can instead select fine, the smallest type size for a given font; small, slightly smaller than the normal size; large, slightly larger than the normal size; very large, slightly larger than the large size; or extra large, the largest type size for a given font. Here's an example of different size changes using the same font.

This is normal size, while this is small.

This is large, AND THIS IS EXTRA LARGE.

(As you can see, changing the type size may sometimes result in a typeface change as well.)

Also within the size category are superscript and subscript, which position characters slightly above or below the normal line of text.

Superscript moves $^{\text{characters up}}$ in a line.
Subscript moves $_{\text{characters down}}$ in a line.

Superscript and subscript come in handy when typing scientific or mathematical information, such as X^{14} or H_2O. (Superscript is automatically used to denote footnotes, as described in Chapter 12.)

The second attribute you can control relates to a font's appearance or typestyle. Each font is assigned a normal appearance. You can instead select italics, where characters are slanted to provide a cursive effect; outline, where characters appear as white and outlined in black; shadow, where characters are printed twice, one slightly to the right of the other to produce a shadow effect; small caps, where characters are lowercase letters printed as if in uppercase, but smaller in size; redline, where characters are marked either with a shaded background, a dotted line under the characters, a vertical bar in the left margin, or in a different color; strikeout, where a solid or dashed line is printed through the characters; bold; underline; and double underline. Here's an example of different styles using the same font:

This is normal, **while this is shadow print.**
THIS IS SMALL CAPS, this is redline, and this
is strikeout. **Bold.** Underline.   Double underline.

(Bold and underline can also be inserted in your text using the BOLD (F6) and UNDERLINE (F8) keys; refer to Chapter 3 for a review of the quick methods for enhancing text with bold or underline. Redline and strikeout can also be inserted with the Compare Document feature, where the screen and disk versions of a document are compared; refer to Chapter 6 for a review of this feature.

To alter an attribute as you type, position the cursor where you want a change in size or appearance to occur and press the FONT (CTRL + F8) key. The Font menu appears:

1 Size; 2 Appearance; 3 Normal; 4 Base Font; 5 Print Color: 0

If you select Size (1 or S), the following menu appears:

1 Suprscpt; 2 Subscpt; 3 Fine; 4 Small; 5 Large; 6 Vry Large;
7 Ext Large: 0

If you select Appearance (2 or A) from the Font menu, this menu appears:

1 Bold; 2 Undrln; 3 Dbl Und; 4 Italc; 5 Outln; 6 Shadw; 7 Sm Cap;
8 Redln; 9 Stkout: 0

Select a size or appearance attribute. Now type the text that you want enhanced with that attribute.

As a final step, you must turn off the special font attribute. You can do so in several ways. One method is to again press the FONT (CTRL + F8) key, select Size (1 or S) or Appearance (2 or A), and then select the attribute again to turn it off. A second method is to simply press the RIGHT ARROW key, which positions the cursor outside the Attribute code. A third method is useful if you have turned on more than one attribute. For instance, perhaps you turned on large size, italics, and boldface. To turn off all three attributes at once, press the FONT (CTRL + F8) key and then select Normal (3 or N). This turns off all attributes for the font, returning it to normal.

To change a font attribute for text you've already typed, use the BLOCK (ALT + F4) key to highlight the portion of text you wish to affect. Then, with **Block on** flashing, press the FONT (CTRL + F8) key. With Block on, WordPerfect displays a special attribute menu:

Attribute: 1 Size; 2 Appearance: 0

Select Size (1 or S) or Appearance (2 or A), and then select the attribute you desire. WordPerfect activates the feature for just the highlighted text and turns Block off automatically.

WordPerfect surrounds the text designated for a different size or appearance attribute with a pair of codes. An On code precedes the text and an Off code follows the text. The codes are

Size Attribute Codes	Appearance Attribute Codes
[SUPRSCPT] [suprscpt]	[BOLD] [bold]
[SUBSCPT] [subscpt]	[UND] [und]
[FINE] [fine]	[DBL UND] [dbl und]
[SMALL] [small]	[ITALC] [italc]
[LARGE] [large]	[OUTLN] [outln]
[VRY LARGE] [vry large]	[SHADW] [shadw]
[EXT LARGE] [ext large]	[SM CAP] [sm cap]
	[REDLN] [redln]
	[STKOUT] [stkout]

How each of these attributes appears on your Typing screen depends on your monitor. On a monochrome monitor, each of the attribute changes may appear brighter than the rest of the text, underlined, highlighted, or blinking. On a color monitor, the attribute changes may appear in a different color. Also, if your computer is equipped with a Ramfont graphics card, then you'll actually be able to view attributes such as italics and different-sized characters right on screen.

Note: With WordPerfect you can change the way that text with font attribute enhancements is displayed on the Typing screen. Refer to the "Display" section of Appendix C for more details.

How each of these attributes appears on the printed page depends on the printer you're using and the currently active font. Font size and appearance attributes are variations of the *current* font. It is often the case that for a particular font, not all the attributes are available on your printer. For instance, for a particular font, different sizes of print and italics may be available, but not shadow, outline, or small caps. You must test these attributes for each font to see what's available.

You can discover which attributes are available on your printer in several ways. One option is to print the printer test document stored on disk under the filename PRINTER.TST. In Chapter 9, you printed PRINTER.TST for the default initial font. Now that you know about font changes, you should print PRINTER.TST for each of the other fonts available for your printer. In other words, retrieve and print PRINTER.TST, change the initial font and print it again, and so on. Another option is to create your own test file. Type some sentences selecting different attributes. Then print that text using different initial fonts.

You may discover that your printer doesn't support certain attributes at all. For instance, some printers don't support double underlining. Others won't support italics, in which case text marked for italics will instead be underlined by the printer.

With the redline attribute, you have a choice as to how the redline marks appear on the printed page. Redline is set up as printer dependent. Once you print PRINTER.TST or a document that includes Redline codes, you'll uncover the default option. You can instead select that redline print as a certain character in the left margin. Or you can select that redline print as a certain character in alternating margins—in the left margin of odd pages and in the right margin of even pages. To change the current method of redline printing for a specific document, make sure that the document is on screen. The cursor can be positioned anywhere. Press the FORMAT (SHIFT + F8) key and select Document (3 or D). The Document Format menu appears as shown in Figure 10-2. Notice that the redline method is "Printer Dependent." Select Redline Method (4 or R), and WordPerfect displays a redline menu:

Redline Method: 1 Printer Dependent; **2** Left; **3** Alternating: **0**

If you select Left (2 or L) or Alternating (3 or A), WordPerfect prompts for the character to be used as the redline character, suggesting the ¦ symbol. Press ENTER to accept that symbol or enter one of your own. Press EXIT (F7) to return to the Typing screen.

If you have a printer that prints in color, you can enhance text not only by changing a font attribute, but by altering the color of text as well. To print in a specified color, position the cursor where you want the color change to take effect in your document. Press the FONT (CTRL + F8) key and then select Print Color (5 or C). The menu shown in Figure 10-4 appears. Select a color option from the 11 predefined colors or create a color of your own by selecting Other (O) and entering the new intensity percentage for red, green, and blue in the three columns on screen. Check your color printer manual to see which colors are supported.

Here's some practice changing font attributes for the document named FINANCE, which is currently on screen. We'll change the font attributes for text already typed and for text as we type.

```
Print Color

                        Primary Color Mixture
                        Red     Green     Blue

        1 - Black        0%       0%       0%
        2 - White      100%     100%     100%
        3 - Red         67%       0%       0%
        4 - Green        0%      67%       0%
        5 - Blue         0%       0%      67%
        6 - Yellow      67%      67%       0%
        7 - Magenta     67%       0%      67%
        8 - Cyan         0%      67%      67%
        9 - Orange      67%      25%       0%
        A - Gray        50%      50%      50%
        N - Brown       67%      33%       0%
        0 - Other

        Current Color    0%       0%       0%


    Selection: 0
```

FIGURE 10-4 Print Color menu

1. Use the BLOCK (ALT + F4) key to highlight the words "venture capitalist," located in the first bulleted paragraph.

2. With Block on, press the FONT (CTRL + F8) key. WordPerfect prompts

   Attribute: 1 Size; 2 Appearance: 0

3. Select Appearance (2 or A). The following menu appears:

   1 Bold; 2 Undrln; 3 Dbl Und; 4 Italc; 5 Outln; 6 Shadw; 7 Sm Cap; 8 Redln; 9 Stkout: 0

4. Select Italics (4 or I). A hidden Italics On code is placed to the left of the block, and an Italics Off code is placed to the right of the block. How italics displays on your screen depends on your monitor.

5. Position the cursor just to the right of the last line in the document.

6. Press the FONT (CTRL + F8) key. With Block off, WordPerfect displays the Font menu:

   1 Size; 2 Appearance; 3 Normal; 4 Base Font; 5 Print Color: 0

7. Select Size (1 or S). The following menu appears:

   1 Suprscpt; 2 Subscpt; 3 Fine; 4 Small; 5 Large; 6 Vry Large; 7 Ext Large: 0

8. Select Small (4 or S).

9. Type the following text:

   He will be sending you a memo regarding his meeting with the

10. Press RIGHT ARROW to end the small-size attribute.

11. Press the FONT (CTRL + F8) key.

12. Select Appearance (2 or A).

13. Select Italics (4 or I).

14. Type **venture capitalist**.

15. Press RIGHT ARROW to end the italics.

16. Press the FONT (CTRL + F8) key.

17. Select Size (1 or S).

18. Select Small (4 or S).

19. To end the sentence, type **by next Friday**.

You have inserted the italic and small-size attributes into your document. You can print the document to see how the attributes will take effect at the printer. An example is shown in Figure 10-5. If you have a monitor with graphics capabilities, you can also use the View Document feature (discussed in Chapter 9) to preview how the font changes and font attribute changes will appear on the printed page before you actually print.

Keep in mind that a font attribute is based on the currently selected font. Therefore, an attribute for one font may appear different than the same attribute for another font. For example, Figure 10-5 shows a printout of FINANCE on an HP LaserJet Series II printer. The bulleted items were printed using a font different from the font used in the rest of the document. Notice that in the first bulleted item, italics for the words "venture capitalist" appear as italics. However, notice that in the last sentence, italics for the words "venture capitalist" appear as underlined text. The italics attribute has a completely different effect depending on the current font.

I spoke to John Samsone on January 3rd about our financial situation. He reported the following highlights:

o   He is meeting with a *venture capitalist* next week who is interested in investing with us.

o   Our debt stands at $159,000 as of December 31st, 10% lower than we anticipated. Financial forecasts project that we'll be out of debt in two years time. Here are the debt figures (in thousands):

Amount Owed	Name of Bank
$48.5	Floyd Interstate
9.8	Center Bank
100.7	Bank of Stevenson

For more detail, call John at (415) 333-9215. He will be sending you a memo regarding his meeting with the venture capitalist by next Friday.

FIGURE 10-5   Printout of FINANCE showing different font changes and font attribute changes

ADJUST THE CHARACTER SPACING

Once you've selected different fonts and font attributes for your text, WordPerfect also offers the ability to refine the spacing between characters and between lines of text. The features available include Line Height, Kerning, Word and Letter Spacing, and Word Spacing Justification Limits. Keep in mind that these features are available to you only if supported by your printer.

Line Height

Line height (also referred to as leading) is the amount of vertical space alloted to each line, measured from the bottom (baseline) of one line to the bottom of the next. WordPerfect assigns a line-height measurement to each font and each font attribute available for your printer. As an example, when you are using a font with the standard type size of 12 points, most printers are assigned a line height equal to approximately 0.16 inch, so that there are six lines of text to one vertical inch of space on a page.

By default, line height is set automatically, meaning it changes for each new font or font attribute in your text. You can also request that your line height be evenly spaced regardless of the fonts or attributes you are using. Move the cursor to where you want to change the line-height setting. Press the FORMAT (SHIFT + F8) key and select Line (1 or L) to display the Line Format menu. Next to the heading "Line Height," WordPerfect indicates the default setting, which is Auto (automatic). Select Line Height (4 or H) and WordPerfect offers two choices:

1 Auto; 2 Fixed: 0

Select Auto (1 or A) and WordPerfect inserts a Line Height code [Ln Height:Auto] that returns line height to the default setting from the cursor position forward in the document. Or select Fixed (2 or F) and WordPerfect displays the current line height, such as 0.16". Press ENTER to accept that suggestion or type in a line-height setting of your own and press ENTER. WordPerfect inserts a Line Height code that indicates the new measurement, such as [Ln Height:0.2"]. Press EXIT (F7) to return to the Typing screen.

Kerning

Kerning allows for reduction in the space between specific pairs of letters. It is commonly used in large-sized fonts to eliminate excessive white space between letters such as the space between the "A" and "V" in "BRAVE." Kerning often makes it easier to read a heading. Be aware, however, that kerning may or may not be available for fonts used with your printer. You can turn on kerning and then print your document to see whether or not it is supported.

Should you wish to attempt kerning, position the cursor where you want the kerning to begin, press the FORMAT (SHIFT + F8) key, select Other (4 or O), and then select Printer Functions (6 or P). The Printer Functions menu appears as shown in Figure 10-6. Select Kerning (1 or K) and then type either **Y** to turn it on or **N** to turn it off. A **[Kern:On]** or **[Kern:Off]** code is inserted at the current cursor position, affecting text from that point forward (assuming that kerning is supported for your printer and the font you're using).

```
Format: Printer Functions

    1 - Kerning                            No

    2 - Printer Command

    3 - Word Spacing                       Optimal
        Letter Spacing                     Optimal

    4 - Word Spacing Justification Limits
        Compressed to (0% - 100%)          60%
        Expanded to (100% - unlimited)     400%




Selection: 0
```

FIGURE 10-6   Printer Functions menu

Word and Letter Spacing

The Word and Letter Spacing feature adjusts the spacing between neighboring words and letters. WordPerfect Corporation has set what it considers to be the optimal spacing between words and letters for each font available with your printer. However, if your printer supports this feature, you can adjust the spacing yourself.

Position the cursor where you want the change in word and/or letter spacing to begin, press the FORMAT (SHIFT + F8) key, select Other (4 or O), and then select Printer functions (6 or P). As shown in Figure 10-6, the default setting is for "Optimal" word and letter spacing. Select Word and Letter Spacing (3 or W) and WordPerfect displays the following menu:

Word Spacing; 1 Normal; 2 Optimal; 3 Percent of Optimal;
4 Set Pitch: 2

In addition to Optimal, your options are Normal, the spacing that looks best according to the printer manufacturer (which, for some printers, is the same as the Optimal setting); Percent of Optimal, which allows you to set your own spacing—100% is comparable to using the Optimal setting, so that numbers less than 100% reduce the space and numbers greater than 100% increase the space; and Set Pitch, which allows you to set spacing at an exact pitch, such as 10 or 12 characters per inch. The pitch setting is then converted by WordPerfect to a percentage of the Optimal setting.

Select an option and, if you selected options 3 or 4, enter in a word spacing measurement. WordPerfect then displays an identical menu for letter spacing. Again select an option and enter a letter spacing measurement if prompted to do so. Now press EXIT (F7) to return to your document.

WordPerfect inserts a code at the current cursor position, such as **[Wrd/Ltr Spacing:Normal,Normal]**, which affects all text from that code forward. You can now print your document to view the result.

Word Spacing Justification Limits

If your document is set with justification on, then WordPerfect assumes that the space between words can be compressed by 60% or expanded by 400% to produce an even right margin. (Refer to Chapter 4 for a review of the Justification feature and how to turn it on or off.) Once these compression and expansion limits are reached, then and only then will WordPerfect adjust spacing between characters. However, assuming that your printer supports it, you can change these compression and expansion limits for a document, fine-tuning justification for your printer.

Position the cursor where you want to change the justification limits, press the FORMAT (SHIFT + F8) key, select Other (4 or O), and then select Printer Functions (6 or P). As shown in Figure 10-6, the default setting is for 60% compression and 400% expansion. Select Word Spacing Justification Limits (4 or W) and then enter numbers representing a compression and expansion percentage. Press EXIT (F7) to return to the document.

WordPerfect inserts a Justification Limitation code into the text listing both percentages, such as **[Just Lim:75,700]**. The larger the percentage, the more flexibility WordPerfect has in adjusting spacing between words. WordPerfect considers an expansion percentage of anything over 999% as an unlimited expansion ability.

INSERT GRAPHICS LINES

WordPerfect has the ability to insert horizontal or vertical graphics lines—of any thickness or shading—anywhere on a page. You can use graphics lines, for example, to separate headings from text, to separate columns, or to border a page. Your printer must support graphics in order to print these lines.

To insert a graphics line, position the cursor where you wish to create a line and press the GRAPHICS (ALT + F9) key. The Graphics menu is displayed:

1 Figure; 2 Table; 3 Text Box; 4 User-defined Box; 5 Line: 0

Select Line (5 or L) and the following menu displays:

1 Horizontal Line; 2 Vertical Line: 0

When you select Horizontal Line (1 or H), the menu shown in Figure 10-7 appears. You can now define the location and dimensions of the horizontal line you desire as follows.

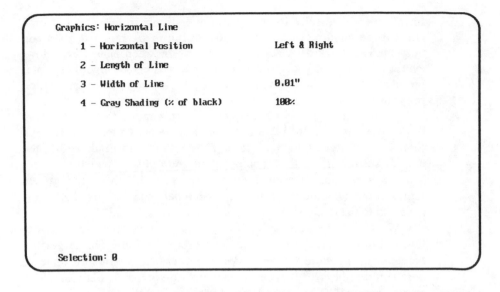

```
Graphics: Horizontal Line

     1 - Horizontal Position          Left & Right

     2 - Length of Line

     3 - Width of Line                0.01"

     4 - Gray Shading (% of black)    100%




Selection: 0
```

FIGURE 10-7   Horizontal Line Graphics menu

- *Horizontal Position*   WordPerfect assumes that you want to
  position the line horizontally beginning at the left margin and
  ending at the right margin, referred to as "Left & Right." Instead, you can position the line beginning at the left margin,
  centered between margins, ending at the right margin, or at a
  specific position from the left edge of the page.

- *Length of Line*   If the horizontal position is set as "Left &
  Right," then the length of line is automatically calculated as the
  distance between the left and right margin. If the horizontal
  position is set to another option, then the line length is set as
  the current cursor position up to the margin specified as the
  horizontal position option. You can accept the suggestion or
  enter a length measurement of your own.

- *Width of Line*   WordPerfect assumes that you want a line 0.01
  inch wide (thick). If you enter a larger measurement, then you
  will be defining a shaded rectangle rather than a line.

- *Gray Shading*   WordPerfect assumes that the shading should be 100% to produce a black line. The lower the percentage entered, the lighter the gray shading.

If you make no changes on the menu shown in Figure 10-7, then Word-Perfect will assume you wish to insert a black line, 0.01 inch thick, from the left margin to the right on the line where the cursor is located, as follows:

When you press EXIT (F7) to return to the Typing screen, the hidden code **[HLine:Left & Right,6.5",0.01",100%]** is inserted (assuming that the distance between the margins is 6.5 inches, as is the case for the default margin settings). If you change any of the options on the Horizontal Line Graphics menu, then the changes are reflected in the hidden code.

```
Graphics: Vertical Line

      1 - Horizontal Position          Left Margin

      2 - Vertical Position            Full Page

      3 - Length of Line

      4 - Width of Line                0.01"

      5 - Gray Shading (% of black)    100%

 Selection: 0
```

FIGURE 10-8   Vertical Line Graphics menu

When you select Vertical Line (2 or V), the menu shown in Figure 10-8 appears. You can now define the location and dimensions of the vertical line as follows:

- *Horizontal Position*   WordPerfect assumes you want to position the line horizontally slightly to the left of the left margin, referred to as "Left Margin." Instead, you can position the line slightly to the right of the right margin, between any two text columns by specifying the number of the first column (refer to Chapter 11 for a discussion of the text column feature), or at a specific position from the left edge of the page.

- *Vertical Position*   WordPerfect assumes that you want to position the line vertically beginning at the top margin and ending at the bottom margin, referred to as "Full Page." Instead, you can position the line beginning at the top margin, ending against the bottom margin, centered between the top and bottom margins, or at a specific position from the top edge of the page.

- *Length of Line*   If the vertical position is set as "Full Page," then the length of line is automatically calculated as the distance between the top and bottom margins. If the vertical position is set to another option, then the line length is set as the current cursor position up to the margin specified as the vertical position option. You can accept the suggestion or enter a length measurement of your own.

- *Width of Line*   WordPerfect assumes that you want a line 0.01 inch wide (thick). If you enter a larger measurement, then you will be defining a shaded rectangle rather than a line.

- *Gray Shading*   WordPerfect assumes that the shading should be 100% to produce a black line. The lower the percentage entered, the lighter the gray shading.

If you make no changes on the menu shown in Figure 10-8, then Word-Perfect will assume you wish to insert a black line, 0.01 inch thick, all the way from the top margin to the bottom margin on the page, just to the left of the left margin.

When you press EXIT (F7) to return to the Typing screen, the hidden code [VLine:Left Margin,Full Page,9"0.01",100%] is inserted (assuming that the distance between the top/bottom margins is 9 inches, as is the case for the default margin settings). If you change any of the options on the Vertical Line Graphics menu, then the changes are reflected in the hidden code.

Be aware that a graphics line—whether horizontal or vertical—is never displayed on the Typing screen. It is displayed on the printed page, or it is displayed using the View Document feature (as described in Chapter 9) providing that you use a monitor that can display graphics. If you insert a graphics line, be careful not to also type text in the same location, or you'll overwrite text with the graphics line when the document is printed.

Also keep in mind that a graphics line will print only if your printer supports graphics. Moreover, even if your printer can print graphics lines, it may not be able to support shading other than 100% (black). If your printer does not support graphics, then an alternative for inserting lines on a page is the Line Draw feature. Line Draw (discussed in Chapter 15) allows you to draw lines and outlines of boxes using special characters.

As an example of inserting graphics lines in text, suppose you wish to create letterhead in WordPerfect where you insert a black line 0.03 inch thick just below your name and address. Proceed as follows:

1. Clear the screen and make sure that the cursor is positioned at the top of the document.

2. Center your (or your company's) name and address. You may wish to select a fancy font or font attribute for the name and address.

3. Position the cursor two blank lines below the address.

4. Press the GRAPHICS (ALT + F9) key. WordPerfect responds with the Graphics menu:

   1 Figure; 2 Table; 3 Text Box; 4 User-defined Box; 5 Line: **0**

5. Select Line (5 or L) and another menu displays:

   1 Horizontal Line; 2 Vertical Line: **0**

6. Select Horizontal Line (1 or H). The full screen menu shown in Figure 10-7 appears.

7. Select Width of Line (3 or W).

8. Type **.03** and press ENTER.

9. Press EXIT (F7) to return to your document.

The hidden code [**HLine:Left & Right,6.5",0.03",100%**] is inserted in the text. The horizontal line is not displayed on the Typing screen. You can see the result of your efforts, however, by printing the

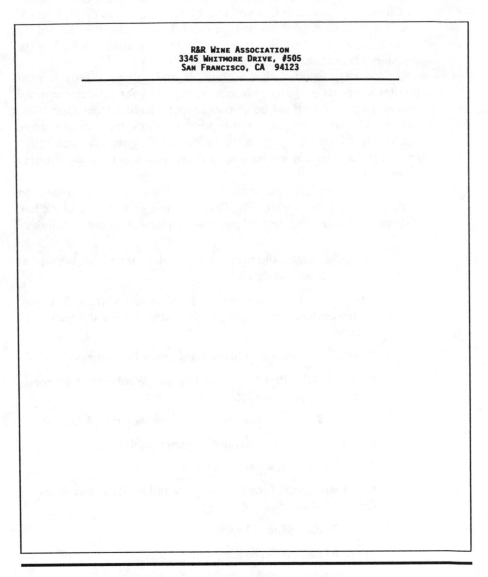

FIGURE 10-9 Letterhead produced using WordPerfect where a graphics line is placed below the address

page or by using the View Document feature (as described in Chapter 9). If you have a printer that supports graphics, you can get results as shown in Figure 10-9.

INSERT GRAPHICS BOXES

In addition to inserting graphics lines, WordPerfect also supports the inclusion of graphics boxes in your text. These boxes can contain either text or graphics images.

There are four different styles of graphics boxes to choose from: figure, table, text, and user-defined. All of them operate basically the same way, offering you the opportunity to keep track of four different categories of graphics boxes. The four graphics box types do, however, have different default settings for how they will appear on the printed page. For instance, figures will be printed with a single-line border around the text or image, while user-defined boxes will be printed with no border. You can, of course, change the default options for any of the graphics box styles, as described farther on in this chapter.

To insert a graphics box, you must position the cursor where you wish to insert a box. This will depend on how you want the box situated on a page. If you want a box associated with a particular paragraph, position the cursor within that paragraph; if your document is edited later on, the graphics box will move with the paragraph. If you want a box treated like any character, position the cursor where you want the box to appear. (You can use the TAB key and the SPACEBAR to position the cursor.) If you want a box placed at a fixed position on the page, position the cursor at the top of that page before any text.

Once you have positioned the cursor, press the GRAPHICS (ALT + F9) key. The Graphics menu is displayed:

    1 Figure; 2 Table; 3 Text Box; 4 User-defined Box; 5 Line: 0

Select from any of the first four options; a menu for that box style appears. For instance, if you selected Figure (1 or F), WordPerfect displays:

    Figure: 1 Create; 2 Edit; 3 New Number; 4 Options: 0

```
Definition: Figure

    1 - Filename

    2 - Caption

    3 - Type                 Paragraph

    4 - Vertical Position     0"

    5 - Horizontal Position   Right

    6 - Size                  3.25" wide x 3.25" (high)

    7 - Wrap Text Around Box   Yes

    8 - Edit




Selection: 0
```

FIGURE 10-10   Figure Definition menu

Select Create (1 or C). WordPerfect displays a full-screen Definition menu for that box style. If the box style is "Figure," for example, then the menu shown in Figure 10-10 displays. You can now define the image, location, and dimensions of the graphics box as follows:

- *Filename*   This option allows you to place a graphics image or a document containing text (which should be less than a page in length) into the graphics box. When you select Filename (1 or F), WordPerfect will prompt for a filename; be sure that you precede the filename with the proper drive or directory if that file is not stored in the default. Press ENTER and the name of that file will appear on the Definition menu.

- *Caption*   WordPerfect assumes you want no caption accompanying a graphics box, but you can add a caption easily by selecting Caption (2 or C). WordPerfect automatically inserts the default caption for that box style and shows it on screen.

Assume that you are creating your first graphics box. For a figure, the default caption style is "Figure 1", for a table, "Table I", for a text or user-defined box, simply "1." WordPerfect assumes that all captions will be boldfaced. If you reveal codes while looking at the caption WordPerfect inserted, you'll discover that the code inserted is **[Box Num]**, no matter what the box style.

You can accept WordPerfect's suggested caption by pressing the EXIT (F7) key. Or you can edit the caption, perhaps adding a space followed by a description of the graphics image. Press EXIT to return to the Definition screen.

- *Type* This option allows you to indicate the type of graphics box you want: paragraph, page, or character. The type of box you select determines how WordPerfect will situate that graphics box on the page and how the box will move if you later edit your text. WordPerfect assumes that you want the box treated as a paragraph type, so that it will remain with the paragraph with which it is associated. (If the paragraph is so close to the bottom of the page that the graphics box cannot fit, the box will be moved to the top of the next page.) Page type treats the box as part of a page, and you can specify exactly where on the page to place the box using the Vertical and Horizontal Position options, described below. Character-type boxes are treated like any other character, so that the box appears exactly where the cursor was positioned when you created the box. (Character boxes are the only type allowed in footnotes and endnotes.)

- *Vertical Position* This option establishes the graphics box's position vertically on the page and this is dependent on the graphics box type.

  If you selected a paragraph-type box, WordPerfect assumes that the box is to be inserted on the line where the cursor was located when you began to create the box. You can instead enter a value measured from the top line of the paragraph. For instance, to start the box even with the first line of the paragraph enter a value of 0".

  If you selected a page-type box, WordPerfect assumes that the box should be aligned with the top margin of the page. You can instead choose that the box occupy the full page, be aligned in the center of the page, be aligned with the bottom margin of the page, or be at a specific position from the top of the page.

If you selected a character-type box, WordPerfect assumes that the text on the same line that follows the box should be aligned with the bottom of the box. You can instead select to align the text with the top or center of the box.

- *Horizontal Position* This option establishes the graphics box's position horizontally on the page, which, like the vertical position, is dependent on the graphics box type.

  If you selected a paragraph-type box, WordPerfect assumes that the box should be inserted at the right margin. You can instead insert the box at the left margin, in the center between the left and right margins, or stretch the box to fill the area from the left to the right margin.

  If you selected a page-type box, WordPerfect assumes you wish to align the box with the right margin. You can instead align the box with the left margin, with the center, or stretch the box to fill the area from the left to the right margin. You can also align the box between text columns. First select a range of columns (such as 1-3) and then align the box with the left margin, with the right margin, with the center, or stretch the box to fill the area from the left to the right margin. (See Chapter 11 for a discussion on creating text columns. When you select to center a graphics box between two columns, text will flow around *both* sides of the box.) You can also set the box at a specific position from the left edge of the page.

  If you selected a character-type box, then the horizontal position is already set by the location of the cursor when you began to create the graphics box.

- *Size* This option sets the height and/or width of the graphics box. The default setting is determined automatically by Word-Perfect based on the shape of the graphics image or text to be inserted in the box and the options you selected for the horizontal and vertical position of the box. You can change the default setting by specifying a particular width, in which case Word-Perfect calculates the height to preserve the graphic image's original shape; specifying a particular height, in which case WordPerfect calculates the width; or by specifying both a width and height.

- *Wrap Text Around Box* WordPerfect assumes that text should always wrap around graphics boxes. You can instead select that text not wrap around graphics boxes, so that the box and the text surrounding it will print in the same location.

- *Edit*   This option has two functions. If the graphics box is empty (that is, you haven't entered a filename) or contains text, then when you select Edit (8 or E), WordPerfect displays a Typing screen for you to enter or edit text. Left and right margins are adjusted to conform with the width of the graphics box. You can enhance text using the Center, Flush Right, Bold, Underline, Base Font, and Font Attribute features, among others. Press EXIT (F7) to return to the Definition screen.

  If the graphics box contains an image, then when you select Edit (8 or E), you can rotate, scale, or move the image, as discussed in the next section.

Once you have decided on the definition for the figure, table, text box, or user-defined box, press EXIT (F7) to return to the Typing screen. A code is inserted in the text at the current cursor position or at the beginning of the current paragraph if the box is defined as a paragraph type. For instance, suppose you just defined your first figure in a document, containing a graphics image that is stored in a file named BOOK.WPG. Then the code inserted is **[Figure: 1;BOOK .WPG]**. Or, if you inserted the same figure but also selected to insert the default caption, then **[Box Num]** is inserted inside the code as follows: **[Figure:1;BOOK.WPG[Box Num]]**. Or suppose you defined your first text box, inserting text directly into the box. The code inserted is **[Text Box:1;;]**.

Once a graphics box is created, what you see on screen depends on the box type you chose. If you created a paragraph or page box, an outline of the box begins to form, which takes full form as soon as you type all the text that will appear around the box. The top of the box outline indicates the box style and number. For instance, Figure 10-11 shows a box outline after the text has been typed around the box. "FIG 1" indicates that this box outline represents Figure 1. If you created a character-type box, then a highlighted rectangle the size of one character appears. With a character type box, you can't see how much space the graphics box will occupy while viewing the Typing screen.

Whatever type of graphics box you create, the text or image inside the box does not appear on the Typing screen. To view the document with the contents of the box, use the View Document feature; however, it takes a monitor that supports graphics to view a box containing a graphics image clearly. You could also print the document; but again, your printer must support graphics to print out a graphics image.

Where do you find a graphics image to insert into a document? One possibility is to use another software package that produces graphics. Table 10-1 lists the graphics formats supported by Word-Perfect. You can create a graphics image using any of the graphics software packages indicated and save it into a WordPerfect-supported format. For instance, you can use Lotus 1-2-3 to create a pie chart and store it on disk in Lotus's PIC format. Or use Harvard Graphics to create a bar graph and store it on disk in CGM format. Or use AutoCAD to draw a diagram and store it on disk in DXF format. Then load WordPerfect and retrieve that pie chart, bar graph, or diagram into a WordPerfect graphics box. (If your graphics software package is not listed in Table 10-1, then you may still be able to bring a graphics image into WordPerfect using GRAB.COM; see Chapter 15.)

If you don't currently own a graphics package, you can still incor-porate graphics images into your documents. WordPerfect has included 30 graphics images on the Fonts/Graphics disk, so that you can get started using graphics right away. These 30 images, all with the file-name extension .WPG, are part of the Publisher's PicturePaks series created by Marketing Graphics Inc., (MGI). Figure 10-12 illustrates all

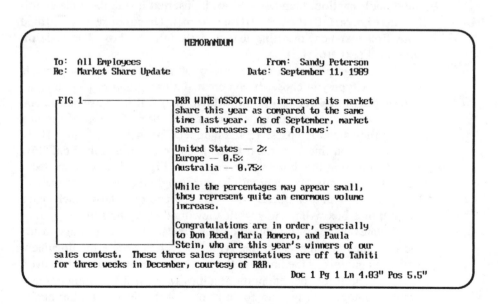

FIGURE 10-11   Figure box outline in the text

WordPerfect-Supported Graphics Format	Graphics Programs*
Computer Graphics MetaFile (CGM)	Freelance Plus, Framework II, Graphwriter, Harvard Graphics, PicturePaks, PlanPerfect (for versions of PlanPerfect before version 4.0, obtain the graphics driver named META.SYS from WordPerfect Corporation)
Dr. Halo PIC Format (DHP)	Dr Halo II
AutoCAD Format (DXF)	AutoCAD
Encapsulated PostScript (EPS)	Adobe Illustrator, Harvard Graphics, Quattro
Hewlett-Packard Graphics Language Plotter File (HPGL)	Harvard Graphics, AutoCAD, IBM CBDS, IBM CATIA, IBM CPG, SlideWrite Plus, Microsoft Chart, VersaCAD, IBM CADAM, IBM GDDM, Graph-in-the Box, DIAGRAM-MASTER, CHARTMASTER, CCS Designer, SignMaster, Diagraph, Generic CAD
GEM Paint Format (IMG)	GEM SCAN, DFI Handy Scanner, Boeing Graph, GEM Paint, Energraphics
Tagged Image File Format (TIFF)	GEM SCAN, DFI Handy Scanner, GEM Paint, Energraphics, SlideWrite Plus, CIES (Compuscan), HP Graphics Gallery, HP Scanning Gallery
Microsoft Windows Paint Format (MSP)	Windows Paint
PC Paintbrush Format (PCX)	PC Paintbrush, SlideWrite Plus, HP Graphics Gallery, HP Scanning Gallery, PicturePaks
Lotus 1-2-3 PIC Format (PIC)	Symphony, VP Planner, SuperCalc 4, Words & Figures, Lotus 1-2-3, Quattro
MacPaint Format (PNTG)	MacPaint
PC Paint Plus Format (PPIC)	PC Paint Plus
WordPerfect Graphics Format (WPG)	PicturePaks

*Some programs can be saved in more than one graphics format

TABLE 10-1   WordPerfect-Supported Graphics Formats

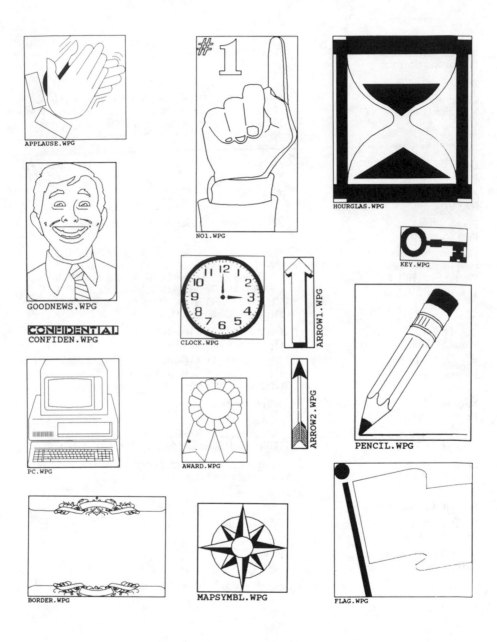

FIGURE 10-12   MGI Publisher's PicturePaks' graphics images included with WordPerfect

FIGURE 10-12   MGI Publisher's PicturePaks' graphics images included with WordPerfect *(continued)*

MEMORANDUM

To: All Employees   From: Sandy Peterson
Re: Market Share Update   Date: September 11, 1989

 R&R WINE ASSOCIATION increased its market
share this year as compared to the same
time last year. As of September, market
share increases were as follows:

United States -- 2%
Europe -- 0.5%
Australia -- 0.75%

While the percentages may appear small,
they represent quite an enormous volume
increase.

Congratulations are in order, especially
to Don Reed, Maria Romero, and Paula
Stein, who are this year's winners of our
sales contest. These three sales representatives are off to Tahiti
for three weeks in December, courtesy of R&R.

FIGURE 10-13   Printout of a document merging text with graphics

30 images. All are ready to be incorporated into a WordPerfect document at any time.

As an example in incorporating graphics images into a document, let's create the document shown in Figure 10-13. The graphics image is one of the PicturePaks images, stored on disk in a file named AP-PLAUSE.WPG. Since the graph needs to stay with the first paragraph, we'll create a paragraph-type box. We'll also place the graphics box at the left margin and reduce the size of the graphics image.

1. On a clear screen, type **MEMORANDUM** as well as the information following "To:," "From:," "Re:," and "Date:," as shown in Figure 10-13. (If you need a refresher on how to center the title or position the "From:" and "Date:" headings flush against the right margin, refer to Chapter 3.)

2. Press ENTER twice to position the cursor where the text of the memorandum is to begin.

3. Type the following paragraph:

   R&R WINE ASSOCIATION increased its market share this year as compared to the same time last year. As of September, market share increases were as follows:

4. Use the UP ARROW and LEFT ARROW keys to position the cursor anywhere within the paragraph you just typed.

5. Press the GRAPHICS (ALT + F9) key. WordPerfect responds with

   1 Figure; 2 Table; 3 Text Box; 4 User-defined Box; 5 Line: 0

6. Select Figure (1 or F). The following menu appears:

   Figure: 1 Create; 2 Edit; 3 New Number; 4 Options: 0

7. Select Create (1 or C). Now the Figure Definition menu appears, as shown in Figure 10-10.

8. Select Filename (1 or F). WordPerfect prompts

   Enter Filename:

9. You must enter the filename APPLAUSE.WPG, preceded by the drive or directory where this image can be found.

   Floppy disk users should insert the Fonts/Graphics disk in drive B, type **B:APPLAUSE.WPG**, and then press ENTER.

   Hard disk users should have the graphics images files with the extension .WPG stored on the hard disk. If you followed the installation instructions described in Appendix A, these files are stored in the directory \WPER on the hard disk. In that case, type **C:\WPER\APPLAUSE.WPG** and press ENTER. (If the graphics images are not found on the hard disk, you can insert the Fonts/Graphics disk in drive A and then enter **A: APPLAUSE.WPG**.

10. Notice that the default setting for the type of graphics box is "paragraph." Thus, this setting requires no modification.

11. Select Vertical Position (4 or V). Because the box is paragraph type, WordPerfect prompts

    Offset from top of paragraph:

and suggests an offset based on the current location of the cursor in relation to the paragraph.

12. Type **0** and press ENTER so that the graphics box lines up evenly with the first sentence of this paragraph.

13. Select Horizontal Position (5 or H). Because the box is paragraph type, WordPerfect prompts

    Horizontal Position: 1 Left; 2 Right; 3 Center; 4 Both Left & Right: 0

14. Select Left (1 or L) to position the box at the left margin.

15. Select Size (6 or S). WordPerfect prompts

    1 Width (auto height); 2 Height (auto width); 3 Both Width & Height: 0

16. Select Height (2 or H). WordPerfect prompts

    Height = 3.41"

    which is the height WordPerfect automatically assigns the graphics box based on the image stored in APPLAUSE.WPG.

17. Type **2.5** and press ENTER. WordPerfect automatically adjusts the width to keep the proper proportions for the graphics image. Your screen will now resemble Figure 10-14.

18. Press EXIT (F7) to register the graphics box and return to your document. The box outline begins to form on screen.

19. Press HOME, HOME, DOWN ARROW to position the cursor at the bottom of the document. The text will readjust, and more of the box outline will form.

20. Type the remainder of the document as shown in Figure 10-13. As you type, the box outline will completely form. (Remember that the graphics image will appear only when printed; your final result on screen will appear as shown in Figure 10-11.)

21. To preview the graphics image within the document, use the View Document feature by pressing PRINT (SHIFT + F7) and selecting View Document (6 or V). The graphics image will display as part of the document.

22. Press EXIT (F7) to return to the Typing screen.

```
Definition: Figure

     1 - Filename              APPLAUSE.WPG (Graphic)

     2 - Caption

     3 - Type                  Paragraph

     4 - Vertical Position     0"

     5 - Horizontal Position   Left

     6 - Size                  2.38" (wide) x 2.5" high

     7 - Wrap Text Around Box  Yes

     8 - Edit




Selection: 0
```

FIGURE 10-14   Figure Definition menu after APPLAUSE.WPG has been sized and positioned

23. Use the SAVE (F10) key to save this document using the file-name MARKETSH.MMO (which stands for market share, memorandum).

If your printer supports graphics, go ahead and print this document. The result is shown in Figure 10-13. On some printers it takes a few moments for the graphics image to be read by the printer before printing begins.

When a document contains both text and graphics, you have the option of printing only the text, only the graphics, or printing the text in one type quality and the graphics in another. (See the "Change Print Options" section in Chapter 9 for more details.) Also, depending on your printer, you may need to increase the memory in your printer to print a page that contains more than one or two graphics images. (If you have insufficient memory, you must first print the text, then print the graphics, and merge the two with scissors and tape or at the copy machine.)

EDIT GRAPHICS BOXES

After you create a graphics box, you can edit its contents or move it at
any time. Position the cursor in the text before the graphics box. Press
the GRAPHICS (ALT + F9) key and then select the menu option corresponding to the style of graphics box you wish to edit—figure, table,
text box, or user-defined box. For a figure, for example, the following
menu appears:

Figure: 1 Create; 2 Edit; 3 New Number; 4 Options: 0

Select Edit (2 or E). WordPerfect asks which graphics box you wish to
edit, suggesting a number. For instance, if you selected to edit a figure,
the prompt that appears may be

Figure number? 2

Type in the number of the figure you wish to edit and press ENTER. The
Definition menu for that graphics box appears on screen, as shown in
Figure 10-14.

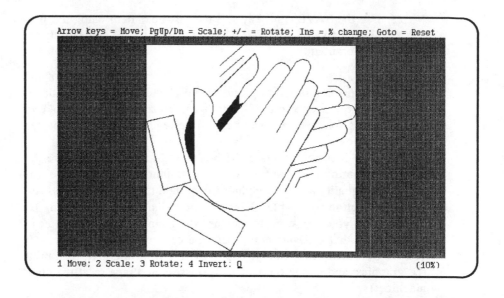

FIGURE 10-15   Graphics Edit screen showing APPLAUSE.WPG

Select any option and edit as you desire. For instance, you can select Filename (1 or F) and enter a new filename, effectively changing the text or graphics image to be inserted in the graphics box. Select Caption (2 or C) and alter the wording of the caption that will appear near the box. Select Vertical Position (4 or V) to alter the graphics box's vertical position on the page.

By selecting Edit (8 or E), you can refine the appearance of the text or graphics image in the box. If your graphics box contains text, the text appears on screen, formatted properly for the margins within that graphics box. Edit the text and press EXIT (F7) to return to the Definition screen for that graphics box. Now you can alter any of the other settings on that screen. Press EXIT (F7) to return to the Typing screen.

If your graphics box contains a graphics image, then when you select Edit (8 or E), the graphics image appears on the Graphics Edit screen, as shown in Figure 10-15. Now you have a variety of options for rotating, scaling, or moving the image *within the graphics box:*

- *Indicate a % Change* This option determines the extent to which the cursor movement keys affect an image for moving, scaling, and rotating (as described below). The default setting is 10%, as indicated in the lower right corner of Figure 10-15. This percentage can be changed to 1%, 5%, or 25% by pressing the INS (INSERT) key repeatedly until the desired percentage appears.

- *Move* This option moves the image horizontally or vertically in the box. Use the arrow keys to move the image by a certain percentage as displayed in the lower right corner of the screen.

  You can also select Move (1 or M) from the menu at the bottom of the screen and enter horizontal and vertical measurements. A positive number (such as 0.3) moves the image up when specifying the vertical movement and to the right when specifying the horizontal movement. A negative number (such as −2) moves the image down when specifying the vertical movement and to the left when specifying the horizontal movement.

- *Scale* This option expands or contracts the image. Press PGUP to expand the image and PGDN to contract the image horizontally and vertically by a certain percentage as displayed in the lower right corner of the screen.

You can also select Scale (2 or S) from the menu at the bottom of the screen and enter vertical (X) and horizontal (Y) scale factors. For instance, to keep the vertical scale as is and to reduce the horizontal scale by half, enter scale X as 100 and scale Y as 50.

- *Rotate*   This option turns the image in a circle. Press the MINUS key (−) on the numeric keypad to rotate the image in a clockwise direction or the PLUS key (+) on the numeric keypad to rotate the image in a counterclockwise direction. The image is rotated based on a certain percentage, as displayed in the lower right corner of the screen.

  You can also select Rotate (3 or R) and enter the number of degrees you wish to rotate the image. For instance, to rotate an image so that it becomes upside down, enter 180 degrees. After you indicate a measurement for the rotation, WordPerfect asks whether you wish to mirror the image. Type Y to mirror the image or N to maintain the image in its usual state. For instance, suppose the image is of an arrow pointing to the right. If you mirror the image, it will point to the left.

- *Invert*   This option switches a bitmap image so that the complementary color of each dot is displayed; black becomes white and white becomes black. This item has an effect only on bitmap images, where images are depicted as a matrix of black dots, and has no effect on line drawings. The graphics images stored on the Fonts/Graphics disk are line drawings and cannot be inverted.

You can also reset the image back to its initial appearance on the Graphics Edit screen by pressing GOTO (CTRL + HOME).

Once you have altered the image on the Graphics Edit screen, press EXIT (F7) to return to the Definition screen for that graphics box. Finally, press EXIT (F7) to return to the Typing screen.

Besides editing the contents or location of a graphics box, you can also alter the box number. Position the cursor in the text where you want the new number to take effect, such as before a certain graphics box. Press the GRAPHICS (ALT + F9) key and then select the menu option corresponding to the style of graphics box you wish to edit—figure, table, text box, or user-defined box. For a figure, for example, the following menu appears:

Figure: 1 Create; 2 Edit; 3 New Number; 4 Options: 0

Select New Number (3 or N). WordPerfect prompts for which number you wish to use. With the figure style, for example WordPerfect prompts

Figure number?

Type in a new number and press ENTER. A code is inserted in the text, renumbering all graphics boxes of the indicated style from the cursor location forward, starting with the new number. For instance, suppose you indicate that you wish to renumber all figures in a document starting with number 5. The code inserted is **[New Fig Num:5]**, and the first figure-style graphics box created below that code will be renumbered as "Figure 5." All subsequent figure-style graphics boxes will be renumbered accordingly. As another example, the code after renumbering a text-style box to number 10 is **[New Txt Num:10]**.

CHANGE GRAPHICS BOX DEFAULT OPTIONS

In addition to adjusting the settings for a particular graphics box, you can alter the default settings assumed for each of the four graphics box styles: figure, table, text box, or user-defined box. The default options are shown in Table 10-2. To change one or more options for a particular box style in a document, position the cursor where you want the changes to take effect.

For instance, position the cursor on the Document Initial Codes screen to alter the options for a particular box style starting at the top of the document. Or position the cursor above Table 5 to change the options for that table and all graphics boxes of the table style that follow. Press the GRAPHICS (ALT + F9) key and then select the menu option corresponding to the style of graphics box you wish to alter— whether a figure, table, text box, or user-defined box. For a figure, the following menu appears:

Figure: 1 Create; 2 Edit; 3 New Number; 4 Options: 0

Select Options (4 or O). A menu, such as that shown in Figure 10-16, appears. Notice in Figure 10-16 that the default settings for the figure-style box options are indicated on the right side of the screen. When

	Figure	Table	Text Box	User-Defined Box
Border Style				
Left	Single	None	None	None
Right	Single	None	None	None
Top	Single	Thick	Thick	None
Bottom	Single	Thick	Thick	None
Outside Border Space				
Left	0.16"	0.16"	0.16"	0.16"
Right	0.16"	0.16"	0.16"	0.16"
Top	0.16"	0.16"	0.16"	0.16"
Bottom	0.16"	0.16"	0.16"	0.16"
Inside Border Space				
Left	0"	0.16"	0.16"	0"
Right	0"	0.16"	0.16"	0"
Top	0"	0.16"	0.16"	0"
Bottom	0"	0.16"	0.16"	0"
Numbering Method				
First Level	Numbers	Roman	Numbers	Numbers
Second Level	Off	Off	Off	Off
Caption Number Style	[BOLD]Figure 1[bold]	[BOLD]Table 1[bold]	[BOLD]1[bold]	[BOLD]1[bold]
Position of Caption	Below box, Outside	Above box, Outside	Below box, Outside	Below box, Outside
Minimum Offset from Paragraph	0"	0"	0"	0"
Gray Shading (% of black)	0%	0%	10%	0%

TABLE 10-2   Default Options for the Four Graphics Box Styles

```
Options:    Figure

        1 - Border Style
                Left                            Single
                Right                           Single
                Top                             Single
                Bottom                          Single
        2 - Outside Border Space
                Left                            0.16"
                Right                           0.16"
                Top                             0.16"
                Bottom                          0.16"
        3 - Inside Border Space
                Left                            0"
                Right                           0"
                Top                             0"
                Bottom                          0"
        4 - First Level Numbering Method        Numbers
        5 - Second Level Numbering Method       Off
        6 - Caption Number Style                [BOLD]Figure 1[bold]
        7 - Position of Caption                 Below box, Outside borders
        8 - Minimum Offset from Paragraph       0"
        9 - Gray Shading (% of black)           0%

Selection: 0
```

FIGURE 10-16   Figure Options menu

you select a different graphics box style, the corresponding default settings are indicated on screen.

The options that you can alter are as follows:

- *Border Style*   This option sets the style for all four borders of the graphics box. The choices are None, Single Line, Double Line, Dashed Line, Dotted Line, Thick Line, or Extra Thick Line.

- *Outside Border Space*   This option sets the amount of space between the borders of the box and the text *outside* the box.

- *Inside Border Space*   This option sets the amount of space between the borders of the box and the image or text *inside* the box.

- *First Level and Second Level Numbering Method*   This option sets the format for the graphics box number to appear in the caption for each box. The choices are Off, Numbers (Arabic), Letters, or Roman Numerals. Letters and Roman numerals are displayed in uppercase for first level numbers and in lowercase for second level numbers. For instance, if you selected Numbers as the first level and Letters as the second level, then the first three figures would be labeled "Figure 1a," "Figure 1b," and "Figure 1c."

• *Caption Number Style* This option sets the style for a graphics box caption. Type **1** where you want the first level number to appear, and type **2** where you want the second level number to appear. For instance, suppose that you selected Numbers as the first level numbering method and Letters as the second level numbering method (as discussed in the bulleted paragraph above). Now you want the figures labeled in boldface as **"Chapter 1, Figure a," "Chapter 1, Figure b,"** and so on. Enter the caption number style as **[BOLD]Chapter 1, Figure 2[bold]**.

• *Position of Caption* This option sets the position of the caption. You have two sets of choices: below or above the graphics box, and outside or inside the graphics box.

• *Mimimum Offset from Paragraph* For a paragraph-style graphics box, this option sets the limit as to the amount of space the graphics box can be offset from the top of the paragraph.

As you've learned, you can specify a certain vertical distance from the top of the paragraph to the top of the graphics box. If necessary, WordPerfect will move the image higher in the paragraph than the vertical distance you specified so that the image can fit on the same page as the text; but it can move the image up only as far as allowed by the Minimum Offset from Paragraph option. When there isn't enough room for the graphics box to fit on the page, even when WordPerfect moves the image up as much as allowed by the Minimum Offset from Paragraph option, the box is moved to the next page.

• *Gray Shading* This option sets the shading within graphics boxes of a particular style. A value of 0% represents no shading. If your printer supports various levels of shading, then a value of 100% represents a black box and you can specify different levels of shading (such as 10%, which is very light gray shading; 20%, which is slightly darker; and so on).

Once you alter any of the default settings, press EXIT (F7) to return to your document. A Graphics Option code is placed at the current cursor position, affecting all graphics boxes of the style you specified from that position forward or until the next Graphics Option code. For instance, the code after altering the options for figure-style graphics boxes is [Fig Opt]; the code after altering text-style boxes is [Txt Opt].

REVIEW EXERCISE

Here's some practice using the special font and graphics features in WordPerfect. Remember, however, that the fonts available and the ability to print graphics both depend on your printer.

1. If it is not currently on screen, retrieve the file MAR-KETSH.MMO, which contains a graphics image.

2. Alter the font attribute for the word "Memorandum" at the top of the document so that it prints in very large letters.

3. On the blank line just below the word "Memorandum," draw a horizontal line that extends from the left margin to the right and is 0.05 inch in thickness. After creating the graphics line (remember that the line will not display on the Typing screen), press ENTER to insert extra white space below the graphics line.

4. Alter the font attribute for the phrase "Congratulations are in order" in the last paragraph so that it prints in small caps. (If small caps are not available with your printer, try another appearance attribute, such as italics or shadow.)

5. Position the figure at the right margin, rather than at the left margin. (*Hint:* Press the GRAPHICS key and then select to edit Figure 1. On the Figure Definition screen, change the Horizontal Position to "Right" instead of "Left." When you press the EXIT key to return to your document, it may appear jumbled. Simply move the cursor down so that WordPerfect will rewrite the screen.

6. You may wish to print your document (results are shown in Figure 10-17).

MEMORANDUM

To: All Employees   From: Sandy Peterson
Re: Market Share Update   Date: September 11, 1989

R&R WINE ASSOCIATION increased its market share this year as compared to the same time last year. As of September, market share increases were as follows:

United States -- 2%
Europe -- 0.5%
Australia -- 0.75%

While the percentages may appear small, they represent quite an enormous volume increase.

CONGRATULATIONS ARE IN ORDER, especially to Don Reed, Maria Romero, and Paula Stein, who are this year's winners of our sales contest. These three sales representatives are off to Tahiti for three weeks in December, courtesy of R&R.

FIGURE 10-17   Printout after completing the review exercise

REVIEW

- Depending on your printer's capabilities, you can select from a number of fonts for printing your document. Use the Initial Font option on the Document Format menu to alter the font for all text, headers, footers, footnotes, and endnotes starting at the top of the document. Use the Base Font option, accessed via the FONT (CTRL + F8) key to alter the font for a portion of text starting at the current cursor position.

- In addition to altering the font for a portion of text, you can alter the size or appearance of that font. The Size and Appearance options are on the FONT (CTRL + F8) key. If the text has yet to be typed, turn on an attribute using the FONT key, type the text, and then press RIGHT ARROW or use the FONT key to turn off that attribute. Or, if the text is already on screen, use the BLOCK (ALT + F4) key to highlight the text before you use the FONT key to select the appropriate attribute.

- WordPerfect offers several features to adjust the spacing between characters and lines, including Line Height, which determines the amount of vertical space allocated to a line (which is set automatically if you don't specify a setting); Kerning, which reduces the space between specific pairs of characters; Word and Letter Spacing, which adjusts the spacing between words and characters; and Word Spacing Justification Limits, which determines how WordPerfect adjusts spacing when justification is on. To use these features, your printer must be able to support them.

- The Line option on the GRAPHICS key lets you draw lines and shade areas on a page. You can specify the horizontal and vertical position of the line, the line's width and length, and the line's shading (blackness). Graphics lines that you insert are never displayed on the Typing screen.

- WordPerfect allows you to define a rectangular area on the page that can contain either text or a graphics image. Four different graphics box types are available: figure, table, text, and user-defined. Each type has different default options for variables such as a box's border style, border space, caption style, and caption position. You can alter these default options in a particular document.

  For each graphics box you create, you can specify not only what the box will contain, but also the box's position on the page, its size on the page, and whether or not you desire a caption. You can also edit a graphics image, thereby rotating, scaling, or inverting the image inside the graphics box.

- WordPerfect provides 30 graphics images that you can use right away in your documents. You can also create an original image using a graphics package. Save your graphics images in a WordPerfect-supported format, and retrieve them into the graphics boxes in a WordPerfect document.

11

CREATING TEXT COLUMNS

Create Newspaper-Style Columns
Move the Cursor in Newspaper Columns
Edit Text in Newspaper Columns
Erase and Change the Column Format
Create Parallel Columns
Move the Cursor in Parallel Columns
Edit Text in Parallel Columns
Review Exercise
Review

In previous chapters, you learned how to type information into tabular columns by changing tab stop locations and working with tab stop keys such as TAB, →INDENT, →INDENT←, ←MARGIN RELEASE, CENTER, and TAB ALIGN. Tabular columns are convenient when you plan to type a table or chart that contains one-line entries, such as

Chou	Seattle	AB-1	34
Goldberg	Seattle	AB-12	2

Tabular columns are also convenient when you plan to type a table that contains one-line entries in all but the last column. In the last column, you can use the →INDENT F4 key to align all text in multiple lines on a tab stop up to a **[HRt]** code, to get results such as

Chou	Seattle	AB-1	34 cases of Chardonnay from container 744; 25 cases of Sauvignon Blanc from 333

However, when you wish to type text in columns where each entry may be many lines long, you will want to take advantage of WordPerfect's Text Column feature. This feature is quite powerful and easy to use. WordPerfect calculates the proper column spacing based on the column widths that you desire. Once you start typing text into a text column, word wrap operates independently in each column, so you can type and let WordPerfect do the job of confining the text to each column. In addition, if you edit the text in one column, the other columns will not become misaligned.

You can create up to 24 columns on a page with the Text Column feature. Discussed in this chapter are the two basic styles of columns that you can select from:

- Newspaper style, where the text flows down the page in each column, as in a magazine or newspaper—each column is independent of the others

- Parallel, where the text reads across the page as in an address or inventory list—a related group of information is kept together in adjacent columns, side by side

You'll learn the four basic steps in creating text columns, and you'll practice editing text and moving the cursor within the columns that you create.

CREATE NEWSPAPER-STYLE COLUMNS

Newspaper-style columns are those in which the text begins at the top of the first column on a page, continues down to the bottom of that column, and then starts at the top of the next column, as shown in

Figure 11-1. You find this type of column in your daily newspapers and in magazines, where you read all of the first column before your eyes move up to the top of the second. A common use for the newspaper-style column is in producing a company newsletter.

There are four basic steps for working with columns (whether newspaper style or parallel): define the columns, turn on the Column feature, type text into the columns, and turn off the Column feature.

Define Columns

The first step in working with newspaper columns is to define your column layout. You must specify the number of columns you desire and the left and right margins of each column. If you desire columns of equal size, WordPerfect can calculate the margins for each column automatically.

To define columns, position the cursor where you want the columns to take effect. For instance, to initiate columns starting at the top of the document, you can position the cursor on the Document Initial Codes screen. If you want to type columns starting in the middle of page 2, position the cursor there. Next press the MATH/COLUMNS (ALT + F7) key. The Math/Columns menu appears:

1 Math On; 2 Math Def; 3 Column On/Off; 4 Column Def: 0

(Though the Math and Column features are accessed with the same function key, they are unrelated. See Chapter 15 for a discussion of the Math feature.) On the Math/Columns menu, select Column Def (4 or D). The Text Column Definition menu appears, as shown in Figure 11-2. You must define your columns by making the following choices:

- *Type (1 or T)*   The default setting for this option is newspaper style. (To indicate a parallel style, choose an option from the Type menu, as described later in this chapter.)

- *Number of Columns (2 or N)*   The default setting for this option is two. To indicate more than two columns, type a number and press ENTER.

R&R WINE ASSOCIATION
EMPLOYEE NEWS

NEW SERVICE OFFERED

All R&R Wine Association employees are now eligible for two valuable company services.

First is the new R&R Money Market Fund. Any percentage of your monthly salary can be automatically invested in the Money Market Fund, an established mutual fund with assets so far of over $1 million. The R&R Money Market Fund is just a part of a larger fund, which is over $45 million strong.

You will earn high yields and enjoy a variety of extras. These include free check writing on your account. The service is unlimited; write as many checks as you need. In addition, there's free reinvestment of your dividends so that your earnings grow faster.

The R&R Money Market Fund is professionally managed by The Thomas Corporation, one of the nation's leading mutual fund companies.

Second, and as a complimentary feature, we now offer a financial planning service, free to all employees. You'll learn how to minimize taxes, what to do about life insurance, and how to handle emergency needs. You'll also be advised on pension plan options.

Why do we offer the Money Market Fund? So that your investments are wise ones, so that you get long-term profit from your earnings at R&R.

Why do we offer the FREE financial planning service? For the same reasons.

To find out more about the benefits of joining our company's Money Market Fund, call Karl Nottingsworth at (415) 666-9444. He's also the person you'll want to speak with about setting up an appointment for financial planning!

WORLD OF WINES

In our last newsletter, we completed a five-part series on wines produced in the United States. Next month, we begin a new series on the wines of Europe. Our first nation in Europe? By popular request, it will be France.

France is most often considered the greatest wine-producing country in the world. The variety of wines grown here is absolutely amazing: the sparkling wines of Champagne, the red wines of Bordeaux, the red and white wines of Burgundy, the sweet wines of Barsac--just to name a few!

You'll learn about all the French wines we ship around the country in our next edition of R&R Wine News.

FIGURE 11-1 Sample of newspaper columns

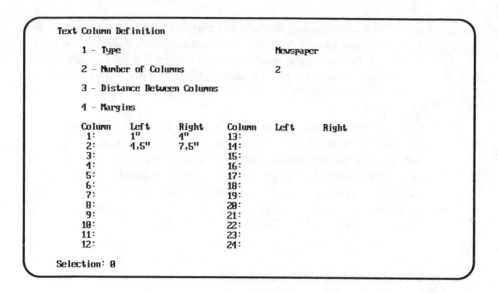

```
Text Column Definition
    1 - Type                         Newspaper
    2 - Number of Columns            2
    3 - Distance Between Columns
    4 - Margins
    Column   Left    Right    Column   Left    Right
      1:      1"      4"        13:
      2:      4.5"    7.5"      14:
      3:                        15:
      4:                        16:
      5:                        17:
      6:                        18:
      7:                        19:
      8:                        20:
      9:                        21:
     10:                        22:
     11:                        23:
     12:                        24:
  Selection: 0
```

FIGURE 11-2   Text Column Definition menu

- *Distance Between Columns (3 or D)*   The default setting is 0.5 inch. To specify another distance, type in a measurement and press ENTER. (This option is useful only if you wish to set all columns at the same width. To set uneven columns, see the next option below.)

- *Margins (4 or M)*   This option is set by default based on your specifications for the Number of Columns and Distance Between Columns options (as described above), taking into account the current left/right margins across the full page. To change the margin settings for individual columns, enter new measurements for each column's left and right margin location.

    You are not limited to the current left/right margins across the full page when setting column margins. For instance, even when the left margin of the page starts at 1 inch, you can start the left margin of the first column at 0.5 inch.

    If you set your own column margins, be sure not to overlap columns and to leave some space between columns so that the columns are easy to read. For instance, if you wish to create two columns and the first has margins of 1 inch and 3.5 inches, you must make sure that the second column starts after position 3.6 inches—somewhere around position 3.8 inches and 4.1 inches would be best to ensure sufficient space between columns for easy reading.

Once all the columns are set, press the EXIT (F7) key or press ENTER to return to the Math/Columns menu. A Column Definition code is inserted at the current cursor position. The Column Definition code indicates how many columns you've specified and what the margins are of each. For instance, if you had set two columns, one with margins of 1 inch and 4 inches and the other with margins of 4.5 inches and 7.5 inches, the code would be [Col Def:2,1",4",4.5",7.5"].

Turn On the Column Feature

You're now ready for step 2—activating the Column feature. From the Math/Columns menu, select Column On/Off (3 or C). This selection is like a toggle switch: when the Column feature is off, this selection turns it on and inserts a [Col On] code. All text that you type following this code will be formatted into columns in whatever format you specified on the Column Definition screen. When the Column feature is active, the status line contains a Column indicator, such as:

Col 1 Doc 1 Pg 2 Ln 1" Pos 1"

Type Text into Columns

The third step in creating columns is to type your text. You should type in newspaper columns as if typing a regular document. Word wrap will be hard at work to ensure that the text remains within the boundaries of the first column.

How WordPerfect starts a new column is analogous to how it starts a new page. After you type 9 inches of text in a column (assuming the default top/bottom margin and page size settings), a Soft Page code [SPg] is automatically inserted, and the cursor jumps to the beginning of the next column. When the last column on a page is full, an [SPg] code is again inserted; but this time, a page bar appears on screen, and the cursor jumps to the beginning of the first column on a new page.

You can also end a column before it would normally end by pressing the HARD PAGE (CTRL + ENTER) key. This forces an end to that column, just as it forces an end to a page when WordPerfect is not in Column mode. A Hard Page code [HPg] is inserted in the text, and the cursor moves up to the top of the next column.

The standard typing features work within columns. For instance, you can press TAB to indent a paragraph to the first tab setting just as you would when you were not in Column mode. If the cursor is at the left margin of a column, you can press the CENTER (SHIFT + F6) key to center a short line of text over that column. Or you can press the FLUSH RIGHT (ALT + F6) key to align a short line of text at the right margin of the column.

Turn Off the Column Feature

The final step is to turn the Column feature off. After you have completed the typing, press the MATH/COLUMNS (ALT + F7) key and select Column On/Off (3 or C). A [Col Off] code is inserted in the text, and the cursor moves down to the left margin below the columns. You can then return to typing text as usual—across the entire line. On the Typing screen, you can tell when the Column feature is no longer active: the status line returns to its standard appearance; for example,

Doc 1 Pg 3 Ln 3.5" Pos 1"

Here's an opportunity to work with newspaper columns. Suppose that your job is to type the monthly R&R Wine Association company newsletter; this month's newletter is shown in Figure 11-1. You will define two evenly spaced columns, with 0.5 inch in between. Proceed as follows:

1. On the first line of a clear screen, center the first line of the title, "R&R WINE ASSOCIATION."

2. On the second line, center the second line of the title, "EMPLOYEE NEWS."

3. Press ENTER four times to insert blank lines.

4. Press the MATH/COLUMNS (ALT + F7) key. WordPerfect responds

   1 Math On; 2 Math Def; 3 Column On/Off; 4 Column Def: 0

5. Select Column Def (4 or D). The screen shown in Figure 11-2 appears. Notice that WordPerfect assumes that you want two newspaper-style columns. WordPerfect also assumes that you want 0.5 inch of space between the columns, as indicated by how WordPerfect calculated the column margins for you. The left column begins at 1 inch, the current left margin for the page. The left column ends at position 4 inches and, because WordPerfect assumes 0.5 inch between columns, the right column begins at position 4.5 inches. The right column ends at 7.5 inches, the current right margin for the page. The default settings are what you desire, so no change is necessary.

6. Press EXIT (F7) to return to the Math/Columns menu:

   1 Math On; 2 Math Def; 3 Column On/Off; 4 Column Def: 0

7. Select Column On/Off (3 or C). As soon as you do, a column indicator appears on the status line to reflect that you're in Column mode. For instance, the status line may read

   Col 1 Doc 1 Pg 1 Ln 2" Pos 1"

   You are now ready to begin typing the first column.

8. Press the CENTER (SHIFT + F6) key, type the title **NEW SER-VICE OFFERED**, and press ENTER twice. Notice that the title is centered over the column rather than over the page, since you're typing within a column.

9. Type the text as shown in Figure 11-1, pressing TAB to indent the first line of each paragraph. Remember that word wrap will keep the text within the margins of that column—you need to press ENTER only to end each paragraph and to insert a blank line between paragraphs.

   Notice that after you type a column 9 inches long, the cursor jumps up to the top of the second column automatically. Continue typing. (If you're a slow typist and don't wish to type the entire text, then you can force a premature page break in the middle of the first column by pressing HARD PAGE (CTRL + ENTER). The cursor moves to the top of the second column. Continue typing part of the second column.)

10. After completing the columns, press the MATH/COLUMNS (ALT + F7) key.

11. Select Column On/Off (3 or C). The cursor jumps to the left margin, below the columns. (If either column ends exactly at the bottom of the first page, the cursor jumps to a new page.) The column indicator disappears. Now you can again type text across the whole width of the page.

In a document, you can turn the Column feature on and off as often as you wish—as long as you have created a column definition. For instance, after typing within columns, you could turn off the Column feature and type some text across the full width of the page. Then you could again press the MATH/COLUMNS (ALT + F7) key and select Column On/Off, to turn the feature on. You could then type a second group of columns and turn the feature off. Figure 11-3 shows a document in which columns were turned on below the title "NEW SERVICE OFFERED," turned off to type a paragraph across the width of the page, and then turned on again below the title "WORLD OF WINES."

When a document with columns is printed, the text in each column is justified on both sides if right justification is on (as shown in Figures 11-1 and 11-3). The printed text has ragged right margins if right justification is set to off. Remember from Chapter 4 that to switch justification on or off, you would position the cursor above the text and use the Line Format menu to insert a [Just On] or [Just Off] code in the text. (Also remember that justification appears on the printed page but not on the Typing screen.)

Because columns are narrower than a full page of text, uneven spacing shows up more in columns. Thus, you might find that hyphenation is especially useful in columns, especially when justification is turned on. One way to work with hyphenation would be to turn it on after you had completed typing the columns. You would move the cursor up above the columns before turning on hyphenation on the Line Format menu. You would then press DOWN ARROW to move the cursor through the columns; WordPerfect would prompt you with those words requiring hyphenation.

R&R WINE ASSOCIATION
EMPLOYEE NEWS

NEW SERVICE OFFERED

All R&R Wine Association employees are now eligible for two valuable company services.

First is the new R&R Money Market Fund. Any percentage of your monthly salary can be automatically invested in the Money Market Fund, an established mutual fund with assets so far of over $1 million. The R&R Money Market Fund is just a part of a larger fund, which is over $45 million strong.

Second, and as a complimentary feature, we now offer a financial planning service, free to all employees. You'll learn how to minimize taxes, what to do about life insurance, and how to handle emergency needs. You'll also be advised on pension plan options.

To find out more about the benefits of joining our company's Money Market Fund, call Karl Nottingsworth at (415) 666-9444. He's also the person you'll want to speak with about setting up an appointment for financial planning!

WORLD OF WINES

In our last newsletter, we completed a five-part series on wines produced in the United States. Next month, we begin a new series on the wines of Europe. Our first nation in Europe? By popular request, it will be France.

France is most often considered the greatest wine-producing country in the world. The variety of wines grown here is absolutely amazing: the sparkling wines of Champagne, the red wines of Bordeaux, the red and white wines of Burgundy, the sweet wines of Barsac--just to name a few!

You'll learn about all the French wines we ship around the country in our next edition of R&R Wine News.

FIGURE 11-3   Sample of two separate sets of newspaper columns

To give your columns a professional look, you may wish to place graphics lines or images between columns. See Chapter 10 for a discussion of how to employ the Graphics feature. If you want the graphics between columns, make sure that the cursor is positioned after the [Col On] code when you press the GRAPHICS (ALT + F9) key.

MOVE THE CURSOR IN NEWSPAPER COLUMNS

In controlling the cursor within columns, page-by-page cursor movement keys such as PGUP and PGDN operate the same whether or not WordPerfect is in Column mode. However, other cursor movement keys are confined to the current column. For instance, HOME, LEFT ARROW moves the cursor to the left edge of the *column,* not the screen. Similarly, HOME, RIGHT ARROW or END moves the cursor to the right edge of the *column.*

There are special cursor movement keys to move the cursor between columns, involving the key combination CTRL + HOME. Remember from Chapter 5 that this combination is referred to as the GOTO key combination. When you press CTRL + HOME, WordPerfect prompts

Go to

If you type a number, the cursor moves to that page.

In Column mode, GOTO in combination with the arrow keys works between columns. To move the cursor one column to the right, press CTRL + HOME, RIGHT ARROW. Similarly, move one column to the left with CTRL + HOME, LEFT ARROW.

You can also move to the very first or last column by pressing HOME one extra time. For instance, suppose that a document has six columns and the cursor is in the third column. If you wish to move to column 1, press CTRL + HOME, HOME, LEFT ARROW. Similarly, if you wish to move to the last column, press CTRL + HOME, HOME, RIGHT ARROW.

There's also a quick way to move to the top or the bottom of the current column: press CTRL + HOME, UP ARROW or CTRL + HOME, DOWN ARROW. Also, if the cursor is at the very end of one column (on the last character), then RIGHT ARROW moves the cursor to the top of the next column, while DOWN ARROW moves the cursor to the top of the same column on the following page.

Here's some practice moving the cursor.

1. Press HOME, HOME, UP ARROW to move to the top of the document on the screen.

2. Press DOWN ARROW until the cursor is inside the columns and **Col 1** appears on the status line.

3. Press CTRL + HOME, DOWN ARROW. The cursor moves to the bottom of column 1.

4. Press END. The cursor moves to the right edge of the column.

5. Press RIGHT ARROW. The cursor moves to the top of column 2.

6. Press CTRL + HOME, DOWN ARROW. Now the cursor is located at the bottom of column 2.

7. Press CTRL + HOME, LEFT ARROW. The cursor moves across to column 1.

8. Press CTRL + HOME, UP ARROW. The cursor returns to the top of column 1.

EDIT TEXT IN NEWSPAPER COLUMNS

Certain editing features operate in columns just as in regular text. The standard deletion keys work the same way, but they are confined to a single column. For instance, the DELETE EOL (CTRL + END) key erases text to the right edge of the column rather than to the right edge of the line. The DELETE EOP (CTRL + PGDN) key erases to the bottom of the column rather than to the bottom of the entire page.

As you insert words, it may appear that the existing text laps over into the next column. When you press DOWN ARROW, the text adjusts. As you add or delete text, the column readjusts. If necessary, the text in other columns shifts up or down as well, just as when you add or delete text during normal editing and the text on each page shifts.

Watch what happens when you delete a paragraph in one of the columns on screen.

1. Position the cursor somewhere within the third paragraph of the first column on the screen, which begins with "You will earn high yields...."

2. Press the MOVE (CTRL + F4) key.

3. Select Paragraph (2 or P). Notice that WordPerfect highlights the paragraph, staying within that column.

4. Select Delete (3 or D). The paragraph is erased. Notice that the following paragraphs shift up to fill in the gap left by the deleted paragraph.

The BLOCK (ALT + F4) key works in Column mode to highlight a chunk of a column. You can perform any of the many features possible after blocking text—copying the block, moving it, saving, printing, and so on. You can use the MOVE (CTRL + F4) key to move a paragraph from one place to another in the usual way.

Note: Chapter 6 describes how WordPerfect allows you to move or copy not only a standard block, but a rectangle or tabular column as well. The Tabular Column option is used for a column aligned on tab stops, but cannot be used for columns created using the Text Column feature. Move or copy words, sentences, or paragraphs in text columns just as you'd move them in standard text.

When you reveal codes in an attempt to check or delete codes within columns, WordPerfect shows only one column at a time and always at the left side of the screen. For instance, Figure 11-4 shows the Reveal Codes screen with the cursor in the first paragraph of column 1. Notice in the bottom window, where codes are displayed, that you can see the [Col Def:] and [Col On] codes, as well as part of the first column; the second column, however, does not appear. The two columns are treated as two separate pages on the Reveal Codes screen.

Certain features are inaccessible when you're typing in columns. For instance, you cannot change margins within columns; you must alter margins above the [Col Def:] code and then redefine the columns to reflect the margin change. Nor can you use the Sort feature (as described in Chapter 15) within columns. And footnotes are inoperative in columns, although endnotes work just fine.

When editing in columns, WordPerfect responds more slowly than when editing normal text. Because the Column feature is quite complicated, WordPerfect has a heavy burden in adjusting the text with each revision you make. If you are planning extensive editing within columns, you can speed up WordPerfect by requesting that it stop display-

```
     NEW SERVICE OFFERED        Market Fund?  So that your
                                investments are wise ones, so
       All R&R Wine Association  that you get long-term profit
   employees are now eligible for  from your earnings at R&R.
   two valuable company services.
                                    Why do we offer the FREE
       First is the new R&R Money  financial planning service?
                                        Col 1 Doc 1 Pg 1 Ln 2.36" Pos 1.5"
{    ▲    ▲    ▲    ▲    ▲    }   {    ▲    ▲    ▲    ▲    ▲    }   ▲    ▲
[Col Def:2,1",4",4.5",7.5"][Col On][Cntr]NEW SERVICE OFFERED[C/N/Flrt][HRt]
[HRt]
[Tab]All R&R Wine Association[SRt]
employees are now eligible for[SRt]
two valuable company services.[HRt]
[HRt]
[Tab]First is the new [UND]R&R Money[SRt]
Market Fund.[und]  Any percentage of[SRt]
your monthly salary can be[SRt]
automatically invested in the[SRt]

Press Reveal Codes to restore screen
```

FIGURE 11-4   Reveal Codes screen: cursor in the left of two newspaper columns

ing the columns side by side. Each column would appear on a separate page, with a page bar between them. Once you'd revised the columns, you could again choose to display columns side by side. The Side-by-Side Columns Display feature is accessed via the Setup menu. Refer to the "Display" section in Appendix C for more details.

ERASE AND CHANGE THE COLUMN FORMAT

WordPerfect's ability to reformat text into and out of newspaper columns is amazing in its flexibility. You can take text that you've already typed and format it into columns. Just position the cursor above the existing text, define the columns so that a **[Col Def:]** code is inserted, and then turn the feature on. When you press DOWN ARROW to adjust the text, it reformats into columns instantly. You should remember to insert a [Col Off] code at the end of the last column.

You can also retrieve text into an already defined column layout. For instance, position the cursor below the [Col Def:] and [Col On] codes that define the columns. Then use the RETRIEVE (SHIFT + F10) key or the LIST FILES (F5) key to retrieve a document. That document is inserted at the current cursor position, automatically formatted into the column layout.

You can cancel the text columns format, too, so that text again appears across the full width of the page. Simply find and erase the [Col Def:] code that defines the column layout. The [Col On] code disappears automatically, and the text readjusts to fill the full width of the page.

You can even insert a brand new [Col Def:] code and then turn on columns. The text would reformat into the brand new column layout that you had defined.

Suppose that you've decided that columns are inappropriate in the document on screen.

1. Press the REVEAL CODES (ALT + F3) key, and hunt down the [Col Def:] code near the top of the document.

2. Position the cursor on the [Col Def:] code and press DEL to erase it, or position the cursor to the right of the code and press BACKSPACE to erase it.

3. Press REVEAL CODES (ALT + F3) to return to the Typing screen. Notice that the text is no longer in a column format.

4. Use the SAVE (F10) key to save the text currently on screen under the filename NEWCOL (standing for newspaper columns)—even though it is no longer formatted into columns. You will reformat this text into columns during the review exercises that conclude this chapter.

CREATE PARALLEL COLUMNS

Parallel-style columns are useful whenever you wish to type columns of text in which information reads *across,* rather than down, the page. Related information is presented in adjacent (parallel) columns that are kept side by side, to get the effect shown in Figure 11-5. For ex-

---

R&R WINE ASSOCIATION: LIST OF MANAGERS

```
Lonnie Chang        Director of the Public        (415) 333-4109
                    Relations Department
                    since 4/12/83.

Tim Fingerman       Distribution Manager,         (415) 549-1101
                    West Coast Region, since
                    6/1/87.  Stationed in
                    Oakland, California.

Paula Garcia        Distribution Manager,         (212) 484-1119
                    East Coast Region, since
                    12/2/82.  Stationed in
                    New York City.

P.J. McClintock     Assistant to the             (415) 333-4401
                    President since 5/13/86.

Sandy Peterson      President since 3/2/82.       (415) 333-4400

John Samsone        Director, Office of          (415) 333-9215
                    Administration, since
                    3/2/82.
```

FIGURE 11-5   Sample of parallel columns

ample, the entry "Lonnie Chang" along with her title and telephone number is considered to be one group of parallel columns. The entries related to "Tim Fingerman" are considered a second group. Word-Perfect automatically inserts a blank line between each group. Parallel style resembles standard tabular columns, except that text can wrap individually in each column.

You can employ parallel columns in two ways. Use the regular Parallel column if either one entry in a group will continue for more than one page or if it doesn't matter to you that one parallel column may be split between two pages. You may wish to use regular Parallel columns, for example, when typing a script.

Use Parallel with Block Protect columns when entries are small and you wish to protect each group of parallel columns from being split between two pages. WordPerfect inserts Block Protection codes so that each group of adjacent columns always remains together. (As described in Chapter 5, the Block Protect feature is also available when text is not in Column mode, to protect a chunk of text from being split by a page break.) Using Block Protect, an entire group is placed on the next page if one column in a group of parallel columns extends beyond a page break. This type of column is convenient to use when you wish to create mailing or inventory lists or the list shown in Figure 11-5, where each group of parallel columns is short.

Follow the same four steps in creating parallel columns as when creating newspaper columns. First insert a **[Col Def:]** code that defines the column layout: press the MATH/COLUMNS (ALT + F7) key, select Column Def (4 or D), and then respond to the menu items on the Text Column Definition screen (Figure 11-2). When defining the Type option, make sure to specify either Parallel or Parallel with Block Protect.

Second, you must turn on the Column feature by selecting Column On/Off (3 or C) from the Math/Columns menu. When you turn on parallel columns, WordPerfect inserts a **[Col On]** code. If you select Parallel with Block Protect, WordPerfect also precedes that code with a **[Block Pro:On]** code, which ensures that related columns across the page are never separated.

The third step is actually typing the text into the columns. As with newspaper columns, you can rely on word wrap to maintain the margins of each column. But in contrast to its use in newspaper columns, the HARD PAGE (CTRL + ENTER) key is used constantly in parallel columns. You must press CTRL + ENTER after completing each entry in a related group of parallel columns. A Hard Page code **[HPg]** is inserted in the text, and the cursor moves up to the top of the next column, where you would type the next entry and press CTRL + ENTER again to continue. In parallel columns, you type each group across the page before moving to the next group.

When you complete the last column of a related group and press CTRL + ENTER, WordPerfect accomplishes many tasks in sequence.

- If you selected Parallel with Block Protect, a **[Block Pro:Off]** code is inserted to designate the end of protection for that group.

- A **[Col Off]** code is inserted to designate the end of columns for that one group.

- The cursor moves to the left margin of a new line, and a **[HRt]** code is inserted so that a blank line is established below the group.

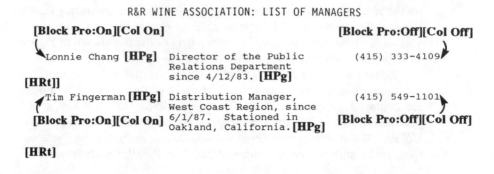

R&R WINE ASSOCIATION: LIST OF MANAGERS

[Block Pro:On][Col On]   **[Block Pro:Off][Col Off]**

Lonnie Chang **[HPg]**   Director of the Public   (415) 333-4109
                          Relations Department
                          since 4/12/83. **[HPg]**
[HRt]]

Tim Fingerman **[HPg]**   Distribution Manager,   (415) 549-1101
                          West Coast Region, since
[Block Pro:On][Col On] 6/1/87. Stationed in   **[Block Pro:Off][Col Off]**
                          Oakland, California. **[HPg]**

[HRt]

FIGURE 11-6   Location of hidden codes in parallel with Block Protect
               columns

- The cursor moves to the left margin of a new line, and, if you
  selected Parallel with Block Protect, a **[Block Pro:On]** code is
  inserted to designate the start of a new group to be protected.

- A **[Col On]** code is inserted in preparation for your typing the
  next group of parallel columns.

All these tasks are accomplished in a split second, and you're ready to
continue typing. Notice in Figure 11-5 that a blank line separates
groups. This line is inserted automatically when you press CTRL +
ENTER after completing the last of a group of parallel columns. Figure
11-6 illustrates where all the codes are inserted around the first two
groups of parallel columns, assuming Block Protect. For parallel
columns without Block Protect, all the same codes are inserted, except
for the **[Block Pro:]** codes.
    The standard typing features work in parallel columns just as in
newspaper columns. For example, use the TAB key to indent the first
line of a paragraph or use the CENTER (SHIFT + F6) key to center text
within one column.
    The fourth step in creating parallel columns is turning off the
Column feature. After you've typed the very last column of the last
group of information, don't press CTRL + ENTER or you'll be inserting
another slew of codes to turn off columns for one group and turn them
on again for a new group. Instead, press the MATH/COLUMNS (ALT +
F7) key and select Column On/Off (3 or C). Now WordPerfect turns off

the feature more permanently, inserting a [**Col Off**] code (and a [**Block Pro:Off**] code if you're using parallel with Block Protect columns) without also inserting another [**Col On**] code.

Here's an opportunity to practice typing the text in Figure 11-5. You'll establish three parallel with Block Protect columns, where the second column will be wider than the other two.

1. Using the EXIT (F7) key, clear the screen of the file named NEWCOL.

2. On the first line of a blank Typing screen, center the title, "R&R WINE ASSOCIATION: LIST OF MANAGERS."

3. Press ENTER three times to insert blank lines.

4. Press the MATH/COLUMNS (ALT + F7) key. WordPerfect responds

   1 Math On; **2** Math Def; **3** Column On/Off; **4** Column Def: **0**

5. Select Column Def (4 or D). The screen shown in Figure 11-2 appears.

6. Select Type (1 or T). The following menu appears:

   Column Type: 1 Newpaper; **2** Parallel; **3** Parallel with Block Protect: **0**

7. Select Parallel with Block Protect (3 or B). Your selection is indicated on screen.

8. Select Number of Columns (2 or N).

9. Type **3** and press ENTER. Again, your selection is indicated on screen.

10. Select Margins (4 or M) so that you can set your own margins, overriding WordPerfect's suggestions.

11. Set margins for the first column: type **1** and press ENTER, and then type **2.5** and press ENTER. (WordPerfect assumes that you wish to enter your column margins in inches, so there's no need to type **1"** or **2.5"**.)

12. Set margins for the second column: type **3** and press ENTER, and then type **5.5** and press ENTER.

13. Set margins for the third column: type **6** and press ENTER, and then type **7.5** and press ENTER.

14. Press EXIT (F7); the Math/Columns menu reappears on screen.

15. Select Column On/Off (3 or C); a column indicator appears on the status line to reflect that you're in Column mode, such as

    Col 1 Doc 1 Pg 1 Ln 1.5" Pos 1"

    You are now ready to begin typing the first group of entries.

16. Type **Lonnie Chang**, and press CTRL + ENTER. The cursor jumps to the next column.

17. Type the following:

    Director of the Public Relations Department since 4/12/83.

    and press CTRL + ENTER.

18. Type the phone number **(415) 333-4109** and press CTRL + ENTER. Notice that the cursor moves down to the left margin two lines below the text of the second column, which is the longest entry.

19. Continue until you have completed typing Figure 11-5; do not, however, press CTRL + ENTER after typing the phone number for the *last* group of entries.

20. After typing the phone number in the last column of the last group, press the MATH/COLUMNS (ALT + F7) key.

21. Select Column On/Off (3 or C). The cursor jumps to the left margin below the columns, and the **Col** indicator disappears. Now you can again type text across the whole width of the page.

MOVE THE CURSOR IN PARALLEL COLUMNS

You can move the cursor left and right between parallel columns in the same fashion as in newspaper columns. That is, if you press CTRL + HOME, LEFT ARROW, the cursor relocates one column to the left, whereas CTRL + HOME, HOME, LEFT ARROW moves the cursor to the first column. Similarly, CTRL + HOME, RIGHT ARROW moves the cursor one column to the right, whereas CTRL + HOME, HOME, RIGHT ARROW moves the cursor to the last column to the right.

You can also move the cursor up or down in parallel columns as in newspaper columns—except that WordPerfect treats each group of parallel columns separately. For example, CTRL + HOME, UP ARROW moves the cursor to the top line of the parallel column where the cursor is located, just below the blank line separating it from the previous group of parallel columns. Also, if the cursor is at the very end of column 1 for one group, RIGHT ARROW moves the cursor to the beginning of column 2 in the same group, while DOWN ARROW moves the cursor to the blank line between two distinct groups of parallel columns. If you press DOWN ARROW again, the cursor moves to column 1 in the next group of parallel columns.

Here's some practice moving the cursor:

1. Press HOME, HOME, UP ARROW to move to the top of the document.

2. Press DOWN ARROW until the cursor is inside the columns (look for **Col 1** to appear on the status line).

3. Press END. The cursor moves to the right edge of the column.

4. Press RIGHT ARROW. The cursor moves to the top of column 2.

5. Press CTRL + HOME, DOWN ARROW. Now the cursor is located at the bottom of column 2 in the first group of parallel columns.

6. Press CTRL + HOME, RIGHT ARROW. The cursor moves across to column 3.

7. Press DOWN ARROW. The cursor moves down to the blank line between the first and second group of parallel columns.

8. Press DOWN ARROW. The cursor moves down to column 3 in the second group of parallel columns.

EDIT TEXT IN PARALLEL COLUMNS

Because there are often many short columns created when you work with parallel columns, editing text is trickier than in newspaper col-

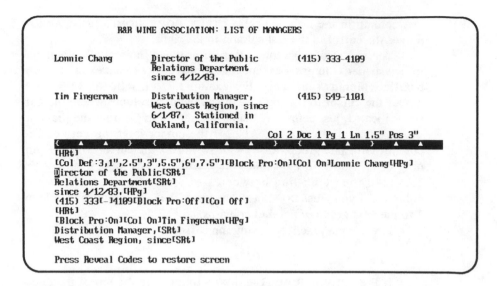

FIGURE 11-7   Reveal Codes screen: cursor in the middle of three Parallel
with Block Protect columns

umns. You must position the cursor precisely, wading through a number of codes on the Reveal Codes screen.

When you reveal codes in an attempt to check or delete codes
within columns, WordPerfect shows the column text only on the left
side of the screen, just as with newspaper columns. But if columns are
short, you may also see part of the preceding column or the next
column. This can be confusing at first.

For instance, Figure 11-7 shows the Reveal Codes screen with the
cursor on the "D" in "Director" in the second column of the first group
of parallel columns. Notice in the bottom window that you can see the
text of all three parallel columns in the group and even part of the next
group. They are all shown as if in one column in the bottom window.
You must find the [HPg] codes to distinguish where one column ends
and another begins within one group of parallel columns. You must
find the [Block Pro:On], [Col On], [Block Pro:Off], and [Col Off]
codes that surround a group of parallel columns to distinguish that
group from a preceding or following group.

If you wish to delete an entire group of parallel columns, make sure that you delete the codes that surround it in addition to the text itself. For instance, suppose that you wish to delete the second group of parallel columns on screen. Remember that these columns are parallel with Block Protect, so that there are Block Protection codes in addition to Column On/Off codes.

1. Position the cursor on the blank line above the "T" in "Tim Fingerman." By positioning the cursor above this group of parallel columns, you're sure to include the [Block Pro:On] and [Col On] codes in your highlighted block.

2. Press the BLOCK (ALT + F4) key.

3. Press DOWN ARROW twice. Since the first column is only one line long, WordPerfect moves the cursor to the [HRt] code below that group, highlighting all of that group's columns, as well as the [Block Pro:Off] and [Col Off] codes that end the group.

4. Press DEL and then type Y to confirm that you want to delete the column. You have effectively deleted the text in the parallel columns along with the accompanying codes.

5. Use the SAVE (F10) key to save this document under the name PARCOL, which stands for PARallel COLumns.

If you wish to insert an entire group of parallel columns, you must position the cursor in the last column of the preceding group on the [Block Pro:Off] code (or on the [Col Off] code if you're using regular parallel columns without Block Protect). This way WordPerfect will insert the proper codes when you press HARD PAGE to begin inserting the new group. For instance, if you wish to list information about another manager below the group of parallel columns pertaining to Sandy Peterson, position the cursor at the end of the column containing his phone number. Then press the REVEAL CODES (ALT + F3) key and position the cursor on the [Block Pro:Off] code, as shown in Figure 11-8. Now you can remain in the Reveal Codes screen or return to the Typing screen. Then press HARD PAGE (CTRL + ENTER) and begin typing the new group of parallel columns. WordPerfect automatically inserts a set of codes for that new group of parallel columns. (You will practice adding a group of parallel columns in the review exercise.)

```
                    New York City.

P.J. McClintock      Assistant to the              (415) 333-4101
                     President since 5/13/86.

Sandy Peterson       President since 3/2/82.       (415) 333-4100_

John Samsone         Director, Office of           (415) 333-9215
                     Administration, since
                     3/2/82.

                                           Col 3 Doc 1 Pg 1 Ln 3.5" Pos 7.4"
{   ▲    ▲    }  {   ▲    ▲    ▲    ▲    }  {   ▲    ▲    }   ▲    ▲
[Block Pro:On][Col On]Sandy Peterson[HPg]
President since 3/2/82.[HPg]
(415) 333[ ]4100[Block Pro:Off][Col Off]
[HRt]
[Block Pro:On][Col On]John Samsone[HPg]
Director, Office of[SRt]
Administration, since[SRt]
3/2/82.[HPg]
(415) 333[ ]9215[Block Pro:Off][Col Off]


Press Reveal Codes to restore screen
```

FIGURE 11-8   Correct cursor position for inserting a new group of Parallel with Block Protect columns

Parallel columns are not as flexible as newspaper columns. Because so many special codes are inserted as you type parallel columns, you don't have the ability to retrieve text into the parallel column format. Nor can you type text first and then later attempt to format the text into parallel columns. So if you want columns side by side on a page, make sure to turn on the Parallel Column feature before typing the text.

REVIEW EXERCISE

Here's some practice using the text you've been typing throughout this chapter. You'll first format already existing text into newspaper columns. Then you'll insert additional information into parallel column format.

1. Press the SWITCH (SHIFT + F3) key to switch to the Doc 2 screen. This screen should be clear. If it's not, press the EXIT (F7) key and type **N** twice to clear the screen.

2. Retrieve the file named NEWCOL (the text that is no longer formatted into newspaper columns).

Suppose that you want to again format the text into two newspaper columns, but this time with the right column wider than the left. Proceed as follows:

3. Position the cursor at the left margin on the line that reads "NEW SERVICE OFFERED," the heading for the first column.

4. Press the MATH/COLUMNS (ALT + F7) key and select Column Def (4 or D). Establish a new column definition for two newspaper columns; the left column will have margins of 1 inch and 3.6 inches, while the right column will have margins of 4 inches and 7.5 inches.

5. Turn on the Column mode.

6. Use the cursor movement keys to move the cursor downward; as you do, watch as the text reformats into the two columns you defined.

7. Print this document. The result (with right justification) is shown in Figure 11-9.

Suppose that you wish to insert another person's name after the information about John Samsone. Continue as follows:

8. Press the SWITCH (SHIFT + F3) key to switch back to the Doc 1 screen. This screen contains the list of managers that you typed in parallel columns format with block protect, saved with the name PARCOL.

9. Position the cursor just to the right of the phone number (415) 333-9215, which is John Samsone's phone number.

10. Reveal codes to make sure that the cursor is on the **[Block Pro:Off]** code.

11. Press HARD PAGE (CTRL + ENTER), and type **George Wilson**

R&R WINE ASSOCIATION
EMPLOYEE NEWS

NEW SERVICE OFFERED

All R&R Wine Association employees are now eligible for two valuable company services.

First is the new R&R Money Market Fund. Any percentage of your monthly salary can be automatically invested in the Money Market Fund, an established mutual fund with assets so far of over $1 million. The R&R Money Market Fund is just a part of a larger fund, which is over $45 million strong.

The R&R Money Market Fund is professionally managed by The Thomas Corporation, one of the nation's leading mutual fund companies.

Second, and as a complimentary feature, we now offer a financial planning service, free to all employees. You'll learn how to minimize taxes, what to do about life insurance, and how to handle emergency needs. You'll also be advised on pension plan options.

Why do we offer the Money Market Fund? So that your investments are wise ones, so that you get long-term profit from your earnings at R&R.

Why do we offer the FREE financial planning

service? For the same reasons.

To find out more about the benefits of joining our company's Money Market Fund, call Karl Nottingsworth at (415) 666-9444. He's also the person you'll want to speak with about setting up an appointment for financial planning!

WORLD OF WINES

In our last newsletter, we completed a five-part series on wines produced in the United States. Next month, we begin a new series on the wines of Europe. Our first nation in Europe? By popular request, it will be France.

France is most often considered the greatest wine-producing country in the world. The variety of wines grown here is absolutely amazing: the sparkling wines of Champagne, the red wines of Bordeaux, the red and white wines of Burgundy, the sweet wines of Barsac--just to name a few!

You'll learn about all the French wines we ship around the country in our next edition of R&R Wine News.

FIGURE 11-9   Practice exercise after text is formatted into two newspaper columns

12. Press HARD PAGE (CTRL + ENTER), and type the following:

    **Distribution Manager, Midwest Region, since 5/4/86. Sta-
    tioned in Chicago, Illinois.**

13. Press HARD PAGE (CTRL + ENTER), and type **(312) 731-2204**

14. Save your practice document for creating parallel columns
    again under the name PARCOL, and save the newspaper
    columns in the Doc 2 window again under the name NEW-
    COL.

REVIEW

- WordPerfect can format text into either of two column styles: newspaper columns, in which text reads down to the bottom of one column and then continues at the top of the next, and parallel columns, in which columns of related information are kept together side by side on the page. When working with parallel columns, you can either work with or without Block Protect. Use Block Protect if the entries are shorter than a page in length and you wish to keep the entries in a group of parallel columns protected from being split by a page break.

- Whether you require newspaper or parallel columns, follow four main steps when working with them: (1) define the column layout; (2) turn Column mode on; (3) type the text; and (4) turn Column mode off. The MATH/COLUMNS (ALT + F7) key is used to define columns and to turn Column mode on and off.

- Within columns, HARD PAGE (CTRL + ENTER) forces the end of one column and the beginning of another. HARD PAGE is used when typing newspaper columns only when you wish to end a short column before reaching the bottom of the page, just as when you wish to end a short page when not in Column mode. HARD PAGE is used constantly when typing parallel columns because you type each entry for one group, which extends *across* columns, before typing entries for the next group.

- A variety of keys move the cursor within and between columns. These are summarized in Table 11-1.

- It is easy to reformat newspaper columns but more difficult to revise the layout for parallel columns. Position the cursor carefully before adding new parallel columns or deleting a group of parallel columns.

Key Combination	Cursor Movement
CTRL + HOME, UP ARROW	Top of current column
CTRL + HOME, DOWN ARROW	Bottom of current column
CTRL + HOME, LEFT ARROW	Preceding column
CTRL + HOME, RIGHT ARROW	Next column
CTRL + HOME, HOME, LEFT ARROW	First column
CTRL + HOME, HOME, RIGHT ARROW	Last column

TABLE 11-1   Cursor Movement in Columns

12

OUTLINING, PARAGRAPH NUMBERING, FOOTNOTING

WordPerfect offers several special numbering features that will save you time. If you create outlines, you can have WordPerfect automatically insert outline numbers for you. Similarly, if you write documents in which you number paragraphs, WordPerfect can insert those paragraph numbers, too.

You can also allow WordPerfect to do the work in incorporating footnotes or endnotes into the text. WordPerfect numbers the notes se-

---

AGENDA: R&R WINE ASSOCIATION BOARD MEETING

I.   Minutes of the last meeting.

II. Reorganization of the Finance Department.

    A.   Who shall fill the position of department manager? Ms. Donna Rainer's name was mentioned previously.

    B.   To whom shall the department manager report?

        1.   The department currently reports to the Vice President.

        2.   The President is currently more involved in the day-to-day operations and restructuring, and works well with Ms. Rainer.

III. Authorization of a new Strategic Plan.

    A.   The original plan, completed by the consulting firm of Burnes and Joseph on May 13th, 1984, is outdated.

    B.   Demographics and consumer preferences have changed significantly over the past five years.

FIGURE 12-1 Sample outline using outline style for numbering

quentially, and the hassle of trying to position footnotes correctly at the bottom of the page is no longer yours; WordPerfect places the footnotes on the page for you and inserts a separator line between the body of the text and the notes.

What these features have in common is that WordPerfect makes sure that the items marked by each feature are *always* numbered properly. If you delete an outline entry, the entire outline is renumbered as required. If you move a paragraph in the text, all the paragraphs are renumbered as necessary. If you insert a footnote, all subsequent footnotes are renumbered to accommodate the insertion. This chapter covers these three timesaving features.

CREATE AN OUTLINE

Before you write a lengthy report, perhaps you first create an outline to organize your thinking and guide you as you write. Or you might write agendas in outline form to make sure that you'll cover all the topics slated for a presentation. Figure 12-1 shows an example of an outline.

Of course, you can create a simple outline without using the Outline feature by simply typing in outline characters (I., II., A., 1., and so on) on your own. However, WordPerfect's Outline feature makes the job a whole lot easier. First, it inserts the outline characters automatically. Second, if you rearrange an outline—add to it, delete from it, or move entries—WordPerfect renumbers the entire outline. Since writing an outline is a fluid, evolving process, the renumbering feature is pure convenience.

WordPerfect inserts an outline character depending on what numbering style you have chosen and which tab stop the cursor is located on. WordPerfect's default for the style of characters is referred to as outline style. There are eight levels in this style; level 1 is at the left margin, and each successive level is located at the next tab stop. The style of characters changes for each of these levels. Level 1, for example, is an uppercase Roman numeral followed by a period. The default styles for all eight levels are

Level 1   I.
Level 2   A.
Level 3   1.
Level 4   a.
Level 5   (1)
Level 6   (a)
Level 7   i)
Level 8   a)

Notice that Figure 12-1 uses the first three levels.

When you're ready to create an outline, you switch on the Outline feature by pressing the DATE/OUTLINE (SHIFT + F5) key and selecting Outline (4 or O). The message **Outline** appears in the lower left corner of the screen, reminding you that the feature is now activated; you are in Outline mode.

Four keys work together to create an outline when the feature is active.

- *ENTER key*   When you press ENTER to insert a Hard Return
  [HRt] code, the cursor moves down a line, and a level-1 outline
  number is automatically inserted on that new line. If you press
  ENTER a second time, the outline number moves down another
  line. (If you press CTRL + ENTER to insert a Hard Page **[HPg]**
  code, a level-1 outline number is also inserted on the new
  page.)

- *TAB key*   With the cursor just to the right of an outline number
  (as in the case just after you press the ENTER key to insert a
  level-1 number), the TAB key moves the outline number one tab
  to the right and increases the numbering style to that of the next
  level.

- *←MARGIN RELEASE (SHIFT + TAB) key*   With the cursor just
  to the right of an outline number, the ←MARGIN RELEASE
  (SHIFT + TAB) key moves the outline number one tab to the left
  and decreases the numbering style to that of the preceding
  level.

- *→INDENT (F4) key*   With the cursor just to the right of an outline number, the →INDENT (F4) key moves the cursor without
  moving the outline number, indenting all lines of text that follow until you again press ENTER. (Alternatively, you can use
  the SPACEBAR to insert space to the right of an outline number
  before typing text, but in this case, only text on the current line
  will be indented.)

When you have completed an outline, you must remember to
switch out of Outline mode; otherwise, an outline number will appear
each time you press ENTER. Turn off the feature the same way you
turned it on: press DATE/OUTLINE (SHIFT + F5) and select Outline (4
or O).

On the screen, it appears as if numbers are inserted into the text,
but if you reveal codes, you will see that what is inserted are actually
[Par Num:Auto] codes. This code means that at each location where
an outline number appears a paragraph number (Par Num) has been inserted automatically (Auto). Because of this code, the outline readjusts
as you add, delete, or move an outline number so that the remaining
entries are numbered in the correct sequence. (The Outline Numbering
feature and the Paragraph Numbering feature—described later in this
chapter—share the same code, so don't let the *paragraph* number code
confuse you; just think of it as an *outline* number code as well.)

Let's produce the outline illustrated in Figure 12-1, to see how the feature operates.

1. On a clear screen, center the title, "AGENDA: R&R WINE ASSOCIATION BOARD MEETING," on the first line, and then press ENTER to move the cursor to the next line.

2. Press the DATE/OUTLINE (SHIFT + F5) key. The following menu appears:

   1 Date Text; 2 Date Code; 3 Date Format; 4 Outline;
   5 Para Num; 6 Define: 0

3. Select Outline (4 or O). The message **Outline** appears on the status line, signifying that you're in Outline mode.

4. Press ENTER. The cursor moves down a line and the number "I." appears on that line.

5. Press the →INDENT (F4) key to indent the first item.

6. Type the following:

   Minutes of the last meeting.

7. Press ENTER twice—once to insert "II." on a new line and a second time to move the outline number down one more line, inserting a blank line.

8. Press the →INDENT (F4) key and type the following:

   Reorganization of the Finance Department.

9. Press ENTER twice, inserting "III."

10. Press TAB. This changes the outline number from level 1 to level 2; an "A." appears.

11. Press the →INDENT (F4) key and type the following:

    Who shall fill the position of department manager? Ms. Donna Rainer's name was mentioned previously.

12. Press ENTER twice, and continue until you complete the outline in Figure 12-1.

13. When the outline is complete, press the DATE/OUTLINE (SHIFT + F5) key and select Outline (4 or O). Now Outline mode is turned off, and the ENTER and other keys return to their usual function.

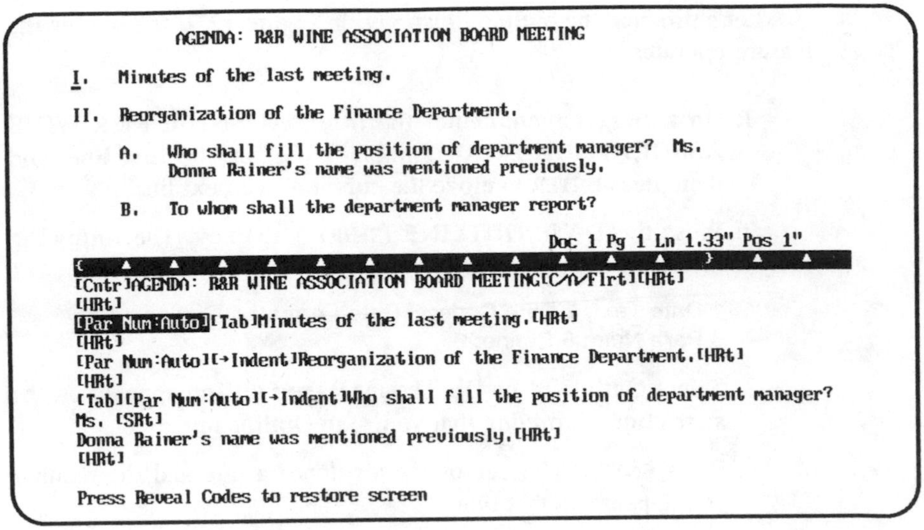

```
         AGENDA: R&R WINE ASSOCIATION BOARD MEETING

I.   Minutes of the last meeting.

II.  Reorganization of the Finance Department.

     A.   Who shall fill the position of department manager?  Ms.
          Donna Rainer's name was mentioned previously.

     B.   To whom shall the department manager report?
                                       Doc 1 Pg 1 Ln 1.33" Pos 1"
```

```
[Cntr]AGENDA: R&R WINE ASSOCIATION BOARD MEETING[C/A/Flrt][HRt]
[HRt]
[Par Num:Auto][Tab]Minutes of the last meeting.[HRt]
[HRt]
[Par Num:Auto][→Indent]Reorganization of the Finance Department.[HRt]
[HRt]
[Tab][Par Num:Auto][→Indent]Who shall fill the position of department manager?
Ms. [SRt]
Donna Rainer's name was mentioned previously.[HRt]
[HRt]

Press Reveal Codes to restore screen
```

FIGURE 12-2 Reveal Codes screen showing Paragraph/Outline number codes

If you reveal codes, you'll see that codes, rather than actual numbers, have been inserted in the text. Figure 12-2 illustrates the Reveal Codes screen with the cursor on the outline number "I." near the top of the document. Notice that where outline numbers are displayed in the top window, **[Par Num:Auto]** codes rather than numbers are displayed in the bottom window.

EDIT AN OUTLINE

An outline can be easily edited. Once you've completed an outline, you can delete an outline number just as you delete any character on screen, using the DEL or BACKSPACE key. You can move the outline number, along with the text that follows, just as you move standard text. To add an outline number, however, you must switch back into Outline mode. (You can also add an outline number without switching into Outline mode by using the Paragraph Numbering feature, described farther on in this chapter.)

You can also change an outline level once you've completed the outline. Edit outline levels when you're in Outline mode by placing the cursor *just to the right* of the outline number and pressing TAB to increase or ←MARGIN RELEASE (SHIFT + TAB) to decrease the outline level. Moreover, you can adjust the outline level when the cursor is located *on* the outline number by pressing TAB to increase or BACK-SPACE to decrease the outline level. This latter method, where you position the cursor on the code before changing the level, also works when you're no longer in Outline mode.

You will find that when you edit outline entries, sometimes the outline numbers on screen do not adjust until you rewrite the screen. You can do so by continuing to press DOWN ARROW or by pressing another cursor movement key, such as PGDN, that relocates the cursor through the outline; each line is renumbered as the cursor moves past it.

You can also rewrite the entire screen without needing to move the cursor. Press the SCREEN (CTRL + F3) key to display the Rewrite menu:

0 Rewrite; 1 Window; 3 Line Draw: 0

Then simply press Rewrite (0 or R) or press ENTER to clear the menu and, at the same time, rewrite the screen.

Let's edit the outline now on screen and observe how WordPerfect renumbers it for you. You are no longer in Outline mode, so you must position the cursor on the outline number in order to increase or decrease the outline level.

1. Position the cursor on the "I." at the beginning of the first outline entry.

2. Press TAB to move the outline number to the next tab stop.

3. Press DOWN ARROW and watch as the outline number on the previous line changes from "I." to "A."

4. Continue to press DOWN ARROW and watch as all the level-1 outline numbers adjust, based on how you edited the first outline entry.

5. Position the cursor back near the top of the document on the "A." of the first outline entry.

6. Press BACKSPACE to move the outline number back to the left margin.

7. Press SCREEN (CTRL + F3) and press ENTER to watch as the level-1 outline numbers readjust, this time without pressing DOWN ARROW through the entire outline.

8. The cursor should now be located on the "I." at the beginning of the first outline entry.

9. Press the DELETE EOL (CTRL + END) key to erase the entire entry.

10. Press SCREEN (CTRL + F3) and press ENTER and watch as the level-1 outline numbers readjust yet again.

DEFINE A NUMBERING STYLE

There are two instances when it becomes necessary to define the numbering style for your outline. First, you must define a numbering style when you want to create two or more independent outlines in the same document. For instance, you may wish to create separate outlines in one document, each beginning with the first number of the first level, "I." If you don't define a new numbering style, WordPerfect will continue numbering a second outline with the number at which the first outline left off.

Second, you must define a numbering style if you want the outline number style to be different from the default. Besides the outline style, which is the default setting, WordPerfect has three other predefined styles: the paragraph style, the legal style, and the bullets style. All four styles are illustrated in Figure 12-3. (Not all printers can print all the symbols used in the bullets style.) In addition, WordPerfect allows you to define your own numbering style, referred to as the user-defined style. For instance, you can choose uppercase letters followed by a period (A., B., C., and so on) as level 1 and lowercase letters followed by a period (a., b., c., and so on) as level 2.

You can define a new style before or after you type the outline. Position the cursor above the outline or above where you're about to type the outline. (Or you can position the cursor on the Document Initial Codes screen to change the style starting at the top of the document.) Next, press the DATE/OUTLINE (SHIFT + F5) key, and select

Outline Style

```
Level 1  I.  II.  ...
Level 2      A.  B.  ...
Level 3          1.  2.  ...
Level 4              a.  b.  ...
Level 5                  (1)  (2)  ...
Level 6                  (a)  (b)  ...
Level 7                       i)  ii)  ...
Level 8                            a)  b)  ...
```

Paragraph Style

```
Level 1  1.  2. ...
Level 2      a.  b.  ...
Level 3          i.  ii.  ...
Level 4              (1)  (2)  ...
Level 5                  (a)  (b)  ...
Level 6                  (i)  (ii)  ...
Level 7                       1)  2)  ...
Level 8                            a)  b)  ...
```

Legal Style

```
Level 1  1  2  ...
Level 2      1.1  1.2  ...
Level 3          1.1.1  1.1.2  ...
Level 4              1.1.1.1  1.1.1.2  ...
Level 5                  1.1.1.1.1  1.1.1.1.2  ...
Level 6                      1.1.1.1.1.1  1.1.1.1.1.2  ...
Level 7                          1.1.1.1.1.1.1  1.1.1.1.1.1.2  ...
Level 8                              1.1.1.1.1.1.1.1  1.1.1.1.1.1.1.2  ...
```

Bullets Style

```
Level 1  ●                        (bullet)
Level 2      O                    (hollow bullet)
Level 3          —                (hyphen)
Level 4              ■            (square bullet)
Level 5                  *        (asterisk)
Level 6                      +    (plus)
Level 7                        •  (small bullet)
Level 8                        x  (lowercase x)
```

FIGURE 12-3 Four predefined numbering styles

Define, (6 or D). The Paragraph Number Definition screen appears, as shown in Figure 12-4. The default is option 3, Outline, though this is difficult to decipher at first. Look at the center of Figure 12-4, next to the category "Current Definition," and you'll see that this style is identical to the style listed next to option 3, Outline.

```
Paragraph Number Definition

    1 - Starting Paragraph Number          1
        (in legal style)

                                         Levels
                           1    2    3    4    5    6    7    8
    2 - Paragraph          1.   a.   i.   (1)  (a)  (i)  1)   a)
    3 - Outline            I.   A.   1.   a.   (1)  (a)  i)   a)
    4 - Legal (1.1.1)      1    .1   .1   .1   .1   .1   .1   .1
    5 - Bullets            •    o    -    ■    *    +    .    x
    6 - User-defined

    Current Definition     I.   A.   1.   a.   (1)  (a)  i)   a)

        Number Style              Punctuation
        1 - Digits                #   - No punctuation
        A - Upper case letters    #.  - Trailing period
        a - Lower case letters    #)  - Trailing parenthesis
        I - Upper case roman      (#) - Enclosing parentheses
        i - Lower case roman      .#  - All levels separated by period
        Other character - Bullet        (e.g.  2.1.3.4)


Selection: 0
```

FIGURE 12-4   Paragraph Number Definition screen

To restart numbering for a new outline, select Starting Paragraph Number (1 or S). Then type **1** (if the number 1 does not appear) and press ENTER if you wish numbering to begin at the beginning, regardless of what numbering style you select, so that, for example, the first entry will be "I." when using the outline style or "•" when using the bullets style. Or, type the outline number and level you wish to start at in legal style characters. For instance, type **2** and press ENTER to begin numbering at "II." (assuming outline style) or type **2.2** and press ENTER to begin numbering at "II., B." or type **2.2.3** and press ENTER to begin numbering at "II., B., 3."

To choose a new numbering style, select Paragraph (2 or P); Outline (3 or O); Legal (4 or L); Bullets (5 or B). Or, select User-defined (6 or U), in which case you must also select a number style and punctuation for each level based on the legend at the bottom of the Paragraph Number Definition menu. For instance, suppose you select User-defined (6 or U); the cursor moves under the heading for level 1. Type **1)** and press ENTER to set level 1 as digits followed by a trailing parenthesis. Or, type **i** and press ENTER to set level 1 as lowercase

Roman with no trailing punctuation. Continue until you've defined a number style and punctuation for each level.

After making selections on the Paragraph Numbering Definition menu, press EXIT (F7) or ENTER. The Date/Outline menu returns to the bottom of the screen. Select another option from this menu or press CANCEL (F1) to clear this menu. When you return the cursor to the Typing screen, a **[Par Num Def]** code is inserted at the current cursor position. (Remember that outline numbering and paragraph numbering use the same code; even though the code seems to imply a *paragraph* number definition, it also governs *outline* numbers.) The code defines a new outline style for all outline numbers farther forward in the document or until the next **[Par Num Def]** code is encountered.

As an example, suppose that you want to alter the numbering style of the text on screen to legal numbering. Here's how to do so:

1. Position the cursor on the blank line above the first outline number. (Alternatively, you can position the cursor on the Document Initial Codes screen, since you wish to alter the numbering style starting at the top of the document.)

2. Press the DATE/OUTLINE (SHIFT + F5) key. The following menu appears:

   1 Date Text; 2 Date Code; 3 Date Format; 4 Outline;
   5 Para Num; 6 Define: 0

3. Select Define (6 or D). The screen shown in Figure 12-4 appears.

4. Select Legal (4 or L) to start the legal numbering style at "1."

5. Press EXIT (F7) to return to the Date/Outline menu.

6. Press CANCEL (F1) to clear the Date/Outline menu and return to the Typing screen.

You have now inserted a **[Par Num Def]** code into the text, redefining the appearance of all the outline numbers. But the screen must be rewritten for this code to take effect. One way to do this is to continue pressing DOWN ARROW and watch as the outline numbers are changed. Or press HOME, HOME, DOWN ARROW to move quickly through the remainder of text to the end of the document. You could also press the SCREEN (CTRL + F3) key and select Rewrite (0 or R) or press ENTER. Now every outline number is rewritten according to the new outline style you defined, as shown in Figure 12-5.

```
      AGENDA: R&R WINE ASSOCIATION BOARD MEETING

1   Reorganization of the Finance Department.

   1.1  Who shall fill the position of department manager?  Ms.
        Donna Rainer's name was mentioned previously.

   1.2  To whom shall the department manager report?

        1.2.1    The department currently reports to the Vice
                 President.

        1.2.2    The President is currently more involved in the
                 day-to-day operations and restructuring, and
                 works well with Ms. Rainer.

2   Authorization of a new Strategic Plan.

   2.1  The original plan, completed by the consulting firm of
        Burnes and Joseph on May 13th, 1984, is outdated.

   2.2  Demographics and consumer preferences have changed
        significantly over the past five years.

                                      Doc 1 Pg 1 Ln 4.83" Pos 1"
```

FIGURE 12-5   Sample outline using legal style for numbering

It may be necessary sometimes to reset tabs to accommodate long legal-style paragraph numbers or Roman numerals. Position the cursor above the numbered paragraphs to reset the tabs, a procedure described in Chapter 4.

Note: In WordPerfect you can permanently change the default numbering style from the outline style to another style. For instance, you can request that WordPerfect assume the bullets style for every document you type unless you specify otherwise. Refer to the "Initial Settings" section of Appendix C for more information.

NUMBER INDIVIDUAL PARAGRAPHS

Paragraph numbering is a close cousin to the Outline feature. The default numbering style for paragraphs is the same as for outlines and is still referred to as outline style:

Level 1	I.
Level 2	A.
Level 3	1.
Level 4	a.
Level 5	(1)
Level 6	(a)
Level 7	i)
Level 8	a)

In addition, you can change that default numbering style just as you do for outlines—using the Define option on the Date/Outline menu. In fact, if your outline is composed of paragraphs, outline entries and numbered paragraphs look just the same.

Then what are the differences? There are two. Unlike outline numbers, paragraph numbers are inserted into a document one by one as you type each paragraph; you must press the DATE/OUTLINE (SHIFT + F5) key each time. In addition, paragraph numbers can be fixed at a certain level irrespective of where on the line that number will appear. For instance, you can insert level-6 numbers, such as (i), (ii), (iii) and so on, at the left margin.

You can insert a paragraph number before or after typing the text of the paragraph. You first position the cursor at the tab stop where you want the paragraph number to appear. Then press the DATE/OUT-LINE (SHIFT + F5) key and select Para Num (5 or P). WordPerfect responds

Paragraph Level (Press Enter for automatic):

Now you can proceed in one of two ways. You can press ENTER, in which case you create an automatic number—WordPerfect assigns a level based on the current cursor location. For instance, if the cursor is at the left margin or before the first tab stop, WordPerfect assigns that paragraph a level-1 number and inserts a **[Par Num:Auto]** code in the text—the same code it inserts when you use the Outline feature. (In essence, this is a second way to insert the same numbering code.) If you later insert or delete tabs in front of a paragraph number, the level will change. You can adjust the level when the cursor is located *on* the paragraph number: press TAB to increase or BACKSPACE to decrease the outline level.

Alternatively, you can type a number from 1 to 8 and then press ENTER, in which case you create a fixed level; you, rather than Word-Perfect, are assigning the level. For instance, if the cursor is at the left margin and you type **5** and press ENTER, the number at that spot will be

---

R&R WINE ASSOCIATION UPDATE

1.   R&R WINE ASSOCIATION increased its market share in the
     United States by 2% this year as compared to the same time
     last year! Congratulations are in order.

2.   Sales this quarter were brisk for European and Australian
     wines. Volumes shipped increased 12% over the same time
     last year.   The Research Department believes that part of
     the increase is due to the weak dollar on international
     markets.

3.   In the United States, there was a noticeable increase in
     consumer preference of Chardonnay over other white wines
     during the past 12 months. This is particularly true in
     California, where Chardonnay is produced in large
     quantities.

FIGURE 12-6   Sample document with numbered paragraphs

a level-5 number. You will have inserted the code **[Par Num:5]** into
the text. That number will remain at level 5, no matter how many tabs
precede it.

Just as with outlining, if you add, delete, or move paragraph numbers, the text will adjust accordingly so that the numbers are in se-
quential order. And if you change the paragraph numbering style, the
paragraphs will be renumbered according to the new style.

As an example, suppose that you wish to number paragraphs with
Arabic numerals—1., 2., 3., and so on—at the left margin. Notice from
Figure 12-3 that this corresponds to the paragraph style. Let's first
define the style on the Paragraph Number Definition screen. Then
we'll insert some paragraph numbers and type the paragraphs shown in
Figure 12-6.

1. Use the EXIT (F7) key to save the document on screen under the filename OUTLINE and to clear the screen. On the clear screen, outline style is again in effect, because it's the default setting.

2. Type and center the title, **R&R WINE ASSOCIATION UP-DATE**, on the first line, and press ENTER twice to insert a blank line.

3. Press the DATE/OUTLINE (SHIFT + F5) key. The following menu appears:

   1 Date Text; 2 Date Code; 3 Date Format; 4 Outline; 5 Para Num; 6 Define: 0   .

4. Select Define (6 or D). The screen shown in Figure 12-4 appears.

5. Select Paragraph (2 or P) to start the paragraph style.

6. Press EXIT (F7) to return to the Date/Outline menu.

7. Select Para Num (5 or P). WordPerfect prompts

   Paragraph Level (Press Enter for Automatic):

8. Press ENTER. A "1.," a level-1 number, appears on screen at the left margin.

9. Press the →INDENT (F4) key, type the first paragraph in Figure 12-6, and press ENTER twice to end the paragraph and insert a blank line.

10. Press the DATE/OUTLINE (SHIFT + F5) key and repeat steps 7 through 9 to type the second and third paragraphs.

11. Use the SAVE (F10) key to save this document using the filename NUMPARA (which stands for NUMbered PARA-graphs). Leave the document on screen.

What if you had wanted to number paragraphs at the left margin with lowercase letters followed by a period, such as a., b., c., and so on? Notice in Figure 12-3 that this is level 2 of the paragraph style. You could have inserted paragraph numbers fixed at level 2.

If you choose, you can align paragraph numbers with the decimal point, rather than the number, on the tab stop. Press the TAB ALIGN (CTRL + F6) key just before you press DATE/OUTLINE (SHIFT + F5) to insert a paragraph number.

Make sure to refer to Chapter 14 if you will be using the Paragraph Numbering feature constantly; you'll learn about shortcuts for inserting Paragraph Numbering codes into your text.

INSERT FOOTNOTES AND ENDNOTES

Legal documents, research articles, and academic papers are commonly peppered with footnotes and endnotes. A footnote is a source citation or a supplementary discussion; a reference mark is inserted in the body of the text, and the footnote itself is placed at the bottom of the page. An endnote is like a footnote except that the endnote's text is placed at a location other than at the bottom of the page—such as compiled with other endnotes at the end of the document.

WordPerfect offers a feature that automatically numbers footnotes and endnotes for you. Footnotes and endnotes are numbered separately so you can include both footnotes and endnotes in the same document. Each note (footnote or endnote) can be from 1 to 16,000 lines long.

For a footnote, WordPerfect automatically allows enough room on a page to accommodate the text of the footnote; gone are the days of trying to calculate the space required at the bottom of the page! (If there is insufficient room to print the text of a footnote on a page, the first 0.5 inch of the footnote text is printed on that page and the rest is printed on the next page.) Endnotes are placed at the end of the document or at another location that you specify. All you need to do is type the text of the note. Should you later insert a new note or delete one, the others are renumbered for you.

WordPerfect has a predefined format for footnotes and endnotes. A sample of footnotes is shown in Figure 12-7. Notice that footnote reference marks appear as superscript text. Footnote text is separated from the main text by a two-inch-long line, and the superscript footnote numbers are placed five spaces from the left margin.

A sample of endnotes is shown in Figure 12-8. Notice that the endnote numbers are not superscript text; they are positioned at the left margin and followed by a period. (However, endnote reference marks *are* superscript text.) The endnotes can be printed wherever the regular text ends at the end of the document; on a separate page at the end of the document, provided that you end the document by pressing CTRL + ENTER to insert a Hard Page code; or anywhere within the document,

R&R WINE ASSOCIATION UPDATE

1.   R&R WINE ASSOCIATION increased its market share in the
     United States by 2% this year as compared to the same time
     last year![1] Congratulations are in order.

2.   Sales this quarter were brisk for European and Australian
     wines. Volumes shipped increased 12% over the same time
     last year. The Research Department believes that part of
     the increase is due to the weak dollar on international
     markets.

3.   In the United States, there was a noticeable increase in
     consumer preference of Chardonnay over other white wines
     during the past 12 months. This is particularly true in
     California, where Chardonnay is produced in large
     quantities.[2]

1. The Eastern Division increased by 1.7%, while the Western
Division increased by 2.2%.

2. Marion Laramy, Wine in the United States, Parker Publishing,
1987, pages 44-45.

FIGURE 12-7   Footnotes within a printed document

---

1. The Eastern Division increased by 1.7%, while the Western
Division increased by 2.2%.

2. Marion Laramy, <u>Wine in the United States,</u> Parker Publishing,
1987, pages 44-45.

FIGURE 12-8   Endnotes at the end of a printed document

provided that you activate the Endnote Placement option, described
farther on in this chapter.

Create Footnotes or Endnotes

Footnotes and endnotes are created in a similar way. You position the
cursor in the main text where you want the note's reference mark to
appear and press the FOOTNOTE (CTRL + F7) key. The following
menu appears:

   1 Footnote; 2 Endnote; 3 Endnote Placement: 0

Now select either Footnote (1 or F) or Endnote (2 or E). Another menu
displays. For instance, if you selected to insert a footnote, you'll view
the following menu:

   Footnote: 1 Create; 2 Edit; 3 New Number; 4 Options: 0

The Endnote menu contains the same four options. Select Create (1 or
C). A special Footnote or Endnote Typing screen appears, with the
reference number already inserted in the upper left corner. Type the
text of the note, inserting any enhancements that you desire, such as
underline, boldface, or a font attribute change. Then press the EXIT
(F7) key to return to the text.

   On the Typing screen, a reference mark appears (though it may not
appear as superscripted on your Typing screen). If you reveal codes,
you'll find that this reference mark is actually a code. The code con-

tains up to the first 50 characters of the footnote's text. For instance, for the first footnote as shown in Figure 12-7, the code reads **[Footnote:1;[Note Num]** The Eastern Division increased by 1.7%, while **th...]**. The [Note Num] within the Footnote code represents the footnote reference mark which appears in the text.

Let's create several footnotes for the document currently on screen.

1. Position the cursor just past the exclamation point (!) that ends the first sentence of the first paragraph.

2. Press the FOOTNOTE (CTRL + F7) key. WordPerfect responds

   1 Footnote; 2 Endnote; 3 Endnote Placement: 0

3. Select Footnote (1 or F) to see the following menu:

   Footnote: 1 Create; 2 Edit; 3 New Number; 4 Options: 0

4. Select Create (1 or C). A Footnote Typing screen appears. Notice that a footnote reference number is automatically inserted for you.

5. Press SPACEBAR once, and type the following:

   The Eastern Division increased by 1.7%, while the Western Division increased by 2.2%.

6. Press the EXIT (F7) key as suggested at the bottom of the screen.

7. Position the cursor at the end of the document, just past the period of the last sentence in the third paragraph.

8. Repeat steps 2 through 4. Now the footnote reference mark inserted is number 2.

9. Press SPACEBAR once, and type the following:

   Marion Laramy, Wine in the United States, Parker Publishing, 1987, pages 44-45.

10. Press the EXIT (F7) key as suggested at the bottom of the Footnote Typing screen.

If you print this document, you'll see the results as shown in Figure 12-7. To print footnotes and endnotes, WordPerfect uses whatever is the selected initial font for your document (unless you inserted a Font or Font Attribute code when typing the text of the footnote or endnote, in which case the font or font attribute you specified is used to print that particular footnote or endnote).

The text of footnotes and endnotes appears on the printed page but is not visible on the Typing screen. To see the contents of a note before printing, you can reveal codes to view the first 50 characters of the note. Or, you can employ the Edit option, described in the next section, to see the text of the entire footnote. Or you can view your footnotes or endnotes by previewing the document on screen using the View Document feature, as described in Chapter 9.

You can insert a new footnote or an endnote anywhere in a document, at any time—all notes will be automatically renumbered for you. For example, let's add a footnote between notes 1 and 2 to see how the footnotes are renumbered.

1. Position the cursor after the period in the last sentence of the second paragraph.

2. Press the FOOTNOTE (CTRL + F7) key. WordPerfect responds

   1 Footnote; 2 Endnote; 3 Endnote Placement: 0

3. Select Footnote (1 or F) to see the following menu:

   Footnote: 1 Create; 2 Edit; 3 New Number; 4 Options: 0

4. Select Create (1 or C). A Footnote Typing screen appears. Notice that a footnote reference number is automatically inserted for you.

5. Press SPACEBAR once, and type the following:

   Paula Fleming, "What's with the Dollar?," The New York Times, May 28, 1987.

6. Press the EXIT (F7) key, as suggested at the bottom of the Footnote Typing screen.

7. Press DOWN ARROW to move the cursor down through the document. Notice that the last footnote is now renumbered for you.

Placement of Footnotes and Endnotes on the Printed Page

The vertical space occupied by footnotes is taken into account as WordPerfect readjusts soft page breaks. WordPerfect counts one blank line which contains the two-inch line separating the footnote text from the main text, one blank line preceding the text of each footnote, and all lines of the footnote text when determining where to break a page. As a result, when you create footnotes, fewer lines of your main text fit on a page.

WordPerfect reserves space at the end of the document for the endnotes, placing them either at the end of the main text or on a separate page if you ended the document by pressing HARD PAGE (CTRL + ENTER).

Alternatively, you can specify where you want endnotes printed. Position the cursor where you wish endnotes to appear when printed. The cursor must be forward from the reference marks for the endnotes you want printed. For instance, if you've created endnotes on pages 1 through 6, then the cursor must be positioned below the last endnote reference mark on page 6 in order for all those endnotes to be printed where you specify; any endnotes cited farther forward in the text will print at the end of the document.

Once the cursor is positioned, press the FOOTNOTE (CTRL + F7) key and select Endnote Placement (3 or P). WordPerfect prompts

Restart endnote numbering? (Y/N) Yes

WordPerfect is asking whether you wish to restart endnote numbering at 1 for all endnotes that follow the current position of the cursor. Type **Y** to begin numbering from the start, or type **N** to continue consecutive endnote numbering. WordPerfect inserts an **[Endnote Placement]** code in the text, followed by an **[HPg]** code so that additional text starts at the top of the next page. If you elected to restart endnote numbering for endnotes below the code, WordPerfect inserts a third code,

[New End Num:1], which dictates that the next endnote will be renumbered to start at number 1. Where the Endnote Placement code is inserted, a special comment displays on screen to remind you that endnotes will be located there when printed:

```
Endnote Placement
It is not known how much space endnotes will occupy here.
Generate to determine.
```

If you wish, you can determine how much vertical space will be occupied by the endnotes as follows: press MARK TEXT (ALT + F5), select Generate (6 or G), and select Generate Table of Contents, Indexes, Automatic References, etc. (5 or G). Then press **Y** to begin the generation of endnotes (as well as any tables, indexes, or automatic references—described in Chapter 15). In moments, the special comment on screen will display as follows:

```
Endnote Placement
```

The comment appears on the Typing screen as only one line in length. However, position the cursor just above the comment, check the Ln indicator on the status line, press RIGHT ARROW to position the cursor on the other side of the comment, and again check the Ln indicator. The status line will indicate how much space is required to print the endnotes. For instance, if the status line reads **Ln 2"** above the comment and reads **Ln 7"** below the comment, this indicates that the endnotes will occupy approximately 5 inches of vertical space on the page.

You can have more than one Endnote Placement code in a document. All endnotes between the code and the previous Endnote Placement code (or the top of the document) are included at the code location when printed.

EDIT FOOTNOTES AND ENDNOTES

To edit or review the text of a footnote or endnote, press the FOOT-NOTE (CTRL + F7) key, select Footnote (1 or F) or Endnote (2 or E), and then select Edit (2 or E). WordPerfect will prompt you for which note you wish to edit, suggesting the first note forward from the current cursor position. For instance, if you will be editing a footnote, WordPerfect may prompt

Footnote number? 1

Press ENTER to accept the suggestion or type in the number of another note you wish to review and press ENTER. That note now appears on screen. You can then use any of the standard editing keys and the BLOCK (ALT + F4) key to revise the text and then press the EXIT (F7) key to return to the Typing screen.

For instance, suppose that you wish to edit the text of the first footnote.

1. Position the cursor at the top of the document.

2. Press the FOOTNOTE (CTRL + F7) key. WordPerfect responds

   1 Footnote; 2 Endnote; 3 Endnote Placement: 0

3. Select Footnote (1 or F) to see the following menu:

   Footnote: 1 Create; 2 Edit; 3 New Number; 4 Options: 0

4. Select Edit (2 or E). WordPerfect prompts

   Footnote number? 1

5. Press ENTER. Footnote number 1 appears on screen, as shown in Figure 12-9.

6. Edit the percent figures in the footnote so that it reads as follows:

   The Eastern Division increased by 1.71%, while the Western Division increased by 2.29%.

7. Press the EXIT (F7) key. When the Typing screen appears, the cursor is repositioned just to the right of footnote number 1.

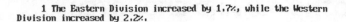

        1 The Eastern Division increased by 1.7%, while the Western
Division increased by 2.2%.

Press Exit when done   Doc 1 Pg 4 Ln 2.19" Pos 1"

FIGURE 12-9   Footnote Typing screen showing text to be edited

You also may decide to delete a note from the text. This is quite
simple. Move the cursor onto the note reference mark in the text and
press DEL. You can also delete by moving the cursor just to the right of
the reference mark and pressing BACKSPACE. When on the Reveal
Codes screen, the footnote or endnote is erased, text and all. When on
the Typing screen, WordPerfect will prompt for you to verify the deletion, such as

Delete [Footnote:1]? (Y/N) No

Type **Y** for yes and the note will be erased, text and all. All remaining
footnotes or endnotes in the text will be renumbered accordingly.

When working with footnotes or endnotes, you may wish to
specify a new starting number. This is useful when you want one
document's numbering to begin where another's left off, as when you
split a long chapter into two separate documents. To indicate a new
starting number, position the cursor in the text before the footnote or
endnote you wish to renumber. Press the FOOTNOTE (CTRL + F7) key,
and select Footnote (1 or F) or Endnote (2 or E). Next, select New

Number (3 or N). WordPerfect prompts for a new note number. Type in the new note number and press ENTER. A code is inserted in the text. For instance, if you reset footnotes to begin at number 20, the code inserted is **[New Ftn Num:20]**. All footnotes following the code would be renumbered sequentially as 21, 22, 23, and so on. Or, if you reset endnotes to begin at number 30, the code inserted is **[New End Num:30]** and all subsequent endnotes would be affected accordingly.

CHANGE FOOTNOTE AND ENDNOTE OPTIONS

You can also alter the defaults that control how footnotes and endnotes appear on the printed page. For instance, you can change the spacing within notes to double spacing; or, instead of using Arabic numerals to reference a footnote in the main text, you can use letters or even other characters, such as the asterisk (*).

To change footnote or endnote options, position the cursor where you want the new option to take effect. For example, place the cursor on page 2 to alter an option starting on that page, or place the cursor on the Document Initial Codes screen (described in Chapter 4) to alter an option starting at the top of the document. Then press the FOOT-NOTE (CTRL + F7) key, select Footnote (1 or F) or Endnote (2 or E), and select Options (4 or O). For footnotes, the menu in Figure 12-10 appears, which indicates the default settings for how footnotes will appear when printed. For endnotes, the menu in Figure 12-11 appears, containing fewer options. The following options are available for either footnotes or endnotes:

- *Spacing Within Notes* This option is preset at 1, for single spacing within the text of the footnotes or endnotes. You can instead select 0.5 for half spacing, 2 for double spacing, and so on.

- *Spacing Between Notes* This option is preset at 0.16 inch so that there is one blank line, 0.16 inch in height, between footnotes or endnotes. You can change that setting; for instance, select 0.15 inch for slightly less space between notes.

```
Footnote Options

    1 - Spacing Within Footnotes          1
              Between Footnotes           0.16"

    2 - Amount of Note to Keep Together   0.5"

    3 - Style for Number in Text          [SUPRSCPT][Note Num][suprscpt]

    4 - Style for Number in Note              [SUPRSCPT][Note Num][suprscpt]

    5 - Footnote Numbering Method         Numbers

    6 - Start Footnote Numbers each Page  No

    7 - Line Separating Text and Footnotes  2-inch Line

    8 - Print Continued Message           No

    9 - Footnotes at Bottom of Page       Yes



Selection: 0
```

FIGURE 12-10   Footnote Options screen

```
Endnote Options

    1 - Spacing Within Endnotes           1
              Between Endnotes            0.16"

    2 - Amount of Endnote to Keep Together  0.5"

    3 - Style for Numbers in Text         [SUPRSCPT][Note Num][suprscpt]

    4 - Style for Numbers in Note         [Note Num].

    5 - Endnote Numbering Method          Numbers







Selection: 0
```

FIGURE 12-11   Endnote Options screen

- *Amount of Note to Keep Together*   This option is preset to keep 0.5 inch of a long footnote or endnote on a page before continuing the note on the next page if WordPerfect has insufficient room to print the note on one page. You can increase or decrease this default setting.

- *Style for Number in Text*   As shown in Figure 12-10 and 12-11, this option is preset with the code string **[SUPRSCPT][Note Num][SuprScpt]**, which means that the note reference mark—whether a number, letter, or character—will print as superscript. You can select a different style, such as removing the Superscript codes or inserting Underline or Boldface codes. (If you accidentally erase the **[Note Num]** code, use the Note Number option on the FOOTNOTE (CTRL + F7) key to reinsert it.)

- *Style for Number in Note*   Footnote numbers are preset to be indented five spaces from the left margin and superscripted. (**[Tab]** and **[→Indent]** codes are not allowed as part of the style, so you must insert spaces instead.) Endnote numbers are preset to be followed by a period, without any indent or superscript. You can insert or delete codes to change the style. (If you accidentally erase the **[Note Num]** code, use the Note Number option on the FOOTNOTE (CTRL + F7) key to reinsert it.)

- *Note Numbering Method*   This option is preset to numbers, which means that footnotes and endnotes will be referenced using numbers. If you select this option, WordPerfect displays the following menu:

1 Numbers; 2 Letters; 3 Characters: 0

Select Letters (2 or L) and WordPerfect will mark footnotes or endnotes in lowercase letters (a,b,c, and so on). Select Characters (3 or C) and WordPerfect allows you to type in up to 20 characters. For instance, if you type in an asterisk (*) as the footnote character, then the first footnote will be marked with one asterisk, the second with two asterisks, and so on. If you type an asterisk and then a pound sign (*#), the first footnote will be marked with one asterisk, the second with one pound sign, the third with two asterisks, the fourth with two pound signs, and so on.

The additional options available for footnotes only are as follows:

- *Start Footnote Numbers each Page*   This option is preset to "No," so that notes are numbered sequentially throughout a document. If you wish the numbering to restart at 1 on every page, you must change this to "Yes" by typing **Y**.

- *Line Separating Text and Footnotes*   This option is preset for a 2-inch line separating the body of the text from the footnotes at the bottom of the page. If you select this option, WordPerfect displays the following menu:

    1 No Line; 2 2-inch Line; 3 Margin to Margin: 0

    Your other choices are to select No Line (1 or N) or Margin to Margin (4 or M), which creates a line that extends from the left to the right margin.

- *Print Continued Message*   This option is preset to "No," so that no message is printed if a footnote is split between two pages. You can instead select "Yes," so that a "(Continued)..." message is printed at the end of the footnote on the first page and at the beginning of where it continues on the next page.

- *Footnotes at Bottom of Page*   This option is preset to "Yes," meaning that even if the page is only partially full, blank lines are inserted so that the notes are printed at the bottom. If you wanted to print footnotes just below the main text on a partially full page, you would change this to "No."

Once you change one or more of the footnote options, press ENTER or EXIT (F7) to return to the Typing screen. For footnotes, a **[Ftn Opt]** code is inserted and will affect all footnotes from the current cursor position forward. For endnotes, the code is **[End Opt]**.

Suppose you want to change the footnote reference marks to letters in the document on screen. In addition, you want a line across the entire page to separate the footnotes from the text. Since you wish to change these options for the entire document, let's do so on the Document Initial Codes screen. (See Chapter 4 if you need a review of the advantages of placing certain codes on the Document Initial Codes screen rather than at the top of a document).

1. With the cursor positioned anywhere in the document, press the FORMAT (SHIFT + F8) key. The Format menu appears.

2. Select Document (3 or D). The Document Format menu appears.

3. Select Initial Codes (2 or C). The Document Initial Codes screen appears.

4. Press the FOOTNOTE (CTRL + F7) key. WordPerfect responds

    1 Footnote; 2 Endnote; 3 Endnote Placement: 0

5. Select Footnote (1 or F) to see the following menu:

    Footnote: 1 Create; 2 Edit; 3 New Number; 4 Options: 0

6. Select Options (4 or O). The Footnote Options screen appears, as shown in Figure 12-10.

7. Select Footnote Numbering Method (5 or M), and then choose Letters (2 or L).

8. Select Line Separating Text and Footnotes (7 or L) and then choose Margin to Margin (3 or M).

9. Press EXIT (F7) to return to the Document Initial Codes screen. You'll see a **[Ftn Opt]** code.

10. Press EXIT (F7) several more times until you return to your document.

11. Press the SCREEN (CTRL + F3) key and press ENTER to rewrite the screen.

12. Use the SAVE (F10) key to resave this document under the name NUMPARA.

Notice that letters now reference the footnotes. Print this page and you'll see that the page prints with letters as footnote reference marks and a separator line across the width of the page. The printed results are shown in Figure 12-12.

Note: In WordPerfect you can permanently change the default footnote or endnote option settings for all new documents that you create, rather than changing the defaults individually for every document. For instance, you may decide that you always want a line extending from margin to margin above footnotes. Refer to the "Initial Settings" section of Appendix C for more information.

R&R WINE ASSOCIATION UPDATE

1.   R&R WINE ASSOCIATION increased its market share in the
      United States by 2% this year as compared to the same time
      last year![a] Congratulations are in order.

2.   Sales this quarter were brisk for European and Australian
      wines. Volumes shipped increased 12% over the same time
      last year. The Research Department believes that part of
      the increase is due to the weak dollar on international
      markets.[b]

3.   In the United States, there was a noticeable increase in
      consumer preference of Chardonnay over other white wines
      during the past 12 months. This is particularly true in
      California, where Chardonnay is produced in large
      quantities.[c]

---

[a] The Eastern Division increased by 1.71%, while the Western
Division increased by 2.29%.

[b] Paula Fleming, "What's with the Dollar?," The New York
Times, May 28, 1987.

[c] Marion Laramy, Wine in the United States, Parker
Publishing, 1987, pages 44-45.

FIGURE 12-12   Printed page after altering the default footnote options

REVIEW EXERCISE

Let's use the document on screen to practice with paragraph number-ing and footnoting. As usual, WordPerfect will always renumber properly after you edit your text.

1. For the document on screen, change the paragraph numbers to the outline style (I., II., III.) rather than the paragraph style. (*Hint:* Since the default *is* the outline style, simply find the **[Par Num Def]** code and erase it.) Watch the numbering style change as you rewrite the text.

2. Suppose you wish to indent the paragraph numbers to the next tab stop. Position the cursor on the number "I." and press TAB. When you press DOWN ARROW, notice that the paragraph num-ber is now "A.," because you've shifted it to level 2. Indent the other paragraph numbers to level 2 as well.

3. Position the cursor just to the right of the percent sign (%) in "increased 12%," which is located in the second paragraph. In-sert the following footnote:

    Actual percent increase is 12.223.

    After you insert the footnote, notice how the two footnotes that follow it are renumbered as soon as you rewrite the screen.

4. Delete the first footnote by positioning the cursor on the foot-note reference mark "a," pressing DEL, and, if you're viewing the Typing screen, typing **Y** to confirm that you wish to delete the footnote. Notice how all the other footnotes are again renumbered after the screen is rewritten.

5. Resave this document under the name NUMPARA.

REVIEW

- You can create outlines with up to eight different outline levels (I., A., 1., a., etc.) by choosing the Outline option after pressing the DATE/OUTLINE (SHIFT + F5) key. Insert outline numbers for level 1 by pressing ENTER; use TAB to move that number to the right and, at the same time, change to one of the other outline levels. An outline will be renumbered if you add, delete, or move entries.

- You can insert individual paragraph numbers by moving to the desired tab stop and selecting the Para Num option after pressing the DATE/OUTLINE (SHIFT + F5) key. Either let WordPerfect insert a number with the level automatically set according to the cursor's location in relation to tab stops, or fix the number at a specific level irrespective of the cursor's position number. Subsequent paragraphs will be renumbered if you add, delete, or move a paragraph.

- For both outlining and paragraph numbering, the default is the outline style. You can select one of three other predefined styles, create a user-defined style, and/or restart the numbering for a second outline or set of paragraph numbers. Insert into the text a Paragraph Number Definition code. This code affects all outline and paragraph numbers forward in the text until the next such code is encountered.

- Press the FOOTNOTE (CTRL + F7) key to insert either a footnote or an endnote. The note's reference mark will appear wherever the cursor is located. The text of the note itself appears not on the Typing screen but on the printed page. You can use the Edit option to revise or simply review the text of a note.

- Delete a footnote or endnote by erasing its reference mark in the body of the text. The remaining notes are renumbered automatically.

- The Footnote/Endnote Option menus provide the ability to change the appearance of your footnotes or endnotes and their accompanying reference numbers.

- WordPerfect assumes that you wish to print endnotes at the end of your document. However, the Endnote Placement feature allows you to specify other locations. All endnotes from the beginning of the document (or from a previous Endnote Placement code) will be printed at that specified location.

13

PRODUCE REPETITIVE DOCUMENTS AND MERGE

Work with Boilerplate Text
Merge with the Keyboard
Merge with a File
Prepare Envelopes and Mailing Labels
Enhance the Merge Process
Review Exercise
Review

WordPerfect offers a variety of sophisticated options for working with repetitive documents. Creating certain documents may entail simply reorganizing standard paragraphs. If so, you can create a system of "boilerplate" files, with each file containing a single or several paragraphs. This lets you retrieve separate files into the document you're currently producing—effectively pasting paragraphs together to produce the document with little actual typing.

Other documents have more in common than just a few select paragraphs. These documents are identical except for bits of information that personalize each one—perhaps a name and an address. The text that changes in each copy of the document is referred to as *variable information*. WordPerfect's Merge feature can quickly create many personalized documents. The Merge feature will accept the variable information directly from the keyboard or from data provided from another file.

In this chapter, you'll learn how to produce repetitive documents quickly and easily. You'll learn first about boilerplating and then about the Merge feature—merging both with the keyboard and with a file. You'll also see how the Merge feature can produce envelopes or mailing labels in minutes. And you'll learn about some special Merge commands for added flexibility. Read on to see that given WordPerfect's power and flexibility, typing the same text over and over is a great waste of time.

WORK WITH BOILERPLATE TEXT

Sometimes the same text appears in a variety of documents, such as a paragraph used frequently in correspondence or a chart included often in promotional materials. Rather than type that text from scratch, you can store it in its own individual file and insert it into any document you're typing. You can think of a collection of these stored paragraphs as a library of boilerplate files, any of which is ready for you to insert into your documents, as needed, without ever retyping.

Create a Boilerplate Paragraph

There are several ways to store boilerplate text on disk. On a clear screen, you can type the text and then store it in its own file, using either the EXIT (F7) or the SAVE (F10) key. If the boilerplate text already exists in a document, you can retrieve that document to the screen and use the Block Save feature, discussed in Chapter 2, to save the boilerplate text in its own file. You would use the BLOCK (ALT + F4) key to highlight the text, press the SAVE (F10) key, type a new filename, and press ENTER. The document on screen would be unaffected, but now the paragraph would be stored in a separate boilerplate file.

The key to creating an effective library of boilerplate files is establishing a logical filenaming system so that it is easy to identify the contents of each file. You should give each boilerplate file a name that reminds you of its contents. For instance, you could name the paragraph most often included first in a letter as BEGIN.LET (standing for BEGINning of LETter), the paragraph that usually concludes a letter as CLOSE.LET, and the paragraph that provides background information on your company as BACK.LET. Or store a whole series of paragraphs named P1, P2, P3, and so on. You may wish to store these boilerplate paragraphs all on one floppy disk or in one directory. Be sure to keep at your desk (or in a file on disk) a list of filenames and a description of the boilerplate text contained in each file.

Here's a practical example, using a paragraph you'd include frequently in promotional material or correspondence if you worked for the R&R Wine Association:

R&R WINE ASSOCIATION, established in 1982, boasts a membership of over 100 outstanding wineries from California, New York, Europe, South America, and Australia. We disseminate information about wine tasting, production, and enjoyment. In addition, we distribute wine produced by our member wineries.

You may remember typing this paragraph as part of the document that you stored on disk under the name SAMPLE. Let's recall the file named SAMPLE and save that one paragraph into its own file to create a boilerplate paragraph.

1. Make sure that the screen is completely clear. If it isn't, press the EXIT (F7) key and then type **N** twice to clear it.

2. Use the RETRIEVE (SHIFT + F10) key to retrieve the file named SAMPLE.

3. Position the cursor on the last page of the document, where you'll find the paragraph that you will save in its own file.

4. Position the cursor on the first "R" in "R&R WINE ASSOCIA-TION."

5. Press the BLOCK (ALT + F4) key and then use the cursor movement keys to highlight the paragraph.

6. Press the SAVE (F10) key. WordPerfect responds

   Block name:

7. Type **BACK.RR** (a name that reminds you that this file will contain BACKground information on the R&R Wine Association) and press ENTER. WordPerfect saves the block independently under that filename.

Nothing on the screen has changed. And yet, you've also created a new, separate file on disk that contains one paragraph. Now this paragraph can be inserted whenever you write a document in which you wish to include background information on the R&R Wine Association.

Insert a Boilerplate Paragraph

You learned in Chapter 2 that WordPerfect retrieves a file without first clearing the screen. That's why, when you want to begin working with a completely different document from the one on screen, you must first remember to use the EXIT (F7) key to clear the screen before you use the RETRIEVE (SHIFT + F10) or LIST FILES (F5) key to retrieve another document.

If you don't clear the screen first, you can combine a boilerplate file with whatever is already on the screen. Simply position the cursor where you want the contents of the boilerplate file inserted. Then proceed in one of two ways. You can press the RETRIEVE (SHIFT + F10) key, type the filename, and press ENTER. Alternatively, you can use the LIST FILES (F5) key to view the List Files screen for a particular drive or directory, position the cursor on the file you wish to retrieve, and select Retrieve (1 or R). When using the List Files screen to retrieve a file onto a screen that already contains text, WordPerfect will prompt asking for verification that you wish to insert the file into the current document on screen. Type **Y** to proceed or type **N** to cancel the Retrieve command.

Once a paragraph has been retrieved, you can continue with the document at hand, typing additional text, editing text, or inserting another boilerplate file. Then you can save the document.

Be cautious if you retrieve boilerplate text onto a clear screen *first,* add additional text, and then attempt to save the document. Word-Perfect will suggest that you save using the name of the boilerplate file that you first retrieved. Be sure that you type in a different filename. If you don't, you may accidentally replace the boilerplate file.

Suppose that you wish to type and store on disk the letter shown in Figure 13-1. Notice that the circled copy in Figure 13-1 is the boilerplate text you just created and stored under the name BACK.RR. You will insert this boilerplate file into the letter, thereby reducing the typing required to produce it.

```
October 15, 1989


Ms. Diane Johnston
334 Glenview Road
Boynton Beach, FL 33436

Dear Ms. Johnston:

This is a response to your letter dated September 21, 1989.  You
asked if the R&R Wine Association is a lobbying organization for
the wine industry.  We are not a lobbying organization.

R&R WINE ASSOCIATION, established in 1982, boasts a membership of
over 100 outstanding wineries from California, New York, Europe,
South America, and Australia. We disseminate information about wine
tasting, production, and enjoyment. In addition, we distribute wine
produced by our member wineries.

I believe you will instead want to contact the Winston Grape
Growers Association of America.  They are located in Baltimore,
Maryland.


Sincerely,                                         Boilerplate text


Donna Jones
Vice President
```

FIGURE 13-1 Sample letter to be typed with the aid of boilerplate text (circled copy)

1. Press the EXIT (F7) key and then type **N** twice to clear the screen.

2. On the clear screen, type the date, the inside address, and the first paragraph of the letter shown in Figure 13-1.

```
October 15, 1989


Ms. Diane Johnston
334 Glenview Road
Boynton Beach, FL 33436


Dear Ms. Johnston:

This is a response to your letter dated September 21, 1989.  You
asked if the R&R Wine Association is a lobbying organization for
the wine industry.  We are not a lobbying organization.

-




                                    Doc 1 Pg 1 Ln 3.5" Pos 1"
```

FIGURE 13-2 Letter just before boilerplate text is inserted

3. Press ENTER twice to end the letter's first paragraph and to insert a blank line, so that your screen resembles Figure 13-2.

4. Press the RETRIEVE (SHIFT + F10) key. WordPerfect responds

   Document to be retrieved:

5. Type **BACK.RR**, and press ENTER. WordPerfect inserts the
   boilerplate paragraph in the letter.

6. Continue typing the remainder of the letter.

7. Use the SAVE (F10) key to store this letter on disk. Because
   you typed text before retrieving the file named BACK.RR,
   WordPerfect makes no filename suggestion, but instead
   prompts

   Document to be saved:

8. Type **JOHNSTON.LET**, and press ENTER. Now you have a
   letter stored on disk, and you still have the boilerplate
   paragraph available for insertion in future documents.

Another candidate for boilerplate is a signature block. For instance, if you had stored on disk the signature block at the bottom of the letter shown in Figure 13-1 (which starts with "Sincerely" and ends with "Vice President"), you could have taken advantage of a second boilerplate file when typing such a letter.

You can also use boilerplates to store commonly used format settings. For instance, suppose that on all the reports you produce, you change the margins and establish a standard header. On a clear screen, you could make these formatting changes. Then before typing any actual text, you could store this document (which contains only codes) in a file, perhaps under the name REP.FMT (which stands for REPort ForMaT). From then on, every time you are ready to create a report, you could retrieve the file named REP.FMT onto a clear screen and then type the text of the report. In this case, however, WordPerfect will suggest the filename REP.FMT the first time you save the report; make sure to save the finished report under a different filename so that you have the file named REP.FMT ready to use when you create a new report. (Also, see Chapter 14 for additional methods for formatting a standard document, such as a report, with ease and swiftness.)

MERGE WITH THE KEYBOARD

The Merge with the Keyboard feature is most useful when you must produce a document time and time again, personalizing it each time, but without needing to store the variable information for later use. Figure 13-3 shows a sample of a memo that the personnel office at R&R Wine Association sends out frequently to different employees. The circled copy is a sample of the type of information that changes from memo to memo. The rest of the memo always stays the same. Using the Merge with the Keyboard feature, WordPerfect can turn the task of producing such a memo into a quick, automated, fill-in-the-blanks job.

Create a Primary File

To use the Merge with the Keyboard feature, you must first create a *primary file*, which contains the text that does not change. In those locations where the document is to be personalized, you insert special

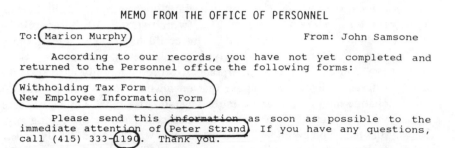

FIGURE 13-3   Sample memo to be produced using the Merge with the
                  Keyboard feature

Merge codes to act as placeholders where the variable information will
later be inserted. The Merge code you insert is ^C (pronounced "Control C"). The "C" stands for "console," another name for the keyboard.
The primary file for the R&R Wine Association's personnel office
memo is shown in Figure 13-4.

You begin a primary file just as you begin any other document:
clear the screen and begin typing the text. Wherever you want to insert
a ^C, press the MERGE CODES (SHIFT + F9) key. WordPerfect will
prompt you with a list of Merge codes. Type **C** and a ^C will be inserted at the current cursor position. Unlike other WordPerfect codes,
Merge codes are displayed on the Typing screen. A word of caution:
make sure not to type the caret symbol and then an uppercase "C" in
an attempt to insert a ^C Merge code. This creates the symbol ^C,
which looks like a Merge code on the Typing screen; but it will not be
treated as a code, and the merge will work improperly.

When you create a primary file, you can edit and format it—
changing margins, tabs, spacing, and so forth—as you would any
standard document. Also, you should check carefully for spelling errors. If you misspell a word, it will appear misspelled every time you
use the primary file to produce a new document. You can use the
Speller feature, described in Chapter 7, to check the primary file for
spelling mistakes before saving it on disk. You should save the document under a name that will remind you that it is not a standard document, but rather a primary file containing Merge Codes. For instance,

```
              MEMO FROM THE OFFICE OF PERSONNEL

To: ^C                                    From: John Sansone

      According to our records, you have not yet completed and
returned to the Personnel office the following forms:

^C

      Please send this information as soon as possible to the
immediate attention of ^C.  If you have any questions, call (415)
333-^C.   Thank you. _




                                     Doc 1 Pg 1 Ln 3" Pos 3.2"
```

FIGURE 13-4   A primary file containing ^C Merge codes

name a primary file beginning with the letters PF or PRI (both standing for Primary File) or with the filename extension .PF or .PRI.

For practice, let's create a primary file to use in producing personalized memos such as the one shown in Figure 13-3.

1. Beginning with a clear screen, press the CENTER (SHIFT + F6) key, press CAPS LOCK, and type

   MEMO FROM THE OFFICE OF PERSONNEL

2. Press CAPS LOCK to switch back to lowercase letters, and press ENTER twice to insert a blank line.

3. Type **To:** and press TAB. You're now at the location where you must insert the first Merge code.

4. Press the MERGE CODES (SHIFT + F9) key. WordPerfect prompts you with

   ^C; ^D; ^E; ^F; ^G; ^N; ^O; ^P; ^Q; ^S; ^T; ^U; ^V:

5. Type C. WordPerfect inserts ^C at the current cursor position.

6. Press the FLUSH RIGHT (ALT + F6) key and type **From: John Samsone**

7. Press ENTER twice to insert a blank line.

8. Press TAB and type the following:

   According to our records, you have not yet completed and returned to the Personnel office the following forms:

9. Press ENTER twice.

10. Press the MERGE CODES (SHIFT + F9) key. WordPerfect prompts you with

    ^C; ^D; ^E; ^F; ^G; ^N; ^O; ^P; ^Q; ^S; ^T; ^U; ^V:

11. Type C. WordPerfect inserts ^C at the current cursor position.

12. Press ENTER twice and type the rest of the memo. Notice in Figure 13-4 that you must insert two more ^C codes in this primary file.

13. Once your screen resembles Figure 13-4, use the EXIT (F7) key to save this file under the name MEMO.PRI (which stands for MEMO, PRImary file), and then clear the screen.

Merge on the Screen

Once you have stored a primary file on disk, you can initiate a merge with the keyboard at any time. You must make sure that the screen is clear. Then press the MERGE/SORT (CTRL + F9) key and select Merge (1 or M). (Though the Merge and Sort features are accessed with the same function key, they are independent. Refer to Chapter 15 for a discussion of the Sort command.) WordPerfect prompts you for the name of a primary file; type in the appropriate filename and press ENTER. Now WordPerfect prompts you for the name of a secondary file; a secondary file is used only for a merge with a file—a feature described later in this chapter; simply press ENTER to bypass this secondary file prompt, signifying to WordPerfect that you wish to perform a merge with the keyboard.

The primary file will appear on screen, and the following message will display at the bottom of the screen, on the status line, to remind you that you have initiated a merge:

* Merging *

WordPerfect will have already located and erased the first ^C code. The cursor will be positioned at that location, and you can fill in variable information directly from the keyboard. When you are done typing the information in that first location in the document, press the MERGE R (F9) key. Now the cursor jumps forward to the next ^C code, erases ^C, and pauses for you to type the personalized information appropriate for this new location. When done typing, again press the MERGE R (F9) key; the cursor jumps to the next ^C code. You should continue until you have completed filling in the last blank where a ^C code previously resided. Then press the MERGE R (F9) key one more time to end the merge process. If you wish to cancel during the course of a merge, press the MERGE CODES (SHIFT + F9) key and type **E**.

After the merge from the keyboard, you are ready to print the document, save it, edit it, or perform any combination of these actions. You can then clear the screen and start the merge process over again to create another personalized memorandum.

Suppose Robert Wambough, an employee at R&R Wine Association, has forgotten to complete several personnel forms. Let's send him a reminder.

1. Make sure that you clear the screen. Then, press the MERGE/SORT (CTRL + F9) key. WordPerfect responds

   1 Merge; 2 Sort; 3 Sort Order: 0

2. Select Merge (1 or M). WordPerfect prompts

   Primary file:

3. Type **MEMO.PRI**, and press ENTER. WordPerfect prompts

   Secondary file:

4. Press ENTER to bypass this prompt. The primary file appears, with the cursor positioned at the first place where you must personalize the memo, as shown in Figure 13-5. Notice that at the bottom of the screen, WordPerfect reminds you that you are merging.

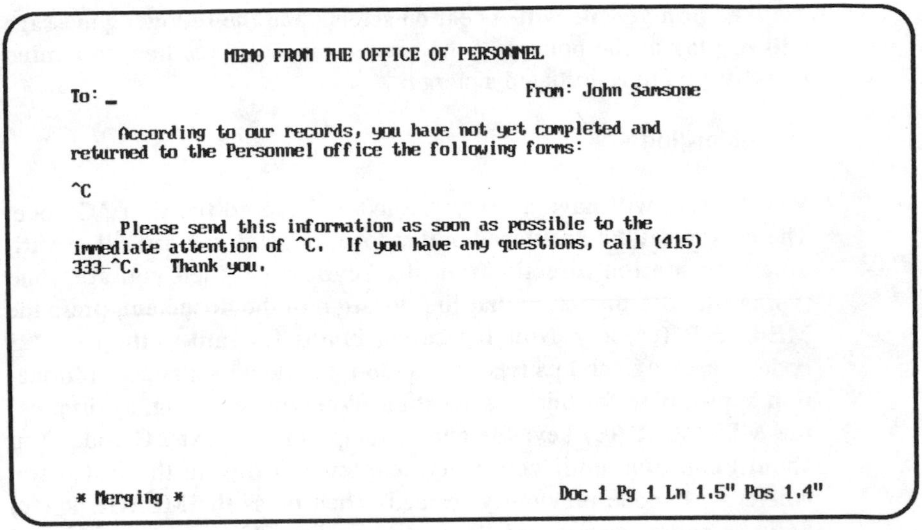

```
                    MEMO FROM THE OFFICE OF PERSONNEL

To: _                                          From: John Sansone

        According to our records, you have not yet completed and
   returned to the Personnel office the following forms:

   ^C

        Please send this information as soon as possible to the
   immediate attention of ^C.  If you have any questions, call (415)
   333-^C.  Thank you.




   * Merging *                              Doc 1 Pg 1 Ln 1.5" Pos 1.4"
```

FIGURE 13-5   The screen during a merge with the keyboard

5. Type **Robert Wambough.**

6. Press the MERGE R (F9) key to continue the merge. Now the cursor moves down to the next preselected place, erases the **^C** code, and pauses for your input.

7. Type **Withholding Tax Form**, and press ENTER so that you can type additional information on the next line.

8. Type **Employee Emergency Form**.

9. Press the MERGE R (F9) key. The cursor moves to the next place for you to type in a name.

10. Type your own name.

11. Press the MERGE R (F9) key. The cursor is positioned for you to type the last four digits of a phone number.

12. Type **9905.**

13. Press the MERGE R (F9) key. The cursor jumps to the bottom of the document; this completes the merge process.

You have completed this memo much faster than if you had to type it from scratch.

Print the document and clear the screen. You're now ready to perform other merges to prepare memos for other forgetful R&R Wine Association employees. After completing just two memos like this one, you'll see how much time and energy the Merge with the Keyboard feature saves you—not to mention the rest it provides for your typing fingers.

MERGE WITH A FILE

The Merge with a File feature is most useful when you must produce and personalize the same document many times, and you wish to store the variable information for later use. Why would you ever wish to save this variable information? You may need, for example, to carry on habitual correspondence with a list of clients or members of a certain organization or committee. In that case, you will want to store the names and addresses of your clients or committee members in a file so that whenever you merge you won't have to type in each name and address over and over again as you do with a merge with the keyboard.

Figure 13-6 shows a letter to be sent to each person on the R&R Wine Association's wine-tasting committee. The circled copy is a sample of the variable information. The rest of the letter always stays the same.

In a merge with a file, you first store the variable information in what's called a *secondary file*. Then you're ready to create a primary file containing the text that stays the same from copy to copy, with special Merge codes inserted in those locations where the document is to be personalized using the variable information in the secondary file.

Create a Secondary File

Figure 13-7 shows a secondary file. It is not standard text; it is merely the information that personalizes each record. A secondary file's vari-

Ms Janice Smith
3559 Biltmore Street
San Francisco, CA 94123

Dear Ms Smith:

Thank you for agreeing to serve on the R&R Wine Association's
California Wine-Tasting Committee.   You are our official
representative from San Francisco!

Our first meeting will be held at the beginning of December in
Monterey, California. I'll be sure to let you know the exact date·
and time as soon as it is confirmed.

I look forward to seeing you soon in Monterey, Janice.

Sincerely,

Lonnie Chang
R&R Wine Association

FIGURE 13-6   Sample letter to be produced using the Merge with a File
                   feature

able information is organized into *records*. A record is one whole set of
related variable information, such as one committee member's name
and address; each record results in the production of one personalized
document. The end of a record is denoted with a ^E Merge code and is
followed by a Hard Page [**HPg**] code which—as you learned in Chapter 5—appears on screen as a row of equal signs. Notice in Figure 13-7
that there are three records. Each record contains information about
one particular person. If you use this secondary file in a merge, the
result will be three separate letters.

Records are broken into separate units called *fields*. A field is one
piece of variable information in a record, such as one committee
member's first name. The field can contain letters, numbers, or both. It
may be only one character long or any number of lines long. Each field
is separated by a ^R Merge code.

Each record must contain the same number of fields, and those
fields must be listed in the same order. Notice in Figure 13-7 that each
record contains seven fields. The first field (referred to as field 1) always contains a title, such as "Mr." or "Ms.," field 2 always contains a
first name, field 3 always contains a last name, field 4 always contains
an address, and so on.

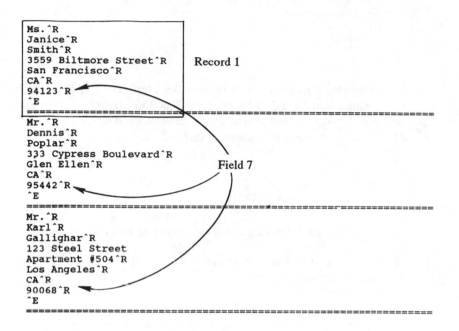

```
Ms.^R
Janice^R
Smith^R
3559 Biltmore Street^R          Record 1
San Francisco^R
CA^R
94123^R
^E
==================================================================
Mr.^R
Dennis^R
Poplar^R
333 Cypress Boulevard^R
Glen Ellen^R                    Field 7
CA^R
95442^R
^E
==================================================================
Mr.^R
Karl^R
Gallighar^R
123 Steel Street
Apartment #504^R
Los Angeles^R
CA^R
90068^R
^E
==================================================================
```

FIGURE 13-7   A secondary file

   Even if you have no information for a field in a given record, you
should still insert the code **^R** to occupy a line so that that record has
the same number of fields as all the others. For instance, suppose you
didn't know Ms. Smith's first name in Figure 13-7. You would enter
her record as follows.

```
Ms.^R
^R
Smith^R
3559 Biltmore Street^R
San Francisco^R
CA^R
94123^R
^E
```

If you forget to insert a **^R** to occupy the blank field 2, WordPerfect will assume that field 2 is Smith, field 3 is 3559 Biltmore, and so on, and you'd get awkward results in the final merged letter addressed to Ms. Smith. For example, instead of this:

```
Ms. Smith
3559 Biltmore Street
San Francisco, CA 94123
```

You could get the following awkward results as an inside address:

```
Ms. Smith 3559 Biltmore Street
San Francisco
CA, 94123
```

A field can, however, have varying numbers of lines. As an example, notice that the addresses in field 4 are one line long for the first two records. But for the last record, field 4 contains a two-line address. This is permissable in WordPerfect; it is the **^R** code, not a hard return, that defines the end of a field.

To create a secondary file, consider the type of variable information you want in your documents. For instance, if only a person's name and address are required to personalize a document, then names and addresses will be the only information typed into a secondary file. But suppose that you run a dentist's office and send bills out every month to your clients. In that case, you will also want to include the amount owed as another field in each record.

Also consider how the variable information should be organized in the secondary file. For instance, if a person's address, city, state, and ZIP code are only used as part of the inside address, then they can be combined into one field, such as in this example:

```
3559 Biltmore Street
San Francisco, CA 94123^R
```

However, if you wish to refer to just the city, the state, or the ZIP code, in addition to using this information as part of the address, you must split the address into separate fields. The following organization would be more suitable:

3559 Biltmore Street^R
San Francisco^R
CA^R
94123^R

This second way of organizing information is used in the secondary file in Figure 13-7, because the final merged result will refer to a committee member's city in both the inside address and within the body of the letter.

Once you've thought about the structure of the variable information, you're ready to type that information into a secondary file. You must start on a clear screen. Type in the first field for the first record and press the MERGE R (F9) key. WordPerfect will insert a ^R code and a hidden **[HRt]** code; the cursor moves to the beginning of the next line, ready for you to type field 2. Type the information for field 2 and again press MERGE R. Continue until you've typed each field for the first record.

After completing an entire record, you must insert a ^E Merge code and a Hard Page code. To do so, press the MERGE CODES (SHIFT + F9) key and type **E**; WordPerfect inserts a ^E code and a hidden **[HPg]** code. Now you are ready to type the second record.

After typing all the records, save the information on disk with a name that reminds you that this is not a standard document, but a secondary file of variable information. For example, name a secondary file beginning with the letters SF or SEC (both standing for Secondary File) or with the filename extension .SF or .SEC.

Suppose that the R&R Wine Association has just organized a wine-tasting committee. In the coming months, numerous letters will be sent to the committee members. Let's create a secondary file containing their names and addresses, as shown in Figure 13-7.

1. Press the EXIT (F7) key, and type **N** twice to clear the screen.

2. Type **Ms.**

3. Press the MERGE R (F9) key. A ^R Merge code is inserted, and the cursor moves down to the next line.

4. Type **Janice** and press the MERGE R (F9) key.

5. Type **Smith**, and press the MERGE R (F9) key.

6. Continue to type the rest of the fields for the first record in Figure 13-7, pressing the MERGE R (F9) key after each.

7. After typing all seven fields, each field followed by a ^R code, press the MERGE CODES (SHIFT + F9) key. WordPerfect displays

   ^C; ^D; ^E; ^F; ^G; ^N; ^O; ^P; ^Q; ^S; ^T; ^U; ^V:

8. Type **E**. WordPerfect inserts ^E at the current cursor position and then inserts a Hard Page code so that a row of equal signs appears across the screen.

9. Continue until you've completed typing the information shown in Figure 13-7 for records 2 and 3.

10. Use the EXIT (F7) key to save this information under the filename WTC.SEC (which stands for "Wine-Tasting Committee, Secondary File"), and then clear the screen.

Create a Primary File

In a merge with a File, the primary file you create contains codes telling WordPerfect precisely where the information corresponding to each field of the secondary file must be inserted. The Merge code you insert in the primary file is ^F*n*^, where the "F" stands for "field" and the "*n*" represents a specific field number. An example of a primary file for a letter to members of the wine-tasting committee is shown in Figure 13-8. The field numbers correspond to the order of fields in the secondary file. For example, notice the line "Dear ^F1^ ^F3^:" in Figure 13-8. If you refer to Figure 13-7, you'll see that this will result in "Dear Ms. Smith:" for the first record and "Dear Mr. Poplar:" for the second.

Typing a primary file for a merge with a file is similar to creating one for a merge with the keyboard. You clear the screen and begin typing the text that stays the same for each copy. Wherever you want to insert a ^F*n*^ code, press the MERGE CODES (SHIFT + F9) key. WordPerfect prompts you with a list of Merge codes; type **F**. WordPerfect then requests a field number; type the appropriate number and press ENTER. WordPerfect inserts that Merge code at the current cursor position. For instance, if you type 5, WordPerfect inserts ^F5^.

```
^F1^ ^F2^ ^F3^
^F4^
^F5^, ^F6^  ^F7^

Dear ^F1^ ^F3^:

Thank you for agreeing to serve on the R&R Wine Association's
California Wine-Tasting Committee.  You are our official
representative from ^F5^!

Our first meeting will be held at the beginning of December in
Monterey, California.  I'll be sure to let you know the exact date
and time as soon as it is confirmed.

I look forward to seeing you soon in Monterey, ^F2^.

Sincerely,


Lonnie Chang
R&R Wine Association

                                    Doc 1 Pg 1 Ln 1" Pos 1"
```

FIGURE 13-8   A primary file containing ^F*n*^ Merge codes

Obviously, the primary file in a merge with a file is set up based on the order of fields in the secondary file. When you create a primary file, you must know which field number corresponds to which item of variable information. One way to do this would be to keep referring to the secondary file, which you can display on the Doc 2 screen, while you create the primary file on the Doc 1 screen. Or you can keep a list of fields by your desk. For example, for the secondary file you just created, you could type up the following list and place it next to your keyboard for whenever you wished to create a new primary file.

Field	Information
1	Title
2	First name
3	Last name
4	Street address
5	City
6	Abbreviation for state
7	ZIP code

Let's create the primary file shown in Figure 13-8.

1. Make sure that the screen is clear. If not, clear the screen using the EXIT (F7) key. You're now at the location where you must insert the first ^F*n*^ Merge code, where a title will be inserted for each person.

2. Press the MERGE CODES (SHIFT + F9) key. WordPerfect prompts

   ^C; ^D; ^E; ^F; ^G; ^N; ^O; ^P; ^Q; ^S; ^T; ^U; ^V:

3. Type **F**. WordPerfect responds with

   Field:

4. Type **1** and press ENTER. WordPerfect inserts **^F1^** at the current cursor position.

5. Since you will want a space separating each person's title and first name in the letter's inside address, press the SPACEBAR once. Now you're ready to type the Merge code where the first name will be inserted in each letter.

6. Press the MERGE CODES (SHIFT + F9) key, type **F**, type **2**, and press ENTER.

7. Press the SPACEBAR once. The cursor is now properly positioned for you to type the next Merge code.

8. Continue inserting codes and text as shown in Figure 13-8.

9. After typing this primary file, check closely for any spelling errors or other typing mistakes; one mistake will show up in as many letters as records contained in your secondary file. You may also wish to perform a spell check.

10. Use the EXIT (F7) key to save the document under the name WTC1.PRI (which stands for "the first PRImary document for the Wine-Tasting Committee"), and then clear the screen.

You can use as many ^F*n*^ codes as you like and in any order in a primary file. Notice in Figure 13-8, for example, that **^F1^**, **^F2^**, **^F3^**, and **^F5^** are each used twice. You don't even need to use all the fields contained in a secondary file. For instance, a secondary file might contain a company name in field 8 and a telephone number in field 9, but since neither of these are used in the primary file shown in Figure 13-8, the codes **^F8^** and **^F9^** would not be inserted in that particular primary file.

When inserting a ^F*n*^ Merge code in a primary file, you can type a question mark after the field number to eliminate the possibility of a blank line in the final merged outcome. For instance, suppose that field 8 is the name of a person's company, which you wish to include below his or her name in the inside address. But suppose that for certain records, there is no company name. In the primary file, enter the inside address as

```
^F1^ ^F2^ ^F3^
^F8?^
^F4^
^F5^, ^F6^ ^F7^
```

Because of the ^F8?^, a record containing the text "ABC Company" as field 8 will be merged as follows:

Ms. Janice Smith
ABC Company
3559 Biltmore Street
San Francisco, CA 94123

On the other hand, another record where field 8 remains blank will be merged like this:

Mr. Dennis Poplar
333 Cypress Boulevard
Glen Ellen, CA 95442

Without the question mark inserted, Mr. Poplar's letter would contain an awkward-looking blank line where field 8 is to be inserted:

Mr. Dennis Poplar

333 Cypress Boulevard
Glen Ellen, CA 95442

Merge on the Screen

Once you have stored a secondary file and a matching primary file on disk, you can initiate a merge with a file. Clear the screen, press the MERGE/SORT (CTRL + F9) key, and select Merge (1 or M). Word-Perfect will prompt you for the name of a primary file; type the appropriate filename and press ENTER. Next, WordPerfect will prompt you for the name of a secondary file; again, type the appropriate filename and press ENTER.

The merge happens on the screen while you wait. (To stop the merge at any time, press the CANCEL (F1) key.) WordPerfect automatically inserts a Hard Page **[HPg]** code after it merges the primary file with one record and before it merges the primary file with the next record. Thus, if you are merging a one-page primary file with ten records in a secondary file, WordPerfect will assemble a document containing ten pages of text—each a separate letter.

When the merge is complete, the cursor is located at the bottom of the document, displaying the letter pertaining to the last record in the secondary file. If you move up to the top of the document, you'll see the letter for the first record. Then continue to press PGDN to view the separate pages.

You have already stored on disk a secondary file containing variable information and a primary file that contains ^**F** codes corresponding to fields in that secondary file. You're now ready to merge these files.

1. On a clear screen, press the MERGE/SORT (CTRL + F9) key. WordPerfect responds

   1 Merge; **2 S**ort; **3 S**ort **O**rder: **0**

2. Select Merge (1 or M). WordPerfect prompts

   Primary file:

3. Type **WTC1.PRI**, and press ENTER. WordPerfect prompts

   Secondary file:

4. Type **WTC.SEC**, and press ENTER. The message * **Merging** * appears at the bottom of the screen.

5. The "Merging" message clears when the merge is completed. The cursor is at the bottom of the merged document.

6. Press HOME, HOME, UP ARROW to move to the top of the document. You're viewing the letter for the first record in the secondary file, the printed results of which are shown in Figure 13-6.

7. Press PGDN to view the second letter.

8. Press PGDN to view the third letter.

Once a merge is complete, the document on screen, which contains the personalized letters, is ready for use. You can edit any of the letters and then either print them or store them on disk. It is usually unnecessary to store the letters on disk. After all, if you want to produce an identical copy of the same letters next week, you can always merge the primary and secondary files again, since both of the files are stored on disk. By printing the merged document and not saving it, you reserve disk space for files that you cannot reproduce so easily.

You can mix and match primary and secondary files. For instance, suppose you create a separate secondary file containing a list of inactive wine-tasting-committee members. You could merge the same primary file named WTC1.PRI (Figure 13-8) with that other secondary file. Or suppose that next month you plan to send another letter to all active members of the wine-tasting committee. In that case, you could create a new primary file containing the text of the new letter, with ^F*n*^ Merge codes in each place where you want to personalize the letters. Store that file on disk, perhaps under the filename WTC2.PRI. You could then perform a merge using WTC2.PRI as the primary file along with WTC.SEC (Figure 13-7) as the secondary file.

PREPARE ENVELOPES AND MAILING LABELS

Once you've used the Merge feature to create hundreds of personalized letters and have printed those letters, your job may not yet be complete. You may still have to produce mailing labels or envelopes so that you can send out those letters. It should not be surprising that WordPerfect can help you with this, too, by performing another merge

You already have stored on disk a secondary file that contains names and addresses. What you must do now is create a primary file for envelopes or labels to merge with that secondary file. The primary file will contain no text; it will simply contain Merge codes in the order that the text in the fields will appear on the envelopes or labels. For instance, a primary file for envelopes or mailing labels corresponding to the fields in the secondary file named WTC.SEC as shown in Figure 13-7 will contain the following.

```
^F1^ ^F2^ ^F3^
^F4^
^F5^, ^F6^ ^F7^
```

You can type these Merge codes on a clear screen and save them, using a file name such as MAILING.PRI that reminds you that this primary file is for your mailing labels or envelopes.

Note: This primary file is used for printing envelopes on any type of printer and for printing mailing labels on all but laser printers. For printing mailing labels on laser printers, a different primary file is required; see the "Sheets of Labels— Two or Three Across" section below for a discussion of printing mailing labels on laser printers.

Once the primary file is stored on disk, clear the screen and perform a merge with MAILING.PRI as the primary file and WTC.SEC as the secondary file. You'll get results such as those shown in Figure 13-9. Notice that a page bar is inserted between the addresses, indicating page breaks; this is because, as you'll remember, WordPerfect inserts a Hard Page code at the end of each separate merged record. Now you're ready to format your merged document and print it—either on envelopes, one-across labels, or two- or three-across labels—as described below.

```
Ms. Janice Smith
3559 Biltmore Street
San Francisco, CA  94123
=======================================================================
Mr. Dennis Poplar
333 Cypress Boulevard
Glen Ellen, CA  95442
=======================================================================
Mr. Karl Gallighar
123 Steel Street
Apartment #584
Los Angeles, CA  90068




                                              Doc 1 Pg 3 Ln 1.5" Pos 3.2"
```

FIGURE 13-9   A merged document for printing envelopes or mailing labels

Envelopes

If you wish to print the addresses on envelopes, press HOME, HOME, UP ARROW to position the cursor at the very top of the merged document containing addresses, such as the one shown in Figure 13-9. Then insert the following format codes at the top of the document:

- *Paper size and type*   Envelope size and type (You must define an envelope form type before you attempt to print envelopes so that WordPerfect knows special instructions in relation to printing envelopes with your printer. See Appendix B for further instructions.)

- *Left and right margins*   4.5 inches as a left margin, 0 inches as a right margin

- *Top and bottom margins*   2.5 inches as a top margin, 0 inches as a bottom margin

(See Chapter 4 to review changing left/right margins, and see Chapter 5 to review modifying the paper size/type and top/bottom margins.)

Now you are ready to turn on your printer. Make sure to have envelopes handy. On some printers, you will have set the envelope type to feed envelopes from a sheet feeder, in which case make sure to stock the sheet feeder with envelopes. On other printers, the only way to print envelopes is by inserting each envelope one at a time; in that case, you will have set the envelope type to pause for you to insert each envelope and then press Go (4 or G) on the Control Printer screen (as described in Chapter 2) to signal WordPerfect to print that envelope.

Continuous Labels—One Across

One-across, continuous-feed labels can be used on many printers, though *not* on laser printers. To print the addresses on one-across, continuous labels, press HOME, HOME, UP ARROW to position the cursor at the very top of the merged document containing addresses, such as the one shown in Figure 13-9. Then insert the following format codes at the top of the document.

- *Paper size and type*   Other size (where you indicate your label size) and labels type (You must define a label form type before you attempt to print a label so that WordPerfect knows special instructions in relation to printing labels; see Appendix B.)

- *Left and right margins*   0.5 inch as a left margin, 0 inches as a right margin

- *Top and bottom margins*   0.25 inch as a top margin, 0 inches as a bottom margin

(These settings may need to be adjusted for your particular printer.)

Now you are ready to turn on your printer and insert the continous labels so that the printhead is lined up with the top of the first label. Then print the merged document to create mailing labels.

Sheets of Labels—Two or Three Across

Labels that are two or three across on a standard-size, 8.5- by 11-inch sheet of paper can be used on a variety of printers, including laser printers. However, the procedure to print labels is quite different depending on whether or not you're using a laser printer.

If you're not using a laser printer, press HOME, HOME, UP ARROW to position the cursor at the very top of the merged document containing addresses, such as the one shown in Figure 13-9. Then, insert the following format codes at the top of the document:

- *Paper size and type*   Other size (where you indicate a width of 8.5 inches, which is actually the width of the sheet, and a height that equals the distance from the top of one label to the top of the next) and labels type (You must define a label form type before you attempt to print a label so that WordPerfect knows special instructions in relation to printing labels; see Appendix B.)

- *Left and right margins*   0.25 inch as a left margin, 0 inches as a right margin

- *Top and bottom margins*   0.25 inch as a top margin, 0 inches as a bottom margin

(These settings may need to be adjusted for your particular printer or the particular sheets of labels that you use.)

Next, format the document into text columns using the MATH/COLUMNS (ALT + F7) key, as described in Chapter 11. (Be sure that you're comfortable with the information in Chapter 11 before you attempt to carry out the following instructions.) Create two or three newspaper-style columns, depending on whether the labels are two or three across, and set the distance between columns as 0 inches to provide the maximum width across each label for an address. Word-Perfect will calculate the proper column margins for you. Turn on the Column feature, and then move the cursor down to rewrite the screen; now the addresses will be formatted into two or three columns. An example for six labels is shown in Figure 13-10.

Now you are ready to turn on your printer and insert a sheet of labels. Print as many pages of the three-column document as there are rows of labels on the sheet. Then insert a new sheet of labels and continue until you've printed as many labels as necessary.

```
Ms. Janice Smith          Mr. Dennis Poplar         Mr. Karl Callighar
3559 Biltmore Street      333 Cypress Boulevard     123 Steel Street
San Francisco, CA  94123  Glen Ellen, CA  95442     Apartment #504
                                                    Los Angeles, CA  90068
============================================================================
Mr. Jose Garcia           Ms. Jaclyn Stein          Ms. Cipi Bloom
1554 Welton Drive         15550 Costa Road          855 Main Street
Oakland, CA  94618        Suite 433                 Suite 50
                          San Jose, CA  95112       Ukiah, CA  95482




                          Col 1 Doc 1 Pg 1 Ln 0.25" Pos 0.25"
```

FIGURE 13-10   A merged document formatted for labels that are three across

If you are using a laser printer, then Figure 13-10 cannot be used for printing labels because Page Break codes will cause only one row of three labels across to print on each sheet of labels. Instead, you must create a special primary file that eliminates Hard Page codes between each row of labels. You must format the primary file *before* you merge, rather than formatting the merged result as is the case with other printers.

To create a primary file for labels using a laser printer, clear the screen and on a clear screen change the top and bottom margins to 0.25 inch. Format the document into text columns using the MATH/COLUMNS (ALT + F7) key, as described in Chapter 11. (Be sure that you're comfortable with the information in Chapter 11 before you attempt to carry out the following instructions.) Create three parallel-style columns with Block Protect if there are two labels across. Or create four parallel-style columns with Block Protect if there are three labels across. The extra column is used to ensure that each row of labels will contain the same number of lines when the primary file is merged; that extra column is the first column and should be only 0.05 inch wide. The remaining columns will be evenly spaced, with the distance between columns set as 0 inches to provide the maximum width across each label for an address. For instance, try the following settings for three labels across:

Column	Left Margin	Right Margin
1	0.25"	0.3"
2	0.3"	3.05"
3	3.05"	5.8"
4	5.8"	8.5"

Turn on the Column feature. Your cursor will be located in column 1. In this first column, press ENTER as many times as the longest address that can fit on a label. For instance, if the longest address that can fit on a label is six lines long, press ENTER six times. Press HARD PAGE (CTRL + ENTER) to move to column 2.

In the second column insert the ^F*n*^ Merge codes that correspond to each person's name and address in the secondary file, and insert one extra line that contains a ^N Merge code (a code described in the next section of this chapter). Insert the ^N code using the same method as you use to insert most other codes: press the MERGE CODES (SHIFT + F9) key and type N. For instance, based on the secondary file shown in Figure 13-7, the codes inserted into column 2 will be

```
^F1^ ^F2^ ^F3^
^F4^
^F5^, ^F6^ ^F7^
^N
```

Press HARD PAGE (CTRL + ENTER) to move to column 3.

In the third column, insert codes identical to those inserted in the second column. Press HARD PAGE (CTRL + ENTER) to move to column 4.

In the fourth column, insert codes like those inserted in the third column, but insert no ^N code. Then, instead of inserting a Hard Page code, use the MATH/COLUMNS (ALT + F7) to turn off the Column feature.

Once the Column feature is off and the cursor returns to the left margin, type the Merge codes ^N^P^P so that the merge will start again, continuing with the next record in the same primary file. (This string of Merge codes is described in the next section of this chapter.) Insert the ^N and ^P codes using the same method as you use to insert most other codes: press the MERGE CODES (SHIFT + F9) key and type N or P. Figure 13-11 shows how the primary file may appear on screen. (The first column is not shown since it is invisible on the Typing screen, containing only Hard Return codes; also, depending on your monitor, you may be unable to see the other three columns at the same time.)

You have now created the primary file. Save this file under a name that reminds you that it is a primary file for your mailing labels on a laser printer—MLLASER.PRI, for example. You can then clear the screen and perform a merge with MLLASER.PRI as the primary file and WTC.SEC as the secondary file. After the merge, the addresses will be formatted into columns, with page breaks appearing after approximately nine rows of labels, which corresponds to the number of rows on your label sheets. Send each page of labels to the printer.

```
        ^F1^  ^F2^  ^F3^      ^F1^  ^F2^  ^F3^      ^F1^  ^F2^  ^F3^
        ^F4^                  ^F4^                  ^F4^
        ^F5^, ^F6^  ^F7^      ^F5^, ^F6^  ^F7^      ^F5^, ^F6^  ^F7^
        ^N                    ^N

    ^N^P^P




                                              Doc 1 Pg 1 Ln 1" Pos 1"
```

FIGURE 13-11   A primary file for mailing labels to be printed on a laser printer

ENHANCE THE MERGE PROCESS

You've thus far worked with four different Merge codes. You used two Merge codes in creating a secondary file: ^R and ^E. You also worked with two Merge codes in a primary file: ^C for the merge from the keyboard and ^Fn^ for the merge from a file.

WordPerfect allows you some added flexibility in the merge process. You can combine ^C and ^Fn^ codes in the same primary file. Perhaps you wish to merge with variable information contained in a secondary file but also wish to have WordPerfect pause at the end of every letter so that you can type in a few extra words from the keyboard. You can insert ^Fn^ codes throughout the primary file and insert a ^C code following the last paragraph, and WordPerfect will merge from the secondary file wherever ^Fn^ codes are located but pause in each letter for input where the ^C code is located. Press the MERGE R (F9) key to continue the merge. WordPerfect will then pause at the bottom of the next letter. This will continue until all records have been merged.

Special Merge Codes

For added flexibility, there are ten additional Merge codes. You insert all the special Merge codes in a document just as you insert the ^C, ^F, and ^E codes—that is, by positioning the cursor, pressing the MERGE CODES (SHIFT + F9) key, and selecting the corresponding letter. Some Merge codes can be inserted in a primary or secondary file on their own; others must be used in combination with other codes. The following are additional Merge codes:

^D	Inserts the current date into the document at the location of ^D during the merge as long as the computer's clock has been set with the correct date. (If not, see Chapter 8 for the method to exit to DOS and enter the date.) For example, you could insert ^D at the top of the primary file shown in Figure 13-8. After the merge, the current date would appear in each letter wherever you inserted that code.
^G*macroname*^G	Directs WordPerfect to execute a macro when the merge is completed. For instance, for a macro named PRINT, you could insert ^GPRINT^G anywhere in a primary file and that macro would execute once all records are merged. (See Chapter 14 for more on what a macro is and what it does.)
^N	Directs WordPerfect to continue the merge using the next record in the secondary file. With certain Merge codes, WordPerfect no longer uses the next record automatically unless instructed, so the ^N code is necessary. Typically, ^N is used in combination with the ^P^P Merge code. (See "Merge Code Combinations" later in this chapter for an example.)
^O*message*^O	Sends a message to the screen reminding you what to type when WordPerfect pauses for your keyboard input during a merge. This code is inserted in a primary file in combination with the Merge code ^C. (See "Merge Code Combinations" later in this chapter for an example.)

^P*filename***^P**	Retrieves another primary file (or just another document, such as a boilerplate file) to the screen and continues the merge process with that new file. If no filename is specified, Word-Perfect continues with the primary file currently being used in the merge. This code is frequently used with the **^N** Merge code. (See "Merge Code Combinations" later in this chapter for an example.)
^Q	Directs WordPerfect to quit the merge whenever this code is encountered. It is handy if you know beforehand where you wish to end a merge. For instance, you could insert a **^Q** code after record 15 in a large secondary file so that only the first 15 records are merged.
^S*filename***^S**	Continues the merge with another secondary file; the primary file now merges with the records of that new secondary file. For example, suppose you create a new secondary file named LIST.SEC. You can insert **^SLIST.SEC^S** at the end of the secondary file named WTC.SEC. After WordPerfect merges the primary file with WTC.SEC, it will automatically begin to merge the same primary file with the secondary file named LIST.SEC.
^T	Types (prints) the merged document directly to the printer. The text prints up to where the **^T** code is inserted; then the printed text is erased from the screen, and the merge continues. (In general, this is used only in combination with other Merge codes, as described in "Merge Code Combinations" later in this chapter.)
^U	Updates the screen so that you can view the current status of the merge. If you place a **^U** code near the bottom of a primary file, you can watch as each letter is created during the merge. This is most useful in a primary document that contains numerous Merge codes, especially **^C** codes, so that you can view the current status of a docu-

ment as WordPerfect pauses for your input from the keyboard.

^V*codes*^V   Protects Merge codes from being acted upon during a merge. The ^V codes disappear, but the protected Merge codes are transferred into the text as if they were standard text. Those Merge codes could then be used in a subsequent merge. For instance, suppose that you place the following sequence of merge codes into a primary file:

```
^F3^^V^R^V
^F2^^V^R^V
California ^V^R^V
^V^E^V
```

During a merge, the ^F*n*^ codes will be acted upon, but the ^R codes will not, since they were sandwiched between the ^V codes. After the merge, the results might be

```
Smith^R
Janice^R
California^R
^E
```

This could then be used as a record in a secondary file for a future merge.

Merge Code Combinations

When you include special Merge codes such as ^P^P or ^N in a file used in a merge, the merge process changes. WordPerfect will no longer make certain basic assumptions, such as that it should insert a hard page after each record is merged. This allows you to determine exactly how the merge is to proceed, but it means that you must insert enough codes to ensure that the merge operates correctly. For certain tasks, you must use special Merge codes in specific combinations and in a specific sequence. The most useful and most frequently used Merge code combinations are the following.

^Omessage**^O^C**   Allows you to insert a message to yourself or someone else as a reminder during the merge process. During a merge, the message will appear on the status line, and the merge will pause so that you can enter whatever is specified by the message. When creating a primary file, make sure that the **^C** code follows the **^O** codes. Figure 13-12 shows an example of the **^O**message**^O^C** sequence in a primary file; Figure 13-13 shows the same file during a merge, with the cursor paused at the first **^C** code. Notice that the bottom left corner of the screen contains the prompt **Type employee's name**, which is the message that had been typed between the first set of **^O** codes.

^N^P^P   Tells WordPerfect not to insert an extra page break after merging with each record. This allows you to create a document in which all the information in the secondary files is merged onto one page rather than onto separate pages. For instance, Figure 13-14 shows an example of a primary file for creating a list of names and locations in California of the wine-tasting committee's members. If this primary file is merged with the secondary file named WTC.SEC, the on-screen result will be the document shown in Figure 13-15.

^T^N^P^P   Allows you to merge directly to the printer instead of to the screen. You would place this sequence of Merge codes at the very bottom of a primary file. After one record is merged, WordPerfect will print the result, clear the screen, and begin to merge the next record. This process will continue to the end of the merge. If you insert this Merge code combination in the primary document, make sure that your printer is turned on and is loaded with paper before you begin a merge.

Suppose that you want to produce a list of the wine-tasting committee's members, such as the one shown in Figure 13-14, that has

```
              MEMO FROM THE OFFICE OF PERSONNEL

To: ^OType employee's name^O^C              From: John Sansone

        According to our records, you have not yet completed and
returned to the Personnel office the following forms:

^OList one form on each line^O^C

        Please send this information as soon as possible to the
immediate attention of ^OName of personnel analyst in charge^O^C.
If you have any questions, call (415) 333-^OLast four digits of
personnel analyst's phone number^O^C.  Thank you.






                                     Doc 1 Pg 1 Ln 1" Pos 1"
```

FIGURE 13-12   A primary file with ^O^O^C Merge code combinations

```
              MEMO FROM THE OFFICE OF PERSONNEL

To:_                                        From: John Sansone

        According to our records, you have not yet completed and
returned to the Personnel office the following forms:

^OList one form on each line^O^C

        Please send this information as soon as possible to the
immediate attention of ^OName of personnel analyst in charge^O^C.
If you have any questions, call (415) 333-^OLast four digits of
personnel analyst's phone number^O^C.  Thank you.




Type employee's name                 Doc 1 Pg 1 Ln 1.5" Pos 1.4"
```

**FIGURE 13-13   The screen during a merge with a message displayed on the
status line**

```
^F1^  ^F2^  ^F3^
^F5^, California

^N^P^P
```

Doc 1 Pg 1 Ln 1" Pos 1"

FIGURE 13-14   A primary file with a ^N^P^P Merge code combination

```
Ms. Janice Smith
San Francisco, California

Mr. Dennis Poplar
Glen Ellen, California

Mr. Karl Gallighar
Los Angeles, California
```

Doc 1 Pg 1 Ln 2.16" Pos 3.3"

FIGURE 13-15   The results of a merge when the primary file contains a
^N^P^P Merge code combination

each person's name and the city in California that each represents. ^F1^, ^F2^, and ^F3^ codes are placed where each person's full name will be inserted. The ^F5^ code corresponds to each person's city. The ^N^P^P code directs WordPerfect to suppress a page break after merging each record and continue with the merge on the same page. Because of the blank line before the ^N^P^P string of Merge codes, you'll find a blank line between each name on the list.

Here's how to proceed using a combination of Merge codes:

1. On a clear screen, press the MERGE CODES (SHIFT + F9) key. WordPerfect prompts

   ^C; ^D; ^E; ^F; ^G; ^N; ^O; ^P; ^Q; ^S; ^T; ^U; ^V:

2. Type F. At the prompt for a field, type **1**, and press ENTER. Press the SPACEBAR once.

3. Press the MERGE CODES (SHIFT + F9) key.

4. Type F. At the prompt, type **2**, and press ENTER. Press the SPACEBAR once.

5. Press the MERGE CODES (SHIFT + F9) key.

6. Type F. At the prompt, type **3**, and press ENTER. Press ENTER again to move down to the next line.

7. Press the MERGE CODES (SHIFT + F9) key.

8. Type F. At the prompt, type **5**, and press ENTER.

9. Type a comma, press the SPACEBAR once, type **California**, and press ENTER twice to insert a blank line.

10. Press the MERGE CODES (SHIFT + F9) key, and type **N**.

11. Press the MERGE CODES (SHIFT + F9) key, and type **P**.

12. Press the MERGE CODES (SHIFT + F9) key, and type **P**. Your screen will resemble the one in Figure 13-14.

13. Use the EXIT (F7) key to save this file under the name REPORT.PRI, and then clear the screen.

You're now ready to merge this primary file with the secondary file you've already created and saved under the name WTC.SEC.

1. On a clear screen, press the MERGE/SORT (CTRL + F9) key. WordPerfect responds

   1 Merge; 2 Sort; 3 Sort Order: 0

2. Select Merge (1 or M). WordPerfect prompts

   Primary file:

3. Type **REPORT.PRI**, and press ENTER. WordPerfect prompts

   Secondary file:

4. Type **WTC.SEC**, and press ENTER. The message * **Merging** * appears at the bottom of the screen.

In moments, you'll get the result shown in Figure 13-15. You're now ready to print this one-page list.

Imagine the time savings of using the Merge feature if there were 50 people on the wine-tasting committee. Once you had created a secondary file for those names, you could then personalize a letter, create a report, and even print mailing labels with the Merge feature. The more you learn about the feature, the more you'll be amazed by its capabilities.

REVIEW EXERCISE

You have created a secondary file that you can now use to personalize many different documents. For practice in merging, in the following steps you'll create a primary document that you will merge with your secondary file to create a new batch of letters to the wine-tasting-committee members.

1. Clear the screen and type a primary file that will produce the document shown in Figure 13-16. The circled copy represents the variable information in each letter. Use the ^D code to have the current date inserted during the merge. Use ^F*n*^ codes to have the addresses, names, and cities inserted during the merge. Save this document under the name WTC2.PRI.

2. Clear the screen and merge the primary file named WTC2.PRI with the secondary file named WTC.SEC.

(DATE)

(INSIDE ADDRESS)

Dear (FIRST NAME):

Thank you for attending R&R Wine Association's first Wine Tasting
meeting. From the response I've gotten, I believe that it was a
huge success.

I look forward to seeing you at our next meeting, (FIRST NAME).
Until then, if my travels take me to (CITY) I'll see if you're
available for a business lunch.

Sincerely,

Lonnie Chang

FIGURE 13-16   Review exercise text

3. Review the letters to make sure that the merge was successful, then print them.

4. Clear the screen and type a primary file that will produce envelopes. (*Hint:* Remember that the primary file for envelopes is just a file of codes in the same structure as the inside address.) Save this file under the name MAILING.PRI.

5. Clear the screen and merge the primary file MAILING.PRI with the secondary file WTC.SEC.

6. Format the resulting merged document so that you can print the addresses on envelopes. (If you don't plan on using your printer to print envelopes, then you may wish to stop the review exercise at this point.)

7. Print the addresses on envelopes.

REVIEW

- When you find yourself typing the same paragraphs in many different documents, establish a collection of boilerplate files: that is, save each paragraph in its own file. When you want to include boilerplate text in a document you're typing, position the cursor where you want the text inserted and use the RETRIEVE (SHIFT + F10) key or the LIST FILES (F5) key to bring in the text.

- The Merge with the Keyboard feature enables you to personalize a standard document or fill out a computer-designed form by inputting information from the keyboard. Create a primary file containing ^C codes at those spots where you want WordPerfect to pause for input. Use the MERGE/SORT (CTRL + F9) key to initiate the merge.

- The Merge with a File feature combines two files to produce personalized documents. The secondary file contains the variable information that personalizes each document. The primary file contains ^F*n*^ codes at those locations where the document is to be personalized with the variable information. Use the MERGE/SORT (CTRL + F9) key to initiate the merge.

- You can easily produce envelopes or mailing labels for records contained in a secondary file. Create a primary file that includes only those fields that correspond to name and address fields for each record in the secondary file. Then perform the merge and format the result so that the addresses will print correctly.

- WordPerfect's Merge feature includes many Merge codes that add flexibility in the merge process. For instance, the ^T Merge code can send a merged document to the printer rather than to the screen. ^D inserts the current date when you merge. And with ^O^O you can create your own messages to function as reminders when you're merging from the keyboard.

14

USING MACROS
AND STYLES

You've learned in previous chapters how to activate sophisticated features such as font changes, text columns, paragraph numbering, and footnoting. As you've seen, it sometimes takes many keystrokes to accomplish a certain task.

You'll learn in this chapter about macros and styles, two features that are the ultimate timesavers! Macros and styles come in handy for word processing chores that you perform on a regular basis.

Macros and styles are similar in that they are both shortcuts; by using a macro or a style, you turn a task that would typically take many keystrokes into one that takes just a few.

But each is most suitable in different types of circumstances. A macro is most appropriate for recording keystrokes that perform a series of commands. For instance, you would create a macro to resave a document on screen, print three copies, change the number of copies back to one, and clear the screen. A style is most appropriate for recording keystrokes that format parts of a document in a certain way. For example, you would create a style for chapter headings so that the headings would be preceded by paragraph numbers, centered, underlined, and printed in italics.

Macros and styles are created and executed in completely different ways. In this chapter, you'll learn first how to define and execute a macro. You'll also learn about some more advanced macro features that allow you to pause a macro for keyboard input or chain several macros together. Next, you'll work with the Styles feature. You'll create a style and use that style in a document. You'll also learn how to create a style library, so that you can store a collection of commonly used styles.

This chapter assumes that you are comfortable with fundamental features discussed in earlier chapters, such as the procedures for changing print options before you print, altering margins, and inserting automatic paragraph numbers. When a feature is mentioned that you haven't yet learned about or that you feel uncomfortable with, be sure to refer to an earlier chapter for a review before reading on.

CREATE A MACRO

A macro is a sequence of keystrokes that WordPerfect stores for you, comparable to the speed-dialing feature on some telephones. With speed dialing, you can have the telephone store a phone number so that instead of having to press ten or more digits to dial someone long distance, you simply press the pound sign (#) and a number. Pressing # and 1 is much easier than dialing 305-734-5555.

Similarly, a macro stores a set of keystrokes, which you execute by pressing just a few keys. For instance, you could create a macro that automatically typed your company's name in a split second. You could write a macro that initiated a merge. Or you could devise a macro that saved a document to disk, sent it to the printer, and cleared the screen—all at the touch of two keys. Create macros only for repetitive tasks, sequences of keystrokes that you press often (just as you reserve speed dialing for telephone numbers you call often), and you're ready to execute them as needed.

When you create or "define" a macro, you actually press each key one by one to record them. Thus, before you define a macro, you must prepare the screen so that you are ready to perform the task at hand. For instance, if the macro you plan to create will print a document from the screen, you must make sure that a document is on the screen and the printer is turned on.

Next, press the MACRO DEFINE (CTRL + F10) key. WordPerfect will respond with

Define macro:

This is WordPerfect's way of asking you for a macro name. You can name a macro in one of three ways:

- Type from one to eight characters and then press ENTER.

- Press the ALT key plus a letter of the alphabet. (As you will soon learn, it is easiest to execute a macro named with the ALT key, so reserve the ALT key for those macros that you use most often but that will not be destructive to your document if you execute accidentally. For instance, don't name a macro that will clear the screen for you ALT + C, or you're liable to accidentally erase the screen in the middle of typing an important document.)

- Press the ENTER key by itself. (As you will soon learn, a macro named with the ENTER key cannot be edited, so reserve the ENTER key for a simple, "quick-and-dirty" macro.)

When you name a macro with one to eight characters or with the ALT key, WordPerfect next prompts for a macro description. Type up to 39 characters describing the macro's purpose and then press ENTER. If you find no need for a macro description to help you later remember the tasks that macro performs simply press ENTER. (If you name a macro with the ENTER key, no such prompt appears.)

Now the message **Macro Def** starts flashing in the lower left corner of the status line. This message serves as a reminder that every key you press from now on will be recorded—just as if you had turned on a tape recorder that recorded everything you said— until you stop the recording. Type the keystrokes exactly as you want them recorded. To signal the end of the macro, again press the MACRO DEFINE (CTRL + F10) key; the **Macro Def** message disappears, and the macro is stored on disk with the extension .WPM. For instance, a macro that you named PRINT will be stored as PRINT.WPM. A macro that you named ALT + A will be stored as ALTA.WPM. The macro that you named with the ENTER key will be stored as WP{WP}.WPM.

What if you make a typing mistake while recording a macro? Press the MACRO DEFINE (CTRL + F10) key to stop recording the macro immediately. Then begin the procedure all over again; press the MACRO DEFINE (CTRL + F10) key and enter the macro name again. WordPerfect will prompt, informing you that a macro by that name has already been defined and asking whether you wish to replace or edit the macro. For a macro named ALT + A, for instance, WordPerfect prompts

ALTA.WPM is Already Defined. 1 Replace; 2 Edit: 0

Select Replace (1 or R), and now record all the keystrokes correctly and press MACRO DEFINE (CTRL + F10) when the recording is finished.

WordPerfect typically stores a macro on disk in the default drive or directory—the same place it stores your document files. But if you later change the default drive/directory, WordPerfect would be unable to locate the macro.

Consequently, you have various options to make sure that macros are always available. If you use a floppy disk system, you may want to store macros on the WordPerfect disk in drive A; that way you'll have access to them no matter which disk is in drive B. To do so, precede the macro name with A:. For instance, when WordPerfect prompts **Define macro:**, type **A:ALTA** or type **A:PRINT3** and press ENTER. If you will be creating so many macros that not all of them can fit on the WordPerfect disk, then continue to store macros on the default drive, drive B, but consider maintaining a disk that stores nothing but macros. That disk can be slipped into drive B just before you create or execute a macro.

If you use a hard disk system, you may wish to store macros in the directory where the WordPerfect program files (such as WP.EXE) are housed. Assuming that the program files are stored in \WPER, then when WordPerfect prompts **Define macro:**, type **C:\WPER\ALTA** or **C:\WPER\PRINT3**. You can also use WordPerfect's Setup menu to specify that all macros be stored in their own directory. For instance, you can create a directory named \WPER\MACROS, where all your macros will be stored, easily accessible no matter what the current default. WordPerfect will always look to that directory for executing macros. See "Location of Auxiliary Files" in Appendix C for more details on specifying a directory for storing and retrieving macros.

Here's a chance to practice creating a macro. Pretend that you work at the R&R Wine Association and you wish to create a macro that types "R&R Wine Association" on command—performing a 20-keystroke task with just 2 keystrokes. Let's name it ALT + R.

1. Position the cursor anywhere on the Typing screen.

2. Press the MACRO DEFINE (CTRL + F10) key. WordPerfect prompts you with

   Define macro:

3. Press ALT + R. WordPerfect prompts

   Description:

4. Type **Inserts "R&R Wine Association"** and press ENTER. The following message flashes on the status line:

   Macro Def

   This message serves to remind you that every keystroke you press from now on will be recorded.

5. Type **R&R Wine Association**.

6. Press the MACRO DEFINE (CTRL + F10) key to end the macro. The **Macro Def** message disappears from the screen, and the macro is stored under the name ALTR.WPM on the default drive/directory.

Here's another macro to practice with, one you'll name without using the ALT key. Suppose that for every letter you write, you print out three copies—one for the person to whom the letter will be sent, one for your boss's files, and one for your own files. Let's create a macro that changes the Number of Copies option on the Print screen to 3, prints out the letter, and then changes the Number of Copies option back to 1. We'll name this macro PRINT3 (which stands for PRINT 3 copies).

1. Position the cursor anywhere on the Typing screen. Make sure that the screen contains some text (such as the phrase "R&R Wine Association" after recording the previous macro), so that WordPerfect will have something to print. Also, turn on the printer and make sure that paper has been inserted properly.

2. Press the MACRO DEFINE (CTRL + F10) key. WordPerfect prompts you with

Define macro:

3. Type **PRINT3**, and press ENTER. WordPerfect prompts you with

Description:

4. Type **Prints 3 copies of page on screen** and press ENTER. The following message flashes on the status line:

Macro Def

This message serves to remind you that every keystroke you press from now on will be recorded.

5. Press the PRINT (SHIFT + F7) key.

6. Select Number of Copies (N), type **3** and press ENTER.

7. Select Page (2 or P). Three copies of the page on screen will print, and you will be returned to the Typing screen.

8. Press the PRINT (SHIFT + F7) key.

9. Select Number of Copies (N), type **1**, and press ENTER. This returns the number to 1 for other documents.

10. Press CANCEL (F1) to return to the Typing screen.

11. Press the MACRO DEFINE (CTRL + F10) key to end the macro. The **Macro Def** message disappears from screen, and the macro is stored under the name PRINT3.WPM in the default drive/directory.

When you press the LIST FILES (F5) key and view a list of files in a drive or directory where macros are stored, you can recognize all the macros by the .WPM extension. Then you can use the Look feature on the List Files menu to display the macro's description—a handy feature if you forget the tasks that a certain macro performs. However, you should never attempt to retrieve a macro; WordPerfect will display an error message.

Suppose you can't remember what the macro named with the ALT + R key combination accomplishes:

1. Use the LIST FILES (F5) key to display a list of files in the default drive/directory.

2. Position the cursor on the file named ALTR.WPM. (If you cannot find the file named ALTR.WPM, then someone may have redirected your macros into a different drive or directory; see "Location of Auxiliary Files" in Appendix C to learn the name of that drive or directory. Then you can use the LIST FILES (F5) key to display a list of files in that different drive/directory.)

3. Select Look (6 or L) or simply press ENTER to activate the Look feature. The following macro description will appear:

   Inserts "R&R Wine Association"

4. Press CANCEL (F1) twice to return to the Typing screen.

EXECUTE A MACRO

Whenever you attempt to execute a macro stored on disk, WordPerfect searches the default drive or directory as well as the drive/directory where the WordPerfect program files are stored (such as WP.EXE). If a certain drive/directory is specified for storing macro files using the Setup menu (as described in Appendix C), then when you attempt to execute a macro, WordPerfect searches that specified drive/directory as well as the one where the WordPerfect program files are stored.

When you are ready to use a macro, you must position the cursor wherever you want the macro execution to begin. What you do next depends on whether you named the macro with the ALT key. If you did, simply press ALT plus the character you named the macro with. If you named the macro with one to eight characters, press the MACRO (ALT + F10) key, type in the macro name, and press ENTER. If you named the macro with only the ENTER key, press the MACRO (ALT + F10) key and press ENTER. In case you wish to stop a macro while it's executing, press the CANCEL (F1) key.

Let's execute the macro named ALTR.WPM:

1. Clear the screen using the EXIT (F7) key and then position the cursor where you want the the R&R Wine Association name to appear.

2. Press ALT + R. In less than a second, the company's name appears on screen.

3. Position the cursor in another location and again press ALT + R. Again, the name appears, much quicker than if you had to type it yourself.

Now let's execute the macro named PRINT3.WPM to print the short document on screen three times. Pretend that you wish to execute the macro at the top of the document.

1. Make sure that your printer is on and that paper is inserted.

2. Press the MACRO (ALT + F10) key. WordPerfect responds with

   Macro:

   prompting you for a macro name.

3. Type **PRINT3**, and press ENTER. Soon three copies of the page on screen will be printed, and the Number of Copies option will be set back to 1. How much easier than hitting the individual keys every time you want three copies of a certain page!

There's a quick way to execute a macro a specific number of times. Before you actually execute the macro, press the ESC key (which was discussed in Chapter 3 as a way to repeat the same keystroke a certain number of times). WordPerfect responds with

Repeat Value = 8

Type the number representing how many times you wish to repeat the macro. Then execute the macro. Here's an example:

1. Press ESC. WordPerfect prompts

   Repeat Value = 8

2. Type **3**. Now the prompt reads

   Repeat Value = 3

3. Press ALT + R. At the current cursor position, the following appears:

R&R Wine AssociationR&R Wine AssociationR&R Wine Association

There's also a way to have a macro execute automatically as soon as a merge is completed. In Chapter 13, you learned about the Merge codes used in a primary file. To execute a macro automatically when a merge is completed, you can insert the macro's name between a pair of ^G^G Merge codes in the primary document. For instance, suppose that once a merge is complete, you wish to print out three copies of the last page of the merged result. You can have this macro execute as soon as a merge is completed by inserting **^GPRINT3^G** anywhere in the primary document used in that merge.

LEARN ABOUT ADVANCED MACRO FEATURES

Macros can be very simple or very complex. So far, you've learned about relatively simple, straightforward macros. Often, these are the most commonly used and can save you much time and give your fingers a rest. But you may want to know about the more advanced macro features described below. Do not attempt these more advanced features until you are comfortable creating and executing basic macros.

Display or Pause During Macro Execution

As you've seen, a macro executes at lightning speed, so fast that you don't see anything but the final result. WordPerfect offers the ability to display the workings of the macro as it is executing. You can also request that WordPerfect pause in the middle of macro execution, so that you can type from the keyboard and then continue the macro. A pause allows you to type different information each time you execute the macro.

Use the key combination CTRL + PGUP to display or pause macro execution. Press this combination while defining a macro wherever you wish the display or pause to occur. For instance, press CTRL + PGUP as the first step in recording keystrokes if you want the entire macro to be displayed during execution. WordPerfect will display the following menu:

1 _P_ause; 2 _D_isplay; 3 _A_ssign; 4 _C_omment: 0

To display the macro from that point on, select Display (2 or D). WordPerfect prompts asking whether or not you wish to display macro execution; type **Y** to turn display on or type **N** to turn display off (the default setting). Now continue defining the macro. You'll be able to watch the progression of the keystrokes each time that you execute the macro; it will no longer be invisible.

To create a pause, a temporary stop in the macro execution, select Pause (1 or P). Type in a sample of the keystrokes to be entered during that pause (a step that can be skipped if your next keystroke in the macro doesn't depend on typing in a sample). Then press ENTER to signal the end of the pause. Now continue defining the macro. When you execute a macro containing a pause, the macro will stop wherever you pressed CTRL + PGUP and selected Pause during macro definition. Type your input and then press ENTER to continue the macro execution.

Chain and Nest Macros

Another advanced feature allows you to chain macros together. In other words, you can write a macro that will execute a second macro— either the same macro or another one—on its own. For instance, you can create a macro that resaves a file on disk and then executes the PRINT3 macro. There are three ways to link macros together:

- A simple macro chain executes another one automatically when the current macro is completed. The last step of the current macro must include the keystrokes to execute the second macro: the MACRO (ALT + F10) key followed by the name of the second macro.

- A repeating macro chain repeats itself over and over until WordPerfect discovers through a search that a search string (a specific phrase or code) is no longer found in the text. The macro can be chained to itself only if a search is part of that macro; otherwise, the macro will repeat over and over until you press the CANCEL (F1) key or until the computer system locks up. The last step in the macro includes the keystrokes to execute the macro over again: the MACRO (ALT + F10) key followed by the name of the current macro.

- A nesting macro executes one macro inside another. Unlike chained macros, the nested macro is executed not when the main macro is completed, but rather at the point where it is encountered in the main macro. The nested macro must have been previously created and stored on disk; also, the nested macro must have been named with the ALT key. Wherever in the main macro you want the nested macro to temporarily take over, insert the keystrokes to execute it: the MACRO (ALT + F10) key followed by the name of the nested macro. Then continue defining the main macro.

Insert Comments in Macros

You can split a macro involving many keystrokes into more readable chunks for editing by inserting comments into the macro. These comments will not affect macro execution, but are helpful when you're attempting to unravel a macro's keystrokes, perhaps to figure out why the macro is not working properly.

For instance, suppose you wish to create a macro that performs a variety of tasks, including changing the default directory and appending some text to a file on disk. Begin recording the macro. Then, before recording the keystrokes that alter the default directory, insert a comment that reads "Change the default directory to \WPER\BUD." Continue with the macro recording and, later on, insert a comment before another set of keystrokes that reads "Append the text on screen to BUDGET.SSM." Continue until you have defined the entire macro.

To insert a comment, define a macro up to the point where you wish to insert the comment. You must be on either the Typing screen or the Reveal Codes screen. Then press CTRL + PGUP. WordPerfect will display the following menu:

1 Pause; 2 Display; 3 Assign; 4 Comment: 0

Select Comment (4 or C) and type in a comment. Then press ENTER and continue defining the macro.

When you later edit a macro that contains comments (editing is described next), the comments will be interspersed among the macro keystrokes wherever you inserted them when creating the macro. Each comment will be preceded by the symbol {;} and will be followed by a tilde (~).

Edit a Macro Stored on Disk

WordPerfect offers the ability to edit a macro that is already stored on disk. Before you edit the macro, you must know the exact keystrokes that you wish to insert. Perform the keystrokes on the Typing screen and jot them down, so that you have a written record of the keystrokes. Then you're ready to edit the macro. Press the MACRO DEFINE (CTRL + F10) key and enter the name of the macro you wish to edit. WordPerfect will prompt, informing you that a macro by that name has already been defined:

PRINT3.WPM is Already Defined. 1 Replace; 2 Edit: 0

Select Edit (2 or E). A Macro Edit screen, as shown in Figure 14-1, will appear.

On the Macro Edit screen, you can select Description (1 or D) and then edit the description. Or, select Action (2 or A), in which case the

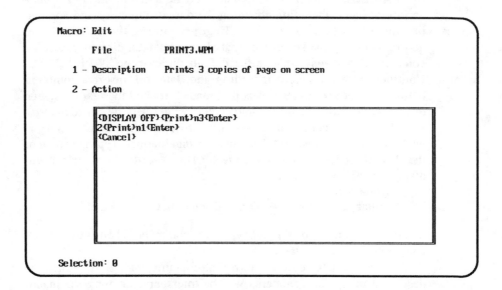

```
Macro: Edit

        File            PRINT3.WPM

1 - Description     Prints 3 copies of page on screen

2 - Action

  ┌─────────────────────────────────────────────────┐
  │ <DISPLAY OFF><Print>n3<Enter>                     │
  │ 2<Print>n1<Enter>                                 │
  │ <Cancel>                                          │
  │                                                   │
  │                                                   │
  │                                                   │
  │                                                   │
  │                                                   │
  └─────────────────────────────────────────────────┘

Selection: 0
```

FIGURE 14-1   Macro Edit screen for a macro named PRINT3

cursor moves inside the double-lined action box that contains the actual keystrokes of the macro. All function key names or editing key names are represented as the key name surrounded by curly braces, such as {Print} to indicate the PRINT (SHIFT + F7) key. Letters and numbers represent either text typed during the macro or a menu item selection. (The keystroke {DISPLAY OFF} is automatically inserted by WordPerfect in each macro to turn off the display of the macro. See the section above if you wish to turn display on.)

In the action box, you can use the cursor movement and editing keys to delete keystrokes and press character or function keys to insert that keystroke; for instance, press CENTER (SHIFT + F6) to insert {Center}. For certain editing and function keys, you must press CTRL + V and then the key to insert the literal keystroke. For instance, press LEFT ARROW to move the cursor to the left when editing, or press CTRL + V, LEFT ARROW to insert the keystroke {Left}. Press CANCEL (F1) to cancel your editing changes, or press CTRL + V, CANCEL to insert the keystroke {Cancel}. Then press EXIT (F7) to register your editing changes and leave the action box.

Here's a simple example. Suppose that after creating the PRINT3.WPM macro, you discover that you want it to print three copies of the full document—whether one page or ten pages in length—and not just three copies of the page where the cursor is located. On the Print Screen, you will want to select Full Document (1 or F) rather than Page (2 or P), after changing the number of copies to 3. Let's edit the macro.

1. Position the cursor anywhere on screen.

2. Press the MACRO DEFINE (CTRL + F10) key. WordPerfect prompts you with

   Define macro:

3. Type **Print3** and press ENTER. Because a macro by that name already exists, WordPerfect prompts you with

   PRINT3.WPM is Already Defined. 1 Replace; 2 Edit: 0

4. Select Edit (2 or E). Now the screen shown in Figure 14-1 appears.

5. Select Description (1 or D).

6. Edit the description to read "Prints 3 copies of full doc on screen," and press ENTER.

7. Select Action (2 or A).

8. Position the cursor on the first character in the second line. This will either be a "2," as shown in Figure 14-1, or it will be a "P," depending on how you selected the Page (2 or P) option when creating the macro.

9. Delete this character and in its place type 1 or F. Either will select the Full Document (1 or F) option on the Print screen once the macro is executed.

10. Press EXIT (F7) to leave the action box.

11. Press EXIT (F7) to exit the Macro Edit screen.

The altered macro is now stored on disk. The next time you execute this macro, WordPerfect will print three copies of the full document.

If you ever wish to erase a macro from the disk rather than edit it, you can do so as you would delete a document file: use the LIST FILES (F5) key to list your files, move the cursor to the name of the macro you wish to delete, and select Delete (2 or D) from the menu at the bottom of the screen.

Programming Language Commands

The ultimate in macro complexity is the Macro programming language available in WordPerfect. This programming language is for those individuals who have basic programming knowledge. The majority of WordPerfect users will never need to learn about and use the Macro programming language, but should know that it does exist. When on the Macro Edit screen (as shown in Figure 14-1), the programming language commands appear when the cursor is in the action box and you press CTRL + PGUP. Now the cursor can be moved from command to command. If the programming language commands appear accidentally, press CANCEL (F1) to return the cursor to the action box without activating any of these programming commands.

For a complete discussion of the Macro programming language commands, and other features such as Assign, which is used when creating complex macros containing programming commands, you can refer to more advanced books on WordPerfect, some of which are recommended at the start of the next chapter.

CREATE A STYLE

A style is a combination of formatting codes and text. For instance, suppose that you produce newsletters once a month where you change top/bottom margins, turn justification off, type the newsletter's banner heading, and format the document into newspaper columns. You can create a style that does this work for you.

In one respect, styles are more limited than macros. A style can only be used to format text on the page. A macro, on the other hand, can be created to format a document and/or to perform a variety of *other tasks* as well, such as changing the default drive/directory, printing a document, or even executing a style.

In another respect, when you do want to format parts of text the same way, styles are more flexible. If you create a style to format chapter headings, for example, and then decide to format the chapter headings differently, you can simply alter the style; all the chapter headings will be updated immediately based on that altered style. If you use a macro to format the chapter headings and then decide to reformat the chapter headings, you must either use the Replace feature or make the changes manually, moving from chapter heading to chapter heading on your own, which is more time consuming.

As with a macro, you first must create a style for a repetitive type of format. That style becomes available for text within the document in which it was created.

To create a style, consider a document's design elements, such as the formatting you desire at the top of the document and the formatting you desire for headings, subheadings, and paragraphs. To create a style for a particular element, position the cursor anywhere in the document for which you wish to create a style. Press the STYLE (ALT + F8) key to display the Styles screen, as shown in Figure 14-2. The middle of the screen is blank as in Figure 14-2 if you have yet to define a style for that document.

Select Create (3 or C) from the menu at the bottom of the screen. The Edit Styles screen, as shown in Figure 14-3, appears. Define the characteristics of the style as follows

```
┌─────────────────────────────────────────────────────────────────┐
│  Styles                                                           │
│    Name          Type  Description                                │
│                                                                   │
│                                                                   │
│                                                                   │
│                                                                   │
│                                                                   │
│                                                                   │
│                                                                   │
│                                                                   │
│    1 On: 2 Off: 3 Create: 4 Edit: 5 Delete: 6 Save: 7 Retrieve: 8 Update: 1  │
└─────────────────────────────────────────────────────────────────┘
```

FIGURE 14-2   Styles screen

```
┌─────────────────────────────────────────────────────────────────┐
│  Styles: Edit                                                     │
│        1 - Name                                                   │
│        2 - Type            Paired                                 │
│        3 - Description                                            │
│        4 - Codes                                                  │
│        5 - Enter           HRt                                    │
│                                                                   │
│                                                                   │
│                                                                   │
│                                                                   │
│                                                                   │
│  Selection: 0                                                     │
└─────────────────────────────────────────────────────────────────┘
```

FIGURE 14-3   Edit Styles screen

- *Name (1 or N)*   Type a name of 11 characters or less and press ENTER.

- *Type (2 or T)*   A menu appears from which you can select two style types:

  Type: 1 P̲aired; 2 O̲pen: 0

  A paired type is for styles that must have a beginning (on) and an end (off), affecting only a specific block of text; an example is a style to format chapter headings. An open type has only a beginning; an example is a style to set the general format for a newsletter starting at the top of the document. The default is for a paired type.

- *Description (3 or D)*   Type a description of up to 54 characters to remind you what the style accomplishes and press ENTER.

- *Codes (4 or C)*   A Reveal Codes screen appears, in which you should type in the text and codes that will make up the style. For an open type, the Reveal Codes screen is blank; type the text and codes in the order you want them to take effect in the text. For a paired type, a comment appears on the Reveal Codes screen. Type the text and codes that begin the style *before* the **[Comment]** code that appears in the bottom window of the screen, and type the text and codes that end the style *after* the **[Comment]** code. Press EXIT (F7) after inserting the text and codes.

- *Enter (5 or E)*   This option is applicable only if you are defining a *paired* type of style. A menu appears from which you can select three different functions for the ENTER key when you actually begin to use the style that is being defined:

  Enter: 1 H̲Rt; 2 Off̲; 3 Off/O̲n: 0

  HRt (1 or H) means that when the style is active pressing the ENTER key inserts a hard return, which is the ENTER key's normal function. Off (2 or F) means that when the style is active pressing the ENTER key turns off the style. Off/On (3 or O) means that when the style is active pressing the ENTER key turns off the style and then immediately turns it on again.

Once the style is defined, press EXIT (F7) to return to the Styles menu. The style will now appear on that menu. Now create additional styles or press EXIT (F7) to return to your document.

```
SALES FIGURES FOR THE WEST COAST

We predict a 15% increase in sales this year.  In the first three
months of this year, the following figures are in from the West
Coast of the United States:

     *    Sales of Chardonnay have sky-rocketed, increasing 58%
          over the same time last year.

     *    Pinot Noir has increased by 11%, a hefty increase, though
          volume  is much smaller for Pinot Noir than Chardonnay.

     *    Chenin Blanc and Cabernet Sauvignon sales have stayed
          about the same.

SALES FIGURES FOR THE EAST COAST

We predict a moderate 4% increase in sales this year.  In the first
three months of this year, the following figures are in from the
East Coast:

                                          Doc 1 Pg 1 Ln 1" Pos 1"
```

FIGURE 14-4   Paragraphs that are formatted with a style

Suppose you're about to type a report, and you want various paragraphs to be underlined and bulleted, using the asterisk as the bullet symbol. An example of the final outcome is shown in Figure 14-4. Let's create a style that can then be applied to paragraphs that you choose. It will be a paired type, since it will affect specific chunks of text, rather than an entire document or large section.

1. On a clear screen, press the STYLE (ALT + F8) key. The Styles screen appears, as shown in Figure 14-2.

2. Select Create (3 or C) to display the Edit Styles screen, as shown in Figure 14-3.

3. Select Name (1 or N), type **Bullets** and press ENTER.

4. Notice that WordPerfect assumes a paired type; so there's no need to select this option.

5. Select Description (3 or D), type **Bulleted Paragraphs** and press ENTER.

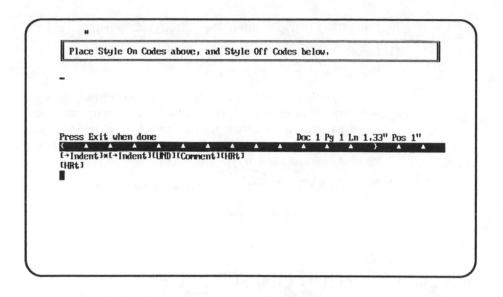

*

| Place Style On Codes above, and Style Off Codes below. |

-

Press Exit when done   Doc 1 Pg 1 Ln 1.33" Pos 1"
{ ▲ ▲ ▲ ▲ ▲ ▲ ▲ ▲ ▲ ▲ ▲ } ▲ ▲
[→Indent]*[→Indent][UND][Comment][HRt]
[HRt]

FIGURE 14-5   Codes inserted for the BULLETS style

6. Select Codes (4 or C) to display a Reveal Codes screen that contains a Comment code. Make sure that the cursor is on the **[Comment]** code, so that what you're about to type will be inserted before the code.

7. To define the formatting for the beginning of each paragraph press →INDENT (F4), type an asterisk (*), press →INDENT (F4), and press the UNDERLINE (F8) key.

8. Press RIGHT ARROW to position the cursor to the right of the **[Comment]** code.

9. To define the formatting for the end of each paragraph press ENTER twice. (Before pressing ENTER, you can also press the UNDERLINE (F8) key to turn off the Underline feature; however, WordPerfect assumes you wish to turn off attributes such as underlining at the end of the style, so this step is not necessary.) Now your screen will appear like the one shown in Figure 14-5.

10. Press EXIT (F7) to return to the Edit Styles Screen.

11. Select Enter (5 or E). WordPerfect prompts

    Enter: 1 HRt; 2 Off; 3 Off/On: 0

    Select Off (2 or F) so that as soon as you press ENTER, the style will turn off automatically. (If you had to type many more bulleted paragraphs in a row than shown in Figure 14-4, you could instead decide to select the Off/On option, so that you'd be ready immediately to type the next paragraph.)

12. Press the EXIT (F7) key twice to return to the Typing screen.

EXECUTE (TURN ON) A STYLE

When you're ready to execute a style, position the cursor where you want the style to take effect. Press the STYLE (ALT + F8) key and then position the Style screen cursor on the name of the style you wish to execute, either by (1) using the arrow keys or (2) pressing the →SEARCH (F2) key to activate a name search, typing the first few letters of the style name until the cursor moves there, and pressing ENTER. Next, select On (1 or O) from the menu at the bottom of the screen. You will be returned to the Typing screen.

For an open style, the process is complete. An Open Style code is inserted in the text. For instance, if the style is named REPORT, then the code inserted is [**Open Style:REPORT**]. Any text you type following the code will be formatted accordingly.

For a paired style, you must also remember to turn off the style. After typing the text to be affected by the style, turn off the style either by (1) again pressing the STYLE (ALT + F8) key, and then selecting Off (2 or F); (2) pressing the RIGHT ARROW key, which positions the cursor outside the Style code; or (3) pressing ENTER, providing that the ENTER key was defined to turn off a style. Style On and Off codes are inserted around the text. For instance, if the style is named BULLETS, then the pair of codes surrounding the text are [**Style On:BULLETS**] and [**Style Off:BULLETS**].

However, in order for a paired style to execute on *already existing text,* you must first highlight that text with the BLOCK (ALT + F4) key. Then press the STYLE (ALT + F8) key, position the cursor on a style name, and select On (1 or O). WordPerfect automatically inserts the Style On and Off codes around the highlighted text.

Here's a chance for you to repeatedly execute the style named BULLETS that you created previously in the document shown in Figure 14-4:

1. On the clear Typing screen where you moments ago created the style, type the heading **SALES FIGURES FOR THE WEST COAST**.

2. Press ENTER twice and type the following paragraph:

   We predict a 15% increase in sales this year. In the first three months of this year, the following figures are in from the West Coast of the United States:

3. Press ENTER twice. Your cursor is now positioned where you want to type a paragraph to be affected by a style.

4. Press the STYLES (ALT + F8) key. The cursor is already positioned on the style named BULLETS, since it is the only style listed.

5. Select On (1 or O).

6. Type the following:

   Sales of Chardonnay have sky-rocketed, increasing 50% over the same time last year.

7. Press ENTER, which has been defined to turn off the style. Two hard returns are inserted because these are the codes you inserted to end the style.

8. Repeat steps 4 through 7, for the two additional bulleted paragraphs shown in Figure 14-4.

9. You may wish to continue typing this document for additional practice. Type the heading and paragraph shown at the bottom of the screen in Figure 14-4 and then use the BULLETS style to format paragraphs that you compose.

A Style code expands to show its contents when you reveal codes and position the cursor on that code. This is convenient when you've inserted a Style code into the text and can't identify the format dictated by that code from the name alone. To see how this works, proceed as follows.

```
SALES FIGURES FOR THE WEST COAST

We predict a 15% increase in sales this year.  In the first three
months of this year, the following figures are in from the West
Coast of the United States:

  _    *    Sales of Chardonnay have sky-rocketed, increasing 58%
            over the same time last year.


                                            Doc 1 Pg 1 Ln 2.33" Pos 1"
[ ▲   ▲    ▲    ▲    ▲    ▲    ▲    ▲      ▲    ▲    ▲  }  ▲    ▲
Coast of the United States:[HRt]
[HRt]
[Style On:Bullets:[→Indent]*[→Indent][UND]]Sales of Chardonnay have sky[-]rocket
ed, increasing 58%[SRt]
over the same time last year.[Style Off:Bullets][Style On:Bullets]Pinot Noir has
 increased by 11%, a hefty increase, though[SRt]
volume  is much smaller for Pinot Noir than Chardonnay.[Style Off:Bullets][Style
 On:Bullets]Chenin Blanc and Cabernet Sauvignon sales have stayed[SRt]
about the same.[Style Off:Bullets][HRt]
SALES FIGURES FOR THE EAST COAST[HRt]

Press Reveal Codes to restore screen
```

FIGURE 14-6   The cursor positioned on a Style On code so that it expands

1. Press the REVEAL CODES (ALT + F3) key to view the Style
   On and Off codes you inserted.

2. Position the cursor on the first Style On code. The code will
   expand to show its contents, as illustrated in Figure 14-6.

3. Position the cursor on a Style Off code to reveal its contents.

4. Press REVEAL CODES (ALT + F3) to return to the Typing
   screen.

EDIT A STYLE

You can edit the format of a style on the Styles screen, but not on the
Typing screen. For instance, suppose that you decide to remove the

asterisks in Figure 14-4 and insert paragraph numbers instead. Try to position the cursor on an asterisk and you'll discover that the task is impossible. The asterisk is part of the Styles On code; the only way to edit it is to edit the style named BULLETS.

To edit a style, return to the Styles screen, position the cursor on the name of the style you wish to edit, and select Edit (4 or E). The Edit Styles screen for that style appears. Now select an item to alter the styles definition. Press EXIT (F7) until you return to the Typing screen.

When you edit a style that has already been executed in a document, the results are truly amazing. The text governed by that style is revised to reflect the editing changes in seconds. As an example, suppose that you decide to alter BULLETS by indenting the bulleted paragraphs one more tab stop to the right and preceding each paragraph with a paragraph number rather than an asterisk.

1. Press the STYLE (ALT + F8) key. The Styles screen appears.

2. Make sure that the cursor is on the style named BULLETS.

3. Select Edit (4 or E) to display the Edit Styles screen.

4. Select Codes (4 or C) to display the codes inserted for the BULLETS style, as shown in Figure 14-5.

5. Check the bottom window to make sure that the cursor is positioned on the first code, [→**Indent**], and press →INDENT (F4) to insert another [→**Indent**] code.

6. Position the cursor on the asterisk.

7. Press DEL to delete the asterisk, press DATE/OUTLINE (SHIFT + F5), select Para Num (5 or P), and press ENTER to insert an automatic paragraph number. Your screen should now resemble Figure 14-7.

8. Press EXIT (F7) until you return to the Typing screen.

In seconds, all the paragraphs governed by the BULLETS style are reformatted; the results are shown in Figure 14-8.

To delete a style, return to the Styles screen, position the cursor on the name of the style you wish to erase, and select Delete (5 or D). WordPerfect then asks for verification. Type **Y** to delete the style or type **N** to abort the command.

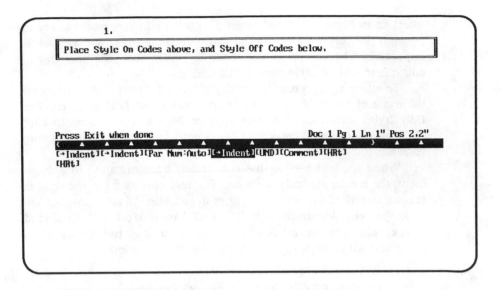

FIGURE 14-7   Codes after editing the BULLETS style

SALES FIGURES FOR THE WEST COAST

We predict a 15% increase in sales this year. In the first three
months of this year, the following figures are in from the West
Coast of the United States:

   1.   Sales of Chardonnay have sky-rocketed, increasing
         58% over the same time last year.

   2.   Pinot Noir has increased by 11%, a hefty increase,
         though volume is much smaller for Pinot Noir than
         Chardonnay.

   3.   Chenin Blanc and Cabernet Sauvignon sales have
         stayed about the same.

SALES FIGURES FOR THE EAST COAST

We predict a moderate 4% increase in sales this year. In the first
three months of this year, the following figures are in from the
East Coast:

                                          Doc 1 Pg 1 Ln 1" Pos 1"

FIGURE 14-8   Sample text after the BULLETS style is edited

MANAGE STYLES BETWEEN DOCUMENTS

When styles are created, they are associated with a specific document. When you save the document on disk, the styles are attached to that file. The next time you retrieve that document and press the STYLES (ALT + F8) key, the Styles screen appears listing those styles.

You can also save and retrieve styles separate from the document to which they are connected. In this way, you can apply styles created in one document to many other documents. For instance, a style you created for use in formatting the January newsletter can then be used when typing future newsletters.

To save a Style screen independently, press the STYLE (ALT + F8) key and select Save (6 or S). Now type a filename, using the same rules for naming files as when storing a document on disk. The Style screen is saved into a blank WordPerfect document, ready to be used in other documents.

To retrieve a Style screen into another document, make sure that the other document is on screen. Press STYLE (ALT + F8), select Retrieve (7 or R), and type in the name of the file containing the styles that you wish to bring into the current document. The retrieved styles are combined with any styles already on screen. If two styles have the same name, WordPerfect will prompt asking whether you wish to replace the existing style with the retrieved style. Type Y to replace or type N to stop the replacement.

You can also establish one of the Style screens that you saved independently as a *style library*. A style library is a collection of styles that will be attached to every new document that you create once the library is established. Reserve the style library for styles that you want to have available for all your documents. See "Location of Auxiliary Files" in Appendix C to learn how to specify one Style screen as a style library.

After you establish a style library, you can also attach this library to a document you created *before* you established the style library. Make sure that the existing document is on screen. Press STYLE (ALT + F8) and select Update (8 or U). The style library will be combined with any styles already on screen. Also use the Update feature if you edit the style library and want the changes reflected on the Style screen for a document you created before the library was edited.

REVIEW EXERCISE

Once you know about macros and styles, you'll want to take some time to think about your repetitive tasks and repetitive formatting needs. Then create your own macros and styles. The time it takes to do so will more than pay for itself in a short while. For additional practice before you start addressing your own, individual needs, try the following:

1. Suppose that after typing certain reports and before printing them, you format them for double spacing and for left/right margins of 2 inches. Create a simple macro that

   - Moves to the top of a document (with HOME, HOME, UP ARROW)

   - Changes the text to double spacing

   - Changes the left and right margins to 2 inches

   - Prints out the full document from the screen

   Name this macro DSMPRINT, which stands for Double Space, Margins, PRINT. (*Hint:* Before you begin recording the macro keystrokes, turn on the printer and type some text on screen so that WordPerfect will have something to print. Proceed slowly when recording the macro keystrokes to reduce the chance of making mistakes. Also, remember to turn off the recording after you send the document on screen to the printer.)

2. Clear the screen and retrieve a single-spaced document, such as JOHNSTON.LET, a letter you created when working with boilerplate text in Chapter 13.

3. Execute the macro named DSMPRINT to format and print this document. (*Hint:* Remember to turn on the printer before you execute this macro.)

4. For the document on screen, create a paired style that will underline and boldface a portion of text. Leave the ENTER key defined with its usual function, inserting a hard return. Name this style UNDBOLD, which stands for UNDerline and BOLDface.

5. Execute the UNDBOLD style several places in the text. For instance, if the file named JOHNSTON.LET is on screen, then

turn on the style for each occurrence of the name R&R Wine Association. (*Hint:* Since the text has already been typed, you must use the BLOCK (ALT + F4) to highlight the text that you wish to be governed by the style.) Then, press the STYLE (ALT + F8) key and turn on the style named UNDBOLD.

6. Resave the document on screen. When you do, the new style that you created will be attached to that document. (If you think that UNDBOLD is a style you will use often, you can also save that style independently into its own file.)

REVIEW

- Create a macro using the MACRO DEFINE (CTRL + F10) key whenever you find yourself typing a certain series of keystrokes over and over again, whether to type a phrase or issue a group of commands. Once you've created a macro, you can let WordPerfect do the repetitive typing for you. The macro is saved on disk with the extension .WPM.

- The macro can be named with the ALT key and a letter, with one to eight characters, or with the ENTER key. How you execute a macro depends on its name. If a macro was named with the ALT key and a letter, simply press ALT plus that letter to execute it. Otherwise, press the MACRO (ALT + F10) key, type the macro's name, and press ENTER.

- Use the repetition counter (the ESC key) before executing a macro when you wish to repeat that macro a specific number of times.

- Macros can involve a complicated series of commands. A macro can include special commands that pause the macro or make it visible. A macro can be linked together with other macros so that one macro automatically begins executing as soon as the first macro is finished or at any time.

- Edit a macro on the Macro Edit screen. You can add or delete various keystrokes to modify the macro.

- Create a style using the STYLE (ALT + F8) key whenever you find yourself formatting certain elements in a document over and over again in the same way. Once you've created a style, you can let WordPerfect do the repetitive formatting for you. If you edit a style, all the text governed by the style is automatically updated to conform to the modifications.

- There are two types of styles: open and paired. When you turn on an open style, the style takes effect for all text that follows the Open Style code. When you turn on a paired style, you must also turn it off; the paired style takes effect for the text that is positioned between the Style On and Style Off codes.

- Styles listed on a Style screen are stored along with the document in which they were created. However, you can save a Style screen independently so that it can be employed in many different documents. You can also establish one Style screen as a style library, which will automatically be attached to every new document that you create.

15

WORDPERFECT EXTRAS

Insert Special Characters
Alter the Keyboard Layout
Learn About Additional Graphics Capabilities
Work with Long Documents
Sort and Select
Use the Math Feature
Transfer Between Software Programs
Review

In previous chapters, you learned about the various features most heavily relied on to manipulate words and produce documents. In addition, WordPerfect can go far beyond the normal bounds of word processing, offering the capabilities to

- Insert special characters, such as mathematical or legal symbols, in a document

- Alter the layout of the keyboard to meet your own special needs

- Import graphics into documents using graphics programs not supported by WordPerfect

- Create line drawings on screen using the cursor movement keys

515

- Insert and update cross-references in a document

- Generate a table of contents, list, index, or table of authorities automatically

- Create a master document so that your work with long documents becomes more manageable

- Sort/select information either line by line or paragraph by paragraph in a document, or record by record in a secondary merge file document

- Calculate totals and the results of formulas in columns and rows

- Convert files between different versions of WordPerfect or between other software packages and WordPerfect

These are some of WordPerfect's most advanced features, which stretch the program's limits far beyond those of a standard word processor.

Should your WordPerfect needs extend to any of the above-mentioned extras, then read on. This chapter provides a general overview of the capabilities of each of WordPerfect's extra features. If you require greater detail on the variations and complexities of any of these extra features, you should know that there are several good sources published by Osborne/McGraw-Hill that go beyond the scope of this book. *WordPerfect: Secrets, Solutions, Shortcuts, Series 5 Edition* (1988), written by this author, offers a thorough explanation of all WordPerfect's features—from basic to advanced—and offers tips and points out traps along the way. Other good sources include *WordPerfect Series 5 Edition: The Complete Reference* (1988) by Karen Acerson and *Advanced WordPerfect, Series 5 Edition* (1988) by Eric Alderman.

INSERT SPECIAL CHARACTERS

With WordPerfect, you are not limited to the keys on the standard keyboard. You can produce other special symbols—for example, the degree symbol (°), the one-half symbol (1/2), the section sign used in legal documents (§), the paragraph sign (¶), and Greek letters such as alpha (α) or beta (β). You can also produce digraphs and diacritical marks such as Æ, á, or ö. In fact, depending on your printer, with WordPerfect you can include a variety of multinational, mathematical, scientific, Greek, and Hebrew symbols in documents—over 1500 special characters in all.

WordPerfect Character Set

In WordPerfect, special characters are separated into thirteen *character sets*. Each character set has a name and a corresponding number, as listed in Table 15-1.

Within a character set are a group of special characters, each of which is assigned a WordPerfect character number. The WordPerfect character number is made up of the character set number, a comma, and a character number from within the set. The special characters and their corresponding WordPerfect character numbers are all listed in two files found on the Conversion disk, CHARACTR.DOC and CHARMAP.TST.

CHARACTR.DOC, which is over 60 pages long, lists the special characters by character set. One special character is displayed on each line, along with a description of that character and its WordPerfect character number. You'll discover, for instance, that • is referred to as the bullet and is WordPerfect character number 4,0. Or, § is the section sign and is WordPerfect character number 4,6. Or, ÷ is the division sign and is WordPerfect character number 6,8.

CHARMAP.TST displays the special characters for each character set in a matrix form and without a written description of each special character, and is therefore only seven pages long. Figure 15-1 shows what will appear on your screen when you first retrieve CHAR-MAP.TST. (The first page of CHARMAP.TST lists the characters in character set 0, the same characters found directly on your keyboard.) With CHARMAP.TST, you must do a bit more work to figure out a special character's WordPerfect character number. Locate a character and add its corresponding row value and its column value together. The row value is usually counted in increments of twenty, such as 0, 20, 40, 60, and so on, or 30, 50, 70, and so on. The column value is any number from 0 to 19. For instance, the exclamation point (!) in Figure 15-1 is part of character set 0 and is at the intersection of row 30 and column 3. Thus, its WordPerfect character number is 0,33.

Name	Character Set #	Contents
ASCII	0	ASCII space through tilde—symbols commonly found on the computer keyboard
Multinational 1	1	Common capitalizable multinational characters, diacritics, and non-capitalizable multinational characters
Multinational 2	2	Rarely used noncapitalizable multinational characters and diacritics
Box Drawing	3	All 81 double/single box drawing characters.
Typographic Symbols	4	Common typographic symbols not found in ASCII
Iconic Symbols	5	Rarely used "picture" (icon) symbols
Math/Scientific	6	Nonextensible, nonoversized math/scientific characters not found in ASCII
Math/Scientific Extension	7	Extensible and oversized math/scientific characters.
Greek	8	Full Greek character set for ancient and modern applications
Hebrew	9	Full Hebrew character set for ancient and modern applications.
Cyrillic	10	Full Cyrillic character set for ancient and modern applications
Japanese Kana	11	Characters for Hiragana or Katakana (the type is determined by the typeface)
User-Defined	12	255 user-definable characters

TABLE 15-1   WordPerfect Character Sets

If you need to insert certain special characters in your document, you must first find out which special characters can be printed by your printer. Some printers can print certain special symbols; with others, you must change the print wheel or font cartridge; and some printers cannot print them at all. The easiest way to test your printer is to retrieve CHARMAP.TST to the screen and print it for each printer available to you. (In Chapter 9 you learned about another test file on the Conversion disk named PRINTER.TST. Retrieve and print CHARMAP.TST in the same way.) Then look through the seven printed pages to discover which special characters will print on your printer.

Once you know that your printer can print a certain symbol, the next step is to type that symbol in your document wherever it's required. In order to type one of these special characters, you must know its WordPerfect character number. Jot down that number after looking at the matrix in CHARMAP.TST or by looking through CHARACTR.DOC.

Once you've discovered a special character's WordPerfect character number, position the cursor in your document where you want the special character to appear. Press the COMPOSE key, which is either CTRL + 2 (the number 2 using the top row of numbers on the keyboard) or CTRL + V. (CTRL + V only operates on the Typing screen, whereas CTRL + 2 operates on a menu as well.) If you press CTRL + 2, no prompt appears on screen. If you press CTRL + V, the following prompt appears.

```
This prints all characters in Character Map 0

     0                   1
     0 1 2 3 4 5 6 7 8 9 0 1 2 3 4 5 6 7 8 9 !

030       ! " # $ % & ' ( ) * + , - . / 0 1 !

050  2 3 4 5 6 7 8 9 : ; < = > ? @ A B C D E !

070  F G H I J K L M N O P Q R S T U V W X Y !

090  Z [ \ ] ^ _ ` a b c d e f g h i j k l m !

110  n o p q r s t u v w x y z { | } ~       !

     0 1 2 3 4 5 6 7 8 9 0 1 2 3 4 5 6 7 8 9 !
     0                   1

This prints all characters in Character Map 1

     0                   1
     0 1 2 3 4 5 6 7 8 9 0 1 2 3 4 5 6 7 8 9 !

C:\WPER\CHARMAP.TST                    Doc 1 Pg 1 Ln 1" Pos 1"
```

FIGURE 15-1   CHARMAP.TST file on screen

Key =

Next, type the special character's WordPerfect character number and press ENTER. For instance, enter **4,6** to insert the section sign, or enter **6,8** to insert the division sign.

When you insert a special character in your document, either that character or a shaded rectangle will appear. Not all special characters can be displayed on screen. Which special characters can be displayed depends on your monitor and whether or not you have a graphics display card inside your computer. If a special character cannot be displayed on screen and a shaded box is shown instead, the special character will still print properly as long as it is supported by your printer.

There may be special characters that you insert in documents quite frequently. If so, consider assigning a special character to key combination. For example, you can assign the degree symbol to the key combination CTRL + D or the section sign to CTRL + S—which is easier than inserting these special characters by pressing CTRL + V, typing a WordPerfect character number, and then pressing ENTER. See the section below that discusses the Keyboard Layout feature for more details on assigning special characters to a key combination.

Digraphs and Diacriticals

When you wish to insert a digraph or diacritical mark, there's a shortcut. A digraph is two vowels or consonants combined to express one sound, such as æ or Æ. A diacritical mark is a symbol that, when combined with a vowel or consonant, expresses a sound that differs from the vowel or consonant alone—for instance, â or é. Instead of finding that digraph or diactrical mark's WordPerfect character number, you can use two characters to create it. Position the cursor in your document where you want the digraph or diacritical mark to appear. Press the COMPOSE key, which is either CTRL + 2 or CTRL + V. If you press CTRL + 2, no prompt appears on screen. If you press CTRL + V, the following prompt appears:

Key =

Type one character of the digraph or the letter to be combined with a diacritical mark, such as A or e. Then type in the second character, such as E or '. WordPerfect inserts the digraph or diacritical mark on screen, such as Æ or á. Remember, however, that whether or not that digraph or diacritical mark displays on screen depends on your monitor. Also, whether or not that digraph or diacritical mark is printed depends on your printer.

You can also use the Overstrike feature to produce digraphs or diacritical marks that your printer might not otherwise produce. The Overstrike feature gives you the ability to print two or more characters in the same position. To use Overstrike, position the cursor in your document where you want the digraph or diacritical mark to appear. Press the FORMAT (SHIFT + F8) key to display the Format menu. Select Other (4 or O) to display the Other Format menu and then select Overstrike (5 or O). WordPerfect prompts

1 Create; 2 Edit: **0**

Select Create (1 or C). WordPerfect prompts

[Ovrstk]

Now type the characters that you wish to print at the same location, and press ENTER. Finally, press EXIT (F7) until you return to the Typing screen.

On the Typing screen, only the last character you typed will appear. For instance, if you typed a', the screen will display only the single quote ('). Reveal codes, however, and you'll find [**Ovrstk:a'**]. Both characters will be printed at the same position. You can also edit the Overstrike code by placing the cursor after the code and following the procedure just described to view the Overstrike menu. Then select Edit (2 or E). After editing the code, press ENTER and EXIT (F7) to return to the Typing screen.

ALTER THE KEYBOARD LAYOUT

WordPerfect offers the ability to reconfigure your keyboard to meet unique needs. You can create a keyboard definition that specifies which key combination will perform a certain feature or task. You can specify which key will do the following:

- *Activate a feature* For instance, on WordPerfect's original keyboard, F1 serves as the CANCEL key. Other software packages, however, reserve the F1 key as the HELP key. So you may wish to set up a new keyboard definition in WordPerfect whereby, among other things, you reassign the F1 key as the HELP key.

- *Insert a special character*   For instance, suppose you frequently type legal documents and insert special characters such as the section sign (§) and paragraph sign (¶). You can set up a keyboard definition whereby all the legal special characters are assigned to certain key combinations. For instance, you'll define a keyboard such that when you press CTRL + S, the section sign is inserted and when you press ALT + P, the paragraph sign is inserted.

- *Execute a macro*   Macros—series of keystrokes that WordPerfect stores for you—are described in Chapter 14. You can write various macros to accomplish repetitive tasks and then set up a keyboard definition whereby you press CTRL plus a letter or a certain function key, or ALT plus a number to execute a given macro.

You can create one or many keyboard definitions. As an example, if you wish to redefine just a few keys for your personal needs, then perhaps establish just one keyboard definition. But if you sometimes type legal documents for which you want certain keys defined one way and sometimes type foreign documents for which you want certain keys defined a second way, then establish two different keyboard definitions.

When a new definition is created, it is stored on disk with the extension .WPK, which stands for WordPerfect Keyboard. You can activate a keyboard definition that you've created at any time while typing or editing a document. You can also return to the *original* keyboard—the one defined by the creators of WordPerfect—at any time.

The WordPerfect package comes with three already-created keyboard definitions, found on the Conversion disk:

- *ALTRNAT.WPK*   Moves the Help feature to the F1 key, the Cancel feature to the ESC key, and the Repeat Value feature to the F3 key.

- *ENHANCED.WPK*   Reassigns more than a dozen keys for moving the cursor or enhancing text. For instance, SHIFT + F11 will turn on italics (useful only for those of you with keyboards containing 12 function keys) and CTRL + DOWN ARROW moves the cursor down to the start of the next sentence.

- *MACROS.WPK*   Assigns a variety of macros to the ALT and CTRL keys.

If you wish to examine any of these three keyboard definitions, floppy disk users should place the Conversion disk in drive B before accessing the Keyboard Layout feature. Hard disk users must specify where these three keyboard definitions are found on the hard disk, as described in the "Location of Auxiliary Files" section of Appendix C, before accessing the Keyboard Layout feature. Now WordPerfect will be able to locate these three keyboard definitions.

To work with the Keyboard Layout feature, press the SETUP (SHIFT + F1) key and select Keyboard Layout (6 or K). A screen as shown in Figure 15-2 appears. Figure 15-2 shows the screen when the three predefined keyboard definitions are available to WordPerfect. If the Conversion disk isn't in the default drive (floppy disk users) or if

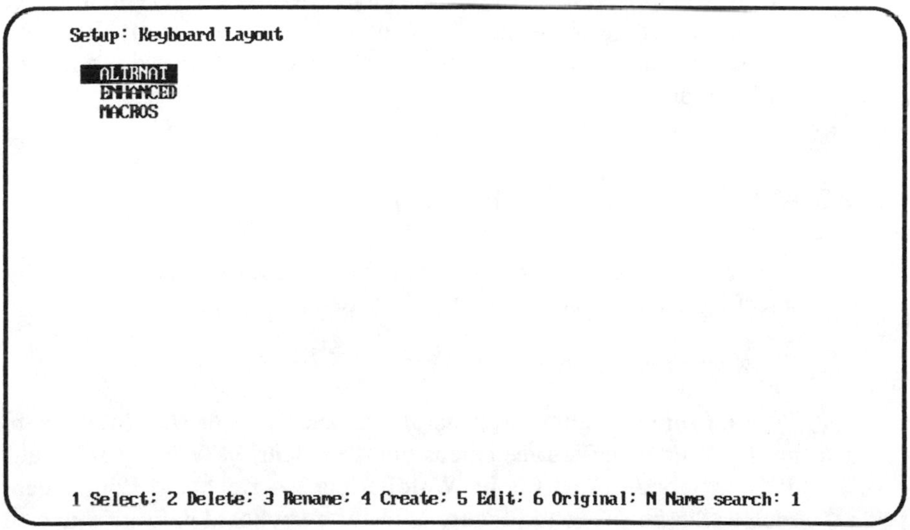

```
Setup: Keyboard Layout

  ALTRNAT
  ENHANCED
  MACROS










 1 Select; 2 Delete; 3 Rename; 4 Create; 5 Edit; 6 Original; N Name search: 1
```

FIGURE 15-2   Keyboard Layout screen listing three predefined keyboard definitions

you haven't indicated to WordPerfect where these keyboard definitions are housed on the hard disk (hard disk users), then there may be no keyboard definitions listed unless you previously created additional keyboard definitions of your own.

The options at the bottom of the Keyboard Layout screen allow you to select a keyboard definition, create a new one, or manage the list of keyboard definitions.

Select a Keyboard Definition or Return to the Original

To activate an already-created definition, display the Keyboard Layout screen. Next, position the cursor on the keyboard definition name that you wish to activate in one of two ways: either use the cursor movement keys or select Name Search (N), type the first characters of the keyboard definition's name, and press ENTER. Now choose Select (1 or S) and press EXIT (F7) to return to the Typing screen.

When you wish to deactivate a certain definition and revert to the original keyboard definition, again display the Keyboard Layout screen, select Original (6 or O), and press EXIT (F7). As an alternative, you can revert to the original keyboard definition directly from the Typing screen: simply press CTRL + 6 (the number 6 on the top row of the keyboard).

Create a Keyboard Definition

Create a keyboard definition from the Keyboard Layout screen by selecting Create (4 or C). WordPerfect then prompts with

Keyboard Filename:

Type a name of eight characters or less and press ENTER. (Make sure not to also type a filename extension; the extension .WPK is automatically assigned to that file by WordPerfect.) A Keyboard Edit screen, such as the one shown in Figure 15-3 for a keyboard definition named LEGAL, will appear on screen. Now your task is to work with a specific key, as part of a keyboard definition. You can select from the menu of options at the bottom of the screen. The first four relate to a key, while the last two options relate to a macro:

- *Edit (1 or E)* This option edits the definition for a specific key or key combination. Position the cursor on a key combination that you wish to edit before selecting this option. The Key Edit screen reappears for the key or key combination you highlighted with the cursor. Once you edit the keystrokes, press EXIT (F7).

- *Delete (2 or D)* This option deletes a definition for a specific key combination. Position the cursor on the key combination you wish to delete before selecting this option. WordPerfect will prompt for confirmation; type **Y** to delete the key combination from the definition.

- *Move (3 or M)* This option moves a key combination's feature or task to a different key. Position the cursor on the key combination before selecting this option.

- *Create (4 or C)* This option assigns a feature or task to a specific key or key combination. WordPerfect will prompt for a

```
Keyboard: Edit
  Name: LEGAL
  Key              Description                    Macro




  Key: 1 Edit: 2 Delete: 3 Move: 4 Create:  Macro: 5 Save: 6 Retrieve: 1
```

FIGURE 15-3 Keyboard Edit screen for a keyboard definition named LEGAL

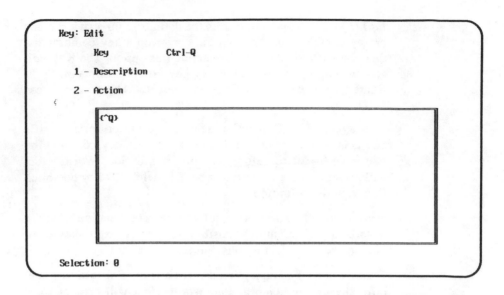

FIGURE 15-4   Key Edit screen for CTRL + Q

key. Type the key or key combination that you wish to define, such as] or CTRL + S or F1 or ALT + P. A Key Edit screen for that key appears, as shown in Figure 15-4 for the key combination CTRL + Q (denoted Ctrl-Q).

When you select Description (1 or D), you can type in an explanation of that key's function for future reference, and press ENTER or EXIT (F7). The description can be up to 39 characters in length.

When you select Action (2 or A), the cursor enters the double-line action box. The key's current function is listed in the action box, such as {^Q} in Figure 15-4, which means that when you press CTRL + Q, ^Q is currently inserted on screen. Type in the exact keystrokes that you want the key to accomplish. For instance, erase the ^Q, press the COMPOSE (CTRL + 2) key, and enter the WordPerfect character number of a special character; this defines CTRL + Q to insert a certain special character. Or erase the ^Q, press the asterisk (*) and then press the →INDENT (F4) key to define a new key that will insert an asterisk and an [→**Indent**] code. Then press EXIT (F7) twice, once to leave the action box and a second time to return to the Keyboard Edit screen; the key combination you just defined is now listed on that screen.

You can define many key combinations for one keyboard definition. Any keys you don't define maintain their original function.

- *Save (5 or S)*   This option saves a key's definition as a file macro so that the macro can be executed like other macros. Position the cursor on the key combination before selecting this option. At WordPerfect's prompt, type in the filename for this macro. The macro will be saved on disk with the extension .WPM, which stands for WordPerfect Macro. The macro can now be executed like any other macro. (Be sure to refer to Chapter 14 for more on macros.)

- *Retrieve (6 or R)*   This option retrieves a previously created macro and assigns that macro to a key combination. Word-Perfect will prompt for a key. Type the key or key combination to which you wish to assign the macro. At WordPerfect's next prompt, type in the macro's filename. Now the macro can be executed either as part of a keyboard definition or using the standard macro executing process.

Once you create a keyboard definition, assigning a variety of keys to specific functions, press EXIT (F7) to return to the Keyboard Layout screen; the name of the newly created keyboard definition will be listed. Remember that you must still choose the Select option if you wish to start using that new keyboard definition.

Manage a Keyboard Definition

You can check the keys that are assigned within a keyboard definition and edit that definition. From the Keyboard Layout screen, position the cursor on the keyboard definition name that you wish to edit either by using the cursor movement keys or by selecting Name Search (N), typing the first characters of the keyboard definition's name, and pressing ENTER. Now select Edit (5 or E). The Keyboard Edit screen for that particular keyboard definition appears. Use the EXIT (F7) key when the editing is complete.

You can also delete or rename a keyboard definition at any time. From the Keyboard Layout screen, position the cursor on the keyboard definition name that you wish to delete or rename. Then select Delete (2 or D) and type **Y** to verify the deletion, or select Rename (3 or R) and type in a new filename for the keyboard definition.

LEARN ABOUT ADDITIONAL GRAPHICS CAPABILITIES

In Chapter 10, you learned about WordPerfect's ability to incorporate graphics lines or graphics boxes into a document. A graphics box can contain text or graphics images created using programs compatible with WordPerfect. If the graphics program you use to create your graphics images is not compatible with WordPerfect, you can use a screen capture program provided by WordPerfect called GRAB.COM. If your printer has no graphics capabilities, you can use the Line Draw feature to create line drawings and see if your printer will print them. Line Draw is also useful when your printer does support graphics but you wish to create a simple line drawing on screen using the cursor movement keys.

Screen Capture Utility

GRAB.COM is a Screen Capture program provided on the Word-Perfect Fonts/Graphics disk. With this program, you can copy any image displayed on screen into a file, which can then be integrated into a WordPerfect document. Given a choice, you'll want to use WordPerfect-supported graphics formats (as described in Chapter 10) rather than GRAB.COM. GRAB.COM captures images of a lesser quality, because the image you capture is only as good as the screen resolution. Nevertheless, it is a useful alternative if your graphics program cannot produce your images in a WordPerfect-supported graphics format.

To use GRAB.COM, you must load it into your computer's memory *before* you load WordPerfect or another software package, so you must be in DOS. Then, if you're a floppy disk user, insert the Fonts/Graphics disk in drive A. At the DOS prompt (A>), type **GRAB** and press ENTER. If you're a hard disk user, change to the hard disk directory where the GRAB.COM program is located. For instance, type **CD \WPER** and press ENTER. Then type **GRAB** and press ENTER.

Now load the graphics program and create the graphics image. When that image is on screen, press ALT + SHIFT + F9. If you hear a two-toned chime, this means you have activated GRAB.COM, the Screen Capture program. (If you hear no such chime, but instead hear a low-pitch buzz, either you are not in Graphics mode, or your monitor cannot support GRAB.COM.) A box is displayed on screen. Use the directional arrow keys to move the box, and use the combination SHIFT plus an arrow key to resize the box. Once the box is properly positioned and sized over the graphics image, press ENTER to store the image; another two-toned chime sounds to signal that the file is being stored. You can press ESC to abort the screen capture.

GRAB.COM saves the image in the default drive/directory in a file named GRAB.WPG. If a file by that name exists, it is stored under GRAB1.WPG (or GRAB2.WPG and so on). The image is now in proper WordPerfect format to be used in a document.

You can then exit the graphics program, load WordPerfect, create a graphics box, and retrieve the file named GRAB.WPG (or GRAB1.WPG, or whatever) into that graphics box—as described in Chapter 10.

Line Draw

In addition to using the Graphics feature, you can also use WordPerfect's Line Draw feature to create illustrations. With Line Draw, you can create simple drawings that contain straight lines and sharp corners right on screen. You can use the arrow keys to produce organizational charts, design graphs, or create a work of art. The lines can be drawn around text either before or after the text is typed. Unlike the Graphics feature, with Line Draw you can see the image you've created right on the Typing screen.

To use the Line Draw feature, position the cursor on the line where you want the drawing to begin, press the SCREEN (CTRL + F3) key, and select Line Draw (2 or L). The Line Draw menu appears:

1 |; 2 ‖; 3 *; 4 Change; 5 Erase; 6 Move: 1   Ln 1" Pos 1"

WordPerfect will assume option 1, meaning that you want to draw with a single straight line. Just start using the UP, DOWN, LEFT, and RIGHT ARROW keys, and an image will form.

The Line Draw menu offers other choices as well. Select option 2, and you can draw with a double line. Option 3 will let you draw lines of asterisks. Select Erase (5 or E) and you retrace your steps to delete lines. Select Move (6 or M) and you can move the cursor without drawing, as if you were picking up a pencil to move it to another spot before continuing.

You can also change the third draw character from an asterisk to another character. Select Change (4 or C), and the following menu appears:

1 ▓: 2 ▐: 3 ▐: 4 ▌: 5 ▪: 6 |: 7 |: 8 ▪: 9 Other: 0

You can select any of these characters to draw with, or you can select Other (9 or O) and choose one of your own from the characters on the keyboard, such as the plus sign (+) or the broken line (I). Figure 15-5 shows a graph drawn by typing graph labels ("Monthly Sales," "Jan," "Feb," "March," and so on) and using three line draw characters—the single line, the asterisk, and the thick dotted line. (The tiny arrows that appear on screen when you use the single or double line, two of which are shown in Figure 15-5, do not appear on the printed page.)

It is usually easier when combining text with graphics to type the text first and then activate Line Draw. Line Draw works in Typeover mode; if you draw over text, the text is replaced by the line. Word-Perfect automatically inserts an **[HRt]** code at the end of each line as you draw.

Should you decide to type text after creating a line drawing, you should switch into Typeover mode first by pressing the INS key. This will ensure that when you type on a line that contains a drawing, you won't disfigure the drawing. Don't type over the drawing or press ENTER on a line that includes a drawing. If you do, you must find and erase the **[HRt]** code to return the drawing to its previous appearance.

Just as with special characters such as § or 1/2, the line draw characters cannot be produced by all printers. You must test your

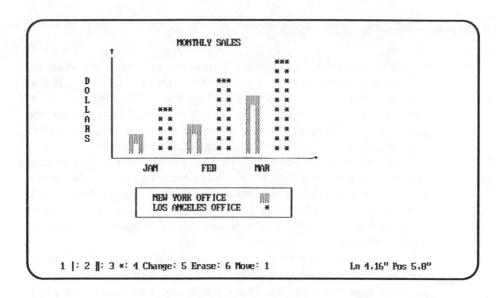

FIGURE 15-5   A graph created with Line Draw using three draw characters

printer's capabilities. One way is to design a line drawing such as the one shown in Figure 15-5 and then print it. Should your printer be unable to print the special line draw characters, you can always draw by using some of the standard keys on your keyboard that all printers can produce, such as the broken line (¦) for vertical lines, the plus sign (+) for box corners, and the minus sign (–) or equal sign (=) for horizontal lines.

WORK WITH LONG DOCUMENTS

WordPerfect offers several powerful features that enable you to manage the text in long documents. These include Automatic References; Generate Tables, Lists, and Indexes; and Master Documents.

Automatic References

Suppose you insert the following phrase in your text: "For more on Chardonnay wines, refer to footnote 14, found on page 33." If you then edit your text so that pages are renumbered and/or edit your footnotes so that they are renumbered, you must manually update the phrase about Chardonnay wines, as well as any other phrase that cites a specific page or footnote number. That's time-consuming.

Instead, employ the Automatic Reference feature. This feature will let you refer to a specific page number, graphics box, footnote, endnote, or outline/paragraph number—called the *target*. Should you later edit your document so that the target becomes a different page or graphics box or footnote, all references can be updated automatically. That's a timesaver.

To create an automatic reference, position the cursor within the referring text wherever you want the reference number to appear. For instance, type **For more on The R&R Wine Association, see page**. Next, press the MARK TEXT (ALT + F5) key and select Auto Ref (1 or R). The Automatic Reference menu displays, as shown in Figure 15-6.

Typically, the referring text and the target will exist in the same document, so that you can select Mark Both Reference and Target (3 or B). WordPerfect wants to know what you are referring to in the text. Is the target a page number? A footnote number? A paragraph number? The menu shown in Figure 15-7 appears. Type in a number that corresponds to your target, such as Page Number (1 or P) if you're referring to a page. Now WordPerfect will prompt based on your target selection. For instance, if you selected a page number, WordPerfect prompts

Move to page; Press Enter.

Position the cursor just past the target and press ENTER. For instance, for a target that's a page number, position the cursor on that page, just past the discussion to which you're referring, and press ENTER. For a target that's a footnote, use the FOOTNOTE (CTRL + F7) key to view the Typing screen for that footnote (see Chapter 12), position the cursor just past the footnote number, and press ENTER.

As a last step, you are asked for a target name. This target name links the referring text to the target. Type a short name. For instance, type **R&R** and press ENTER.

You are returned to your phrase in the text. That phrase now appears with the reference number; such as, "For more on The R&R

```
Mark Text: Automatic Reference

     1 - Mark Reference

     2 - Mark Target

     3 - Mark Both Reference and Target

Selection: 0
```

FIGURE 15-6   Automatic Reference menu

```
Tie Reference to:

     1 - Page Number

     2 - Paragraph/Outline Number

     3 - Footnote Number

     4 - Endnote Number

     5 - Graphics Box Number

After selecting a reference type, go to the location of the item you want to
reference in your document and press Enter to mark it as the "target".

Selection: 0
```

FIGURE 15-7   Tie Reference to menu

Wine Association, see page 23." But the reference number 23 is really a code. Reveal Codes and you will view the following: "For more on The R&R Wine Association, see page **[Ref(R&R):Pg** 23]." This code is called a Reference code, where the target name is R&R and the reference number is 23. The target, too, contains a code. For instance, just below a discussion of the R&R Wine Association on page 23, you may find the code **[Target**(R&R)].

If you later edit the document, the location of text related to the R&R Wine Association may move from page 23 to another page, perhaps page 19. In that case, you should direct WordPerfect to generate (update) the automatic references before you save or print the document. To do so, press the MARK TEXT (ALT + F5) key, select Generate (6 or G), and then select Generate Tables, Indexes, Automatic References, etc. (5 or G). Type **Y** at WordPerfect's prompt to verify that you wish to generate (update) all automatic references (as well as tables, lists, and indexes, which are discussed farther on in this chapter). Now the phrase in the text will read: "For more on The R&R Wine Association, see page 19."

Besides marking a reference and target at the same time, you can also mark them separately. For instance, suppose that you plan to create many references to the same target. Begin your phrase in the text where you'll refer to a target and on the Automatic Reference menu (Figure 15-6), select Mark Reference (1 or R) to mark the referring text. Once you insert a Reference code, a question mark (?) will appear instead of a reference number. Repeat for each reference you wish to make in the text. Later, position the cursor at the target location, return to the Automatic Reference menu, and select Mark Target (2 or T) to insert a Target code. Use the same target name for all Reference codes and Target codes that are linked together. Remember to generate (update) the automatic references, as described above, to replace each question mark with the proper reference number.

Generate Tables, Lists, and Indexes

In a dissertation, book, legal brief, or other long document, the author often prepares reference aids to help the reader easily find information in that document. WordPerfect offers assistance when you need to create reference aids, which include an index (like the one at the back of this book), a table of contents (like the one at the front of this book), up to nine separate lists (of illustrations, graphs, maps, and such), and up to 16 sections of a table of authorities (which lists various cases, regulations, and cases cited in a legal document). Best of all, if you let WordPerfect create these reference aids for you, they can be updated by WordPerfect when you later edit your text.

The procedure for producing any of these reference aids is basically the same: (1) mark the text that will be included; (2) define the style of the reference aid; and (3) generate the reference aid.

MARK TEXT   You must insert codes around phrases in the text that you want incorporated in a particular reference aid. This is called marking the text. Suppose that you want to mark a heading to be included in a table of contents. Use the BLOCK (ALT + F4) key to highlight the heading. Then press the MARK TEXT (ALT + F5) key. With Block on, the following menu appears:

Mark for: 1 ToC; 2 List; 3 Index; 4 ToA: 0

Select the option that corresponds to the reference aid for which you are marking the text; for instance, select ToC (1 or C) to mark the heading for a table of contents. Then WordPerfect will ask you how that highlighted text should be treated:

- For a table of contents, WordPerfect asks for the table of contents level. Think of the table of contents as having a structure similar to that of an outline: level-one text starts at the left margin, level two is indented one tab stop, and so on.

- For a list, WordPerfect asks you for which list the text should be marked. For example, suppose you were creating one list of illustrations related to white wines and another list for red wines. The first could be identified as list 1, and the second could be list 2.

- For an index, WordPerfect asks for the index heading and subheading. For instance, one entry in an index might be

  White Wines

     Chardonnay

     Chenin Blanc

  The heading would be "White Wines," and the subheadings would be "Chardonnay" and "Chenin Blanc."

- For a table of authorities, WordPerfect prompts for that citation's section number. For instance, perhaps your table of authorities will have two sections: statutes and cases. Section 1 could be statutes, and section 2 could be cases.

The citation is then displayed on the screen. You can edit how it will appear in the table of authorities and then press the EXIT (F7) key.

Finally, WordPerfect will ask for the citation's short form, which will serve as a nickname. If you mark that citation again in the text, you can use the short form instead of editing the full citation again.

Each time that you mark a phrase to be included in a reference aid, codes are placed around that phrase. For instance, suppose you marked the heading "Sales Figures for the West Coast" as a level-2 entry in a table of contents. The heading would be surrounded with a pair of hidden codes as follows: **[Mark:ToC,2]**Sales Figures for the West Coast**[EndMark:ToC,2]**. Of course, those codes can be viewed only on the Reveal Codes screen.

You also have a feature available to mark text quickly for an index. You may have a number of words or phrases that appear sprinkled throughout a document. Instead of marking each phrase individually, you can create a *concordance file*, which is a document containing those common phrases that you want included in an index. On a clear screen, type the phrases, one on each line, and then save this document under a name that reminds you it's a concordance file. WordPerfect will ask for the name of the concordance file when you define the index (the procedure to define a reference aid follows). When Word-Perfect creates (generates) the index, it will search the document for those phrases contained in the concordance file and include the corresponding page numbers in the index. The phrases are assumed to be headings unless you mark those phrases in the concordance file—in the same way that you mark phrases in a document—as subheadings. Creating a concordance file does not exclude you from also marking phrases individually in the text. WordPerfect will compile both into an index when generated. But a concordance file does free you from having to mark the same phrase over and over again in the text.

DEFINE THE REFERENCE AID'S STYLE   Your next step is to define the table, list, or index that you wish to create. Position the cursor where you want that reference aid to appear. For an index, the cursor must be positioned at the end of the document. When WordPerfect generates an index, it looks backward in the text for marked phrases, so any marked phrases that are forward from the cursor will not be included. For the other reference aids, the cursor can be located anywhere in the document. For instance, you can position the cursor on a separate page at the end of the document to ensure that the page-reference numbers are correct when you generate the aid. In this way, you can always renumber the page on which the reference aid is located after you generate it. For instance, you can number the page containing a table of contents as page i, even though it is located at the end of the document. (See Chapter 5 for directions on renumbering pages). Alternatively, you can position the cursor on a separate page at the front of the document; however, you must remember to renumber your pages *before* you actually generate the reference aid so that the page-reference numbers are correct.

With the cursor located in the document where you want a reference aid to be generated, press the MARK TEXT (ALT + F5) key. With Block off, a different menu appears:

1 Auto Ref; 2 Subdoc; 3 Index; 4 ToA Short Form; 5 Define;
6 Generate: 0

Select Define (5 or D), choose the option corresponding to the reference aid you wish to define, and then follow WordPerfect's prompt to define the reference aid. In a document you can generate more than one list and multiple sections in a table of authorities, so each list and table of authorities section must be defined separately.

For a specific list, table of contents, or index, you are given the opportunity to determine how page numbers should appear once generated. Figure 15-8 shows a sample of the five numbering styles available. With a table of contents, you can also determine how many levels should be generated and whether entries in the last level should be placed together on the same line, separated by semicolons—referred to as wrapped format. With an index, you also have the opportunity to indicate a filename for a concordance file that you may have created.

For a table of authorities, a menu screen appears where you decide whether (1) the page numbers (which will always appear at the right margin on the page) should be preceded by dot leaders, (2) the table should include underlining, and (3) a blank line should be inserted between authorities.

A Definition Mark code is placed in the text. For instance, suppose you just defined list 1, where the numbering style will be flush

1 - No page numbers:

Sales Figures for the West Coast

Sales Figures for the East Coast

2 - Page numbers follow entries:

Sales Figures for the West Coast 5

Sales Figures for the East Coast 5

3 - Page numbers follow entries in parentheses:

Sales Figures for the West Coast (5)

Sales Figures for the East Coast (5)

4 - Flush right page numbers:

Sales Figures for the West Coast   5

Sales Figures for the East Coast   5

5 - Flush right page numbers with dot leaders:

Sales Figures for the West Coast 5

Sales Figures for the East Coast 5

FIGURE 15-8   Numbering styles available for a list, index, or table of contents

right page numbers (option 4); the code inserted is **[Def Mark: List,1:4]**. Or suppose that you defined section 3 of a table of authorities; the code inserted is **[Def Mark:ToA,3]**.

GENERATE THE REFERENCE AID   The hard work is now over. You simply press a few keys and sit back while the table, list, or index is generated. With the cursor located anywhere in the document, press the MARK TEXT (ALT + F5) key, select Generate (6 or G), and select Generate Tables, Indexes, Automatic References, etc. (5 or G). At WordPerfect's prompt, type **Y** to continue with the generation (where all reference aids as well as automatic references are updated) or type **N** to abort the command. Depending on the length of your document, the generation process could take several minutes.

```
                    TABLE OF CONTENTS


Introduction . . . . . . . . . . . . . . . . . . . . . . . .  1

Wine Sales . . . . . . . . . . . . . . . . . . . . . . . . .  3
        Sales Figures for the West Coast. . . . . . . . . . .  5
        Sales Figures for the East Coast. . . . . . . . . . .  5

Future Projections . . . . . . . . . . . . . . . . . . . . .  7
        West Coast. . . . . . . . . . . . . . . . . . . . . .  8
                Short-term . . . . . . . . . . . . . . . . . .  9
                Long-term. . . . . . . . . . . . . . . . . . .  9
        East Coast. . . . . . . . . . . . . . . . . . . . . . 11
                Short-term . . . . . . . . . . . . . . . . . . 12
                Long-term. . . . . . . . . . . . . . . . . . . 12

Conclusions. . . . . . . . . . . . . . . . . . . . . . . . . 14




                                    Doc 1 Pg 1 Ln 1" Pos 1"
```

FIGURE 15-9   A table of contents

After the table, index, or list is generated, you can put on the finishing touches. For example, if you put a title at the top of a table of contents that you defined as having three levels with flush right page numbers and dot leaders, you'd have a result like that shown in Figure 15-9.

Master Documents

The Master Document feature aids you in working with a long document. You can store separate parts of a long document in individual files, referred to as *subdocuments*. Then you can create a main document that links all the subdocuments together, referred to as the *master document*. You can edit each subdocument separately, so that editing becomes more manageable. At the same time, you can work with them as a whole via the master document for tasks that require the documents be treated as one, such as printing or generating a comprehensive table of contents, table of authorities, index, or list. And all numbering features found in the subdocuments—such as footnotes, endnotes, paragraph numbering, automatic referencing, and page numbering—will operate consecutively when the subdocuments are linked to the master.

The master document is basically a small file consisting of text and links to each subdocument. Suppose, for instance, you are writing a book. Each chapter can be stored on disk as a separate subdocument, using filenames such as CHAP1, CHAP2, and so on. The master document may include a title page, reference aids such as a table of contents, an introduction, and links to each chapter.

To work with the Master Document feature, you can first type and save all the subdocuments on disk, or you can create the master document first and then create the subdocuments later. When you're ready to create the master document, start typing on a clear screen just as you would for beginning any document. In the location where you want to incorporate a subdocument, press the MARK TEXT (ALT + F5) key and select Subdoc (2 or S). WordPerfect prompts

Subdoc Filename:

Enter the name of the file to be placed at that location, including the drive and/or directory in which it can be found if different from the default, such as **C:\WPER\CHAP1**. A comment box is inserted in the text, such as

```
Subdoc: C:\WPER\CHAP1
```

If you reveal codes, you'll see that the box represents a Subdocument code **[Subdoc:C:\WPER\CHAP1]**. This code links the master to the subdocument named CHAP1 (which is housed on the hard disk (drive C) in the directory named \WPER). It acts as a placeholder for the actual text found in that file.

Continue until all subdocuments have been linked to the master. The master document may contain very little text—just a string of Subdocument codes, one on each line. You can also separate each Subdocument code with a hard page (CTRL + ENTER) so that, when printed, each subdocument will begin on a separate page. Save the file using a filename that will remind you that it is a master document. For example, name the master document BOOK or MASTER or BOOK .MAS.

When you're ready to print the document in its entirety, including all the subdocument text, you must expand the master document. (You can also expand the master before generating a table, list, or index, but you don't have to; WordPerfect will do so automatically when you generate.)

To expand the master document, retrieve it to the screen. Press the MARK TEXT (ALT + F5) key, select Generate (6 or G), and select Expand Master Document (3 or E). In moments, the text of the subdocuments will be incorporated into the master, each bordered by a pair of comment boxes. For instance, the boxes around Chapter 1 will appear as follows:

```
Subdoc Start: C:\WPER\CHAP1
```

Located here would be the text of Chapter 1.

```
Subdoc End: C:\WPER\CHAP1
```

If you reveal codes, you'll see that the boxes represent two Subdocument codes [Subdoc Start:C:\WPER\CHAP1] and [Subdoc End:C:\WPER\CHAP1]. (Should WordPerfect be unable to locate a subdocument on disk during the expansion process, WordPerfect will prompt asking whether you wish to continue. Type Y to do so, even though a certain subdocument cannot be expanded, or type N to stop the expansion with that subdocument.)

After printing, you can again condense the master into its short form. To do so, press the MARK TEXT (ALT + F5) key, select Generate (6 or G), and select Condense Master Document (4 or C). WordPerfect has no idea whether you edited any of the text of the subdocuments while the master was expanded, and so responds with the prompt

Save Subdocs (Y/N)? Yes

Type Y if you made any editing changes in any of the subdocuments, in which case WordPerfect will then prompt asking whether you wish to replace the version of each separate subdocument on disk with the version on screen. Type N if you made no changes to the subdocuments or don't wish to save any changes made. The master will then collapse into its short form. Remember to condense a master document again before resaving it on disk, so that the master takes up the least amount of disk space possible.

SORT AND SELECT

WordPerfect offers some of the same capabilities for use in your documents as a traditional data base manager. You can rearrange text in a specific order, either alphabetically or numerically; this is referred to as a sort. Or you can isolate information that meets certain conditions, such as those names that begin with the letter "P" or those lines that contain the name "San Francisco"—this is referred to as a select. You can even sort and select at the same time; for instance, you could select the names of people who live in San Francisco and sort those names alphabetically.

You can sort or select text in three ways. First, you can sort or select individual lines. An example of a document appropriate for a line sort is shown in Figure 15-10. Each line is referred to as an individual record. Within records, text typed at the left margin is referred to as field 1. Text aligned on the next tab stop is referred to as field 2. (In Figure 15-10, for example, field 2 contains first names.) Text aligned on the next tab stop would be in field 3, and so on.

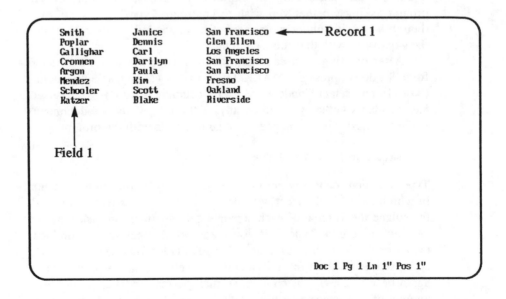

FIGURE 15-10   A document to be sorted by line

```
        Chenin Blanc wines are white and usually range from semi-sweet
   to semi-dry.

        Cabernet Sauvignon is a red grape.  The wines have a
   complexity that often comes from the oak barrels in which the wine
   is aged.

        Pinot Noir is light, and is often thought to lack the flavor
   and elegance of other fine reds.  Winemakers have been
   experimenting with this variety, and Gamay Beaujolais is one of its
   clones.

        Chardonnay is a successful white wine variety.  Chardonnays
   can be rich, full-bodied, and complex.




                                    Doc 1 Pg 1 Ln 1" Pos 1"
```

FIGURE 15-11   A document to be sorted by paragraph

Besides working with lines, you can also sort or select paragraphs, such as those in Figure 15-11. Here, each record is an entire paragraph. Fields are again defined based on whether text is aligned on tab stops. The paragraphs in Figure 15-11 are considered to be in field 2, since the first line of each paragraph is indented into the first tab stop. If the paragraphs had started flush against the left margin, they would have been in field 1.

Finally, you can sort or select information in a secondary merge file. As described in Chapter 13, the end of a record in a secondary merge file is signified by a ^E code and fields within each record are separated by ^R codes. Figure 15-12 shows two records in a secondary file; each contains seven fields.

It's a good idea to store a copy of a document on disk before you attempt to sort or select; that way, in case you sorted or selected in a way you disliked, or if you got unexpected results, you would still have the original document intact on disk. Especially when you're first learning how to use the Sort command, *save a copy on disk first!*

```
Ms.^R
Janice^R
Smith^R
3559 Biltmore Street^R
San Francisco^R
CA^R
94123^R
^E
===================================================================
Mr.^R
Dennis^R
Poplar^R
333 Cypress Boulevard^R
Glen Ellen^R
CA^R
95442^R
^E
===================================================================



                                              Doc 1 Pg 1 Ln 1" Pos 1"
```

FIGURE 15-12   A secondary merge file, which WordPerfect can sort

Sort by Line Using the Standard Defaults

If you wish to perform a sort only (without using the select function), and if you wish to sort by the first word in each line of a document, then the procedure is quick and easy. Press the MERGE/SORT (CTRL + F9) key and select Sort (2 or S). WordPerfect will prompt you with

Input file to sort: (Screen)

WordPerfect assumes that the file you wish to sort is the one currently on screen. Press ENTER to verify. If the file is on disk, type the name of the file you wish to sort and then press ENTER. Next, WordPerfect will prompt you with

Output file to sort: (Screen)

WordPerfect assumes that the results of the file should be shown on screen. Press ENTER to accept the default, sorting to the screen. Alternatively, you can type the name of a file that the results should be sent

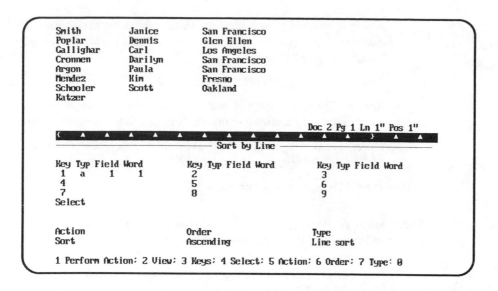

FIGURE 5-13 Sort by Line menu

to and then press ENTER, in which case the screen will not change after the sort; you'll have to retrieve the named file to see the results.

Next, the screen splits into two windows. The top window shows the first ten lines of the file you are about to sort; the bottom window shows the Sort by Line menu. Figure 15-13 shows the Sort by Line menu when WordPerfect is about to sort a document containing names and cities. Notice that there are seven options at the bottom of the figure.

The first option, Perform Action (1 or P), executes the sort or the select, according to the directions specified under the headings on the Sort screen. WordPerfect starts with certain assumptions about how you want the sort or the select to occur. The headings on the Sort screen indicate that if you maintained all of WordPerfect's defaults, the following will occur when you select Perform Action:

- *Key Typ Field Word* The sort will be based on only one key (only key number 1 is defined). As you can see under this heading in Figure 15-13, the key is defined as alphanumeric ("a") and is the first word of the first field. "Alphanumeric" means that you wish either to sort words or to sort numbers of equal length (such as ZIP codes).

- *Select*   No selection criteria are defined.

- *Action*   The command will sort only; no items will be selected. (Sort is the only alternative until selection criteria are defined.)

- *Order*   Text will be sorted in ascending order, which means "A" to "Z" for letters and smallest to largest for numbers.

- *Type*   The sort will occur line by line.

These settings are appropriate for sorting a document such as that shown in Figure 15-10. Here's how to perform this basic sort.

1. On a clear screen, set tabs so that there are only two tab stops, at positions 2.5" and 4.0".

2. Type the document as shown in Figure 15-10, making sure to align first names and cities on tab stops so that they are in separate fields. For instance, type **Smith**, press TAB, type **Janice**, press TAB, type **San Francisco**, and press ENTER. Then continue with the other lines in this list.

3. Use the SAVE (F10) key to save this document under the name SORTTEST.

4. Press the MERGE/SORT (CTRL + F9) key.

5. Select Sort (2 or S).

6. Press ENTER twice to verify that both the input and output are to be on the screen. After a moment, the Sort menu appears, as shown in Figure 15-13.

7. Select Perform Action (1 or P). The lines in the document are rearranged by last name, from "A" to "Z."

8. If you wish, save this document again under the same filename.

Sometimes you may wish to sort or select only a portion of a document. For instance, perhaps you wish to sort a list of names on page 2 of a multipage document. In that case, first highlight the list you wish to sort, using the BLOCK (ALT + F4) key. Then press the

MERGE/SORT (CTRL + F9) key, and the Sort menu will appear. When you select option 1, Perform Action, WordPerfect will sort only the highlighted portion of the document.

Change the Sort Defaults

What if you wish to sort the records in the document in Figure 15-10 by city name, which is field 3? Or in descending order, "Z" to "A"? What if the document you wish to sort is organized not in lines but in paragraphs, as in Figure 15-11? What if it is a secondary merge file, as in Figure 15-12? Or what if you wish to activate the Select command so that you can extract only certain information from the document? If so, you must change the defaults on the Sort menu *before* pressing option 1, Perform Action. The Sort menu's other options are described below:

- *View (2 or V)* This option allows you to temporarily position the cursor in the top window, where the text that you wish to sort is located. You can then use the arrow keys to scroll through the document, viewing ten lines at a time, to check the document before continuing with the sort. You can view the text, but you cannot edit it. Pressing the EXIT (F7) key returns the cursor to the bottom window to continue with the sort.

- *Keys (3 or K)* This option allows you to specify what text you wish to sort or select by. You can, for example, define two keys in a sort—key 1 could be last name and key 2 could be first name. That way, if two people had the same last name, Word-Perfect would perform a second-level sort for those two records by their first names. Or you can define another key to be used in a selection. For example, you could select only those people who lived in San Francisco and then sort them by last and first names. Always define the sort keys first—as key 1, key 2, and so on—and then define the select keys. You can define a maximum of nine keys.

  For a line sort, you must define a key as a specific word in a specific field, and you must indicate whether that word is alphanumeric (such as a last name or a ZIP code) or numeric (such as a dollar amount). Because a record in a paragraph or a secondary merge file can contain more than one line, you must also specify that word's line for a paragraph or merge sort.

For example, suppose that for Figure 15-13 you wish to sort by first name (which is field 2) if two people have the same last name. You would define key 1 as last name, which is the default setting:

Key	Typ	Field	Word
1	a	1	1

You would provide the following definition for key 2:

Key	Typ	Field	Word
2	a	2	1

Or suppose that you no longer wish to sort by last name; instead, you wish to sort by city. Then you must redefine key 1:

Key	Typ	Field	Word
1	a	3	1

If you were sorting paragraphs or a merge file instead of lines, WordPerfect would request not only a type, a field, and a word, but a line as well.

- *Select (4 or S)* This option allows you to specify a selection statement. For instance, you could select only those people in the list in Figure 15-10 who resided in San Francisco. Or you could select only those terms in Figure 15-11 that began with the letter "C" or only those records in a secondary merge file with a ZIP code of 94123. When you performed the action, those records that met the statement's condition would remain on screen; the other records would disappear.

  A selection statement is an equation in which you include one or more keys and then indicate what criteria those keys must meet for a record to be selected. There are eight symbols you can use in the equations; they are shown in Table 15-2.

  For instance, suppose you had defined key 1 as the first word of the city (as above), and wish to select only those lines in which the city is San Francisco. The selection statement you type is

  key1=San

  Suppose that key 2 is defined as first name. To select those lines in which the city is San Francisco and the first name is Dennis, the statement is

  key1=San * key2=Dennis

Comparison Symbol	Meaning
=	equal to
< >	not equal to
>	greater than
>=	greater than or equal to
<	less than
<=	less than or equal to
+	OR (connects two key conditions together so that either condition can be true for a record to be selected)
*	AND (connects two key conditions together so that both must be true for a record to be selected)

TABLE 15-2   Symbols Used in a Selection Statement

- *Action (5 or A)*   This option specifies whether you wish to sort, select, or sort and select at the same time. If nothing is typed under the "Select" heading, then your only option is to sort. If you had entered an equation under the heading, WordPerfect assumes that you wish to sort and select. You can instead decide only to select without sorting.

- *Order (6 or O)*   For a sort, this option lets you choose between ascending order (A,B,C for letters and 1,2,3 for numbers) or descending order (Z,Y,X for letters and 100,99,98 for numbers).

- *Type (7 or T)*   This option specifies the type of sort you desire. WordPerfect assumes a line sort, as indicated under the heading "Type." So, for a line sort, it would be unnecessary to alter the default. But if your text were organized in paragraphs, you must change the type to a sort by paragraph; for a secondary file, you must change to a merge sort.

Once you change any of the defaults, they remain set for the entire working session or until you change them again. So each time you sort or select, make sure to check under each heading before performing the action.

USE THE MATH FEATURE

With WordPerfect's Math feature, you can type an invoice, calculate your yearly budget, or produce a cost estimate without running to a calculator to figure totals. WordPerfect will do the calculations for you. You can add up to 24 math columns on a page, where a math column contains numbers aligned on a tab stop. The Math feature will operate only if the numbers you wish to add are aligned on tab stops. Therefore, you cannot type your first column of numbers at the left margin, although you can enter labels there.

You can calculate subtotals, totals, and grand totals in columns. In addition, with a bit more preparation, you can add, subtract, multiply, or divide across rows (lines).

Add Numbers Using the Standard Defaults

WordPerfect starts out with three basic assumptions about your use of the Math feature: that you wish to calculate only in columns, that the results of the calculations should show two digits after the decimal point, and that negative values should be displayed in parentheses. If these defaults are correct, you're almost ready to type your math columns.

But you must first complete two tasks. To begin, you must set tab stops for the columns you wish to create; you should be sure to set tab stops where you want the decimal points in the columns to be aligned. Second, you must turn on the Math feature. Move the cursor to the line where you want the math columns to begin, press the MATH/COLUMNS (ALT + F7) key, and select Math On (1 or M). The hidden code **[Math On]** is inserted in the document, and the message **Math** appears in the lower left corner of the screen.

Now you're ready to type your text and numbers. Each time you press TAB to move to the next column, WordPerfect will prompt you with

Align char = .MATH

This is similar to the prompt you see when you use the TAB ALIGN (CTRL + F6) key; it informs you that when you type a number with a decimal point, the decimal will be aligned at the tab stop. (If there is no decimal point in the number you are typing, that number will be aligned flush right on the tab stop).

There will be some places where you will want a calculation to appear instead of a number. In those places, you type in one of the following math operators:

Operator	Calculation	Description
+	Subtotal	Numbers directly above the operator are added
=	Total	Subtotals above the operator are added
*	Grand Total	Totals above the operator are added

When you have finished typing the math document, your screen may look like Figure 15-14, which shows columns containing a mix of text, numbers, and math operators as place holders where the calculated numbers will appear.

After you've completed typing the math columns, you must turn off the Math feature. You should make sure that the cursor is below the last number or math operator in the columns; then press the MATH/COLUMNS (ALT + F7) key and select Math Off (1 or M). A [Math Off] code is inserted, and the message **Math** disappears from the screen.

Your last step is to perform the calculations wherever math operators are located. To do so, position the cursor anywhere within the math columns. The message **Math** will reappear whenever the cursor is between the [Math On] and [Math Off] codes. Press the MATH/COLUMNS (ALT + F7) key and select Calculate (2 or C). In moments, you'll get results like those shown in Figure 15-15.

After you calculate, the math operators continue to display next to the calculated subtotal, total, or grand total, but they will not appear on the printed document. Leave those math operators in your document so that if you choose you can change any number in a column and calculate again.

```
                  Jan      Feb      Mar

      East Coast

        Cabernet      33.8     20.1     22.3
        Chardonnay    44.5     55.2     33.8
        Chenin Blanc  20.3     24.3     33.1
        Pinot Noir    10.5     12.8     14.2

        Subtotal        +        +        +

      West Coast

        Cabernet      22.9     25.4     23.3
        Chardonnay    60.5     85.2     77.9
        Chenin Blanc  22.2     18.3     36.1
        Pinot Noir     9.0      4.5      8.2

        Subtotal        +        +        +


      TOTAL             =        =        =


      Math                              Doc 1 Pg 1 Ln 1" Pos 1"
```

FIGURE 15-14   Sample of a document containing math columns

```
                  Jan      Feb      Mar

      East Coast

        Cabernet      33.8     20.1     22.3
        Chardonnay    44.5     55.2     33.8
        Chenin Blanc  20.3     24.3     33.1
        Pinot Noir    10.5     12.8     14.2

        Subtotal    109.10+  112.40+  103.40+

      West Coast

        Cabernet      22.9     25.4     23.3
        Chardonnay    60.5     85.2     77.9
        Chenin Blanc  22.2     18.3     36.1
        Pinot Noir     9.0      4.5      8.2

        Subtotal    114.60+  133.40+  145.50+


      TOTAL         223.70=  245.80=  248.90=


      Math                              Doc 1 Pg 1 Ln 1" Pos 1"
```

FIGURE 15-15   Math document after calculating

```
Math Definition          Use arrow keys to position cursor

Columns                  A B C D E F G H I J K L M N O P Q R S T U V W X

Type                     2 2 2 2 2 2 2 2 2 2 2 2 2 2 2 2 2 2 2 2 2 2 2 2

Negative Numbers         ( ( ( ( ( ( ( ( ( ( ( ( ( ( ( ( ( ( ( ( ( ( ( (

Number of Digits to      2 2 2 2 2 2 2 2 2 2 2 2 2 2 2 2 2 2 2 2 2 2 2 2
  the Right (0-4)

Calculation   1
  Formulas    2
              3
              4

Type of Column:
    0 = Calculation    1 = Text    2 = Numeric    3 = Total

Negative Numbers
    ( = Parentheses (50.00)        - = Minus Sign  -50.00


Press Exit when done
```

FIGURE 15-16   Math Definition screen

Change the Default Math Settings

You may wish to alter some of WordPerfect's defaults. For example, perhaps you want to have one digit after the decimal rather than two. You may want each total to appear in a column just to the right of the totaled numbers. Or you may want to calculate across lines. If that's the case, then after you reset tabs but *before* you turn on the Math feature, you must create a new math definition, which will serve to override the default math settings. Press the MATH/COLUMNS (ALT + F7) key and select Math Def (2 or E). The Math Definition screen shown in Figure 15-16 appears.

On this screen, you can define each column separately. Your first math column is referred to as column A, the second is column B, and so on. (Remember that column A is not the information typed at the left margin, but the information typed at the first tab stop.) For each column, you can define the following:

- *Type*   The default is 2, which, from the legend at the bottom of the screen, you can see is a numeric column. Other choices are 1, Text columns, for when you wish to fill a column with words rather than numbers; 3, Total column, a column devoted to the calculated totals of the column to the left; and 0, Calculation columns, for when you wish to calculate across lines.

- *Negative numbers*   The default is for parentheses around a calculation that results in a negative number, as in (50). Alternatively, you can select a minus sign preceding a negative number, as in −50.

- *Number of digits to the right* The default is for two digits after the decimal point; you can select from zero to four. For instance, if you wanted the results of calculations to show only one place after the decimal, you would change the setting to 1 for each column.

- *Calculation formulas*   The default is for no calculations across rows. You can instead insert up to four formulas for calculations across rows, using the following symbols:

+	addition	−	subtraction
*	multiplication	/	division

For instance, assume that you are working with five math columns. Column B will contain totals of the numbers in column A. Similarly, column D will contain totals of the numbers in column C. If you want column E to reflect the results of column B minus column D, you must type **0** for column E under the heading "Type." The cursor will jump down to the first line by the heading "Calculation Formulas"; type **B-D** and press ENTER. Figure 15-17 shows the resulting Math Definition screen. (Notice that type, number of digits, and a calculation formula have also been changed on this screen.)

In addition, there are four special formulas you can use when calculating across rows. These special formulas must be entered on their own and not as a part of a larger formula. These formulas and their meanings are

+	add the numbers in all numeric columns
+/	calculate the average of all numeric columns
=	add the numbers in all total columns
=/	calculate the average of all total columns

```
Math Definition          Use arrow keys to position cursor

Columns                  A B C D E F G H I J K L M N O P Q R S T U U W X

Type                     2 3 2 3 0 2 2 2 2 2 2 2 2 2 2 2 2 2 2 2 2 2 2 2

Negative Numbers         ( ( ( ( ( ( ( ( ( ( ( ( ( ( ( ( ( ( ( ( ( ( ( (

Number of Digits to      1 1 1 1 1 2 2 2 2 2 2 2 2 2 2 2 2 2 2 2 2 2 2 2
  the Right (0-4)

Calculation    1    E    B-D
  Formulas     2
               3
               4

Type of Column:
     0 = Calculation    1 = Text     2 = Numeric    3 = Total

Negative Numbers
     ( = Parentheses (50.00)         - = Minus Sign  -50.00


Press Exit when done
```

FIGURE 15-17   Math Definition screen with the defaults changed for columns
A through E

For instance, suppose that you are working with four math columns
and you want column D to be the average of columns A, B, and C. Assume that columns A, B, and C have all been defined as numeric
columns. You must type **0** for column D at the setting "Type." The cursor will jump to the setting "Calculation Formulas," where you will
type **+/** and press ENTER.

When you exit the Math Definition screen and return to the
Typing screen, WordPerfect will insert a **[Math Def]** code. All math
columns typed below that code will be affected by that Math Definition code. The Math/Columns menu will remain on screen; you would
select Math On (1 or M). You would then be ready to type the math
columns. You should proceed as usual; that is, press TAB to move from
column to column. Type in a number or insert math operators (+, =, or
*) where you want the calculated subtotals, totals, or grand totals to
appear. If you had defined a total column, you should be sure to insert
the math operators in that total column and not in the numeric
columns. Whenever you press TAB to move to a column defined as a
calculation column, an exclamation point (!) will appear. You should

	January, 1989	January, 1988	Increase
East Coast			
Cabernet	33.8	25.5	
Chardonnay	41.5	41.5	
Chenin Blanc	28.3	18.5	
Pinot Noir	18.5	18.7	
Subtotal	+	+	!
West Coast			
Cabernet	22.9	24.3	
Chardonnay	68.5	48.2	
Chenin Blanc	22.2	19.4	
Pinot Noir	9.8	8.1	
Subtotal	+	+	!
TOTAL	=	=	!
Math		Doc 1 Pg 1 Ln 1.5" Pos 1"	

FIGURE 15-18   Math document based on the math definition shown in Figure 15-17

leave that operator wherever you desire calculations but erase the exclamation point where you didn't want a calculation to appear. Like the other math operators, the exclamation point does not appear on the printed page.

After typing the math columns, you should remember to turn off the Math feature by pressing the MATH/COLUMNS (ALT + F7) key and selecting Math Off (1 or M). Figure 15-18 shows how a document might look after you had completed typing it; it is based on the math definition shown in Figure 15-17. Your final step is to position the cursor back within the math columns and calculate by pressing the MATH/COLUMNS (ALT + F7) key and selecting Calculate (2 or C).

TRANSFER BETWEEN SOFTWARE PROGRAMS

WordPerfect interacts easily with other software packages. First, Version 5.0 is equipped so that files created in Version 5.0 can be used with earlier versions. Second, WordPerfect comes with a program named CONVERT.EXE, which can transform files between other popular word processing packages (such as WordStar and MultiMate), spreadsheet packages (such as Lotus 1-2-3), or database managers (such as dBASE) and WordPerfect. Third, WordPerfect can work with text files written in ASCII, which is like a universal language; in this way, ASCII (DOS) text files can be used as the intermediary between WordPerfect and other products.

Switch Between WordPerfect Versions 5.0 and 4.2

For those of you who recently upgraded to Version 5.0, no special process is required to use documents created with Version 4.2. Simply load Version 5.0, retrieve any document, edit the document as usual, and save it as usual—by using the SAVE (F10) or the EXIT (F7) key. The document is saved into Version 5.0 format. You may have to manually edit certain format codes so that they operate properly in version 5.0.

On the other hand, Version 5.0 documents should not be retrieved when you are using Version 4.2. Suppose that you use Version 5.0 but the person across town who will be editing your documents uses Version 4.2. In that case, you must store your documents on disk in Version 4.2 format for that other person. Using Version 5.0 and with your document on screen, press the TEXT IN/OUT (CTRL + F5) key and select Save WP 4.2 (4 or W). A prompt will appear requesting a filename. Type a filename and press ENTER to store the file on disk in Version 4.2 format. It is a good idea to type a new filename when saving a file in Version 4.2 format; you will thus maintain one copy of the file in Version 5.0 format whenever you use the SAVE (F10) or the EXIT (F7) key and a separate copy in Version 4.2 format when you use the TEXT IN/OUT (CTRL + F5) key.

Use the Convert Program

A program named CONVERT.EXE, which resides on the WordPerfect Learning disk, transforms files from certain other formats into Word-Perfect, and vice versa. Files that contain documents (such as letters written using WordStar) can be transferred into WordPerfect's document file format, while those containing records (such as lists of names and addresses entered in dBASE) can be transferred into Word-Perfect's secondary file format so that they can be used in a merge operation. In addition, Convert also changes WordPerfect files into other formats.

The following document files can be transferred to or from Word-Perfect with Convert:

- WordStar 3.3

- MultiMate 3.22

- WordPerfect 4.2

- Files that are in Revisable-Form-Text or Final-Form-Text format, such as IBM word processing packages on IBM mainframes and microcomputers (DisplayWrite, DisplayWrite 3, and DisplayWrite 4 enable you to tranfer files into this format.)

- Files that are in Navy DIF format

The following can be transferred into WordPerfect secondary merge files:

- Mail merge files (created using WordStar or dBASE, among others)

- Spreadsheet DIF files (Lotus 1-2-3 files can be transferred into this format to work with Convert.)

You can also convert a WordPerfect secondary merge file into spreadsheet DIF format so that it can be used with Lotus 1-2-3. Fields become cells and records become rows.

Finally, the Convert program can change a file from 8-bit to 7-bit format and vice versa to aid you in sending WordPerfect documents electronically via a modem.

```
Name of Input File? b:doc
Name of Output File? b:doc2


1 WordPerfect to another format
2 Revisable-Form-Text (IBM DCA Format) to WordPerfect
3 Navy DIF Standard to WordPerfect
4 WordStar 3.3 to WordPerfect
5 MultiMate 3.22 to WordPerfect
6 Seven-Bit Transfer Format to WordPerfect
7 WordPerfect 4.2 to WordPerfect 5.0
8 Mail Merge to WordPerfect Secondary Merge
9 WordPerfect Secondary Merge to Spreadsheet DIF
A Spreadsheet DIF to WordPerfect Secondary Merge

Enter number of Conversion desired_
```

FIGURE 15-19   The Convert program main menu

If you had a document on disk in one of the formats mentioned above and you wished to convert it into WordPerfect format, or if you wanted to convert a WordPerfect document to one of these formats, then start at the DOS prompt. If you have already loaded WordPerfect, you must exit WordPerfect. Floppy disk users should then place the Conversion disk in drive A and type **A:CONVERT** and press ENTER. Hard disk users should have the file named CONVERT.EXE on the hard disk (in the same directory as the WordPerfect program, if you followed the installation procedures described in Appendix A); in that case, use the change directory command to switch to the directory where it is stored (for instance, enter **CD \WPER**), type **CONVERT**, and press ENTER.

After the Convert program has been loaded, WordPerfect will first ask for an input file name. This is the name of the file you wish to convert. Type the filename, including the drive or directory where it is found (for example, B:DOC, or C:\BILL\DOC), and press ENTER. Next, WordPerfect will ask for the name of the output file, the file where the converted document should be stored—the name must be different from that of the input file. Type a name and press ENTER; now the menu shown in Figure 15-19 will appear (assuming that the input file is B:DOC and the output file is B:DOC2). From here, select an option for the type of conversion you desire and then respond to WordPerfect's prompts or press the CANCEL (F1) key to abort the conversion. (If you select option 1, to convert from WordPerfect to another format, a second screen will appear, providing you with choices for the output file format.)

If you converted a file into WordPerfect format, you are now ready to load WordPerfect and retrieve the output document (such as DOC2). If you converted to another software package, you could load that other package and retrieve the output document. Be aware that certain sophisticated formatting features won't translate correctly; you will want to reformat the document. For instance, if the document you converted had been typed in columns, the conversion into columns may not work properly, and you may have to reformat the document into columns manually.

Transfer Files Using DOS (ASCII) Text Files

Another way that WordPerfect interacts with other software packages is by importing a DOS (ASCII) text file into WordPerfect or by exporting a WordPerfect file into a DOS (ASCII) text file. DOS text files are written using only those ASCII (American Standard Code for Information Interchange) codes that most software programs can understand. These files contain straight text, spaces, and little else—they are stripped down, containing no special formatting codes for underlining, boldface, margin changes, and the like. Thus, they are often used as the intermediary between different computer programs. This is a way to work in WordPerfect with files created by software packages not supported by the Convert program.

To import (retrieve) a DOS text file into WordPerfect, you must clear the WordPerfect Typing screen, press the TEXT IN/OUT (CTRL + F5) key, and select Dos Text (1 or T). The following Dos Text menu appears:

1 Save; 2 Retrieve (CR/LF to [HRt]); 3 Retrieve (CR/LF to [SRt] in HZone): 0

Select option 2 to retrieve the text file and have each line end with a Hard Return code; this is appropriate when retrieving files that you do not want to word wrap. Select option 3 to retrieve the text file and have each line that ends within the hyphenation zone end with a soft return; this is appropriate when retrieving files that you wish to then reformat within WordPerfect. Lines within paragraphs will end with **[SRt]** codes rather than with **[HRt]** codes so that paragraphs will readjust when you edit the text.

There's another option for importing, as well—this one found on the List Files screen. When viewing a list of files after pressing the LIST FILES (F5) key, position the cursor on the DOS text file and select Text In (5 or T). A hard return is inserted at the end of each line—identical to selecting option 2 on the Dos Text menu.

To export (save) a WordPerfect document into ASCII format, you must make sure that the document is on screen. Then press the TEXT IN/OUT (CTRL + F5) key, select Dos Text (1 or T), and select Save (1 or S). You must then type a filename and press ENTER; type a new filename so that you can preserve the original copy of your file in WordPerfect format. WordPerfect will save that file on disk, stripping it of all special formatting so that the file could be used with another software package.

As an alternative for exporting, you can press the TEXT IN/OUT (CTRL + F5) key and select Save Generic (3 or G) and enter a filename. This is most appropriate when you plan to use the text in another word processing program. More of the special formatting will be preserved. For instance, text that had been centered will remain so because spaces will be inserted around the centered text. Also, soft returns will be converted into spaces.

WordPerfect's ability to import and export DOS text files is convenient for those of you who create DOS batch files. For instance, Appendix A describes how you can create a batch file in DOS to aid you in loading WordPerfect. You can work with a batch file from within WordPerfect. For example, suppose you wish to revise the batch file named AUTOEXEC.BAT. You could use the TEXT IN/OUT (CTRL + F5) key to retrieve that file (selecting option 2 on the Dos Text menu so that each line ends with a hard return) and then edit the file using WordPerfect's standard editing features. After editing, you would use the TEXT IN/OUT (CTRL + F5) key to save the batch file again in DOS text format. Those of you who have attempted to edit batch files by rewriting them from scratch or by using EDLIN, DOS's own editor, will find the TEXT IN/OUT (CTRL + F5) key a convenient alternative.

REVIEW

- Depending on the capabilities of your printer, you can produce documents that contain special characters used in mathematical, legal, foreign, or technical text. The Compose feature allows you to type special characters with just a few keystrokes. The Overstrike feature lets you type two or more characters in the same location.

- WordPerfect allows you to change the layout of the keyboard, so that you can tailor the keyboard to your special needs. Using the Keyboard Layout feature, you can, for instance, redefine the keyboard so that the key combination CTRL + S produces the section symbol (§) and the key combination SHIFT + F12 executes a print macro.

- You can take further advantage of WordPerfect's graphics abilities, originally described in Chapter 10. The GRAB.COM program lets you incorporate graphics images into your documents from programs not directly compatible with WordPerfect. The Line Draw feature lets you draw lines and boxes on screen with sharp corners to create organizational charts or graphs. You create horizontal and vertical lines using the arrow keys as your "paintbrush."

- WordPerfect can aid in the production of a long document, such as a book, thesis, annual report, or legal brief. The Automatic Reference feature allows you to create and update references in a document, such as "See Footnote 2, page 44." The Master Document feature helps you work more easily with lengthy documents by creating a small file consisting of subdocuments and text. The Generate Tables, Lists, and Indexes feature automatically generates reference aids, including tables of contents, tables of authorities, lists, and indexes.

- WordPerfect has some data base management capabilities. The Sort feature can sort text in alphabetical or numerical order, whether that text is a list organized by line, a group of paragraphs, or a secondary file used in a merge. And it can select specific text, such as all names that begin with the letter "B" or all records in a secondary file with the ZIP code 90046.

- With the Math feature, you can add or subtract numbers in a column. And you can calculate across a row based on a formula.

- You can transfer files between different versions of WordPerfect or between another software package and WordPerfect. The CONVERT.EXE program allows you to take files from certain other programs, such as WordStar, and convert them to WordPerfect format so that you could use WordPerfect for all your word processing needs. And you can save a file into WordPerfect version 4.2 format or transfer files to and from standard ASCII format, a universal computer language, using the TEXT IN/OUT (CTRL + F5) key.

APPENDIXES

Installing WordPerfect
Selecting Printers
The Setup Menu
Getting Additional Support

A

INSTALLING
WORDPERFECT

Installation for Floppy Disk Users
Installation for Hard Disk Users
Startup (Slash) Options

Before you attempt to use the disks that come inside the WordPerfect package, you must prepare them to operate on your computer equipment, a process referred to as installation. Installation is the first thing you should do after you purchase WordPerfect and rip open its plastic wrapping. You need to install the program only once; you or anyone who uses your computer will then be ready to use WordPerfect thereafter.

By installing, you make it more convenient to start up Word-Perfect. You can set up your computer system so that WordPerfect loads by just pressing a few keystrokes.

You must also install WordPerfect because floppy disks— including those on which the WordPerfect program is stored—are fallible. If you accidentally bend a disk, that disk will be ruined. Or a disk might no longer operate because of a mechanical problem. As a precaution, you install WordPerfect so that you have a second copy of the program. If you're a floppy disk user, you place that second copy on another set of floppy disks and use that second set whenever you start up WordPerfect on your computer. If you're a hard disk user, you place that second copy on your hard disk and use the hard disk whenever you start up WordPerfect on your computer. The original WordPerfect disks—the ones that come inside the WordPerfect package—should be stored in a safe place, remaining available should human or mechanical error cause your working copy (either on floppies or on your hard disk) to malfunction.

This appendix describes how to install WordPerfect. The process is different for floppy and hard disk users; thus, the procedure is described separately for each. At the end of the chapter, you will also learn about special options for starting up WordPerfect. Depending on your computer equipment and your computer needs, you may wish to take advantage of one or more of these options.

After you've installed WordPerfect, you'll be ready to type and edit documents on screen. Turn to "Getting Started" for a basic lesson on starting up and using WordPerfect with your computer equipment and then begin with Chapter 1, where you'll type several WordPerfect documents.

Be aware that after installing WordPerfect, you will need to perform one more installation-type task before you can actually print your documents. You must inform WordPerfect of the printer(s) attached to your computer, so WordPerfect knows how to print your documents. This procedure is described in Appendix B.

INSTALLATION FOR FLOPPY DISK USERS

The five main steps for installing WordPerfect are (1) start or boot up your computer, (2) format blank disks so that they're ready to accept information, (3) copy the WordPerfect program onto the blank disks, (4) create a special file named CONFIG.SYS so that WordPerfect will run properly, and (5) write a batch file to start up WordPerfect for you. You don't have to necessarily write a batch file, but it is recommended. A batch file contains a set of commands that automate the process of starting up WordPerfect—saving you time. Once a batch file is created, you can start up WordPerfect any time by inserting the proper disk and simply turning on your computer.

Boot Up Your Computer

Booting up your computer means to turn it on and start up the Disk Operating System (DOS), the program that is essential to the operation of your computer. To do so, perform the following steps:

1. Find your DOS disk. There are different versions of DOS. You must have DOS 2.0 or higher, such as Version 2.1, 3.0, 3.1, 3.2, and so on, to work properly with WordPerfect. (Your DOS disk label may read "MS-DOS" or "PC-DOS"; both are acceptable.)

2. Place the DOS disk in drive A and close the disk drive door. When you have two disk drives (which is required for using WordPerfect), drive A is usually the disk drive on the left or on the top.

3. Turn on the computer. (Depending on your equipment, you may also have to turn on your monitor separately.) Now wait for a minute or so—the computer takes a bit of time to start up.

4. For some of you, the computer will respond with a request for the current date; type it in. For example, if today's date is December 9, 1988, type **12-09-88**. If you make a typing mistake, press the BACKSPACE key to erase the error and then type the correct character. The BACKSPACE key is marked with the word "BACKSPACE" or with a long, straight arrow pointing to the left: ←. (The date and time will be entered for you automatically if your computer is equipped with an internal clock.)

5. If you typed in the date, now press the ENTER key. The ENTER key is marked with the word "ENTER" or "RETURN" or with a crooked arrow pointing to the left: ↵.

6. For some of you, the computer responds with a request for the current time; type it in. The computer works on a 24-hour clock. For example, if the current time is 4:30 P.M., type **16:30**.

7. If you typed in the time, now press the ENTER key.

You should now see on screen an uppercase "A" followed by a greater than symbol: A>. This is referred to as the DOS prompt and indicates that DOS is loaded and waiting for your instructions. The "A" means that the instructions will involve drive A.

Format Blank Disks

You are now ready to format blank disks so that they can store a copy of the WordPerfect program. You must format one blank disk for each disk in the WordPerfect package. In addition, you will format two extra disks—one that will store WordPerfect's help files and one that you can use as your first data disk, a disk that will store the first documents you create using WordPerfect. (For instance, if you use 5 1/4-inch double-density floppy disks—which are typical on IBM PC or compatible computers—then make sure to format 14 disks.) The last disk will be formatted specially; the computer's operating system (DOS) will be stored on it so that both WordPerfect and DOS can be started from a single disk.

When you format a disk, any information previously stored on that disk is wiped out. Therefore, be *sure* to format only brand new, blank disks or those that don't have anything you wish to preserve stored on them. Follow these steps to format a disk:

1. With the DOS disk still in drive A, insert a blank disk into drive B and close the disk drive door.

2. Type **format b:** (upper- or lowercase makes no difference when typing commands in DOS). The screen shows

   A>format b:

   (Remember to use the BACKSPACE key if you make a typing mistake.)

3. Press ENTER. DOS prompts you to place a blank disk in drive B.

4. Since a blank disk is already in drive B, simply press ENTER to format the disk.

5. Once the disk has been formatted, you will be asked whether you wish to format another. Type **Y** for yes and press ENTER.

6. Insert a new blank disk in drive B and press ENTER.

7. Repeat steps 5 and 6 until you have formatted one blank disk for each disk in the WordPerfect package, plus one extra disk to serve as a data disk. For instance, if you use 5 1/4-inch double-density floppy disks (which are typical on IBM PC or compatible computers), then make sure to format 13 disks.

8. After you have formatted these 13 disks, DOS again asks whether you wish to format another. Type N for no.

9. Insert the one unformatted blank disk that remains into drive B, and close the disk drive door.

10. Type **format b:/s**. (The "/s" that you type directs the computer to place part of DOS on that disk after the disk is formatted.) The screen shows

    A>format b:/s

11. Press ENTER. DOS prompts you to place a blank disk in drive B.

12. Since the final blank disk is already in drive B, simply press ENTER to format the disk and to insert a part of DOS on that disk so that it becomes "bootable," meaning that with it you can boot up your computer.

13. When the disk has been formatted, DOS asks whether you wish to format another. Type N for no and press ENTER. Leave the formatted disk that contains a part of DOS in drive B.

Copy the WordPerfect Files

Now you're ready to copy WordPerfect onto these formatted disks so that you have working copies of the WordPerfect program.

1. Remove the DOS disk from drive A and insert the disk labeled "WordPerfect 1." (If instead of 5 1/4-inch disks you use 3 1/2-inch disks, then insert the disk labeled "WordPerfect 1/Word-Perfect 2.") The newly formatted disk that contains DOS should still be in drive B.

2. Type **copy wp.exe b:**. The screen shows

    A>copy wp.exe b:

3. Press ENTER. WordPerfect's main program file named WP.EXE is copied onto the disk in drive B.

4. Remove the disk in drive B. Fill out a label for the new working copy of this WordPerfect disk. For instance, if you use 5 1/4-inch floppy disks, write on the label "WordPerfect 1—Working Copy" and then affix the label to the disk. If the label is already on the disk, write gently using a felt-tip pen so as not to puncture the disk.

5. Insert another blank formatted disk in drive B. The original WordPerfect 1 disk should still be in drive A.

6. Type **copy *.fil b:**. The screen shows

   A>copy *.fil b:

7. Press ENTER. The WordPerfect Help files are copied onto the disk in drive B.

8. Remove the disks in drive A and B. Fill out a label for the new working copy of the WordPerfect Help files. For instance, label the disk "WordPerfect Help."

9. Insert the WordPerfect 2 disk in drive A and another blank formatted disk in drive B. (If you're a 3 1/2-inch-disk user, place the working copy of the WordPerfect 1/WordPerfect 2 disk back in drive B instead of inserting a blank formatted disk.)

10. Type **copy *.* b:**. The screen shows

    A>copy *.* b:

    (If you're a 3 1/2-inch disk user, then you should instead type **copy wp.fil** and press ENTER and then type **copy *.?rs** and press ENTER. In this way, you copy only selective files. Now skip to step 12 below.)

11. Press ENTER. One by one, all the files from the WordPerfect disk are transferred onto the working copy.

12. Remove the disks in drives A and B, fill out a label for the new working copy of the WordPerfect disk (for example, label the disk "WordPerfect 2—Working Copy").

13. Repeat steps 9 through 12 until the rest of the WordPerfect disks have been copied onto formatted disks and the working disks have been labeled. (If you're a 3 1/2-inch-disk user, also repeat steps 9 through 12, but ignore the information in paren-

theses in steps 9 and 10 for the rest of the WordPerfect disks.) You can label the last formatted disk as your data disk. For instance, label this last disk as "Data Disk 1."

14. Place the original WordPerfect disks in a safe place for storage. Use only the working copies with your computer; if a working copy gets lost or damaged or wears out, you can always make a new set of working copies from the originals.

Table A-1 provides a list of the WordPerfect program files on each disk and the purpose that each serves.

Create the CONFIG.SYS File

WordPerfect operates properly only if you create a special file called CONFIG.SYS that you store on the working copy of your WordPerfect 1 disk (or on whatever disk you use to start up your computer). This file must contain the command FILES=20 so that the computer knows how many files can remain open at one time, a necessity for running WordPerfect. Follow the instructions below to create such a file:

1. Insert your working copy of the WordPerfect 1 disk (or WordPerfect 1/WordPerfect 2 disk if you use 3 1/2-inch disks) into drive A.

2. Type **copy config.sys+con config.sys**. The screen shows

   A>copy config.sys+con config.sys

3. Press ENTER. WordPerfect responds with the message "CON."

4. Type **files=20** and press ENTER.

5. Press CTRL + Z (which means to hold down on the CTRL key and, while holding it down, type Z) and press ENTER.

The computer will inform you that one file has been copied. The CONFIG.SYS file is now on the WordPerfect 1 disk.

WordPerfect 1 Disk

WP.EXE	WordPerfect Program File
WPHELP.FIL	WordPerfect Help File
WPHELP2.FIL	WordPerfect Help File

WordPerfect 2 Disk

KEYS.MRS	Keyboard Macro Resource File
STANDARD.PRS	Text Mode Preview and Standard Printer Resource File
WP.FIL	Contains a part of the WordPerfect code
WP.MRS	Macro Resource File
WPSMALL.DRS	Driver Resource File (contains the IBM character set when viewing a document)

Speller Disk

WP{WP}US.LEX	Main and Common Word Lists (U.S. English Dictionary)
SPELL.EXE	Speller Utility

Thesaurus Disk

WP{WP}US.THS	Thesaurus List

Learning Disk

TUTOR.COM	Tutorial
LEARN.BAT	Batch File to Initiate Tutorial on a Floppy Disk System
INSTALL.EXE	Auto-Install Program
*.STY	Styles for WordPerfect Workbook
*.TUT	Tutorial Files
*.WKB	Learning Files for WordPerfect Workbook
*.WPG	Graphics Images for WordPerfect Workbook
*.WPM	Macros for WordPerfect Workbook

TABLE A-1   WordPerfect Files

PTR Program Disk

PTR.EXE	Printer Program Utility
PTR.HLP	Printer Program Help File

Conversion Disk

CURSOR.COM	Cursor Utility
CHARACTR.DOC	WordPerfect Character Set Documentation
CHARMAP.TST	Character Set Printer Test
CONVERT.EXE	Convert Program
FC.*	Font Conversion Program and Documentation
GRAPHCNV.EXE	Graphics Convert Program
LIBRARY.STY	Style Library Example
MACROCNV.EXE	Macros Convert Program (converts Version 4.2 macros into Version 5)
ORDERWPG.DOC	Graphics Ordering Information
PRINTER.TST	WordPerfect Features Printer Test
README	DOS Text File of Additions to the Conversion Disk
STANDARD.CRS	Conversion Resource File (converts Version 4.2 documents into Version 5)
*.WPK	WordPerfect Keyboard Definition Examples

Fonts/Graphics Disk

EGA*.FRS	Character Sets for EGA Monitors
GRAB.COM	Screen Capture Utility
HRF*.FRS	Fonts for Hercules RamFonts Graphics Cards
WP.DRS	Driver Resource File (contains character set for hard disk systems)
*.WPD	Graphics Driver File for Specific Monitors
*.WPG	30 Graphics (Clip-Art) Images

Printer 1, 2, 3, 4 Disks

*.ALL	Printer Driver Files
README	DOS Text File of Additional Printer Drive Files Available

TABLE A-1 WordPerfect Files (*continued*)

Files Created During a WordPerfect Session

WP}WP{.*	Overflow, Print Buffer, Sort, and other temporary files (stored on the drive where WP.EXE is located or on the drive specified with the /D startup option), which are deleted when you exit WordPerfect
*.BK!	Original Backup Files
*.CRS	Document Conversion Files
*.PRS	Printer Definition Files
*.WPK	Keyboard Definition Files
*.WPM	Macro Files
WP{WP}.BK#	Timed Backup Files
WP{WP}US.SUP	Supplementary Dictionary File
WP{WP}.SET	Setup File (stored where WP.EXE is located, contains all the changes to the WordPerfect default settings)

TABLE A-1   WordPerfect Files (*continued*)

Write a Batch File to Load WordPerfect

You are now ready to write a set of instructions using DOS so that you can start up WordPerfect quickly from now on. (The batch file is a recommended convenience, not a necessity. You can always load WordPerfect directly from the DOS prompt without using a batch file. The chapter entitled "Getting Started" shows how to load WordPerfect either with or without a batch file.)

The following instructions help you create the most commonly used batch file, one that automates the following tasks: (1) pausing for you to set the computer's date and time each time you load Word-Perfect; (2) setting the default drive, which is the drive for saving and retrieving files, to drive B, where the data disk is found; (3) loading WordPerfect automatically; and (4) changing the default drive back to drive A when you exit WordPerfect.

Note: If your computer is equipped with a battery-operated clock, you don't need to have the batch file pause for you to enter the computer's date and time, so skip steps 3 and 4 below. (You may need to include a command that accesses your computer's clock program instead of steps 3 and 4. For instance, you may need to type **astclock** and press ENTER. Then you'll also have to copy the file named ASTCLOCK onto the WordPerfect 1 disk for the batch file to operate properly.)

1. The working copy of the WordPerfect 1 disk should still be in drive A; if not, reinsert it.

2. Type **copy con: autoexec.bat** and press ENTER.

3. Type **date** and press ENTER.

4. Type **time** and press ENTER.

5. Type **b:** and press ENTER.

6. Type **a:wp** and press ENTER. (Instead of typing just **a:wp**, you can type a slightly different line to take advantage of WordPerfect's special startup options. For instance, you can type **a:wp/r** so that each time WordPerfect is loaded, the **/r** option will be activated, causing WordPerfect to operate faster. See this appendix's last section for details on the startup options.)

7. Type **a:** and press ENTER.

8. Press CTRL + Z; that is, hold down the CTRL key and type **Z**. Now your screen reads as follows:

```
A>copy con: autoexec.bat
date
time
b:
a:wp
a:
^Z
```

9. Press ENTER. In moments, the computer tells you that one file has been copied. You have just created a batch file.

The batch file you just created lets you load WordPerfect with ease! From now on, all you have to do to start up WordPerfect is insert the WordPerfect 1 disk (the working copy, of course) in drive A, turn on the computer, and respond to the date and time prompts (if you don't have an internal clock). WordPerfect will begin loading automatically.

Turn now to the chapter entitled "Getting Started" at the front of this book for step-by-step instructions on starting and using Word-Perfect.

INSTALLATION FOR HARD DISK USERS

The six main steps for installing WordPerfect are (1) start or boot up your computer; (2) create separate directories on your hard disk so that the information you store on it will be neatly organized; (3) copy the WordPerfect program files into the directories just created; (4) create (or modify) a special file named CONFIG.SYS so that WordPerfect will run properly; (5) write a batch file to automate the procedure for loading WordPerfect, which is optional; and (6) if necessary, change the AUTOEXEC.BAT file on your hard disk to indicate the directory where the WordPerfect program files are stored.

The WordPerfect program offers an Auto-Install program that can perform steps 2 through 4 for you. If you want the flexibility to create directories with a name of your own choosing and copy the Word-Perfect program files yourself, then you can bypass the Auto-Install program and install manually. Both the auto and manual methods are described in the following pages.

If you wish to store documents on floppy disks rather than on your hard disk, you may also wish to format blank floppy disks as a final step, which is also described below.

Boot Up Your Computer

Booting up your computer means to turn it on and start up the Disk Operating System (DOS)—the program that is essential to the operation of your computer. DOS is stored on your hard disk. To boot up your computer, perform the following steps:

1. Turn on the computer. (Depending on your equipment, you may have to turn on your monitor separately.) Now wait for a minute or so—the computer takes a bit of time to start up.

2. For some of you, the computer responds with a request for the current date; type it in. For example, if today's date is December 9, 1988, type **12-09-88**. If you make a typing mistake, press the BACKSPACE key to erase the error and then type the correct character. The BACKSPACE key is marked with the word "BACKSPACE" or with a long, straight arrow pointing to the left: ←. (The date and time will be entered for you automatically if your computer is equipped with an internal clock.)

3. If you typed in the date, press the ENTER key. The ENTER key is marked with the word "ENTER" or "RETURN" or with a crooked arrow pointing to the left: ⏎.

4. For some of you, the computer responds with a request for the current time; type it in. The computer works on a 24-hour clock, so if the current time is 4:30 P.M., type **16:30**.

5. If you typed in the time, press the ENTER key.

You should now see on screen an uppercase "C" followed by a greater than symbol: **C>**. This is referred to as the DOS prompt, indicating that DOS is loaded and waiting for your instructions. The "C" means that the instructions will involve drive C, the hard disk. (Some of you may instead see a prompt such as **C:\>**.)

Create Directories and Copy the WordPerfect Files

Why create directories? A hard disk, like a floppy disk, stores information. But a hard disk stores many times more information than a floppy. It is common practice to divide a hard disk into directories (like file drawers in a filing cabinet) to keep the information stored on the hard disk logically organized. Therefore, your next task is to create directories on the hard disk in which you will store the WordPerfect program and the documents (data files) that you create. Then you will copy the WordPerfect files into those directories. You can do so either using WordPerfect's Auto-Install program or on your own.

USE AUTO INSTALL   WordPerfect's Auto-Install program will perform the following for you:

- Create a directory named \WP50 and another directory named \WP50\LEARN

- Copy the WordPerfect program files from the WordPerfect 1, WordPerfect 2, Fonts/Graphics, Speller, Thesaurus, and PTR Program disks into \WP50

- Copy the files from the Learning disk into \WP50\LEARN

- Alter the file named CONFIG.SYS file on your hard disk so that your computer runs WordPerfect properly (The command "Files=20" will be inserted in that file, and your original CONFIG.SYS file will be renamed CONFIGS.OLD. If the file named CONFIG.SYS does not exist on your hard disk, it will be created.)

If you wish to use Auto-Install, then proceed as follows:

1. Insert the WordPerfect Learning disk into drive A.

2. At the DOS prompt, type **a:**. The screen reads

   C>a:

3. Press ENTER. Now the DOS prompt on screen reads

   A>

   (Some of you may instead see a prompt such as A:\>.)

4. Type **install** and press ENTER. The Auto-Install program will begin in moments.

5. Respond to each question that is displayed on screen, typing **Y** for yes or **N** for no. WordPerfect will prompt for a yes or no before copying each WordPerfect disk. WordPerfect will also inform you when to insert a certain disk in drive A so that files can be copied from drive A to the hard disk.

6. When the Auto-Install is complete, place the original WordPerfect disks in a safe place for storage. Use only the hard disk to load WordPerfect; if something goes awry with the WordPerfect program on the hard disk, you can always run Auto-Install again to copy from the originals. (You will need to have

the Printer 1 through Printer 4 disks available when you define printers in Appendix B.)

Once the Auto-Install program is complete, you should create a separate directory where you will store your data files, such as a directory named \WP50\DATA. By creating a separate directory for your documents, you protect the WordPerfect program from being accidentally tampered with or erased as you create and edit your documents. To do so from DOS:

1. At the DOS prompt, type **c:** and press ENTER. Now the DOS prompt will read C> or C:\>.

2. Type **md \wp50\data** and press ENTER.

(See Chapter 8 for the procedure to create directories from *within* WordPerfect.)

WordPerfect's Auto-Install program does *not* copy the contents of the Printer 1, Printer 2, Printer 3, Printer 4, or Conversion disks onto the hard disk. Storing the Printer disks on the hard disk is not advised; they merely take up disk space and are unnecessary once you define your printer(s) (as described in Appendix B). However, you may wish to store files from the Conversion disk onto the hard disk. For instance, if you think you'll need to transfer files from other software packages to WordPerfect (as discussed in Chapter 15), then it will be more convenient to store the file named CONVERT.EXE on the hard disk. If you want to test your printer capabilities (as discussed in Chapter 9), you may decide that it's preferable to copy PRINTER.TST. If you wish to work with special characters (as described in Chapter 15), then the files named CHARACTR.DOC and CHARMAP.TST are important.

If your hard disk has available disk space and you wish to copy certain files from the Conversion disk, follow these steps:

1. Place the Conversion disk in drive A.

2. Type **cd \wp50** and press ENTER to change to the directory where the WordPerfect program files are housed.

3. To copy all the files from the Conversion disk onto the hard disk, type **copy a:*.*** and press ENTER.

   Alternatively, you can copy just a few files. For instance, type **copy a:printer.tst** and press ENTER to copy that one file.

Refer to Table A-1 for a list of files housed on the Conversion as well as on the other WordPerfect disks.

4. Type **cd ** and press ENTER to leave the special WordPerfect directory and return to the root directory.

Note: Throughout this book, the directory assumed for where the WordPerfect program files are stored is \WPER, and the directory assumed for where your documents are stored is \WPER\DATA, which is the case if you install WordPerfect manually as described below. For those of you who installed WordPerfect using Auto-Install, substitute the names \WP50 and \WP50\DATA.

CREATE DIRECTORIES AND COPY THE WORDPERFECT FILES MANUALLY   If you decide not to use Auto-Install, you must create directories and copy the WordPerfect files onto the hard disk manually.

1. At the DOS prompt, type **cd ** (upper- or lowercase makes no difference when typing DOS commands). The screen shows

    C>cd\

2. Press ENTER. This ensures that you are in the main (root) directory on the hard disk.

3. To create a new directory to house the WordPerfect files, type **md \wper**. The screen shows

    C>md \wper

4. Press ENTER. A new directory called WPER is created.

5. To create a new directory to house the WordPerfect learning files (sample files that you can use along with the WordPerfect Workbook provided with the WordPerfect package), type **md \wper\learn**. The screen shows

    C>md \wper\learn

6. Press ENTER. A new directory named \WPER\LEARN is created.

7. To create a new directory to house your data files (the documents you create using WordPerfect), type **md \wper\data**. The screen shows

C>md \wper\data

8. Press ENTER. A new directory named \WPER\DATA is created.

You have thus created a directory named \WPER and two sub-directories within \WPER, \WPER\LEARN and \WPER\DATA. If you can imagine your hard disk organized in a treelike structure, the Word-Perfect directories you created can be represented as follows:

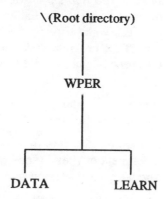

\ (Root directory)

WPER

DATA   LEARN

(Refer to Chapter 8 for a further discussion on working with directories.)

Now you are ready to copy some of the files on the WordPerfect disks to the \WPER directory and other files to the \WPER\LEARN directory. (You will store files in the \WPER\DATA directory when you begin to create and save your own files.)

1. Type **cd \wper** to switch to the WPER directory. The screen shows

   C>cd \wper

2. Press ENTER.

3. Insert the WordPerfect 1 disk into drive A (the drive on the left or on the top—or perhaps the only floppy disk drive you have) and close the disk drive door.

4. Type copy **a:*.*.** The screen shows

   C>copy a:*.*

   or

C:\WPER>copy a:*.*

5. Press ENTER. All the program files on the floppy disk will be copied to the \WPER directory on the hard disk.

6. Repeat steps 4 and 5 after inserting the WordPerfect 2, Speller, Thesaurus, Fonts/Graphics, PTR Program, and Conversion disks. (Refer to Table A-1 to see whether you need to copy certain disks or certain files on certain disks onto the hard disk. For instance, if you don't plan to create or modify a printer definition, which is highly probable assuming that your printer and WordPerfect work properly together, don't copy any of the files from the PTR Program disk onto the hard disk. That way you reserve space on your hard disk for files you will use more frequently.)

7. Type **cd \wper\learn** and press ENTER. This switches you to the \WPER\LEARN directory.

8. Insert the Learning disk into drive A. The Learning disk contains an assortment of files for use with the tutorial and WordPerfect Workbook (as discussed in Appendix D).

9. Type **copy a:*.*.** The screen shows

C>copy a:*.*

or

C:\WPER\LEARN>copy a:*.*

10. Press ENTER. All the files on the Learning disk are copied to the \WPER\LEARN directory.

11. Type **cd ** and press ENTER to return to the main (root) hard-disk directory.

12. Place the original WordPerfect disks in a safe place for storage. Use only the hard disk to load WordPerfect; if something goes awry with the WordPerfect program on the hard disk, you can always copy these files onto the hard disk again from the originals. (The Printer disks are not copied to the hard disk at this time; instead, a portion of what's on the disks will be copied to the hard disk during printer selection, a procedure described in Appendix B. You will need to have the Printer 1 through Printer 4 disks available when you define printers in Appendix B.)

If you wish, you can organize your hard disk differently. For example, you can copy the Speller disk and Thesaurus disk files into another directory. If you do, however, you must notify WordPerfect where these files are located by using the Setup menu (see Appendix C for details).

Create the CONFIG.SYS File

WordPerfect operates properly only if you create a special file called CONFIG.SYS that you store on the hard disk. This file must contain the command "Files=20" so that the computer knows how many files can remain open at one time. If you used Auto-Install, this file has been created for you already, and you can skip to the next section, "Write a Batch File." If you installed WordPerfect manually (or you installed WordPerfect using Auto-Install but wish to enhance the CONFIG.SYS file), then proceed as follows:

1. Type **cd ** and press ENTER to ensure that you're in the main directory on the hard disk.

2. Type **type config.sys** and press ENTER.

3. If a list of commands appears on screen and one of those commands reads FILES=20 (or more, such as FILES=30), then your CONFIG.SYS file needs no adjusting. In that case, skip to the next section, "Write a Batch File."

   If the message "File Not Found" appears or if a list of commands appears that does not include FILES=20 (or more), then move on to step 4 below.

4. Type **copy config.sys+con config.sys.** The screen shows

   C>copy config.sys+con config.sys

5. Press ENTER. DOS responds with the message "CON."

6. Type **files=20** and press ENTER. (You can also type other commands and press ENTER if you wish to enhance your CONFIG.SYS file.)

7. Press CTRL + Z (which means to hold down the CTRL key and, while holding it down, type **Z**) and press ENTER.

If no file existed, then one will be created. If the file named CON-FIG.SYS previously existed, then the FILES=20 command is added to the existing file.

Write a Batch File to Load WordPerfect

You are now ready to write a set of DOS instructions so that you can start up WordPerfect quickly from now on. (The batch file is a recommended convenience, not a necessity. You can always load Word-Perfect directly from the DOS prompt without using a batch file. The chapter entitled "Getting Started" shows how to load WordPerfect either with or without a batch file.)

The following instructions help you create the most commonly used batch file, one that automates the following tasks: (1) setting the default directory, which is the directory for saving and retrieving files, to be \WPER\DATA (or \WP50\DATA if you used Auto-Install); (2) loading WordPerfect automatically; and (3) changing the default directory back to the root when you exit WordPerfect.

1. Type **cd ** and press ENTER. This ensures that you are in the main (root) directory.

2. Type **copy con: wp5.bat** and press ENTER.

3. Type **cd \wper\data** and press ENTER. (If you used Auto-Install, type **cd \wp50\data** and press ENTER.)

4. For those of you who use DOS Version 2.X (that is, Version 2.0 or 2.1), type **wp**, and press ENTER.

   For those of you who use DOS Version 3.X or higher (that is, Version 3.0, 3.1, and so on), type **\wper\wp** and press ENTER. (If you used Auto-Install, type **\wp50\wp** and press ENTER.)

   (Instead of typing just **wp** (Version 2.X) or **\wper\wp** (Version 3.X), you can type a slightly different line to take advantage of special startup options in WordPerfect. For instance, you can type **wp/r** (Version 2.X) or **\wper\wp/r** (Version 3.X or higher) so that each time WordPerfect is loaded, the **/r** option will be activated, causing WordPerfect to operate faster. See this appendix's last section for details on the startup options.)

5. Type **cd ** and press ENTER.

6. Press CTRL + Z; that is, hold down the CTRL key and type **Z**. Now your screen may read as follows:

```
C>copy con: wp5.bat
cd \wper\data
wp
cd \
^Z
```

7. Press ENTER. In moments, the computer tells you that one file has been copied. You have just created a batch file.

Change the AUTOEXEC.BAT File

The batch file you just created changes the default directory so that when you start up WordPerfect, files are automatically saved to and retrieved from a special directory named \WPER\DATA. But the WordPerfect program is in another directory. If you are a DOS Version 2.X user or you wish to use WordPerfect's tutorial program (described in Appendix D), then, as a final step, you must indicate to WordPerfect where to find the WordPerfect program and the WordPerfect tutorial. You use the Path command to do so, putting that command into another batch file named AUTOEXEC.BAT, which is a special batch file that is executed automatically when your computer is first turned on. (If you are a DOS Version 3.X user and don't wish to ever use the tutorial, then skip to the last two paragraphs of this section; it is unnecessary for you to create a Path command because of the way that you wrote the batch file in the previous section.)

1. Type **cd ** and press ENTER. This ensures that you are in the main (root) directory.

2. Type **type autoexec.bat** and press ENTER.

3. If the message "File Not Found" appears, then you need to create an AUTOEXEC.BAT file. Proceed to step 4 immediately.

   If, instead, the computer responds with a list of commands, then a file named AUTOEXEC.BAT does exist. In that case, you must insert or alter the Path command contained in that file to include the location of the WordPerfect program. Before you proceed to step 4, write down on a sheet of paper the commands that are displayed on screen. For instance, you may write down the following:

```
date
time
prompt $p$g
path c:\;c:\123;c:\db
```

Perhaps the AUTOEXEC.BAT contains only one command:

```
path c:\;c:\dos
```

Whatever the commands, write them down.

4. Type **copy con: autoexec.bat** and press ENTER.

5. If no AUTOEXEC.BAT existed (so that you viewed the message "File Not Found" in step 3), then proceed as follows to create a basic AUTOEXEC.BAT file:

   • If your computer is not equipped with an internal clock, type **date** and press ENTER, and type **time** and press ENTER.

   • Next type **path c:\;c:\wper;c:\wper\learn** and press ENTER. (If you used Auto-Install, substitute \wp50 wherever you see \wper.)

   • Then type **prompt pg** and press ENTER. (This is an optional but convenient command; it displays the current directory at the DOS prompt.)

   If an AUTOEXEC.BAT file existed previously (the contents of which you jotted down on a piece of paper), then type each command just as it was listed originally. However, alter the Path command by adding the following to the end of the command: c:\wper;c:\wper\learn. (If you used Auto-Install, remember to substitute \wp50 wherever you see \wper.) For example, suppose the path command previously read:

```
path c:\;c:\123;c:\db
```

Now type it as

```
path c:\;c:\123;c:\db;c:\wper;c:\wper\learn
```

Then finish typing the rest of the commands that existed in the original AUTOEXEC.BAT file. Make sure to press ENTER after typing each command. (If no Path command previously existed then insert one as the last command which reads

path c:\;c:\wper;c:\wper\learn

and press ENTER.)

6. Press CTRL + Z; that is, hold down the CTRL key and type Z. Now, assuming the most basic AUTOEXEC.BAT file, your screen reads as follows:

```
C>copy con: autoexec.bat
 path c:\;c:\wper;c:\wper\learn
 prompt $p$g
 ^Z
```

7. Press ENTER. In moments, the computer tells you that one file has been copied. You have just created (or modified) the AUTOEXEC.BAT file, which contains the Path command so that WordPerfect will load easily for you.

The batch file you just created lets you load WordPerfect with ease! From now on, all you have to do to start up WordPerfect is turn on the computer, type **wp5**, and press ENTER. WordPerfect will begin loading for you automatically.

Turn now to the chapter entitled "Getting Started" at the front of this book for step-by-step instructions on starting and using Word-Perfect.

Format Blank Floppy Disks

You can always change the default directory from within WordPerfect so that you can save certain files in one directory and other files in another directory. Or you can change the default drive from within WordPerfect so that you save files on a floppy disk in drive A rather than on the hard disk. Chapter 8 describes how to change the default drive and directory.

If you want to store some files on floppy disks, you must first format a floppy disk so that it is available for storing files. (When you format a disk, any information previously stored on that disk is wiped out. Therefore, be sure to format only brand new, blank disks or those that have nothing you wish to keep stored on them.) Proceed as follows:

1. Insert a blank disk into drive A, and close the disk drive door.

2. At the DOS prompt, type **format a:** (upper- or lowercase makes no difference when typing commands in DOS). The screen shows

   C>format a:

3. Press ENTER. WordPerfect prompts you to place a blank disk in drive A. (Make sure that when you type the word "format," you always follow that command with a space and then "a:"— otherwise, you're liable to wipe out all the information stored on your hard disk!)

4. Since a blank disk is already in drive A, simply press ENTER to format the disk.

5. Once the disk has been formatted, you will be asked whether you wish to format another disk. You can type **Y** for yes, insert a new disk, and then repeat steps 3 and 4. Or type **N** for no, which exits you from the format command.

STARTUP (SLASH) OPTIONS

Depending on your equipment and needs, it may be advantageous to load WordPerfect in a slightly different way. Usually, the command that triggers WordPerfect to load is "wp." (If you're using a hard disk, then the command may be preceded by the directory where WordPerfect is housed, such as "\wper\wp.")

Instead of "wp," you can add the forward slash symbol (/) followed by various characters to activate options that make a session more productive. For instance, you can load WordPerfect by typing **wp/r** or **wp/d-b:**. The options take effect only until the next time you load WordPerfect. You can also include one or more startup options in your batch file in place of "wp," so that they are activated automatically each time you load WordPerfect. (The procedure to write a batch file is discussed for floppy and hard disk users earlier in this appendix.) The various startup options are described below.

Option 1—Speed Up the Program with Expanded Memory

As you now know, WordPerfect is loaded into RAM before you begin a session. Yet, the computer must still refer to the WordPerfect program on the disk drive from time to time. You can tell when the computer is referring to a disk drive: the indicator light on your disk drive is illuminated.

One reason that WordPerfect refers to the disk is that some detailed program instructions are not loaded into RAM when you load WordPerfect. The computer must refer to the disk periodically for further information, slowing down the processing time of the computer. Whether a hard or floppy disk user, you can avoid the slowdown if your computer's RAM is large enough. If your computer is equipped with *expanded* memory (which means more than 640Kb) and at least 300K of RAM is unused, you can even load the more detailed instructions into RAM. To do so, instead of typing **wp** at the DOS prompt to load WordPerfect, you can invoke what is called the /r (pronounced "slash r") option by typing **wp/r**. You can also include this option in a batch file.

This will load *all* the WordPerfect instructions—even the more detailed set—into RAM. As a result, WordPerfect will be able to execute commands more quickly for you.

Conversely, you can inhibit the use of expanded memory when using WordPerfect by using the /ne option. Type **wp/ne** at the DOS prompt.

Option 2—Redirect Temporary Files

WordPerfect often creates temporary files as you make requests and stores those temporary files on whatever drive/directory the Word-Perfect program is stored. These are WordPerfect's own housekeeping duties. As a result, floppy disk users must keep the WordPerfect disk in drive A even after exercising the /r option. You can direct WordPerfect to perform housekeeping functions on another drive or directory, however, by using the /d option.

To use this option, type **wp/d** followed by a hyphen and the new drive or directory. For example, say you wanted to redirect housekeeping to the B drive. To load WordPerfect, you would type **wp/d-b:**. You can also include this option in a batch file. (If you redirect the temporary files to drive B, you must make sure that the disk in drive B has enough room to store those temporary files—64K is usually sufficient.)

A floppy disk user who employs the /d option in conjunction with the /r option can remove the WordPerfect 2 disk from drive A for most of the working session. That will cut down on the constant swapping of disks, allowing you, for example, to keep the Help disk in drive A to have access to the Help facility.

Option 3—Load WordPerfect and a Commonly Used File Simultaneously

Say that you'll be working on the same document every day for the next week. You can specify a filename, preceded by the drive or directory where it is stored, so that the document and WordPerfect are loaded together. If your document is in a file called JONES and is stored on the floppy disk in drive B, type **wp b:jones** at the DOS prompt. (No slash is typed for this startup option.) As soon as Word-Perfect appears on the screen, the file named JONES is retrieved for editing. You can also include this option in a batch file.

As another example, if your document is in a file named CEO1.MMO and is stored on the hard disk in the directory \WPER\DATA, then type **wp c:\wper\data\ceo1.mmo** at the DOS prompt to load WordPerfect and retrieve CEO1.MMO.

Option 4—Load WordPerfect and a Commonly Used Macro Simultaneously

A macro is a fast way to store phrases or execute keystrokes that you use often (as explained in Chapter 14). If you wish to start a macro as soon as you load WordPerfect, then specify that macro as you load WordPerfect. Type **wp/m** followed by a hyphen and the macro name.

(Precede the macro name with the drive or directory where it is stored if the macro is not located where the WordPerfect program files are stored.) For instance, if your macro is named START and is stored where the WordPerfect program is stored, then type **wp/m-start** at the DOS prompt. The macro will be activated as soon as WordPerfect appears on the screen. You can also include this option in a batch file.

As another example, if the macro is named DONNA and is stored in the directory \WPER\MAC, then type **wp/m-\wper\mac\donna** at the DOS prompt to load WordPerfect and execute DONNA.

Option 5—Improve WordPerfect's Performance on Certain Types of Computers

Use the /i option if you are using DOS Version 2.0 or 2.1 and if Word-Perfect cannot locate the program file named WP.FIL when you attempt to load WordPerfect. At the DOS prompt, type **wp/i**.

Use the /nf (nonflash) option if your screen goes blank periodically or windowing programs are resident in RAM when you use WordPerfect. At the DOS prompt, type **wp/nf**.

Use the /nc option to disable the Cursor Speed feature (as described in Appendix C). This is important when you're working with equipment or a TSR (terminate and stay resident) program that conflicts with the Cursor Speed feature. Sometimes, WordPerfect won't load without invoking this option. At the DOS prompt, type **wp/nc**.

Use the /nk option to disable enhanced keyboard commands. This is important when you're working with equipment or a TSR program and, after loading, WordPerfect locks up or the keyboard freezes. Your problems should clear up if, at the DOS prompt, you type **wp/nk**.

Use the /ss (screen size) option to set the screen size of your monitor when WordPerfect cannot automatically discern the correct size. Type **wp/ss** followed by a hyphen and the rows and columns displayed by your monitor. For example, suppose that your monitor displays 66 rows and 80 columns (as the Genius monitor does). At the DOS prompt, type **wp/ss-66,80**.

All of these options can also be included in a batch file.

Option 6—Return to the Default Setting

When you purchase WordPerfect, certain settings are provided as defaults by WordPerfect Corporation. For instance, WordPerfect sets the left/right/top/bottom margins all at 1 inch. Realizing, however, that individuals have different needs, the designers of WordPerfect provided the ability to change those defaults via the Setup menu (described in Appendix C).

Once you change the defaults, you can load WordPerfect and restore the original default settings for a particular working session with the /x option. At the DOS prompt, type **wp/x**. When you exit Word-Perfect and later load WordPerfect *without* the /x option, the previous changes that you initiated using the Setup menu will be restored.

Option 7—Combine More than One Slash Option

You can combine any or all of the options mentioned above. For example, say you used a floppy disk system with 1 megabyte RAM, which means you have enough memory to exercise the /r option. Also say you decided to redirect all temporary files to the disk in drive B so that you could place the Speller disk in drive A for the majority of your working session.

To load WordPerfect, you would type **wp/r/d-b:**. You could also include this combination of options in a batch file.

B

SELECTING PRINTERS

Create Printer Definition Files
Select a Printer

There are hundreds of brands of printers on the market today— Epson, Hewlett-Packard, Toshiba, Okidata, and more—with different models under each brand name. WordPerfect can work with hundreds of different printers. However, you must inform WordPerfect which printer or printers you are using before you attempt to print your documents. If you don't, WordPerfect cannot work with the printer effectively; your documents will print with strange characters or in an odd format or not at all.

When you indicate to WordPerfect which printer you intend to use, instructions for that printer, called a printer definition, are taken from the Printer 1, Printer 2, Printer 3, or Printer 4 disk (depending on where the information for that printer is located) and stored alongside the WordPerfect program. You can create many printer definitions for many printers.

Besides indicating to WordPerfect your brand of printer, you must edit WordPerfect's standard settings for that printer definition, adapting the printer file to your equipment setup. That printer is then available to be selected for any document you produce. This chapter describes the basic steps for defining and selecting a printer.

CREATE PRINTER DEFINITION FILES

Printer files telling WordPerfect how to operate with various printers are housed with the extension .ALL on separate disks that come with the WordPerfect package—Printer 1, Printer 2, Printer 3, and Printer 4. You must create a printer definition file for each printer you plan to use. When you do, WordPerfect creates an individual file with a .PRS extension (which stands for Printer ReSource file) for that one printer, which is thereafter used whenever you wish to print a document using that printer. For example, HPLASEII.PRS would hold the printer definition for the HP LaserJet Series II printer.

For each printer attached to your computer, take note of both the brand and the number. For example, don't just note Epson—look at the printer or the manual to see whether you have an Epson FX-100, MX-100, or whatever. Then follow these steps to create new printer files for the printers that you will use with WordPerfect:

1. If you haven't already done so, load WordPerfect so that the Typing screen is displayed, as described in the chapter entitled "Getting Started."

2. If you use a floppy disk system, insert the Printer 1 disk into drive B.

    If you use a hard disk system and have not copied the files from the Printer 1, 2, 3, and 4 disks onto the hard disk, insert the Printer 1 disk into drive A or B.

3. Press PRINT (SHIFT + F7) to display the Print screen, as shown in Figure B-1.

    Notice in Figure B-1 that no printer is listed next to the Select Printer option. This means that no printer has yet been selected. (If your Print screen has a printer listed next to the Select Printer option, then a printer has already been defined and selected for your computer. If that printer is correct, you are ready to print your documents; otherwise, continue with the instructions below.)

4. Choose Select Printer (S). The Select Printer screen appears, as shown in Figure B-2 (assuming that no printers have yet been defined).

5. From the menu at the bottom of the screen, select Additional Printers (2 or A). For hard disk users who copied the printer

```
Print

     1 – Full Document
     2 – Page
     3 – Document on Disk
     4 – Control Printer
     5 – Type Through
     6 – View Document
     7 – Initialize Printer

Options

     S – Select Printer
     B – Binding                    0"
     N – Number of Copies           1
     G – Graphics Quality           Medium
     T – Text Quality               High




Selection: 0
```

FIGURE B-1   Print screen

```
Print: Select Printer
















1 Select: 2 Additional Printers: 3 Edit: 4 Copy: 5 Delete: 6 Help: 7 Update: 1
```

FIGURE B-2   Select Printer screen

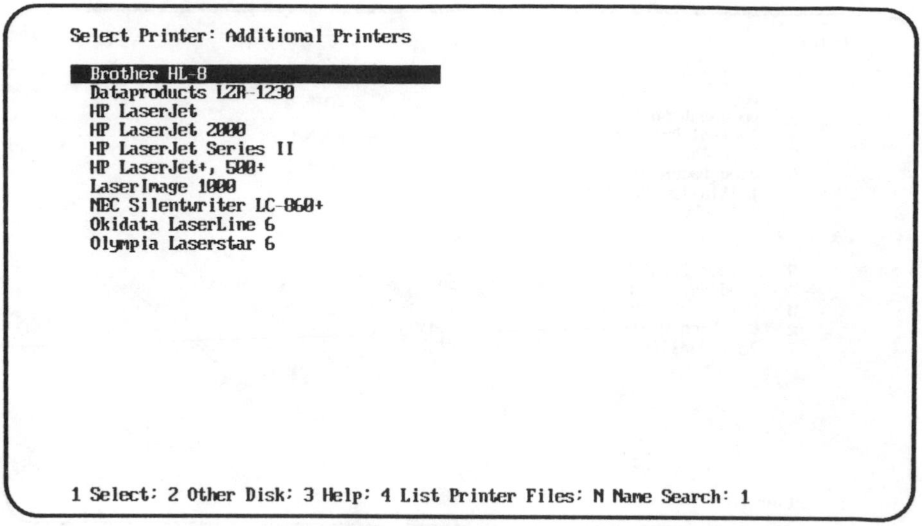

```
Select Printer: Additional Printers

 Brother HL-8
 Dataproducts LZR-1230
 HP LaserJet
 HP LaserJet 2000
 HP LaserJet Series II
 HP LaserJet+, 500+
 LaserImage 1000
 NEC Silentwriter LC-860+
 Okidata LaserLine 6
 Olympia Laserstar 6




 1 Select: 2 Other Disk: 3 Help: 4 List Printer Files: N Name Search: 1
```

FIGURE B-3   Additional Printers screen

files onto the hard disk in the same directory where the Word-
Perfect program is stored, the Additional Printers screen appears. The cursor highlights the first printer name on that list
and a new menu appears at the bottom of the screen. An example is shown in Figure B-3.

If WordPerfect can't find the files with an extension of
.ALL, WordPerfect indicates that the printer files are not
found. In that case, select Other Disk (2 or O), and Word-
Perfect prompts

Directory for printer files:

Type the drive letter where the printer files are located followed by a colon, such as **A:** or **B:**. Then press ENTER. (If the
printer files are found in another directory on the hard disk,
type the directory name, such as **\WPER\PTRS**, and press
ENTER.) Now you'll see a screen like the one shown in Figure
B-3.

6. Move the cursor to the name of your printer either by (1) using the cursor movement keys (such as DOWN ARROW, UP ARROW, PAGE DOWN, and PAGE UP); or (2) typing N to initiate the Name Search feature, typing the name of the printer, and, as soon as the cursor moves directly to that printer, pressing ENTER to leave the Name Search feature.

   If you can't find your printer on the list that WordPerfect is displaying, insert another Printer disk (such as the Printer 2 disk), again select Other Disk (2 or O), type in the name of the drive or directory where you inserted the other Printer disk, and press ENTER to view a different list of printers. If the name of the printer is still not shown, repeat the process with another Printer disk (such as the Printer 3 or Printer 4 disk). Then position the cursor on the printer attached to your computer.

   Note: If your printer is not listed on *any* of the Printer disks, then you can try a printer definition for a similar printer, such as an Epson printer if you use a dot matrix printer, or a Diablo or NEC if you use a daisy wheel printer. You can also create a printer definition for a standard printer, discussed at the end of this section. Or you can request that WordPerfect send you a driver for your printer; call WordPerfect toll free at 1-800-321-4566.

7. Choose Select (1 or S) or simply press ENTER to define the printer that your cursor is highlighting. A filename with the extension .PRS displays at the bottom of the screen. This is WordPerfect's suggestion for a printer definition filename.

8. Press ENTER to accept the displayed name. Or, if you wish to store the printer definition under a different name, enter a name of your own (with an extension of .PRS) and press ENTER. WordPerfect now displays a Printer Helps and Hints screen, which lists the printer's special features and limitations, if any.

9. Read over the Helps and Hints screen and then press EXIT (F7). WordPerfect updates the fonts for that printer and then displays the Select Printer Edit screen for that printer. An example is shown in Figure B-4 for the HP LaserJet Series II printer.

10. Read over the Select Printer Edit screen to decide whether you need to make changes to that printer's standard settings to adapt it to any special setup or equipment you may have.

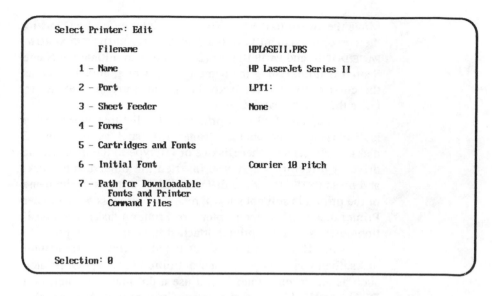

```
Select Printer: Edit

        Filename                    HPLASEII.PRS

    1 - Name                        HP LaserJet Series II

    2 - Port                        LPT1:

    3 - Sheet Feeder                None

    4 - Forms

    5 - Cartridges and Fonts

    6 - Initial Font               Courier 10 pitch

    7 - Path for Downloadable
        Fonts and Printer
        Command Files




Selection: 0
```

FIGURE B-4   Select Printer Edit screen

You can edit the settings now or later on. To edit the settings now, select the options you wish to alter and enter the changes. (See the next section, "Edit Printer Settings," for an explanation of each option on this screen.)

11. Press EXIT (F7) to store the printer definition you just created on disk in a file with the extension .PRS.

12. Repeat steps 5 through 11 for additional printers for which you wish to create printer definition files.

Whenever you create a new printer definition file, that printer will appear thereafter on the Select Printer screen (Figure B-2), so that you can select to use that printer definition for printing your documents.

At any time, you can view a list of your .PRS files. From the Select Printer screen, select Additional Printers (2 or A) to return to the Additional Printers screen (figure B-3 shows an example) and choose List Printer Files (4 or L). One file is shown on this list that you did not create but that resides on the WordPerfect 2 disk (and, if

you are a hard disk user, you copied onto the hard disk): STAN-
DARD.PRS. This file contains a printer driver for a standard ("vanil-
la") printer, allowing you to print text on any printer (but not
necessarily in proper format for your specific printer). You can select
the standard printer by choosing Select (1 or S); the standard printer
will be added to those listed on the Print screen.

Other options on the Select Printer menu besides Additional
Printers (2 or A) include Select (1 or S), described in this chapter's last
section as a method for selecting one of the defined printers; Edit (3 or
E), enabling you to edit the settings for a particular printer, as
described in the next section; Copy (4 or C), which enables you to
copy an existing printer definition to a file with a different filename
(but also with the extension .PRS), so that the new file can be edited
while retaining the old file; Delete (5 or D), allowing you to erase a
printer definition from disk; Help (6 or H), which displays the Printer
Hints and Helps screen for that printer (a screen that first displays
when you create a .PRS file for your printer); or Update (7 or U),
which lets you replace a printer definition with a new copy from the
.ALL file.

Edit Printer Settings

Once you have created a printer file for a certain printer, you should
then change its standard settings, tailoring them to your equipment.
Check your printer manual to find out whether your printer works with
a parallel or a serial port. If your printer is serial, then you must gather
information from your printer manual on baud rate, parity (none, odd,
or even), stop bits (1 or 2), and data bits (7 or 8).

Also, decide how your paper (forms) will be fed to the printer,
either (1) continuously, meaning either that you use a laser printer with
only one paper tray or you use one long ream of paper, where the
pages are separated by perforations; (2) manually, meaning that each
sheet of paper is hand fed; (3) by a sheet feeder. To use a sheet feeder,
you must know its brand name and the number of paper bins. (You
may decide to sometimes feed paper manually and other times to use
continuous forms, in which case, you can create two separate printer
definitions for one printer.)

Then, if you're not already viewing the Select Printer Edit screen
for a particular printer (an example is shown in Figure B-4 for the HP
LaserJet Series II printer), press PRINT (F7), choose Select Printer (S),
position the cursor on the name of the printer file that you wish to edit,

and press Edit (3 or E). The options on the Select Printer Edit screen are as described below.

NAME This printer setting specifies the name that is listed for that printer whenever you display the Select Printer screen. You can change this name, making it more descriptive, by choosing Name (1 or N) and typing up to 36 characters. Then press ENTER.

PORT This setting indicates the type and number of the port (plug) on the back of the computer to which the printer is attached. When you select Port (2 or P), a menu appears as follows:

> **Port: 1 LPT 1; 2 LPT 2; 3 LPT 3; 4 COM 1; 5 COM 2; 6 COM 3; 7 COM 4; 8 Other: 0**

LPT 1 through LPT 3 imply a parallel printer, where the number indicates the parallel plug to which your printer is attached. If your printer is a parallel printer, generally it is plugged into LPT 1, the default setting. COM 1 through COM 4 indicate a serial printer, where the number indicates the serial plug to which your printer is attached. When you specify a port for a serial printer, WordPerfect prompts for the printer's baud, parity, stop bits, character length, and whether the XON/XOFF protocol is on or off. See your printer manual for the appropriate settings.

SHEET FEEDER If you use a sheet feeder that automatically feeds paper into the printer, use this option to define it. Select Sheet Feeder (3 or S). A Sheet Feeder screen appears, listing possible sheet feeder brands for that printer. (If this screen does not appear, then WordPerfect does not have access to the Printer disk containing the original driver for your printer, which is contained in the file with an extension of .ALL. WordPerfect prompts **Directory for printer files**:. Insert the correct Printer disk in drive A or B, and then type **A:** or **B:** and press ENTER; if the printer files is on the hard disk, type the correct directory and press ENTER.)

Move the cursor to highlight your sheet feeder brand and press ENTER. A Helps and Hints screen appears for that brand. Read the information provided, and then press EXIT (F7) to return to the Select Printer Edit screen. (You should then make sure to use the Forms option, described below, to indicate the location of the available forms in the sheet feeder.)

FORMS This setting defines the characteristics of the forms you plan
to use with the printer. WordPerfect uses this information when it encounters a Paper Size/Type code in your document (as described in
Chapter 5) and assumes the standard form type if no code is inserted in
your document.

When you select Forms (4 or F), the Select Printer Forms screen
appears, an example of which is shown in Figure B-5. WordPerfect has
already defined several forms for you. For instance, Figure B-5 indicates that WordPerfect Corporation has defined the Envelope, Standard, and [ALL OTHERS] form types for the HP LaserJet Series II
printer. (The [ALL OTHERS] option is used if you insert a Paper
Size/Type code in your document for a paper type that is unavailable,
meaning that the type you indicated in the code hasn't been defined.)
You can delete a form by positioning the cursor and selecting Delete (2
or D). You can add a form to that list by selecting Add (1 or A). You
can edit a form by positioning the cursor and selecting Edit (3 or E).

If you select to add a form, WordPerfect displays a menu as shown
in Figure B-6. This screen lists seven basic form types, an [ALL

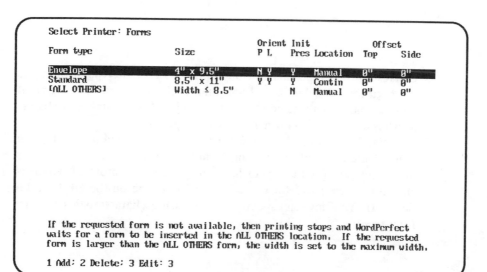

FIGURE B-5 Select Printer Forms screen

```
Select Printer: Form Type
      1 - Standard

      2 - Bond

      3 - Letterhead

      4 - Labels

      5 - Envelope

      6 - Transparency

      7 - Cardstock

      8 - [ALL OTHERS]

      9 - Other




Selection: 1
```

FIGURE B-6   Select Printer Form Type screen

OTHERS] form type, and an Other option. Select the type of form you are defining; or select Other and then indicate a form type name of your choosing. This name will carry along with it a number of characteristics of the form on which you will be printing.

Whether you selected to add a form and indicated a form type or you selected to edit an existing form type, the Select Printer Forms menu appears for that specific form type, an example of which is shown in Figure B-7 for the envelope form type on the HP LaserJet Series II. You now can specify the following characteristics for that form type:

- *Size*   This option sets the dimensions of the paper type you are defining. You can choose from several commonly used dimen-

```
Select Printer: Forms

        Filename                HPLASEII.PRS

        Form Type               Envelope

    1 - Form Size               4" x 9.5"

    2 - Orientation             Landscape

    3 - Initially Present       Yes

    4 - Location                Manual

    5 - Page Offsets - Top      0"
                       Side     0"




Selection: 0
```

FIGURE B-7   Select Printer Forms screen for a specific form type (envelope) on the HP LaserJet Series II Printer

sions or select Other and enter a specific height and width of your choosing to match the size of the form you are defining.

- *Orientation*   This option sets the direction in which the characters will print, of importance in printers where you are unable to insert the paper sideways into the printer and thus, must tell the printer to print sideways on the form. *Portrait* orientation prints lines parallel to how the form is inserted into the printer. *Landscape* orientation prints lines perpendicular to how the form is inserted into the printer (sideways), for printing envelopes or printing documents across the width of a page.

  Notice, for example, that the orientation for the envelope in Figure B-7 is landscape. This is because, with an HP LaserJet Series II printer, an envelope can only be inserted with its narrow end first, which is perpendicular to how you want it to actually print.

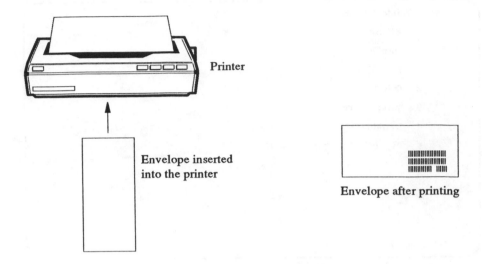

Printer

Envelope inserted
into the printer

Envelope after printing

- *Initially Present*   This option sets whether the form is in the printer when you begin to print, or whether you want Word-Perfect to stop the print job and prompt you to insert the form. (If you indicate that the form is not initially present, then when WordPerfect encounters the Paper Size/Type code for the form type you are defining, WordPerfect will sound a beep. You must then select Control Printer (4 or C) on the Print screen and select Go (4 or G) to signal WordPerfect that it can start print-ing, as discussed in Chapter 2.)

- *Location*   This option sets where and how the form will be fed into the printer, either continuously, manually, or from a specific bin in a sheet feeder. For instance, select continuous if you use continuous feed paper on a dot matrix or daisy wheel printer or if paper is fed through a single tray on a laser printer. Select manual if you plan to feed each sheet of paper manually. Select sheet feeder if you defined a sheet feeder for use with your printer.

  (If you select the location as manually fed, also referred to as hand-fed, then when you request that WordPerfect print a document, WordPerfect will sound a beep before printing each page. You must then insert paper in the printer, select Control Printer (4 or C) on the Print screen, and then select Go (4 or G);

this signals Wordperfect that paper is in the printer and it can start printing. This procedure is discussed step-by-step in Chapter 2.)

- *Page Offsets* This option sets whether forms are fed into the printer at different horizontal and vertical positions than Word-Perfect otherwise assumes. For instance, if your sheet feeder inserts envelopes 1 inch from the normal starting position of the printhead, then you should specify that offset. You can specify a top edge offset and/or a side offset, either in a positive number (such as 1 inch) for forms inserted with their top edge above the printhead or their left edge to the right of the printhead or a negative number (such as −1 inch) for forms inserted with their top edge below the printhead or their left edge to the left of the printhead.

Next, press ENTER or EXIT (F7) to return to the Select Printer Forms screen, which lists all forms defined for your printer, including the form you just defined. You can define a number of forms for the same printer. For instance, if you use a sheet feeder, you will want to define a form type for each sheet feeder bin. If you plan to feed both envelopes and labels into your printer, create envelope and label form types and set the appropriate characteristics for each.

When you have defined all the forms you will use for your printer, press EXIT (F7) to return to the Select Printer Edit screen.

CARTRIDGES AND FONTS If your printer allows you to insert different print cartridges or download font files so that you have a variety of extra fonts available for printing, use this setting to list all possible cartridges or fonts you plan to use with your printer. WordPerfect uses this information when it encounters a Font Change code in your document (see Chapter 10).

When you select Cartridges and Fonts (5 or C) and if your printer has other cartridges or fonts, the Select Printer Cartridges and Fonts screen appears; an example is shown in Figure B-8. (If this screen does not appear, even though other cartridges and fonts are available for your printer, it is because WordPerfect does not have access to the Printer disk containing the original driver for your printer. Word-Perfect prompts **Directory for printer files:**. Insert the correct Printer disk in drive A or B, type **A:** or **B:**, and press ENTER. If the printer file is on the hard disk, type the correct directory and press ENTER.) Under the heading "Font Category," the Select Printer Cartridges and Fonts

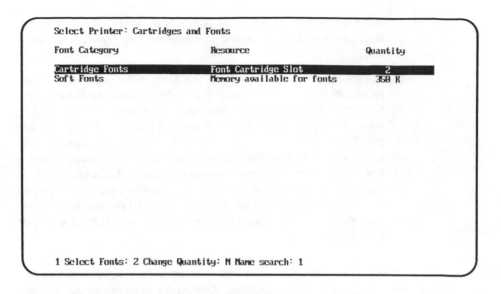

```
Select Printer: Cartridges and Fonts

Font Category              Resource                    Quantity

Cartridge Fonts            Font Cartridge Slot             2
Soft Fonts                 Memory available for fonts     350 K












1 Select Fonts: 2 Change Quantity: N Name search: 1
```

FIGURE B-8   Select Printer Cartridges and Fonts screen

screen indicates whether your printer uses cartridge fonts, print wheels, and/or soft (downloadable) font files, each as a separate option. Under the heading "Resource," the screen indicates where the fonts are loaded from (such as from the printhead or from a cartridge slot) and under the heading "Quantity," the screen indicates the number of slots available for cartridges, the print wheels that can be used, or the amount of memory available for downloadable font files.

To indicate that you have added more slots or memory than is preset for your printer, move the cursor to the appropriate font category, select Change Quantity (2 or Q), and enter the appropriate number.

To select available fonts, move the cursor to the font category of your choice and choose Select Fonts (1 or S) or simply press ENTER. A list of the available cartridges or fonts for that font category appears. Move the cursor to a cartridge or font you want to use with your printer, and then, depending on the instructions at the bottom of the screen, choose one of the following options:

- Press * to mark it as Present When Print Job Begins, which means that the cartridge or font is in a slot or in the printer memory when you start a print job. Fonts marked with this option are downloaded when you select the Initialize Printer option on the Print menu (see Chapter 9). Also, for printers where fonts cannot be swapped, memory is automatically decreased when you mark a font with *.

- Press PLUS to mark it as Can be Loaded (Unloaded) During Print Job, which means that WordPerfect will load (or unload) the font or ask you to insert (or remove) the cartridge during a print job. For printers where fonts cannot be swapped, fonts can only be loaded during a print job or unloaded afterwards. If fonts can be swapped, fonts can be loaded or unloaded during a print job.

- Press both * and PLUS (the + key), in which case WordPerfect downloads the font and, if necessary, unloads it to load another font. That font is then reloaded at the end of the print job.

Continue to mark all fonts that you wish to use (or until memory is almost used up), and then press EXIT (F7) to return to the Select Printer Cartridges and Fonts screen. Press EXIT (F7) again to return to the Select Printer Edit screen.

INITIAL FONT   This setting specifies the default font for the printer you are defining. WordPerfect uses this font when it prints a document, unless a Font Change code is inserted in the document to override the initial font (see Chapter 10).

When you select Initial Font (6 or I), the Select Printer Initial Font screen appears, which lists the possible fonts available for your printer (including built-in fonts and those you marked with the Cartridges and Fonts option, described above). To select a font, move the cursor to the font of your choice in one of two ways: either use the cursor movement keys or type N to activate the Name Search option, type the first letters of the font name until the cursor moves there, and press ENTER to turn off Name Search. Then, with the cursor highlighting the font of your choice, choose Select (1 or S) or simply press ENTER. An asterisk is inserted next to that font, indicating that it has been chosen as the initial font, and you are immediately returned to the Select Printer Edit screen.

PATH FOR DOWNLOADABLE FONTS AND PRINTER COMMANDS
This setting indicates the drive/directory where WordPerfect should look for downloadable font files and printer command files. When you select Path for Downloadable Fonts and Printer Commands (7 or D), you should then enter a drive/directory. For instance, if all downloadable fonts are stored on the hard disk in a directory named \WPER\FONTS, enter **C:\WPER\FONTS**.

SELECT A PRINTER

After you've defined the printers you will be using with WordPerfect, you can select a printer for printing one or more documents. The printer you select remains the currently selected printer until you select a new printer.

Make sure to select a printer *before* you attempt to print a document in WordPerfect. To do so, follow these steps:

1. Press the PRINT (SHIFT + F7) key.

2. Choose Select Printer (S) to display the previously defined printers. If an asterisk does not appear in front of one of the printers listed, then no printer has been selected.

3. Position the cursor on the name of the printer you wish to designate as the selected printer.

4. Choose Select (1 or S) or press ENTER to select that printer. You are returned to the Print screen.

5. Choose an option on the Print menu to print a document, or press EXIT (F7) to exit the Print screen.

Once a printer has been selected, you are ready to turn to the chapters that instruct you in printing in WordPerfect. (See Chapter 2 for more on the basics of printing documents and Chapter 9 for various print options and enhancements.)

Keep in mind that whenever you save a document the currently selected printer is saved with the document. When the document is printed, WordPerfect changes to that saved printer selection for printing—even if the currently selected printer is different.

C

THE SETUP MENU

Backup
Cursor Speed
Display
Fast Save, Unformatted
Initial Settings
Keyboard Layout
Location of Auxiliary Files
Units of Measure

The designers who wrote WordPerfect made certain assumptions about how the program would operate once it is loaded. For example, they determined that once saved, a document's filename should appear on the left side of the status line—one of WordPerfect's Display options. They preset all margins at 1 inch and right justification to on—two of WordPerfect's Initial Settings options. They decided to specify the cursor position on the status line in inches—one of the Units of Measure options.

Realizing that different individuals have different desires and needs, however, the designers also provided the ability to permanently change these and other options via what's called the Setup menu, so that you can customize the program for your equipment or special formatting needs.

You can access the Setup menu at any time while you are working on the Typing screen or the Reveal Codes screen. Simply press the SETUP (SHIFT + F1) key. The menu shown in Figure C-1 appears, with

```
Setup
      1 - Backup
      2 - Cursor Speed                30 cps
      3 - Display
      4 - Fast Save (unformatted)      No
      5 - Initial Settings
      6 - Keyboard Layout
      7 - Location of Auxiliary Files
      8 - Units of Measure




   Selection: 0
```

FIGURE C-1   Setup menu

a list of the eight Setup options that can be altered. After you alter the Setup menu and press EXIT (F7) to return to the Typing screen, the changes are saved on disk in a special file named WP{WP}.SET. These changes take effect for each new document you create in the current working session and each time that you start up WordPerfect thereafter—or until you alter them again. (If you wish to change initial settings temporarily, for just a single document, then you can do so using the FORMAT (SHIFT + F8) key, as explained in Chapters 4 and 5.)

This chapter will explain each of the eight options on the Setup menu. You'll learn how to tailor WordPerfect's defaults to your own needs.

BACKUP

Select Backup (1 or B) on the Setup menu and WordPerfect displays the screen shown in Figure C-2. On this screen, WordPerfect offers two features to help protect your documents from disaster: Timed Backup and Original Backup. Both are initially inactive. You can choose to activate one or both of them.

Timed Backup instructs WordPerfect to save whatever document is currently on screen (and thus in RAM) to a temporary backup file on disk at specified time intervals. For instance, you can activate Timed Backup to save a file to disk every 15 minutes. That way, if you experience a machine or power failure—when all information in RAM disappears—you can reload WordPerfect and retrieve the temporary backup file. You will lose, at most, only 15 minutes of work. Consider activating this feature if you are forgetful about saving your documents periodically to disk using the SAVE (F10) key.

```
Setup: Backup

      Timed backup files are deleted when you exit WP normally.  If you
      have a power or machine failure, you will find the backup file in the
      backup directory indicated in Setup: Location of Auxiliary Files.

      Backup Directory

   1 - Timed Document Backup          No
       Minutes Between Backups        30


      Original backup will save the original document with a .BK! extension
      whenever you replace it during a Save or Exit.

   2 - Original Document Backup       No




Selection: 0
```

FIGURE C-2   Setup Backup screen

Turn on the Timed Document Backup option by selecting Timed Document Backup (1 or T) and then typing **Y**. WordPerfect inserts the word "Yes" next to the heading "Timed Document Backup," and then moves down to the heading "Minutes Between Backups," suggesting 30 minutes. Type a number and press ENTER (or simply press ENTER if you wish to leave the backup at 30-minute intervals). Press ENTER to return to the Backup screen or press EXIT (F7) to return to the Typing (or Reveal Codes) screen.

Once the Timed Backup option is active, text on the Doc 1 Typing screen is stored at the time interval specified in a temporary file named WP{WP}.BK1. If you're currently working on a document in the Doc 2 Typing screen, that text is stored in a temporary file named WP{WP}.BK2. After the first backup, a document is saved again at the time interval specified only if the document is modified. For example, suppose you have indicated a time interval as every 30 minutes and are now typing a memo on the Doc 1 screen. After 30 minutes, WordPerfect backs up the document in the Doc 1 screen, creating a file named WP{WP}.BK1. The following message appears momentarily at the bottom of the WordPerfect screen:

* Please Wait *

When the message clears, the document has been backed up. Every 30 minutes thereafter, WordPerfect updates WP{WP}.BK1 provided that you have edited what is on screen during that time. You can specify a directory where timed backup files are to be stored, using the Location of Auxiliary Files option on the Setup menu, described later in this appendix. If you do not specify a directory, temporary files will be stored on the same drive/directory where WordPerfect's main program file (WP.EXE) is found.

WordPerfect deletes the temporary backup files when you exit from WordPerfect using the EXIT (F7) key. If instead you experience a power or machine failure, the backup files remain on disk; when you reload WordPerfect, you can retrieve WP{WP}.BK1 or WP{WP}.BK2 and continue working. Assuming Timed Backup is still active, Word-Perfect will prompt with the following the first time the backup is to be stored on disk after you reload:

Old backup file exists: 1 Rename; 2 Delete

Select Rename (1 or R) to rename the old backup file with a different name, so that WordPerfect can save the *new* backup using the filename

WP{WP}.BK1. If you no longer need the text stored in the old backup file, select Delete (2 or D) to delete it.

For the WordPerfect user who experiences frequent power failures or who is a fast typist, consider indicating a more frequent time interval than every 30 minutes—perhaps every 10 or 15 minutes (or even more frequently). While this will slow down the operations of Word-Perfect each time a document is backed up, a power or machine failure will cost you, at most, only 10 or 15 minutes of work.

Keep in mind that the Timed Document Backup feature is *not a substitute* for saving a document with a name of your choosing using the SAVE (F10) or EXIT (F7) keys. (See Chapter 2 for more on saving documents to disk.) Since WordPerfect deletes the temporary files when you exit WordPerfect normally, Timed Backup is *only* of value in case of a power or machine failure.

The second backup feature is Original Backup. Original Backup instructs WordPerfect to save the original file on disk each time you replace it with the document on screen. The original copy is saved with the extension .BK! (and remains on disk even when you exit normally from WordPerfect). You activate the Original Backup option from the Backup screen (Figure C-2) by selecting Original Document Backup (2 or O) and typing Y. WordPerfect inserts the word "Yes" next to the heading "Original Document Backup." Press ENTER to return to the Backup screen or press EXIT (F7) to return to the Typing screen.

As an example of how Original Backup operates once activated, suppose that you type and save a document on the disk in drive B with the filename MEMO. You then edit the document and save it again with the same filename. When you save, WordPerfect prompts

Replace B:\MEMO? (Y/N) No

If you type Y, the old version of MEMO will be saved under the name MEMO.BK!, and the edited version will be stored under the name MEMO. The next time you edit and save the document, the contents of MEMO will be transferred to MEMO.BK! as a backup, and the edited version will again be stored under the name MEMO.

Those of you who have used WordStar, which automatically backs up an original, are familar with the advantage of the Original Backup option—it safeguards against your replacing a file inadvertently. Should you replace a file accidentally, you can simply retrieve that same file with the extension .BK! and not lose any text that you typed.

If you elect to activate the Original Backup feature, realize that files with the same name but a different extension share the same original backup file. For example, if you have files named MEMO.1 and MEMO.2, only one backup file will be created. Thus, if you use this feature, consider naming all your documents such that the first part of each filename—the eight characters that precede the period—is unique (such as MEMO1 and MEMO2) so that each can be assigned its own original backup file.

CURSOR SPEED

Most keys on the computer keyboard repeat when they are held down. (Keys on the keyboard that commonly do not repeat when held down include CTRL, ALT, SHIFT, CAPS LOCK, and NUM LOCK.) By default, WordPerfect is set up to repeat 30 times for every 1 second you hold down a key (30 characters per second), as shown in Figure C-1. Select Cursor Speed (2 or C) on the Setup menu, and WordPerfect allows you to increase or decrease the rate at which keys repeat. WordPerfect prompts with the following menu:

Characters Per Second: 1 15; 2 20; 3 30; 4 40; 5 50; 6 Normal: 0

Select a menu option to change the cursor speed, or select Normal (6 or N) to return to your keyboard's normal cursor speed, which is usually 10 characters per second. If the Cursor Speed feature does not work properly on your computer or conflicts with a TSR (Terminate and Stay Resident) program, select the Normal option to avoid any incompatibilities. Once you select an option, the Characters Per Second menu clears. You can then press ENTER or EXIT (F7) to return to the Typing screen.

You may wish to experiment with the Cursor Speed feature to see which setting you prefer. One way to do so uses the cursor movement keys. For instance, at the default of 30 characters per second, position the cursor at the beginning of a sentence and hold down the RIGHT ARROW key until the cursor moves to the end of the sentence. Then change the cursor speed, and again move the cursor through a sentence using the RIGHT ARROW key. You'll quickly find which speed is most comfortable for you. You may find that faster isn't always better—a faster cursor speed often results in your overshooting the location where you want to position the cursor.

DISPLAY

Select Display (3 or D) on the Setup menu and WordPerfect displays the screen shown in Figure C-3. The Display options alter how text and menus are exhibited on screen as you work in WordPerfect. The options available are as follows:

Automatically Format and Rewrite

The default setting is "Yes," meaning that WordPerfect will format the text on screen as you edit to abide by current margins, tabs, and so on. You can request that WordPerfect stop the automatic reformatting of text by selecting Automatically Format and Rewrite (1 or A) and then typing N, so that WordPerfect inserts "No" next to this option; now WordPerfect will only format and rewrite text as you scroll through a

```
Setup: Display

     1 - Automatically Format and Rewrite    Yes

     2 - Colors/Fonts/Attributes

     3 - Display Document Comments            Yes

     4 - Filename on the Status Line          Yes

     5 - Graphics Screen Type                 IBM EGA 640x350 16 color

     6 - Hard Return Display Character

     7 - Menu Letter Display                  BOLD

     8 - Side-by-side Columns Display         Yes

     9 - View Document in Black & White       No



Selection: 0
```

FIGURE C-3   Setup Display screen

document or when you press the SCREEN (CTRL + F3) key and select Rewrite (0 or R).

Colors/Fonts/Attributes

WordPerfect supports numerous monitors and display cards, including Monochrome, CGA, PC 3270, Black and White, EGA Color or Monochrome, VGA Color or Monochrome, 8514/A, MCGA, Hercules Graphics Card, and Hercules Graphics Card plus RamFont. You can change the characteristics, colors, and/or fonts by which normal text and text with attributes (such as boldfaced or superscripted text) appear on screen. The text can be displayed differently on the Doc 1 screen and the Doc 2 screen. The choices available to you for displaying on-screen text depend on your computer monitor and display card. Select Colors/Fonts/Attributes (2 or C) and the following choices are available.

MONOCHROME MONITORS   The Attributes screen contains seven columns. The left column of this screen lists the possible attributes with which text can appear on screen: Normal (without any special attributes); Blocked (when text is within the boundaries of a phrase with "Block on"); with one of the sixteen size and appearance attributes found on the FONT (CTRL + F8) key (such as Underline, Strikeout, Bold, Double Underline, Small Caps, and so on); Bold and Underline (text that is both boldfaced and underlined at the same time); and Other Combinations (such as text that is underlined and in small caps at the same time or that is boldfaced and double underlined at the same time). The middle columns each indicate which of your monitor capabilities (Blink, Bold, Blocked, Underline, or Normal) will be activated for each of the attributes. The last column shows you a sample of the result of your selection for a particular attribute. Here's an example for three attributes on the Attributes screen:

Attribute	Blink	Bold	Blocked	Underline	Normal	Sample
Normal	N	N	N	N	Y	Sample
Underline	N	N	N	Y	N	<u>Sample</u>
Bold	N	Y	N	N	N	**Sample**

For each attribute, move the cursor across the appropriate row to each capability, and press **Y** to turn on the capability, **N** to turn off the capability, or the SPACEBAR to switch Y to N or N to Y. You can turn on more than one capability for an attribute; for instance, select both blink and bold. (You may not be able to turn on or off certain attributes which are reserved for your display card; WordPerfect will skip over attributes that you are unable to change.)

CGA/PC AND 3270/MCGA MONITORS   (or EGA monitors that have insufficient memory on the display card to use the font capabilities or have EGA in a mode that displays more than 25 lines on screen) The Colors/Fonts screen contains two options. Select Fast Text Display (2 or F) to determine whether you want WordPerfect to speed up text display. Then type **Y** or **N**. If you select "Yes" to activate fast text display, you may find that snow (static) appears on the Typing screen, in which case you will want to change this option to "No." (If the setting for this option is predefined as N/A, then the setting cannot be changed for your monitor.)

Select Screen colors (1 or S) to choose your monitor's colors for specific attributes. At the top, WordPerfect lists 16 colors that are available to be displayed on your screen, along with their corresponding letters. Below this are four columns. The left column lists the possible attributes with which text might appear on screen—the same as for monochrome monitors (above). The middle two columns each indicate by letter the foreground and background colors that should be used for each of the attributes. The last column shows a sample of the result of your selection for a particular attribute.

Here's an example for three attributes on the screen (the samples are not shown below since this book will not display text in colors other than black):

Attribute	Foreground	Background	Sample
Normal	H	B	
Underline	H	A	
Bold	P	B	

For each attribute, move the cursor across the appropriate row and type a letter key to select a color for the screen's background and foreground. For instance, you can select white as your foreground color and black as your background color for normal text, and light blue as your foreground color and black as your background color for underlined text. (You may not be able to turn on or off certain attributes which are reserved for your display card; WordPerfect will skip over attributes that you are unable to change.)

```
Setup: Colors/Fonts

    1 - Screen Colors

    2 - Italics Font, 8 Foreground Colors

   *3 - Underline Font, 8 Foreground Colors

    4 - Small Caps Font, 8 Foreground Colors

    5 - 512 Characters, 8 Foreground Colors

    6 - Normal Font Only, 16 Foreground Colors







Selection: 0
```

FIGURE C-4   Setup Colors/Fonts screen for EGA/VGA monitors

EGA/VGA MONITORS   The Colors/Fonts screen contains six options, as shown in Figure C-4. Options 2 through 6 are your font options. Select one of these font options; an asterisk appears next to the selected option. (If you have a Hercules RamFont display card, your choices include whether or not to display 6 or 12 fonts, rather than only 1 font as on the EGA.) Should an asterisk not appear, there is a problem loading that font; copy all WordPerfect files ending with .FNT to the same directory as where WP.EXE is located. If you select

- *The Italics, Underline, or Small Caps Font*   You can choose to see one of these fonts and/or choose from 8 colors on screen.

- *512 Characters*   You can increase the number of displayable characters in the current font from 256 to 512 (which is useful if your documents frequently contain special characters, as described in Chapter 15) and can choose from 8 colors on screen.

• *Normal Font Only* No special fonts will be shown on screen, but 16 foreground colors are available to choose from.

Next, select Screen colors (1 or S), to select your monitor's fonts and colors for specific attributes pertaining to the font option that you selected. At the top, WordPerfect lists 8 colors (or 16 colors if you selected font option 6) that are available to be displayed on your screen, along with their corresponding letters. Below this are five columns (or four columns if you selected font option 5 or 6). The left column lists the possible attributes with which text can appear on screen—the same as for monochrome monitors (above). The next column (which appears only if you selected font options 2, 3, or 4) lists whether the font you selected will be activated for each attribute. The following two columns each indicate by letter the foreground and background colors that should be used for each of the attributes. The last column shows a sample of each attribute.

Here's an example for three attributes on the screen, assuming that you selected font option 2, 3, or 4 (the samples are not shown below since this book will not display text in colors other than black):

Attribute	Font	Foreground	Background	Sample
Normal	N	H	B	
Underline	Y	H	A	
Bold	N	P	B	

For each attribute, move the cursor across the appropriate row and type **Y** or **N** to select whether or not the font should be activated (not applicable if you selected font options 5 or 6) and then a letter key to select a color for the screen's background and foreground. For instance, you can select no font, white as your foreground color and black as your background color for normal text; and activate the font and select light blue as your foreground color and black as your background color for underlined text. (You may not be able to turn on or off certain attributes which are reserved for your display card; WordPerfect will skip over attributes that you are unable to change.)

(If you have a Hercules RamFont card, then first select Screen Attributes (1 or S) and indicate which of your monitor capabilities should be activated for each of the attributes. You can select Reverse Video, Bold, Underline, Strikeout, or the following fonts: Normal (1); Double Underline (2); Italics (3); Small Caps (4); Outline (5); Subscript (6); Superscript (7); Fine Print (8); Small Print (9); Large Print (A); Very Large Print (B); Extra Large Print (C). When done selecting attributes, select Foreground/Background Colors (5 or F) and select a number from 1 to 64 to change the colors.)

Whatever type of monitor you use, once you select how characters will display on the first document screen (i.e., the Doc 1 or Doc 2 screen), press SWITCH (SHIFT + F3) to then assign characteristics to attributes on the other document screen. Repeat the same procedure as described above or, if you want the Doc 1 screen and Doc 2 screen to display colors, fonts, and attributes in the same way, simply press the MOVE (CTRL + F4) key; the attributes are copied from the other document screen into the current one.

Finally, press EXIT (F7) to save your selections and to return to the Display Menu. (Remember that any changes you make affect how attributes are shown on the screen, but not how they appear on the printed page.) The changes take effect immediately.

Display Document Comments

The default setting is "Yes," meaning that if you insert a comment into your text (as described in Chapter 3), WordPerfect will display the comment on screen in a double-line box. You can instead request that WordPerfect conceal comments by selecting Display Document Comments (3 or D) and typing **N**, so that WordPerfect inserts "No" for this option; now comments inserted in any of your documents will be hidden on the Typing screen, and you will only know that a comment exists when you see the code [**Comment**] on the Reveal Codes screen.

Filename on the Status Line

The default setting for this option is "Yes," meaning that once you save a file on disk, the file's path (drive/directory where it is stored) and filename appears on the status line when that file is on screen. You can decide to suppress the filename by selecting Filename on the Status Line (4 or F) and typing **N**, so that WordPerfect displays "No" for this option.

Graphics Screen Type

WordPerfect automatically selects a graphics driver for your monitor and display card when you start the program. Figure C-3, for example, shows that WordPerfect has detected an IBM EGA monitor, with 640 x 350 resolution, and 16 colors available.

If WordPerfect has selected the wrong graphics driver or if you have a special situation such as two monitors running on the same computer, then you can indicate a different option by selecting Graphics Screen Type (5 or G). WordPerfect displays a list of screen types. Position the cursor on the correct option and press ENTER. If your graphics screen type is not shown in this list, you will need to copy the driver file for your graphics screen (with an extension of .WPD) from the Fonts/Graphics disk to the directory where WP.EXE is located. Then return to the Setup menu and select the Graphics Screen Type option.

Hard Return Display Character

WordPerfect assumes that you want a hard return displayed as a space on the Typing screen (that is, the code is invisible unless you switch to the Reveal Codes screen, where you can view the accompanying [HRt] code). If you want a character other than a space displayed on the Typing screen, then select Hard Return Display Character (6 or H) on the Setup Display menu and type the character you want to use, such as] or >. To have the hard return displayed as a shaded box on screen (■), press a function key. To have the hard return displayed as a special character, such as » or ▬, you can use the Compose feature (see Chapter 15) to insert that character on screen. The new display character is shown on the Display Menu. If you change your mind and want no character to represent a hard return, then you can again select Hard Return Display Character (6 or H), and press the SPACEBAR.

Menu Letter Display

WordPerfect is designed with mnemonic menus, so that in addition to selecting a feature with a number, you can type the mnemonic letter. WordPerfect assumes that you want the mnemonic letter displayed on screen in bold. Instead, you can select to display the mnemonic letter with another attribute, such as underline (which is how mnemonic letters are displayed on line menus in this book so that they are easy to spot). Select Menu Letter Display (7 or M) on the Display Setup menu, and WordPerfect prompts

> 1 Size; 2 Appearance; 3 Normal: 0

These are the same three options on the Font menu when you press the FONT (CTRL + F8) key. Now you can select Size (1 or S) or Appearance (2 or A) to select a size or appearance attribute for the menu letter display. The attribute that you select is shown on the Display menu. Select Normal (3 or N) if you want the mnemonic letter to display as normal text—implying that you plan to select all features with a number, rather than with the mnemonic letter. Your choice for how the mnemonic letter is displayed takes effect for both the Doc 1 and Doc 2 screens.

Side-by-Side Columns Display

The default setting is "Yes," meaning that columns you create with the Text Columns feature (as described in Chapter 11) are displayed side by side, as they appear on the printed page. You can decide to display each column on a separate page by selecting Side-by-Side Columns Display (8 or S) on the Setup Display menu and typing N, so that WordPerfect displays "No" for this option. This is useful for speeding up performance when editing documents containing extensive text column format. (Even when columns are displayed on separate pages on screen, they still appear side by side on the printed page.)

View Document in Black and White

The default setting for this option is "No." You can instead force printed text colors to be shown in black and white when previewing text using the View Document feature by selecting View Document in Black & White (9 or V) and typing **Y**.

FAST SAVE, UNFORMATTED

As shown in Figure C-1, the default setting for Fast Save is "No," meaning that whenever you press SAVE (F10) or EXIT (F7) and store a document on disk, WordPerfect will save the document as formatted. Instead, you can request that WordPerfect save without formatting. Select Fast Save (4 or F) on the Setup menu, and type **Y**, so that Word-Perfect inserts "Yes" on the Setup menu; now WordPerfect will save the on-screen document to disk without formatting the document.

By activating the Fast Save option, you reduce the time it takes to save a document. But be aware that a document cannot be printed from disk unless it is formatted; a document can be printed from disk when Fast Save has been activated only if you press HOME, HOME, DOWN ARROW to format the document just before saving it. Otherwise, you must retrieve the document and print it from screen.

There are, therefore, tradeoffs in activating the Fast Save option. If you typically print documents from screen, consider activating the Fast Save option; this will save you time when saving. Just remember to press HOME, HOME, DOWN ARROW before saving documents that you wish to print from disk in the future. On the other hand, if you typical-ly print documents from disk, consider leaving the Fast Save option set as "No."

INITIAL SETTINGS

Select Initial Settings (5 or 1), on the Setup menu and WordPerfect dis-plays the screen shown in Figure C-5. On this screen WordPerfect of-fers features to change format settings as well as print and beep options. These options are as follows:

- *Beep Options*   WordPerfect can sound a beep to alert you when one of the following messages appears on the status line: (1) an error message, such as **ERROR: File not found**; (2) the mes-

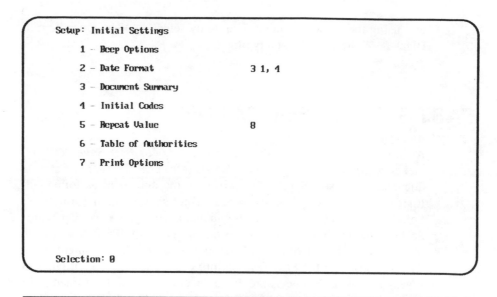

```
Setup: Initial Settings
     1 - Beep Options
     2 - Date Format              3 1, 4
     3 - Document Summary
     4 - Initial Codes
     5 - Repeat Value             8
     6 - Table of Authorities
     7 - Print Options




Selection: 0
```

FIGURE C-5   Setup Initial Settings screen

sage that prompts for hyphenation, which begins **Position Hyphen; Press ESC**; or (3) the message indicating that the search string was not found during a Search or Replace operation, * **Not Found** *.

When you select Beep Options (1 or B), a Setup Beep Options screen appears indicating the current default settings. The default setting is for a beep to sound during hyphenation, but not on an error or search failure. Select an item from this Beep Options menu and press **Y** to turn on the option or **N** to turn off the option. Then press ENTER to return to the Initial Settings screen or EXIT (F7) to return to the Typing screen.

- *Date Format*   Chapter 3 describes the Date feature, which can insert today's date (or time) automatically for you. Figure C-5 shows that WordPerfect assumes that you want to display the date as "3 1, 4" (where the number 3 represents the month as a word, the number 1 represents the day of the month, and the number 4 represents the year with all 4 digits shown, as in May 5, 1989 or September 26, 1989).

You can change the default style for the date format by selecting Date Format (2 or D). The Date Format menu appears on which you can make a change and then press ENTER or EXIT (F7) to return to the Initial Settings screen. Refer to Chapter 3 for more on the Date Format menu (and how you can change the style for the date format for just one working session using the DATE/OUTLINE key).

- *Document Summary*   As described in Chapter 8, WordPerfect provides the opportunity to create a document summary, which will be attached to a specific document when it is saved as a file on disk. You can decide on two default settings regarding summaries: (1) whether a document summary form is automatically displayed when you press SAVE or EXIT to store a new document for the very first time (the default setting is "No"); and (2) the subject search text, which is the pre-selected phrase used by WordPerfect to find the subject of a document (the default is "RE:").

   To alter these settings, select Document Summary (3 or S). WordPerfect displays the Setup Document Summary menu. Select Create on Save/Exit (1 or C) and type Y to have Word-Perfect prompt you for a document summary when one does not already exist as you press SAVE or EXIT. You may also select Subject Search Text (2 or S) and enter a search string that you commonly use (such as "SUBJECT:" or "TOPIC") to identify the subject of your document. Be sure to refer to Chapter 8 for a fuller explanation of the Document Summary feature.

- *Initial Codes*   Every time you clear the screen and are ready to begin typing a new document, WordPerfect makes certain assumptions about how the new document should be formatted. For instance, the default left, right, top, and bottom margin settings are 1 inch. The default line spacing is single. The default justification is for justification on (meaning both the left and right margins will be justified). These initial settings can be changed *from document to document* by inserting format codes, as explained in Chapter 4 and other chapters.

   But what if you find yourself changing a specific format setting in the same way *for every document?* You can change that default permanently, tailoring the initial format codes to those you use most often. WordPerfect will then assume the new default every time you begin typing a document.

   As a general rule, don't change the Setup menu unless you

find yourself altering a format setting in the same way for almost all your documents.

To alter the default format settings, select Initial Codes (4
or I). WordPerfect displays the Setup Initial Codes screen,
which is similar to a clear Reveal Codes screen. If the bottom
window on screen is completely blank, this indicates that all
the default settings as set up by WordPerfect Corporation are in
effect (the default format settings are listed in Chapters 4 and
5). If format codes are displayed, then you or some other user
has already altered some of the initial format settings.

To change any setting, insert format codes just as you
would on the Typing screen for a specific document. For example, if you wish to change right justification from on to off
as the default, press FORMAT (SHIFT + F8), Line (1 or L), Justification (3 or J), type N, and press EXIT (F7)—just as you
would to turn off justification in a specific document. If you
want the margin defaults to change, press FORMAT (SHIFT +
F8) and proceed to change margins as if in a document. If you
wish to alter WordPerfect's assumptions on footnote options
(such as the spacing between each footnote), press FOOTNOTE
(CTRL + F7), Footnote (1 or F), Options (4 or O), and when the
Footnote Options screen appears, make any changes you
desire—as you would in a document. The codes will display
only in the bottom window on the screen (just as they appear
only in the bottom window on the Reveal Codes screen within a
document). Then press EXIT (F7) to return to the Initial Settings screen.

Once you change the default format settings, those new
settings will affect new documents that you create from that
point on. Of course, any of the newly defined default settings
can still be changed in a particular document; when you're
typing a document and display the Document Initial Settings
screen (as described in Chapter 4), the default initial settings
can be seen, edited, or eliminated for that one document.

Be aware, however, that any change to the default format
settings will have no effect on preexisting documents. That's
because an invisible document prefix (packet of information) is
saved with every document you store on disk. The invisible
packet includes those codes on the Document Initial Codes
screen which, unless altered, are derived from those found on
the Setup Initial Codes screen at the time the document is first
created. For example, suppose that you created and stored on

disk one document using the default left/right margin settings of 1 inch. If you then use the Setup menu to alter the default to 2 inches, that first document will remain with margins of 1 inch, even though the left/right margin settings for all future documents will be defaulted at 2 inches.

- *Repeat Value*   You can change the number of times that the ESC key repeats a keystroke. The ESC key is used to repeat a character, cursor movement, or macro. By default, when you press ESC, WordPerfect prompts

Repeat Value = 8

This means that the next keystroke you press will repeat eight times. You can permanently change the default value for this feature by selecting Repeat Value (5 or R), typing a number, and pressing ENTER. (You can also override the default setting of the repeat value for a specific working session when viewing the Typing or Reveal Codes screen by pressing ESC, typing a number, and pressing ENTER; see Chapter 3 for details.)

- *Table of Authorities*   As described in Chapter 15, WordPerfect can generate a table of authorities for you. You can decide on three default settings regarding the style for Table of Authorities entries when generated: (1) whether a dot leader should precede the page location of each authority (the default setting is "Yes"); (2) whether to allow underlining in the generated table (the default setting is "No"); and (3) whether to insert blank lines between authorities (the default setting is "Yes").

   To alter these settings, select Table of Authorities (6 or A). WordPerfect displays the Setup Table of Authorities menu. Select an option and type **Y** or **N**. (You can also change these settings for a specific document, rather than change the default.) Be sure to refer to Chapter 15 for a fuller explanation of the Table of Authorities feature.

- *Print Options*   As described in Chapter 9, you can select from various print options before printing a document. These include Binding Width, which WordPerfect assumes is 0 inches; Number of Copies, which WordPerfect assumes is 1; Graphics Quality, which WordPerfect assumes is medium; and Text Quality, which WordPerfect assumes is high.

   To alter these settings permanently, select Print Options (7 or P). WordPerfect displays the Setup Print Options menu.

```
Setup: Location of Auxiliary Files

     1 - Backup Directory

     2 - Hyphenation Module(s)

     3 - Keyboard/Macro Files

     4 - Main Dictionary(s)

     5 - Printer Files                    C:\WPER

     6 - Style Library Filename

     7 - Supplementary Dictionary(s)

     8 - Thesaurus




Selection: 0
```

FIGURE C-6   Setup Location of Auxiliary Files screen

Select an option and enter the appropriate setting to establish a
new default for that option. Be sure to refer to Chapter 9 for a
fuller discussion of the print options and for the method to alter
these options for specific print jobs.

KEYBOARD LAYOUT

With the Keyboard Layout feature, you can create or edit a keyboard
definition, where a keyboard definition specifies which key should be
chosen to perform a certain task or feature. You can set up your own
keyboard definition whereby a feature is activated by pressing a key of
your choosing, a special character is inserted on screen by pressing a
key of your choosing, or a macro is executed by pressing a key of your
choosing. Chapter 15 discusses this feature.

LOCATION OF AUXILIARY FILES

Select Location of Auxiliary Files (7 or L), and WordPerfect displays the menu shown in Figure C-6. On this menu, you specify where certain auxiliary files are located on disk. In most cases, if you do not specify a location for auxiliary files, WordPerfect assumes that these files are located either in the default drive/directory or wherever the main WordPerfect program file (WP.EXE) is housed:

- *Backup Directory* Timed backup files (described previously in this chapter) will be stored in this directory.

- *Hyphenation Module(s)* WP{WP}US.HYL is located in this directory. The hyphenation module is optional—you can purchase it separately from WordPerfect Corporation, as mentioned in Chapter 4. When you specify a default path for the hyphenation modules, the message **Hyphenation (c) copyright Soft-Art, Inc., 1988** appears momentarily.

- *Keyboard/Macro Files* Keyboard files (with the extension .WPK), macro files (with the extension .WPM), and macro resource files (with the extension .MRS) are stored in this directory. Refer to Chapter 14 for more on the Macros feature and Chapter 15 for more on the Keyboard Layout feature.

- *Main Dictionary(s)* The WP{WP}US.LEX file (or another main dictionary file, such as a file for another language) is located here. This file contains the dictionary of words used to spell check a document. See Chapter 7 for more on the Spell feature.

- *Printer Files* Files with the extension .ALL and .PRS are located in this directory. .ALL files are those originally housed on the Printer 1 through Printer 4 disks, containing printer drivers for a variety of printers. .PRS files are created when you define a printer to work with WordPerfect (as described in Appendix B). WordPerfect assumes that these files are stored in the same directory where WP.EXE is housed unless you specify otherwise using this option.

- *Style Library Filename* The path and filename for the file that acts as your style library is stored in this directory. Note that this is the only option on the Location of Auxiliary Files menu where you must indicate not only a directory, but a specific *filename* as well. For instance, suppose you wish to establish as your style library the file named STYLE.LIB, which is stored on the hard disk in the subdirectory \WPER. You would enter the following as the style library file: C:\WPER\STYLE.LIB. See Chapter 14 for more on the Styles feature.

- *Supplementary Dictionary(s)*   The WP{WP}US.SUP file and other supplementary dictionary files are located in this directory. See Chapter 7 for more on the Spell feature.

- *Thesaurus*   The WP{WP}US.THS file (or another thesaurus file that you use, such as a file for another language) is located in this directory. This file contains the thesaurus used when you press THESAURUS (ALT + F1). See Chapter 7 for more on the Thesaurus feature.

By specifying a location for your auxiliary files, you can arrange a hard disk's WordPerfect files into their own directories. For instance, if you specify a keyboard/macro files directory, then whenever you create a keyboard definition or macro, WordPerfect automatically stores the file in the directory you specified. And, when you activate a keyboard definition or invoke a macro, WordPerfect looks to that directory to find the definition or macro. Therefore, you can keep all keyboard definitions and macros separate from your document files, and thus maintain a well-organized filing system.

Keep in mind that on the Location of Auxiliary Files menu, you indicate a drive/directory for all items except for item 6, Style Library Filename, where you indicate a drive/directory *and filename*.

UNITS OF MEASURE

Numerous features in WordPerfect involve some type of measurement. WordPerfect allows you to display all measurements in either inches, centimeters, points, or Version 4.2 units, which are the lines and columns units used by WordPerfect Version 4.2 users.

As set up by WordPerfect Corporation, WordPerfect assumes that you want measurements displayed in inches. For instance, margins and tab settings on the Line Format menu are shown in inches (such as 1"). When you change margins or tabs, WordPerfect assumes inches. The

```
Setup: Units of Measure

     1 - Display and Entry of Numbers          "
             for Margins, Tabs, etc.

     2 - Status Line Display                   "


  Legend:

     " = inches
     i = inches
     c = centimeters
     p = points
     w = 1200ths of an inch
     u = WordPerfect 4.2 Units (Lines/Columns)




  Selection: 0
```

FIGURE C-7   Setup Units of Measure screen

format code inserted into the text also displays the measurement in inches, such as **[L/R Mar:2",1.5"]**.

Furthermore, WordPerfect assumes that you want the Ln and Pos indicators on the status line to display in inches, so that the status line may read

Doc 1 Pg 4 Ln 2.5" Pos 1"

You can alter the way measurements are displayed and/or change the way the cursor position is displayed on the status line. Select Units of Measure (8 or U) on the Setup menu, and WordPerfect shows the menu illustrated in Figure C-7. Your units of measurement options are

- *Inches indicated with "*   The default setting for both items.

- *Inches indicated with i* For example, if you selected Status Line Display (2 or S) and typed **i** the status line would then read

  Doc 1 Pg 4 Ln 2.5i Pos 1i

- *Centimeters* For example, if you selected Status Line Display (2 or S) and typed **c**, the status line would then read

  Doc 1 Pg 4 Ln 6.36c Pos 2.54c

- *Points* (This is a commonly used measurement in the publishing industry.) For example, if you selected Status Line Display (2 or S) and typed **p**, the status line would then read

  Doc 1 Pg 4 Ln 180.5p Pos 72p

  In WordPerfect, points equal 1/72 inch. You should know that in publishing, points equal 1/72.27 inch, a 0.4% difference which is small but nevertheless significant when doing precise work.

- *1200ths of an inch* For example, if you selected Status Line Display (2 or S) and typed **w**, the status line would then read

  Doc 1 Pg 1 Ln 1200w Pos 1200w

- *Version 4.2 units* With this option, vertical measurements are represented as lines and horizontal measurements as column positions. For example, if you selected Status Line Display (2 or S) and typed **u** the status line would then read

  Doc 1 Pg 4 Ln 1 Pos 10

  When you select Version 4.2 units, the size of a line or column varies based on the size of the font you are using in your document. Should you decide to work with the status line in version 4.2 units, you must keep in mind that the Ln number indicates a distance from the top *margin,* while for the other units of measure, this indicates a distance from the top *edge of the page.*

No matter what measurement you decide to use as your default, you do not have to enter measurements in the selected unit. You can still enter a measurement in another unit of measure as long as it is followed by a letter to indicate the units—i or " for inches, c for centimeters, p for points, w for 1200ths of an inch, h for Version 4.2

horizontal units, v for Version 4.2 vertical units. For instance, suppose that you selected that all display and entry of numbers will be in inches. You can indicate a left margin of 2.5c (centimeters), 90p (points), or 15h (Version 4.2 horizontal units) and WordPerfect will convert your entry into inches. If, instead, you simply enter 2, then WordPerfect assumes that you are specifying 2 inches.

Depending on the document you are working on, you may wish to change the units of measure frequently. For instance, you may wish to switch into points when producing a newsletter and to inches for standard documents.

You can also select the status line in one unit of measure and the display and entry of numbers in a different unit of measure.

D

GETTING ADDITIONAL SUPPORT

As a beginning user, you may encounter some frustration in becoming accustomed to how WordPerfect operates. Just remember that you're not alone. Many thousands of people use WordPerfect daily and have numerous questions as they learn about new WordPerfect features.

Whatever you do, don't work with WordPerfect in a vacuum. Establish a support network for yourself. If you know someone who uses WordPerfect, start sharing information; you'll both expand your comfort with and knowledge of WordPerfect.

In addition, there are many formal sources of assistance, whether you desire additional instruction on WordPerfect or you need help answering specific questions related to a particularly complicated document or your computer equipment. Here are some suggestions:

- For more practice with a variety of features, the WordPerfect package contains a workbook and a tutorial.

    The WordPerfect Workbook includes 32 lessons. Start a lesson by loading WordPerfect. Floppy disk users should then place the Learning disk in drive B. Hard disk users should change to the default directory on the hard disk where the learning files are stored, such as \WPER\LEARN. (Chapter 8 describes how to change the default directory from within

637

WordPerfect.) Then begin reading the workbook.

The tutorial offers additional practice in the basics, such as using the keyboard, formatting a document, moving text, and using some of the more advanced features. To access the tutorial, you must be in DOS and not in WordPerfect. Floppy disk users should place the WordPerfect 1 disk in drive A and the WordPerfect Learning disk in drive B. At the DOS prompt A>, type **B:** and press ENTER. Next, type **learn** and press ENTER to access the tutorial. Hard disk users should change to the directory where the learning files are stored. For instance, suppose that the learning files are in the directory named \WPER\LEARN; at the DOS prompt, type **cd \wper\learn** and press ENTER. Then type **tutor** and press ENTER to start the tutorial. (Hard disk users: if the tutorial doesn't begin, then you may need to alter the file named AUTOEXEC.BAT on your hard disk to indicate to DOS with the Path command where the tutorial files are stored on disk; see Appendix A.)

Once in the tutorial, you can select which features you wish to learn more about. Just read the screen and follow the instructions provided.

- For a more in-depth understanding of advanced WordPerfect features, look to other books by Osborne/McGraw-Hill, available at your local bookstore. Several of these are listed at the start of Chapter 15.

  For a free catalog of all Osborne/McGraw-Hill offerings, fill out and return the card at the back of this book, or write to Osborne/McGraw-Hill, 2600 Tenth Street, Berkeley, California 94710.

- For help using WordPerfect with your particular equipment, your computer dealer may have the answer.

- For a better understanding of your computer and various software packages, there are user groups devoted to your brand of computer. If you have an IBM PC, for example, there may be an IBM PC user group in your area in which you can meet other people who use WordPerfect and exchange information. User groups' names and addresses are listed in regional and national computer magazines.

- For a user group devoted exclusively to WordPerfect Corporation products, there's the WordPerfect Support Group in Baltimore, Maryland. But you don't need to live in Baltimore to get their support. They produce a newsletter called "The Word-Perfectionist," which is a great source for general information and tips on WordPerfect and other WordPerfect Corporation products. In addition, the Support Group operates an electronic mail bulletin board service (for those of you with a modem), through which members can share ideas and information. You can join by writing to the following address:

WordPerfect Support Group
P.O. Box 1577
Baltimore, MD 21203

To subscribe to "The WordPerfectionist," you can also call the following toll-free number: 800 USA-GROUP. You can access the bulletin board service from CompuServe (an on-line service) by typing **GO WPSG**.

Also, check local magazines for a WordPerfect support group in your area. For instance, Seattle, Washington, has its own WordPerfect user group.

- For answers to specific questions on WordPerfect, look to WordPerfect Corporation. Their telephone support is frequently hailed as the best in the business. Over 200 people staff the telephones in Customer Support, ready to answer your questions about installation, printers, or general items on all Word-Perfect Corporation products. They are extremely responsive once you get through to them, but you may be placed on hold during peak hours (11:00 A.M. to 3:00 P.M. mountain time). The Customer Support toll-free number is different depending on your needs:

Specific Topic	Toll-Free Number
WordPerfect Version 5 Installation	(800) 533-9605
General Questions	(800) 321-3349
Printer Support	(800) 541-5097
Graphics	(800) 321-3383
Features	(800) 541-5096
WordPerfect Networks	(800) 321-3389

Additional toll-free telephone numbers are available for information on other WordPerfect products, such as WordPerfect Library, WordPerfect Office, DataPerfect, and so on. For a recording of all toll-free numbers, dial (800) 321-5906. Service hours are 7:00 A.M. to 6:00 P.M. mountain time during weekdays and 8:00 A.M. to noon on Saturdays. If the person you speak to can't answer your question, he or she will usually find someone who can or refer you to another department.

When you call, make sure that you're at your computer, with WordPerfect loaded. That way you can duplicate the problem you're encountering keystroke-by-keystroke for the Customer Support representative.

Alternatively, you can write to the Customer Support Department. The address is

WordPerfect Corporation
Attention: Customer Support Department
1555 North Technology Way
Orem, UT 84057

When you write, include a full explanation of the problem you're encountering, the equipment you use, and the version and release date of your WordPerfect program. (Your Word-Perfect program's release date will appear in the upper right corner of the computer screen when you press the HELP (F3) key while in WordPerfect.)

- For special information pertaining to your particular release of WordPerfect, check to see if any of your WordPerfect disks contains a file named README. WordPerfect Corporation continually improves its product, even between the introduction of new versions. When minor changes are made for a version already on the market, the changes for new releases of that version are often documented in a file named README. Use the LIST FILES (F5) key while in WordPerfect to see if a file named README is listed (see Chapter 2 for a discussion of the LIST FILES key). If it is, you can look at or print out its contents. It may give you information on changes made to your copy of WordPerfect or specific files now included on a certain disk.

TRADEMARKS

Adobe™	Adobe Systems, Inc.
AT®	International Business Machines Corporation
AutoCAD®	CADAM
CBDS™	International Business Machines Corporation
CDDM™	International Business Machines Corporation
CHART-MASTER®	Ashton-Tate/used under license from Chartmasters, Inc.
CPG™	International Business Machines Corporation
dBASE®	Ashton-Tate
Diablo®	Xerox Corporation
DIAGRAM-MASTER®	Decision Resources, Inc./Ashton-Tate
DisplayWrite™	International Business Machines Corporation
Dr. Halo™	IMSI
EnerGraphics™	Enertronics Research, Incorporated
Epson®	Seiko Epson Corporation
Epson FX-100™	Epson America, Inc.
Epson MX-100™	Epson America, Inc.
Framework II®	Ashton-Tate
Freelance® Plus	Lotus Development Corporation
GEM®	Digital Research, Incorporated
Generic CADD™	Generic Software, Inc.
Genius™	DataMate
Graph-in-the-Box®	New England Software
Graphwriter®	Lotus Development Corporation
Harvard™	Software Publishing Corporation
Helvetica®	Linotype Co.
Hercules®	Hercules Computer Technology
Hewlett-Packard®	Hewlett-Packard Company
HP™	Hewlett-Packard Company
HP Scanning Gallery™	Hewlett-Packard Company
HP Graphics Gallery™	Hewlett-Packard Company
IBM®	International Business Machines Corporation

INDEX

Command Card
Basic WordPerfect Features

CURSOR CONTROL

Character left	←
Character right	→
Line up	↑
Line down	↓
Word Left	CTRL + ←
Word Right	CTRL + →
Left end of line	HOME, HOME, ←
Right end of line	HOME, HOME, → or END
Left end of screen	HOME, ←
Right end of screen	HOME, →
Top of screen	HOME, ↑ or – (numeric keypad)
Bottom of screen	HOME, ↓ or + (numeric keypad)
Top of current page	CTRL + HOME, ↑
Bottom of current page	CTRL + HOME, ↓
Top of page number	CTRL + HOME, *pagenumber*
Top of previous page	PGUP
Top of next page	PGDN
Beginning of document	HOME, HOME, ↑
End of document	HOME, HOME, ↓

DELETE TEXT/CODES

Character left of cursor	BACKSPACE
Character at cursor	DEL
Word at cursor	CTRL + BACKSPACE
Characters right of cursor to end of line	DELETE EOL (CTRL + END)
Characters right of cursor to end of page	DELETE EOP (CTRL + PGDN)
Sentence, paragraph, page	CTRL + F4
Block	Block text DEL, Y
Undelete	F1, 1

SAVE DOCUMENT

And Remain in Document
1. F10
2. Enter filename
3. Y/N (if resaving)

And Clear the Screen
1. F7, Y
2. Enter filename
3. Y/N (if resaving)
4. N

And Exit WordPerfect
1. F7, Y
2. Enter filename
3. Y/N (if resaving)
4. Y

BLOCK TEXT/CODES
1. Cursor on first character
2. ALT + F4
3. Cursor on last character

RETRIEVE DOCUMENT

Directly
1. SHIFT + F10
2. Enter filename

From List Files
1. F5, Enter drive/directory
2. Highlight file, 1

PRINT

Text from Screen
1. Position cursor
2. SHIFT + F7
3. 1 for full document, 2 for page

Block from Screen
1. Block text
2. SHIFT + F7, Y

Document from Disk
1. SHIFT + F7, 3
2. Enter document name
3. Enter range of pages

Document from List Files (Disk)
1. F5, enter directory
2. Highlight file, 4
3. Enter range of pages

Cancel Print Job
1. SHIFT + F7, **4, 1**
2. Enter print job number

CENTER (OR FLUSH RIGHT)
1. Position cursor
2. SHIFT + F6 (or ALT + F6)

UNDERLINE (OR BOLD)

While Typing
1. F8 (or F6)
2. Type text
3. F8 (or F6)

Existing Text
1. Block text
2. F8 (or F6)

CHANGE LINE SPACING
1. Position cursor
2. SHIFT + F8, **1, 6**
3. Enter spacing, F7

RESET MARGINS

Left/right
1. Position cursor
2. SHIFT + F8, **1, 7**
3. Enter margins, F7

Top/bottom
1. Position cursor
2. SHIFT + F8, **2, 5**
3. Enter margins, F7

RESET TABS
1. Position cursor
2. SHIFT + F8, **1, 8**
3. Clear Tab(s)
4. Set tab(s), F7, F7

SEARCH TEXT/CODES
1. Position cursor, F2
2. Type search string, F2

REPLACE TEXT/CODES
1. Position cursor
2. ALT + F2, Y/N for confirmation
3. Type search string, F2
4. Type replace string, F2

INSERT HEADERS (OR FOOTERS)
1. Position cursor at top of page
2. SHIFT + F8, **2, 3 (or 4)**
3. Select **1** or **2** for type of header (or footer)
4. Select frequency
5. Type the text, F7, F7

INSERT PAGE NUMBERS
1. Position cursor at top of page
2. SHIFT + F8, **2, 7**
3. Select page number position, F7

MOVE (OR COPY)

Sentence, Paragraph, Page
1. Position cursor
2. CTRL + F4, **1 or 2 or 3**
3. **1 (or 2)**
4. Position cursor, ENTER

Block of Text
1. Block text
2. CTRL + F4, **1**
3. **1 (or 2)**
4. Position cursor, ENTER

CHECK SPELLING
1. Position cursor
2. Insert Speller (floppy disk users)
3. CTRL + F2, **1**
4. **1** for word, **2** for page, **3** for document
5. Respond to menu options

USE THESAURUS
1. Position cursor on word
2. Insert Thesaurus (floppy disk users)
3. ALT + F1
4. Respond to menu options

IF YOU ENJOYED THIS BOOK . . .

help us stay in touch with your needs and interests by filling out and returning the survey card below. Your opinions are important, and will help us to continue to publish the kinds of books you need, when you need them.

What brand of computer(s) do you own or use? ☐ At work ☐ At school ☐ At home

Where do you use your computer the most?

What topics would you like to see covered in future books by Osborne/McGraw-Hill?

How many other computer books do you own?

Why did you choose this book?
- ☐ Best coverage of the subject.
- ☐ Recognized the author from previous work.
- ☐ Liked the price.
- ☐ Other

Where did you find this book?
- ☐ Bookstore
- ☐ Computer/software store
- ☐ Department store
- ☐ Advertisement
- ☐ Catalog

Where did you hear about this book?
- ☐ Book review.
- ☐ Osborne catalog.
- ☐ Advertisement in:
- ☐ Found by browsing in store.
- ☐ Found/recommended in library
- ☐ Other

- ☐ Required textbook
- ☐ Library
- ☐ Gift
- ☐ Other

Where should we send your FREE catalog?

NAME

ADDRESS

358-1 CITY _____ STATE _____ ZIP

BUSINESS REPLY MAIL

FIRST CLASS   PERMIT NO. 3111   Berkeley, CA

Postage will be paid by addressee

Osborne **McGraw-Hill**

2600 Tenth Street
Berkeley, California 94710